AN INTRODUCTION TO BUDDHISM

In this new edition of the bestselling *Introduction to Buddhism*, Peter Harvey provides a comprehensive introduction to the development of the Buddhist tradition in both Asia and the West. Extensively revised and fully updated, this new edition draws on recent scholarship in the field, and explores the tensions and continuities between the different forms of Buddhism. Harvey critiques and corrects some common misconceptions and mistranslations, and discusses key concepts that have often been over-simplified and over-generalized.

The volume includes detailed references to scriptures and secondary literature, an updated bibliography and a section on web resources. Key terms are given in Pali and Sanskrit, and Tibetan words are transliterated in the most easily pronounceable form. This truly accessible account is an ideal coursebook for students of religion, Asian philosophy and Asian studies, and is also a useful reference for readers wanting an overview of Buddhism and its beliefs.

PETER HARVEY is Emeritus Professor of Buddhist Studies at the University of Sunderland. He is the author of *An Introduction to Buddhist Ethics: Foundations, Values and Issues* (Cambridge, 2000) and *The Selfless Mind: Personality, Consciousness and Nirvana in Early Buddhism* (Curzon, 1995). He is editor of the *Buddhist Studies Review* and one of the two founders of the UK Association for Buddhist Studies.

Frontispiece: The 'Peace Pagoda' in Battersea Park, London

AN INTRODUCTION TO BUDDHISM

Teachings, History and Practices

SECOND EDITION

PETER HARVEY

CAMBRIDGE
UNIVERSITY PRESS

CAMBRIDGE
UNIVERSITY PRESS

University Printing House, Cambridge CB2 8BS, United Kingdom

Cambridge University Press is part of the University of Cambridge.

It furthers the University's mission by disseminating knowledge in the pursuit of education, learning and research at the highest international levels of excellence.

www.cambridge.org
Information on this title: www.cambridge.org/9780521859424

First edition published 1990, reprinted twenty times.
Second edition first published 2013
6th printing 2017

Printed in the United Kingdom by Clays, St Ives plc

A catalogue record for this publication is available from the British Library

Library of Congress Cataloguing in Publication data
Harvey, Peter (Brian Peter)
An introduction to Buddhism : teachings, history and practices / Peter Harvey. – Second edition.
pages cm
Includes bibliographical references and index.
ISBN 978-0-521-85942-4
1. Buddhism. I. Title.
BQ4022.H37 2012
294.3–dc23
2012021011

ISBN 978-0-521-85942-4 Hardback
ISBN 978-0-521-67674-8 Paperback

May any karmic fruitfulness *(puñña)* generated by writing this work be for the benefit of my parents, wife and daughter, all who read this book, and indeed all beings.

Namo tassa Bhagavato Arahato Sammā-sambuddhassa
Honour to the Blessed One, *Arahat*,
perfectly and completely Awakened One!

The author (second from the right) accompanied by two Samatha Trust teachers at a festival at Ratanagiri Vihāra, Northumberland, UK, giving alms to Ajahn Sumedho, then head of the Forest Sangha.

Contents

Illustrations

Tables

Preface to the Second Edition, and Acknowledgements

The first edition of this book has sold over 55,000 copies since its publication in 1990, and has translations in French, Italian and Spanish. It has been used as a textbook from MA level down to secondary school level.

The book was aimed to give a balanced overview of the panorama of Buddhisms in the world, for students, Buddhists and the general public. As a writer, I was an 'insider' to Buddhism looking outwards to help others look inside its many 'rooms'. My own starting point was as: a scholar of Theravāda Buddhism who was mainly used to working with textual material, someone whose first degree was in philosophy, who had taught a university course on Buddhism for a number of years, a practising Theravāda Buddhist, and a meditation teacher in the Samatha Trust tradition. In order to write an introduction to Buddhism as a whole, I had to broaden beyond my base in exploring the textual sources of Mahāyāna Buddhism, and historical and anthropological accounts of *all* traditions. My background meant that I wrote as an 'insider' to various strands of Theravāda Buddhism, but as a sympathetic 'outsider' to Mahāyāna traditions and even some strands of Theravāda.

My aims in the new edition are as in the first edition, though now also including a greater willingness to explore tensions as well as continuities between the different forms of Buddhism:

1. to present as comprehensive an overview of Buddhism as possible;
2. to introduce key ideas/practices/developments, linking them to textual citations, where relevant;
3. to show their relationship to other ideas and practices of the same tradition;
4. to show their parallels in other Buddhist traditions;
5. to present the diversities within Buddhism, but in a way which allows the reader to see how one thing led to another: the continuities, and thus the

uniting common threads that run through the tapestry of Buddhism, sometimes with a similar end attained by different means;
6. to nevertheless explore some tensions between the different forms of Buddhism;
7. to show how Buddhism works as a set of *practices*, not just a set of beliefs;
8. to show the overall dynamics of how Buddhism 'works';
9. to include a good range of illustrations, from all the traditions;
10. to convey something of the emotional tone or 'flavour(s)' of Buddhism;
11. to emphasize aspects of Buddhism that particularly help to illuminate Buddhism as it is now, showing the relevance of historical developments to the present.

The focus is on the main developments, ideas and practices, and their relationships, seeking a breadth of coverage with interlinked shafts of depth, and to convey Buddhism's nature as a living tradition.

This second edition has been thoroughly revised throughout. It gives detailed references to both scriptures and secondary literature, the bibliography is updated and a section on web resources is added, which is also available online at www.cambridge.org/harvey. It provides both Pali and Sanskrit versions of key terms, uses Pinyin forms for Chinese terms (with Wade-Giles forms given on first use), with pronounceable forms used for Tibetan names and terms (with the Wylie transcription forms given on first use). When an italicized foreign term is used in the plural, an unitalicized s is added, for clarity.

Throughout, more explanations and clarifications have been added. In Chapter 2 and elsewhere, 'karmic fruitfulness' is used as a translation for *puñña*, rather than the common but rather limp 'merit'. In Chapter 3, the *ariya-sacca*s are translated and explained as 'True Realities for the Spiritually Ennobled', rather than 'Noble Truths' or 'Holy Truths', with *dukkha* as 'the painful'/'painful' and *anattā* as 'non-Self' rather than 'not-self'. Also, a section on '*Nirvāṇa* as an object of insight' has been added. In Chapter 4, there is a new section on 'The three aspirations, *Jātaka*s and *Avadāna*s', and more attention is given to the heritage of the school that has become known as the 'Theravāda', in part to more clearly differentiate it from early Buddhism.

In Chapter 5, attention is given to the varying senses of the key term 'emptiness' in Mahāyāna thought, as for example in the self-emptiness and other-emptiness debate in Tibetan Buddhism, and in developments of Tathāgata-garbha thought in East Asian Buddhism. In Chapter 6, more attention is given to differentiating the different kinds of *Bodhisattva*, and the section on Tantra is considerably expanded.

Chapter 7 now includes a section on esoteric or 'tantric' Southern Buddhism. Chapter 8 traces several uniting concerns through the devotional activities it explores. Chapter 9 draws on research from my *Introduction to Buddhist Ethics*. Chapter 10 includes updated material on the revival of the *bhikkhunī* ordination line in the Theravāda. Chapter 11, on meditation, has been restructured and developed in more depth. It now includes sections on 'Qualities to be developed by meditation', 'The contributions of *samatha* and *vipassanā* meditation in Southern Buddhism', 'Some recent methods of *vipassanā* practice', 'The *cakras* and the "six yogas of Nāropa"', 'Sexual yoga', 'Mahāmudrā', 'Dzogch'en' and 'Zen in action: straightforward mind at all times'.

Chapter 12, on Buddhism in modern Asia, has been considerably updated, for example to include material on the Dhammakāya and Santi Asoke movements in Thailand, the interaction of Buddhism and spirit religion in Sri Lanka, and in Japan, the 'Critical Buddhism' debate and the Nichiren Shōshū/Sōka Gakkai split. Chapter 13, on Buddhism beyond Asia, has been extensively updated, and with new sections on 'The internet, films and music', 'Immigration' and 'Categories of Buddhists, and their characteristics and numbers'. Both Chapters 12 and 13 contain many new tables, and both include material on 'Engaged Buddhism'.

I would like to express my gratitude to Lance S. Cousins, now of Wolfson College, Oxford, for his very valuable comments on a draft of the first edition of this work, and Paul Harrison, of Stanford University, for his various comments on this edition.

I would also like to thank: Russell Webb for information on Buddhism in Europe; Cathy Cantwell, of Oxford University, for her comments on tantric material; my students Mary Jaksch, of the New Zealand Diamond Sangha, for help in understanding *kōans*, and Aigo Pedro Castro Sánchez, author of *Las Eseñanzas de Dōgen*, for help in understanding the use of the term *Mahāsattva*; Jane Caple, of Leeds University, for information on numbers of Northern Buddhists in China; Ajahn Tiradhammo for his comments on the chapter on the *Saṅgha*; and Stewart McFarlaine, formerly of Lancaster University, for his help with some points on Eastern Buddhism.

A Note on Language and Pronunciation

Most of the foreign words in this work are from Pali and Sanskrit, which are closely related languages of ancient India. Pali is the scriptural, liturgical and scholarly language of Southern (Theravāda) Buddhism, one of the three main cultural traditions of Buddhism. Sanskrit, or rather 'Buddhist Hybrid Sanskrit', is the language in which many of the scriptures and scholarly treatises of Mahāyāna Buddhism came to be written in India. Northern and Eastern Buddhism, where the Mahāyāna form of Buddhism predominates, generally use the Tibetan or Chinese translations of these texts. Many works on Buddhism give only Sanskrit versions of words, but this is artificial as Sanskrit is no longer used by Buddhists (except in Nepal), but Pali is still much in use. This work therefore uses the Pali version of terms (followed in brackets on first use by the Sanskrit) for most of early Buddhism, for Southern Buddhism, and when discussing Buddhism in general. Sanskrit versions are used when particularly discussing Mahāyāna forms of Buddhism, for some early schools which also came to use Sanskrit, and when discussing Hinduism. The Sanskrit term '*Stūpa*', referring to a relic mound, is also used in preference to the less well-known Pali term '*Thūpa*'; the same applies to '*Nirvāṇa*' rather than '*Nibbāna*'. An unitalicized Sanskrit '*karma*' is also used instead of Pali '*kamma*', as it is now also an English word. In many cases, Pali and Sanskrit terms are spelt the same. Where the spellings are different, the Pali spelling is the simpler one.

Both Pali and Sanskrit have more than twenty-six letters, so to write them in the Roman alphabet means that this needs to be expanded by the use of diacritical marks. Once the specific sounds of the letters are known, Pali and Sanskrit words are then pronounced as they are written, unlike English ones. It is therefore worth taking account of the diacritical marks, as they give a clear guide to pronunciation. The letters are pronounced as follows:

1. ***a*** is short and flat, like the *u* in 'hut' or 'utter'
   i is short, like *i* in 'bit'
   u is like *u* in 'put', or *oo* in 'foot'

e is like *e* in 'bed', only pronounced long
o is long, like *o* in 'note' (or, before more than one consonant, more like *o* in 'not' or 'odd').

2. A bar over a vowel makes it long:
   ā is like *a* in 'barn'
   ī is like *ee* in 'beet'
   ū is like *u* in 'brute'.
3. Sanskrit also has the vowels *ai* and *au*, respectively pronounced like the 'ai' in aisle and 'ow' in vow. Thus Jain rhymes with line, not with Jane.
4. When there is a dot under a letter (*ṭ, ḍ, ṇ, ṣ, ṛ, ḷ*), this means that it is a 'cerebral' letter. Imagine a dot on the roof of one's mouth that one must touch with one's tongue when saying these letters. This produces a characteristically 'Indian' sound. It also makes *ṣ* into a *sh* sound, and *ṛ* into *ri*.
5. The Sanskrit letter *ḥ* represents an aspiration of the preceding vowel: an 'h' sound followed by a slight echo of the vowel, e.g. *duḥkha* as *duh*[u]*kha*.
6. *ś* is like a normal *sh* sound.
7. Aspirated consonants (***kh, gh, ch, jh, ṭh, ḍh, th, dh, ph, bh***) are accompanied by a strong breath-pulse from the chest, as when uttering English consonants very emphatically. For example:
   ch is like *ch-h* in 'church-hall'
   th is like *t-h* in 'hot-house'
   ph is like *p-h* in 'cup-handle'
   When aspirated consonants occur as part of a consonant cluster, the aspiration comes at the end of the cluster.
8. ***c*** is like *ch* in 'choose'.
9. ***ñ*** is like *ny* in 'canyon', ***ññ*** is like *nnyy*.
10. ***ṃ*** is a pure nasal sound, made when the mouth is closed but air escapes through the nose, with the vocal chords vibrating; it approximates to *ng*.
11. ***ṅ*** is an *ng*, nasal sound said from the mouth, rather than the nose.
12. ***v*** may be somewhat similar to English *v* when at the start of a word, or between vowels, but like *w* when combined with another consonant.
13. Double consonants are always pronounced long, for example *nn* is as in 'unnecessary'.

All other letters are pronounced as in English.

ō is used to denote a long *o* in Japanese (as in 'note', rather than 'not').

For Tibetan words, the full transcription, according to the Wylie system, is given in brackets on first use, but otherwise, including in the index, a form that gives a better indication of pronunciation is given, as in Samuel (1993: 617–34).

For Chinese, the modern Pinyin system of romanization is used, followed, on first use, by the form in the older Wade-Giles system. A few things to note in Pinyin:

j has no equivalent in English, but is like an unaspirated *q*.

q has no equivalent in English, but is like *ch*eek, with lips spread wide with *ee*, and the tongue curled downwards to touch back of the teeth, and strong aspiration.

x has no equivalent in English, but is like *sh*e, with the lips spread and the tip of the tongue curled downwards and stuck to the back of the teeth when saying *ee*.

zh is like *ch* as a sound between *ch*oke, *j*oke and *tr*ue.

z is between su*ds* and ca*ts*.

c is like *ts* in ca*ts*.

Abbreviations

Note that below:
Th. = a text of Pali Canon or later Theravādin literature
My. = a Mahāyāna text in Sanskrit, Chinese or Tibetan

A.	*Aṅguttara Nikāya* (Th.); (tr. F. L. Woodward and E. M. Hare) *The Book of Gradual Sayings*, 5 vols., London, PTS, 1932–6; (tr. Bhikkhu Bodhi) *The Numerical Discourses of the Buddha: A Complete Translation of the Aṅguttara Nikāya*, one vol., Boston, Wisdom, 2012; (tr. Nyanaponika Thera and Bhikkhu Bodhi) *Numerical Discourses of the Buddha*, New York and Oxford, Altamara, 1999: partial translation in one vol.
A-a.	*Aṅguttara Nikāya Aṭṭhakathā* (*Manorathapūraṇī*) (Th.): commentary on *A.*
AKB.	*Abhidharma-kośa-bhāṣya* [of Vasubandhu – mostly Sarvāstivāda]; (tr. L. M. Pruden, from L. de La Vallée Poussin's French translation) *Abhidharmakośa-bhāṣyam* 4 vols., Berkeley, Asian Humanities Press, 1991.
Asl.	*Aṭṭhasālinī* (Th.): commentary on the *Dhs.*; (tr. Pe Maung Tin) *The Expositor*, 2 vols. London, PTS, 1920 and 1921.
Asta.	*Aṣṭasāhasrikā Prajñāpāramitā Sūtra* (My.); (tr. E. Conze) *The Perfection of Wisdom in Eight Thousand Lines, and its Verse Summary*, Bolinas, Four Seasons Foundation, 1973.
Bca.	*Bodhicaryāvatāra* of Śāntideva (My.); (tr. K. Crosby and A. Skilton) *Śāntideva: The Bodhicaryāvatāra*, Oxford and New York, Oxford University Press.
BCE	Before the Christian Era.
BM.	S. Shaw, *Buddhist Meditation: An Anthology from the Pāli Canon*, London and New York, Routledge, 2006.

BP.	D. S. Lopez, Jr, ed., *Buddhism in Practice* [anthology], Princeton, N.J., Princeton University Press, 1995, cited by text number.
BPS	Buddhist Publication Society.
BS1.	E. Conze, *Buddhist Scriptures* [anthology], Harmondsworth, Penguin, 1959.
BS2.	D. S. Lopez, *Buddhist Scriptures* [anthology], London and New York, Penguin, 2004, cited by text number.
BSR.	*Buddhist Studies Review.*
BT.	W. T. de Bary, ed., *The Buddhist Tradition in India, China and Japan* [anthology], New York, The Modern Library, 1969; repr. New York, Random House, 1992.
BTTA.	E. Conze, ed., *Buddhist Texts Through the Ages*, Oxford, Cassirer, 1954; repr. Oxford, One World, 1995, cited by text number.
Bvms.	*Buddhavaṃsa* (Th.); (tr. I. B. Horner) in *Minor Anthologies*, Vol. III, London, PTS, 1975. Also includes translation of *Cariyā-piṭaka.*
BW.	Bhikkhu Bodhi, *The Buddha's Words: An Anthology of Discourses from the Pali Canon*, Boston, Wisdom, 2005.
c.	*Circa.*
CE	Christian Era.
Ch.	Chinese.
D.	*Dīgha Nikāya* (Th.); (tr. T. W. and C. A. F. Rhys Davids) *Dialogues of the Buddha*, 3 vols., London, PTS, 1899–1921; (tr. M. Walshe) *Long Discourses of the Buddha*, 2nd revised edition, Boston, Wisdom, 1996, one vol.
D-a.	*Dīgha Nikāya Aṭṭhakathā* (*Sumaṅgalavilāsinī*) (Th.): commentary on *D.*
Dhp.	*Dhammapada* (Th.); (tr. K. R. Norman) *The Word of the Doctrine*, London, PTS, 1997; (tr. V. Roebuck) *The Dhammapada*, London, Penguin, 2010. Buddharakkhita and Ṭhānissaro translations on Access to Insight website.
Dhp-a.	*Dhammapada Aṭṭhakathā*, commentary on *Dhp* (Th.); (tr. E. W. Burlingame) *Buddhist Legends*, 3 vols., Harvard Oriental Series, Cambridge, Mass., Harvard University Press, 1921; repr. London, PTS, 1995.

Dhs. — *Dhamma-saṅgaṇī* (Th.); (tr. C. A. F. Rhys Davids) *A Buddhist Manual of Psychological Ethics*, London, PTS, 1900, 3rd edn, 1993.

EB. — J. S. Strong, *The Experience of Buddhism: Sources and Interpretations*, 2nd edn, Belmont, Calif., Wadsworth, 2002, cited by text number.

f. — Founded.

FWBO — Friends of the Western Buddhist Order.

It. — *Itivuttaka* (Th.); (tr. P. Masefield) *The Itivuttaka*, London, PTS, 2001.

Jap. — Japanese.

Jat. — *Jātaka with Commentary* (Th.); (tr. by various hands under E. B. Cowell) *The Jātaka or Stories of the Buddha's Former Births*, 6 vols., London, PTS, 1895–1907. S. Shaw, *The Jātakas: Birth Stories of the Bodhisatta*, New Delhi, Penguin, 2006, translates 26 of the *Jātakas*.

JBE — *Journal of Buddhist Ethics*.

JIABS — *Journal of the International Association of Buddhist Studies*.

Khp. — *Khuddaka-pāṭha* (Th.); (tr. with its commentary, Bhikkhu Ñāṇamoli) *Minor Readings and Illustrator*, London, PTS, 1960.

Khp-a. — Commentary on *Khp.*: see last item for translation.

Kor. — Korean.

Kvu. — *Kathāvatthu* (Th.); (tr. S. Z. Aung and C. A. F. Rhys Davids) *Points of Controversy*, London, PTS, 1915.

Kvu-a. — *Kathāvatthu Aṭṭhakathā* (*Pañcappakaraṇa-atthakathā*) (Th.): commentary on *Kvu.*; (tr. B. C. Law) *The Debates Commentary*, London, PTS, 1940.

Lanka. — *Laṅkāvatāra Sūtra* (My.); (tr. D. T. Suzuki) *The Lankavatara Sutra*, London, Routledge and Kegan Paul, 1932; repr. Delhi, MB, 2003.

Lotus Sūtra — *Saddharma-puṇḍarīka Sūtra* (My.); (tr. H. Kern, from Sanskrit) *The Saddharma-puṇḍarīka* or *The Lotus of the True Law*, Sacred Books of the East, Vol. XXI, Oxford, Clarendon Press, 1884; repr. Delhi, MB, 1968; (tr. B. Kato *et al.*, from Chinese) *The Threefold Lotus Sūtra*, New York and Tokyo, Weatherhill/Kosei, 1975; repr. Tokyo, Kosei Shuppan-Sha, 1998.

M. — *Majjhima Nikāya* (Th.); (tr. I. B. Horner) *Middle Length Sayings*, 3 vols., London, PTS, 1954–9; (tr. Bhikkhu Ñāṇamoli and Bhikkhu Bodhi) *The Middle Length Discourses of the Buddha*, one vol., Boston, Wisdom, 1995.

M-a. — *Majjhima Nikāya Aṭṭhakathā (Papañcasūdanī)* (Th.); commentary on *M.*

MB — Motilal Banarsidass (publisher).

MBS — Mahā Bodhi Society.

Miln. — *Milindapañha* (Th.); (tr. I. B. Horner) *Milinda's Questions*, 2 vols., London, PTS, 1963 and 1964.

Mmk. — *(Mūla-)madhyamaka-kārikā* [of Nāgārjuna] (My.); (tr. K. K. Inada) *Nāgārjuna: A Translation of his Mūlamadhyamaka-kārikā, with an Introductory Essay* [and Sanskrit text], Tokyo, Hokuseido Press, 1970; repr. Delhi, Sri Satguru, 1993; (tr. J. Garfield, from Tibetan) 1995, *The Fundamental Wisdom of the Middle Way: Nāgārjuna's Mūla-madhyamakakārikā*, Oxford, Oxford University Press.

Ms. — *Mahāyāna-saṃgraha* [of Asaṅga] (My.); (tr. J. P. Keenan) *The Summary of the Great Vehicle, by Bodhisattva Asaṅga*, Berkeley, Numata Center for Buddhist Translation and Research, 1992.

Mv. — *Madhyānta-vibhāga* [of Asaṅga/Maitreya] (My.); (tr. S. Anacker) in his *Seven Works of Vasubandhu*, Delhi, MB, 1984; (tr. T. A. Kochumuttom) Chapter 1 is translated in his *Buddhist Doctrine of Experience*, Delhi, MB, 1982.

Mvkb. — *Madhyānta-vibhāga-kārikā-bhāṣya* [of Vasubandhu] (My.); (tr. S. Anacker) in his *Seven Works of Vasubandhu*, Delhi, MB, 1984; (tr. T. A. Kochumuttom) Chapter 1 is translated in his *Buddhist Doctrine of Experience*, Delhi, MB, 1982.

Mvm. — *Mahāvaṃsa* (Th.); (tr. W. Geiger) *The Mahāvaṃsa or Great Chronicle of Ceylon*, London, PTS, 1964.

Mvs. — *Mahāvastu* [of the Lokottaravāda school]; (tr. J. J. Jones) *The Mahāvastu, Translated from the Buddhist Sanskrit*, 3 vols., London, PTS, 1949–56.

MW. — R. Bucknell and C. Kang, eds., *The Meditative Way: Readings in the Theory and Practice of Buddhist Meditation*, Richmond, Surrey, Curzon Press, 1997.

n.d. — No date.

Ndk. — *Nidānakathā* (Th.); (tr. N. A. Jayawickrama) *The Story of the Buddha (Jātaka-nidāna)*, Oxford, PTS, 2002.

Panca. — *Pañcaviṃśati-sāhasrikā Prajñāpāramitā Sūtra* (My.); (tr. E. Conze) *The Large Sutra on Perfect Wisdom*, London, Luzac & Co., 1961–4; repr. Delhi, MB, 1979, and Berkeley, Calif., University of California Press, 1985.

Patis. — *Paṭisambhidāmagga* (Th.); (tr. Bhikkhu Ñāṇamoli) *The Path of Discrimination*, London, PTS, 1982.

Plat. — *The Platform Sutra of the Sixth Patriarch* (My.) (tr. from Chinese by P. B. Yampolsky), New York, Columbia University Press, 1967.

pron. — Pronounced.

PTS — Pali Text Society.

Pv. — *Petavatthu* (Th.); (tr. H. S. Gehman) 'Stories of the Departed', in *The Minor Anthologies of the Pali Canon Part IV*, I. B. Horner and H. S. Gehman, London, PTS, 1974.

repr. — Reprint.

Rv. — *Ratnagotra-vibhāga* [of Asaṅga/Maitreya, or Sthiramati/Sāramati] (My.); (tr. from Sanskrit by J. Takasaki) *A Study of the Ratnagotravibhāga (Uttaratantra): Being a Treatise on the Tathāgatagarbha Theory of Mahāyāna Buddhism*, Rome, Series Orientales Rome XXIII, 1966; (tr. from Tibetan by J. Kongtrul and K. T. Gyamtso) *Buddha Nature: The Mahayana Uttara Shastra with Commentary*, Ithaca, N.Y., Snow Lion, 2000.

S. — *Saṃyutta Nikāya* (Th.); (tr. Bhikkhu Bodhi) *The Connected Discourses of the Buddha*, one vol., Boston, Wisdom, 2005.

S-a. — *Saṃyutta Nikāya Aṭṭhakathā* (*Sāratthappakāsinī*) (Th.); commentary on *S.*

SB. — R. Gethin, *Sayings of the Buddha: A Selection of Suttas from the Pali Nikāyas*, Oxford and New York, Oxford University Press, 2008.

Skt — Sanskrit.

Sn. — *Sutta-nipāta* (Th.); (tr. K. R. Norman) *The Group of Discourses*, in paperback *The Rhinoceros Horn and Other Early Buddhist Poems*, London, PTS, 1984; (tr. K. R. Norman) *The Group of Discourses*, Vol. II, London, PTS, 1992 revised translation with introduction and notes.

Sn-a.	*Sutta-nipāta Aṭṭhakathā* (*Paramatthajotikā* II) (Th.); commentary on *Sn.*
Srim.	*Śrīmālā-devī Siṃhanāda Sūtra* (My.); (tr. A. & H. Wayman) *The Lion's Roar of Queen Śrīmālā*, New York and London, Columbia University Press, 1974; repr. Delhi, MB, 1989.
Ss.	*Śikṣā-samuccaya* [of Śāntideva] (My.); (tr. C. Bendall and W. H. D. Rouse) *Śikṣā-samuccaya: A Compendium of Buddhist Doctrine Compiled by Śāntideva Chiefly from the Early Mahāyāna Sūtras*, London, 1922; repr. Delhi, MB, 1971.
Svb.	*Suvarṇa-bhāsottama Sūtra* (My.); (tr. R. E. Emmerick) *The Sūtra of Golden Light*, London, Luzac and Co., 1970; references to text, not translation pagination.
Thag.	*Thera-gāthā* (Th.); (tr. K. R. Norman) *Elders' Verses*, Vol. I, London, PTS, 1969.
Thig.	*Therī-gāthā* (Th.); (tr. K. R. Norman) *Elders' Verses*, Vol. II, London, PTS, 1971.
Tib.	Tibetan.
Trims.	*Triṃśatikā-kārikā* (or *Triṃśikā*) [of Vasubandhu] (My.); see under *Mv.* for translations.
Tsn.	*Trisvabhāva-nirdeśa* [of Vasubandhu] (My.); see under *Mv.* for translations.
Ud.	*Udāna* (Th.); (tr. P. Masefield) *The Udāna*, London, PTS, 1994.
Vc.	*Vajracchedikā Prajñāpāramitā Sūtra* (My.); (tr. and explained by E. Conze) in *Buddhist Wisdom Books: The Diamond Sutra and the Heart Sutra*, London, George Allen and Unwin, 1958; repr. as *Buddhist Wisdom*, New York, Vintage, 2001; *Vajracchedikā Prajñāpāramitā*, 2nd edn, Rome, Istituto Italiano per il Medio de Estremo Oriente, 1974.
Vibh.	*Vibhaṅga* (Th.); (tr. U. Thittila) *The Book of Analysis*, London, PTS, 1969.
Vibh-a.	Commentary on *Vibh.* (Th.); (tr. Ñāṇamoli) *Dispeller of Delusion*, 2 vols., London, PTS, 1988 and 1989.
Vigv.	*Vigraha-vyāvartanī* [of Nāgārjuna] (My.); (tr. J. Westerhoff) *The Dispeller of Disputes*, Oxford, Oxford University Press, 2010.

Vims.	*Viṃśatikā-kārikā* [of Vasubandhu] (My.); see under *Mv.* for translations.
Vin.	*Vinaya Piṭaka* (Th.); (tr. I. B. Horner) *The Book of the Discipline*, 6 vols., London, PTS, 1938–66.
Vism.	*Visuddhimagga* [of Buddhaghosa] (Th.); (tr. Bhikkhu Ñāṇamoli), *The Path of Purification: Visuddhimagga*, Onalaska, Wash., BPS Pariyatti, 1999.
Vrtti.	*Viṃśatikā-vṛtti* [of Vasubandhu] (My.); see under *Mv.* for translations.
Vv.	*Vimāna-vatthu* (Th.); (tr. I. B. Horner) 'Stories of the Mansions', in *The Minor Anthologies of the Pali Canon Part IV*, I. B. Horner and H. S. Gehman, London, PTS, 1974.
Vv-a.	*Vimāna-vatthu Aṭṭhakathā (Paramatthadīpanī III)* (Th.); commentary on *Vv.*

Most of these works are still in print; reprints have only been mentioned where the publisher differs from the original one. Translations published by the PTS are from the editions of the text published by them. Other translations are from various editions. Translations given in this book are not necessarily the same as those in the cited translations, particularly in the case of translations from Pali. For a detailed listing of Buddhist texts and their translations, see Williams and Tribe (2000: 230–48).

Reference is generally to volume and page number of the text in Pali; but for *Dhp., Sn., Thag.* and *Thig.*, it is to verse number, and Mahāyāna works other than *Sūtras* are referred to by chapter and verse number. For *Kvu.*, reference is either to the page number or the number of the 'book' and the discussion point within it. *Dhs., Plat.* and *Vc.* are referred to by section (sec.) number in text.

The page numbers of the relevant edition of an original text are generally given in brackets in its translation, or at the top of the page. In translations of the Pali Canon, the volume number of the translation generally corresponds to the volume of the PTS edition of the texts, except that *Middle Length Sayings* I translates only the first 338 pages of *M.* I, the rest being part of *Middle Length Sayings* II. Also, *Vin.* III and IV are translated respectively as *Book of the Discipline*, Vols. I plus II (pp. 1–163), and II (pp. 164–416) plus III, with *Vin.* I and II as *Book of the Discipline*, Vols. IV and V, and *Vin.* V is *Book of the Discipline* VI. Moreover, in *Book of the Discipline* I–V, the number indicating the Pali page number shows where the relevant page *ends*, rather than begins, as is usual in other translations.

Note that a very useful source for translations of many Pali texts is *Access to Insight*: www.accesstoinsight.org/tipitaka. It references texts by *Sutta* number, or section and *Sutta* number, but also gives, in brackets, the volume and page number of the start of the relevant text in Pali (PTS edition).

Introduction

The history of Buddhism spans almost 2,500 years from its origin in India with Siddhattha Gotama (Pali, Skt Siddhārtha Gautama), through its spread to most parts of Asia and, in the twentieth and twenty-first centuries, to the West. Richard Gombrich holds that the Buddha was 'one of the most brilliant and original thinkers of all time' (2009: vii), whose 'ideas should form part of the education of every child, the world over', which 'would make the world a more civilized place, both gentler and more intelligent' (Gombrich, 2009: 1), and with Buddhism, at least in numerical terms, as 'the greatest movement in the entire history of human ideas' (Gombrich, 2009: 194). While its fortunes have waxed and waned over the ages, over half of the present world population live in areas where it is, or has been, a dominant cultural force.

The English term 'Buddhism' correctly indicates that the religion is characterized by a devotion to 'the Buddha', 'Buddhas' or 'buddha-hood'. 'Buddha' is not a proper name, but a descriptive title meaning 'Awakened One' or 'Enlightened One'. This implies that most people are seen, in a spiritual sense, as being asleep – unaware of how things really are. As 'Buddha' is a title, it should not be used as a name, as in, for example, 'Buddha taught that . . .'. In many contexts, 'the Buddha' is specific enough, meaning the Buddha known to history, Gotama. From its earliest times, though, the Buddhist tradition has postulated other Buddhas who have lived on earth in distant past ages, or who will do so in the future. The later tradition also postulated the existence of many Buddhas currently existing in other parts of the universe. All such Buddhas, known as *sammā-sambuddhas* (Skt *samyak-sambuddhas*), or 'perfect fully Awakened Ones', are nevertheless seen as occurring only rarely within the vast and ancient cosmos. More common are those who are 'buddhas' in a lesser sense, who have awakened to the nature of reality by practising in accordance with the guidance of a perfect Buddha such as Gotama. The Tibetan tradition also recognizes certain humans as manifestations on earth of Buddhas of other world-systems.

As 'Buddha' does not refer to a unique individual, Buddhism is less focused on the person of its founder than is, for example, Christianity. The emphasis in Buddhism is on the *teachings* of the Buddha(s), and the 'awakening' of human personality that these are seen to lead to. Nevertheless, Buddhists do show great reverence to Gotama as a supreme teacher and an exemplar of the ultimate goal that all strive for, so that probably more images of him exist than of any other historical figure.

In its long history, Buddhism has used a variety of teachings and means to help people first develop a calmer, more integrated and compassionate personality, and then 'wake up' from restricting delusions: delusions which cause attachment and thus suffering for an individual and those he or she interacts with. The guide for this process of transformation has been the '*Dhamma*' (Skt *Dharma*): the patterns of reality and cosmic law-orderliness discovered by the Buddha(s), Buddhist teachings, the Buddhist path of practice, and the goal of Buddhism, the timeless *Nirvāṇa* (Pali *Nibbāna*). Buddhism thus essentially consists of understanding, practising and realizing *Dhamma*.

The most important bearers of the Buddhist tradition have been the monks and nuns who make up the Buddhist *Saṅgha* or 'Community'. From approximately a hundred years after the death of Gotama, certain differences arose in the *Saṅgha*, which gradually led to the development of a number of monastic fraternities (*nikāyas*), each following a slightly different monastic code, and to different schools of thought (*vādas*). All branches of the *Saṅgha* trace their ordination-line back to one or other of the early fraternities; but of the early schools of thought, only that which became known as the Theravāda has continued to this day. Its name indicates that it purports to follow the 'teaching' of the 'Elders' (Pali *Thera*, Skt *Sthavira*) of the first schism (see p. 90). While it has not remained static, it has kept close to what we know of the early teachings of Buddhism, and preserved their emphasis on attaining liberation by one's own efforts, using the *Dhamma* as guide. Around the beginning of the Christian era, a movement began which led to a new style of Buddhism known as the Mahāyāna, or 'Great Vehicle'. This has been more overtly innovative, so that for many centuries, Indian Mahāyānists continued to compose new scriptures. The Mahāyāna is characterized by a more overt emphasis on compassion, devotion to a number of holy saviour beings, and several sophisticated philosophies, developed by extending the implications of the earlier teachings. In the course of time, in India and beyond, the Mahāyāna produced many schools of its own, such as Zen. One group of these which developed by the sixth century in India, and is sometimes seen as separate from the

Mahāyāna, is known as the Mantranaya, or the 'Path of *Mantras*'. It is mostly the same as the Mahāyāna in its doctrines, but developed a range of powerful new *practices* to attain the goals of the Mahāyāna, such as the meditative repetitions of sacred words of power (*mantras*) and complex visualization practices. It is based on *tantras* or complex systems of ritual, symbolism and meditation, and its form from the late seventh century is known as the Vajrayāna, or 'Vehicle of the Thunderbolt'.

Our knowledge of the teachings of the Buddha is based on several canons of scripture, which derive from the early *Saṅgha*'s oral transmission of bodies of teachings agreed on at several councils. The Theravādin 'Pali Canon' is preserved in the Pali language, which is based upon a dialect close to that spoken by the Buddha, Old Māgadhī. It is the most complete extant early canon, and contains some of the earliest material. Most of its teachings are in fact the common property of all Buddhist schools, being simply the teachings which the Theravādins preserved from the early common stock. While parts of the Pali Canon clearly originated after the time of the Buddha, much must derive from his teachings. There is an overall harmony to the Canon, suggesting 'authorship' of its system of thought by one mind. Given that the Buddha taught for forty-five years, some signs of development in teachings may simply reflect changes during this period. Some promising attempts at relative dating rely on criteria of style, and comparisons of related texts in different canons are now producing good results. These canons gradually diverged as different floating oral traditions were drawn on, and systematizing texts peculiar to each school were added. Many of the minor differences within and between canons, however, can be seen to be due to the way in which oral traditions always produce several different permutations of essentially the same story or teachings.

The early canons contain a section on *Vinaya*, or monastic discipline, one on *Suttas* (Skt *Sūtras*), or 'discourses' of the Buddha, and some contain one on *Abhidhamma* (Skt *Abhidharma*), or 'further teachings', which systematizes the *Sutta*-teachings in the form of detailed analyses of human experience. The main teachings of Buddhism are contained in the *Suttas*, which in the Pali Canon are divided into five *Nikāyas* or 'Collections', the first four (sixteen volumes) generally being the older. In other early canons, the five divisions paralleling the *Nikāyas* are called *Āgamas*. The Pali Canon was one of the earliest to be written down, this being in Sri Lanka in around 20 BCE, after which little, if any, new material was added to it. There are also sections of six non-Theravādin early canons preserved in Chinese and Tibetan translations, fragments of a Sanskrit Canon still existing in Nepal, and odd texts in various languages of India and Central Asia found in Tibet, Central Asia and Japan.

The extensive non-canonical Pali literature includes additional *Abhidhamma* works, historical chronicles, and many volumes of commentaries. An extremely clear introduction to many points of Buddhist doctrine is the *Milindapañha* ('Milinda's Questions'), which purports to record conversations between a Buddhist monk and Milinda (Menander; *c.* 155–130 BCE), a king of Greek ancestry. Another is the *Visuddhimagga* ('Path of Purification'), a very influential Theravāda compendium of meditation practices and doctrine, written by Buddhaghosa (fifth century CE).

Mahāyāna texts were composed from around the first century BCE, originating as written, not oral, works. In time, they were recorded in a form of the Indian prestige language, Sanskrit. While many are attributed to the Buddha, their form and content clearly show that they were later restatements and extensions of the Buddha's message. The main sources for our understanding of Mahāyāna teachings are the very extensive Chinese and Tibetan Buddhist Canons. While most of the Pali Canon has been translated into English, only selected texts from these have been translated into Western languages, though much progress is being made. For some details on the three main extant Canons, see Appendix I.

While Buddhism is now only a minority religion within the borders of modern India, its spread beyond India means that it is currently found in three main cultural areas. These are those of: 'Southern Buddhism', where the Theravāda school is found, along with some elements incorporated from the Mahāyāna; 'Eastern Buddhism', where the Chinese transmission of Mahāyāna Buddhism is found; and the area of Tibetan culture, 'Northern Buddhism', which is the heir of late Indian Buddhism, where the Mantranaya/Vajrayāna version of the Mahāyāna is the dominant form. One can see these as like the three main branches of the 'tree' of Buddhism, though as all parts of a tree are genetically identical, this underplays the differences that have developed within Buddhism over time. Yet one can trace a series of transformations linking early and later forms in a causal continuum; just as Buddhism says that a person in one life and the next rebirth is 'neither (unchangingly) the same nor (completely) different', this can be said of the various forms of Buddhism that have evolved. A better image than branches of a tree is branches of a large 'family'. There are 'family resemblances' across all three branches, though certain features and forms are more typical of, and sometimes unique to, one of the three branches. The fifth edition (2005) of the Robinson and Johnson book *The Buddhist Religion* was retitled *Buddhist Religions*, to emphasize how the three main cultural forms of Buddhism are in a sense different 'worlds'. Yet this downplays the continuities and the many connections in the vast network of Buddhism.

Buddhism's concentration on the essentials of spiritual development has meant that it has been able to co-exist both with other major religions and with popular folk traditions which catered for people's desire for a variety of rituals. There has hardly ever been a 'wholly Buddhist' society, if this means a kind of religious one-party state. Buddhism has been very good at adapting to different cultures while guarding its own somewhat fluid borders by a critical tolerance of other traditions. Its style has been to offer invitations to several levels of spiritual practice for those who have been ready to commit themselves. In Southern Buddhist lands, worship of pre-Buddhist nature gods has continued, while, especially in Sri Lanka, Buddhists also worship gods whose cults are Indian in origin. Most Buddhists would not see this as a betrayal of Buddhism, but just an attempt to interact with minor powers of the cosmos for some worldly advantage: like a person asking a member of parliament to try and help him. In Northern Buddhism, a similar relationship exists with the indigenous Bön religion of Tibet. In China, Taiwan, Korea and Vietnam, Buddhism has co-existed with Confucianism – more a system of social philosophy than a religion, the Daoist religion and much folk religion. People would often partake of elements of all these traditions. In Japan, Buddhism has existed alongside the indigenous nature-orientated religion of Shintō, and the Confucianism that it brought with it from China. Traditionally, people would be married by Shintō rites and buried with Buddhist ones. In China (which now includes Tibet), North Korea, Vietnam and Laos, Buddhism exists under Communist governments. Chinese Communists persecuted Buddhism and vandalized its temples during the Cultural Revolution (1966–76), but the government has since been easing up on it, so as to allow a gentle resurgence in China proper, and a continuation of the very strong Buddhist culture of Tibet. The religion remains oppressed in North Korea, but is reasonably strong in Laos and Vietnam. In Mongolia, regions of the Russian Federation, and Cambodia, Buddhism is strengthening after previous Communist periods.

The number of Buddhists in the world is as follows (see Chapter 12 for detailed breakdowns): Southern Buddhism, 150 million; Northern Buddhism 18.2 million; Eastern Buddhism, approximately 360 million. There are also around 7 million Buddhists outside Asia (see Chapter 13). This gives an overall total of around 535 million Buddhists in the world – 7.8 per cent of the total 2010 world population of 6,852 million – though in East Asia, there are at least another 200 million who relate to Buddhism to a fair extent.

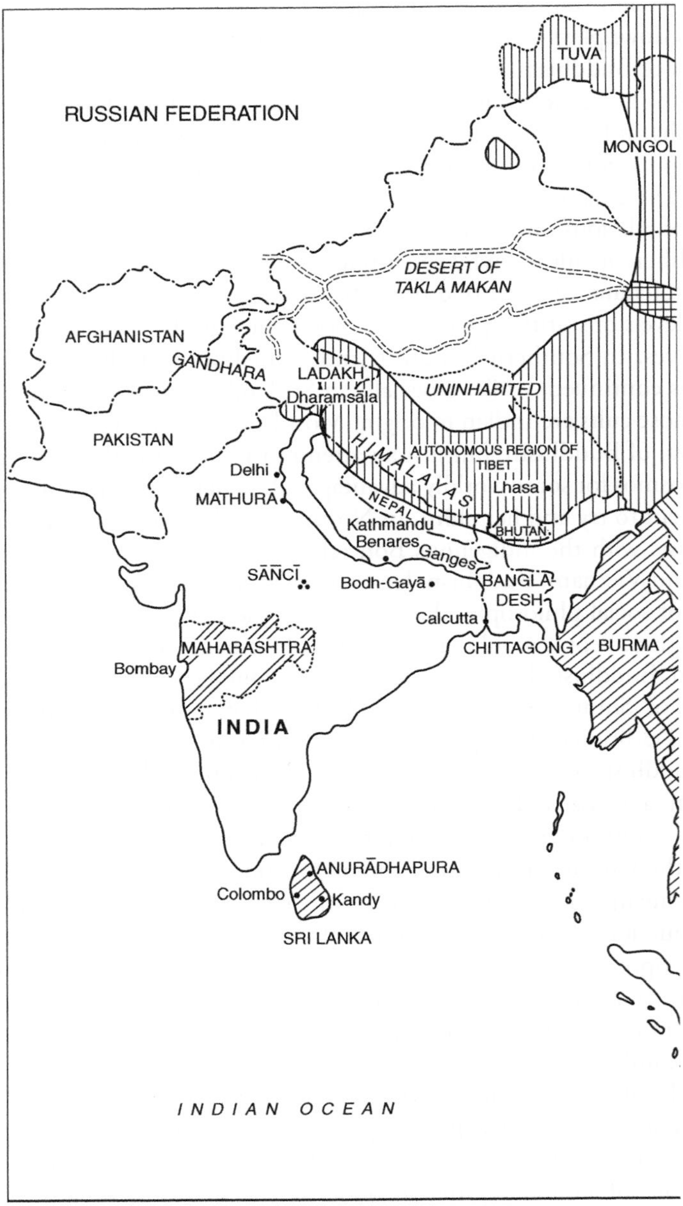

Map 1: Current location of Buddhism in Asia.

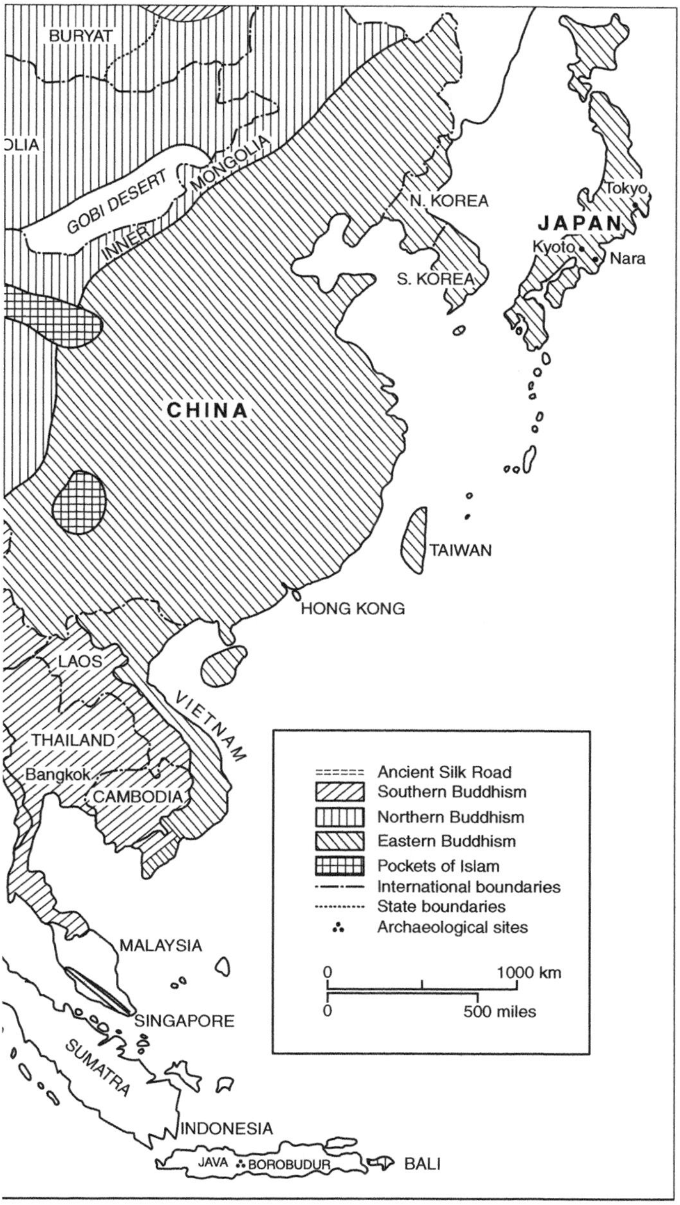
BURYAT
OLIA
GOBI DESERT
INNER
MONGOLIA
N. KOREA
S. KOREA
JAPAN
Tokyo
Kyoto
Nara
CHINA
TAIWAN
HONG KONG
LAOS
VIETNAM
THAILAND
Bangkok
CAMBODIA
MALAYSIA
SINGAPORE
SUMATRA
INDONESIA
JAVA
BOROBUDUR
BALI
Ancient Silk Road
Southern Buddhism
Northern Buddhism
Eastern Buddhism
Pockets of Islam
International boundaries
State boundaries
Archaeological sites
0
1000 km
0
500 miles

CHAPTER I

The Buddha and his Indian Context

Indian culture has not been as concerned with recording precise dates as have Chinese or Graeco-Roman cultures, so datings cannot always be arrived at with accuracy. All sources agree that Gotama was eighty when he died (e.g. *D*.II.100), and the Pali sources of Theravāda Buddhism say that this was '218' years before the inauguration of the reign of the Buddhist emperor Asoka (Skt Aśoka): the 'long chronology'. Sanskrit sources preserved in East Asia have a 'short chronology', with his death '100' years or so before Asoka's inauguration. Based on a traditional date of the inauguration, Pali sources see Gotama's dates as 623–543 BCE. However, references in Asokan edicts to named Hellenistic kings have meant that modern scholars have put the inauguration at *c.* 268 BCE (giving *c.* 566–486 BCE for Gotama) or, more recently, anywhere between 267 and 280 BCE. Richard Gombrich[1] has argued that '218' and '100' are best seen as approximate numbers, and sees 136 as more likely, based on figures associated with a lineage of Buddhist teachers in the *Dīpavaṃsa*, a chronicle of Sri Lanka – with the '218' in this text (6.1) as from its misunderstanding of figures in its earlier part. With various margins of error, Gombrich sees Gotama's death as between 422 and 399 BCE, with *c.* 404 as most likely, giving his dates as *c.* 484–404 BCE.

BACKGROUND TO THE LIFE OF THE BUDDHA[2]

Brahmanism

The Buddha taught in the region of the Ganges basin in north-east India, where the dominant religion was Brahmanism, administered by priests

[1] 1991–1992 and 2000, cf. Cousins, 1996c, Harvey, 2007d: 105b–107a.

[2] For early Indian religion, see: Basham, 2005: 234–58, 289–300; Flood, 1996: 30–102; and Olivelle, 1996.

known as Brahmins (*Brāhmaṇas*). Later, around 200 BCE, this tradition began to develop into the religion now known as Hinduism. Brahmanism had entered the north-west of the Indian sub-continent from around 1500 BCE, brought by a nomadic people who seem to have come from an area now in eastern Turkey, southern Russia and northern Iran. In this area, people spoke a postulated Aryan (Skt *Ārya*) language – the basis of a number of 'Indo-European' languages spread by migration from there to India, Iran, Greece, Italy and other parts of Western Europe. The form of the language spoken in India was Sanskrit (from which Pali is derived), which is thus linked, through Greek and Latin, to modern European languages. The influx of the Aryans seems to have overlapped with the decline of the Indus Valley Civilization, a sophisticated city-based culture which had existed in the region of Pakistan since around 2500 BCE. The religion of the Aryans was based on the *Veda*, a body of 'revealed' oral teachings and hymns: the *Ṛg Veda Saṃhitā* (*c.* 1500–1200 BCE), three other *Veda Saṃhitās*, and later compositions known as *Brāhmaṇas* and *Upaniṣads*. The Aryans worshipped 'thirty-three' mostly male gods known as *devas*, or 'illustrious ones': anthropomorphized principles seen as active in nature, the cosmos and human life. The central rite of the religion was one in which the priests sang the praises of a particular *deva* and offered him sacrifices by placing them in a sacrificial fire. In return, they hoped for such boons as health, increase in cattle, and immortality in the afterlife with the *devas*. In the *Brāhmaṇas* (*c.* 1000–800 BCE), animal sacrifices came to be added to the earlier offerings, such as grain and milk. The enunciation of the sacred sacrificial verses, known as *mantras*, was also seen as manipulating a sacred power called *Brahman*, so that the ritual was regarded as actually coercing the *devas* into sustaining the order of the cosmos and giving what was wanted. The great responsibility of the priests in this regard was reflected in them placing themselves at the head of what was regarded as a divinely ordained hierarchy of four social classes, the others being those of the *Kṣatriyas* (Pali *Khattiyas*) or warrior-leaders of society in peace or war, the *Vaiśyas* (Pali *Vessas*), or cattle-rearers and cultivators, and the *Śūdras* (Pali *Suddas*), or servants. A person's membership of one of these four *varṇas*, or 'complexions' of humanity, was seen as determined by birth; in later Hinduism the system incorporated thousands of lesser social groupings and became known as the *jāti*, or caste, system. Members of the top three *varṇas* were seen as *āryans*, or 'noble ones', and seen as socially superior due to the claimed purity of their descent.

Brahmins learnt of yogic techniques of meditation, physical isolation, fasting, celibacy and asceticism from ascetics whose traditions may have gone back to the Indus Valley Civilization. Such techniques were found to be useful as spiritual preparations for performing the sacrifice. Some Brahmins then retired to the forest and used them as a way of actually carrying out the sacrifice in an internalized, visualized form. The *Upaniṣads* were composed out of the teachings of the more orthodox of these forest dwellers. Of these, the pre-Buddhist ones are the *Bṛhadāraṇyaka* and *Chāndogya* (seventh to sixth centuries BCE) and probably the *Taittirīya, Aitareya* and *Kauṣītaki* (sixth to fifth centuries BCE). In these, *Brahman* is seen as the substance underlying the whole cosmos, and as identical with the *Ātman*, the universal Self which the yogic element of the Indian tradition had sought deep within the mind. By true knowledge of this identity, it was held that a person could attain liberation from reincarnation after death, and merge back into *Brahman*. The idea of reincarnation seems to have developed as an extension of the idea, found in the *Brāhmaṇas*, that the power of a person's sacrificial action might be insufficient to lead to an afterlife that did not end in another death. The *Upaniṣads*, perhaps due to some non-Aryan influence, saw such a death as being followed by reincarnation as a human or animal. Non-Aryan influence was probably more certain in developing the idea that it was the quality of a person's *karma*, or 'action', that determined the nature of their reincarnation in an insecure earthly form; previously, '*karma*' had only referred to sacrificial action. Nevertheless, Brahmanism continued to see karma in largely ritual terms, and actions were judged relative to a person's *varṇa*, their station in society. Gombrich argues that the Buddha's central teachings came in response to those of the early *Upaniṣads*, notably the *Bṛhadāraṇyaka*, especially its ideas on *Ātman* (1996: 31). Moreover, in Buddhism the ethical quality of the impulse behind an action was the key to its being good or bad, rather than its conformity with ritual norms (2006: 67–70; 2009: 19–44).

A key term of Brahmanical thought was *Dharma*, seen as the divinely ordained order of the universe and human society, as seen in the specific duties (*dharmas*) assigned to each *varṇa*. *Dharma* includes both how things are (cf. a 'law' of physics) and how they should be (cf. a legal 'law'); it is the existent ideal standard (cf. the standard metre rule in Paris). In Buddhism, *Dharma* (Pali *Dhamma*) is also a central term. Here, the emphasis is not on fixed social duties, but primarily on the nature of reality, practices aiding understanding of this and practices informed by an understanding of this, all aiding a person to live a happier life and to move closer to liberation. Interest in the *Dharma* of things, their basic pattern or order, is also seen in the early Indian concern with enumerating the various elements of a person and the cosmos. In Buddhism, one sees this in various analytical lists, such as the six elements (earth, water, fire, wind, space and consciousness), or five rebirth realms.

At the time of the Buddha, most Brahmins aimed at attaining the heaven of the creator god Brahmā (also known as Prajāpati) by means of truthfulness, study of the Vedic teachings, and either sacrifice or austerities. Some were saintly, but others seem to have been haughty and wealthy, supporting themselves by putting on large, expensive and bloody sacrifices, often paid for by kings. At its popular level, Brahmanism incorporated practices based on protective magic spells, and pre-Brahmanical spirit-worship no doubt continued.

The Samaṇas

The time of the Buddha was one of changing social conditions, where the traditions of small kin-based communities were being undermined as these were swallowed up by expanding kingdoms, such as those of Magadha and Kosala (Gombrich, 2006: 49–60). A number of cities had developed which were the centres of administration and of developing organized trade, based on a money economy. The ideas expressed in the *Upaniṣads* were starting to filter out into the wider intellectual community and were being hotly debated, both by Brahmins and by *Samaṇas* (Skt *Śramaṇas*), wandering 'renunciant' thinkers who were somewhat akin to the early Greek philosophers and mystics. The *Samaṇas* rejected the Vedic tradition and wandered free of family ties, living by alms, in order to think, debate and investigate. Many came from the new urban centres, where old certainties were being questioned, and increasing disease from population-concentration may have posed the universal problem of human suffering in a relatively stark form. They therefore sought to find a basis of true and lasting happiness beyond change and insecurity.

In its origin, Buddhism was a *Samaṇa*-movement. Its description and assessment of the other *Samaṇa* groups are contained in the *Sāmaññaphala Sutta* (*D*.1.47–86 (*SB*.5–36)). One of the major *Samaṇa* groups comprised the Jains. Jainism was founded, or at least led in the Buddha's day, by Vardhamāna the Mahāvīra, or 'Great Hero'. It teaches that all things, even stones, are alive, each containing a *Jīva*, or 'Life-principle'. These are seen as individually distinct, rather like the Western idea of a 'soul' but unlike the universal *Ātman* of the *Upaniṣads*, and to be naturally bright, omniscient and blissful. The aim of Jainism is to liberate one's *Jīva* from the round of rebirths by freeing it from being weighed down by an encrustation of karma, seen as a kind of subtle matter. The methods of doing so are

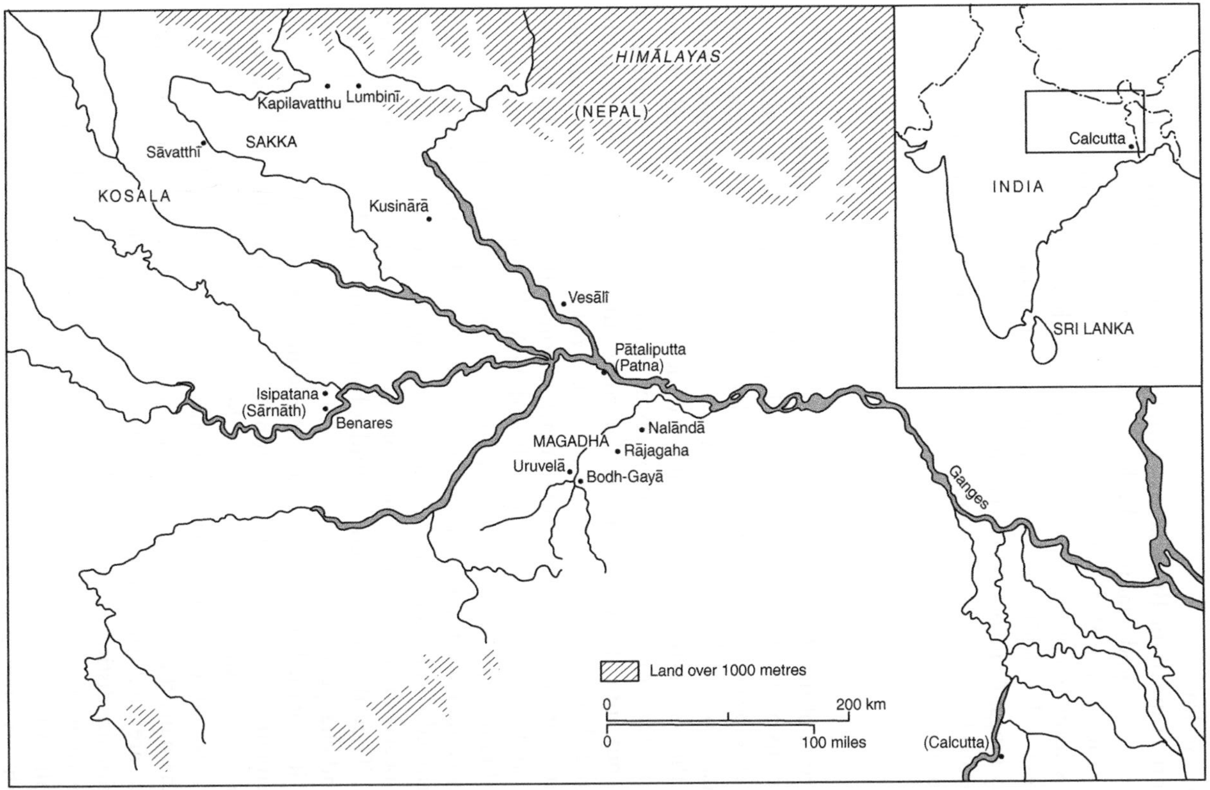

Map 2: The region where the Buddha lived and taught.

primarily austerities such as fasting, going unwashed and pulling out the hair, so as to wear out the results of previous karma, and self-restraint, total non-violence to any form of life, and vegetarianism, so as to avoid the generation of new karma. The free-will of the *Jīva* is emphasized, though even actions such as unintentionally killing an insect are held to generate karma. While the Buddha agreed with the Jains on such matters as rebirth and non-violence, he saw their theory of karma as somewhat mechanical and inflexible, and opposed their asceticism as too extreme.[3]

A group of *Samaṇas* that rivalled the Buddhists and Jains in their early centuries was that of the Ājīvikas (Basham, 1981). Their founder was Makkhali Gosāla (Skt Maskarin Gośāla), but according to the Pali tradition they also drew on ideas from Pūraṇa Kassapa (Skt Purṇa Kāśyapa) and Pakuddha Kaccāyana (Skt Kakuda Kātyāyana). Gosāla's key doctrine was that *niyati*, or impersonal 'destiny', governed all, such that humans had no ability to affect their future lives by their karma: actions were not freely done, but were determined by *niyati*. Gosāla thus believed in rebirth, but *not* in the principle of karma as that which regulates the level of a person's rebirth. The 'Life-principles' of living beings are driven by *niyati* alone through a fixed progression of types of rebirths, from a low form of animal to an advanced human who becomes an Ājīvika ascetic. The Ājīvikas practised rigorous asceticism such as fasting, nakedness and perhaps also disfiguring initiations, and aimed to die by self-starvation (as Vardhamāna in fact did), as a fitting way to end their last rebirth. Both Vardhamāna, who had originally been on good terms with Gosāla, and the Buddha criticized Ājīvika fatalism as a pernicious denial of human potential and responsibility.

Two other small groups of *Samaṇas* were the Materialists and the Skeptics. According to the Pali tradition, in the Buddha's day their main spokesmen were, respectively, Ajita Kesa-Kambalī (Skt Ajita Keśa-kambalin) and Sañjaya Belaṭṭhaputta (Skt Sañjayī Vairaṭiputra). The Materialists' aim was to lead an abstemious, balanced life which enjoyed simple pleasures and the satisfaction of human relationships. They denied any kind of self other than one which could be directly perceived, and held that this was annihilated at death. They therefore denied the idea of rebirth, and also those of karma and *niyati*. Each act was seen as a spontaneous event without karmic effects, and spiritual progression was not seen as possible. The Buddha characterized the Materialists' theory as the extreme view of 'annihilationism', and saw most other views of the day as some form of the opposite extreme, 'eternalism', which says that what survives death is some

[3] Gombrich, 2009: 45–60 discusses Jain antecedents to some Buddhist ideas.

eternal Self or Life-principle. The Skeptics responded to the welter of conflicting theories on religious and philosophical issues, and the consequent arguments, by avoiding commitment to *any* point of view, so as to preserve peace of mind. They held that knowledge on such matters was impossible, and would not even commit themselves to saying that other people's views were wrong. The Buddha saw this evasive stance as 'eel-wriggling', though he shared the wish to step aside from the 'jungle' of conflicting views, and avoid dogmatic assertions built on flimsy grounds. This common emphasis is perhaps reflected in the fact that the Buddha's two chief disciples, Sāriputta (Skt Śāriputra) and Moggallāna (Skt Maudgalyāyana), were originally Skeptics. The Buddha also shared the Materialists' emphasis on experience as the source of knowledge, and thus shared a critical evaluation of current beliefs on rebirth, karma and Self. He saw the Materialists and Skeptics as going too far, however, in denying or doubting the principles of karma and rebirth, which he held were shown to be true by (meditative) experience (*M.*I.402). Buddhism, then, did not uncritically absorb belief in karma and rebirth from existing Indian culture, as is sometimes held. These ideas were very much up for debate at the time.

THE LIFE OF THE BUDDHA[4]

We know that Gotama was born in the small republic of the Sakka (Skt Śākya) people, which straddles the present border with Nepal and had Kapilavatthu (Skt Kapilavastu) as its capital. From his birth among these people, Gotama is known in Mahāyāna tradition as Śākya-muni, 'the Śākyan sage'. The republic was not Brahmanized, and rule was by a council of household-heads, perhaps qualified by age or social standing. Gotama was born to one of these rulers, so that he described himself as a *Kṣatriya* when talking to Brahmins, and later tradition saw him as the son of a king.

In the early Buddhist texts, there is no *continuous* life of the Buddha, as these concentrated on his teachings. Only later, between 200 BCE and 200 CE, did a growing interest in the Buddha's person lead to various schools producing continuous 'biographies', which drew on scattered accounts in the existing *Sutta* and *Vinaya* collections, and floating oral traditions. These 'biographies' include the Lokattaravādin *Mahāvastu* (*Mvs.*; first century CE), the Mahāyānized Sarvāstivādin *Lalitavistara* (Bays, 1983; from the first century CE), Aśvaghoṣa's poem, the *Buddhacarita* (Johnston, 1972, (*BS1*.34–66); second century CE), and the Theravādin *Nidānakathā*

[4] On this, see: Ñāṇamoli, 2003; Ray, 1994: 44–78; Strong, 2001; Thomas, 1949.

(*Ndk.*; second or third century CE). The details of these are in general agreement, but while they must clearly be based around historical facts, they also contain legendary and mythological embellishments, and it is often not possible to sort out one from the other. While the bare historical basis of the traditional biography will never be known, as it stands it gives a great insight into Buddhism by enabling us to see what the *meaning* of the Buddha's life is to Buddhists: what lessons it is held to contain.

The traditional biography does not begin with Gotama's birth, but with what went before it, in his many lives as a *Bodhisatta*, a being (Pali *satta*) who is dedicated to attaining *bodhi*: 'enlightenment', 'awakening', buddhahood. At *bodhi*, there arises 'vision, knowledge, wisdom, true knowledge, and light' (*S*.v.422) and '*bodhi*' is related to '*bujjhati*', 'understands', in the sense of 'rising from the slumber of the continuum of the (moral and spiritual) defilements' (*Asl.*217). As an 'awakening', *bodhi* is not the awakening *of* something, that is, a beginning of something, but a final awakening *from* delusion etc. '*Bodhi-satta*' was originally equivalent to Sanskrit '*bodhi-sakta*', meaning 'one bound for/seeking/directed towards awakening', though in time it came to be Sanskritized as '*Bodhi-sattva*', a 'being (for) awakening'.

It is held that a 'hundred thousand eons and four incalculable periods ago', in one of his past lives, Gotama was an ascetic named Sumedha (or Megha) who met and was inspired by a previous Buddha, Dīpaṅkara (Skt Dīpaṃkara).[5] He therefore resolved to strive for Buddhahood, by becoming a *Bodhisatta*. Sumedha knew that, while he could become an enlightened disciple of Dīpaṅkara, an *Arahat*, the path he had chosen instead would take many lives to complete. It would, however, culminate in his becoming a perfect Buddha, one who would bring benefit to countless beings by rediscovering and teaching the timeless truths of *Dhamma* in a period when they had been forgotten by the human race (*Bvms.*2A.56). He then spent many lives, as a human, animal and god, building up the moral and spiritual perfections necessary for Buddhahood. These lives are described in what are known as *Jātaka* stories (*Jat.*, e.g. *BS1*.24–30). Over the eons, he also met other past Buddhas (Collins, 2010: 126–71; Harvey, 2007d: 161a–165a); the *Dīgha Nikāya* names six (*D*.II.2–9), and the *Buddhavaṃsa*, twenty-three. In his penultimate life he was born in the Tusita (Skt Tuṣita) heaven, the realm of the 'delighted' gods. This is said to be the realm where the *Bodhisatta* Metteyya (Skt Maitreya) now lives, ready for a future period in human history when Buddhism will have become extinct, and he can become the next Buddha.[6]

5 *Bvms.* ch. 2; *Ndk.*1–19 (*BTTA*.72); *Mvs.* 1.231–9 (*BS1*.19–24); *Divyāvadāna* 246–53 (*EB*.1.4.1).
6 *D*.III.76; *BTTA*.22; *BS1*.238–42; *BS2*.12; *EB*.1.9.

It is said that Gotama chose the time in human history in which to be reborn for the last time (*Ndk*.48–9), with the *Suttas* saying that he was 'mindful and fully aware' when he was conceived in his mother's womb (*M*.III.119 (*BW*.50–4)).

The early texts clearly see the conception and the other key events of Gotama's life, such as his birth, awakening, first sermon and death, as events of cosmic importance; for at all of them they say that light spread throughout the world and the earth shook. *Ndk*.50 relates that at the time of the conception, Mahāmāyā, his mother, dreamt that she was transported to the Himālayas where a being in the form of an auspicious white elephant entered her right side. On recounting this dream to her husband, Suddhodana (Skt Śuddhodana), he had it interpreted by sixty-four Brahmins. They explained that it indicated that his wife had conceived a son with a great destiny ahead of him. Either he would stay at home with his father and go on to become a *Cakkavattin* (Skt *Cakravartin*), a compassionate Universal Emperor – which the *Suttas* say that he had been in many previous lives (*A*.IV.89) – or he would leave home and become a great religious teacher, a Buddha.

This paralleling of a *Cakkavattin*[7] and a Buddha is also made in relation to other events of Gotama's life, and indicates the idea of a Buddha having universal spiritual 'sovereignty' – i.e. influence – over humans and gods. It also indicates that Gotama renounced the option of political power in becoming a Buddha. He certainly had no political pretensions, as Muhammad had, and was not seen as a political threat by the rulers of his day, as was Jesus. He did, however, teach kings and give teachings on how best to govern a realm.

Ndk.52–3 relates that, near the end of her pregnancy, Mahāmāyā journeyed from Kapilavatthu to the home of her relatives to give birth, as was the custom. On the way, she and her party passed the pleasant Lumbinī grove, where she stopped to enjoy the flowers and birdsong. Here she went into labour and, holding on to a Sāl tree, gave birth standing up. The birth of Gotama under a tree fits the pattern of the other key events in his life: attaining awakening under another tree, giving his first sermon in an animal (perhaps deer) park, and dying between two trees. This suggests his liking for simple natural environments where he could be in harmony with all forms of life. The *Sutta* accounts say that the baby was set down on the ground by four gods, and that a warm and cool stream of water appeared

[7] For example at *D*.II.142, 169–99 (*SB*.98–115), III.142–79; *A*.I.109–10 (*BW*.115–16); Harvey, 2007d: 153a–155a.

from the sky as a water-libation for mother and child. He immediately stood, walked seven paces, scanned in all directions, and said in a noble voice that he was the foremost being in the world, and that this would be his last rebirth (*M*.III.123).

As his mother had died a week after giving birth (*M*.III.122), Gotama was brought up by his father's second wife, Mahāmāya's sister, Mahāpajāpatī (Skt Mahāprajāpatī). The *Suttas* say little on his early life, except that it was one of lily pools, fine clothes and fragrances, with female musicians as attendants in his three mansions (*A*.I.145). The later biographies portray him as having been an eager, intelligent and compassionate youth. They relate that his father was keen that he should stay at home to become a great king, and so surrounded him with luxuries to ensure that he remained attached to the worldly life. At sixteen, he was married, and at twenty-nine had a son named Rāhula. In Theravāda texts, his wife is generally called 'Mother of Rāhula' (Rāhula-mātā, *Ndk*.58), but other names used in these and other texts are Bhaddakaccā, Bimbā-devī, Yaśodharā and Gopā.[8]

The renunciation and quest for awakening

It was from a pleasant and wealthy background, then, that Gotama renounced the worldly life and set out on his religious quest. The lead-up to this crucial transition is described in different ways in the early and later texts. The *Suttas* portray it as the result of a long consideration. Even from his sheltered existence, he became aware of the facts of ageing, sickness and death. Realizing that even he was not immune from these, the 'vanities' of youth, health and life left him (*A*.I.145–6). He therefore set out to find the 'unborn, unageing, undecaying, deathless, sorrowless, undefiled, uttermost security from bondage – *Nirvāṇa*' (*M*.I.163). He realized, though, that:

> Household life is crowded and dusty; going forth [into the life of a wandering *Samaṇa*] is wide open. It is not easy, living life in a household, to lead a holy-life as utterly perfect as a polished shell. Suppose I were to shave off my hair and beard, put on saffron garments, and go forth from home into homelessness? (*M*.I.240)

The later texts say that the transition occurred at the age of twenty-nine, just after the birth of his son (*Ndk*.61–3),[9] portraying it as arising from a sudden realization rather than from a gradual reflection. In this, they follow

[8] Harvey, 2007d: 117a–121a; for a nineteenth-century Thai text 'Bimbā's Lament', see *BP*.43.

[9] Though the Sarvāstivāda tradition (*EB*.I.3) has Rāhula being conceived on the night of the renunciation, thus ensuring Gotama's family line is continued.

the model of a *Sutta* story of a previous Buddha (*D*.II.22–9), which sees the lives of all Buddhas as following a recurring pattern (*dhammatā*). *Ndk*.58–9 relates that, on three consecutive days, Gotama visited one of his parks in his chariot. His father had had the streets cleared of unpleasant sights, but the gods ensured that he saw an age-worn man, a sick man and a corpse. He was amazed at these new sights, and his charioteer explained to him that ageing, sickness and death came to all people, thus putting him in a state of agitation at the nature of life. In this way, the texts portray an example of the human confrontation with frailty and mortality; for while these facts are 'known' to us all, a clear realization and acceptance of them often does come as a novel and disturbing insight. On a fourth trip to his park, Gotama saw a saffron-robed *Samaṇa* with a shaven head and a calm demeanour, the sight of whom inspired him to adopt such a life-style. That night, he left his palace, taking a long last look at his son, who lay in his sleeping wife's arms, knowing it would be difficult for him to leave if she awoke. His renunciation of family life stands as a symbolic precedent for the monastic life of Buddhist monks and nuns.

The Buddhist tradition sees his leaving of his family as done for the benefit of all beings; moreover, after he became a Buddha, he is said to have returned to his home town and taught his family, with his son ordaining under him as a novice monk, and his father becoming a 'non-returner' (*Ndk*.91–2): one with liberating insight just less than that of the *Arahat* (Skt *Arhat*; see p. 86). After his father's death, his stepmother, Mahāpajāpatī becomes a nun who goes on to become an *Arahat*, and whose death is compared to that of the Buddha (*BP*.9). It is also said in the Theravāda commentaries that his ex-wife ordained as a nun (*Jat*.II.392–3), and she may be identical with the nun known as Bhaddakaccānā, seen as the nun who was pre-eminent in 'higher knowledges' (such as memory of past lives; *A*.I.25).

The *Suttas* say that Gotama sought out teachers from whom he could learn spiritual techniques, going first to Āḷāra Kālāma (Skt Arāḍa Kālāma).[10] Gotama soon mastered his teachings and then enquired after the meditational state on which they were based. This was the 'sphere of nothingness', a mystical trance probably attained by yogic concentration, in which the mind goes beyond any apparent object and dwells on the remaining 'nothingness'. After Gotama quickly learnt to enter this state, Āḷāra offered him joint leadership of his group of disciples, but he turned down the offer

[10] *M*.I.160–75 (*BW*.54–9, 69–75; *BS*2.14); see also M.II.91–7 (*SB*.173–94).

as he felt that, while he had attained a refined inner calmness, he had not yet attained awakening and the end of suffering.

He then went to another yoga teacher, Uddaka Rāmaputta (Skt Udraka Rāmaputra), and again quickly grasped his doctrine and entered the meditational state on which it was based, the 'sphere of neither-perception-nor-non-perception'. This went beyond the previous state to a level of mental stilling where consciousness is so attenuated as to hardly exist. In response, Uddaka acknowledged him as even his own teacher, for only his dead father, Rāma, had previously attained this state. Again Gotama passed up a chance of leadership and influence on the grounds that he had not yet reached his goal. Nevertheless, he later incorporated both the mystical states he had attained into his own meditational system, as possible ways to calm and purify the mind in preparation for developing liberating insight. He in fact taught a great variety of meditational methods, adapting some from the existing yogic tradition, and can be seen as having been one of India's greatest practitioners of meditation.

After having experimented with one of the methods of religious practice current in his day, Gotama went on to try another: ascetic self-mortification. The *Suttas* tell that he settled in a woodland grove at Uruvelā (Skt Uruvilvā) and resolved to strive earnestly to overcome attachment to sensual pleasures by intense effort, trying to dominate such tendencies by force of will (*M*.I.240–6). He practised non-breathing meditations, though they produced fierce headaches, stomach pains, and burning heat all over his body. He reduced his food intake to a few drops of bean soup a day, till he became so emaciated that he could hardly stand and his body hair fell out. At this point, he felt that it was not possible for anyone to go further on the path of asceticism and still live. Nevertheless, though he had developed clarity of mind and energy, his body and mind were pained and untranquil, so that he could not carry on with his quest. He therefore abandoned his practice of harsh asceticism, which the later texts (*Ndk*.67) say lasted for six years.

At this point, he might have abandoned his quest as hopeless, but he thought 'might there be another path to awakening?' (*M*.I.246). He then remembered a meditative state that he had once spontaneously entered, sitting at the foot of a tree while his father was working (the commentary says: ceremonially ploughing). He recollected that this state, known as the 'first *jhāna*' (Skt *dhyāna*), was beyond involvement in sense-pleasures, which he had been attempting to conquer by painful asceticism, but was accompanied by deep calm, blissful joy and tranquil happiness. He remembered having wondered whether it was a path to awakening, and as he now saw that it was, he resolved to use it. The above sequence, of course, implies that the two mystical states he had earlier attained were not entered via the *jhānas*, although this became the route to them in the Buddhist meditative system, where they are the top two of four 'formless' (*arūpa*) attainments.

When Gotama took sustaining food to prepare himself for attaining *jhāna*, his five companions in asceticism shunned him in disgust, seeing him as having abandoned their shared quest and taken to luxurious living. One *Sutta* (*Sn*.425–49) outlines a temptation sequence which the later texts (*Ndk*.72–4) put at this juncture. It refers to a Satan-like figure known as Māra, a deity who has won his place by previous good works, but who uses his power to entrap people in sensual desire and attachment, so as to stay within his realm of influence (Ling, 1962). This is the round of rebirth and repeated death, so that Māra is seen as the embodiment of both sense-desire and death. Māra came to the emaciated ascetic with honeyed words. He urged him to abandon his quest and take up a more conventional religious life of sacrifice and good works, so as to generate good karma. In response, Gotama replied that he had no need of more good karma, and scorned the 'squadrons' of Māra: sense-desire, jealousy, hunger and thirst, craving, dullness and lethargy, cowardice, fear of commitment, belittling others, obstinate insensitivity and self-praise. Māra then retreated in defeat.

This account, clearly portraying the final inner struggle of Gotama, gains dramatic colour in the later texts, where Māra's 'army' of spiritual faults bore witness to the fact that he had done many charitable acts in previous lives. Taunting Gotama that he had no-one to bear witness to *his* good deeds, Māra tried to use the power derived from his own good karma to throw Gotama off the spot where he was sitting. Gotama did not move, however, but meditated on the spiritual perfections that he had developed over many previous lives, knowing that he had a right to the spot where he sat. He then touched the earth for it to bear witness to the good karma he had generated in past lives. The earth quaked, and the earth goddess appeared, wringing from her hair a flood of water, accumulated in the past when Gotama had formalized good deeds by a simple ritual of water-pouring (Strong, 2001: 72). At the quaking and flood, Māra and his army fled. This 'conquest of Māra' is commemorated as a victory over evil by countless images and paintings. These show Gotama, as in Plate 1, seated cross-legged in meditation with his right hand touching the earth: the 'conquest of Māra' (Pali *māra-vijaya*) or 'earth-witness' (Skt *bhūmi-sparśa*) gesture.

The idea of the earth goddess acting as witness to Gotama's perfections is suggestive of the spiritual need to be mindfully 'earthed'. Indeed in his

Plate 1: A nineteenth-century Burmese image, showing Gotama at his 'conquest of Māra', just prior to his awakening.

spiritual quest, it is notable that Gotama turned to a path of *mindful awareness of the body*, especially breathing, to induce joyful *jhāna*, rather than *not attending to* the physical in formless states or trying to *forcefully repress* the body and its needs in the painful ascetic way.

The awakening and after

Free of spiritual hindrances, Gotama then developed deep meditations as a prelude to his awakening, seated under a species of tree which later became known as the *Bodhi*, or 'Awakening' tree. The *Sutta* account (*M*.I.247–9 (*BW*.64–7)) describes how he entered the first *jhāna*, and then gradually deepened his state of concentrated calm till he reached the fourth *jhāna*, a state of great equanimity, mental brightness and purity. Based on this state, he went on to develop, in the course of the three watches of the moonlit night, the 'threefold knowledge': memory of many of his countless previous lives, seeing the rebirth of others according to their karma, and knowing the destruction of the *āsavas* (Skt *āśravas*) – spiritual 'taints' or 'cankers' which fester in the mind and keep it unawakened. The third knowledge, completed at dawn, brought the perfect awakening he had been seeking, so that he was now, at the age of thirty-five, a Buddha, with joyful direct experience of the unconditioned *Nirvāṇa*, beyond ageing, sickness and death.

The Canonical account (*Vin*.I.1–8; *M*.I.167–70) then says that the new Buddha stayed under or near the *Bodhi*-tree for four or more weeks, at the place now called Bodh-Gayā. After meditatively reflecting on his awakening, he pondered the possibility of teaching others, but thought that the *Dhamma* he had experienced was so profound, subtle and 'beyond the sphere of reason', that others would be too subject to attachment to be able to understand it. At this, the compassionate god Brahmā Sahampati – whom the Buddhist tradition saw as a long-lived 'non-returner' who had been taught by a previous Buddha (*S*.V.232–3; *Sn-a*.476) – became alarmed at the thought that a fully awakened person had arisen in the world, but that he might not share his rare and precious wisdom with others. He therefore appeared before the Buddha and respectfully asked him to teach, for 'there are beings with little dust in their eyes who, not hearing the *Dhamma*, are decaying'. The Buddha then used his mind-reading powers to survey the world and determine that some people were spiritually mature enough to understand his message, and so decided to teach. The entreaty of the compassionate Brahmā is seen by Buddhists as the stimulus for the unfolding of the Buddha's compassion, the necessary complement to his awakened wisdom for his role as a perfect Buddha, a 'teacher of gods and humans'. The words attributed to Sahampati are now used as a Theravāda chant to formally request a monk to teach.

Gotama wished to teach his two yoga teachers first of all, but gods informed him that they were now dead, a fact which he then confirmed by his meditative awareness. He therefore decided to teach his former companions in asceticism. Intuiting that they were currently in the animal park at Isipatana (Skt Ṛṣipatana; now called Sārnāth) near Varanasi (Benares), he set out to walk there, a journey of about one hundred miles.

The first sermon and the spread of the teachings

The Canonical account (*Vin*.I.8–21) relates that, on arriving at the animal park, his five former companions saw him in the distance, and resolved to snub him as a spiritual failure. As he approached, however, they saw that a great change had come over him and, in spite of themselves, respectfully greeted him and washed his feet. At first they addressed him as an equal, but the Buddha insisted that he was a *Tathāgata*, a 'Thus-gone' or 'One-attuned-to-reality' (cf. *A*.II.23–4 (*BW*.421–3)), who had found the Deathless and could therefore be their teacher. After he twice repeated his affirmation, to overcome their hesitation, the ascetics acknowledged that he had a new-found assurance and were willing to be taught by him.

Gotama, usually referred to as the 'Lord' or 'Blessed One' (*Bhagavat*) in the *Sutta*s, then gave his first sermon. This commenced with the idea that there is a 'middle way' for those who have gone forth from the home life, a way which avoids both the extremes of devotion to mere sense-pleasures and devotion to ascetic self-torment. Gotama had himself previously experienced both of these spiritual dead-ends. The middle way which he had found to lead to awakening was the *Ariya* (Skt *Ārya*), or Noble, Eight-factored Path (*Magga*, Skt *Mārga*). He then continued with the kernel of his message, on the four True Realities for the Spiritually Ennobled (generally translated as 'Noble Truths'), which are four crucial dimensions of existence: the painful aspects of life; craving as the key cause of rebirth and these associated mental and physical pains; the cessation of these from the cessation of craving; and the way of practice leading to this cessation, the Noble Eight-factored Path. He then emphasized the liberating effect on him of his full insight into and appropriate responses to these realities, such that he was now a Buddha.

As a result of this instruction, one member of Gotama's audience, Koṇḍañña (Skt Kauṇḍinya), gained experiential insight into the four True Realities, so that Gotama joyfully affirmed his understanding. This insight is described as the gaining of the stainless '*Dhamma*-eye', by which Koṇḍañña 'sees', 'attains' and 'plunges into' the *Dhamma*, free from all doubt in the Buddha's teachings. This is a person's first spiritual breakthrough, involving the first glimpse of *Nirvāṇa*. In most cases, as with Koṇḍañña, it makes a person a 'stream-enterer': one who has entered the path that will ensure the full attainment of *Nirvāṇa* within seven lives at most. Koṇḍañña's gaining of the *Dhamma*-eye is clearly seen as the climax of the first sermon, for as soon as it occurs, the exultant message is rapidly transmitted up through various levels of gods that 'the supreme *Dhamma*-wheel' had been set in motion by the 'Blessed One', and could not be stopped by any power: an era of the spiritual influence of the *Dhamma* had begun. The 'Setting in motion of the *Dhamma*-wheel' (*Dhamma-cakka-ppavattana*, Skt *Dharma-cakra-pravartana*) thus became the title of the *Sutta* of the first sermon (*S*.V.420–4).

After Koṇḍañña was ordained, thus becoming the first member of the monastic *Saṅgha*, the Buddha gave more extensive explanations of his teachings to the other four ascetics, so that, one by one, they attained the *Dhamma*-eye and were then ordained. Later the Buddha gave his 'second' sermon (see p. 58), at which his disciples all attained the full experience of *Nirvāṇa* – as he himself had done at his awakening – so as to become *Arahats*.

Other disciples, monastic and lay, followed, so that soon there were sixty-one *Arahats*, including the Buddha. Having such a body of awakened monk-disciples, the Buddha sent them out on a mission to spread the *Dhamma*: 'Walk, monks, on tour for the blessing of the manyfolk, for the happiness of the manyfolk, out of compassion for the world, for the welfare, the blessing, the happiness of gods and humans' (*Vin*.I.21 (*BTTA*.7)). As the teaching spread, Gotama in time gained his two chief disciples: Sāriputta, famed for his wisdom and ability to teach, and Moggallāna, famed for his psychic powers developed by meditation.[11] At some point during his life, Gotama initiated an order of nuns (see pp. 298–9), this being said to be in response to the repeated requests of his stepmother Mahāpajāpatī, and the suggestion of his faithful attendant monk Ānanda (*Vin*.II.253–83 (*BTTA*.3)).

The Canon gives only incidental reference to events between the sending out of the sixty *Arahats* and the last year of the Buddha's life. The general picture conveyed is that he spent his long teaching career wandering on foot, with few possessions, around the Ganges basin region. Though he was of a contemplative nature, loving the solitude of natural surroundings, he was generally accompanied by many disciples and spent much of his time in or near the new towns and cities, especially Sāvatthī, Rājagaha and Vesālī (Skt Śrāvastī, Rājagṛha, Vāiśalī). Here, there were many people of a questioning nature looking for a new spiritual outlook. The commentary to the *Thera-gāthā* and *Therī-gāthā* describes the background of 328 monks

[11] For stories of his converting some key disciples, see *BTTA*.1; *EB*.2.1.1/3/5/6.

and nuns (Gombrich, 2006: 56; Gokhale, 1994: 61) and indicates that over two-thirds came from urban areas. It also indicates that, as to their social backgrounds, 41 per cent were Brahmin, 23 per cent *Kṣatriya*, 30 per cent *Vaiśya*, 3 per cent *Śūdra*, and 3 per cent 'outcaste' (below the *Śūdra*s in the Brahmanical hierarchy). Of these, the Brahmins do not generally appear to have been traditional village priests, but urban dwellers perhaps employed as state officials. State officials and merchants were the dominant groups in urban society, but neither had an established niche in the *varṇa* system (though merchants later came to be seen as *Vaiśya*s). These groups, whose achievements depended on personal effort, seem to have been particularly attracted to the Buddha's message, which addressed people as individuals in charge of their own moral and spiritual destiny, rather than as members of the *varṇa* system (Gombrich 2006: 79–83); respect should be based on moral and spiritual worth, not birth: it had to be earned (*Sn*.136). The Buddha taught all who came to him without distinction: men, women, rich merchants, servants, Brahmins, craftsmen, ascetics, kings and courtesans, and made a point of insisting that social background was irrelevant to the position of individuals within the *Saṅgha* (*A*.IV.202). He also urged his disciples to teach in the local languages or dialects of their hearers (*Vin*. II.139). In contrast, the Brahmins taught in Sanskrit, which had by now become unintelligible to those who had not studied it, and only made the Vedic teachings available to males of the top three *varṇa*s.

The Buddha's charisma and powers

The early texts portray the Buddha as a charismatic, humanitarian teacher who inspired many people. He even elicited a response from animals: for it is said that an elephant once looked after him by bringing him water when he was spending a period alone in the forest (*Vin*.I.352). A person who bore enmity towards him, however, was his cousin Devadatta, one of his monks. Jealous of his influence, Devadatta once suggested that the ageing Buddha should let him lead the *Saṅgha*, and then plotted to kill him when the request was turned down (*Vin*.II.191–5). In one attempt on his life, Devadatta asked his friend, Prince Ajātasattu (Skt Ajātaśatru), to send soldiers to waylay and assassinate the Buddha. Sixteen soldiers in turn went to do this, but all were too afraid to do so, and became the Buddha's disciples instead. In another attempt, the fierce man-killing elephant Nālāgiri was let loose on the road on which the Buddha was travelling. As the elephant charged, the Buddha calmly stood his ground and suffused the elephant with the power of his lovingkindness, so that it stopped and bowed its head, letting the Buddha stroke and tame it.

In gaining hearers for his message, the Buddha did not always rely on his charisma, reputation and powers of persuasion. Occasionally he had recourse to his psychic powers, though he forbade the mere display of these by his disciples (*Vin.*II.112). The results of such powers are not seen as supernatural miracles, but as the supernormal products of the great inner power of certain meditations. A late Canonical passage (*Patis.*I.125) describes his 'marvel of the pairs', which later legendary material ascribes to the Buddha while staying at Sāvatthī (*Dhp*-a.III.204–16): he rose into the air and produced both fire and water from different parts of his body. Occasionally, he used his powers to heal one of his devout supporters physically, such as bringing a long and very painful childbirth to an end (*Ud.*15–16), or curing a wound without leaving even a scar (*Vin.*I.216–18). The Buddha generally regarded psychic powers as dangerous, however, as they could encourage attachment and self-glorification. In a strange parallel to the temptation of Jesus in the desert, it is said that he rebuffed Māra's temptation to turn the Himālayas into gold (*S.*I.116).

The passing away of the Buddha

The *Mahāparinibbāna Sutta*[12] deals with the last year of the Buddha's life. During this period, he suffered an illness, and Ānanda asked about the fate of the *Saṅgha* after his death, clearly wondering who would lead it. In reply, the Buddha said that he had taught the *Dhamma* without holding anything back, and that the *Saṅgha* depended on the *Dhamma*, not on any leader, even himself.[13] Members of the *Saṅgha* should look to their own self-reliant practice, with the clearly taught *Dhamma* as guide: with themselves and the *Dhamma* as 'island' and 'refuge' (*D.*II.100). Later the Buddha specified that, after his death, the *Saṅgha* should take both the *Dhamma* and monastic discipline (*Vinaya*) as their 'teacher' (*D.*II.154).

Though unwell for the last three months of his life, the Buddha continued to wander on foot, his journey ending in the small village of Kusinārā (Skt Kuśunagarī). When asked what his funeral arrangements should be, he said that this was the concern of the laity, not the *Saṅgha*, but that his body should be treated like that of a *Cakkavattin* emperor. It should be wrapped

[12] *D.*II.72–167 (*SB.*37–97); *EB.*1.7 is from a parallel Sanskrit text.

[13] Though several texts of north-west India came to talk of Mahākāśyapa (Pali Mahākassapa) as having been the Budda's successor (Ray, 1994: 105–18).

in cloth, placed in a coffin and cremated. The relics remaining should then be placed in a *Stūpa* (Pali *Thūpa*), or burial mound, at a place where four roads meet. He then said, 'When people place a garland, fragrance or paste there, or make respectful salutations, or bring peace to their hearts, that will contribute to their long-lasting welfare and happiness' (*D*.II.142). After his cremation, the Buddha's relics were placed in eight *Stūpas* (*EB*.1.1), with the bowl used to collect the relics and the ashes of the funeral fire in two more. Such *Stūpas*, which could alternatively contain relics of *Arahats*, later became the focus of much devotion.

Even on his death-bed, the Buddha continued to teach. A wanderer asked whether other *Samaṇa* leaders had attained true knowledge. Rather than say that their religious systems were wrong and his right, the Buddha simply indicated that the crucial ingredient of any such system was the Noble Eight-factored Path: only then could it lead to full Arahatship. He saw such a Path as absent from other teachings that he knew of.

Not long after this, the Buddha asked his monks if any had final questions that they wanted answering before he died. When they were silent, he sensitively said that, if they were silent simply out of reverence for him, they should have a friend ask their question. They remained silent. Seeing that they all had a good understanding of his teachings, he therefore gave his final words: 'It is the nature of conditioned things to decay, but if you are attentive, you will succeed!' (*D*.II.156). He then made his exit from the world, in the fearless, calm and self-controlled state of meditation. He passed into the first *jhāna*, and then by degrees through the three other *jhānas*, the four 'formless' mystical states, and then the 'cessation of perception and feeling' (see pp. 331–2). He then gradually descended back to the first *jhāna*, moved back up to the fourth *jhāna*, and passed away from there (*D*.II.156). Buddhists see this event not so much as a 'death' as a passing into the Deathless, *Nirvāṇa*.

THE NATURE AND ROLE OF THE BUDDHA

The *Suttas* contain some very 'human' information on the Buddha, such as getting backache after a long teaching session (*D*.III.209). In the *Mahāparinibbāna Sutta*, we find the eighty-year-old Buddha expressing 'weariness' at the prospect of being asked about the rebirth-destiny of *every* person who has died in a locality (*D*.II.93); saying he was old and worn out and only knowing comfort when in a deep meditation (*D*.II.100); in his final illness, being extremely thirsty, and insisting on immediately being given water (*D*.II.128–9). However, elsewhere in the same text the Buddha crosses the

Ganges by means of his psychic power (*D*.II.89); he says that, if he asked, he could have lived on 'for a *kappa*, or the remainder of one' (*D*.II.103), with *kappa* (Skt *kalpa*) generally meaning 'eon', but possibly here the maximum human life-span of around 100 years; when he lies down between two *Sāl* trees, where he will die, these burst into unseasonal blossom in homage to him, and divine music is heard in the sky (*D*.II.137–8); gods from ten regions of the universe assemble to witness the great event of a Buddha's passing into final *Nirvāṇa* at death (*parinibbāna*, Skt *parinirvāṇa*;[14] *D*.II.138–9); gods prevent his funeral pyre from igniting until the senior disciple Mahākassapa (Skt Mahākāśyapa) arrives at the site (*D*.II.163).

Thus, while modern Theravādins sometimes say that the Buddha was 'a human being, pure and simple' (Rahula, 1974: 1), such remarks have to be taken in context. They are usually intended to contrast the Buddha with Jesus, seen as the 'Son of God', and to counter the Mahāyāna view of the Buddha's nature, which sees it as far above the human. These remarks may also be due to a modernist, somewhat demythologized view of the Buddha. In the Pali Canon, Gotama was seen as *born* a human, though one with extraordinary abilities due to the perfections built up in his long *Bodhisatta* career. Once he had attained awakening, though, he could no longer be called a 'human', as he had perfected and transcended his humanness. This idea is reflected in a *Sutta* passage where the Buddha is asked whether he is (literally 'will be') a god (*deva*) or a human (*A*.II.37–9 (*BTTA*.105)). In reply, he said that he had gone beyond the deep-rooted unconscious traits that would make him a god or human, and was therefore to be seen as a *Buddha*, one who had grown up in the world but who had now gone beyond it, as a lotus grows from the water but blossoms above it, unsoiled.

The mysterious nature of a Buddha is indicated by the Buddha's chiding of a monk who had too much uncritical faith in him, so as to be always following him round: 'Hush, Vakkali! What is there for you in seeking this vile visible body? Vakkali, whoever sees *Dhamma*, sees me; whoever sees me, sees *Dhamma*' (*S*.III.120). This close link between the Buddha and *Dhamma* is reinforced by another *Sutta* passage, which says that a *Tathāgata* can be designated as 'one having *Dhamma* as body' (*Dhamma-kāya*; Harrison, 1992: 50) and who is '*Dhamma*-become' (*Dhamma-bhūta*; *D*.III.84). These terms indicate that a Buddha has fully exemplified the *Dhamma*, in the sense of the Path, in his personality or 'body'. Moreover, he

[14] The term *parinibbāna/parinirvāṇa* is sometimes also used for the attaining of *Nirvāṇa* in life (the verbal equivalent *parinibbāyati* is often used this way), but has more typically, and especially in modern usage, come to refer particularly to an *Arahat*'s or Buddha's attaining final *Nirvāṇa* at death.

has fully realized *Dhamma* in the supreme sense by his experience of *Nirvāṇa*, the equivalent of the supreme *Dhamma* (*A*.I.156 and 158). The *Arahat* is no different in these respects, for he is described as 'become the supreme' (*brahma-bhūta*, *S*.III.83), a term which is used as an equivalent to '*Dhamma*-become' in the above passage. Any awakened person is one who is 'deep, immeasurable, hard-to-fathom as is the great ocean' (*M*.I.487). Having 'become *Dhamma*', their awakened nature can only really be fathomed by one who has 'seen' *Dhamma* with the '*Dhamma*-eye' of stream-entry. While Christians see Jesus as God-become-human, then, Buddhists see the Buddha (and *Arahat*s) as human-become-*Dhamma*.

In the early Buddhist texts, the Buddha is himself said to be an *Arahat*, and to be in most respects like other *Arahat*s. Any *Arahat*'s experience of *Nirvāṇa* is the same; however, a perfect Buddha is seen as having more extensive knowledge than other *Arahat*s. While not omniscient in the sense of continuously and uninterruptedly knowing everything (*M*.II.126–7), it is said that he could remember as far back into his countless previous lives as he wished, and know how any being was reborn, in accordance with their karma (*M*.I.482). Other *Arahat*s had limitations on such powers, or may not even have developed them (*S*.II.122–3; *M*.I.477). A perfect Buddha is seen as one who can come to know anything knowable (*A*.II.25); he just needs to turn his mind to it (*Miln*.102, 106). What he teaches is just a small portion of his huge knowledge (*S*.V.438 (*BW*.360–1)), for he only teaches what is both true and spiritually useful (*M*.I.395; Harvey, 1995b).

A second key difference between a Buddha and an *Arahat* is that a Buddha is someone who, by his own efforts, rediscovers the Path after it has been lost to human society (*S*.II.105–7 (*BW*.69)). Having discovered it for himself, he skilfully makes it known to others so that they can fully practise it for themselves and so become *Arahat*s (*S*.III.64–5 (*BW*.413–14)). He is a rediscoverer and teacher of timeless realities (*A*.I.286–7). As founder of a monastic *Saṅgha*, and propounder of the rules of conduct binding on its members, a Buddha also fulfils a role akin to that of 'law-giver'.

THE NATURE AND STYLE OF THE BUDDHA'S TEACHING

The Buddha's style of teaching was generally one of skilful adaptation to the mood and concerns of his hearers, responding to the questions and even the non-verbalized thoughts of his audience and taking cues from events (Gombrich, 2009: 161–79). By means of a dialogue with his questioners, he gradually moved them towards sharing something of his own insight into reality. When Brahmins asked him about how to attain union with the god

Brahmā after death, he said this could be attained by meditative development of deep lovingkindness and compassion, rather than by bloody Vedic sacrifices (*D*.I.235–52). He often gave old terms new meanings, for example talking of the *Arahat* as the 'true Brahmin' (*Dhp*.383–423), and using the term *ariya*, equivalent to the Sanskrit term for the 'noble' Aryan people, in the sense of spiritually noble or ennobled.

The Buddha treated questions in a careful, analytic way. Some he answered directly, others he answered after first analysing them so as to clarify the nature of the question. Some he answered with a counter-question, to reveal concealed motives and presuppositions; others again he 'set aside' as question-begging and fraught with misconceptions (*A*.II.46). He did not mind if others disagreed with him, but censured misinterpretations of what he taught. He showed even-mindedness when gaining disciples. A general, Sīha (Skt Siṃha), who was a great supporter of Jain monks, once decided to become a lay disciple, but the Buddha advised him that such a prominent person as himself should carefully consider before changing his religious allegiances (*Vin*.I.236 (*BTTA*.2)). When he still wished to do so, and wanted to support *Buddhist* monks, the Buddha advised him that he should still support Jain monks, too.

The Buddha emphasized that one should not mistake belief for knowledge,[15] and the importance of self-reliance and the experiential testing-out of all teachings, including his own (*M*.I.317–20 (*BW*.93–6)). Only occasionally, for example before his first sermon, did he use his authority, but this was not to force people to agree with him, but to get them to listen so that they could then gain understanding. He also advised his disciples not to react emotionally when they heard people speaking in blame or praise of him, but to assess calmly the degree to which what was said was true or false (*D*.I.3). He was well aware of the many conflicting doctrines of his day, a time of intellectual ferment. Rejecting teachings based on authoritative tradition, or mere rational speculation, he emphasized the examination and analysis of actual experience. When he spoke to the confused Kālāma people,[16] after many teachers had visited them praising their own teachings and disparaging those of others, he said:

> you should not go along with something because of what you have been told, because of authority, because of tradition, because of accordance with a transmitted text, on the grounds of reason, on the grounds of logic, because of analytic thought, because of abstract theoretic pondering, because of the appearance of the speaker,

[15] *M*.II.168–77 (*BW*.96–103; Harvey 2009b: 179–81).

[16] *Kālāma Sutta*, *A*.I.188–93 (*BW*.88–9; *SB*.251–6; Harvey 2009b: 176–8).

or because some ascetic is your teacher. When you know for yourselves that particular qualities are unwholesome, blameworthy, censured by the wise, and lead to harm and suffering when taken on and pursued, then you should give them up. (*A*.I.189 (*SB*.252))

Accordingly, they should see that greed, hatred and delusion (lack of mental clarity), which lead to behaviour that harms others, are to be avoided, and non-greed (generosity and renunciation), non-hatred (lovingkindness and compassion) and non-delusion (clarity of mind and wisdom) are to be engaged in. By implication, teachings which discourage the former and encourage the latter are worth following.

The Buddha emphasized that his teachings had a practical purpose, and should not be blindly clung to. He likened the *Dhamma* to a raft made by a man seeking to cross from the dangerous hither shore of a river, representing the conditioned world, to the peaceful further shore, representing *Nirvāṇa* (*M*.I.134–5 (*BTTA*.77; *SB*.160–1)). He then rhetorically asked whether such a man, on reaching the other shore, should lift up the raft and carry it around with him there. He therefore said, '*Dhamma* is for crossing over, not for retaining'. That is, a follower should not grasp at Buddhist ideas and practices, but *use* them for their intended purpose, and should know that a person who has accomplished their goal does not carry them as an identity to defend. Many ordinary Buddhists, though, do have a strong attachment to Buddhism.

While the Buddha was critical of blind faith, he did not deny a role for soundly based faith or 'trustful confidence' (*saddhā*, Skt *śraddhā*); for to test out his teachings, a person has to have at least some initial trust in them. The early texts envisage a process of listening, which arouses *saddhā*, leading to practice, and thus to partial confirmation of the teachings, and thus to deeper *saddhā* and deeper practice until the heart of the teachings is directly experienced (*M*.II.171–6). A person then becomes an *Arahat*, one whose confidence is rooted in insight. Even in Theravāda Buddhism, which often has a rather rational, unemotional image, a very deep faith in the Buddha, *Dhamma* and *Saṅgha* is common. Ideally, this is based on the fact that some part of the Buddha's path has been found to be uplifting, thus inspiring confidence in the rest. Many people, though, simply have a calm and joyful faith (*pasāda*, Skt *prasāda*) inspired by the example of those who are well established on the Path.

CHAPTER 2

Early Buddhist Teachings: Rebirth and Karma

In this and the following chapter, the central doctrines of early Buddhism, as presented primarily in the Pali Canon, will be outlined, along with some of their later applications. While the Mahāyāna developed a new orientation towards some of these early teachings, and new doctrines of its own, such developments can only be understood against the background of these teachings. In the Theravāda, they have remained the guiding framework for all new developments.

In a sense, Buddhism begins and ends with the Buddha's awakening experience, for this is the ultimate source of Buddhist teachings, and these are a guide towards moral and spiritual development culminating in an experience of a like nature. At his awakening, the Buddha gained direct knowledge of rebirth, karma and the four 'True Realities for the Spiritually Ennobled'. All of the central teachings of early Buddhism can be arranged under one or other of these three heads.

REBIRTH AND COSMOLOGY

One word used to refer to the cycle of rebirths is *saṃsāra*, 'wandering on', which indicates that the process is seen as long and often aimless. It is not just said that we have had 'many' past lives, but that we have had *innumerable* ones. On the night of his awakening, the Buddha is said to have remembered more than a hundred thousand (*M*.I.22). The Buddhist view, in fact, is that there is no known beginning to the cycle of rebirths and the world: 'Inconceivable is any beginning of this *saṃsāra*; an earliest point is not discerned of beings who, obstructed by spiritual ignorance and fettered by craving, run and wander on' (*S*.II.178 (*BW*.37–40)). However far back in time one goes, there must have been prior causes for whatever beings existed at that time. Hence, it should not be said that the Buddha remembered 'all' his past lives.

The earliest the Buddha is specifically said to have remembered is ninety-one 'eons' ago (*M.*I.483). An 'eon' (*kappa*, Skt *kalpa*) is a vast unit of time used for measuring the coming and going of world-systems. The physical universe is said to consist of countless world-systems spread out through space, each seen as having a central mountain (Meru) surrounded by four continents and smaller islands, which came to be seen as all on a flat disc (e.g. *Vism.*205–6). They also exist in thousandfold clusters, galactic groupings of these clusters, and super-galactic groupings of these galaxies (*A.*I.227). Within this vast universe, with no known limit, are other inhabited worlds where beings also go through the cycle of rebirths. Just as beings go through a series of lives, so do world-systems: they develop, remain for a period, come to an end and are absent, then are followed by another. Each phase takes an 'incalculable' eon, and the whole cycle takes a 'great' eon (Harvey, 2007d: 161a–165a). The huge magnitude of this period is indicated by various suggestive images. For example, if there were a seven-mile-high mountain of solid granite, and once a century it was stroked with a piece of fine cloth, it would be worn away before a great eon would pass (*S.*II.181–2). Nevertheless, more eons have passed than there are grains of sand on the banks of the river Ganges (*S.*II.183–4)!

The cycle of rebirths – of *puna-bbhava*, or re-becoming – is thus seen as involving innumerable lives over vast stretches of time. If the cycle only involved human rebirths, it would be hard for a Buddhist to explain the human population explosion. As it is, though, the cycle is seen to involve many other forms of life, such as animals, so that readjustment between populations is quite feasible. This then introduces the idea of different realms of rebirth (*BS*2.1; *EB*.I.5.2).

The first two of these realms are those of humans and the animal kingdom. The latter includes sentient creatures as simple as insects. Plants are not included, though they are seen as having a very rudimentary consciousness, in the form of sensitivity to touch (*Vin.*I.155–6). There are also realms of beings who are not (normally) visible. One of these is the realm of *petas* (Skt *preta*), the 'departed' (*BS*2.4). As these are seen as having bodies made of only 'subtle' matter, such a rebirth does not involve 're-incarnation', that is, getting a gross physical body again. *Petas* are seen as frustrated ghostly beings who inhabit the fringes of the human world due to their strong earthly attachments, not unlike the ghosts of Western literature. One type of *peta*, generally known as a 'hungry ghost', is portrayed as having a huge stomach, racked by hunger, and a tiny neck that allows little sustenance to pass.

The worst realm is the hell realm (*niraya*), comprising a number of hellish rebirths (*BS1*.224–6). These are described as involving experiences of being burnt up, cut up, frozen or eaten alive, yet being revived to re-experience these (e.g. *M.*III.183). They are, then, realms in which a tortured consciousness experiences abominable nightmares, where every object of the senses appears repulsive and ugly (*S.*IV.126). Some hells are worse than others, but all are seen as appropriate to the evil deeds which led to them. While life in the hells is measured in millions of years, *no* rebirth is eternal, so a being from hell will in time reach the human level again.

The animal, *peta* and hell realms are the lower rebirths, where beings suffer more than human beings. The higher, more fortunate realms of rebirth are those of humans and *devas*, 'illustrious ones' or gods. Together these make up the five realms. Sometimes this becomes six, by dividing the gods into two types: gods proper and *asuras*, or 'titans', seen as proud, fierce, power-hungry divine beings (counted among the lower rebirths). Gods proper are said to live in twenty-six heavens, which are grouped according to a threefold classification of rebirths. The lowest of these is the 'realm of sense-desire' (*kāma-dhātu*), which encompasses all the rebirths mentioned so far, including the six lowest heavens. In all of these realms, beings perceive sensory objects in such a way as to particularly notice their qualities of desirability or undesirability. More subtle than and 'above' the realm of sense-desire is the 'realm of (pure, elemental) form' (*rūpa-dhātu*). Here dwell more refined gods, who are known in general as *brahmās*, in contrast to the *devas* proper of the six lower heavens. In the realm of form there are said to be sixteen heavens of a progressively refined and calm nature. Beings at this level of existence are aware of objects in a pure way devoid of sensuous desire, and are without the senses of touch, taste and smell. They suffer from other attachments and limitations, however. More refined than the form realm is the 'formless realm' (*arūpa-dhātu*, Skt *ārūpya-dhātu*), which is comprised of the four most refined types of rebirth. They are purely mental 'spheres' (*āyatana*) completely devoid of anything having even subtle shape or form. They are named after the characteristic states of consciousness of the *brahmās* reborn 'there'. In the first, they have the experience of 'infinite space'; in the second they dwell on the 'infinite consciousness' which can contemplate infinite space; in the third, they experience the apparent 'nothingness' of their level of existence; in the last, their resting state of consciousness is so subtle that their sphere is that of 'neither-perception-nor-non-perception'. This last rebirth, the 'summit of existence', constitutes the highest and most subtle form of life in the cosmos, with a huge life-span of 84,000 eons; and yet even this eventually ends in death. Under the teacher Uddaka Rāmaputta, Gotama is said to have attained a meditation which would have led to rebirth in this realm, but rejected it as falling short of his goal (see p. 19). All these rebirth realms parallel the kinds of human mental states and actions that are seen to lead to them; hence Buddhism has a kind of 'psycho-cosmology' (Gethin, 1997, and 1998: 112–32).

Among the six sense-desire heavens are several significant ones. The second heaven up is that of the Tāvatiṃsa (Skt Trāyastriṃśa) gods, the 'thirty-three' gods of the pre-Buddhist Vedic pantheon. The chief Vedic god, Indra, often known as Sakka (Skt Śakra) in Buddhist texts, is said to have become a 'stream-enterer' and thus a protector of Buddhism (*D*.II.288). The fourth heaven is that of the Tusita (Skt Tuṣita; 'Contented') gods, being the realm in which *Bodhisattas* spend their penultimate life, and in which Metteyya (Skt Maitreya), set to be the next Buddha, now dwells. On the fringes of the sixth heaven dwells the tempter Māra (*M-a*.I.33–4). The structure of things is such that there will nearly always be a Māra in a world-system, but the particular incumbents of this kind of cosmic position are born and die, as in the case of all other gods (Ling, 1962). They can perhaps be likened to particular people who hold an office such as that of mayor. As a Māra dwells in a heaven, he has good karma behind him, but like the 'Satan' of Christianity, who is seen as a fallen angel, his previous goodness has gone awry. Like a charismatic but ego-driven cult-leader, he uses his powers to try to manipulate other beings to be under his sway, rather than to help them.

The top five form heavens are known as the 'pure abodes' (*suddhāvāsa*, Skt *śuddhāvāsa*), and are only attainable by persons, known as non-returners, who are almost *Arahats*. The remaining eleven form heavens parallel the four meditative *jhānas*, and are reached by people who have mastered such a state during life, which 'tunes' their minds into a certain level of existence. Of the beings of these heavens, perhaps the most significant is Great Brahmā, who dwells in the upper heaven of the first *jhāna*, whose sphere of influence takes in one thousand 'world-systems' (*D*. II.261), and whose life-span is one great eon. In the bottom two form heavens dwell the ministers and retinue of Great Brahmā.

The essential details of the levels of rebirth are as follows, with the figures in brackets being the length of life in them:[1]

Formless realm. Four types of purely mental rebirths, the spheres of:

- Neither-perception-nor-non-perception (84,000 eons), Nothingness (60,000 eons), Infinite Consciousness (40,000 eons), Infinite Space (20,000 eons).

[1] *Vibh*.422–6; *A*.II.128–9 (*BW*.216–18); Gethin, 1998: 112–19.

Form realm. Heavens paralleling the:

- Fourth *jhāna*: the five pure abodes (16, 8, 4, 2, 1 thousand eons), Unconscious Beings (500 eons), heaven of Great Reward (500 eons).
- Third *jhāna*: heavens of Complete Beauty (64 eons), Boundless Beauty (32 eons), Limited Beauty (16 eons).
- Second *jhāna*: heavens of Streaming Radiance (8 eons), Boundless Radiance (4 eons), Limited Radiance (2 eons).
- First *jhāna*: heavens of Great Brahmā (1 eon), Brahmā's Ministers (half an eon), Brahmā's Retinue (one-third of an eon).

Sense-desire realm:

- The six *deva* heavens, of: Masters of the Creations of Others (16,000 divine years (d.y.)), Those Who Delight in Creating (enjoyable objects) (8,000 d.y.), The Contented (4,000 d.y.), The Yāma Gods (2,000 d.y.), The Thirty-three Gods (1,000 d.y.), The Gods of the Four Kings (500 d.y.).
- Human beings.
- Bad rebirth realms: *asuras*, hungry ghosts, animals, hell-beings (life-spans unspecified).

It is emphasized that the experience of time is relative, so that in the lowest heaven, fifty human years pass in one divine 'day', and in 500 divine 'years', nine million human years pass. In the sixth heaven, 1,600 human years pass in one 'day', and 9,216 million human years pass in the life-span there.

The questions of a creator God and the origins of human life

Buddhism sees no need for a creator of the universe, as it postulates no ultimate beginning to it, and regards it as sustained by natural laws (Nyanaponika, 1981). Moreover, if there were a creator of the world, he would be regarded as responsible for the suffering which is found throughout it (*Jat*.v.238). The nearest thing to God in the early texts is the Great Brahmā of our world-system, who was seen by some Brahmins as having created the world. While the Buddha regarded him as a long-lived glorious being, he still saw him as mistaken in his belief that he was an all-powerful creator. A *Sutta* passage in fact recounts why he had this belief (*D*.1.18). Periodically, a physical world-system and the lower heavens associated with it come to an end. At this time, beings from these lower levels are generally reborn as gods of 'Streaming Radiance' (Ābhassara, Skt Ābhāsvara). After a long period, the three lowest form heavens appear, and a Streaming Radiance god dies and is reborn there as a Great Brahmā. After some time, he becomes lonely and longs for the presence of others. Soon his wish is fulfilled, simply because other Streaming Radiance gods die and happen to be reborn, due to their karma, as his ministers and retinue. Not remembering his previous life, Great Brahmā therefore thinks, 'I am Brahmā, Great Brahmā . . . the All-seeing, the Controller, the Lord, the Maker, the Creator . . . these other beings are my creation'. His ministers and retinue agree with this erroneous conclusion, and when one of them eventually dies and is reborn as a human, he develops the power to remember his previous life, and consequently teaches that Great Brahmā is the eternal creator of all beings. This account is an ironic allusion to a passage at *Bṛhadāraṇyaka Upaniṣad* 1.4.1–3, in which the divine Self (*Ātman*; elsewhere identified with *Brahman*, the power sustaining the universe) creates other beings as he wishes not to be alone. Another ironic story illustrates a Great Brahmā's limitations. A monk with a philosophical question, about the transcending of all worlds, meditates so as to be able to contact gods and ask them his question. None of the gods from the lowest heaven up to that of the retinue of Brahmā can help him, but he is assured that Great Brahmā will be able to do so. Yet when asked the question, Great Brahmā only replies with his proud assertion of his creatorship. After responding three times in this way, he takes the monk on one side and says that he could not disillusion his retinue by publicly admitting that he did not know the answer; the monk had best go to the Buddha, who would surely know it (*D*.I.215–23). A Great Brahmā is thus seen as inferior to the Buddha in wisdom. While such ideas can be seen to satirically undermine Brahmanical ones (cf. Gombrich, 1996: 65–95; 2009: 180–92), they also put in place an alternative explanatory narrative.

While being kind and compassionate, none of the *brahmās* are world-creators, so there is no theological problem of evil in early Buddhism: the problem of how an all-powerful, all-knowing, all-loving God could create a world in which evil and suffering exist. As we will see, though (p. 141), something akin to this problem is found in some strands of Mahāyāna Buddhism.

The nearest thing to a creation story in Buddhism is its account of how beings come to populate a world-system as it starts up in a new cycle of existence. The *Aggañña Sutta*[2] says that, at this time, gods of Streaming Radiance die and are reborn hovering over the re-evolving physical world, then an expanse of water in complete darkness. The reborn beings are seen as sexless, self-luminous and still semi-divine. After a long time, a crust of 'savoury earth' spreads out on the waters, and a greedy being tastes it and craves for it. This primeval act of desire and eating is imitated by others, till

[2] *D*.III.80–98 (*SB*.116–28); cf. *EB*.3.3.2 and *BTTA*.206.

the beings lose their self-luminosity, become more solid and proud of their appearance, and so eventually develop into two sexes. Their environment is rich in food, but the more they greedily gather in its bounty, the less it gives: an idea which we can now see as having ecological implications. Eventually the notion of private property develops, and theft, lying and violence come in its train. By now recognizably human, the people then form a social contract to choose a king who will rule over them and punish wrongdoers. Thus goes the Buddhist account of a 'fall', due to greed and pride, and of the development of sexuality, human beings and society.

The implications of the rebirth perspective

The Buddhist perspective on rebirth is that it is not a pleasant affair (S.II.179–80 (*BW*.218–19)), but that all unenlightened people are reborn whether they like it or not, and whether they believe in rebirth or not. The process of life and rebirth has no inherent purpose; for it was not designed and created by anyone. Thus, for example, one is not reborn '*so as* to be able to spiritually learn'; rebirth may provide an opportunity for spiritually learning, but this is a fortunate side-effect of it. While one's life is not seen as *given* a 'purpose' by a designing God, one can *oneself* give one's life a purpose, based on understanding the nature of life, its possibilities and problems. Accordingly, sensible aims are: to avoid causing suffering for oneself and others in this life; to gain relatively pleasant rebirths through good actions; ultimately to transcend rebirths altogether; and to help others to do so. Most Buddhists therefore aim for attaining a heavenly or a human rebirth, with the *Arahat*'s liberating experience of *Nirvāṇa* as the long-term goal; heavens are *this* side of salvation, with *Nirvāṇa* as beyond the limitations of both earthly and heavenly existence. The goal of full Buddhahood is an even higher goal, which is emphasized in Mahāyāna Buddhism.

Within the round of rebirths, all beings are part of the same cycle of lives. Each human being has been an animal, ghost, hell-being and god in the past, and is likely to be so again at some time in the future. Any form of suffering one witnesses in another human or other being has been undergone by oneself at some time (*S*.II.186): thus one should not cling to rebirths and should have compassion for other sentient beings. In one's innumerable past lives, the law of averages dictates that most beings one comes across, however one might dislike them now, have at some time been a close relative or friend (*S*.II.189–90), so that lovingkindness towards them is appropriate.

Such teachings, of course, urge a kindness and non-violence towards all forms of life. Humans are part of the same cycle of lives as other beings, and are not separated from them by a huge gulf. Nevertheless, the more complex and developed a being is, the worse it is to harm or kill it; so it is worse to kill a human than an animal (*M-a.*I.198 (*BS1*.70–1); Harvey, 2000: 52). In the lower realms, there is much suffering and little freedom of action. In the heavens, the primarily happy lives of the gods tend to make them complacent, and they may also think they are eternal, without need of liberation. The human realm is a middle realm: there is enough suffering to motivate humans to seek to transcend it by spiritual development, and enough freedom to be able to act on this aspiration. It is thus the most favourable realm for spiritual development.

A human rebirth is relatively rare, however (*A.*I.35). While the human population has been increasing, there are still many more animals, birds, fishes and insects, for example. Mahāyāna Buddhists talk of having attained a 'precious human rebirth' (Guenther, 1971: 14–29; *BS2*.2; cf. *D.*III.263–4): a marvellous opportunity for spiritual growth that should be used wisely and respected in others. As it may be cut short at any time by death, it should not be frittered away.

KARMA[3]

The movement of beings between rebirths is not a haphazard process but is ordered and governed by the law of karma: the principle that beings are reborn according to the nature and quality of their past actions; they are 'heir' to their actions (*M.*III.203). All intentional actions, good or bad, *matter*; for they leave a trace on the psyche which will lead to future results. It is said in the Tibetan tradition[4] that acts of hatred and violence tend to lead to rebirth in a hell, acts bound up with delusion and confusion tend to lead to rebirth as an animal, and acts of greed tend to lead to rebirth as a ghost. A person's actions mould their consciousness, making them into a certain kind of person, so that when they die their outer form tends to correspond to the type of nature that has been developed. If bad actions are not serious enough to lead to a lower rebirth, or after having already done so, they affect the nature of a human rebirth: stinginess leads to being poor, injuring beings leads to frequent illnesses, and anger leads to being ugly – an extension of the process whereby an angry person gradually develops ugly features during their present life (*M.*III.203–6 (*BW*.161–6)). Poor, ill or ugly

[3] On this, see: *BS2*.3; Harvey, 2000: 14–31, 61–6; Ñāṇamoli and Khantipālo, 1993; Nyanaponika, 1990; Payutto, 1993; Nyanatiloka, 1994; Samuel, 1993: 199–222.

[4] Gampopa's 'Jewel Ornament of Liberation' (Guenther, 1971: 79), citing Nāgārjuna's *Ratnāvalī*.

people are not to be presently blamed for their condition, however, for the actions of a past life are behind them, and the important thing is how they act and others treat them now. Living an ethical life is said to variously lead to: wealth, through diligence; a good reputation; self-confidence in all kinds of company, without fear of reproach or punishment; dying without anxiety, and rebirth in a happy world (*D*.ɪɪ.86), as a human or sense-desire realm god. It also gives a good basis for developing the meditative calm of *jhāna*, which then tends to rebirth in a corresponding heaven, as well as preparing the mind for insight. In order to attain *Nirvāṇa*, a person must be able to perform a transcendental action, namely the attainment of deep insight into reality (*A*.ɪɪ.230–2 (*BW*.155–6)).

The law of karma is seen as a natural law inherent in the nature of things, like a law of physics. It is not operated by a God, and indeed the gods are themselves under its sway. Good and bad rebirths are not, therefore, seen as 'rewards' and 'punishments', but as simply the natural results of certain kinds of action. Karma is often likened to a seed, and the two words for a karmic result, *vipāka* and *phala*, respectively mean 'ripening' and 'fruit'. An action is thus like a seed which will sooner or later, as part of a natural maturation process, result in certain fruits accruing to the doer of the action: just as one may get tasty edible fruits or inedible bitter ones, depending on what seeds one plants. The Christian expression 'as one sows, so one will reap' exactly fits this.

What determines the nature of a karmic 'seed' is the will or intention behind an act: 'It is will (*cetanā*), O monks, that I call karma; having willed, one acts through body, speech or mind' (*A*.ɪɪɪ.415). It is the psychological impulse behind an action that is 'karma', that which sets going a chain of causes culminating in a karmic fruit. So if someone says of some event in their life 'it's my karma', a more accurate use of Buddhist terminology would be to say 'it's the result of my karma'. Actions, moreover, must be intentional if they are to generate karmic results: accidentally treading on an insect does not have such an effect, as the Jains believe. Nevertheless, thinking of doing some bad action is itself a bad (mental) karma, especially when one gives energy to such a thought, rather than just letting it pass. Deliberately letting go of such a thought is a good mental karma. Regretting a past bad (or good) action, and resolving not to do it again lessens its karmic result as it reduces the psychological impetus from the act. However, while painful feelings at the thought of a past act may be part of its karmic result, entertaining heavy guilt feelings is seen as associated with (self-)hatred, and as being an anguished state which is not conducive to calm, clarity and thus spiritual improvement.

While belief in the law of karma can sometimes degenerate into a form of fatalism, the Buddha emphasized that deterministic fate (*niyati*) and karma are very different concepts; for the idea of karma stresses the importance of human action and its effects: people make their own 'destiny' by their actions. Moreover, not everything that happens to a person is seen as due to karma. It is said that unpleasant feelings or illnesses can arise from a variety of causes: 'originating from bile, phlegm, or wind, from union (of bodily humours), born from seasonal changes, born from disruptive circumstances, due to exertion [of oneself or another person], or born of the fruition of karma' (*S*.IV.230–31 and *A*.V.110). While all volitional actions are seen as having karmic results, this does not mean that all that happens is a karmic result; karma is one cause among many in life. In part, this is simple logic: because A is a cause of B, this does not mean that B is *only ever* caused by A; drowning is a cause of death, but not all deaths are due to drowning. Further, the Buddha criticized not only theories which saw all experiences and associated actions as due to past karma, but also those which saw them as due to the diktat of a God, or to pure chance (*A*.I.173; *M*.II.214).

The aspects of life which are seen as the result of past karma include one's form of rebirth, social class at birth, general character, some of the crucial good and bad things which happen to one, and even the way one experiences the world. Out of the mass of sense-data, one only ever gets 'edited highlights' of what lies around one. Some people tend to notice pleasant things, while others tend to notice unpleasant things; these differences are said to be due to karma. Results of past actions do not include *present* intentional actions, however, though karmic results may influence the type of action that a person tends to think of doing.

As a person never knows what aspect of any situation may have been determined by karma, difficult situations are not to be passively accepted, but one should do one's best to improve them; only when things happen in spite of efforts to avert them might they be put down to past karma. If the situation can be averted or changed, fine, but then any anxiety or suffering it led to still may be seen as due to past karma. As an aid to planning courses of action in a karma-influenced world, many traditional Buddhists use divination methods such as astrology at certain points in their lives, so as to try to gauge what their karma has in store for them. The idea of the influence of karma, while not fatalistic, does encourage a person to live patiently with a situation. Rather than making new bad karma by getting angry with society or other people, blaming them for one's lot, this can be viewed as the result of one's own actions of the past. This attitude arises from one taking responsibility for the shape of one's life. As do people of other religions, however, Buddhists sometimes have an idea of fate, in parallel with their idea of karma, or they may even use past karma as an excuse for continuing with present bad karma.

It is mostly at the human level that good and bad actions are performed. The gods generally have little scope for doing either good or evil, and most simply enjoy the results of the previous good actions which led to their existence. Animals, ghosts and hell-beings have little freedom for intentional good or bad actions, though the higher animals can sometimes act virtuously, if not in a self-consciously moral way. How a human chooses to act is of pivotal importance: freedom of choice brings the possibility of both great good and great evil.

Beings in the lower rebirths generally just reap the results of particular previous bad actions. When these results come to an end, the results of some previous good actions may well then come to fruition and buoy up the being to some better form of life, and sooner or later they reach the human level again. This illustrates that karma does not bring results just in the next life: an action is said to have effects later in the present life, the next life and also in some subsequent ones (*A*.III.415).

The law of karma is not regarded as rigid and mechanical, but as the flexible, fluid and dynamic outworking of the fruits of actions. The full details of its working out, in specific instances, are said to be 'unthinkable' (*acinteyya*, Skt *acintya*) to all but a Buddha (*A*.IV.77). A moral life is not necessarily immediately followed by a good rebirth, if a strong evil action of a past life has not yet brought its results, or a dying person regrets having done good. Similarly, an immoral life is not necessarily immediately followed by a bad rebirth (*M*.III.209–15 (*SB*.195–204)). The appropriate results will come in time, however (*Dhp*.71).

In Buddhism, one should avoid actions criticized by the wise (*A*.I.89) and a 'good' action is generally referred to as *kusala* (Skt *kuśala*): informed by wisdom and thus 'skilful' in producing an uplifting mental state in the doer, or 'wholesome' in that it involves a healthy state of mind (Cousins, 1996b; Harvey, 2000: 42–3; 2011). A 'bad' action is *akusala*: 'unskilful/unwholesome'. Key criteria for an action being 'unskilful' are its being conducive to the harm of oneself, of others, or of both (*M*.I.415–16), and its being 'destructive of intuitive wisdom, associated with distress, not conducive to *Nirvāṇa*' (*M*.I.115). Correspondingly, a 'skilful' action does not conduce to any such harm, but does conduce to the growth of wholesome states of mind (*M*.II.114). The 'harm' to oneself which is relevant here is spiritual harm, or material harm if this arises from self-hatred. In other respects, an act which benefits others at the expense of material harm to oneself is certainly not unskilful.

Unskilful and skilful actions naturally arise from different motivating impulses (*M.*I.46–7), which colour the nature of the volition behind an action. Thus one should avoid 'corrupt and harmful actions of unskilful volition, with painful (immediate) consequences, (karmically) ripening in pain', and do 'beneficial actions of skilful volition, with happy consequences, ripening in happiness' (*A.*V.292–7). The three possible motivating 'roots' of unskilful action are: (i) greed (*lobha*), which covers a range of states from mild longing up to full-blown lust, avarice, fame-seeking and dogmatic clinging to ideas; (ii) hatred (*dosa*, Skt *dveṣa*), which covers mild irritation through to burning anger and resentment, and (iii) delusion (*moha*), as in stupidity, confusion, bewilderment, dull states of mind, ingrained misperception, specious doubt on moral and spiritual matters, and turning away from reality by veiling it from oneself. The opposites of these are the three 'roots' of skilful action: (i) non-greed, covering states from small generous impulses through to a strong urge for renunciation of worldly pleasures; (ii) non-hatred, covering friendliness through to forbearance in the face of great provocation, and deep lovingkindness and compassion for all beings, and (iii) non-delusion, covering clarity of mind through to the deepest insight into reality. While phrased negatively, these three are more than the mere *lack* of their opposites. They are positive states in the form of anti-greed, anti-hatred and anti-delusion.

Generating and sharing karmic fruitfulness or 'merit'

Good actions are said to be 'beautiful' (*kalyāṇa*) and to be, or have the quality of, *puñña* (Skt *puṇya*), which term is either an adjective or noun. As an adjective, Cousins sees it as the 'fortune-bringing or auspicious quality of an action' (1996b: 153), while as a noun 'it is applied either to an act which brings good fortune or to the happy result in the future of such an act' (1996b: 155). Thus we see:

> Monks, do not be afraid of *puññas*; this, monks, is a designation for happiness, for what is pleasant, charming, dear and delightful, that is to say, *puññas*. I myself know that the ripening of *puññas* done for a long time are experienced for a long time as pleasant, charming, dear and delightful. (*It.*14–15, cf. *A.*IV.88–9)

Puñña is usually, rather limply, translated as 'meritorious' (adjective) or 'merit' (noun). However, 'meritorious' implies being deserving of reward, praise or gratitude, but *puñña* refers to something with a natural power of its own to produce happy results; it does not depend on anyone to give out what is due to the 'deserving'. In Christian theology, 'merit' refers to a good deed seen to have a claim to a future reward from a graceful God, an idea that ill fits Buddhism. A *puñña* action is 'auspicious', 'fortunate' or 'fruitful', as it purifies the mind and thus leads to future good fortune (McDermott, 1984: 31–58). The Sanskrit word *puṇya* may derive from the root *puṣ*, meaning 'to thrive, flourish, prosper', or *pū*, 'to make clean or clear or pure or bright', hence a Theravādin commentary explains *puñña* by saying 'it cleanses and purifies the life-continuity' (*Vv-a*.10; Bodhi, 1990). A further reservation on 'merit' for *puñña* is that, in normal English usage, to say something 'has merit' is often to damn it with faint praise, while in Buddhism, acts of *puñña* are seen as uplifting and admirable. The effect of the translation 'merit' is to produce a flattened, dispirited image of this aspect of Buddhism. Admittedly, *puñña* alone will not bring awakening, as wisdom is needed for this, but it does help prepare the ground for this.

As the noun *puñña* refers to the power of good actions as seeds for future happy fruits, an appropriate translation is '(an act of) karmic fruitfulness', with 'karmically fruitful' as the adjective. The *Saṅgha* is described as the best 'field of *puñña*', that is, the best group of people to 'plant' a gift 'in' in terms of good results of the gift, hence 'like fields are the *Arahats*; the givers are like farmers. The gift is like the seed, [and] from this arises the fruit' (*Pv*.I.1). In defence of the above translation, while karmic fruit/results can be of either good *or* bad actions, and *puñña* relates only to good actions, the English word 'fruit' can also mean only edible, pleasant fruit such as apples, without referring to inedible, unpleasant ones.

The opposite of *puñña* is *apuñña*, which one can accordingly see as meaning '(an act of) karmic harm' or 'karmically harmful', that is, producing no pleasant fruits, but only bitter ones. A synonym for *apuñña* is *pāpa*, which, while often translated as 'evil' or 'bad', really means that which is 'infertile', 'barren', 'harmful' (Cousins, 1996: 156) or 'bringing ill fortune'.

Buddhists are keen to perform 'karmically fruitful' actions; for *puñña* is an unlosable 'treasure', unlike physical goods (*Khp*.7). The early texts refer to three 'bases for effecting karmic fruitfulness' (*puñña-kiriya-vatthus*): giving (*dāna* – especially by giving alms to monks), moral virtue (*sīla*) and meditative cultivation of skilful qualities (*bhāvanā*) (*D*.II.218). Later texts add: showing respect, helpful activity, sharing karmic fruitfulness, rejoicing at the karmic fruitfulness of others, teaching *Dhamma*, listening to *Dhamma*, and straightening out one's views (*D-a*.III.999). Any act of giving is seen as karmically fruitful, even giving in the hope of some return, or giving purely to get the karmic result of giving. A purer motive, however, is seen as leading to a better karmic result. Thus it is particularly good to give from motives such as the appreciation of a gift as helping to support a holy way of life, or of the calm and joy that giving naturally brings (*A*.IV.60–3). While a large gift is generally seen as more auspicious than a small one, purity of mind can also make up for the smallness of a gift, for 'where there is a heart of calm and joyful faith (*citta-pasāde*), no gift is small' (*Jat*.II.85). Indeed, a person with nothing to give can act auspiciously by simply rejoicing at another person's giving. In Theravāda lands, this is expressed by uttering of the ritual expression *sādhu*, meaning 'it is good!', when others give. The same principle, of course, logically implies that if one verbally or mentally applauds someone else's unwholesome action, one is performing an unwholesome action oneself.

In Theravāda tradition, a karmically fruitful act may not only be performed by empathizing (*anumodanā*) with someone else's auspicious deed, but also by the auspicious quality of an act (*patti* – what has been gained) being transferred to or shared with another being. This practice may have originated as a Buddhist adaptation of the Brahmanical *śrāddha* ceremony, in which gifts were seen as transferred to deceased relatives by giving them to Brahmins at memorial rites at various intervals after a death in the family. In an early text, a Brahmin asks the Buddha if *śrāddha* rites bring benefit to the dead, and the Buddha replies that the dead will benefit only if reborn as *petas*, for these ghostly beings live either on the putrid food of their realm or on what is provided by gifts from relatives and friends (*A*.V.269–72; *EB*.2.5.3). The *Petavatthu*, a late Canonical text, accordingly describes a number of instances where a gift is given in the name of a suffering *peta*, so that they attain rebirth as a god due to the karmic fruitfulness of the giving. Theravāda rites for the dead therefore include the feeding of monks and the transference of the karmic fruitfulness ('merit') to the deceased, or whatever other ancestors may be *petas*, in the hope that this will ease their lot as *petas* or help them to a better rebirth. This is done especially seven days after a death, but also in yearly memorial services. Another early text has the Buddha say that it is wise to support monks and to dedicate the gift to the local gods, so that they will look with favour on the donor (*D*.II.88). Accordingly, Theravāda donations to monks often conclude with a verse transferring the karmic fruitfulness of the gift to gods. The latter are seen as having less opportunity to do auspicious deeds themselves, but can benefit from transferred karmic fruitfulness, which helps maintain them in their divine rebirth; in return, it is hoped that they will use whatever powers they have to aid and protect Buddhism and the person making the donation. A boy ordaining as a novice or full monk will also share the karmic fruitfulness of this act with his mother. Here, her karmic fruitfulness will come from both the act of 'giving up' her son to the monkhood, and her rejoicing at his auspicious act.

Given the Buddhist stress on the idea that a person can only generate karmic fruitfulness by their own deeds, the idea of 'transferring' it is potentially anomalous. To avoid such an anomaly, the Theravādin commentaries, dating from the fifth century CE or earlier, developed an orthodox interpretation, and Tibetan Buddhists have a similar idea. This is that no karmic fruitfulness is actually transferred, but that the food, etc. donated to monks is dedicated, by the performer of the auspicious donation, to an ancestor or god, so that the donation is done on their behalf, with their property. Provided that they assent to this donation-by-proxy by rejoicing at it, they themselves generate karmic fruitfulness. By a living being affirming someone else's action as good, particularly if it is done on their behalf, they directly perform a positive mental action of their own.

The idea of sharing karmic fruitfulness helps to modify any tendency in the karma doctrine to encouraging people to 'amass' karmic fruitfulness for themselves, like a kind of non-physical money in the bank. Karmic fruitfulness can and should be shared with others. Giving, for example, generates karmic fruitfulness; then when this is shared with others, there is another generous act which generates more karmic fruitfulness: the more karmic fruitfulness is shared, the more there is of it – unlike with money or material goods – and happiness increases in the world! Sharing karmic fruitfulness is a way of spreading the karmic benefits of good deeds to others, as a gesture of goodwill. This is expressed in the traditional simile to explain such sharing: lighting many lamps from one.

BELIEF IN REBIRTH AND KARMA

While Buddhism holds that the existence of rebirth and the life-to-life efficacy of karma can be confirmed by experiences in deep meditation, most Buddhists have not attained these. They therefore only have *belief* in these principles, not direct knowledge of their truth, and use these beliefs to provide a perspective on life and action in it. Buddhism, though, emphasizes the need to differentiate between what one *believes* and what one actually *knows* (*M*.II.171). Beliefs are candidates for knowledge but are not the same as it, and may be false. Even when true, one does not oneself *know* this if one has not experientially confirmed it. One's belief may be relatively well based, but still be partial and relatively distorted.

Nevertheless, while it is best to *know* for oneself, to *believe* what is true is better than to believe what is false. For Buddhism, karma and rebirth are seen as realities whose actuality is affirmed by a very reliable source: the Buddha and certain of his disciples. Their claim to knowledge on these matters is generally trusted because of their reliability on other more easily testable matters. Some Western Buddhists see rebirth as a kind of 'optional extra' in Buddhism. For them, it may be, but the evidence is that it clearly was not so for the Buddha:

> Since there actually is another world [any world other than the present human one, i.e. different rebirth realms], one who holds the view 'there is no other world' has wrong view . . . Since there actually is another world, one who says 'there is no other world' is opposing those *Arahats* who know the other world. (*M*.I.402)

That said, part of the working out of karma is said to come in this life, and people can observe that the results of good and bad actions very often catch up with a person even during one life. In a similar way, an aspect of the rebirth doctrine relates to what can be observed in one life. Probably from the time of earliest Buddhism, rebirth was seen both as a process which takes place after death, and also as a process taking place during life. That is, one is constantly changing during life, 'reborn' as a relatively 'different' person according to one's mood, the task one is involved in, or the people one is relating to. Depending on how one acts, one may experience 'heavenly' or 'hellish' states of mind. The Buddhist would say that it is reasonable to suppose that this process of change, determined especially by the nature of one's actions, does not abruptly stop at death, but carries on. In two early texts (*M*.I.403; *A*.I.193), the Buddha says that to believe in karma and rebirth, and accordingly live a moral life, will lead to a good rebirth *if* rebirths exist. If rebirths do not exist, nothing will have been lost, and the person will in any case have been praised for their conduct by wise people. The 'best bet' is thus to believe in and act on these principles. Moreover, one who has lived a moral life and is non-attached will not be afraid of death (*A*.II.173–6 (*SB*.256–8)). Past karma also offers perhaps the only religiously satisfactory explanation of the repeated sufferings of people who have done nothing to warrant it in this life.

Modern Buddhists also point to certain data which apparently supports the theory of rebirth. Much of this has been researched by Professor Ian Stevenson, an American psychiatrist who has published the results of his investigations in such works as *20 Cases Suggestive of Reincarnation* (1974).[5] These detail studies of young children, from places such as India, Sri Lanka,

[5] See also Stevenson, 1987 and the research of Erlendur Haraldsson: http://notendur.hi.is/erlendur/english.

the Lebanon, Brazil and Alaska, who spontaneously speak as if they have recall of a past human life. In the typical case, the child starts referring, not long after he or she can talk, to events, relations and possessions that he had when he was 'big'. These 'memories' generally fade as the child grows up. The previous personality is often locatable as having lived some way away, unknown to the child's family, and to have died not long before the child was conceived. The child often knows intimate details of the person's life, has similar character traits, and can even recognize past 'relatives' in a crowd, correctly name them, and react to them with strong and appropriate emotion. Sometimes, birthmarks correspond in location and even appearance to wounds or surgical incisions associated with the previous personality's death. Stevenson holds, after much probing analysis of the more impressive cases, that explanations such as fraud, wish-fulfilling fantasy, overhearing information about a dead person, or telepathy, are inadequate. He therefore regards rebirth as probably the best hypothesis to explain these cases, though possession would also explain some. It is unlikely that such cases are a purely modern phenomenon, and it seems reasonable to suppose that their occurrence in the past has helped sustain belief in rebirth in Buddhist cultures.

While teachings on karma and rebirth are an important part of Buddhist belief, they are not the *most* crucial, nor the most specifically Buddhist. They act, though, as the lead-up to, and motivator for, the most important teachings, those on the four True Realities for the Spiritually Ennobled. When teaching laypersons, the Buddha frequently began with a 'step-by-step discourse':

> that is, i) talk on giving, talk on moral virtue, talk on the heaven worlds; ii) he made known the danger, the inferior nature of and tendency to defilement in sense-pleasures, and the advantage of renouncing them [by moral discipline, meditative calming, and perhaps ordination]. When the Blessed One knew that the householder Upāli's mind was ready, open, without hindrances, inspired and confident, then he expounded to him the elevated *Dhamma*-teaching of the Buddhas: the painful, its origin, its cessation, the path. (*M*.I.379–80)

Here, the teaching on the True Realities for the Spiritually Ennobled is an 'elevated' one, or one 'particular' to Buddhas, which is given after a two-stage progressive teaching on more preparatory matters. The teachings of the 'step-by-step discourse' and the four True Realities correspond, respectively, to two levels of 'right view', or 'right understanding' of reality (*M*.III.72). The first is belief that: giving is worthwhile; what one does *matters* and has an effect on one's future; this world is not unreal, and one goes on to another world after death; it is good to respect parents, who establish one in this world; some of the worlds one can be reborn in (e.g. some heavens) are populated by beings that come into existence spontaneously, without parents; spiritual development is a real possibility, actualized by some people, and it can lead, in deep meditation, to memory of past rebirths in a variety of worlds, and awareness of how others are reborn in such worlds. This is the precise opposite of the view ascribed to the materialist Ajita Kesakambalī (*D*.I.55).

The second level of right view is wisdom and insight which directly perceives the True Realities. As it leads beyond suffering and rebirth in any world, it is seen as transcendent (*lokuttara*, Skt *lokottara*) and truly Noble (*ariya*). The first type is seen as ordinary (*lokiya*, Skt *laukika*), as it supports actions leading to good rebirths. Practice based on ordinary right view is seen as creating a good basis for the additional development of wisdom. Thus the overall path of Buddhism is seen as a training which gradually moves towards the profounder teachings, just as the ocean bottom shelves down gradually from the shore into the depths (*A*.IV.200–1), though insights may then come suddenly. Many Buddhists may not get beyond the shallows, but the invitation and opportunity to go deeper are always there.

CHAPTER 3

Early Buddhist Teachings: The Four True Realities for the Spiritually Ennobled

What are generally known as the four 'Noble Truths' (Pali *ariya-sacca*, Skt *ārya-satya*) are the focus of what *Vin*.I.10–12 portrays as the first sermon of the Buddha: the *Dhamma-cakka-ppavattana Sutta*.[1] As found in the early *Sutta* (Skt *Sūtra*) collections known as the *Nikāyas* or *Āgamas*, the *ariya-saccas* are subjects of an advanced teaching intended for those who have, by the 'step-by-step' discourse (see p. 48), been spiritually prepared to have them pointed out. If the mind is not calm and receptive, talk of *dukkha* (Skt *duḥkha*) – the mental and physical pains of life, and the painful, stressful, unsatisfactory aspects of life that engender these – may be too disturbing, leading to states such as depression, denial and self-distracting tactics. The Buddha's own discovery of the *ariya-saccas* was from the fourth *jhāna* (Skt *dhyāna*), a state of profound meditative calm (*M*.I.249). The Mahāyāna later came to see the teachings on the *ariya-saccas* as themselves preliminary to higher teachings – but there is none of this in the *Nikāyas* or *Āgamas*. In these, they are not teachings to go beyond, or unproblematic simple teachings, but about deep realities to be seen by direct insight (*S*.V.442–3 (*BW*.362–3)), and then responded to in appropriate ways.

The translation of *ariya-sacca* as 'Noble Truth' (e.g. Anderson, 1999), while well established in English-language literature on Buddhism, is the 'least likely' of the possible meanings (Norman, 1997: 16). To unpack and translate this compound, one needs to look at the meanings of each word, and then how they are related. The term *sacca* (Skt *satya*) is regularly used in the sense of 'truth', but also to mean a 'reality', a genuinely real existent. In pre-Buddhist works, *Chāndogya Upaniṣad* 6.15.3 sees the universal Self as *satya*, and *Bṛhadāraṇyaka Upaniṣad* 2.3 talks of two forms of *Brahman*: *sat*, which is mortal, and *tyam*, which is immortal, with 2.3.6

[1] *S*.V.420–4 (*BW*.75–8, *SB*.243–6, Harvey 2007a); Skt *Dharma-cakra-pravartana Sūtra* (*EB*.1.6).

implying that the latter is 'the real behind the real [*sayasya satyam iti*]' (Olivelle, 1996: 28), that is, *satya* encompasses all reality, which is twofold in its nature. There is also a connection to *sat*, meaning existence.

As regards the meaning of (*ariya-*)'*sacca*' in the Buddha's first sermon, there are three reasons why it cannot here mean 'truth'. First, it is said that the second *ariya-sacca* is to be abandoned (*S*.v.422): surely, one would not want to abandon a 'truth', but one might well want to abandon a problematic 'reality'. Secondly, it is said that the Buddha understood, '"This is the *dukkha ariya-sacca*"', not 'The *ariya-sacca* "This is *dukkha*"', which would be the case if *sacca* here meant a *truth* whose content was expressed in words in quote marks. Thirdly, in some *Sutta*s (e.g. *S*.v.425), the first *ariya-sacca* is explained by identifying it with a kind of existent (the five bundles of grasping-fuel – see below), not by asserting a form of words that could be seen as a 'truth'. In normal English usage, the only things that can be 'truths' are propositions, that is, something that is expressed in words (spoken, written, thought). Something *said* about *dukkha*, even just 'this is *dukkha*', can be a 'truth', but *dukkha* itself can only be a true, genuine *reality*. Hence 'true reality' is here best for *sacca*, which still keeps a clear connection to 'truth' as the other meaning of *sacca*.

What of the term *ariya*? As a noun, this means 'noble one'. In Brahmanism, the term referred to members of the top three of the four social classes, denoting purity of descent and social superiority (see p. 9). In Buddhism it is used in a spiritual sense: the Buddha is 'the noble one' (*S*.v.435) and other 'noble ones' are those who are partially or fully awakened, and those well established on the path to these states (see pp. 86–7). To make clear the spiritual sense of the term, and that being a 'noble one' is an attainment rather than something one is born to, the translation 'the spiritually ennobled' seems most apposite: a person who has been uplifted and purified by deep insight into reality. As an adjective, *ariya* means 'noble', hence the Buddhist path, the practice of which makes ordinary people into noble ones, is itself said to be 'noble'.

While a 'truth' might be 'noble' or, for those who have insight into it, 'ennobling', the case is different when *sacca* means a 'true reality'. As one of the *ariya-sacca*s, the origin of *dukkha*, is to be abandoned, this can hardly be 'noble' or 'ennobling'. *Ariya*, then, must here mean 'the spiritually ennobled'. An *ariya-sacca* must thus be a 'true reality for the spiritually ennobled' (Harvey, 2007a, 2009a). The four of these are the most significant categories of existence, that only the spiritually ennobled recognize the full import of. Correct identification of them, and deep insight into their nature, is what makes a person spiritually ennobled. Of course, teachings *about* these true realities are still seen as truths, but such teachings are not themselves the *ariya-sacca*s.

The four True Realities for the Spiritually Ennobled form the structural framework for all higher teachings of early Buddhism. They are: (i) *dukkha*, 'the painful', encompassing the various forms of 'pain', gross or subtle, physical or mental, that we are all subject to, along with painful things that engender these; (ii) the origination (*samudaya*, i.e. cause) of *dukkha*, namely craving (*taṇhā*, Skt *tṛṣṇā*); (iii) the cessation (*nirodha*) of *dukkha* by the cessation of craving (this cessation being equivalent to *Nirvāṇa*); and (iv) the path (*magga*, Skt *mārga*) that leads to this cessation. The first sermon says that the first of the four is 'to be fully understood'; the second is 'to be abandoned'; the third is 'to be personally experienced'; the fourth is 'to be developed/cultivated'. To 'believe in' the *ariya-sacca*s may play a part, but not the most important one.

The same fourfold structure of ideas (x, origination of x, its cessation, path to its cessation) is also applied to a range of other phenomena, such as the experienced world (*loka*; *S*.I.62). This structure may also have been influenced by, or itself influenced, the practice of early Indian doctors: (i) diagnose an illness, (ii) identify its cause, (iii) determine whether it is curable, and (iv) outline a course of treatment to cure it. The first True Reality is the metaphorical 'illness' of *dukkha* (*Vibh-a*.88), and the Buddha is seen as fulfilling the role of a spiritual physician. Having 'cured' himself of *dukkha*, he worked to help others to do likewise. The problem of suffering had prompted his own quest for awakening, and its solution naturally became the focus of his teachings. He sometimes summarized these by saying simply, 'Both in the past and now, I set forth just this: *dukkha* and the cessation of *dukkha*' (e.g. *M*.I.140).

THE FIRST TRUE REALITY FOR THE SPIRITUALLY ENNOBLED: THE PAINFUL

In his first sermon, the Buddha said this on the first True Reality:

> Now *this*, monks, for the spiritually ennobled, is the painful (*dukkha*) true reality (*ariya-sacca*): [i] birth is painful, ageing is painful, illness is painful, death is painful; [ii] sorrow, lamentation, (physical) pain, unhappiness and distress are painful; [iii] union with what is disliked is painful; separation from what is liked is painful; not to get what one wants is painful; [iv] in brief, the five bundles of grasping-fuel are painful. [numbers added]

The word *dukkha* has been translated in many ways, with 'suffering' as the most common, so that the above passage is generally translated, 'Now this, monks, is the noble truth of suffering: birth is suffering. . .', but 'suffering' is only an appropriate translation in a general, inexact sense. The English word 'suffering' is a noun (as in 'his suffering is intense'), a present participle (as in 'he is suffering from malaria') or an adjective (as in 'the suffering refugees'). If one translates 'birth is suffering', it does not make sense to take 'suffering' as a noun, as it is not the case that birth etc. are themselves *forms of* suffering – they can only be occasions for the arising of the experience of suffering, things which often entail it. But nor can 'suffering' be here meant as a present participle – it is not something that birth *is doing*; and as an adjective 'suffering' only applies to people. In the passage on the first True Reality, *dukkha* in 'birth is *dukkha. . .*' *is* an adjective, as shown by the fact that the grammatical gender changes according to the word it qualifies, and 'painful' is a translation which properly reflects this.

In fact, the basic everyday meaning of *dukkha* as a noun is 'pain' as opposed to 'pleasure' (*sukha*). These, with neither-*dukkha*-nor-*sukha*, are the three kinds of feeling (*vedanā*), with *dukkha* explained as covering both physical pain – *dukkha* in the narrowest sense – and unhappiness (*domanassa*), mental pain (*S*.v.209–10). Similarly, in English, 'pain' refers not just to physical pain, but also to mental distress, both of these being covered by the second part of the phrase the 'pleasures and pains of life'. One also talks of 'it pains me to say this, but. . .' and of difficult situations or persons as 'a pain' – clearly in the sense of a mental pain, not a physical one. In the first sermon, something to which the adjective *dukkha* is applied is 'painful' in the sense of being in some way troublesome or problematic, either obviously (e.g. physical pain, not getting what one wants) or only on investigation (e.g. being born). It applies to all those things which are unpleasant, stressful, unsatisfactory, imperfect and which we would like to be otherwise. Those things that have these qualities can then be described as 'the painful', which seems to be the meaning of the '*dukkha*' that is explained above as 'birth is painful. . .'. Here 'the painful' means both mental or physical pains and the aspects of life that engender these.

The first features described as 'painful' in the above quote (i) are basic biological aspects of being alive, each of which can be traumatic (*BW*.20–36). The *dukkha* of these is compounded by the rebirth perspective of Buddhism, for this involves repeated re-birth, re-ageing, re-sickness and re-death. The second set of features refer to physical or mental pain that arises from the vicissitudes of life. The third set of features point to the fact that we can never wholly succeed in keeping away things, people and

upādāna-kkhandha is also part of this fire imagery (1996: 66–8; 2009: 111–28). The *upādāna-kkhandhas*, then, can each be seen as a 'bundle of fuel' (1996: 67) which 'burns' with the 'fires' of *dukkha* and its causes (*S*.II.19–20). They are each sustaining objects of, or fuel *for*, grasping (cf. Ṭhānissaro, 1999a: ch. 2). The translation 'bundles of grasping-fuel' captures these nuances.

That the spiritually ennobled see even the factors making up a person as *dukkha* shows that their understanding of reality is rather different from that of ordinary people (who are also unlikely to see being born as *dukkha*). Hence it is said that while the world sees the flow of agreeable sense-objects as pleasurable, and the ending of this as *dukkha*, the spiritually ennobled see the transcending of the *khandhas* and sense-objects as what is truly pleasurable (*Sn*.759–62 and *S*.IV.127): *Nirvāṇa* as the blissful state beyond all conditioned phenomena of the round of rebirths.

To aid understanding of *dukkha*, Buddhism gives details of each of the five factors into which it analyses personality. All but the first of these 'bundles' are mental in nature; for they lack any physical 'form':

1. *Rūpa* '(material) form'. This refers to the material aspect of existence, whether in the outer world or in the body of a living being. It is said to be comprised of four basic elements or forces, and forms of subtle, sensitive matter derived from these. The four basics are solidity (literally 'earth'), cohesion ('water'), heat ('fire') and motion ('wind'). From the interaction of these, the body of flesh, blood, bones, etc. is composed.
2. *Vedanā* or 'feeling'. This is the hedonic tone or 'taste' of any experience: pleasant, painful (*dukkha*) or neutral. It includes both sensations arising from the body and mental feelings of happiness, unhappiness or indifference.
3. *Saññā* (Skt *saṃjñā*), which processes sensory and mental objects, so as to classify and label them, for example as 'yellow', 'a man' or 'fear'. It is 'perception', 'cognition', mental labelling, recognition and interpretation – including misinterpretation – of objects. Without it, a person might be conscious but would be unable to know *what* he was conscious of.
4. The *saṅkhāras* (Skt *saṃskāra*), or 'constructing activities' (also rendered as 'volitional activities', 'mental formations' and 'karmic activities'). These comprise a number of processes which initiate action or direct, mould and give shape to character. The most characteristic one is *cetanā*, 'will' or 'volition', which is identified with karma (see p. 40). There are processes which are ingredients of all mind-states, such as sensory stimulation and attention, ones which intensify such states, such as energy, joy or desire-to-do, ones which are ethically 'skilful', such as

mindfulness and a sense of moral integrity, and 'unskilful' ones, such as greed, hatred and delusion.

5. *Viññāṇa* (Skt *vijñāna*), '(discriminative) consciousness'. This includes both the basic awareness of a sensory or mental object, and the discrimination of its aspects or parts, which are actually recognized by *saññā*. One might thus also see it as perceptual 'discernment'. It is of six types according to whether it is conditioned by eye, ear, nose, tongue, body or mind-organ. It is also known as *citta*, the central focus of personality, which can be seen as 'mind', 'heart' or 'thought'. This is essentially a 'mind-set' or 'mentality'; some aspects of which alter from moment to moment, but others recur and are equivalent to a person's character. Its form at any moment is set up by the other mental *khandhas*, but in turn it goes on to determine their pattern of arising, in a process of constant interaction.

Much Buddhist practice is concerned with the purification, development and harmonious integration of the five 'bundles' that make up personality, through the cultivation of virtue and meditation. In time, however, the fivefold analysis is used to enable a meditator to gradually transcend the naïve perception – with respect to 'himself' or 'another' – of a unitary 'person' or 'self'. In place of this, there is set up the contemplation of a person as a cluster of changing physical and mental processes, or *dhammas* (Skt *dharma*), thus undermining grasping and attachment, which are key causes of suffering.

Phenomena as impermanent and non-Self[2]

Though the first sermon emphasizes *dukkha*, this is in fact only one of three related characteristics or 'marks' of the five *khandhas*. These fundamental 'three marks' (*ti-lakkhaṇa*, Skt *tri-lakṣaṇa*) of all conditioned phenomena are that they are impermanent (*anicca*, Skt *anitya*), painful (*dukkha*, Skt *duḥkha*), and non-Self (*anattā*, Skt *anātman*).[3] Buddhism emphasizes that change and impermanence are fundamental features of *everything*, bar *Nirvāṇa*. Mountains wear down, material goods wear out or are lost or stolen, and all beings, even gods, age and die (*M*.II.65–82 (*BW*.207–13); *EB*.3.2.1). The gross form of the body changes relatively slowly, but the matter which composes it is replaced as one eats, excretes and sheds skin cells. As regards the mind, character patterns may be relatively persistent,

[2] See Collins, 1982; Harvey, 1995a: 17–108, and 2009b: 265–74.
[3] E.g. *S*.III.44–5 (*BW*.342–3), *S*.IV.46–7 (*SB*.224–5), *S*.IV.133–5 (*BW*.346–7).

but feelings, moods, ideas, etc. can be observed to constantly change. The ephemeral and deceptive nature of the *khandhas* is expressed in a passage which says that they are 'devoid, hollow' as: 'Material form is like a lump of foam, and feeling is like a bubble; perception is like a mirage, and the constructing activities are like a banana tree [lacking a core, like an onion]; consciousness is like a [magician's] illusion' (*S*.III.142 (*BW*.343–5); *SB*.220–2).

It is because of the fact that things are impermanent that they are also *dukkha*. Because they are impermanent and in some sense painful, moreover, they are to be seen as *anattā*, non-Self. When something is said to be *anattā*, the kind of 'self' it is seen not to be is clearly one that would be permanent and free from all pain, however subtle – so as to be happy, self-secure, independent. While Pali and Sanskrit do not have capital letters, in English it is useful to signal such a concept with a capital: *S*elf.

The term *anattā* is nearly always a noun,[4] in the form of the word for Self, *attā* (Skt *ātman*), prefaced by the negative prefix *an*, meaning that what is *anattā* is nothing to do with 'self' in a certain sense: it is not a Self – it is not-Self – nor what pertains or belongs to such a thing (*attaniya*, *S*.III.33–4; *S*.IV.54), as 'mine', or what contains Self or is contained in it (*M*.I.300; *S*.III.127–32). It is 'empty (*suñña*, Skt *śūnya*) of Self or what pertains to Self' (*S*.IV.54 (*BTTA*.81; *BW*.347)). While *anattā* is often rendered simply as 'not-Self', this translation captures only part of its meaning, as it misses out the aspect of not being anything that pertains to a Self, which 'non-Self' includes.

The important teaching on this was introduced by the Buddha in his second sermon, the *Anatta-lakkhaṇa Sutta* (*Vin*.I.13–14; *S*.III.66–8 (*BSI*.118; *BW*.341–2)). Here he explained, with respect to each of the five *khandhas*, that if it were truly Self, it would not 'tend to sickness', and it would be totally controllable at will, which it is not. Moreover, as each *khandha* is impermanent, *dukkha* and of a nature to change, it is inappropriate to consider it as 'This is mine, this am I, this is my Self'.

In the Buddha's day, the spiritual quest was largely seen as the search for identifying and liberating a person's true Self. Such an entity was postulated as a person's permanent inner nature, the source of true happiness and the autonomous 'inner controller' (Skt *antaryamin*) of a person's actions, inner elements and faculties. It would also need to be in full control of itself. In Brahmanism, this *ātman* was seen as a universal Self identical with *Brahman*, while in Jainism, for example, it was seen as the individual 'Life-principle' (*jīva*). The Buddha argued that anything subject to change,

[4] Occasionally, *anattā* it is an adjective meaning 'without Self'.

anything involved with the disharmony of mental pain, anything not autonomous and totally controllable by its own or an owner's wishes, could not be such a perfect true Self or what in any way pertained or belonged to it. Moreover, to take anything as being such is to lay the basis for much suffering; for what one fondly takes as one's permanent, essential Self, or its secure possession, all actually changes in undesired ways. While the *Upaniṣads* recognized many things as being not-Self, they felt that a real, true Self could be found. They held that when it was found, and known to be identical to *Brahman*, the basis of everything, this would bring liberation. In the Buddhist *Suttas*, though, literally everything is seen as non-Self, even *Nirvāṇa*. When this is known, then liberation – *Nirvāṇa* – is attained by total non-attachment. Thus both the *Upaniṣads* and the Buddhist *Suttas* see many things as not-Self, but the *Suttas* apply it, indeed non-Self, to *everything*.

The teaching on phenomena as non-Self is not only intended to undermine the Brahmanical or Jain concepts of Self, but also much more commonly held conceptions and deep-rooted feelings of I-ness. To feel that, however much one changes in life from childhood onwards, some essential part remains constant and unchanged as the 'real me', is to have a belief in a permanent Self. To act as if only *other* people die, and to ignore the inevitability of one's own death, is to act as if one had a permanent Self. To relate changing mental phenomena to a substantial self which 'owns' them – '*I* am worried . . . happy . . . angry' – is to have such a Self-concept. To build an identity based on one's bodily appearance or abilities, or on one's sensitivities, ideas and beliefs, actions or intelligence etc. is to take them as part of an 'I'.

The non-Self teaching can easily be misunderstood and misdescribed; so it is important to see what it is saying. The Buddha accepted many conventional usages of the word 'self' (also *attā*), as in 'yourself' and 'myself'. These he saw as simply convenient ways of referring to a particular collection of mental and physical states. But within such a conventional, empirical self, he taught that no permanent, substantial, independent, metaphysical Self could be found. This is well explained by an early nun, Vajirā:[5] just as the word 'chariot' is used to denote a collection of items in functional relationship, but not a special part of a chariot, so the conventional term 'a being' is properly used to refer to the five *khandhas* relating together. None of the *khandhas* is a 'being' or 'Self', but these are simply conventional labels used to denote the collection of functioning *khandhas*.

[5] *S.*I.135 (*EB.*3.2.3), cf. *Miln.*25–8 (*BS1.*147–9; *EB.*3.2.2).

The non-Self teaching does not deny that there is continuity of character in life, and to some extent from life to life. But persistent character traits are merely due to the repeated occurrence of certain *citta*s, or 'mind-sets'. The *citta* as a whole is sometimes talked of as an (empirical) 'self' (e.g. *Dhp*.160 with 35), but while such character traits may be long-lasting, they can and do change, and are thus impermanent, and so 'non-Self', insubstantial. A 'person' is a collection of rapidly changing and interacting mental and physical processes, with character patterns re-occurring over some time. Only partial control can be exercised over these processes: so they often change in undesired ways, leading to suffering. Impermanent, they cannot be a permanent Self. Being 'painful', they cannot be an autonomous true 'I', which would contain nothing that was out of harmony with itself.

While *Nirvāṇa* is beyond impermanence and *dukkha*, it is still non-Self. This is made clear in a recurring passage (e.g. at *A*.I.286–7), which says that all *saṅkhāras*, here meaning conditioned phenomena, are impermanent and *dukkha*, but that 'all *dhammas*' are non-Self. '*Dhamma*' (Skt *dharma*) is a word with many meanings in Buddhism, but here it refers to any basic component of reality. Most are conditioned, but *Nirvāṇa* is the unconditioned *dhamma* (*A*.II.34); both conditioned and unconditioned *dhamma*s are non-Self. While *Nirvāṇa* is beyond change and suffering, it has nothing in it which could support the feeling of I-ness; for this can only arise with respect to the *khandhas*, and it is not even a truly valid feeling here (*D*.II.66–8; Harvey, 1995a: 31–3).

That said, it should be noted that, while 'all *dhamma*s are *anattā*' – 'everything is non-Self' – clearly implies that there is no Self, the word *anattā* does not *itself* mean 'no-Self', that is, does not itself mean 'there is no Self'. It simply means that what it is applied to is not a Self or what pertains to it. Moreover, the non-Self teaching is not in *itself* a denial of the existence of a permanent self; it is primarily a practical teaching aimed at the overcoming of attachment. Indeed, when directly asked if 'self' (in an unspecified sense) exists or not, the Buddha was silent, as he did not want either to affirm a permanent Self, or confuse his questioner by not accepting self in any sense (*S*.IV.400–1 (*EB*.3.2.4)). A philosophical denial of 'Self' is just a view, a theory, which may be agreed with or not. It does not necessarily get one to examine all the things that one actually *does* identify with, consciously or unconsciously, as Self or essentially 'mine'. This examination, in a calm, meditative context, is what the 'non-Self' teaching aims at. It is not so much a conceptual idea as something to be *done*, applied to actual experience, so that the meditator actually *sees* that '*all dhamma*s are non-Self'. A mere philosophical denial does not encourage this, and may actually mean that a person sees no need for it.

While the *Suttas* have no place for a metaphysical Self, seeing things as *non-Self* is clearly regarded as playing a vital soteriological role. The concept of 'Self', and the associated deep-rooted feeling of 'I am', are being utilized for a spiritual end. The non-Self teaching can in fact be seen as a brilliant device which uses a deep-seated human aspiration, ultimately *illusory*, to overcome the negative products of such an illusion. Identification, whether conscious or unconscious, with something as 'what I truly and permanently am', or as inherently 'mine', is a source of attachment; such attachment leads to frustration and a sense of loss when what one identifies with changes and becomes other than one desires. The deep-rooted idea of 'Self', though, is not to be attacked, but used as a measuring rod against which all phenomena should be compared: so as to see them as falling short of the perfections implied in the idea of Self. This is to be done through a rigorous experiential examination of the phenomena that we *do* identify with as 'Self', 'I' or 'mine': as each of these is examined, but is seen to actually be non-Self, falling short of the ideal, the intended result is that one should let go of any attachment to such a thing. In doing this, a person finally comes to see *everything* as non-Self, thereby destroying all attachment and attaining *Nirvāṇa*. In this process, it is not necessary to give any philosophical 'denial' of Self; the idea simply withers away, as it is seen that no actual instance of such a thing can be found anywhere (*M.*I.138 (*SB.*161–5)). One can, then, perhaps see the Self idea as fulfilling a role akin to a rocket which boosts a payload into space, against the force of gravity. It provides the force to drive the mind out of the 'gravity field' of attachment to the *khandhas*. Having done so, it then 'falls away and is burnt up', as itself an empty concept, part of the unsatisfactory *khandhas*.

Just as *anattā* is sometimes translated as 'no-self', it is sometimes translated as 'no-soul', but while Buddhism does not accept a 'soul' in the sense of an immortal essence of a person, 'soul' in the sense of that which gives life to the body is not denied: the presence of the flux of discriminative consciousness (*viññāṇa*) plus 'vitality' (*āyu*) and 'heat' fulfil this role (*M.*I.296). 'Soul' can also mean the moral and emotional part of a person, and in this sense could be seen to correspond to *citta*, a term which covers both 'mind' and 'heart', in the sense of the centre of emotions. Again, 'soul' can refer to a person viewed as embodying moral or intellectual qualities, as when one refers to 'the great souls of antiquity'. This is echoed in the Buddhist term *mahattā*, 'great selves' (*It.*28–9) – strong, spiritually developed people – which term resurfaced in recent times in the title *mahātma*, 'great soul', applied to the Hindu teacher Gandhi. The term can also refer to energy and spirit, as found in good art or

Buddhism, then, sees the basic root of the pain and stress of life as spiritual ignorance, rather than sin, which is a wilful turning away from a creator God. Indeed, it can be regarded as having a doctrine of something like 'original sinlessness'. While the mind is seen as containing many unskilful tendencies with deep roots, 'below' these roots it is free from active taints: 'Monks, this mind (*citta*) is brightly shining (*pabhassara*, Skt *prabhāsvara*), but it is defiled by adventitious defilements' (*A*.I.10). That is, the deepest layer of the mind is bright, and pure (though not yet immune from being obscured by defilements). This represents, in effect, the potentiality for attaining *Nirvāṇa* – but defilements arise through the mind's inept modes of interaction with the world. Even a newborn child is not seen as having a wholly pure mind, however, for it is said to have unskilful latent tendencies (*anusaya*, Skt *anuśaya*) which are carried over from a previous life (*M*.I.433). In the calm of deep meditation, the depth-radiance of the mind is experienced at a conscious level, as the process of meditation suspends the defiling five hindrances, just as a smelter purifies gold-ore so as to attain pure gold (*S*.V.92). More than a temporary undefiled state of mind is necessary for awakening, however. For this, there must be destruction of the four 'taints' or 'cankers' (*āsava*, Skt *āśrava*): the most deeply rooted spiritual faults, which are likened to festering sores, leeching off energy from the mind, or intoxicating influxes on the mind. These are the taints of (i) sense-desire, (ii) attachment to 'being' and to a prized identity, (iii) views, and (iv) spiritual ignorance, which are all seen as conditioning, and being conditioned by, spiritual ignorance (*M*.I.54–5).

The second *nidāna*, 'constructing activities' or 'karmic activities' (*saṅkhāra*, Skt *saṃskāra*) are expressed in both karmically harmful and karmically fruitful actions of body, speech and mind.[9] In a person who has destroyed spiritual ignorance, actions no longer have the power to 'construct' any karmic results. Prior to that, actions can be karmically fruitful if they are based on *some* degree of insight into reality, such as the principles of karma or impermanence. The main 'constructing activity' is will (*cetanā*), that which initiates actions. As it is conditioned, but not rigidly determined in a fixed pattern by past events, it has a relative freedom (Harvey, 2007c). For example, the arising of anger need not lead on to angry behaviour, if a person becomes watchfully aware of it, so as to lessen its

[9] Plus in 'imperturbable' constructing activities, leading to rebirth in the formless realms and their neutral feeling-tone. These are listed separately from the karmically fruitful ones, which lead to experiences of happiness.

power. This is because the act of mindfulness brings about a change in the current conditions operating in the mind.

Constructing activities condition '(discriminative) consciousness' (*viññāṇa*, Skt *vijñāna*): for actions generate tendencies whose momentum tends to make a person become aware of, or think of, certain objects. For example, if one has decided (a mental action) to look for a certain article to buy, one's mind will automatically notice related things, such as advertisements and 'for sale' notices, which were previously not even mentally registered. 'That which we will, and that which we intend to do, and that for which we have a latent tendency, this is an object for the persistence of consciousness. If there is an object, there is a support for consciousness' (*S*.II.65 (*BW*.357–8)). What one is conscious of, and thus the form of one's consciousness, depends on one's volitions and tendencies. As consciousness is also conditioned by its objects (and the sense-organs), the version of Conditioned Arising at *D*.II.63 gives name-and-form, that is, mental and physical phenomena as objects, as the first link in the chain, followed by consciousness and on through the remaining links as in the standard version (Harvey, 1995a: 124–8).

The most important context in which constructing activities condition consciousness is in the generation of consciousness in a future life: for it is said that the 'evolving' or 'conducive' (*saṃvattanika*) consciousness is the crucial link between rebirths (*M*.II.262). At death, the momentum set up by constructing activities (and craving) is not cut off, but impels the evolving flux of consciousness to spill over beyond one life and help spark off another. Conditioned Arising here provides a 'middle' way of understanding which avoids the extremes of 'eternalism' and 'annihilationism': the survival of an eternal Self, or the total annihilation of a person at death (cf. *It*.43–4 (*BW*.215–16)). Of a person in two consecutive rebirths, it is said, 'He is not [unchangingly] the same and he is not [completely] different' (*Miln*.40 (*BSI*.149–51)). No unchanging 'being' passes over from one life to another, but the death of a being leads to the continuation of the life process in another context, like the lighting of one lamp from another (*Miln*.71). The 'later' being is a continuation, or evolute of the 'earlier' one on which he is causally dependent. They are linked by the flux of consciousness and the accompanying seeds of karmic results, so that the character of one is a development of the character of the 'other'. After death, a changing personality flux flows on. Given long enough, this may become *very* different from how one is now: and yet what will be then will have developed out of how one is, and acts, now.

The fourth *nidāna* is 'mind-and-body', literally 'name-and-form' (*nāma-rūpa*), consisting of feeling, perception, will, stimulation and attention ('mind/naming'), and the physical elements ('body/form') (*S*.II.3). As such, it can be seen primarily as the 'sentient body': the body and accompanying mental states which provide sentience. This develops once the flux of consciousness 'descends' into the womb (*D*.II.62–3), when there has also been intercourse at the right time of the month (*M*.I.265–6). Outside the womb, the fully developed sentient body continues unless consciousness is cut off (*D*.II.63): for consciousness, vitality and heat make a body alive and sensitive (*M*.I.295–6). Together, consciousness and name-and-form encompass all five *khandhas* of personality, and the interaction between them is seen to be the crux of the process of life and suffering:

> Indeed, consciousness turns back round onto name-and-form, it does not go beyond. Only in this way can one be born, or grow old, or die, or fall away from one's past existence, or be reborn: that is to say, insofar as consciousness is conditioned by name-and-form, name-and-form is conditioned by consciousness, the six sense-bases are conditioned by name-and-form . . . (*D*.II.32)

The next *nidāna* is the six sense-bases (*āyatana*), which are the five physical sense-organs and the mind-organ (*mano*), the latter being seen as that which is sensitive to mental objects, that is, objects of memory, thought, imagination and the input of the five senses. These six are conditioned by the sentient body as they can only exist in a living organism. Now Buddhism emphasizes that, whatever the external physical world is like, the 'world' (*loka*) of our actual lived experience is one built up from the input of the five senses, interpreted by the mind-organ (*S*.IV.95). As this interpretation is, for most people, influenced by spiritual ignorance, our 'lived world' is skewed and not in harmony with reality. Such a world is fraught with unsatisfactoriness, but it is conditioned and can be transcended: 'I declare that this fathom-long carcase, which is percipient and endowed with mind-organ, contains the world, and the origin of the world, and the cessation of the world [*Nirvāṇa*], and the way leading to the cessation of the world' (*S*.I.62 (*SB*.209–10)). This can be seen as about the four True Realities for the Spiritually Ennobled, with 'the world' replacing '*dukkha*'.

The following *nidāna*s show how the world of suffering is built up (*S*.II.73–4 (*BW*.358–9)). Only if there are sense-bases can there be 'stimulation' (*phassa*, Skt *sparśa*) of these: the coming together of a sense-base, its object and the appropriate kind of consciousness. While often translated as 'contact', this translation does not properly indicate the involvement of consciousness in *phassa*. When there is stimulation, feeling (*vedanā*) arises. Depending on what feelings arise, there is craving (*taṇhā*), to enjoy, prolong or get rid of them. Indeed the latent tendencies to attachment, aversion or confused ignorance may become active (*M.*III.285). While one cannot help what feelings arise, the extent of craving in response to them is modifiable. Craving is thus one of the two weak points in the twelvefold chain, the other being spiritual ignorance (*Vism.*523–6). The Buddhist path aims to undermine craving by moral discipline and meditative calming, and then destroy craving and ignorance by the development of wisdom.

From a 'thirst' for something arises 'grasping' (*upādāna*) at it, a more active involvement with and clinging to the object of craving. Such grasping may be for sense-pleasures, for views, for rules and observances (as sufficient for attaining awakening) or doctrines of a Self (*M.*I.50–1). Grasping then leads on to 'becoming' (*bhava*), that is, a particular kind of character or nature that is crystallizing into a certain mode of being. The Theravādin *Abhidhamma* explains this as having two aspects: 'karma-becoming', that is, karmically fruitful and harmful volitions, and 'resultant-becoming', existence in some world as a result of grasping and karma (*Vibh.*137). Such a world is primarily meant as a new rebirth but, arguably, it can also be seen as applying to a 'world' in this life, that is, a developed identity or a situation one finds oneself in as a result of one's grasping and actions. 'Becoming' may also have been intended to refer to an 'intermediate becoming' (*antarā-bhava*), a period of transition between rebirths. About half the pre-Mahāyāna schools, including the Theravādins, held that the moment of death was immediately followed by the moment of conception, with *no* intervening period. The other schools, and later the Mahāyāna, believed in such an existence. Some *Sutta* passages seem to indicate that the earliest Buddhists believed in it. One refers to a time when a being has laid aside one body and has not yet arisen in another (*S.*IV.399–400). Another refers to a subtle-bodied *gandhabba*, or spirit-being, as needing to be present if sexual intercourse is to lead to conception (*M.*I.265–6; Harvey 1995a: 98–108).

Any 'becoming' and its impelling energies and inclinations to seek 'more' is seen to naturally lead on to birth (*jāti*), in the sense of the very start of a rebirth, conception. It might additionally be interpreted, on a different time-scale, as referring to the constant re-arising, during life, of the processes comprising the five *khandhas*. Once birth has arisen, 'ageing and death', and various other *dukkha* states follow. While saying that birth is the cause of death may sound rather simplistic, in Buddhism it is a very significant statement; for there is an alternative to being born. This is to attain *Nirvāṇa*, so bringing an end to the process of rebirth and redeath. *Nirvāṇa* is not subject to time and change, and so is known as the 'unborn'; as it is not born it cannot die, and so it is also known as the 'deathless'. To attain this state, all phenomena subject to birth – the *khandhas* and *nidānas* – must be transcended by means of non-attachment.

Of the twelve *nidānas*, those actively contributing to the arising of *dukkha* are spiritual ignorance, the constructing activities, craving, grasping, and karma-becoming, the others being results of these (*Vism*.579–81). Note that it is never said that the last *nidāna*, ageing and death, is a condition for the first, ignorance. Nevertheless, people may wrongly think this because the Tibetan 'Wheel of Life' (Bechert and Gombrich, 1984: 29; Gethin, 1998: 158) has the twelve *nidānas* around its rim, so that the first and last are shown next to each other.

As a general point on Conditioned Arising, it should be noted that it presents a 'middle' way of understanding that echoes the Buddhist path as a 'middle way' of practice. This idea was to be greatly influential on later forms of Buddhism – such as the Mādhyamika, or 'Middle Way' school – all of which sought to best express the true 'middle' way of understanding reality. In the early texts, the notion is seen in the idea of Conditioned Arising as avoiding the extremes of both 'eternalism' and 'annihilationism' as regards the fate of a person after death (see above). It also avoids the extremes of substantialism – seeing the experienced world as existing here and now in a solid, essential way – and nihilism – seeing it as purely an illusion, non-existent. Rather, the experienced world is a constantly arising and passing away flow of processes. This is seen in a passage explaining the deeper meaning of 'right view', the first factor of the Noble Eight-factored Path.[10] This explains that truly seeing how the experienced world originates, through the links of Conditioned Arising, shows it is wrong to hold to its 'non-existence', while seeing its cessation, that is, the Nirvāṇic cessation of the links, shows it is wrong to hold to its substantial 'existence'. One with right view is not 'shackled by bias, clinging and insistence' or 'affirming "my Self"', and 'has no doubt or uncertainty that what arises is only arising *dukkha*, and that what ceases is only ceasing *dukkha*' (and what is *dukkha* is also non-Self).

It is also said that Conditioned Arising is a 'middle' way of being that shows the error of the views that 'all is one' and 'all is a diversity' (*S*.II.77). The first of these is exemplified by the Upaniṣadic idea that everything is *Brahman*, and indeed in some popular Western presentations of Buddhism.

[10] *Kaccāyanagotta Sutta*: *S*.II.17 (*BW*.356–7); cf. *EB*.3.2.5.

The second sees reality as a collection of separately existing, independent entities. Conditioned Arising, though, is a network of processes which could not exist apart from each other, yet are not the same as each other.

THE THIRD TRUE REALITY FOR THE SPIRITUALLY ENNOBLED: THE CESSATION OF THE PAINFUL – *NIRVĀṆA*

The third True Reality is described in the first sermon as follows:

Now *this*, monks, for the spiritually ennobled, is the ceasing-of-the-painful true reality. It is the remainderless fading away and cessation of that same craving, the giving up and relinquishing of it, freedom from it, non-reliance on it.

That is, the ending of thirst for the 'next thing', so as to give full attention to what is here, now; abandoning attachments to past, present or future; freedom that comes from contentment; not relying on craving so that the mind does not fixate on anything, adhering to it, roosting there. When craving and other related causes thus come to an end, *dukkha* ceases. This is equivalent to *Nirvāṇa* (Pali *Nibbāna*), also known as the 'unconditioned' or 'unconstructed' (*asaṅkhata*, Skt *asaṃskṛta*), the ultimate goal of Buddhism (Collins, 2010). As an initial spur to striving for *Nirvāṇa*, craving for it may play a role (*A*.II.145; Webster, 2005: 134–5), but this helps in the overcoming of other cravings, is generally replaced by a wholesome aspiration, and is completely eradicated in the full experience of *Nirvāṇa*: *Nirvāṇa* is only attained when there is total non-attachment and letting go.

Nirvāṇa literally means 'extinction' or 'quenching', being the word used for the 'extinction' of a fire. The 'fires' of which *Nirvāṇa* is the extinction are described in the 'Fire sermon' (*S*.IV.19–20 (*BW*.346; *SB*.222–4)). This teaches that everything internal and external to a person is 'burning' with the 'fires' of attachment, hatred (*rāga, dosa* (Skt *dveṣa*)) and delusion (*moha*) and of birth, ageing and death. Here the 'fires' refer both to the causes of *dukkha* and to *dukkha* itself. Attachment (i.e. sensual and other forms of lust) and hatred are closely related to craving for things and craving to be rid of things, and delusion is synonymous with spiritual ignorance. *Nirvāṇa* during life is frequently defined as the destruction of these three 'fires' or defilements (e.g. *S*.IV.251 (*BW*.364; *EB*.3.4.1)). When one who has destroyed these dies, he or she cannot be reborn and so is totally beyond the remaining 'fires' of birth, ageing and death, having attained final *Nirvāṇa*.

Both during life and beyond death, *Nirvāṇa* pertains to the *Arahat*, one who has direct knowledge that he or she has destroyed the four 'taints' (see

p. 68). *Nirvāṇa* in life is described as 'with remainder of what is grasped at' (*sa-upādi-sesa*, Skt *sopadhi-śeṣa*), meaning that the *khandhas*, the result of past grasping, still remain for him. *Nirvāṇa* beyond death is described as 'without remainder of what is grasped at' (*an-upādi-sesa*, Skt *nir-upadhi-śeṣa*), (*It*.38–9 (*BTTA*.97, *BW*.366–7)).

Nirvāṇa *during life*

It is often thought that *Nirvāṇa* during life is an ever-present state of the *Arahat*, but it would seem that this cannot be so (Harvey, 1995a: 180–97). As *Nirvāṇa* is synonymous with the cessation of all that is *dukkha*, and *Nirvāṇa* during life is not seen as inferior to *Nirvāṇa* beyond death in any respect (*Sn*.876–7), it cannot be ever-present; for the *Arahat* will at some time experience physical pain. Moreover, simply to walk down the road is to have such conditioned states as feeling and consciousness occurring. As the cessation of *dukkha* involves the stopping of each of the *nidāna*s and *khandhas*, *Nirvāṇa* lies beyond the occurrence of such states. One must therefore see *Nirvāṇa* during life as a specific experience, in which the defilements are destroyed forever, and in which there is a temporary stopping of all conditioned states (*Sn*.732–9). Such a destruction-of-defilements is clearly a transcendent, timeless experience, for it is said to be 'deathless' (*S*.v.8) and 'unconditioned' (*S*.iv.362). During life or beyond death, *Nirvāṇa* is the unconditioned cessation of all unsatisfactory, conditioned phenomena. During life, it is where these phenomena stop, followed by their recurrence in the arising of normal experiences of the world; once attained, this stopping can be returned to. Beyond death, it is where they stop for good.

Descriptions of the Nirvāṇic experience stress its 'otherness', placing it beyond all limited concepts and ordinary categories of thought. This is clearly shown in a description at *Ud*.80 (*BTTA*.95; *BW*.365–6) that begins by firmly asserting the existence of that which lies beyond all *dukkha*. It then says that this is a sphere where there are neither the four physical elements, nor the four formless mystical states or corresponding heavenly levels of rebirth where only mental phenomena exist (see p. 34). This indicates that it is beyond mind-and-body (*nāma-rūpa*). Further, it is said to be beyond this world or any other world of rebirth, and beyond the arising and ceasing of phenomena in the process of life and rebirth. It is without any 'support' (*patiṭṭhā*) on which it depends, and is without any mental 'object' (*ārammaṇa*). In the face of *Nirvāṇa*, words falter, for language is a product of human needs in this world, and has few resources with which to deal with that which transcends all worlds. *Nirvāṇa*, it is said, is an aspect of the *Dhamma* which is 'difficult to understand ... beyond abstract reasoning, subtle' (*Vin.*I.4). The most accurate and least misleading descriptions are negative, saying what it is *not*. Thus, above, there is an affirmation of existence followed by a string of negations. Most synonyms of *Nirvāṇa* are also negative: the stopping of *dukkha*, the unborn, the unbecome, the unmade (*Ud.*81 (*BW.*366)), the deathless, stopping (*nirodha*), non-attachment (*virāga*).

Positive descriptions of *Nirvāṇa* are generally of a poetic, suggestive nature. Thus it is said to be: the 'further shore' (beyond this 'shore' of life and its pains, *M.*I.134–5 (*BTTA.*77)); the '[cool] cave of shelter' (a powerful image of peace and rest in the hot Indian climate). Certain positive descriptions give a less poetic indication of its nature. It is the 'calming (*samatha*) of all constructing activities' (*Vin.*I.5), the 'highest bliss', the very opposite of *dukkha* (*M.*I.508). It is 'timeless' (*A.*I.158), for it is beyond time (*Miln.*323), and so is permanent and eternal (*Kvu.*121). *S.*IV.368–73 (*BW.*364–5) emphasizes the goal as 'the unconditioned', then adds many synonyms for this, including: the taintless, the true reality (*sacca*), the beyond, the very-hard-to-see, the undecaying, the non-manifestive (*anidassana*), the unelaborated (*nippapañca*), the peaceful, the sublime, the amazing, freedom, the unclinging, the island (amidst the flood), the refuge.

Though it is approached and attained by the Noble Eight-factored Path, *Nirvāṇa* is not caused by it, being unconditioned. Thus the last two True Realities are not (iii) the end of *dukkha*, (iv) the path that causes this end, but (iii) the end of *dukkha* from the end of its cause, (iv) the path that leads to this end. The Path is the best of all conditioned states (*A.*II.34 (*BW.*168–9)), and *Nirvāṇa* is related to the Path as a mountain is related to a path which leads up to it.[11] In general, Buddhism sees it as more appropriate to describe this Path than to try and precisely describe its goal.

Nevertheless, certain passages in the *Sutta*s hint that *Nirvāṇa* may be a radically transformed state of consciousness (*viññāṇa*):

> The consciousness which is non-manifestive [like space], endless,
> accessible from all sides [or: wholly radiant]:
> *Here* it is that solidity, cohesion, heat and motion have no footing,
> Here long and short, coarse and fine, foul and lovely [have no footing],
> Here it is that name (*nāma*) and form (*rūpa*) stop without remainder:
> By the stopping of consciousness, [all] this stops here. (*D.*I.223)

[11] *Miln.*269 (*BTTA.*98, *BS1.*157–9, *EB.*3.4.2).

Like *Ud.*80, above, this describes a state beyond the four physical elements, where name-and-form are transcended. As the heart of Conditioned Arising is the mutual conditioning of consciousness and name-and-form, this state is where this interaction ceases: from the stopping of consciousness, name-and-form stops. Consciousness is not non-existent when it stops, however: for it is said to be non-manifestive and endless, and like a sunbeam that is not obstructed by any object in its path (*S.*II.103). One passage on the stopping (*nirodha*) of the *nidāna* of consciousness (*S.*III.54–5) says that a monk abandons attachment for each of the five *khandhas*, such that there is no longer any object (*ārammaṇa*) or support (*patiṭṭhā*) for consciousness; consciousness is thus 'unsupported' (*apatiṭṭhita*, Skt *apratiṣṭhita*) and free of constructing activities, so that it is released, steadfast, content, undisturbed, and attains *Nirvāṇa*. This description, of a 'stopped' consciousness which is unsupported by any mental object, where name-and-form/mind-and-body are transcended, seems to accord well with the above *Ud.*80 description of *Nirvāṇa*.

To say that *Nirvāṇa* is unconditioned, objectless consciousness indicates something of its nature, but does not penetrate far into its mystery. For it seems impossible to imagine what awareness devoid of any object would be like. As regards the 'stopping' of mind-and-body, as a state occurring during life, this is perhaps to be understood as one where all mental processes (including ordinary consciousness) temporarily cease, and the matter of the body is seen as so ephemeral as not to signify a 'body'. A passage at *M.*I.329–30 which parallels *D.*I.223 says that the non-manifestive (*anidassana*) consciousness 'is not reached by the solidness of solidity, by the cohesiveness of cohesion'. The analysis of *Nirvāṇa* as objectless consciousness, though, is the author's own interpretation (Harvey, 1995a: 198–226). The Theravādin tradition sees *Nirvāṇa* as 'objectless' (*Dhs.*1408), but regards 'consciousness' as *always* having an object. *D.*I.223 is thus interpreted as concerning *Nirvāṇa* as to-be-known-by-consciousness: *Nirvāṇa* is itself the object of the *Arahat*'s consciousness (*Patis.*II.143–5).

The Arahat[12]

Some further light is shed on *Nirvāṇa* during life by examining the nature of the *Arahat*[13] (Skt *Arhat*), one who has attained the Nirvāṇic experience and

[12] See *EB.*3.5.2, *SB.*265–6, *BW.*406–13, Katz, 1982; Ray, 1994: 79–150.

[13] Books use either '*Arahat*' or '*Arahant*' as the Pali form. The first is the form that appears in compounds while the second is its stem form.

been radically transformed by it. The full experience of *Nirvāṇa* destroys attachment, hatred and delusion forever. As a person becomes an *Arahat* in this experience (which is then immediately known by a reviewing knowledge), the destruction of these three defilements is given both as the definition of *Nirvāṇa* during life and of 'Arahatness' (*Arahatta*; *S*.IV.252).

The word *Arahat* means 'worthy one', that is, worthy of great respect. He or she is one who has fully completed spiritual training, is fully endowed with all factors of the Path, and has quenched the 'fires' of the defilements. He has overcome the 'disease' of *dukkha* and attained complete mental health (*A*.II.143). Such a perfected one is described as follows: 'Calm is his mind, calm is his speech, calm is his behaviour who, rightly knowing, is wholly freed, perfectly peaceful and equipoised' (*Dhp*.96). The calm actions of the *Arahat* are such that he no longer creates karmic results leading to rebirths. They are just pure spontaneous actions without any future fruit. The balanced detachment of the *Arahat*'s mind is such that, while he may experience physical pain (perhaps as a result of past karma), no mental anguish at this can arise (*Miln*.44–5). He and the almost-enlightened non-returner are free of aversion to physical pain, and so add no mental pain in response to it (*S*.IV.208–9). This is because he does not identify with the pain as 'mine', but simply sees it as a non-Self passing phenomenon. As is said in the second century CE *Avadāna-śataka* (II.384; Dayal, 1932: 15), 'the sky and the palm of his hand were the same to his mind'. Even faced with the threat of death, the *Arahat* is unruffled. In this situation, the *Arahat* Adhimutta disconcerted some potential assailants by fearlessly asking why he should be perturbed at the prospect of the end of the constituents of 'his' personality: he had no thought of an 'I' being here, but just saw a stream of changing phenomena (*Thag*.715–16). This so impressed the robbers threatening him that they became Adhimutta's disciples. Anyone who shows any hint of fear, conceit or any other negative states cannot be an *Arahat* (*M*.I.317, cf. *Vism*.634–5), and if the Buddha, or one of his *Arahat* disciples who can read minds, examines and talks with someone who claims to be an *Arahat*, they can tell whether or not their claim is true (*A*.V.155–6).

Though free of fear and craving, the *Arahat* should not be thought of as apathetic or emotionless. The uprooting of negative emotions eradicates restrictions on such qualities as mindful alertness, lovingkindness and compassion. *Arahats* are not all alike, either; for some were noted for specific abilities: in teaching, in psychic powers based on meditation, in explaining concisely phrased teachings, or in living an ascetic life-style (*A*.I.23–5). While the *Arahat* is one who has seen through the delusion of a permanent Self or I, he or she nevertheless has an empirical self, or character, which is very well developed in virtue, meditative calm and wisdom (Harvey, 1995a: 54–63): he is 'one of developed self' (*bhāvit-attā, It.*79), a 'great self' (*mahattā*; *A.*I.249; *It.*28–9), not a psychologically 'small' person. Yet in such a self he sees no Self, no substantial 'I': he has no 'I am' conceit (*S.*III.83–4 (*BTTA.*14; *BW.*412–13)). An *Arahat* has a strong mind, 'like a thunderbolt' (*A.*I.124), in which flashes of insight arise, and he has fully developed the 'seven factors of awakening' (*bojjhaṅga*, Skt *bodhyaṅga)*: mindfulness, investigation of *Dhamma*, vigour, joy, tranquillity, mental unification and equanimity (*Thag.*161 with *D.*III.106). He is not attracted or repelled by anything, but is 'independent, not infatuated, freed, released, and dwells with a mind that is made to be without barriers' (*M.*III.29).

Nirvāṇa *beyond death*

At the death of an *Arahat* or Buddha, the 'grasped at' personality factors come to an end. This raises the question of what happens to an awakened person beyond death: does he still exist? The Buddha was often asked this question of the state of a *Tathāgata*, here meaning a Buddha or *Arahat*, after death: could it be said that he 'is' (*hoti*), that he 'is not' (being annihilated), that he 'both is and is not', or that he 'neither is nor is not'? These were part of a small set of 'undetermined questions' which the Buddha set aside without answering (*S.*IV.373–400). One reason for this was that he saw speculating over them as a time-wasting diversion from spiritual practice. When one monk told him that he would leave the *Saṅgha* unless he was given answers to these questions, the Buddha gave a simile to show how foolish he was: if a man was shot by a poisoned arrow but refused to let a doctor cure him until he knew everything about who shot the arrow, and what the arrow was made of, such a man would soon die (*M.*I.426–31 (*BW.*230–3; *SB.*168–72)). The Buddha then said that he had clearly explained *dukkha* and the way beyond it, but that asking the undetermined questions was not connected with, nor conducive to, *Nirvāṇa*. This accords with his saying that he taught only what was both true and spiritually useful (*M.*I.395).

Besides these practical considerations, the Buddha also clearly saw the undetermined questions as having a misconception built into them. Like the innocent man who was asked 'have you stopped beating your wife?', he could not rightly reply either 'yes' or 'no' to them. The Buddha explained that the questions were always asked by people who saw a permanent Self as somehow related to the five *khandhas* (see pp. 64–5), but that he did not answer the questions because he had no such view (*S.*IV.395). That is, his questioners were asking about the fate of an awakened substantial *Self* after death, and as no such thing could be found during life, it was meaningless to discuss its state after death.

Setting aside this misconception, how might one understand the state of the awakened person beyond death? Is he to be seen as annihilated with the ending of the five *khandhas*? Such a view, equivalent to the second undetermined question, is seen as particularly pernicious, however: for it is emphasized that all that ends at death is *dukkha* (*S*.III.109–12). Some light is shed on the situation by a passage in which the Buddha discusses the undetermined questions on a *Tathāgata*, equating these with questions on whether an awakened monk 'arises' (i.e. is reborn), or not, etc. after death (*M*.I.486–7). Here he says that, while one would know whether a burning fire had gone out, one could not meaningfully ask what direction the quenched fire had gone in: east, west, south or north. He then stresses that a *Tathāgata* (even in life) is 'deep, immeasurable, hard-to-fathom as is the great ocean'.[14] While to a Western-educated person, an extinct fire goes nowhere because it does not exist, the Buddha's audience in ancient India would generally have thought of an extinguished fire as going back into a non-manifested state as latent heat (e.g. *A*.III.340–1). The simile of the extinct fire thus suggests that the state of an awakened person after death is one which is beyond normal comprehension, not that it is a state of nothingness: 'There exists no measuring of one who has gone out [like a flame]. That by which he could be referred to no longer exists for him. When all phenomena are removed, then all ways of describing have also been removed' (*Sn*.1076). Similarly, it is said that the questions on the *Tathāgata* are set aside because, beyond his death, there are absolutely no grounds for saying that he is with or without a body, with or without perception, or neither with nor without perception (*S*.IV.402).

Having destroyed all causes of rebirth, a *Tathāgata* cannot be reborn in any way, such as in the very refined and subtle 'sphere of neither-perception-nor-non-perception'. While he is not annihilated at death, it can't be said he 'is' anything. 'His' indefinable state must be seen as 'beyond' rather than 'after' death, for it must be beyond existence in time. As to what that state is, all that it can be is: *Nirvāṇa*, the cessation of conditioned phenomena. The nearest hint at what this might be, beyond death, is a passage on Godhika, who had attained *Nirvāṇa* at the very point of death (*S*.I.121–2). Seeing a smokiness going in the four directions, the Buddha said that this was Māra seeking out where Godhika's consciousness

[14] *BW*.367–9; *BTTA*.107, cf. 110–11, 119.

was 'supported', that is, where he was reborn. The Buddha affirmed that Māra's quest was in vain, however, for 'with an unsupported consciousness, the clansman Godhika has attained *Nirvāṇa*'. As an 'unsupported' consciousness is no longer conditioned by constructing activities or any objects (as argued above), it must be unconditioned and beyond *dukkha*, no longer a *khandha*. As all that ends at death are the 'grasped at' *khandhas*, equivalent to *dukkha*, there seems to be no reason why such a mysterious consciousness should end at death too.

However one interprets the situation, the Theravāda tradition emphasizes that the Buddha, since his death, is beyond contact with the world and cannot respond to prayer or worship (*Miln.* 95–100). Nevertheless, something of his *power* is seen to remain in the world, to be drawn on by both chanting and practising his teachings (*Dhamma*), and even through the bodily relics which remained after his cremation. One commentary says that 5,000 years after the *parinibbāna* (Skt *parinirvāṇa*), or passing into *Nirvāṇa* at death of the Buddha, the practice of Buddhism will have disappeared, such that the period of Gotama Buddha's influence will have ended. All his relics will then travel to the foot of the tree under which he attained awakening, and disappear in a flash of light (*Vibh-a.*433; *BTTA.*22). This is known as the *parinibbāna* of the relics.

Nirvāṇa *as an object of insight*

As well as the aspects of an *Arahat*'s *Nirvāṇa* discussed above, *Nirvāṇa* is also seen, in the early texts, as something that can be known as an object of mind by the *Arahat* and other Noble ones (Harvey, 1986, 1995a: 193–7). At stream-entry, a person gains his first 'glimpse' of *Nirvāṇa*, for he gains the *Dhamma*-eye and 'sees' the *Dhamma* which is *Nirvāṇa* (see pp. 23–4, 29 and 86). The *Nirvāṇa* which he sees must be none other than the timeless, unconditioned realm which the *Arahat* finally 'enters' at death, and which he also periodically fully experiences during life. *Nirvāṇa*, indeed, is seen as existing whether or not anyone attains it, as is shown by the assertion that, if it were not for the existence of the unborn, unconditioned, it would not be possible to leave behind born, conditioned, *dukkha* phenomena (*It.*37, *Ud.*81). One could perhaps say that the *Arahat*'s *full* experience of *Nirvāṇa* during life, with *Nirvāṇa* as not simply a known object, is one of 'participating in' that unborn, unconditioned blissful reality.

Nirvāṇa as an object of insight is known when one 'focuses mind on the deathless element: "This is the peaceful, this is the sublime, that is, the stilling of all constructing activities, the relinquishing of all attachments, the destruction of craving, non-attachment, stopping, *Nirvāṇa*'" (*M.*I.436, cf. *A.*V.321–6). A term for this state seems to be the concentration (*samādhi*) or deliverance of mind (*ceto-vimutti*) that is 'signless' (*animitta*), in which one attends to no perceptual 'signs', or perceptual indications, even those of the most subtle meditative state, but attends to the 'signless element' (*M.*I.296). A passage at *A.*V.318–19 (Harvey, 1995a: 195–6) says that in seeing beyond a range of perceptual signs, for example 'earth'/solidity, and perceiving 'This is the peaceful . . . *Nirvāṇa*', 'a monk's concentration is of such a sort that in solidity, he is not percipient of solidity', and likewise of any other physical element or subtle spiritual state. Solidity is perceived, as it were, as empty of 'solidity'; perception does not latch onto a 'sign' as a basis for seeing solidity *as* solidity. Rather, the mind perceives the signless, *Nirvāṇa*. Yet to fully attain *Nirvāṇa*, even this sublime but conditioned perception must be let go of (*M.*III.108).

Once Arahatship is attained, the liberated person's unshakeable deliverance of mind (*Nirvāṇa*) is 'empty' of attachment, hatred and delusion (*M.*I.297–8 (*BTTA.*82)), and may be contemplated as such. *Nirvāṇa* is thus known as 'the empty' (*suññata*, Skt *śūnyatā*: 'emptiness'), and is known in this aspect through contemplation of phenomena as 'empty of Self or what pertains to Self'.

THE FOURTH TRUE REALITY FOR THE SPIRITUALLY ENNOBLED: THE PATH TO THE CESSATION OF THE PAINFUL

In the first sermon, the Buddha has this to say on the Path:

> Monks, these two extremes should not be followed by one gone forth [into the renunciant life]. What two? That which is this pursuit of sensual happiness in sensual pleasures, which is low, vulgar, the way of the ordinary person, ignoble, not connected to the goal; and that which is this pursuit of self-mortification, which is painful, ignoble, not connected to the goal. Monks, without veering towards either of these two extremes, the *Tathāgata* has awakened to the middle way (*majjhimā paṭipadā*, Skt *madhyama pratipad*), which gives rise to vision, which gives rise to knowledge, which leads to peace, to higher knowledge, to full awakening, to *Nirvāṇa*.
>
> And what, monks, is that middle way. . .? It is just this noble eight-factored path (*ariya aṭṭhaṅgika magga*, Skt *āryāṣṭāṅgika mārga*). . .
>
> Now *this*, monks, for the spiritually ennobled, is the true reality which is the way leading to the cessation of the painful. It is this noble eight-factored path, that is to say, [1] right view, [2] right resolve, [3] right speech, [4] right action, [5] right livelihood, [6] right effort, [7] right mindfulness, [8] right mental unification. (numbers added)

The Noble Eight-factored Path is a middle way that avoids a life of pursuing either sense-pleasures or harsh asceticism, and it leads to the cessation of *dukkha* (Bodhi, 1994; Gethin, 2001: 190–226). As later chapters will deal with the details of Buddhist practice, this section will be confined to a general outline of the Path and its dynamics, and the stages of sanctity reached by it.

The Path has eight factors (*aṅga*), each described as right or perfect (*sammā*, Skt *samyak; S.*v.8–10 (*BW*.239–40)). These factors are also grouped into three sections (*M.*I.301). Factors 1–2 pertain to *paññā* (Skt *prajñā*), or wisdom; factors 3–5 pertain to *sīla* (Skt *śīla*), moral virtue; factors 6–8 pertain to *samādhi*, meditation. The eight factors exist at two basic levels, the ordinary (*lokiya*, Skt *laukika*), and the transcendent (*lokuttara*, Skt *lokottara*) or Noble (see p. 49), so that there is both an ordinary and a Noble Eight-factored Path (*M.*III.71–8); see Table 1.

In the Table, the key difference between the ordinary and Noble Paths can be seen to arise from the different forms of right view. The order of the eight Path-factors is seen as that of a natural progression, with one factor following on from the one before it. Right view comes first (*S.*v.2) because it knows the right and wrong form of each of the eight factors; it also counteracts spiritual ignorance, the first factor in Conditioned Arising (*S.*v.1–2 (*SB*.226)). From the cool knowing of right view blossoms right resolve, a right way of thinking/aspiring, which has a balancing warmth. From this, a person's speech becomes improved, and thus his or her action. Once he is working on right action, it becomes natural to incline towards a virtuous livelihood. With this as basis, there can be progress in right effort. This facilitates the development of right mindfulness, whose clarity then allows the development of the calm of meditative concentration. Neither the ordinary nor the Noble Path is to be understood as a single progression from the first to eighth factor, however. Right effort and mindfulness work with right view to support the development of all the Path-factors (*M.*III.72–5): the Path-factors mutually support each other to allow a gradual deepening of the way in which the Path is trodden. Each Path-factor is a skilful state to be cultivated; it progressively wears away its opposite 'wrong' factor, until all unskilful states are destroyed.

In most contexts (e.g. *D.*II.91), moral virtue, meditation and wisdom are given in this order, which is different from the order in which the Path-factors are grouped in Table 1. This may be in part because the former is the order in which people tend to work on the aspects of the ordinary Path. The wisdom derived from this then leads to the breakthrough which is the wisdom at the start of the Noble Path. Once this is attained, stream-enterers have completely fulfilled moral virtue, then non-returners (see below) have

Table 1 *Factors of the Eight-factored Path*

Wisdom

1. **Right view** (*sammā-diṭṭhi*, Skt *samyag-dṛṣṭi*):
   i) at the 'ordinary' level: belief in the principles of karma and rebirth, making a person take full responsibility for his actions (see pp. 48–9). It also includes intellectual and preliminary experiential understanding of the four True Realities for the Spiritually Ennobled;
   ii) at the Noble or 'transcendent' level, as right seeing: transformative direct insight into the True Realities and Conditioned Arising (*M*.I.46–55 (*BW*.323–35), Ñāṇamoli and Bodhi, 1991) in the form of the faculty of wisdom that sees the flux of conditioned reality and, beyond it, *Nirvāṇa*.
2. **Right resolve** (*sammā-saṅkappa*, Skt *samyak-saṃkalpa*): A '*saṅkappa*' is seen as springing from what one focuses perception on, and to potentially lead on to desire-to-do, yearning and seeking something out (*S*.II.143), reminiscent of the *saṃkalpa* or preparatory resolve that the Brahmins made before carrying out a sacrificial ritual. It concerns the emotions and aspirations and is:
   i) at the 'ordinary' level, resolve for: a) *nekkhamma* (Skt *naiṣkāmya*), peaceful 'renunciation' or 'non-sensuality', and away from sense-pleasures (*kāmas*); b) non-ill-will, equivalent to lovingkindness, and away from ill-will; c) non-cruelty, equivalent to compassion, and away from cruelty.
   ii) at the Noble level: focused mental application (*vitakka*, Skt *vitarka*) in accord with right seeing. It is seen to both spring from and aid right view, both being part of wisdom. It aids right view as it is a repeated application of the mind to an object of contemplation, so that this can be rightly seen and understood, in a deep and discerning way, to be impermanent, *dukkha*, non-Self.

Moral virtue: i) at the 'ordinary' level, these factors are well established; ii) at the Noble level, they are the natural virtue of one in a deep state of insight.

3. **Right speech** (*sammā-vācā*, Skt *samyag-vācā*): abstaining from false speech, divisive speech, harsh speech and frivolous speech (see pp. 276–7).
4. **Right action** (*sammā-kammanta*, Skt *samyak-karmanta*): abstaining from onslaught on living beings, taking what is not given and wrong conduct in regard to sensual pleasures (see pp. 269–76).
5. **Right livelihood** (*sammā-ājīva*, Skt *samyag-ājīva*): making one's living in such a way as to avoid causing suffering to others (human or animal) through cheating them (*M*.III.75) or by physically harming or killing them: avoiding 'trade in weapons, living beings, meat, alcoholic drink, or poison' (*A*.III.208).

Meditation: the level of practice shifts to the Noble level once Noble right seeing guides them.

6. **Right effort** (*sammā-vāyāma*, Skt *samyag-vyāyāma*): a) avoiding the arising of unwholesome states (e.g. greed, hatred or delusion); b) undermining unwholesome states which have arisen; c) developing wholesome states, as in meditation; d) maintaining wholesome states which have arisen.
7. **Right mindfulness** (*sammā-sati*, Skt *samyak-smṛti*): practising the four applications of mindfulness (*satipaṭṭhāna*, Skt *smṛty-upasthāna*; see pp. 321–4) – alert, mindful observation of the qualities and changing nature of: a) body (including breathing); b) feeling; c) states of mind; d) *dhammas*: basic patterns in the flow of experience, such as: the five *khandhas*, the five hindrances, the four True Realities, and the seven factors of awakening.

Table 1 (*cont.*)

8. **Right concentration/mental unification** (*sammā-samādhi*, Skt *samyak-samādhi*): states of calm, peace and mental clarity arising from intently focusing the mind on one or other meditation object. These are concentrat*ed* states, rather than the act of concentrat*ing*, which pertains more to right effort. They are states in which the mind's energies have been unified, in the form of the four *jhāna*s (Skt *dhyāna*), lucid meditative trances (see pp. 329–31).

also completely fulfilled meditation, and *Arahat*s have also completely fulfilled wisdom (*A*.I.231–2).

Accordingly, the Path can be seen to develop as follows. Influenced by good and inspiring examples, a person's first commitment will be to develop virtue, a generous and self-controlled way of life for the benefit of self and others. To motivate this, he or she will have some degree of preliminary understanding, ordinary right view, in the form of some acquaintance with the Buddhist outlook and an aspiration to apply it, expressed as *saddhā* (Skt *śraddhā*), trustful confidence or faith. With virtue as the indispensable basis for further progress, some meditation may be attempted. With appropriate application, this will lead to the mind becoming calmer, stronger and clearer. This will allow experiential understanding of the *Dhamma* to develop – intent but calm concentration aids insight to penetrate subtle truths – so that deeper wisdom arises. From this, virtue is strengthened, becoming a basis for further progress in meditation and wisdom. With each more refined development of the virtue–meditation–wisdom sequence, the Path spirals up to a higher level. In time, the Noble level of the Path may be reached, in one practising for the realization of stream-entry. The Noble Path is the convergence of all eight path-factors in a state of strong insight into the 'three marks' (see p. 57), especially impermanence (*S*.III.225); it forms a skilful method of approach, free of spiritual hindrances and open to experiencing direct insight into the True Realities for the Spiritually Ennobled. In the *Sutta*s the Noble Path lasts an unspecified time and, once it has arisen, it guarantees attaining stream-entry at some time in the present life (*S*.III.225 (*BW*.393)). In the later *Abhidhamma* period (see p. 92), it came to be seen as lasting only for either one (Theravāda) or fifteen (Sarvāstivāda) moments, in which *Nirvāṇa* is directly seen, being immediately followed by becoming a stream-enterer. In effect, this sees only the culminating moment(s) of the *Sutta* Noble Path as the true Noble Path. The ordinary and then Noble Path are then used for subsequent spiritual breakthroughs, up to Arahatship. The form of the Path which immediately leads up to becoming an *Arahat* has two extra factors, right knowledge (*sammā-ñāṇa*, Skt *samyag-jñāna*) and right freedom (*sammā-vimutti*, Skt *samyag-vimukti*), making it ten-factored (*M.*III.76).

Most people, including most Buddhists, have not yet experienced the Noble Path, and are known as *puthujjanas* (Skt *pṛthagjana*), 'ordinary persons'. They are seen as, in a sense, 'deranged' (*Vibh-a.*186), as they lack the mental balance of those endowed with the Noble Path, the eight kinds of 'Noble (*ariya*) persons' (*S.*V.202)[15] who make up the Noble *Saṅgha* (*D.*III.227). The first seven Noble persons are called 'trainees' (*sekha*, Skt *saikṣa*), the *Arahat* is *asekha*, one beyond training.

The first Noble person is one 'practising for the realization of the fruit which is stream-entry' (*A.*IV.293). He or she is either a *Dhamma*-follower, particularly strong in wisdom, or a faith-follower, whose strength is faith in the Buddha, though he is not lacking in wisdom. Either of the two goes on to become the next kind of Noble person, the stream-enterer (*sotāpanna*, Skt *srotāpanna*), respectively as a *Dhamma*-attained or faith-freed person (*M.*I.477–9 (*BW.*390–2)). The stream-enterer gains a first glimpse of *Nirvāṇa* and so knows that the Noble Eight-factored Path is definitely the 'stream' that leads there (*S.*V.347–8). He is sure to become an *Arahat* within seven lives (*S.*II.133–4 (*BW.*394)) and is free from rebirths as a hell-being, animal, ghost or *asura*, as he has completely destroyed the first three of ten spiritual 'fetters' (*S.*V.357). The first fetter is 'Self-identity view' (see pp. 64–5), destroyed by deep insight into the four True Realities for the Spiritually Ennobled and Conditioned Arising. The second is vacillation in commitment to the three refuges and the worth of morality. The stream-enterer thus has unwavering confidence in the refuges and unblemished morality (*S.*V.343–4 (*BW.*394–5) and *A.*I.235). This is because he has 'seen' and 'plunged into' the *Dhamma* (*M.*I.380), giving him trust in *Dhamma* and in the '*Dhamma*-become' Buddha (see pp. 28–9), and is himself a member of the Noble *Saṅgha*, whether lay or a member of the monastic *Saṅgha*. The third fetter destroyed is grasping at rules and observances, for although his morality is naturally pure, he knows that this alone is insufficient to attain *Nirvāṇa* (*M.*I.192–7 (*BW.*233–7)), and is not fixedly attached to any ways of doing things.

The attainment of stream-entry is often seen in the arising of the '*Dhamma*-eye' (e.g. *S.*II.133–4), though this may also refer to an initial breakthrough at a higher level of the Path, without the intermediary state

[15] And see *A.*IV.292, *S.*V.202 and *M.*I.140–2 at *BW.*385–6.

of stream-entry (Anderson, 1999: 138). Passages on the arising of the '*Dhamma*-eye' (e.g. *D*.I.110) first talk of a person being given the two-stage 'step-by-step discourse' (see p. 48) so as to be poised for a break-through, intently open to the truth, and then hearing the teaching on the Four True Realities for the Spiritually Ennobled. Then: 'the *Dhamma*-eye, dustless, stainless arose to him that: "whatever is of the nature to arise (*samudaya-dhamma*), all that is of the nature to stop (*nirodha-dhamma*)"', so that the hearer becomes one who has 'seen *Dhamma*, attained to *Dhamma*, known *Dhamma*, fathomed/plunged into *Dhamma*'. With a new sense of clarity of vision, he goes for refuge to the Buddha, *Dhamma* and *Saṅgha* (if this has not already been done), and becomes a lay follower, or ordains as a monk or nun (if he or she has not done so already).

What, then, is it to 'see' *Dhamma* with the '*Dhamma*-eye'? At *S*. III.135, a monk wanting to 'see' *Dhamma* is given a teaching on Conditioned Arising and its stopping, such that *Dhamma* was 'penetrated' by him. Indeed, insight into phenomena as 'of the nature to arise' can be seen as knowledge of Conditioned *Arising*, and insight into them as 'of the nature to stop' can be seen as knowledge of *Nirvāṇa*, the *stopping* of all the links of Conditioned Arising (*S*.II.70). Such insight would be focused on the arising (*samudaya*) of *dukkha* from craving, and its stopping with the stopping of craving, the focus of the Buddha's first sermon. Indeed at the end of the Buddha's first sermon, the *Dhamma*-eye arose to one of the ascetics that the Buddha was teaching.

After stream-entry, by deepening his insight, a person may become one practising for the realization of once-returning, and then a once-returner (*sakadāgāmin*, Skt *sakṛdāgāmin*). A once-returner can only be reborn once in the sense-desire world, as a human or lower god. Any other rebirths will be in the higher heavens. This is because he has destroyed the unsubtle forms of the next two fetters, sensual desire and ill-will, as well as unsubtle forms of delusion. The next Noble persons are the ones practising for the realization of non-returning, and the non-returner (*anāgāmin*). The non-returner (*BW*.396–402) has destroyed even subtle sensuous desire and ill-will, so that great equanimity is the tone of his experience, and he cannot be reborn in the sense-desire world. His insight is not quite sufficient for him to become an *Arahat*, and if he does not manage to become one later in life, or even in the between-lives period (Harvey, 1995a: 100–2), he is reborn in one of the heavens of the form or formless realms. In particular, he may be reborn once or more within the five 'pure abodes', the most refined heavens in the form world, and where only non-returners can be reborn. In such rebirths, he matures his insight till he becomes a long-lived *Arahat*-god.

The final two Noble persons are the one practising for the realization of Arahatness, and the *Arahat* himself. The *Arahat* destroys all the five remaining fetters: attachment to the form and formless worlds, the 'I am' conceit, perhaps now in the form of lingering spiritual pride, restlessness and spiritual ignorance. These are destroyed by the Ten-factored Path, which brings *dukkha* and all rebirths to an end in the blissful experience of *Nirvāṇa*. The Buddha said that among his disciples, the more advanced Noble persons were rarer: there were more non-returners than *Arahats*, more once-returners than non-returners, and more stream-enterers than once-returners (*S*.v.406). All of the latter three would later become *Arahats*, though.

CHAPTER 4

Early Developments in Buddhism

THE EARLY *SAṄGHA*

The *Saṅgha* (Skt *Saṃgha*), in the sense of the 'Community' of monks and nuns with the Buddha as its teacher, originated as one of the groups of *Samaṇas*. These suspended their wandering existence during the three months of the rainy season, and for the Buddhist *Samaṇas* this 'rains' (*Vassa*, Skt *Varṣa*) period became a time of intensified religious practice, with greater contact with the public at large. They also tended to return to the same places at *Vassa*, such as parks donated by wealthy lay patrons, and these locations then became the basis for a more settled communal way of life. In this way, the Buddhists invented monastic life, which was a middle way between the life of the solitary Jain renouncers, and that of the Brahmin householders.

The monastic discipline (*Vinaya*) developed by the Buddha was designed to shape the *Saṅgha* as an ideal community, with the optimum conditions for spiritual growth. Its sustaining power is shown by the fact that no human institution has had such a long-lasting continuous existence, along with such a wide diffusion, as the Buddhist *Saṅgha*. The Buddha advocated frequent meetings of each local *Saṅgha*, with the aim of reaching a unanimous consensus in matters of common concern (*D*.II.76–7). If necessary, there was also provision for voting and majority rule (*Vin*.II.84).

Just after the Buddha's passing away (*c.* 404 BCE), a 'communal recitation' (council) of 500 *Arahats* was held at Rājagaha (Skt Rājagṛha, *Vin*.II.284–7) to agree the contents of the *Dhamma* and *Vinaya* which the Buddha had left as 'teacher' (*D*.II.154).[1] Ānanda, the Buddha's faithful attendant monk, recited the *Suttas*, such that each begins: 'Thus have I heard'. The monk Upāli recited the *Vinaya*. The claim that the whole of the present *Vinaya* and *Sutta* sections of scripture were recited then is probably an exaggeration.

[1] See Berkwitz, 2010: 42–6 on early councils.

Perhaps seventy years after the first 'communal recitation', a second was held at Vesālī (Skt Vaiśālī), this being to censure certain monks whose conduct was seen as lax on ten points, such as their accepting money (*Vin*.II.294–307). If these points were not already against the formal *Vinaya*, they were made so then. Sixteen or more years later, perhaps at a further council, at Pāṭaliputta (Skt Pāṭaliputra), the first schism in the previously unified *Saṅgha* occurred; other such schisms followed. The causes of these were generally disagreements over monastic discipline, though the points of *Vinaya* which separated the early monastic fraternities (*nikāyas*) often arose from variant developments in geographically separated communities, rather than from actual disagreements. Discussion of points of doctrine also led to the development of different interpretative schools of thought (*vādas*). Originally, these could not be a cause of schism, as the only *opinion* a monk could be condemned for was the persistent claim that sensual behaviour is not an obstacle to be overcome (*Vin*.IV.133–6). Early on, it seems that adherents of a particular school of thought could be found among members of various monastic fraternities, but perhaps by the second century BCE monastic fraternities started to become known for the specific doctrinal interpretations common among their members. By around 100 CE at least, schisms could occur over points of doctrine, and the distinction between a 'fraternity' and a 'school' faded. While members of different monastic fraternities could not take part in official *Saṅgha* business together, they often shared the same monasteries, and studied each others' doctrines. The laity was probably not very concerned about the differences between the fraternities or schools.

The cause of the first schism is not agreed. The Theravāda tradition says that it was caused by the defeated party at the council of Vesālī.[2] It cannot have been over the ten lax practices, however, as both of the fraternities which emerged from the schism agreed in condemning these. Other traditions, such as the Sarvāstivāda, say that the cause was doctrinal, concerning five points put forward by the monk Mahādeva. This dispute was probably a later one, however, and became projected back as the cause of the first schism. Jan Nattier and Charles Prebish (1976–7) have shown that the probable cause of the schism was an attempt to slightly expand the number of monastic rules. Concern for monastic rigour and unity may have caused one section of the *Saṅgha* to incorporate some new rules in the section of the *Vinaya* on deportment, dress and behaviour in public of the monks. This may have been to turn previous *de facto* practices into *de jure* rules, so as

[2] As stated in the fourth-century CE *Dīpavaṃsa* (V.1–54 (*EB*.3.6.1)).

to properly train new members of the *Saṅgha*. As the reformists seem to have been based in regions of India where Buddhism was spreading, this would have been important to them. The reformist section could not win over the more conservative majority, so that agreement could not be reached, and a schism ensued. The reformists called themselves the Sthaviras (Pali Thera), the Elders.[3] The majority called themselves the Mahāsāṃghikas, or those 'Belonging to the Universal *Saṅgha*'.

THE *ABHIDHAMMA*

In the third century BCE, a few schools added works of *Abhidhamma* (Skt *Abhidharma*) to their canons of teachings, developing them from *Mātikās* (Skt *Mātṛkā*), or tabulated summaries of topics, which may have originated with the Buddha (Gethin, 1998: 202–23).[4] The *Abhidhammas* of the different schools differed appreciably in details, but all aimed to present the teachings of the *Suttas* systematically, along with interpretations which drew out their implications. Other schools in time expressed their views in extra-canonical treatises. The *Abhidhamma* literature sought to avoid the inexactitudes of colloquial conventional language, as is sometimes found in the *Suttas*, and state everything in psycho-philosophically exact language, on 'ultimate realities' (*paramattha-sacca*, Skt *paramartha-satya*). In doing this, it analysed reality into a sequence of micro-moments, so that it could also analyse what happens in any of these.

The *Abhidhamma* performs two main tasks. On the one hand, it refines the *khandha* type of analysis so as to give a fine-grained enumeration and characterization of all the *dhammas* (Skt *dharma*), basic patterns or basic processes, which are experienced as making up the flow of mental and physical phenomena. This can be seen as an extension of mindfulness of *dhammas* in the *Suttas* on the four applications of mindfulness (*D*.II.290–315; *M*.I.55–63); these *dhammas* being: the five hindrances, five *khandhas*, six senses and their objects, seven factors of awakening, and four True Realities for the Spiritually Ennobled. On the other hand, the *Abhidhamma* refines the doctrine of Conditioned Arising by showing how the basic patterns condition each other in a web of complex ways. The first task is carried out in, for example, the first three books of the Theravādin *Abhidhamma*: the

[3] Later the terms Sthāvira or Sthāvirīya (Pali Theriya) were sometimes used, and Theriya and Theravādin came to be used as equivalents by the Theravādins.

[4] For more on *Abhidhamma*, see: Berkwitz, 2010: 61–7; Chapple, 1996; Guenther, 1976; Mendis, 1985; Nyanaponika, 1965; Ratnayaka, 1981; Ronkin, 2005; Rowlands, 1982; van Gorkom, 1990.

Dhamma-saṅgaṇī (*Dhs*, 'Enumeration of *Dhammas*'), the *Vibhaṅga* (*Vibh*, '(Book of) Analysis') and *Dhātu-kathā* ('Discourse on Elements'). The second is carried out in its seventh, and probably latest book, the six-volume *Paṭṭhāna* ('Conditional Relations'), which goes into great detail on how particular *dhammas* are interrelated by one or more of twenty-four kinds of conditional relationships. The fourth book, the *Puggala-paññatti* ('Concept of Persons'), discusses various character-types and levels of spiritual development. While this literature has sometimes been seen as dry and scholastic, it is a spiritual psychology with a very practical purpose. It gives a detailed knowledge of the working of the mind, and thus can guide a person in meditative development; it also facilitates the proper understanding of personality as an interaction of impermanent, unsatisfactory, ownerless and insubstantial events. In some ways, it is like a detailed, careful analysis of the subtle nature of music: notes, their relationships and how they may be combined.

The *Abhidhamma*, except in discussing character-types, analyses 'persons' and 'things' down into a number of *dhammas* that, as viewed in the light of the Buddha's teaching, or *Dhamma*, are basic facts of experience: interdependent basic patterns within the overall Basic Pattern (*Dhamma*) of the nature of reality. Each *dhamma* (other than *Nirvāṇa*, which is beyond change) is seen as a patterned process consisting of a stream of momentary events of a particular kind. The term '*dhamma*' is used both for such a type of process and the specific events it comprises. By the early centuries CE, existence came to be seen as consisting of the interaction of a limited number of *dhammas*: including *Nirvāṇa*, eighty-two according to the Theravāda school, and seventy-five in the Sarvāstivāda. These were seen as the constituents of reality: not exactly its 'building-blocks', which is too static an image, but its component processes. Some attention is given to the types of physical processes: the four basic elements (see p. 56) and matter such as the sensitive part of sense-organs or the visible aspect of objects (a further twenty-four *dhammas* in the Theravāda schema). However, most attention is focused on the mind. In the Theravādin *Abhidhamma*, this is said to consist, at any micro-moment, of some form of the *dhamma* 'consciousness' or 'mind' (*citta*) along with various 'mental states' (*cetasika*, Skt *caitasika* or *caitta*), these being some form of feeling and perception, and some of the fifty constructing activities. Included as forms of *citta* are the five sense-consciousnesses, mind-consciousness (*mano-viññāṇa*), and mind-organ-element (*mano-dhātu*) (*Dhs*.1187), which are together seen as constituting the *khandha* of consciousness (*Vibh*.54). *Citta* is also of many modes (eighty-nine in all) according to whether it is, for example, ethically skilful, unskilful or the result of previous ethically active states. As later systematized in the *Abhidhammattha-saṅgaha* (Bodhi, 1993; Wijeratne and Gethin, 2002), perhaps dating from the seventh century CE, the 'mental states' are divided into: those which accompany all *citta*s (7); those which can accompany any, intensifying them (6); those which accompany some or all unskilful *citta*s or their karmic results (14); and those which accompany some or all skilful ones or their karmic results (25). The precise cluster of 'mental states' accompanying a moment of *citta* signifies its nature. At each instant in time, another cluster of *citta*-with-*cetasika*s arises, thus accounting for the subtle moment-to-moment changes in a person's experience.

The *Paṭṭhāna*, along with the *Miln*.299–300, also develops the idea of *bhavaṅga*, a mode of *citta* which is seen as the resting state of consciousness, as exists in dreamless sleep.[5] Equivalent to the 'brightly shining mind' (see p. 68), this level of mental functioning is seen as being constantly flicked in and out of during waking consciousness. After a few moments of *bhavaṅga*, other types of *citta* follow, which turn towards some sense-object, such as a visual shape, come to know it and then give some skilful or unskilful response. The mind then flicks back into the *bhavaṅga* level before turning towards the same or another sense-object, such as a sound. Thus one does not see and hear strictly simultaneously, but the mind rapidly dances between *bhavaṅga* and the senses and mind-organ, building up a picture of the world like that built up by the moving dot on a television screen.

The *Abhidhamma*'s focus on momentary realities leads to seeing the full power of the transcendent, Noble Eight-factored Path as lasting for a very short time (see p. 84). The Theravāda sees each of the 'Path' states, immediately after which a person becomes a stream-enterer, once-returner, non-returner and *Arahat*, as lasting only one moment each. The Sarvāstivāda sees these as lasting fifteen moments each. The Noble Eight-factored Path is, on this kind of view, an achieved state, rather than something a person practises. All practice is done at the level of the ordinary Eight-factored Path (see pp. 82–3). When this culminates in the Noble Path, a person is immediately aware of *Nirvāṇa*.

THE EARLY SCHOOLS AND THEIR DOCTRINES

Within the monastic fraternities originating from the Sthaviras of the first schism, three systematic schools of thought (*vāda*s) developed during the third century BCE: the Pudgalavāda (Pali Puggalavāda), Sarvāstivāda (Pali

[5] Collins, 1982: 225–47; Gethin, 1994, 1998: 215–18; Harvey, 1995a: 145–8, 160–6, 252–8.

Sabbatthivāda) and Vibhajyavāda (Pali Vibhajjavāda).[6] The fraternities originating from the Mahāsāṃghikas were more doctrinally open, and so drew on ideas from these *vādas*, and later took to Mahāyāna ideas more readily.

The Pudgalavādins, or 'Personalists', were dissatisfied with the doctrinal non-acceptance of any kind of substantial self.[7] While other schools saw *Sutta* references to the 'person' as merely a conventional way of referring to the collection of *khandhas*, which were empty of any Self-essence, they saw the 'person' as being just as real as the *khandhas*: a kind of subtle Self which, being an organic whole that included them, was neither the same as nor distinct from them. Over time, it was neither identical nor different, neither eternal nor non-eternal. Though criticized by all other Buddhist schools, the Pudgalavādins were quite successful, and in the seventh century CE, under the patronage of the emperor Harṣa, a quarter of Indian monks belonged to their school. Notable fraternities that followed the Pudgalavādin line were the Vātsīputrīyas and the Saṃmatīyas. They later died out, however, and only a few short texts of theirs survive.

The Sarvāstivādins, or 'Pan-realists',[8] became the dominant school in north India, especially in the north-west under the patronage of Kaniṣka I, who ruled in the late first or early second century CE. From here, they became influential in Central Asia, on the route to China. Their canonical *Abhidharma* survives in Chinese translation. They became known for their view that not only present *dharmas* exist, but also past and future ones. They argued that knowledge of past and future must have objects which are existent, and that the past *dharmas* must exist in order to explain how past karma affects the present. They also saw positive and negative dispositions as existent even when their conscious expressions were absent. Their opponents argued that only present *dharmas* exist, and that the effect-producing impetus of past karma continues in the present. The Sarvāstivādins held that past and future *dharmas* differ from things which are pure illusions, and from conceptual labels for groups of *dharmas*, in that they each have a specific 'own-nature' (Skt *svabhāva*), a unique defining characteristic that is intrinsic to it and is present whenever, and however, it exists (Williams, 2009: 68). There was a related tendency to reify them as fundamental and indivisible ultimate realities. They were seen as primary

[6] For the name of a school, -vāda is used, and -vādin for a follower of one. For an overview of the early schools, see: Berkwitz, 2010: 51–61.

[7] *BS1*.192–7; Conze, 1967: 123–30; Cousins, 1994; Harvey, 1995a: 34–8; Williams and Tribe, 2000: 92–6.

[8] Bastow, 1995; Conze, 1967: 137–41; Gethin, 1998: 220–1; Willemen *et al.*, 1998; Williams and Tribe, 2000: 83–7; *EB*.3.6.2.

existents (*dravya-sat*), while everyday realities such as trees and people were seen as 'secondary', 'conceptual' ones (*prajñapti-sat*). For example, the only reality that a 'person' has is that of the cluster of *dharmas* that the conceptual label 'person' applies to. Moreover, that which binds *dharmas* together in a 'person' was itself a *dharma*, known as *prāpti*, or 'possession'.

Among those who were ordained in the Sarvāstivāda fraternity, some were critical of its *Abhidharma* ideas, and looked to the *Sūtras* (Pali *Sutta*) in support of their own interpretations. Those with this critical perspective, which may have also been shared by some from other fraternities, were known as Sautrāntikas.[9] They argued that many of the *dharmas* of the Sarvāstivādins were not separate ultimate realities, and that the idea of them somehow existing in the past, present and future made them virtually permanent and independent things: more with an inherent 'own-existence' than just 'own-nature'. Sautrāntikas developed theories of their own, but regarded these as provisional explanatory devices, rather than as descriptions of the ultimate nature of things. One such notion was that, while there was no ultimate reality 'possession', the fact that individuals had or lacked certain dispositions could be explained by saying that their body–mind complex contained certain 'seeds', or tendencies.

A council was held in around 100 CE, under Kaniṣka I, and the Sarvāstivādins claimed that this was to decide between different interpretations of their *Abhidharma*. The second century then saw the production of the *Mahāvibhāṣā* which, in the form of a commentary on the first book of their *Abhidharma*, the *Jñāna-prasthāna*, discussed different interpretations. In general, it supported the views of Vasumitra, who held that conditioned *dharmas* simply move from a 'future' state, to a momentary manifestation in the 'present', when they carry out the characteristic activity of the relevant *dharma*, to a 'past' state. Past and future *dharmas* exist in a non-active way. In all this, their inner nature does not change. The orthodox Sarvāstivādins took their stand on the *Mahāvibhāṣā*, and so were often known as Vaibhāṣikas. In the fourth century, a masterly survey of their thought was elaborated by Vasubandhu in his *Abhidharma-kośa* (Berkwitz, 2010: 109–11). He then produced a commentary on this, the *Abhidharma-kośa-bhāṣya (AKB.)*, in which the *Abhidharma-kośa* itself is embedded, which included a critique of aspects of it that drew on some Sautrāntika ideas. His initial work, however, remained the classic statement of *Abhidharma* in north India. Included in it were certain speculations on the meaning of a Buddha's

[9] Conze, 1967: 141–3; Gethin, 1998: 221–2; Williams and Tribe, 2000: 87–90.

'*Dharma*-body' (see p. 167), seeing it as a term for both the powers, abilities and perfections developed by a Buddha, and his purified inner nature.

While the Sarvāstivādins were not much represented in south India, this was an area where the Vibhajyavādins, or 'Distinctionists', were strong. Cousins comments that they: 'were the school predominant in Ceylon and Gandhāra [north-west] at an early date, as well as being present, if not predominant, in other parts of Central Asia, China, South India and South-east Asia by around the third century CE at the latest. No other school had a comparable spread at this date' (2001: 169). This school of thought was followed by the ancestors of four of the fraternities active in the early centuries CE (Cousins, 2001: 132): (i) the Dharmaguptakas (Pali Dhammaguttikas), who came to be located mainly in the north-west of the Indian sub-continent and on the trade routes to China (and whose *Vinaya* is still used in China); (ii) the Kāśyapīyas (Pali Kassapiyas), probably in the same area; (iii) the Mahīśāsakas (Pali Mahiṃsāsakas), there and in part of mainland India; (iv) the Tāmraparṇīyas (Pali Tambapaṇṇiyas), 'those from the island of Laṅkā', who were strongly established in Ceylon[10] but also active in the Andhra region (south-east) and other parts of south India. The latter were later called the Theravāda, Pali for 'school of the Elders'; by implication, the Elders (Pali *Thera*, Skt *Sthavira*) of the first schism. The Theravāda survived in south India till the seventeenth century, and then withdrew to its base in Ceylon. All other pre-Mahāyāna schools of thought eventually died out in India, though certain ones were studied by some of the Mahāyānists of Northern and Eastern Buddhism. In Japan, the small Kusha school still exists, based on study of the *Abhidharma-kośa*.

The Theravāda tradition holds that, during the reign of the emperor Asoka, a council was held at Pāṭaliputta in around 250 BCE, at the end of which Tissa Moggaliputta composed the *Kathāvatthu* (*Kvu*), a 'Book of Discourses' arguing against the views of other schools. This work, the fifth book of the Vibhajyavāda/Theravāda *Abhidhamma*, was probably added to in the subsequent two centuries. The Vibhajyavādins distinguished between the real existence of present *dhammas*, and non-existent past or future ones (e.g. *Kvu*.I.6–8), and largely resisted the tendency to reify *dhammas*, retaining the older, more experiential understanding of their nature. They insisted on the uniqueness of *Nirvāṇa* as the sole unconditioned *dhamma*. The Sarvāstivādins also included space in this category, and somewhat devalued *Nirvāṇa* by making it simply one among many timeless metaphysical realities. The Vibhajyavādin view (e.g. at *Kvu*.VI.1–6, XIX.3–5)

[10] Now known, as a state, as Sri Lanka.

is that, as the unconditioned is beyond space and time, it cannot have any divisions within it.

Another of their characteristic doctrines is that, at stream-entry, insight into the four True Realities for the Spiritually Ennobled does not come gradually, in a series of separate thought-moments (as the Sarvāstivādins held), but simultaneously, in one thought moment (*Kvu*.II.9; *Patis*.II.105–6). As the first reality is *dukkha*, and the third is the stopping of *dukkha*, or *Nirvāṇa*, this view might be seen to imply that the conditioned world of *dukkha* is not ultimately different from unconditioned *Nirvāṇa*. As unconditioned, *Nirvāṇa* can have no spatial or temporal relationship to *anything*, even by negation: no place or time can be nearer to or further from it. It is not separate from the conditioned world, but is, as it were, always available to be experienced. As it is also the stopping of conditioned *dhammas*, this seems to imply that, ultimately, these are not *fundamentally* real. This connects with some of the things said of the 'signless' concentration (see pp. 80–1).

An important idea in this period was that of the three 'gateways to liberation' (*vimokha-mukha*, Skt *vimokṣa-mukha*; Conze, 1967: 59–71): the 'signless' (*animitta*, Skt *ānimitta*), the 'aim-free' (*appaṇihita*, Skt *apraṇihita)* and 'the empty' (*suññata*) or 'emptiness' (Skt *śūnyatā*). These are referred to in the *Abhidharma-kośa-bhāṣya* (e.g. *AKB*.VIII.23e–26d), and in the *Paṭisambhidāmagga*, an early Vibhajyavādin systematizing text contained in the Pali Canon. The latter explains that insight into phenomena as impermanent leads to the first gateway, insight into phenomena as *dukkha* leads to the second, and insight into phenomena as non-Self, or empty of Self or what pertains to Self, leads to the third (*Patis*.II.58). The three liberations know *Nirvāṇa* under three aspects, as:

- The 'signless' as it is devoid of signs indicative of anything graspable; it is the profound realm which is beyond all particular, limited, conditioned phenomena, which are all subject to constant change: in the signless liberation, constructed phenomena are seen as 'limited and circumscribed' (*Patis*.II.48) by their ephemeral nature.
- The 'aim-free' as it lies beyond goal-directedness concerning conditioned phenomena, which are all *dukkha*, so that there is a profound letting go.
- The 'empty' as it is an open spaciousness beyond concepts, being known in this aspect by deep insight into everything as non-Self, which is utterly free of all 'settling on' of phenomena as 'Self', 'I', 'mine' or 'permanent', etc. (*Patis*.II.67–8). *Nirvāṇa* is void of any ground for notions of 'I' – these can only arise from grasping at the *khandhas* – and is empty of attachment, hatred and delusion.

The discussion of various ways in which something can be 'empty/an empty thing (*suññaṃ*)' at *Patis*.II.177–83 shows that anything's lacking something is its being 'empty' of it, whether it is phenomena's lack of Self or permanence, or renunciation's lack of sensual desire. But *Nirvāṇa*, the 'supreme empty thing', is that *which lacks* conditioned states or craving. If x is seen as empty of y, then the term '*suñña*' as an adjective refers to x's *quality of lacking* y, and as a noun can refer to *x itself*, as the thing *that lacks* y. This distinction is relevant to some of the later Mahāyāna uses of the term 'emptiness' (*śūnyatā*).

The notion of *svabhāva* (Pali *sabhāva*) does occur in the Vibhajyavāda/ Theravāda as well as Sarvāstivāda tradition, but in a different sense than there: as simply 'own-nature' rather than as also an implied 'own-existence'. The *Atthasālinī*, the commentary on the first book of the *Abhidhamma*, explains *dhammas* thus: 'They are *dhammas* because they uphold their own own-nature. They are *dhammas* because they are upheld by conditions or they are upheld according to their own-nature' (*Asl*.39). Here 'own-nature' would appear to mean a characteristic nature, which is not something inherent in a *dhamma* as a separate ultimate reality, but arises due to the supporting conditions of both other *dhammas* and previous occurrences of that *dhamma*. This is of significance as it makes the Mahāyāna critique of the Sarvāstivādin's notion of *svabhāva* largely irrelevant to the Theravāda.

The Vibhajyavādins argued against the view, held by the Sarvāstivādins and Pudgalavādins, that some *Arahats* could regress from their state after temporarily attaining it (*Kvu*.I.2). For the Vibhajyavādins, such a person was not yet a true *Arahat*. They also argued against related points which became known as the 'five points of Mahādeva' (Cousins, 1991), the earliest reference to which is in their *Kathāvatthu* (II.1–5). The first point is that, even though all *Arahats* are free of sensual desire, a Māra god can cause the bodies of some male *Arahats* to emit semen when asleep; those with full mastery of meditative accomplishments are immune from this. The second point is that, as an *Arahat* may be ignorant of matters such as a person's name, he may lack a certain kind of *ñāṇa* (Skt *jñāṇa*), or insight. In their original form, in which the present fifth point was probably replaced by the idea that some *Arahats* could regress, the 'five points' were probably *Abhidhamma* debating points, used to sharpen up people's understanding of certain issues and distinctions. They may well originally have been propounded by the Sarvāstivāda school.

The monastic traditions of all surviving forms of Buddhism go back to fraternities descended from the Sthaviras of the first schism, which means that much less is known of the Mahāsāṃghika ones (Williams and Tribe, 2000: 94–6). The doctrines ascribed to them by others are described in relatively late texts, of the early centuries CE. These broadly differentiate a northern and southern branch, the Ekavyavahārika and Caitīya fraternities (which perhaps divided in the second century BCE). Whoever originated the 'five points of Mahādeva', they became associated with the 'Mahāsāṃghikas', or more specifically with the Caitīya branch. This may have been originated by the monk Mahādeva, who seems to have propounded a new formulation of the points. Some scholars have held that Mahādeva's points imply a 'downgrading' of an *Arahat* relative to a perfect Buddha. This seems to be incorrect, however. Only a slight 'downgrading' is implied, and this applies to one kind of *Arahat* relative to another. The first kind has only a limited attainment of the meditative state of *jhāna* (Skt *dhyāna*), and lacks the higher knowledges which can be developed using these as a basis. The second has these higher knowledges, and can use them so as to be 'skilled in the states of others': he knows the inner states and needs of others, and can use this knowledge in compassionately helping them. Mahādeva's points are thus associated with an increased emphasis on altruistic action, as became central to the Mahāyāna.

As regards actual Mahāsāṃghika texts, some of their *Sūtra* collection and all of their *Vinaya* survive in Chinese translation. In a language approximating to Sanskrit, there survives a text known as the *Mahāvastu(-avadāna)*, which purports to be a *Vinaya* work. It describes itself as a work of the Lokottaravāda, or 'Transcendentalist' school, which is probably the same as the Ekavyavahārikas or 'One-utterancers'. The latter held that *all* the utterances of the Buddha were concerned with what was transcendent (cf. *EB*.3.6.3). The *Mahāvastu* (*Mvs.*) grew over a number of centuries, perhaps beginning in the late second century BCE. While its outlook has often been seen as foreshadowing certain Mahāyāna ideas, it has itself been shown to incorporate whole passages from early Mahāyāna scriptures, and may have been influenced by Mahāyāna concepts up to as late as the fifth century CE. It sees Gautama as 'transcendental' even before his Buddhahood. He leaves the Tuṣita heaven in a mind-created body to bestow his blessings on the world (see p. 15), and though highly spiritually developed, he pretends to start from the beginning, making 'mistakes' such as asceticism (*Mvs*.I.169–70). As a Buddha, he is an omniscient being who is ever in meditation. No dust sticks to his feet, and he is never tired. He eats out of mere conformity with the world, and so as to give others a chance to do karmically fruitful actions by giving him alms food. For such a world-transcending being, it was felt that all incidents in his life must have occurred for a special reason. The *Mahāvastu* thus gives much attention to the Buddha's biography, and also includes many *Jātaka* tales. In examining his development to Buddhahood, a series of ten stages of the *Bodhisattva* (Pali *Bodhisatta*) career were outlined. This idea was also important in the Mahāyāna, though the details are different. Unlike the Mahāyāna, the Transcendentalists still saw the goal for most people as Arahatship, the way of the *Bodhisattva* being for extraordinary individuals.

THE THREE ASPIRATIONS, *JĀTAKAS* AND *AVADĀNAS*

Among the early schools, one of three kinds of aspiration came to be espoused by dedicated practitioners. These were to aim to become awakened as a *sāvaka-buddha* (Skt *śrāvaka-buddha*), a *pacceka-buddha* (Skt *pratyeka-buddha*) or a *sammā-sambuddha* (Skt *samyak-sambuddha*) (Gethin, 1998: 32–4). The first is an 'awakened disciple': an *Arahat*, one liberated by practising under the guidance of a perfect Buddha such as Gotama; this attainment might be in this or a future life. The second is a 'solitary awakened one', someone who attains awakening by their own efforts, often by practising in the forest (Ray, 1994: 213–50), in a phase of history when the teachings of a perfect Buddha are unavailable, and teaches others only in a minimal way. The term may have originally been *pacceya-buddha*, meaning 'one awakened by a cause', such as insight into the limited nature of conditioned reality coming from seeing a withered leaf fall (Harvey, 2007d: 600a–602b). Their insight is seen as greater than that of an *Arahat*. The third kind of *buddha* is the 'perfectly and completely awakened one', usually referred to simply as Buddhas or perfect Buddhas. These are beings who have the ability to rediscover the *Dhamma* when it has become lost to human society, and teach it in many skilful ways, to the benefit of many others (see pp. 15, 30). The first aspiration was the most common in the early schools, but a few aspired to, and took vows to attain, the higher goals, which were seen to take many more lives to attain (Harvey, 2007d: 83a–87b; Ratnayaka, 1985). All three goals were seen to require the development of certain moral and spiritual perfections (*pāramī*, Skt *pāramitā*), respectively to an ordinary, higher or supreme level (Bodhi, 1996).

These perfections were particularly associated with the *Bodhisatta*, enabling him to become a perfect Buddha. They were seen as illustrated in the *Jātakas*, or 'Birth Stories' (*Jat.*), which told of the (usually) great deeds, in past lives of the being that was to become the Buddha Gotama (Appleton, 2010). Each such story tells of a life when, as a human, animal or god, he did some inspiring deed of generosity, kindness or wisdom, or facilitated these in others. At the end of each story, key characters are identified with the Buddha or his key disciples or relatives. The verses are canonical, but in general only make sense in the context of the commentarial narrative in which they are embedded.

While the *Jātakas* helped inspire people to emulate the Buddha, the *Avadānas* or 'Stories of Actions and Their Results' emphasized the power of devotion to him (*BP*.11). These developed from the second century BCE. They include the *Apadāna*, of the Pali Canon, the Sarvāstivādin *Avadānaśataka* (*BS2*.17) and *Divyāvadāna* (Rotman, 2008), and the Lokottaravādin *Mahāvastu-avadāna*. These give stories on past lives of *Arahats* and the Buddha, emphasizing the powerful spiritual benefit of having done service (*adhikāra*) to past Buddhas or their relics. Buddhas and their relics were seen as potent 'fields of karmic fruitfulness' (see p. 44), such that an act of devotion to them could generate a huge amount of good karma. Moreover, making a connection to a Buddha in this way was seen as a crucial prerequisite for future awakening. A related idea is that of the Buddha-field (Skt *Buddha-kṣetra*, Pali *Buddha-khetta*), a Buddha's domain or sphere of influence, and these came to be seen in some schools as countless in number, spread among the even greater number of world-systems in the universe (*Mvs*.1.121–5). As later expressed in the *Visuddhimagga* of Buddhaghosa (*Vism*.414 (*BTTA*.120)), our Buddha has a threefold Buddha-field: that of his birth – the ten thousand world-systems that shook at his birth and later significant events in his life; that of his authority – the hundred thousand million world-systems where certain *parittas*, or protective chants (see pp. 249–50) have power; that of his knowledge, which is immeasurable.

EMPEROR ASOKA AND BUDDHISM

During the reign of the emperor Asoka (Skt Aśoka, *c*. 268–239 BCE), Buddhism spread more widely, reaching most of the Indian sub-continent, and also beyond, thus becoming a 'world religion'. The Magadhan empire which Asoka inherited included most of modern India except the far south: the largest in the sub-continent until its conquest by the British. Asoka adopted the social ethic of Buddhism as the guiding principle of his rule, and has been seen by Buddhists as the model of a compassionate Buddhist ruler. The most important sources for our knowledge of him are his numerous edicts, as promulgated on rocks and stone pillars in a variety of languages.[11]

[11] *EB*.2.6.3; *BT*.51–4; Dhammika, 1993; Nikam and McKeon, 1959.

The Buddha seems to have had a liking for the semi-democratic republics of his day, but he was aware of the rising power of kingdoms. His ideals of kingship came from (i) his view that the first king in human society was elected by his people so as to preserve social harmony (p. 38), and (ii) his ideas on compassionate *Cakkavattin* rulers of the past, who ruled with great concern for *Dhamma*, in the sense of morality and social justice (e.g. *D*.III.58–9). At the start of his reign, Asoka seems to have been content to carry on the policy of his forebears, which saw it as the duty of a ruler to expand his realm by force, according to a 'might is right' philosophy.[12] While Asoka had already become a nominal Buddhist in around 260 BCE, the full implications of his new faith do not seem to have hit home until after his bloody conquest of the Kaliṅga region, in the following year. In an edict after this episode, he evinced great remorse at the carnage he had caused, and expressed the desire to govern, please and protect his subjects according to *Dhamma*. He now felt that it was his duty to improve the quality of his subjects' lives, so as to provide a sound framework for their following a moral and religious way of life, Buddhist or otherwise. He inaugurated public works, such as wells and rest-houses for travellers, supported medical aid for humans and animals, and gave aid for the fostering of such measures in regions beyond his empire. *Dhamma*-officials were appointed to encourage virtue, look after old people and orphans, and ensure equal judicial standards throughout the empire. While Asoka retained some judicial beatings, he abolished torture and, perhaps, the death penalty (Norman, 1975). Released prisoners were given some short-term financial help, and encouraged to generate karmic fruitfulness for their future lives.

Asoka's concern for the moral improvement of his people was partly expressed in legislation, but more often in attempts to persuade people to live a better life. A prime value encouraged in his edicts was *ahiṃsā*, or 'non-injury': a key emphasis of both Buddhism and other Indian traditions. While he kept his army as a deterrent to invasion, Asoka gave up conquest. Hunting trips, the sport of kings, were replaced by pilgrimages to sites associated with the Buddha (*EB*.I.2). In time, the large royal household became completely vegetarian. Brahmanical animal sacrifice was banned in the capital, and a wide range of non-food animals, birds and fishes were protected. Generosity towards *Samaṇas*, Brahmins and the aged was urged. Respect for these and parents, good behaviour towards friends and relatives,

[12] Spelt out in the Brahmanical *Artha Śāstra* of Kauṭilya, of around 300 BCE. Later legends, in such texts as the *Aśokāvadāna* (Strong, 2008), portray Asoka turning from an early 'black' period to a later 'white' one, under the influence of Buddhism.

and good treatment of servants was praised. Mercy, truthfulness, sexual purity, gentleness and contentment were recommended. The lay-orientation of Asoka's values is shown by the fact that the edicts refer to a harmonious society and heavenly rebirth as the goal of a good life lived according to *Dhamma*, making no mention of *Nirvāṇa* (Basham, 1982).

Asoka gave Buddhism a central place in his empire, just as the Roman emperor Constantine (ruled 306–37 CE) did for Christianity. Nevertheless, he supported not only Buddhist monks and nuns, but also Brahmins, Jain wanderers, and Ājīvika ascetics, in accordance with a pattern that later Buddhist and Hindu rulers also followed. At a time when different religions were in competition for converts, he urged mutual respect and tolerance. He saw all religious traditions as contributing in some way to spiritual development, and his twelfth rock edict holds that a common basis for religions is that praising one's own tradition and criticizing others should be held in check: for religious wrangling brings harm both to one's own and others' religions, while mutual respect strengthens both (Nikam and McKeon, 1959: 51–2). Though the Theravāda and Sarvāstivāda schools both claim a special association with Asoka, he was probably not partial to any one Buddhist school, and he discouraged schism. He was, however, interested in the purity of the *Saṅgha*, and may have assisted in the purging of lax monks.

In his pilgrimages to Buddhist sites, Asoka erected shrines and memorial pillars. According to later legendary accounts, he also opened up the original ten *Stūpas* and distributed their relics in many new ones throughout India, thus helping to popularize the cult of devotion at *Stūpas*. During his reign, Buddhist missionary activity was considerable. Theravādin sources record that the monk Tissa Moggaliputta sent out parties of monks to a number of 'border areas'. Asokan edicts also record that the emperor sent out embassies to a number of foreign lands; for he wished to spread the ideals he followed: a 'conquest by *Dhamma*' rather than a military conquest. To the north-west, embassies were sent as far as Syria, Egypt and Macedonia, though there is no record of their having arrived there. To the east, they went to 'Suvaṇṇa-bhūmi', probably the Mon country of lower Burma or central Thailand. To the south, they went to south Indian kingdoms and also to the island of Ceylon. The relationship between the missions and the embassies is not clear, but monks could well have accompanied the embassies, and there was clearly co-operation in the case of Ceylon. Here, in around 250 BCE, a mission headed by Asoka's own son, the *Arahat* monk Mahinda (*EB*.6.1.1), was very successful in implanting what was to become known as the Theravāda form of Buddhism.

DEVOTION AND SYMBOLISM IN EARLY BUDDHISM[13]

Asoka's espousal of Buddhism helped it to develop as a popular religion. The faith-orientated developments that this involved were a complement to the wisdom-orientation expressed in the works of *Abhidhamma*. One can see these as having appealed, respectively, to the kinds of people who might become faith-followers and *Dhamma*-followers (see p. 85). Prior to the popularization of the *Stūpa*-cult,[14] it is probable that the main focus of devotion was the tree under which the Buddha attained awakening, and others grown from its cuttings or seeds. These became known as *Bodhi*, or 'Awakening' trees, and were greatly revered, both as reminders of the Buddha's awakening and as tangible links with his great spiritual powers. Building on pre-Buddhist tree-worship, devotion at such a tree was expressed by making offerings such as flowers at an altar at its base, by tying pennants to it, and watering it. Clockwise circumambulation was also performed, an act which signified that what was walked around symbolized something ideally at the centre of a person's life.

The Buddhist *Stūpa* probably developed from pre-Buddhist burial mounds for kings, heroes and saints, which go back into prehistory in many cultures. They became important in Buddhism due to the holy relics (Pali *sarīra*, Skt *śarīra*) they contained, their symbolizing the Buddha and his *parinirvāṇa* (passing into final *Nirvāṇa* at death), and in some cases their location at significant sites. Relics (see p. 27) were an important focus of devotion in early Buddhism, and have remained so since then (Harvey, 2007d: 133a–137b; Strong, 2004). The importance of devotion to them was emphasized in the *Avadānas*. Relics placed in *Stūpas* are said to have been those of Gotama, *Arahats* and even of past Buddhas. Having been part of the body of an awakened being, they were considered to have been infused with something of the power-for-goodness of an awakened mind, and to bring blessings to those who expressed devotion in their vicinity. Where funerary relics could not be found, hair or possessions of holy beings, copies of bodily relics or possessions, or Buddhist texts came to be used in their place (*BP*.28).

The best-preserved ancient Buddhist *Stūpa*, dating from the first century CE in its present form, is at Sāñcī in central India (see Figure 1, and Bechert and Gombrich, 1984: 64–5). It was built over a *Stūpa* dating from the third

[13] On early Buddhist symbols, see Berkwitz, 2010: 27–32, Harvey, 1990 and 2007d: 107a–116b. For an overview of Buddhist art, see Fisher, 1993.

[14] On which, see Ray, 1994: 324–57.

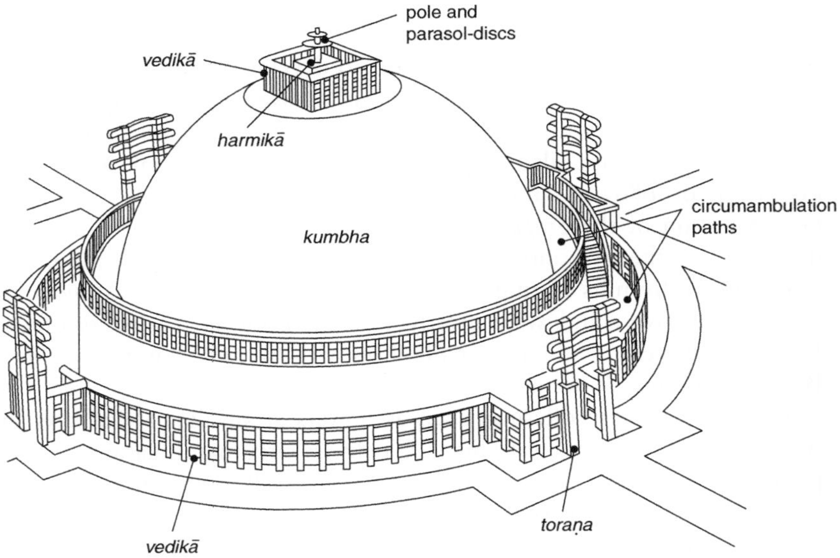

Figure 1: Sāñcī *Stūpa*.

century BCE, which may have been built or embellished by Asoka. The four gateways, or *toraṇas*, place the *Stūpa* symbolically at a crossroads, as the Buddha had specified, perhaps to indicate the openness and universality of the *Dhamma*. Carved reliefs on the gateways depict *Jātaka* tales, along with symbolic indications of previous Buddhas and events in Gotama's final life. The circular *vedikā*, or railing, marks off the site dedicated to the *Stūpa*, and encloses the first of two paths for circumambulation (*pradakṣiṇā-patha*). The *Stūpa* dome, referred to in early texts as the *kumbha* or 'pot', is the outermost container of the relics. It is associated with an Indian symbol known as the 'vase of plenty', and symbolically acts as a reminder of an enlightened being as 'full' of uplifting *Dhamma*.

On top of the Sāñcī *Stūpa* is a pole and discs, which represent ceremonial parasols. As parasols were used as insignia of royalty in India, their inclusion on *Stūpas* can be seen as a way of symbolizing the spiritual sovereignty of the Buddha. The kingly connection probably derives from the ancient custom of rulers sitting under a sacred tree at the centre of a community to administer justice, with mobile parasols later replacing such shading trees. The parasol-structure on *Stūpas* also seems to have symbolized the Buddhist sacred tree, which in turn symbolized awakening. This is suggested by a second-century BCE stone relief of a *Stūpa* which shows it surmounted by a tree with parasol-shaped leaves. The structure at the base of the pole and discs has also been found, on a number of *Stūpa*s, to have resembled the design of *Bodhi*-tree enclosures.

In later *Stūpa*s, the top part fused into a spire, and several platforms were often added under the dome to elevate it in an honorific way. It then became possible to see each layer of the structure as symbolizing a particular set of spiritual qualities, such as the 'four right efforts' (see p. 83), with the spire symbolizing the powers and knowledge of a Buddha. *Stūpas* are now often known by the term 'Pagoda', probably a corruption of *Dagaba* ('relic-container'), the term used in Sri Lanka, which derives from Pali *dhātu-gabbha*, 'container (of the Buddha)-elements'.

A notable feature of early representations of Gotama, even before his awakening, is that he is only shown by symbols (Bechert and Gombrich, 1984: 19), such as a *Dhamma*-wheel above an empty throne with footprints in front of it: a significant space suggesting the calm and stillness of the Buddha's mind, and *Nirvāṇa* as the supreme 'emptiness'. This must have been due to the feeling that the profound nature of one nearing or having attained Buddhahood could not be adequately represented by a human form. Even contemporary Brahmanism only portrayed minor gods in non-symbolic ways.

In time, the absence of the long-dead Buddha was keenly felt, and there arose a need for a representation of him in human form to act as a more personalized focus of devotion. The development of Buddha-images, in the second century CE,[15] was preceded by the practice of visualizing the Buddha's form, as seen at *Sn*.1140–2, where a monk reverently keeps a clear image of the Buddha in mind (Williams, 2009: 209–10). This was one way to practise mindful recollection of the Buddha and his qualities (Pali *Buddhānussati*, Skt *Buddhānusmṛti*). The period when images developed was also one in which a change in mood was affecting all Indian religions, leading to the portrayal of the founder of Jainism, and of major Hindu gods, as focuses of *bhakti*, or warm 'loving devotion'. In Buddhism, this change had also led to the compositions of more thorough sacred biographies of the Buddha, and contributed to the origin of the Mahāyāna.

The craftsmen who made the first Buddha-images drew on the tradition that Gotama had been born with the 'thirty-two characteristics of a Great Man', which indicated that he would become either a Buddha or a *Cakkavattin*. These bodily features are described as karmic results of specific

[15] *EB*.1.8 gives a late passage claiming that the first Buddha-image was made in the Buddha's lifetime.

spiritual perfections built up in past lives (*D*.III.142–78). The most obvious one shown on Buddha-images is Gotama's 'turbaned-head' (Skt *uṣṇīṣa*, Pali *unhīsa*), meaning that he had a head shaped like a royal turban, or that one with spiritual vision could see a royal turban on his head. However interpreted, artistic portrayals first hid it under a top-knot of hair, and then showed it as a protuberance on the top of the head. The *Suttas* see it as a result of previous moral and spiritual prominence; later texts see it as a kind of 'wisdom bump' to accommodate a Buddha's supreme wisdom. A feature of Buddha-images not among the 'characteristics' is the elongated ear-lobes. These signify Gotama's 'royal' upbringing, when he wore heavy gold ear-rings, and thus his renunciation of the option of political greatness. They may also be seen as a common symbol for nobility of character, or indicative of the Buddha's 'divine ear', a meditation-based psychic ability.

Buddha-images seem to have been first produced within the empire of Kaniṣka I, which was in the region of modern Afghanistan, Pakistan and north-west India. This occurred at about the same time in Gandhāra, a western region in which the images were influenced by Hellenistic Greek art, and in the Indian city of Mathurā. While the early images were somewhat faltering as spiritual statements, in time the craftsmen were able to express many spiritual qualities in stone. Early Buddha-images were also made in Āndhradeśa, a region of south-east India which had Amarāvatī as its capital. The earliest extant images from here were made about a century after the earliest ones surviving from Mathurā and Gandhāra. They developed what became the standard way of showing the Buddha's head and hair, in which the *uṣṇīṣa*, undisguised by a mound of hair, is clearly portrayed as part of the head, and the whole scalp is covered in small snail-shell spirals of hair, recalling one of the 'thirty-two characteristics', that of the body hair curling in rings to the right. Later Buddha-images developed by an interaction of the three styles described above, and by sculptors improving their art. It was in the Gupta period (320–540 CE) that the classical Buddha-image was produced in India. A fine example of such an image is shown in Plate 2. It has life, vigour and grace, and its features suggest joy, compassion, wisdom, serenity and meditative concentration. It expresses qualities attained by someone at the goal of Buddhism, and was intended to help stimulate the growth of such qualities in one who contemplated it.

Images of the Buddha came to show him in a variety of positions – seated cross-legged, standing, walking or lying down on his right side in sleep or on his deathbed – and with a variety of hand-gestures, especially showing him turning the *Dhamma*-wheel, reasoning, urging fearlessness, meditating or touching the earth just before his awakening (see p. 21). These were to show

Plate 2: An image from Sārnāth, showing the Buddha making the gesture of 'Setting in motion the *Dhamma*-wheel', symbolizing his first sermon (fifth or sixth century CE).

him at different key events in his life, show different sides of his nature, and of course to be focuses for inspiring devotion.

THE RISE OF THE MAHĀYĀNA

The movement which became known as the Mahāyāna started to arise some time between 150 BCE and 100 CE, as the culmination of various earlier developments (Williams, 2009: 21–44). Its origin is not associated with any named individual, nor was it uniquely linked to any early school or fraternity, though it drew on both Mahāsāṃghika and Sarvāstivādin trends, and its philosophical ideas in India both built on and critiqued Sarvāstivāda *Abhidharma*, as a kind of 'Sarvāstivāda-plus'. It may have arisen at around the same time in the south-east and north-west. Reginald Ray suggests it started among forest meditators of the south-east and was then taken up especially in the north-west (1994: 251–92, 404–17). It had three main ingredients: first, a wholehearted adoption of the *Bodhisattva* path, which various early schools had outlined; secondly, a new cosmology arising from visualization practices devoutly directed at the Buddha as a glorified, transcendent being. These first two relate, respectively, to the concerns of the *Jātakas* and *Avadānas*. Thirdly, a new perspective on *Abhidharma*, which derived from meditative insight into the deep 'emptiness' of phenomena (see p. 81) and led to a new philosophical outlook. These three ingredients respectively emphasize compassion, faith and wisdom. There developed a new orientation to traditional Buddhist teachings and an upsurge of novel interpretations, whose gradual systematization established the Mahāyāna as a movement with an identity of its own.

The Mahāyāna emerges into history as a loose confederation of groups, each associated with one or more of a number of new *Sūtras* (Pali *Suttas*). These attained a written form, in Middle Indian dialects, very soon after they were composed. Scribal amendments then gradually transformed their language into 'Buddhist Hybrid Sanskrit', which approximated to classical Sanskrit, the prestige language of India. The texts were often added to over time, as seen by their different versions in Chinese translations, some of which are earlier in form than surviving Sanskrit versions. As the ideas of the different *Sūtras* were drawn on, later Mahāyānists integrated their ideas and systematized them in various competing ways, depending on which text was seen to contain the highest, fullest truth. This process continued in the lands of Northern and Eastern Buddhism, which also took on differing broad emphases of their own.

Anyone accepting the new literature as genuine *Sūtras* – authoritative discourses of the Buddha – thereby belonged to the new movement. This did not necessitate monks and nuns abandoning their old fraternities, as they continued to follow the monastic discipline of the fraternities in which they had been ordained. The Mahāyānists remained a minority among Indian Buddhists for some time, though in the seventh century, perhaps half of the 200,000 or more monks counted by the Chinese pilgrim Xuanzang (Hsüan-tsang) were Mahāyānist (Williams, 2009: 44).

Traditionalists denied that the new literature was 'the word of the Buddha' (*Buddha-vacana*), like the early *Suttas*. This early material did include teachings and inspired utterances of the Buddha's major disciples, but these were accepted as 'the word of the Buddha' as he had agreed with the teachings, or because of his general praise for such disciples. Even after these were all dead, some remembered material was added to the *Suttas* if it harmonized well with the existing corpus in style and content. The new *Sūtras* were very different in style and tone, but were defended as 'the word of the Buddha' through various devices.[16] First, they were seen as inspired utterances coming from the Buddha, now seen as still contactable through meditative visions and vivid dreams. Secondly, they were seen as the products of the same kind of perfect wisdom which was the basis of the Buddha's own teaching of *Dharma* (Pali *Dhamma*) (*Asta*.4). Thirdly, in later Mahāyāna, they were seen as teachings hidden by the Buddha in the world of serpent-deities (*nāgas*), until there were humans capable of seeing the deeper implications of his message, who would recover the teachings by means of meditative powers. Each explanation saw the *Sūtras* as arising, directly or indirectly, from meditative experiences. Nevertheless, they take the form of dialogues between the 'historical' Buddha and his disciples and gods.

The initial new *Sūtras* were regarded as the second 'turning of the *Dharma*-wheel' (see p. 24), a deeper level of teaching than the early *Suttas*, with the Buddha's *Bodhisattva* disciples portrayed as wiser than his *Arhat* (Pali *Arahat*) disciples. Because of the liberating truth the *Sūtras* were seen to contain, there was said to be a huge amount of karmic fruitfulness in copying them out, and disseminating, reciting, expounding, understanding, practising and even ritually venerating them. Such claims suggest defensiveness on the part of a new, small movement trying to establish itself. Some of the Mahāyāna *Sūtras* may have been in part produced by the new breed of charismatic *Dharma*-preachers who championed them (Kent, 1982). These

[16] McQueen, 1981 and 1982; Williams, 2009: 38–44.

monks, and some laypeople, directed their preaching both within and beyond the existing Buddhist community, to win converts. This they did by extolling the virtues of perfect Buddhahood, so as to elicit a conversion experience of profound psychological effect. This was the 'arising of the thought of awakening (*bodhi-citta*)', the heartfelt aspiration to strive for full Buddhahood, by means of the *Bodhisattva* path.

The new perspective on scriptural legitimacy led to the Mahāyāna having an open, ongoing 'revelation', which produced a huge outpouring of new *Sūtras* in India in the period up to around 650 CE. These were composed anonymously, often by a number of authors elaborating a basic text, to produce works frequently running to hundreds of pages in length. In contrast, the early *Suttas* are ninety-five printed pages long at most, and often only run to a page or two. In certain early *Suttas* such as the *Mahā-samaya* (*D*.II.253–62), the Buddha is a glorious spiritual being surrounded by countless gods and hundreds of disciples. The Mahāyāna *Sūtras* developed this style. In them, the Buddha uses hyperbolic language and paradox, and makes known many heavenly Buddhas and high-level heavenly *Bodhisattvas*, existing in many regions of the universe. A number of these saviour beings, Buddhas and in time *Bodhisattvas*, became objects of devotion and prayer, and greatly added to the appeal and missionary success of the Mahāyāna.

The nature of the Mahāyāna and its attitude to earlier schools

At first, the new movement was called the *Bodhisattva-yāna*, or '(Spiritual) Vehicle of the *Bodhisattva*'. This was in contradistinction to the 'Vehicle of the Disciple' (*Śrāvaka-yāna*) and 'Vehicle of the Solitary Buddha' (*Pratyeka-buddha-yāna*), which respectively aimed to become *Arhats* and *Pratyeka-buddhas* (see p. 99). As the new movement responded to criticisms from those who did not accept the new *Sūtras* (*BP*.34), it increasingly stressed the superiority of the *Bodhisattva-yāna*, and referred to it as the *Mahā-yāna*: the 'Great Vehicle', or 'Vehicle (Leading to) the Great' (Williams, 2009: 267). The other 'vehicles' were disparaged as being the 'Inferior Vehicle', or *Hīna-yāna* (*BSI*.197–211, from the *Lotus Sūtra*). The 'greatness' of the new vehicle was seen to lie in three areas: its compassionate motivation, directed at the salvation of countless beings; the profundity of the wisdom it cultivated; and its superior goal, omniscient Buddhahood.

Prior to its first translation into Chinese in 286 CE, the *Sūtra* known as the *Saddharma-puṇḍarīka*, or 'Lotus of the True *Dharma*' ('*Lotus*' for short) developed a perspective which, while hostile to the 'Hīnayāna', sought to portray it as incorporated in and completed by the Mahāyāna (Williams, 2009: 149–61). Chapter 2 of the *Sūtra* achieves this accommodation by what was to become a central Mahāyāna concept, that of *upāya-kauśalya*: skill (*kauśalya*) in means (*upāya*), or skilful means. This built on the old ideas of the Buddha's adept teaching methods, in which he adapted the contents of his teaching to the temperament and level of understanding of his audience. This was by simply selecting his specific teaching from a harmonious body of teachings. Now he was seen as having given different levels of teaching which might actually appear as conflicting, for the 'higher' level required the undoing of certain over-simplified lessons of the 'lower' level. While the Buddha's ultimate message was that *all* can become omniscient Buddhas, this would have been too unbelievable and confusing to give as a preliminary teaching (*BT*.85–90). For the 'ignorant with low dispositions', he therefore begins by teaching on the four True Realities for the Spiritually Ennobled, setting out the goal as attaining *Nirvāṇa* by becoming an *Arhat*. The *Arhat* is seen as still having a subtle pride, and as lacking in compassion in his hope of escaping the round of rebirths, thus leaving unenlightened beings to fend for themselves. For those who were prepared to listen further, the Buddha then teaches that the true *Nirvāṇa* is attained at Buddhahood, and that all can attain this, even the *Arhats*, who currently think that they have already reached the goal. The Buddha has just 'one vehicle' (*eka-yāna*), the all-inclusive Buddha-vehicle, but he uses his 'skilful means' to show this by means of three: the vehicles of the Disciple, Solitary Buddha, and *Bodhisattva*. He holds out to people whichever of them corresponds to their inclinations and aspirations, but once he has got them to develop spiritually, he gives them all the supreme Buddha-vehicle (*EB*.4.1). As the *Bodhisattva* path leads to Buddhahood, it seems hard to differentiate the *Bodhisattva* and Buddha-vehicles. Not all Mahāyāna *Sūtras* follow this 'one vehicle' perspective; indeed most, such as the *Ugraparipṛcchā* (Nattier, 2003), follow a 'three vehicle' (*tri-yāna*) one in which *Arhats* do not develop further. Others, such as the *Aṣṭsāhasrikā Prajñāpāramitā*, emphasize the importance of *Bodhisattvas* not falling back so as to seek the lesser goal of Arhatship.

According to the standards of Arhatship preserved by schools such as the Theravāda, the charge that the *Arhat* is proud and selfish is absurd. By definition, he or she is one who has finally destroyed the 'I am' conceit, the root of all egoism and selfishness. He is also described as imbued with lovingkindness and as compassionately teaching others. The Theravāda still acknowledges that the long path to Buddhahood, over many many lives, is the loftiest practice, as it aims at the salvation of countless beings (*Vism*.13).

Hence the late fourteenth-century *Dasa-bodhisatt'uppattikathā*, or 'Account of the Arising of Ten *Bodhisattvas*', talks in glowing terms of Metteyya and nine following *Bodhisattvas*. Nevertheless, while the *Bodhisattva* path has been and is practised by a few Theravādins (often laypeople), it is seen as a way for the heroic few only. Most, though, have gratefully made use of Gotama Buddha's teachings so as to move towards Arhatship, whether this be attained in the present life or a future one.

The Mahāyāna, though, urged as many men and women as possible to join the heroic few treading the demanding *Bodhisattva* path. Even so, the stereotype of the Mahāyāna as being more open to lay aspirations does not seem straightforwardly applicable to the early Mahāyāna (Berkwitz, 2010: 71–5). In early Chinese translations of Mahāyāna texts, the lay *Bodhisattva* is expected to live a life free of attachment to family, and to aim to ordain as soon as possible (Harrison, 1987; *BS*2.29). In much of this, he is akin to the ideal devout lay disciple in the Pali *Suttas* (e.g. *A*.IV.208–21). He might reach an advanced spiritual stage, but so might a layperson in the Theravāda tradition, say. Nevertheless, lay practitioners do play a prominent part in several important Mahāyāna *Sūtras*, such as the *Vimalakīrti-nirdeśa*.[17]

The call to the *Bodhisattva* path was inspired by the vision that the huge universe will always be in need of perfect Buddhas. The person entering this path aspired to be a compassionate, self-sacrificing hero (Nattier, 2003). His path would be long, as he would need to build up moral and spiritual perfections not only for his own exalted state of Buddhahood, but also so as to be able to aid others altruistically by teaching, good deeds, transference of karmic fruitfulness and offering response to prayers. While compassion had always been an important part of the Buddhist path (see pp. 24, 83), it was now more strongly emphasized, as the motivating factor for the whole *Bodhisattva* path.

Over the centuries, many monks studied and practised according to both the Śrāvakayāna and Mahāyāna; not infrequently, both were present in the same monastery. The Chinese, in fact, did not come to clearly differentiate the Mahāyāna as a separate movement until late in the fourth century. Moreover, in Eastern and Northern Buddhism, the term 'Hīnayāna' came to be mostly used to refer to the lower level of spiritual motivation and practice which prepared for the Mahāyāna level. It is in any case a mistake to equate the 'Hīnayāna' with the Theravāda fraternity, both because the term is a disparaging one not accepted by Theravādins, and also because it was used to refer to any person who did not accept the Mahāyāna *Sūtras* as

[17] Lamotte, 1976; *BT*.271–6; *EB*.4.4.4.

authoritative. Such persons could come from any of the ordination fraternities, while perhaps living with others who did accept these new *Sūtras* to some extent. Moreover, these fraternities also included a *Bodhisattva* path, so it is incorrect to see them as purely Śrāvakayāna in nature. That said, those Theravādins who were resistant to accepting the new, Mahāyāna *Sūtras* in time became the dominant voice in their tradition.

In talking of those Buddhists who did not accept the Mahāyāna *Sūtras*, one is faced with the problem of finding a convenient label for them. The pejorative term 'Hīnayāna' is inappropriate (Katz, 1980), and the term 'Theravāda' refers to only one of the traditions which originated prior to the rise of the Mahāyāna movement, and whose members were critical of the new texts to some degree. 'Śrāvakayāna' is a useful term, though one must remember that fraternities which were mainly Śrāvakayāna in orientation also contained some who took the *Bodhisattva* path, either set within a doctrinal context that did not include ideas from the new *Sūtras*, or who used these texts and their ideas. So fraternities 'which emphasized the Śrāvakayāna' is better. Some use the term 'Mainstream' Buddhism to denote non-Mahāyānists (Williams and Tribe, 2000: 210; *EB*.88–9); but while the Mahāyānists were not the 'mainstream' in India, they became the 'mainstream' in places such as Tibet, China and Japan.

One thing is clear, though: one cannot understand the Mahāyāna in isolation from what came before it. One also needs to understand Mahāyāna rhetoric and self-justification in its context so as to be wary of over-generalizations based on it, and beware of imposing either Western notions of religious differences, or ideals of twentieth-century lay-orientated Japanese Buddhism, onto early Indian Buddhism. The broad Mahāyāna movement originated gradually, unlike the Protestant Reformation, and it was not lay-led, as Japanese scholars have sometimes argued.

CHAPTER 5

Mahāyāna Philosophies: The Varieties of Emptiness

The Mahāyāna *kind of motivation*, of compassionately aspiring for perfect Buddhahood, is typically set within a framework of Mahāyāna *doctrine*. One should not forget, however, that such motivation has also existed in a minority of those whose doctrinal framework has been that of one of the early schools, such as the Theravāda. There are also those whose doctrinal context is Mahāyāna, but who aim for worldly protection, or a good rebirth, or their own liberation, so as to not (yet) have a motivation-level that is Mahāyāna.

The Mahāyāna doctrinal perspective is expressed in both *Sūtras* and a number of *Śāstras*, 'treatises' written by named authors. These systematically present the outlook of particular Mahāyāna schools, based on the *Sūtras*, logic and meditational experience. Each school is associated with a particular group of *Sūtras*, whose meaning it sees as fully explicit (*nītārtha*); other *Sūtras* may be regarded as in need of interpretation (*neyārtha*). In India, the Mahāyāna developed two main philosophical schools: the Mādhyamika, and later the Yogācāra. Both have been key influences on Northern and Eastern Buddhism.

THE PERFECTION OF WISDOM LITERATURE AND THE MĀDHYAMIKA SCHOOL

Sources and writers

The Mādhyamika school was also known as the Śūnyatā-vāda, the 'Emptiness Teaching', for its key concept is that of 'emptiness', also central to the *Prajñā-pāramitā*, or 'Perfection of Wisdom' *Sūtras* (*BTTA*.141–8). Among these is the oldest extant Mahāyāna text, the *Aṣṭasāhasrikā (Asta.)*, or '8,000 Verse' Perfection of Wisdom *Sūtra*. Originating in the first centuries BCE and CE, its contents were expanded, in the period to 300 CE, to form works of 18,000, 25,000 (*Panca.*) and 100,000 verses. Short versions were also composed. The 300 verse *Vajracchedikā* (*Vc.* (*BS1*.164–8; *BS2*.51)), or 'Diamond-cutter' may date from 300 to 500 CE, though in some form may have existed in the early phase of this literature. The one-page *Hṛdaya*, or 'Heart' Perfection of Wisdom *Sūtra*[1] dates from after 300. Jan Nattier[2] has argued that it was composed in China as a condensation of ideas in the 100,000 verse version, then introduced into India, perhaps by the pilgrim-monk Xuanzang, and translated into Sanskrit, as Indian Mahāyānists recognized its great merits. The 300 to 500 CE period also saw the composition of the *Abhisamayālaṃkāra*, attributed to the *Bodhisattva* Maitreya, an exegetical work much used in Tibet.

The Mādhyamika school was founded by Nāgārjuna (*c.* 150–250 CE), a south Indian monk, philosopher and mystic. The school's foundation-document is his *(Mūla)-madhyamaka-kārikā*, 'Verses on the (Fundamentals of) the Middle Way' (*Mmk.*). This argues for what Nāgārjuna sees as the true 'Middle Way' of the Buddha (see p. 69), seeking to convince those not accepting the Mahāyāna *Sūtras* that the early scriptures, properly understood, lead to seeing that everything is 'empty' of both inherent, independent existence and inherent nature (an essence) (Westerhoff, 2009). Many other works are attributed to Nāgārjuna, though several were probably by later writers of the same name. Among the more reliable attributions (Williams, 2009: 64–5) is the *Vigraha-vyāvartanī*, 'Averting the Arguments' (*Vigv.*), which critiques objections to his ideas. While his outlook seems close to that of the Perfection of Wisdom *Sūtras*, he does not quote from them or refer to the 'Mahāyāna' or *'Bodhisattva'* in the *Madhyamaka-kārikā*. It was left to his other works, if authentic, or his key disciples, Āryadeva (*BP*.32) and Nāga, to make such explicit connections.

Buddhapālita (*c.* 470–540) and then Bhāvaviveka[3] (*c.* 490–570) built up the popularity of the school. The latter improved its logical methods, drawing on the ideas of the Buddhist logician Dignāga (*c.* 480–540) and developed a new interpretation of Nāgārjuna's ideas, thus forming the Svātantrika-Mādhyamika school.[4] Its interpretation was then disputed by Candrakīrti (late sixth century), who built on the work of Buddhapālita to found the Prāsaṅgika-Mādhyamika school as a definitive statement of Mādhyamika. Candrakīrti's ideas are expressed in such works as his commentary on the *Madhyamaka-kārikā*, the *Prasannapadā*, or 'Clear-worded', and Śāntideva (*c.* 650–750) drew on this perspective in his *Bodhicaryāvatāra*

[1] *BS1*.162–4; *EB*.4.2.2; Conze, 1958 contains both this and the *Diamond-cutter*.
[2] 1992; cf. Williams, 2009: 48–9, 284. [3] Also known as Bhavya and Bhāviveka.
[4] Also known in Tibet as the Sautrāntika-Mādhyamika.

(*Bca*.; *BP*.14; Berkwitz, 2010: 121–5), an influential overview of the path of the Mahāyāna *Bodhisattva*. Śāntarakṣita (*c*. 680–740) and his pupil Kamalaśīla (*c*. 700–50) also added some Yogācāra ideas to those of the Svātantrika-Mādhyamika, thus forming the Yogācāra-Mādhyamika school. The above later Mādhyamika writers had a great influence in Tibet, but were unknown in China, where the Mādhyamika had a less lasting influence. The Chinese version of the Mādhyamika was the Sanlun, or Three Treatise, school, founded by the great translator Kumārajīva (334–413).

The Śūnyatāvādin orientation

The Perfection of Wisdom literature extols wisdom (*prajñā*) and also the other transcendent 'perfections' (*pāramitā*) involved in the *Bodhisattva* path. While it and Nāgārjuna's works were clearly for intellectuals, they re-emphasized the Buddha's rejection of all speculative 'views', claiming that *Abhidharma* analytical thinking could lead to a subtle form of intellectual grasping: the idea that one had 'grasped' the true nature of reality in a neat set of concepts. In later Zen, such an endeavour was seen as like trying to catch a slippery catfish in a equally slippery gourd. The new literature also saw, in the *Abhidharma*'s contrasting of *Nirvāṇa* with the conditioned *dharmas* that make up a 'person', the basis of a subtle form of spiritual self-seeking: the desire to 'attain' *Nirvāṇa* for oneself, to *get* something one did not already have; in Sarvāstivādin terms, to have it linked to one by the *dharma* 'possession' (*prāpti*). The new texts sought to re-emphasize that the goal was to be attained by totally 'letting go', so as to produce a thought, or state of consciousness (*citta*), transcending any sensory or mental object as support (cf. p. 76): 'the *Bodhisattva* . . . should produce an unsupported thought, i.e. a thought which is nowhere supported, a thought unsupported by sights, sounds, smells, tastes, touchables, or mind objects' (*Vc*. sec. 10c).

Empty dharmas *and Conditioned Arising*

A key Perfection of Wisdom criticism of *Abhidharma* thought – primarily Sarvāstivādin – was that it did not go far enough in understanding that everything is non-Self (Skt *anātman*), or 'empty' (*śūnya*) of Self (see pp. 58 and 81). It understood the 'absence of Self in persons' (*pudgala-nairātmya*), but when it analysed 'persons' down into *dharmas*, each with an inherent 'own-nature' (*svabhāva*; see pp. 93–4), it was seen not to have understood the 'absence of Self(-nature) in *dharmas*' (*dharma-nairātmya*): that they are essence-less. The Perfection of Wisdom literature holds that a *dharma* (and also an ordinary 'thing') is not an ultimate fact in its own right, for it cannot be anything by 'itself'; its arising and very nature are dependent on other *dharma*s, which are in turn dependent on others, etc.: it is 'empty' of any *svabhāva*. Edward Conze explains that for the Perfection of Wisdom, *svabhāva* means: 'Natural or inherent condition of something existing through its own power alone, having an invariable and inalienable mark, and having an immutable essence. In its "own-being" a thing is just itself, and not merely as it is relative to ourselves, or to other things' (*Asta.* transl., p. 320). Paul Williams argues that while the term meant 'inherent nature' for the Sarvāstivādins, in the Mādhyamika, it underwent a subtle shift in meaning, to '"intrinsic existence" (or "inherent existence") in the sense of a causally independent, fundamentally real existence' (Williams, 2009: 68); that is, its meaning was still seen to include 'inherent nature', but this was seen to also imply 'inherent existence'. Aspects of the critique of inherent existence are then seen to imply a critique of the idea of inherent nature.

Nāgārjuna's critique of the notion of *svabhāva* (*Mmk.* ch.15) argues that anything which arises according to conditions, as all phenomena do, can have no inherent existence/nature; for what it is depends on what conditions it. Moreover, if there is nothing with inherent existence, that is, self-existence, there can be nothing with 'other-existence' (*para-bhāva*), that is, something which is dependent for its existence and nature on something *else* which has self-existence. So there is not anything with a true, substantially existent nature (*bhāva*); hence no non-existent (*abhāva*), in the sense of a true existent that has gone out of existence. Like Nāgārjuna, the Perfection of Wisdom literature therefore regards all *dharma*s as like a dream or magical illusion (*māyā*) (*BTTA*.166; cf. p. 58). This does not mean that they are simply unreal. Their ungraspable nature is, rather, wholly different from what it seems, like the trick of a conjurer; or, we might now say, like an illusion in a 'virtual reality' electronic medium – except that all components of the medium would also be seen as perceptual illusions too . . . There is something there in experience, and one can describe it well in terms of *dharma*s, so it is wrong to deny these exist; yet they do not have substantial existence either. What we experience does not exist in an absolute sense, but only in a relative way, as a passing interdependent phenomenon. The nature of *dharma*s lies in between absolute 'non-existence' and substantial 'existence', in accordance with an early *Sutta* passage[5] quoted by Nāgārjuna (*Mmk*.15.7; cf. *EB*.4.2.3). This is what Nāgārjuna means by the

[5] *S*.II.17 (see p. 72), known in Sanskrit as the *Kātyāyanāvavāda Sūtra*.

'Middle Way'. He argues that something with inherent existence would substantially exist and be eternal; to believe in such an entity is to hold to the eternalist view, while to believe that such a thing could go out of existence is to hold to the annihilationist view; both these views being condemned by the Buddha.

The Mādhyamika interpretation of Conditioned Arising sees it as meaning that phenomena are not only mutually dependent for their 'arising' in time, but are so in their very nature. Thus they cannot really be spoken of as separately identifiable entities which interact. By 'itself', a thing is nothing. It is what it is only in relation to other things, and they are what they are in relation to it and yet other things. In his examination of the process of seeing (*Mmk*. ch. 3), Nāgārjuna argues that there is no activity of vision which is presently not seeing. Therefore, one cannot say that there is something, 'vision', which may then go on to perform the separate action 'seeing': 'vision' and 'seeing' are mutually dependent, and cannot be separately identified. As the Perfection of Wisdom literature would paradoxically put it, vision is 'empty of' vision. There is, then, no real activity 'vision' which 'sees'. But if vision does not see, then non-vision certainly does not see, so how can one identify a 'seer' who is characterized by his 'seeing'? Without a seer, how can there be anything seen? All such concepts, and the more general ones of subject and object, are meaningful only in relationship to each other. Similarly, what is short depends on what is long; for long and short are correlative concepts. By such reasoning, Nāgārjuna even says that the 'unconditioned' (traditionally a term for *Nirvāṇa*) is conceptually dependent on the conditioned, its opposite (*Mmk*.7.33).

As illusion-like and empty, *dharmas* are not to be seen as ultimately existing existents/processes (Williams and Tribe, 2000: 100–01). No 'bedrock existence', so to speak, can be found – even *Nirvāṇa* – but fully knowing and accepting this gives one, so to speak, a bedrock.

Tibetan writers of the Gelugpa school (see p. 208), who follow the Prāsaṅgika-Mādhyamika view, thus see a threefold aspect to something's being empty of *svabhāva*:

1. Things (e.g. persons, moods, tables, mountains) that can be analysed into their parts – which may be themselves further analysable – lack *svabhāva* as they are dependent on those parts (be these physical or mental), and have no true existence of their own, in this sense lacking both inherent existence and inherent nature.
2. *Dharmas*, which is what one reaches by rigorous analysis into parts, are dependent on other *dharmas* for their arising; they lack *svabhāva* as they are not independent, hence are lacking in inherent *existence*.

3. Both everyday things and *dharmas* are also dependent on imputation by mental designation, in relation to other things or *dharmas*: they lack an inherent *nature*, one 'from their own side'. Even *Nirvāṇa* is dependent in this sense.

Abhidharmists would all agree with point 1. They would agree with point 2, as long as this only concerned conditioned *dharmas*, not *Nirvāṇa*; though the Sarvāstivādin idea of *dharmas*, as in some sense existing timelessly, compromised the idea of *dharmas* other than *Nirvāṇa* being dependent. It is on point 3 that there is more of a break made with *Abhidharma* ideas. It should be noted, though, that there is a suggestion of 3 in the Vibhajyāvāda/Theravāda idea that *duḥkha* (Pali *dukkha*), conditioned phenomena, can be known in the same moment that their stopping, *Nirvāṇa*, is known (see p. 96).

Conventional truth and language

The Mādhyamika school holds that confusion over the nature of phenomena arises because people do not understand how the Buddha taught according to two levels of truth or reality: 'conventional truth/reality' (*saṃvṛti-satya*) and profound 'ultimate truth/reality' (*paramārtha-satya*) (*Mmk*.24.8–9). The concept of two levels of truth already existed in *Abhidharma*. There, 'conventional truths' were those expressed using terms such as 'person' and 'thing'; 'ultimate truth' is more exact, expressed by talking of *dharmas*, ultimate realities. For the Mādhyamika writers, however, talk of *dharmas* is just another kind of provisional, conventional truth. Such conventional truths should not be confused with ultimate truths, that is, truths about supposedly essential, ultimate realities; to see them like this is delusion.[6] The real ultimate truth is that all things discussed in terms of conventional truth are empty of ultimate, essential reality; they are, indeed, *conventional*. Seeing them thus is wisdom, leading to *non-attachment* to conventional realities, but a greatly enhanced ability to *skilfully work with* them.

To think that because a word exists, there must be some real self-enclosed entity in the extra-linguistic world that it refers to, is to make the mistake of reification: turning words into things. Ordinary language references to such things as 'self', 'space', 'time', 'road', 'thought' or 'hunger' do not mean that reality includes any of these as essential entities: they are simply useful concepts in certain contexts. For the Mādhyamikas, true statements at the

[6] *Mmk*.24.8–10; Williams, 2009: 76–9.

conventional level are 'true' because humans agree to use concepts in certain ways; because of linguistic conventions. 'Ice is cold' is true because 'ice' is a term used to describe a form of 'water' which is experienced as 'cold'. The terms of language arise because, from the continuous flux of experience, discriminating conceptualization (*prapañca*) abstracts various segments and takes them to be separate entities or qualities, with fixed natures. These then become focuses of attachment. The language-constructs (*prajñapti*) which are labels for them are interrelated in many ways. They gain their meaning from how they are used, in relationship to other concepts, not by referring to objective referents existing outside language.[7] Yet while language determines how we experience the world, it does not bring things into existence; it too is a dependent, empty phenomenon. A particular 'thing' enters the human world by being discriminated through a name or concept, but this exists in relation to a 'something' to which it is applied: both 'name' and perceived 'form' exist in relationship to each other (*Mmk*. ch. 5).

Emptiness

In the Śūnyatāvādin perspective, each phenomenon lacks an inherent nature, and so all are said to share an empty 'non-nature' as their 'nature' (*Asta*.192). Thus one *dharma* cannot ultimately be distinguished from another: the notion of the 'sameness' of *dharmas*. Their shared 'nature' is 'emptiness' (*śūnyatā*). As the *Heart Sūtra* says, 'whatsoever is material form, that is emptiness, and whatsoever is emptiness, that is material form' (and similarly for the other four 'bundles' making up a 'person'). 'Emptiness', though, is not some ultimate basis and substance of the world, like the *Brahman* of the *Upaniṣads*. It implies that no such self-existent substance exists: the world is a web of fluxing, interdependent, baseless phenomena. Nāgārjuna, in fact, equates emptiness with the principle of Conditioned Arising; for this logically leads to it:

> Whatever is conditioned arising,
> That is explained to be emptiness.
> That, being a dependent designation (*prajñapti*).
> Is itself the middle way (*pratipat . . . madhyamā*). (*Mmk*.24.18)

Emptiness, then, is an adjectival quality of '*dharmas*', their dependent non-ultimacy, not a substance which composes them. It is neither a thing

[7] This view is reminiscent of the later philosophy of Ludwig Wittgenstein (1889–1951), which critiqued his earlier idea that language works by 'picturing' facts in the world.

nor is it nothingness; rather it refers to the essencelessness of reality, which cannot be captured by concepts, with their tendency to breed reification.

Some have seen modern physics as containing parallels to this perspective (Wallace, 2003). When the 'solid' objects of common-sense reality were first analysed, they were seen to consist of empty space and protons, neutrons and electrons. Classical physics saw these as hard, indivisible particles, the ultimate building-blocks of matter; but further analysis showed them to consist of a whole range of odd particles such as 'quarks', whose nature is bound up with the forces through which they interact. Matter turns out to be a mysterious field of interaction, with 'particles' not being real separate entities, but provisional conceptual designations.

Critics from the early schools saw the emptiness teaching as implying that the four True Realities for the Spiritually Ennobled were themselves empty, thus subverting the Buddha's teaching. In reply, Nāgārjuna argued that it is the notion of *dharmas*-with-inherent-nature – and hence inherent existence – which subverts the teachings on the four True Realities (*Mmk.* ch.24; *EB*.4.3.1). If *duḥkha* had inherent existence, it would be causeless and eternal, and could never be brought to an end. If the Path had inherent existence, it could never be gradually developed to perfection in a person; for he or she would either have it or not have it. In a world of entities with inherent existence, all change and activity would be impossible; everything would be static and eternal. It is because everything is empty that there can be activity, including spiritual development. An analogy, here, is that the decimal number system would collapse without the quantity zero.[8]

Skilful means and the transcending of views

Nāgārjuna emphasizes that ultimate truth, indicated by talk of emptiness, completes rather than subverts conventional truth. Indeed, it can be understood only if the conventional teachings on the four True Realities for the Spiritually Ennobled have been understood (*Mmk.* ch.24.10). This relates to the concept of 'skilful means', which in the Śūnyatāvādin perspective is developed to mean that *all* Buddhist teachings – including Śūnyatāvādin ones – should be regarded as provisional devices that can at most hint at or indirectly indicate ultimate truth. The teachings, especially on Conditioned Arising, are simply to induce in people a skilful frame of mind: one in which

[8] A concept which derives from India, with the term 'zero' coming, via the Arabic *ṣifr*, from the term *śūnya*, empty.

there can be insight into that which transcends all such teachings – the inexpressible empty-of-essence nature of things.

Nāgārjuna's method in the *Madhyamaka-kārikā* is to criticize all views and theories about ultimate entities or principles. This he does by showing that their necessary consequences (*prasaṅga*) contradict either the views themselves, which are thus reduced to absurdity, or experience. Moreover, he seeks to show that *all* logically possible views on specific topics, such as motion and time (*Mmk.* chs.2 and 19), are untenable; that our notions of them are self-contradictory inasmuch as we take such things as realities in themselves. In this, he uses his method of 'four-cornered (*catuṣkoti*) negation', the device of examining and refuting all the four logically possible alternatives on a topic: x is y, x is non-y, x is both y and non-y, x is neither y nor non-y.

In chapter 1, he examines theories on causality. The first of the logical possible views on this is 'self-production': that an effect arises from a cause ultimately identical with itself, part of the same underlying substance (as in the Hindu Sāṃkhya school[9]). This would lead to pointless self-duplication, however, and if a thing reproduced itself, there would be nothing to stop it continuing to do so for ever. The world is not observed to be like this. If the same substance is said to manifest itself differently only when conditions are appropriate, '*self*-production' has already been given up.

The second possibility, 'other-production', is that, ultimately, an effect arises from a cause that is inherently 'other' than it, with a different inherent nature. This is seen as an *Abhidharma* view, to the extent that it is said in this that both a *dharma* and the *dharmas* that condition it have specific own-natures or essences, which are thus essentially *different* from each other. Here, Nāgārjuna argues that, if really distinct entities existed, all would be equally 'different', so anything could 'cause' anything. A cause and its (supposedly different) effect may always occur together,[10] but to point this out is to *explain* nothing about how causality works. What is inherently 'other' than something cannot be its cause. A 'cause' is not a 'cause' in itself, then, but only in relation to its 'effect' (*Mmk.*1.5). *If* cause and effect were essentially different entities, there could not be a link between them. This is an instance of a general problem: a relation of *any* sort has to (i) *connect* two terms, unifying them, and (ii) to connect *two* terms, differentiating them. A relation cannot obtain between essential entities which are either identical

[9] The Sāṃkhya saw all things in the world as different forms of one underlying substance, *prakṛti* (nature).

[10] In the words of the Scottish empiricist philosopher David Hume (1711–76), being 'constantly conjoined'.

with or different from each other. All essentialist views 'freeze' reality into bits, identical with (as in 'self-production') or different from each other (as in 'other-production'), but then cannot coherently account for how these bits interact to form the world as it is experienced. As emphasized in early Buddhism, Conditioned Arising avoids the extremes of everything being a single unity and it being an unconnected diversity (see pp. 72–3).

The third theory is that causality involves both 'self-production' and 'other-production'. If this means that some parts of the cause and effect are the same, and some are different, the problems of the first two views apply. If it means that all of the cause is both the same as and different from all of the effect, this is impossible. The final possibility is that things originate by neither 'self-production' nor 'other-production': spontaneously, without a cause. But if this were true, everything would be an unpredictable chaos, which it is not.

The fourth view, note, is not that of Nāgārjuna. His 'position' seems to be that at the conventional, phenomenal level, causality can be observed, with 'one' thing (with the support of other conditions) causing 'another' to originate; yet none of the logically possible theories of causality can explain how it 'works'. This is because, at the ultimate level, no real 'things' can be found which 'originate'; no things exist with inherent existence, 'they' *only* exist conventionally. Moreover, no supposed 'cause' has an actual power to make something else happen; effects arise from a combination of various conditions, with none of them 'making' the effect happen. As argued by Jay Garfield (*Mmk*. transl., pp. 103–23), Nāgārjuna sees causality as simply a matter of observed regularities in an essence-free world; one cannot actually go further or deeper than this, except by explaining one kind of regularity in nature by reference to a wider or more general form of regularity. For example an explosion may be explained by reference to the presence of a source of combustion, an explosive gas and oxygen; the quality of an explosive gas can be explained by reference to its chemical make-up, and this can be explained by reference to the physical make-up of atoms, etc.

The Mādhyamikas' talk of emptiness, then, is intended as the antidote to *all* theories: 'Emptiness is proclaimed by the victorious ones (Buddhas) as the refutation of all views; but those who hold "emptiness" as a view are called incurable' (*Mmk*.13.8; cf. *BS*2.38, vv.6–7). Nāgārjuna examines the views of others to provide a form of spiritual therapy, to help liberate people from all constricting viewpoints. In doing this, he claims not to have any presuppositions of his own, but to work with those of his opponents in a kind of logical judo, using conventional logic. The insights which this produces are also to be deepened by meditative contemplation of phenomena.

The Svātantrika-Mādhyamika school held that logic itself is not empty, but has an autonomous existence (*svatantra*), such that valid positive statements can be made from a Mādhyamika perspective. The inferences made at the conventional level are a real bridge to at least some aspects of ultimate truth. The Prāsaṅgika school, on the other hand, emphasized that the Mādhyamika contained only a negative dialectic, to disprove the views of others, and that to understand ultimate truth is to know the limits of logic, words and concepts, culminating in a direct, non-conceptual experience. This seems to accord with the Perfection of Wisdom *Sūtras*, which certainly sought to avoid setting up any views, or indeed to 'say' anything: 'There is nothing at all to understand, nothing at all to understand. For nothing in particular has been indicated, nothing in particular has been explained' (*Asta*.38; cf. *EB*.4.4.4; *BT*.271–6).

Ultimate truth and thusness

At the ultimate level, even talk of 'emptiness' is to be finally given up: as the things which are said to be empty do not ultimately exist, one cannot even say that 'they' are 'empty' (*Mmk*.22.11): 'the emptiness of all *dharmas* is empty of that emptiness' (*Panca*.196). The ultimate truth, then, is that there are no ultimate realities; existence is inconceivable and inexpressible as it has no ultimate ground: 'When the domain of thought ceases, that which can be stated ceases' (*Mmk*.18.7). The Perfection of Wisdom literature contains an elusive series of subtle allusions to that which lies beyond words. An indicator which it uses for this is the notion of *tathatā:* 'thusness' or 'suchness'. The thusness of something, equivalent to its emptiness, is its very as-it-is-ness, what it is such as it is, without conceptually adding anything to it or taking anything away from its actuality: it is simply '*thus*: . . .'. Thusness is 'immutable and unchangeable, undiscriminated, undifferentiated', it belongs to nowhere, is neither past, present nor future, and the same thusness is found in all *dharmas* (*Asta*.307). 'True reality' (*tattva*) is 'not conditioned by something else, peaceful, not elaborated by conceptual proliferation (*prapañca*)' (*Mmk*.18.9; as is also typically said of *Nirvāṇa*). Ultimate truth is known when spiritual ignorance is transcended and the limitations of language are totally seen through, with no further generation of, or attachment to, dream-like linguistic constructs, just perfect even-mindedness (*Mmk*.25.24). Empty, conditioned phenomena are seen as worthless and are thus no longer constructed, so that insight into ultimate truth is attaining the bliss of *Nirvāṇa*.

Nirvāṇa *and* saṃsāra

In Śūnyatāvādin thought, the *Nirvāṇa* which is thus attained is not seen as a *dharma* different from *dharmas* of *saṃsāra*, the conditioned world of suffering and rebirths: 'there is not the slightest bit of difference between the two' (*Mmk*.25.20; *EB*.4.3.1). How can this be? The very fact of the 'unconditioned' *Nirvāṇa* being contrasted, at the conventional level, to *saṃsāra*, makes its nature a *relational* one, such that it is empty of inherent nature. *Nirvāṇa*, indeed, was held to be 'the empty' (Pali *suññata*) even by the early schools of Buddhism, in the sense of being empty of defilements, known through seeing all as empty of Self, and being beyond conceptualization in any positive terms (see pp. 81, 96). For Nāgārjuna, the conditioned and the unconditioned cannot, then, be differentiated because 'both' are found to 'be' emptiness: Selflessness, essencelessness, free of any essentially existing defilements. What is more, while *Nirvāṇa* is seen by all schools of Buddhism as 'unborn', 'deathless' and not impermanent, in the Śūnyatāvādin perspective, conditioned *dharmas* can be similarly described. This is because, if they lack inherent existence, and do not exist as such, they cannot be said to 'originate' or 'cease' (*Mmk*.7.33); their thusness is not subject to arising or ceasing, but is constant (*Mahāprajñāpāramitā Sūtra* (*BTTA*.148)). Consequently, they cannot be said to be impermanent (not that they are permanent): they remain 'unoriginated' (the *Heart Sūtra*), 'unborn', and without differentiation from *Nirvāṇa*. Thus *Nirvāṇa* is not attained by the eradication of anything real, namely defilements, but by the non-construction of the conditioned world of *saṃsāra*:[11] for 'all *dharmas* are unthinkable . . . equal to the unequalled. For they are *Tathāgata-dharmas*' (*Asta*.280), and 'the thusness of all *dharmas* and the thusness of the *Tathāgata* are simply this one single thusness' (*Asta*.512). *Nirvāṇa* and *saṃsāra* are not two separate realities, but the field of emptiness, seen by either spiritual ignorance or true knowledge (*Mmk*.25.9). As the *Heart Sūtra* again says, 'In emptiness there is neither material form, nor feeling, nor perception, nor constructing activities, nor consciousness . . . There is no *duḥkha*, no origination, no stopping, no path'. When the emptiness of the five 'bundles' of a 'person' is seen, they as essentially existing entities 'disappear' – though as conventional realities, they remain.

The idea that *Nirvāṇa* and *saṃsāra* are non-different plays a central role in the Perfection of Wisdom perspective. Once 'established', there followed

[11] Cf. the Theravāda view, that when the Path brings realization of *Nirvāṇa*, this is not the ending of past defilements, which no longer exist, or of present ones, which are incompatible with it; it is the stopping of the production of any future defilements, and their effects (*Vibh-a*.299–300).

other conclusions with consequences for the whole of Mahāyāna thought. Most importantly, the *Bodhisattva* need not seek to escape *saṃsāra* to attain *Nirvāṇa*. He can tirelessly work to aid 'suffering beings', sustained by the idea that *Nirvāṇa* is, so to speak, something already present in *saṃsāra*. As an advanced *Bodhisattva*, he directly experiences this non-duality of *saṃsāra* and *Nirvāṇa*, this realization being fully matured when Buddhahood – *Nirvāṇa* in the highest sense – is reached. The nature of Buddhahood, 'Buddhaness' (*buddhatā*), is of course emptiness, as is the nature of everything. Because of this, all beings are seen to have a nature which is non-different from Buddhaness. Without this, how could ordinary frail beings eventually become omniscient Buddhas?

Self-emptiness and other-emptiness

The implications of the above were seen in two kinds of ways within Mahāyāna traditions. In Tibet, these are called 'self-emptiness' (*rang stong*, pronounced *rang dong*) and 'other-emptiness' (*gzhan stong*, pronounced *zhen dong*).[12] The first is the perspective of the Gelugpa school (see p. 208), which takes the line of the Prāsaṅgika-Mādhyamika. It sees the emptiness teaching as a 'non-affirming negative', on the lack of inherent nature/existence in anything. As beings are empty of a fixed Self, and their minds empty of inherent nature, they are capable of ultimate change and are not ultimately different from *Nirvāṇa*. Their defilements (attachment, hatred and delusion, etc.), which sustain *saṃsāra*, are also empty of inherent existence, and so can be transcended. This is seen initially through reasoning, then the result of this reasoning is the focus of meditative concentration, leading on to a non-conceptual direct insight into emptiness, at the path of seeing, at the start of the path of the Noble *Bodhisattva*. Along this path, as the perfections are developed, the tendency of ordinary perception to habitually see things in a non-empty way is gradually purified away.

The 'other-emptiness' view is held by people mainly linked to the Nyingmapa and Kagyüpa schools, drawing on ideas of the now extinct Jonangpa school (see p. 208). This perspective sometimes calls itself the 'Great Mādhyamika'. In this view, the most important referent of the term 'emptiness' is a self-existent, unchanging reality that pervades all phenomena (*BS2*.52). Like *Nirvāṇa* as seen by the early schools (see pp. 81, 96), it is 'emptiness' in being empty of defilements – empty of what is other than it; however, this does not mean it is empty of its own positive qualities; rather

[12] Williams, 2009: 112–15; Powers, 2007a.

it is full of Buddha-qualities. Knowing the limits of concepts does not just show the limitations of conventional truths, it reveals the true, underlying absolute reality that is known in a non-conceptual way: emptiness, the radiant, non-dual consciousness of a Buddha. The task of beings, then, is not to 'attain' something that they do not already possess, but to *uncover* and know their Buddhaness. The task of the *Bodhisattva* is to skilfully help them in this. This view sees this ultimate emptiness as the *Tathāgata-garbha* (see below).

In the self-emptiness view, the ultimate truth is that there is no ultimate reality, no reality with an inherent nature/existence; there are just non-ultimate conventional realities. Seeing *Nirvāṇa* is seeing emptiness, in the sense of seeing that everything is empty of ultimacy. In the other-emptiness view, while conventional realities are still seen as empty of ultimacy, there is seen to be an ultimate reality, emptiness, which is a positive reality, but is empty of defilements. This is the basis of everything. The self-emptiness view is akin to ideas in early Buddhism in finding no ultimate basis that is the support of everything else. The other-emptiness view is akin to ideas in early Buddhism in seeing *Nirvāṇa* as a reality in its own right, but unlike it in seeing this reality as the basis of everything, much like the *Ātman-Brahman* of the *Upaniṣads*.

The differences between these perspectives echoes the fact that in early Buddhism, the quality of being 'empty' (Pali *suñña*, Skt. *śūnya*) referred to a certain kind of lack, while 'the empty' (*suññaṃ/suññata*) referred to a reality that *has* a certain kind of lack. 'Emptiness' (Pali *suññatā*) sometimes refers to a quality of lack (e.g. *M*.III.105), though the *Arhat*'s liberated mind is an emptiness that is that which *is empty of* attachment, hatred and delusion (*S*.IV.297). As will be seen below, the term 'emptiness' has a range of meanings in the Mahāyāna. When the term is used, one always needs to try to discern if it refers to a kind of lack – and if so, what kind (e.g. of inherent nature) – or to a positive reality that is lacking in certain negative features.

THE YOGĀCĀRA SCHOOL

Sources and writers

Ideas of the Yogācāra school were probably first adumbrated in the early strata of the *Yogācāra-bhūmi-śāstra*, attributed to Asaṅga (310–90?) but with ideas predating him (Williams, 2009: 85–7). They are also rooted in the ideas of certain *Sūtras* which began to appear in the third century CE. The most important is the *Saṃdhinirmocana* ('Freeing the Underlying

Meaning'; Powers, 1995). The *Sūtra* sees itself as a 'third turning of the *Dharma*-wheel', surpassing the first two 'turnings': the teachings on the four True Realities for the Spiritually Ennobled, and the Perfection of Wisdom *Sūtras*. The *Mahāyāna-abhidharma Sūtra* is another such text. The influential *Laṅkāvatāra* ('Descent into Laṅkā') *Sūtra* (*Lanka.*), which gradually developed from around 300 CE, also contains many Yogācāra ideas in its unsystematic summary of Mahāyāna teachings.

The Yogācāra was founded as a separate school by Asaṅga, seen by tradition as a monk ordained in the Vibhajyavādin Mahīśāsaka fraternity. His 'teacher' was one Maitreyanātha, or Maitreya, who may have been a human teacher, or seen by Asaṅga as the heavenly *Bodhisattva* Maitreya. In time, Asaṅga converted his half-brother to the Mahāyāna: Vasubandhu, seen as the Vasubandhu who composed the Sarvāstivādin *Abhidharma-kośa* and its *bhāṣya* (see p. 94). The scholarly debate as to whether the two Vasubandhus were actually the same person is as yet unresolved, though one can see a line of development from the *bhāṣya* to some ideas of the Yogācāra Vasubandhu (Berkwitz, 2010: 108–9; Williams, 2009: 301–2).

Asaṅga's works (Williams, 2009: 87) include the *Mahāyāna-saṃgraha* ('Compendium of the Mahāyāna': *Ms.*), the *Abhidharma-samuccaya* ('Collection of *Abhidharma*'), this being a Yogācāra version of the *Abhidharma*, and a commentary on the *Saṃdhinirmocana Sūtra*. Several other works associated with Asaṅga are attributed by either Chinese or Tibetan tradition to 'Maitreya', in the sense that this *Bodhisattva* inspired Asaṅga to write them. The most philosophically important of these is the *Madhyānta-vibhāga* ('Discrimination between the Middle and Extremes': *Mv.*). Vasubandhu's most important works are: the *Triṃśatikā-kārikā* or *Triṃśikā* ('Thirty Verses': *Trims.*); the *Viṃśatikā-kārikā* ('Twenty Verses': *Vims.*) and his commentary on this, the *Viṃśatikā-vṛtti* (*Vrtti.*); the *Tri-svabhāva-nirdeśa* ('Exposition of the Three Natures': *Tsn.*) and his commentary on the *Madhyānta-vibhāga*, the *Madhyānta-vibhāga-kārikā-bhāṣya* (*Mvkb.*). In the sixth century lived two important Yogācāra teachers, Sthiramati and Dharmapāla, with the ideas of the latter being taken to China by Xuanzang, founder of the Faxiang (Fa-hsiang) school. Also associated with the Yogācāra are the logicians and epistemologists Dignāga (fifth to sixth century) and Dharmakīrti (*c.* 530–600; *BS*2.21; Berkwitz, 2010: 117–21).

The Yogācāra orientation

Asaṅga and Vasubandhu not only developed the characteristic ideas of the Yogācāra school, but also sought to systematize and synthesize all the strands of the Mahāyāna along with some Śrāvakayāna ideas. While Vasubandhu was primarily a theoretician, and gave the school its classical form, Asaṅga's writings were deeply rooted in the practice of *dhyāna* (Pali *jhāna*), or meditative trance. Accordingly, 'Yogācāra' means the 'Practice of Yoga', referring to the *Bodhisattva*'s path of meditative development. While the Mādhyamikas and Yogācāras had their philosophical differences, they both had Buddhahood as their goal, and can be seen as being complementary in their approaches. The Mādhyamikas had an analytical, dialectic approach to reality, emphasizing *prajñā* (wisdom); the Yogācāras emphasized *samādhi* (meditative concentration) and the withdrawal of the mind from sensory phenomena. Just as the early Buddhists sought to transcend limiting attachment by seeing phenomena as impermanent, painful and non-Self, so the Mādhyamikas sought this by seeing them as 'empty' of inherent nature/existence, and the Yogācāras sought it by seeing perceived phenomena as mental constructions. The withdrawal of the mind from sensory phenomena in the Yogācāra seems related to what in early Buddhism is described as the apprehension of *Nirvāṇa* as the 'signless' (*animitta*) – that which is devoid of indications which the mind can latch on to or interpret (see p. 96) – just as the Mādhyamika path is related to seeing *Nirvāṇa* as 'the empty'.

The Mādhyamikas regarded the normal experience of the world as a product of conceptual constructions, but had not concerned themselves with the psychological details of this process. The Yogācāras addressed this question and related ones. For example, if the Sarvāstivādin idea of past *dharmas* as still existing is not acceptable, how are memories and the effects of past karma transmitted over time, if a being is composed of a stream of momentary events, as described in the *Abhidharma*? Here, the Yogācāra answer built on those of earlier schools, such as the Sautrāntikas, who had posited a series of momentary karmic 'seeds' reproducing themselves over time, and the Vibhajyavādins (and later Theravādins), who had posited *bhavaṅga* consciousness (see p. 92), which gave continuity to personality even through dreamless sleep. In continuing to wrestle with such questions, the Yogācāras developed a new *Abhidharma* literature set within a Mahāyāna framework (Guenther, 1976).

Central to the Yogācāra is an emphasis on consciousness; indeed an alternative later name for the school was Vijñānavāda, the 'Consciousness Teaching'. In early Buddhism (see p. 69), the flux of consciousness is seen as the crucial link between rebirths, and a transformed state of consciousness is associated with *Nirvāṇa*. The perceiving mind is also that which interprets experience so as to construct a 'world', and can be the basis for experiencing the world-transcending *Nirvāṇa*. 'The world is led by mind/thought' (*A*.II.177). In the Yogācāra, the role of the mind in constructing the world is so emphasized that all concepts of an external physical reality are rejected: the perceived world is seen as 'representation-only' (*vijñapti-mātra*) or 'mind/thought-only' (*citta-mātra*). In this, the Yogācāras went one step beyond the Sautrāntikas' theory, in which objects were seen as real, but were only known by inference from the representations that they caused in the mind.

The Yogācāra and the Mādhyamika views of each other

Both the Mādhyamikas and the Yogācāras saw themselves as preserving the Buddhist Middle Way between the extremes of nihilism (everything is unreal) and substantialism (substantial entities exist, see p. 72). The Yogācāras criticized the Mādhyamikas for tending towards nihilism, with phenomena supported by nothing but other unsupported phenomena, while the Mādhyamikas criticized the Yogācāras for tending towards substantialism, setting up mind as an ultimate entity when all was equally 'empty' of inherent existence/nature. The Mādhyamika assessment is reflected in a fifth-century schema, later used in Tibet, which grades the key schools according to their grasp of the truth: (i) Vaibhāṣika Sarvāstivāda, (ii) Sautrāntika, (iii) Citta-mātra (Yogācāra), (iv) Mādhyamika. To reach the Mādhyamika level, however, the other schools had to be progressively studied. Moreover, the Yogācāra-Mādhyamika later developed as a powerful syncretistic school: the Yogācāra emphasis on how the experienced world was a mental construct accorded with the Mādhyamika idea that things were 'empty' in part because they were dependent on imputation by mental designation. The 'substantialism' of the Yogācāras is in fact more apparent than real, as their theories on mind are essentially tentative devices, 'skilful means' to be used in conjunction with a series of meditations in leading the practitioner beyond all mental constructions, including all theories, to a direct experience of the true nature of reality. For them, one who cannot get beyond words and theories is like someone who mistakes a fingertip for the thing that it is pointing at, such as the moon (*Lanka*.196–7 and 224) – an image that is common in Zen Buddhism.

The Yogācāra view of the role and nature of consciousness

In previous *Abhidharma*, consciousness (Skt *vijñāna*, Pali *viññāṇa*) or *citta* (thought/mind/heart) was seen to be of seven types: consciousness related to each of the five physical senses, mind-consciousness, and mind-organ (Skt *manas*, Pali *mano*; *Dhs*.1187; *AKB*.I.16), with the latter processing the input from the senses, often in a way skewed by the 'I am' conceit. *Manas* was seen by the Yogācāras as a process of subliminal thought, which organizes data from the six consciousnesses into the experience of a meaningful world, according to set categories (cf. *M*.I.295; *M*.III.216–17). It contains the basis both for correct judgements and misperception of reality, and for both skilful and unskilful karma, which are generated by volitions accompanying the six consciousnesses (*Triṃs*. v. 6). As a basis for misperceptions, it is called *kliṣṭa-manas*, defiled or afflicted mind. As in earlier *Abhidharma*, each instance of a type of *citta* is seen as a momentary event, accompanied by an appropriate collection of 'mental states' (Skt *caitta* or *caitasika*, Pali *cetasika; Triṃs*. vv. 3–4).

Manas and the six consciousnesses represent only the surface of the mind, which is active and oriented towards 'objects'. There is, though, an additional eighth form of consciousness, which is the *āśraya*, or 'basis' of the rest; it is their fundamental root.[13] Devoid of purposive activity and only indistinctly aware of objects, it is an underlying unconscious level of mind known as *ālaya-vijñāna*, the 'storehouse consciousness'. The *Laṅkāvatāra Sūtra* (*Lanka*.46–7, cf. 38–9) sees the seven active consciousnesses as related to the *ālaya* as waves are related to the ocean: they are not really separate from it, but are simply perturbations in it. These perturbations do not affect the ever-still depths of the ocean-like *ālaya*, though. Asaṅga equates the *ālaya* with what the *Mahāyāna-abhidharma Sūtra* calls the 'Realm (or principle, *dhātu*) without beginning in time, which is the common basis of all *dharmas*' (*Ms*. ch. 2). It is similar to the Theravādin *bhavaṅga* consciousness (see p. 92), except that the *ālaya* is seen to be simultaneous with the other forms of consciousness (Waldron, 2003: 106, 112), while *bhavaṅga* is the intermittent resting state of mind-consciousness.

When a person performs actions, or karmas, traces are left on his unconscious: 'seeds' of future karmic effects sink into the *ālaya*, a receptacle which actively stores them, ready to later mature. The *ālaya* consists of a series of *cittas* (*Triṃs*. v. 4), accompanied by both karmic 'seeds' and the 'seeds' of potential defilements and memories. These all reproduce themselves over time, thus accounting for the continuity of personality through death and periods of unconsciousness, when the seven active consciousnesses are absent (*Triṃs*. v. 16).

[13] *EB*.4.3.3 (*Triṃs*.1–19); Waldron, 2003; Williams, 2009: 97–100.

The *ālaya* is also said to contain some intrinsically pure 'seeds', the source of religious striving.[14] They arise from the profound depths of the *ālaya*, the *param-ālaya* or '*ālaya* which is beyond' (*Lanka*.272). In the Shelun school, the earliest Chinese version of the Yogācāra, this is designated as a ninth, 'immaculate' (*amala*), consciousness. This school saw the immaculate consciousness as beyond the dualisms of subject and object, existence and non-existence, and as the *Dharma-dhātu*, the '*Dharma*-realm/principle',[15] or as 'thusness', equivalent to emptiness and *Nirvāṇa*. It also regarded it as beyond the individual unconscious, and as a universal reality which lies 'within' all beings. The other Yogācāra school in China, the Faxiang, saw immaculate consciousness as simply the *ālaya* when freed of the defiled aspects of it (Williams, 2009: 99).

Ālaya acts as the basis of the active consciousnesses by actually projecting them out of itself. The Yogācāra, then, regards a person's perception of the world as a product of the unconscious mind. This notion is related to the observation that, in any situation, we only really notice what our mind is attuned to perceive, be this something that interests us, threatens us, excites us or disgusts us. We only ever get 'edited highlights' of the possible field of perception. What we perceive is clearly related to our nature, which is the product, among other things, of our previous actions (cf. pp. 41 and 69). That perception is not just a question of passively 'seeing what is there' is demonstrated by the many examples, in psychology books on perception, of ambiguous figures that can be 'seen' in different ways. It is also illustrated by the way in which one may take some time to recognize the subject of a photograph taken at an odd angle or in odd lighting. Once it is 'seen', though, it is hard *not* to recognize it. The Yogācāras emphasized this kind of thing to such an extent that perception is regarded as essentially a process of imagining, in which the mind generates mental constructions that are perceived as a world.

The Yogācāra philosophy explains the 'mechanics' of the process of construction as follows. Within the *ālaya*, the karmic 'seeds' are matured by the subtle influence of *vāsanā*s or perfuming 'impressions' generated by ingrained attachment to mental constructions.[16] The 'seeds' then ripen in

[14] The Sautrāntikas also talked of an indestructible 'seed' of 'goodness' as the source of Nirvāṇic striving, and the Theravādins equated *bhavaṅga* consciousness with the 'brightly shining' *citta* referred to at *A*.I.10 (see p. 68).

[15] In early Buddhism, '*Dharma-dhātu*' referred to principles discovered by the Buddha: Conditioned Arising and the four True Realities for the Spiritually Ennobled (e.g. *S*.II.56–7), and the three marks (*A*.I.286): basic patterns of reality awakened to by the Buddha (*S*.II.25).

[16] The terminology of 'seeds' and 'impressions' having already been developed by the Sautrāntikas.

the form of the flow of experiences which consists of *manas* and the six consciousnesses, each orientated to its own type of 'object', of which it is a 'representation' (*vijñapti*) (*Lanka*.44, and *Trims*. v. 2). *Manas* splits the seamless flow of experience into an experiencing 'subject' and an experienced 'object', or 'grasper' and the 'graspable'. Building on this, it then generates other forms of delusory discrimination (*vikalpa*). In this process, language plays a large role. It is suffused with the subject/object distinction and provides concepts under which 'significant' forms (*nimitta*) can be separated out from the flow of experience and named, as supposedly fixed entities, such as 'a wheel' (*Lanka*.226).

While all that is actually experienced is consciousness and its mental concomitants, then, discrimination produces the fiction that these are experiences undergone by an 'inner' subject, and are of a separate 'external' world, along with 'inner' feelings and emotions. For the Yogācāra, the flow of experiences is actually neither 'internal' nor 'external' – it just is. A rough analogy is afforded by the situation of interacting with a computer-generated virtual-reality world (cf. p. 117), where the viewer is led 'around' an apparently three-dimensional space through a seamless series of two-dimensional on-screen images, and may also identify with one of the characters depicted, as also happens when watching a television programme. The analogy is, of course, imperfect. It still contains a watcher of the computer- or TV-screen, whereas in the Yogācāra view the watcher 'himself' is like the on-screen picture! *Manas* takes the supposed 'subject' as a real permanent Self or I, partly due to a confused awareness of the *ālaya* which is its basis. This I-delusion is then the source of cravings related to 'objects', and of a variety of volitions which generate karmic 'seeds' – to be stored in the *ālaya* until they ripen into the future flow of experience. Thus the cycle of life and lives continues, with *ālaya* and *manas* mutually conditioning each other.

The world as 'thought-only'

The Yogācāra view has been generally taken as a form of philosophical idealism, which denies the reality of the material world and asserts that reality is mental. It can certainly sound idealist: 'Visible entities are not found, the external world is merely thought/mind (*citta*) seen as a multiplicity [of objects]; body, property and environment – these I call thought-only (*citta-mātra*)' (*Lanka*.154; cf. *BTTA*.183). The intention of the school, though, is not to propound a mere philosophical viewpoint, but to develop a perspective which will facilitate awakening. In doing this, it develops many tentative theories which aim to articulate what is immediately experienced, and rejects theories which go beyond this to discuss a 'material world'. If an extra-mental reality exists, we never experience it. Our actual 'world' is merely 'thought' (and its mental accompaniments) or a 'representation' (*vijñapti*), produced by consciousness. Conscious experience may contain some shadowy reflection of extra-mental existences, but is so massively conditioned by mental constructs that it is these that must be the focus of analysis and spiritual change.[17]

To support this view, meditative experience is appealed to. In this, concentration on an object can generate a mental image such as a coloured disc of light, which in time becomes more vivid and clear than objects seen with the open eyes (see p. 326). Asaṅga argues that, however real such images appear, they are clearly nothing apart from thought/mind. If this applies to experiences had in a calm, less deluded state, how much more does it apply to ordinary experience? He also argues that, as some advanced meditators can change earth into water, then these are not really outside the mind. Moreover, dreams show that one can have pleasant and unpleasant 'sensory' impressions when there is no real object to cause them (*Ms*.2.27.1–8 (*BTTA*.184)).

This perspective is not taken to mean that we all inhabit totally private worlds. The similarity in people's karmic 'seeds' means that our 'worlds' have much in common, though different types of being are seen as perceiving the 'same object' very differently: while humans see a river as a source of washing and drinking, for fish it is just their home environment, and for 'hungry ghosts' it is a stream of pus and excrement which cannot assuage their ravaging thirst (*Ms*.2.4). Note that this idea does imply that there is an extra-mental 'something' that is being perceived differently. Moreover, what one being does can help or harm another; Vasubandhu asserts that this is not through the action of material bodies and physically produced speech, but by one being's mental 'representations' causing an effect in those of another. While beings are, as far as we know, only streams of mental phenomena, these do interact (*Vims*. vv. 18–20) – as must also be so for people to partake of language, which the Yogācāra sees as shaping experience.

The three natures

While the Mādhyamikas talk in terms of 'two levels of truth', a central Yogācāra concept is that of three apparent 'natures' – the three *svabhāvas*

[17] A side-effect of this is that non-karmic kinds of causality are neglected: everything experienced is seen as due to karma (including how other beings affect one).

(*EB*.4.3.2). Each is a perspective on experience which concerns both a type of real or supposed knowledge, and a degree of reality that this knowledge relates to. As in the Mādhyamika, the intention is to move from one's ordinary, vitiated experience to that of the highest degree of truth or reality. For the Yogācāras, there is also an intermediary level of reality, though the Mādhyamikas regarded this as an impossible mix of reality and unreality.

The first of the three 'natures' is the *parikalpita*, the '(mentally) constructed' or 'imagined'. This is what is structured by the subject/object discrimination: the common-sense world of self, people and things, and 'objects' of thought such as mental and physical *dharmas*, all wrongly seen as having real permanent essences ('own-nature'). Its 'degree' of reality is zero: it is just an illusory appearance. As a kind of 'knowledge', it is taken in by the illusion, engrossed in the perceptual signs (*nimitta*) that are its general forms, as well as related details (*Lanka*.67). It is the world of 'conventional usage' (*vyavahāra*; *Trims*. v. 23) mediated by language.

The second 'nature' is the *paratantra*, the 'other-dependent'. This is the level of relative reality, in the form of the flow of changing mental phenomena (i.e. *dharmas* properly understood), arising dependent on one another according to the principle of Conditioned Arising as in the system of eight forms of *citta* and accompanying mental states (*Mv*.1.9–10). It also refers to the relative knowledge which comprehends these phenomena as mutually dependent and impermanent. It is not the highest level of reality, however, for it is the very process which generates the subject/object duality and so projects the 'constructed' nature: it is the 'construction of the unreal' (*abhūta-parikalpa; Tsn*. v. 4).

The third and highest 'nature' is the *parinispanna*, the 'absolutely accomplished'. This is the absolutely real level, devoid of the subject/object duality, in which knowledge is perfected due to directly knowing the world as 'representation only'. While the 'constructed' is like the water in a mirage, and the 'other-dependent' is like the mirage itself, the 'absolutely accomplished' is like the complete lack of real water in the mirage. Or the first is like the illusory hairs seen by a person with cataracts, the second is like that which produces these illusions, and the third is like the unconfused objects seen by one with sound eyes.[18]

Because it knows that the imaginary 'constructed' is empty of a real 'nature', and that the interdependent phenomena of the 'other-dependent' level are also individually empty of an inherent 'nature' (as in Mādhyamika thought), the 'absolutely accomplished' is knowledge of the very empty

[18] *Saṃdhinirmocana Sūtra* (Taisho 16, p. 693 a–b), as cited by Keenan, 1982: 11.

'nature' of all phenomena: emptiness. This 'nature' is also known as thusness (*tathatā*), the inconceivable as-it-is-ness of reality. As the knowledge which knows it has totally transcended the subject/object illusion, it *is* the very thusness which it knows. Thusness is the very nature of reality and the three 'natures' are just three different perspectives on it, of varying degrees of adequacy (*Tsn.* vv. 18–21).

While the Mādhyamikas use the term 'emptiness' to denote simply the absence of inherent nature/existence in phenomena, the Yogācāras also see 'emptiness' as a term for something that is positively existing – in the form of the non-dual nature of the 'other-dependent' nature. Reality, understood according to the true Middle Way, is empty of duality but not empty of existence; it is that which is empty. The 'other-dependent', 'construction of the unreal', is not totally unreal, but exists 'within' emptiness, being neither separate from nor identical to it, just as impermanent things are neither separate from nor identical to impermanence (*Mvkb.* ch. 1, vv. 3 and 14). It has an 'ineffable (*anabhilāpya*) nature' known only by Buddhas (*Vrtti.* v. 10).

The Yogācāra path and goal

The first two natures are the basis of defilements and thus of suffering. The Yogācāra path therefore aims to understand the dualistic 'constructed' so as to undermine the aspect of the 'other-dependent' which is its basis, until this is finally cleansed away from it, to leave the 'absolutely accomplished'. In deep meditative calm, the mind gradually overcomes the tendency to interpret experiences as indicating external 'objects'. As this tendency wanes, consciousness still tends to be grasped at as a real 'subject', more real than 'objects'. Finally, the full realization of 'representation-only' comes when the utter transcending of any 'object' leads to the collapse of any notion of 'subject', which is merely its dualistic contrast (*Tsn.* v. 36). Thus arises the experience of transcendent knowledge, which is an undifferentiated unity, beyond the subject/object duality and concepts of any kind, even 'thought'. It is thought which is no longer what is usually meant by 'thought', as it is without object, contentless.[19] This is the realization of the 'absolutely accomplished', and is said to be perception of the 'unlimitedness' of the *Dharma*-realm, awakening (*bodhi*) (*Tsn.* vv. 37–8).

The path to *Nirvāṇa* is a gradual development of virtue, meditative concentration, and insight into the emptiness of 'other-dependent'

[19] *Trims.* vv. 28–9 and commentary (*BTTA*.181; cf. p. 116).

phenomena. The final attainment comes suddenly,[20] however, as a momentous spiritual transition, a shattering upheaval which takes place at the root of the mind – in *ālaya* in its form as *manas*. This event is known as the 'reversal of the basis' (*āśraya-parāvṛtti*). It is where the usual flow of the worldly mind suddenly stops, so that the six sensory consciousnesses no longer present information.[21] Having stopped discriminating 'objects' in the flow of the six consciousnesses, *manas* 'turns round' from these and attains direct, intuitive, noble knowledge (*ārya-jñāna*) of *ālaya* as its basis. Due to this, *ālaya* is no longer capable of carrying karmic 'seeds', the source of the consciousness of 'objects', as its deluding nature is seen through. The intuition thus penetrates to the non-dual depths of *ālaya*, the *Dharma*-realm which is ultimate reality, so that everything is seen as 'thought-only' in the highest sense. In the mirror of *manas*, the unknowing *ālaya* has gained knowledge of its inner nature, so that *Nirvāṇa* is 'the *ālaya*-consciousness which is realized inwardly, after a reversal has taken place' (*Lanka*.62). *Nirvāṇa*, then, is the transfiguration of *saṃsāra*, not its abolition: as in the Mādhyamika, 'there is no difference between *saṃsāra* and *Nirvāṇa*' (*Lanka*.61).

An advanced *Bodhisattva* who has experienced *Nirvāṇa* does not rest content with this. He turns again to *saṃsāra* in the service of others, which the *Mahāyāna-saṃgraha* calls his 'non-abiding' (*apratiṣṭhita*) *Nirvāṇa*, not clinging either to *saṃsāra* or to *Nirvāṇa* as something supposedly separate from this (Nagao, 1991). He does this by meditatively sending forth a seemingly physical 'mind-made body' (*Ms*.2.27.8 ((*BTTA*.184)) – which is like a conjurer's magical illusion and no more an external physical object than anything else – in which he tunes in to and perceives the apparent 'world' of those he is seeking to aid. *Lanka*.136–7 describes how an (eighth-stage) *Bodhisattva*, having attained 'reversal', enters a meditative concentration in which he attains two forms of mind-made body. With the first of these, he can travel at will to the presence of any heavenly Buddha in his 'Buddha-land', while in the second, he can take on the form of a variety of classes of beings, so as to work among them and help them towards liberation. Here one sees Yogācāra philosophical ideas connecting up with central Mahāyāna concerns.

Purity and defilement

The Yogācāras reflected much on the relationship between a 'pure' ultimate reality and a defiled, impure *saṃsāra* found 'within' it. 'Reversal' does not

[20] As does Arhatship in the early schools. [21] Cf. the 'signless' deliverance (pp. 81 and 96).

bring about a change in ultimate reality; for what is changeable is impermanent. Its purity is intrinsic to it: 'As is pure gold, water free from dirt, the sky without a cloud, so it is pure when detached from imagination' (*Lanka*.131). 'Emptiness' is seen as undefiled due to its very nature, the brightly shining state of the transcendental *citta*, but this purity is hidden by adventitious defilements (*Mv*.1.23, cf. p. 68). Vasubandhu comments that the existence of these alien defilements (at the 'other-dependent' level) explains why people do not attain liberation without effort, while the shining nature of ultimate reality explains why the effort to attain purity will not be fruitless. He also comments (on *Mv*.5.21): 'The *Dharma*-realm, being like space, is pure by nature, and the duality "pure" and "impure" is only adventitious, arriving later'. That is, only in contrast to 'impure' defilements is the ultimate reality 'pure'; in itself it is beyond all such dualities.

TATHĀGATA-GARBHA THOUGHT

According to the Chinese tradition, Indian Mahāyāna thought consisted of the Mādhyamika, Yogācāra and 'Tathāgata-garbha' schools. The Indian and Tibetan traditions did not count the latter strand of thought as a separate philosophical school, though: for it originated in the period between the origin of the Mādhyamika and Yogācāra, its ideas were in some ways intermediary between theirs, and they both drew on these ideas. Moreover, there were no great Indian teachers associated with this strand of thought. This was probably because it was not intended as a well-worked-out system, but arose among those seeking to articulate and support aspects of religious practice. Nevertheless, it made an important contribution to Mahāyāna thought.[22]

Tathāgata-garbha sources

The earliest known Tathāgata-garbha text was the *Tathāgata-garbha Sūtra* (*BP*.7), composed *c*. 200–250 CE. The most important one, however, is the *Śrīmālā-devī-siṃhanāda Sūtra* (*Srim*.), 'The *Sūtra* on the Lion's Roar of Queen Śrīmālā', composed between 250 and 350 CE. Also important is the single extant Sanskrit treatise on the *Tathāgata-garbha*. This is known as the *Ratnagotra-vibhāga* (*Rv*.), 'An Analysis of the Jewels and Lineages', or *Uttara-tantra*, 'The Treatise on the Supreme'. The Chinese tradition

[22] Keenan, 1982; Ruegg, 1969, 1989a and 1989b; Williams, 2009: 103–28.

attributes this to a Sthiramati/Sāramati; the Tibetan tradition less plausibly attributes it to the *Bodhisattva* Maitreya, via Asaṅga. This text, which quotes liberally from the *Śrīmālā-devī-siṃhanāda Sūtra*, was probably composed soon after it. The (Mahāyāna) *Mahāparinirvāṇa Sutra*,[23] a text which exists in various versions and which was influential in China, also contains many relevant ideas. The *Laṅkāvatāra Sūtra* (*Lanka.*) assimilates Tathāgata-garbha thought to the Yogācāra viewpoint, and this assimilation is developed further in a text which was a widely used summary of the Mahāyāna in China. This is the *Dasheng qixinlun* (*Ta-sh'eng ch'i-hsin lun*), 'The Treatise on the Awakening of Faith in the Mahāyāna', composed, or possibly translated, around 550 CE.

The Tathāgata-garbha

The first word in the term *Tathāgata-garbha* literally means 'Thus-gone' or 'Thus-come', a term for a Buddha as one who is attuned to reality, while the second basically means either an embryo, or a womb or other container. Tibetan translations are based on the first meaning of *garbha*, while Chinese ones are based on the second. *Tathāgata-garbha* thus means something like 'embryonic Buddha' or 'matrix of a Buddha', though the earliest meaning may have been a reference to beings as 'containing a Buddha'. This 'embryo' is seen as existing within all living beings, indicating that, however deluded or defiled they are, they can mature into Buddhas. The *Tathāgata-garbha*, then, represents the 'Buddha-potential' within all beings. In the *Tathāgata-garbha Sūtra*, it is affirmed by the Buddha to be 'complete with virtues and not different from myself'. It is an emptiness which is itself full of possibilities; it is resplendent with the qualities of Buddhahood, beginningless, unchanging and permanent (*Rv.* vv. 51, 84). It is beyond duality, having the nature of thought and the intrinsic purity of a jewel, space or water (*Rv.* vv. 28, 30, 49). It is brightly shining with lucid clarity (*Rv.* v. 170) and is 'by nature brightly shining and pure' (*Lanka.*77). Beings are seen as ignorant of this great inner treasure, but the Buddha reveals it to them so as to encourage them in spiritual development. Moreover, it is the *Tathāgata-garbha* which responds to spiritual teachings and aspires for *Nirvāṇa* (*Srim.* ch. 13; *EB*.4.3.5). In some ways, this approach can be seen as an echo of the early idea of seeing *Nirvāṇa* as 'the aim-free' or 'wishless' (see p. 96): if one already has the supreme, what more could one wish for?

[23] A very different text from the Theravādin *Mahāparinibbāna Sutta*, and its Sanskrit parallels of other early schools.

The Tathāgata-garbha *and the defilements*

In the *Tathāgata-garbha Sūtra* and *Ratnagotra-vibhāga* (vv. 96–8 (*BTTA*.169)), a number of metaphors are used to illustrate the relationship between the intrinsically pure *Tathāgata-garbha* and the 'stains of adventitious defilements' – greed, hatred, delusion, etc. – which are said to obscure it. It is both like a Buddha-image wrapped in tattered rags, which suggests an unchanging perfection which has simply to be uncovered, and also like the shoots of a great tree piercing through the fruit from which it grows, suggesting that it is a potential in need of cultivation. Indeed it is to be seen as both 'since beginningless time naturally present' and 'perfected through proper cultivation' (*Rv.* v. 149). While these may be seen as in tension, perhaps the intention is to indicate that one must *first* uncover the *Tathāgata-garbha*, as a Buddha-potential, and *then* mature it to Buddhahood by activating qualities implicit within it. The *Ratnagotra-vibhāga* sees the *Tathāgata-garbha* as already present, 'the immaculate true nature to which nothing need be added and from which nothing need be taken' (*Rv.* v. 113). Yet it has to be separated from accompanying impurities, just as gold-ore has to be refined so as to bring out and manifest the intrinsic purity of gold. In *Bodhisattvas*, it is partly purified, and in Buddhas, it is wholly purified (*Rv.* v. 47).

The *Mahāparinirvāṇa Sūtra* sometimes suggests that the *Tathāgata-garbha* is an already existent intrinsically pure essence, and sometimes that it is a specific seed-potency of future purity. That said, in a perspective which has in its background the Sarvāstivādin idea that future *dharmas* in some sense exist, the distinction between a potential for future Buddhahood and an existent Buddhahood that one just needs to uncover, is lessened. As argued by Ming-Wood Liu (1982), while the *Sūtra* says that sentient beings definitely 'have' the *Tathāgata-garbha*, which is identical to the eternal unconditioned nature of a *Tathāgata*, *Nirvāṇa*, they only 'have' it in a future sense. They have the ability to become Buddhas when the right conditions of spiritual practice come into play, just as milk has the potential to become cream or butter when treated in the right way, but does not already 'contain' cream or butter. A man may loosely say that he 'has butter' if he has some milk to churn, but he still has to churn it. For sentient beings, the Buddha-nature is existent in the future, but not in the present (Liu 1982: 73–4). Yet as sentient beings, with minds, they are ever-capable of becoming Buddhas. Liu thus reads the overall message of the *Sūtra* as that sentient beings are capable of awakening because they lack a fixed, definitive nature (1982: 84). This, in effect, is how the Mādhyamika school understands the

Tathāgata-garbha: as a way of talking about emptiness of inherent nature, which thus allows ultimate change (see p. 126). This interpretation, however, is not generally how the *Tathāgata-garbha* was understood in East Asia, where it often came to be seen as a pre-existent reality waiting to be uncovered.[24]

The latest sections of the *Mahāparinirvāṇa Sūtra* translated into Chinese are notable for the idea that everyone, including very wicked people – *icchantikas* or 'decadents' – will eventually become Buddhas, due to their *Tathāgata-garbha* (*EB*.8.3). This refuted the idea, found in some strands of Yogācāra thought such as the Faxiang school, that such people were incapable of any kind of enlightenment because their storehouse-consciousnesses lacked the pure seeds that would enable this (Williams, 2009: 98 and 107).

If the *Tathāgata-garbha* is the pure basis of successful spiritual striving, however, it is necessary to account for the existence of the alien defilements which hold living beings back from awakening. How do they co-exist in a being? The *Ratnagotra-vibhāga* sees the defilements as a 'shell' as beginningless as the 'stainless nature of mind' that it covers (v. 129). The *Śrīmālā-devī-siṃhanāda Sūtra* says that defilements are ultimately rooted in beginningless ignorance, but that only a Buddha can comprehend how the mind, whose inner nature is the intrinsically pure *Tathāgata-garbha*, can be in *any way* associated with defilements. Here, in fact, one can see a Buddhist version of the problem of evil: from where does evil originate? Buddhism avoids the 'theological' problem of evil (see p. 37), but a similar problem arises here. This is because the *Tathāgata-garbha* is seen as the eternal foundation and support of both the unconditioned, including 'inconceivable Buddha qualities' (*Srim*. ch. 13), and the conditioned world of *saṃsāra*. Quoting from the *Mahāyāna-abhidharma Sūtra*, the *Ratnagotra-vibhāga* (ch. 9: Takasaki transl., p. 291) equates the *Tathāgata-garbha* with the *Dharma*-realm/ principle' (*dhātu*) which is described thus (cf. p. 131): 'The Realm is without beginning in time / It is the common basis (*āśraya*) of all *dharmas* / Because it exists, there also exist / All places of rebirth and full attainment of *Nirvāṇa*.' This was probably not meant in the sense that there is a single, universal basis for the whole universe – for the *Tathāgata-garbha Sūtra* refers to a plurality of *Tathāgata-garbhas* – but in the sense that the minds of sentient beings are what sustain the round of rebirths, and also have a potential which makes possible the realization of *Nirvāṇa*.

[24] The idea that one can already be a Buddha, yet not know this, is not without its problems. The Mahāyāna emphasizes that Buddhas are omniscient, so if one is a Buddha, one should already know this!

Making the *Tathāgata-garbha* the basis of all clearly implies that it is also the basis of the defilements and ignorance. The *Ratnagotra-vibhāga* supports this implication by saying that karma and the defilements are based on unwise attention (which perceives the conditioned world as permanent and substantial); that this is based on 'the mind's purity', but that this 'true nature of mind' is itself without any further basis (*Rv.* vv. 56–7). *Lanka.*220 actually says that the *Tathāgata-garbha* 'holds within it the cause for both skilful and unskilful actions, and by it all forms of existence are produced. Like an actor it takes on a variety of forms'.[25] In the final analysis, though, the Tathāgata-garbha texts seek to avoid any notion that genuine evil comes from the pure *Tathāgata-garbha*. Thus the defilements are seen as insubstantial, unreal, but as imagined by the deluded mind. This is seen by the fact that the true *Nirvāṇa*, Buddhahood, is not regarded as the extinction of anything (the defilements), but as the '*Dharma*-body' or *Tathāgata* (*Srim.* chs. 5 and 8). This already exists, for, 'covered' by defilements, it is the *Tathāgata-garbha.*[26] As in the Mādhyamika and Yogācāra, awakening is not realized by destroying real defilements, but simply by not originating illusory ones, and the illusory suffering to which they lead. Why these illusions should be imagined is still not explained, however: only a Buddha can know.

Tathāgata-garbha thought in relation to the Mādhyamika and Yogācāra

Both the Tathāgata-garbha writers and the Yogācāras assign a more positive meaning to 'emptiness' than is (explicitly) found in classical Mādhyamika. The *Tathāgata-garbha* is equated with 'emptiness', and is said to be empty of and separate from all defilements, but not empty of or separate from 'the inconceivable Buddha-qualities, more numerous than the sands of the Ganges' (*Srim.* ch. 9). This sets up a dichotomy between unreal defilements, and the truly real Buddha-qualities. This perspective differs from the Yogācāra one, where there are *three* levels of reality, the three *svabhāvas*. Thus the Tathāgata-garbha writers hold there to be two levels of reality, like the Mādhyamikas, but hold a more substantivist view of the highest reality than the Mādhyamikas.

In both the Mādhyamika/Perfection of Wisdom and the Yogācāra is found the notion of the 'brightly shining *citta*', which ultimately derives

[25] Cf. empathy – knowing how another being feels – makes possible both compassion and deliberate cruelty.
[26] Though in other texts, the *Tathāgata-garbha* is itself spoken of as what is obscured by defilements.

from an early *Sutta* (see p. 68) and is a key Tathāgata-garbha concept. In the Perfection of Wisdom literature, it is said of the 'thought of awakening' (*bodhi-citta*),[27] 'That thought is no thought, since by nature it is brightly shining', and that it is a state of 'no-mindedness' (*acittatā*) which is beyond existence and non-existence (*Asta*.5–6). This equates the brightly shining *citta* with the *bodhi-citta*, which Tathāgata-garbha literature sees as arising when a person becomes aware of the *Tathāgata-garbha* within. Nevertheless, the Perfection of Wisdom passage sees the brightly shining mind as empty of the own-nature of mind, and does not set it up as the basis of the world. In both Tathāgata-garbha thought and the Yogācāra, an aspect of mind *is* set up as the basis for both the conditioned world and attainment of the unconditioned. For the Tathāgata-garbha writers, this basis was the shining *Tathāgata-garbha*, while for the Yogācāras it was the depths of the *ālaya-vijñāna*.

It is notable that the *Ratnagotra-vibhāga* quotes from the *Mahāyāna-abhidharma Sūtra*, a Yogācāra text, and that another early Yogācāra text, the *Mahāyāna-sūtrālaṃkāra*, emphasizes the brightly shining mind, which it says is the nature of the *Tathāgata* and a *garbha* that all beings have. These facts suggest a particular affinity between Tathāgata-garbha and Yogācāra thought. It may well be that they developed in similar circles (Keenan, 1982). While the Tathāgata-garbha writers retained an emphasis on the intrinsic purity of the mind, the Yogācāras moved on to explain the arising and working of defiled, empirical consciousness. In this, the origin of defilement, termed 'the construction of the unreal', was accorded a greater reality than in Tathāgata-garbha thought. In the *Laṅkāvatāra Sūtra*, the two strands of thought are united, for it is actually said that the *ālaya-vijñāna* is also known as the *Tathāgata-garbha* (*Lanka*.221).

A final problem is that *Lanka*.77–8 describes the *Tathāgata-garbha* as 'hidden in the body of every being like a gem of great value . . . it is eternal, permanent'. Given this description, how then does it differ from a permanent Self, which Buddhism had never accepted?[28] The texts seem somewhat ambivalent on this. On the one hand, the *Dharma*-body, the fully mature *Tathāgata-garbha*, is the perfection of permanence and of Self (*Srim*. ch. 12). On the other, while the *Tathāgata-garbha* may seem like either a Self or eternal creator to the ignorant, it is not so, for it is the same as emptiness

[27] In general, a term for the compassionate aspiration for Buddhahood, so as to be able to greatly help others, but it is also used for the mind-state which knows emptiness.

[28] The Self-like nature of the *Tathāgata-garbha* is an echo of the Pudgalavādins' idea of a mysterious inner 'person': see p. 93.

(*Lanka*.78). It may be Self-like, but is not a true Self, in the sense of an 'I': 'The Buddha is neither a Self nor the *skandha*s (Pali *khandha*), he is knowledge free from evil taints' (*Lanka*.358).

The Tathāgata-garbha *and the self-emptiness versus other-emptiness debate*

This Tibetan debate on the nature of 'emptiness' (see pp. 126–7) is of particular relevance to the *Tathāgata-garbha* (Powers, 2007a; Williams, 2009: 112–15). Those of the other-emptiness view see the other-empty pure reality as the *Tathāgata-garbha*, interpreted as a pre-existent reality that just needs uncovering: it is a radiance that is empty of defilements. Those of the self-emptiness view regard talk of '*Tathāgata-garbha*' as simply a way of saying that emptiness of inherent nature of the minds of beings means that they are capable of ultimate change, so that they can become Buddhas. The latter view downplays the idea of the radiance of the mind, uncovered in meditation, as the specific seed of future Buddhahood, whereas the other-emptiness view is contentious in holding that the *Tathāgata-garbha* does not and need not change, being an already present perfect Buddhahood that only needs to be uncovered.

In Tibet, the other-emptiness approach is seen, for example, in the approach of *Dzogch'en*, as found in the Nyingmapa school (see p. 205). This 'Great Perfection' practice is seen by its adepts as a wholly self-sufficient 'spontaneously perfect' way leading to a sudden realization of one's primordial perfection and wisdom. The approach is seen as one of simply allowing radiant clarity, the true nature of mind, to manifest itself. This involves allowing thoughts to come and go as they will, without attachment for – or rejection of – them or their objects, so as to be able to focus on the radiance in the thought-flow itself. By such a practice, the adept develops the ability to let his flow of thought-trains gradually and naturally slow down. At a certain point in this development, the flow suddenly stops, as true non-attraction and non-aversion to thought arises in a spontaneous instant, with the mind resting in a state of pure awareness (*rig pa*[29]), thusness, empty of constructing 'objects', motionless. This is seen as the sudden attainment of enlightenment, the unproduced spontaneous perfection of the primordial Buddha Samantabhadra, personification of the '*Dharma*-body' – or at least a foretaste of this. The *self*-emptiness approach to enlightenment, though, is a more gradualist one.

[29] Skt *vidyā*, opposite of *avidyā*, spiritual ignorance.

East Asian developments

In China, the *Tathāgata-garbha* was often called *Foxing* (*Fo-hsing*), the 'Buddha-nature'.[30] The influential *Dasheng qixinlun*, the 'Awakening of Faith in the Mahāyāna', saw this as a universal 'One Mind', an Absolute that is the basis of the whole universe, thus giving it a cosmological role (Williams, 2009: 115–19). The Tiantai (T'ien-t'ai) monk Zhanran (Chan-jan, 711–82 CE) argued that the Buddha-nature is the immutable mind at the base of all phenomena, even soil and dust. Dōgen (1200–53), founder of Sōtō Zen in Japan, saw the whole phenomenal world not as *manifesting* or *containing* the Buddha-nature, the ultimate, but as *being* it (Williams, 2009: 119–22). While such texts as the *Mahāparinirvāṇa Sūtra* had denied that walls and stones had the Buddha-nature, he asserted they, like all else, *were* it. The whole changing flux of empty phenomena was nothing but the Buddha-nature, within which it was not possible to designate anything as 'non-sentient'.

In the twentieth century, a group of Japanese Sōtō Zen scholars[31] developed a view known as 'Critical Buddhism' (see p. 407) that strongly critiques a range of elements of Japanese Buddhism grouped under the heading of what they call '*dhātu-vāda*': a monistic view which sees everything as based on one fundamental substantial foundation. A key aspect of this is the idea of Buddha-nature, and related Japanese 'original/inherent enlightenment thought' (Jap. *hongaku shisō*; (*BT*.191–2)). The Critical Buddhists see such ideas as non-Buddhist, due to being out of tune with the teachings of non-Self and Conditioned Arising, which they see as *the* defining essence of 'true Buddhism': they regard all else in Buddhism as questionable (Hubbard and Swanson, 1997; Williams, 2009: 122–5).

THE *AVATAṂSAKA SŪTRA* AND THE HUAYAN SCHOOL

While Tathāgata-garbha thought was perceived by the Chinese as a third school of Indian Mahāyāna philosophy, the Chinese themselves developed the Huayan (Hua-yen) school, based on the *Avataṃsaka*, or 'Flower Ornament' *Sūtra* (Ch. *Huayan jing*). This is a huge work, many of whose chapters circulated as separate *Sūtras*. Some were translated into Chinese in the second century CE, but the whole was translated in the fifth and then, in a slightly longer form, in the seventh century. A translation also exists in

30 Though it also seems equivalent to Skt *Buddhatā*, Buddha-ness.

31 They are less critical of Dōgen than of other Japanese Buddhists.

Tibetan. The most important books, both surviving in Sanskrit, are the *Daśa-bhūmika Sūtra*, on the 'Ten Stages' of the *Bodhisattva* path, and the *Gaṇḍavyūha*, or 'Grand Array' *Sūtra*, which makes up more than a quarter of the whole *Avataṃsaka* (Cleary, 1985, 1989, 1991; Williams, 2009: 132–8).

The *Avataṃsaka* as a whole deals with: the stages of development and qualities of the *Bodhisattvas*; religious practices; the nature and glories of Buddhahood; visionary descriptions of worlds; and the nature of reality. It contains rhythmic repetitions, a flow of images and shifting perspectives intended to expand horizons and awareness, and a cosmic vision of the deep interrelationship of everything. The *Gaṇḍavyūha*, its culmination, is a literary masterpiece dealing with the spiritual pilgrimage of the youth Sudhana, who is sent by the Buddha on a journey to fifty-two teachers to learn the secrets of the *Bodhisattva* path.[32] The journey begins with the Buddha in a pavilion in an Indian grove, which by meditation he causes to merge with him and expand to encompass the whole universe, and countless *Bodhisattvas* from immeasurably distant worlds appear on the scene. These *Bodhisattvas* have such powers as being able to expand their bodies to the ends of the universe, as the Buddha has done. As Sudhana embarks on his pilgrimage, the world in which he moves is not the common-sense everyday world, but the world seen through the eye of wisdom, full of marvellous wonders. Near his journey's end, he comes to the *Bodhisattva* Maitreya, who shows him the huge tower of the Buddha Vairocana ('The Resplendent One'). This is described as the abode of all *Bodhisattvas*, meaning that it represents the universe as seen by their wisdom and compassion. Sudhana enters the tower, where he finds a wondrous world, as vast as space, full of countless paths, palaces, banners and trees, all made of jewels, along with countless mirrors, burning lamps and singing birds:

This is the abode of all those who make one *kalpa* (eon) enter into all *kalpas* and all *kalpas* into one *kalpa* . . . who make one *dharma* enter into all *dharmas* and all *dharmas* into one *dharma*, and yet without each being annihilated . . . who manifest themselves in all worlds without moving a hair's breadth from the place where they are . . . This is the abode of those who go about everywhere in the *Dharma*-realm, unattached, depending on nothing, with no habitation, burden-free, like the wind blowing in the air, leaving no track of their wanderings . . . [For such beings] in one particle of dust is seen the entire ocean of worlds, beings and *kalpas*, numbering as many as all the particles of dust that are in existence, and this fusion takes place with no obstruction whatever . . . While abiding here they also perceive that the

[32] The stages of Sudhana's journey are depicted on many of the friezes of the huge Borobudur *Stūpa-maṇḍala* on the island of Java, Indonesia.

principle of sameness prevails in all beings, in all *dharmas*, in all the Buddhas, in all the worlds . . . (Suzuki, 1970c: 120–1, 125, 131, 132; cf. *EB*.4.3.6)

The visionary world described in this *Sūtra* is in some ways reminiscent of, though more wondrous than, the mythological bejewelled city of a *Cakravartin* emperor described in an early *Sutta*, the *Mahāsudassana* (*D*.II.169–98). It is not intended as a mere play of the imagination, but is an attempt to convey, through a series of images for contemplation, an insight into the 'unthinkable' (*acintya*) nature of reality. The heart of this insight is the notion of the 'interpenetration' of all existences. This grows out of the notion of emptiness, that things are what they are because of their relationship to other things, in a web of interdependence. It is also an expression of the consequent 'sameness' (*samatā*) of things. The *Sūtra* depicts a world of light and jewels; for jewels are such that light passes through them and reflects from them; each ray of light, which does not interfere with other rays of light, represents a line of dependence between interdependent existences which lack own-nature (are 'transparent'). The Huayan master Fazang (Fa-tsang, 643–712) thus illustrated the interpenetration of all things by an image drawn from the *Avataṃsaka Sūtra*: the jewel-net of the god Indra, wherein each jewel in the net reflects every other one, including their reflections of each jewel, and so on to infinity (Cook, 1989: 214). The world of Vairocana's Tower is the transcendental *Dharma*-realm, the realm where insight penetrates into the mutual interfusion of everything, seeing into the thusness of things. The *Dharma*-realm is not different from the *loka-dhātu*, the worldly-realm of 'separate' phenomena, but is its true nature, interpenetrating it. The *Dharma*-realm is the totality of the interpenetrating web of existence. In each part of this whole, the whole is present, and in the whole, each part is a necessary ingredient. Just as any part of a three-dimensional holographic image of a thing contains the whole image, each part of the *Dharma*-realm, each item of existence, reflects and includes each and every other part; for all are interdependent. Any bit of the universe shows what the universe as a whole is. And yet each item of existence remains what it is, without obstruction from the other items – indeed it cannot be what it is without its relationship with them. Here is a holistic, organic vision of things, a kind of 'cosmic ecology' (Cook, 1989: 214) in which the entire universe of space and time is present in a particle of dust. Thus the *Sūtra* says: 'Every living being and every minute thing is significant, since even the tiniest thing contains the whole mystery'. As a Chan saying extracted from book 20 of the *Avataṃsaka Sūtra* says, 'Mind, Buddha and all sentient beings, these are no different' (Cleary, 1983: 188).

Ideas of 'emptiness' are used in Huayan, and other schools influenced by it, not just as the antidote to all views, but as the ground for a positive appreciation of the concrete realities of nature, as part of a harmonious organic unity. In tune with the Chinese love of harmony and nature, every item of existence is seen as worthy of respect and honour; for all is the 'body' of Vairocana Buddha, as also taught by Kūkai (774–835), the Japanese founder of the tantric Shingon school. Logically, this includes all that early Buddhism saw as '*duḥkha*', but while these views are very different, they have in common the values of awareness and non-attachment.

In systematizing the *Avataṃsaka Sūtra*'s message, Huayan thought combines many ideas from earlier Mahāyāna thought, and is influenced by the ideas of indigenous Chinese Daoism (Taoism), especially that everything is a form of a fluid ultimate reality, the '*Dao*' (*Tao*). Using a well-established pair of Chinese ideas, the *Dharma*-realm is said to be the underlying 'principle' or 'noumenon' (Ch. *li*) which interpenetrates 'phenomena' (*shi* (*shih*)) as they do each other. As Sengzhao (Sêng-chao, 384–414) had put it, 'Heaven and earth and I are of the same root, the ten-thousand things and I are of one substance' (Suzuki, 1959: 353). Phenomena are empty, but are not unreal; for they are no different from *li*. Phenomena are seen as radically interrelated, and thus empty of inherent nature, much as in Mādhyamika thought, but as well as this 'horizontal' relationship between phenomena, there is also their 'vertical' relationship with *li*, the *Tathāgata-garbha* conceived as like the ever-malleable *Dao*. All phenomena are actual forms of this, as illustrated by Fazang's 'Treatise on the Golden Lion' (*BT*.168–72). In this, the phenomena of the world are like the parts of a golden lion, all of which are made of the same malleable gold, being forms of it (Williams, 2009: 141–4). The choice of a golden object in the treatise is probably not accidental: the intrinsic brightness of gold is no doubt an allusion to the intrinsic brightness of the Buddha-nature, and to the meditative mind, to which it is related. This idea of an underlying substance to things is very different, though, from how Indian Mādhyamika saw things, for it is rather like the *Brahman* of the *Upaniṣads*, which was also seen as the basis and substance composing everything. Yet *li* is not static and unchanging, but fluid and without any fixed form, like the *Dao*. It is a kind of 'emptiness', but now in the sense of something which is empty of fixed form, and so full of countless possibilities. It is empty of defilements, but not of an intrinsic radiance; it has a bright openness, a natural purity to which no defilements can stick, so to speak – though defilements are of course included in the phenomena that are the forms of *li*. Phenomena interpenetrate each other, through deep interdependence, and are also in a sense identical with each other, as they are all forms of *li*. They are also each the unique cause of the totality of existence, the *Dharma*-realm, as without a particular phenomenon, the totality would not only lack one item, but also lack the multiple effects that this brings to the whole. As each phenomenon is also the cause of the whole, they are also identical in this respect.

Such ideas are explored by Francis Cook (1977), though he tends to see only a Mādhyamika sense of 'emptiness' in Huayan thought. In their writings, Huayan authors sought to argue for their perspective, though their arguments are often obscure and mix valid and very debatable points. Perhaps what they were trying to say is very difficult to adequately verbalize. Perhaps they sometimes wrongly conflated different kinds of ideas, such as different kinds of 'emptiness'. Perhaps something of both of these. Perhaps what look like arguments are intended more as guidance in meditation.

Huayan ideas had implications for how the Buddhist path was seen, for the very start of the path, the arising of faith, was seen as in a sense identical with its goal (Williams, 2009: 144–5). This may reflect, in part, the fact that the first time meditation really starts to work for someone, this opens up for them a whole vista of possibilities. There is then a sense in which practice after this time is a question of unpacking and exploring what has already been obscurely felt/seen. There is, here, a parallel to the tantric idea of using the goal (visualized as a holy being) as a key aspect of the path (see p. 189).

In Huayan, practice involves being aware of one's Buddha-nature and acting as far as possible like a Buddha, until this becomes a natural and spontaneous way of being (*BT*.192–3). Its kind of speculative mysticism provided the philosophical perspective that imbues much of Chan/Zen Buddhism, and today its ideas are much emphasized by the 'Order of Interbeing'[33] of the monk Thich Nhat Hanh, of the Vietnamese Chan tradition (known as Thien). An illustration he often uses (e.g. 1991) is that in a sheet of paper are the tree its fibres came from, the sun and rain that sustained this, the logger that cut it down and all he depended on, and ourselves as part of a deeply interdependent world in which all items 'inter-are' with all others.

A COMPARATIVE OVERVIEW OF MAHĀYĀNA PHILOSOPHIES AND THEIR IDEAS OF 'EMPTINESS'

Looking back over the philosophies discussed in this chapter, one can see a range of meanings given to the word 'emptiness', reflecting the different

[33] www.orderofinterbeing.org

concerns and perspectives of the relevant texts, authors and schools. Broadly speaking:

- For the Mādhyamikas, 'emptiness' is a quality shared by *all* phenomena: their lack of inherent nature and inherent existence, with no underlying shared substance to them, either.
- For the Yogācāras, the mental phenomena of the other-dependent nature, which is all one directly knows to exist, are individually empty in a Mādhyamika sense, but there is an additional sense of 'emptiness' as meaning the lack of a real subject/object duality in this mental flow, and this 'emptiness' is also a name for the positive reality, not empty of itself, which lacks this.
- In Tathāgata-garbha texts, the Mādhyamika sense of emptiness may apply to conditioned phenomena, but the most important sense of 'emptiness' is the pure and changeless *Tathāgata-garbha*, the supreme empty thing which is empty of real defilements, but full of Buddha-qualities and the basis of all actions of beings.
- For the Huayan school, while the Mādhyamika sense of emptiness applies to individual phenomena, they are forms of an underlying substance, the *Dharma*-realm, *Tathāgata-garbha*, One Mind, *li*, which is 'emptiness' in the sense of that which lacks any *fixed* nature, being fluid and infinitely malleable, like the *Dao*. This underlying principle is not multiple in nature, one per each being, but is a single universal principle at the root of the entire universe.

CHAPTER 6

Mahāyāna Holy Beings, and Tantric Buddhism

THE PATH OF THE *BODHISATTVA*

A '*Bodhisattva*' (see p. 15) is a 'being of/for awakening', that is, one dedicated to attaining *bodhi* – 'awakening', 'enlightenment' or 'buddhahood'. One who aims at the *bodhi* of a perfect Buddha, rather than of a *Pratyeka-buddha* or *Arhat* (see p. 99), was sometimes also called a *Mahāsattva*, a Great Being, or one directed towards the Great, that is, perfect Buddhahood (Harrison, 2000: 174–5; Williams, 2009: 55) – though the term '*Bodhisattva*' on its own is usually understood in this sense. The Mahāyāna is focused on this kind of *Bodhisattva*, one on the path to perfect Buddhahood, whose task is to compassionately help beings while maturing his or her own wisdom (*BT*.83–5; *BTTA*.124–7).

Wisdom, compassion and skilful means

In his wisdom (*prajñā*), the Mahāyāna *Bodhisattva* knows that there are no 'beings', just fluxes of '*dharmas*' that lack inherent existence (*BTTA*.157), but his 'skilful means' enables him to reconcile this wisdom with his compassion (*karuṇā*). This urges him to work for the salvation of all beings, for such empty fluxes do experience 'themselves' as 'suffering beings' (*Vc.* sec. 3).

Wisdom itself aids compassion in a number of ways. Ultimately, it leads to becoming an omniscient Buddha, who can teach and aid beings in countless ways. It also ensures that compassionate action is appropriate, effective and not covertly self-seeking. The *Bodhisattva* can also rub shoulders with wrongdoers, in an effort to 'reach' them, as with the lay *Bodhisattva* Vimalakīrti (*BT*.271–6), as he knows that their bad characteristics are not inherently existent. Any potential pride at the good he does is tempered by the reflection that his karmic fruitfulness is also 'empty' (*Vc.* sec. 8).

Most importantly, wisdom strengthens the feeling of solidarity with others, by insight into the 'sameness of beings': 'self' and 'others' being equally empty, there is no ultimate difference between them. Śāntideva (*c.* 650–750) persuasively draws on the idea of emptiness of inherent existence/nature to argue that indifference to the suffering of 'others' is as absurd as indifference to one's 'own' suffering. In his *Śikṣā-samuccaya* (*Ss.*) he argues that 'self' and 'other' are relative terms, like 'this bank' and 'the further bank' of a river: neither bank is, of itself, the 'further' bank. If one says that one should not protect another from pain, as it does not hurt oneself, then why does one seek to avert the pain of, or to bring positive benefit to, 'oneself' later in this life or in future lives? One will not be unchangingly *the same* being then (*Ss.*315). Body and mind consist of a changing series of states. We each, by habit, call these 'I', but why not use this notion as regards 'other' beings? Thus one should strive to prevent suffering in *any* being (*Ss.*316). Compassion for others does not bring pain to oneself, it makes possible joy based on awareness of others' being delivered from suffering. Karmic fruitfulness is to be rejoiced in, whoever generates it. Thus the *Bodhisattva* should constantly identify with others (*Ss.*317). In his *Bodhicaryāvatāra* (*Bca.*), Śāntideva says that, realizing that all are equal in wanting happiness and not wanting pain, one should protect others as one protects oneself, for suffering is just suffering, whoever it conventionally 'belongs' to (ultimately it is ownerless, not being the possession of any Self): what is so special about me and 'my' suffering (*Bca.*VIII.90–96, cf. 103)?

Just as wisdom aids compassion, compassion aids wisdom's undercutting of self-centredness, by motivating a life of self-sacrifice and active service for others. The *Upāya-kauśalya* (Skill in Means) *Sūtra* (Tatz, 1994: 73–6) and Śāntideva (*Ss.*168) assert that the *Bodhisattva* may even do a deed leading to hell, if this is a necessary part of helping someone else and giving them a more wholesome outlook on life (see p. 271; Harvey, 2000: 134–40). The great flexibility that the doctrine of skilful means gave the Mahāyāna, however, is guarded from becoming licence by its association with compassion, purifying meditations, and belief in the results of karma.

The Mahāyāna brought about a 'shift in the centre of gravity of Buddhist ethics' (Keown, 1992: 142), with a new emphasis on moral virtue 'as a dynamic other-regarding quality, rather than primarily concerned with personal development and self-control' (Keown, 1992: 131). The concept of ethical action (*śīla*; Pali *sīla*) became broadened so as to no longer be seen as simply one component of the path; in the widest sense it encompassed the whole of it. In such texts as Asaṅga's (310–90?) *Mahāyāna-saṃgraha* and *Bodhisattva-bhūmi*,[1] it came to be seen as comprising:

[1] Part of the *Yogācāra-bhūmi*, attributed as a whole to Asaṅga or his teacher, but with some parts perhaps predating them.

1. The ethics of 'restraint or vow (*saṃvara*)', through both the precepts of lay morality (abstention from harming others) and the monastic code, both termed *prātimokṣa*.[2]
2. The ethics of 'collecting wholesome/skilful states' (*kuśala-dharma-saṃgraha*), through the practice of the *Bodhisattva* perfections.
3. The ethics of 'working for the welfare of beings' (*sattvārtha-kriyā*), through active help for them.

The first was seen as the foundation for the other two, but as needing them to supplement it. A *śrāvaka*, one dedicated to becoming an *Arhat*, was seen as neglecting the welfare of other beings, only practising (i): disengaging from evil (Tatz, 1986: 69–70). A *Bodhisattva* also practises (ii) and (iii): engaging in good (Tatz, 1986: 87). That said, (ii) concerns the development of positive qualities and actions that are mostly shared with the Eight-factored Path, and a concern to help others is certainly not absent in Southern Buddhism, for example.[3] That said, the dedication of one's karmic fruitfulness to future Buddhahood is something that only the Mahāyāna emphasizes, and compassion takes centre place in it (Tatz, 1986: 48–9).

The ethics of benefiting sentient beings is ministering to the needs of others by: nursing those who are ill; advising on how to attain worldly and transcendent goals; gratitude for help received and returning it; protection from wild animals, kings, robbers and the elements; comforting those stricken by calamities; giving to the destitute; attracting disciples by friendliness and then attracting material support for them; amenability to the (non-harmful) desires of others; applauding and pointing out others' good qualities; compassionately humbling, punishing or banishing others in order to make them give up unwholesome ways and take to wholesome ones; using psychic powers to show the results of unwholesome actions in hells etc., and generally inspiring and teaching others (Tatz, 1986: 50; cf. *BT*.91). Practical help should also include such things as guiding the blind, teaching sign language to the deaf, and giving hospitality to weary travellers (Tatz, 1986: 54–5). In its other-regarding orientation, the Mahāyāna *Bodhisattva* ideal shares an emphasis on compassion with the early Buddhist idea of the Universal Emperor (*Cakravartin*; see pp. 16 and 101).

The perfections and stages of the Bodhisattva

The *Bodhisattva* path begins with the arising of the *bodhi-citta*, the aspiration to strive for Buddhahood for its own sake, and for the sake of helping

[2] Pali *pāṭimokkha*: a term reserved in the Theravāda for monastic precepts.
[3] So the characterization of the *śrāvaka* as only focused on avoiding evil seems unfair.

suffering beings (*EB*.4.4.2). For this momentous event to occur, a person requires karmic fruitfulness and knowledge, generated by moral and spiritual practice in the present and past lives, combined with devotion and reflections on the sufferings of beings and the need for Buddhas.

A series of meditations are used to arouse the *bodhi-citta* (Wayman, 1991: 45–57), which work with the early Buddhist set of four *brahma-vihāras*, or 'divine abidings': lovingkindness, compassion, empathetic joy, and equanimity. First of all, equanimity is developed towards all beings, as an unbiased impartiality, based on the realization that current enemies may in time become friends, and vice versa. Next, the meditator develops lovingkindness by reflecting on the kindness that his mother has shown him, then reflecting that in the long round of rebirths, even neutral strangers and enemies have been his mothers in previous lives (see p. 38). Hence he aspires for the happiness of all beings: the 'great lovingkindness' (*mahā-maitrī*). He then develops compassion by similar reflections prefaced by visualization of the pitiful lot of a condemned criminal or animal about to be slaughtered, reflecting that his present mother and all past mothers have experienced many kinds of such suffering in the realms of rebirth. Thus arises the aspiration to lead all beings from such sufferings, the 'great compassion' (*mahā-karuṇā*). Finally, there is the development of empathetic joy, rejoicing at the present happiness of beings, particularly enemies. Additionally, there may be practice of the 'exchange of self for others'. This is advocated by Śāntideva at *Bca*.VII.16, VIII.120,[4] in which a person looks on another, lowly, person as 'I' and on himself as he would on someone else. Fully identifying with the other person and his outlook, he sees himself through the other person's eyes, perhaps as proud and uncaring. He focuses his ambitions on that person, and whatever indifference he normally has to others is focused on himself (*Bca*.VIII.140–54).

The initial 'arising of the thought of awakening' (*bodhi-citt'otpāda*), as a resolve, is known as the 'aspiration-thought' (*praṇiddhi-citta*); when it is put into practice, it is known as the 'implementation-thought' (*prasthāna-citta*; *Bca*.I.15). Even the resolve alone, without implementation, is seen as generating much karmic fruitfulness and as wearing out much past bad karma (*Ss*.II). The *bodhi-citta* is seen as the seed of all the qualities of Buddhahood, and a precious and glorious event which reorientates a person's whole being.

After the arising of the *bodhi-citta*, a person takes various *Bodhisattva* vows (*praṇidhāna*) in the presence of others who live by them, or with all

[4] See also Wayman, 1991: 59–61.

Buddhas and *Bodhisattvas* as witness (*BS2*.43). Some are general vows: to overcome innumerable defilements, attain incomparable Buddhahood, and to save all beings; others may be to help beings in more specific ways. The vow to save all beings (or at least as many as possible) is made more credible and less overly ambitious by the notion that beings already have 'Buddhaness', or the *Tathāgata-garbha*, and it is made non-egoistic by the notion that beings are not ultimately different from the *Bodhisattva*. Such vows are not taken lightly, however. They are seen to become a powerful autonomous force within the psyche and to bring very bad karmic results if broken. Even in the Sarvāstivādin tradition, the *Bodhisattva* path was seen to last three 'incalculables', each of these consisting of a thousand million million great eons, each of which is the time from when a world-system began to the start of the next one.[5] This figure was also the most common one quoted in the Mahāyāna (*BS1*.30–33; Dayal, 1932: 76–9), though a figure of thirty-three incalculables is also found. The hugely long nature of the *Bodhisattva* path helps explain why it is seen as so compassionate to set out on, for the path to Arhatship, while still challenging, is much quicker. The longer path will bring benefit to more beings, though.

The *Bodhisattva* path is practised by developing a number of 'perfections' (*pāramitā*) and progressing through the ten *Bodhisattva* 'stages' (*bhūmi*).[6] Six 'perfections' (*EB*.4.4) are described in the Perfection of Wisdom literature, though another four were later added to co-ordinate with the last four of the stages. The stages are described in such works as the *Bodhisattva-bhūmi* and the *Daśa-bhūmika Sūtra*, first translated into Chinese in 297 CE. The *Daśa-bhūmika Sūtra* talks of the first *Bodhisattva* stage as beginning with the arising of the *bodhi-citta*, but Tibetan Buddhists use a model from the works of Kamalaśīla (*c.* 700–750) and Atiśa (982–1054), which add various preliminaries, drawing on the Sarvāstivādin schema of paths or *mārgas* (Gethin, 1998: 194–8, 230). In the Mahāyāna, these are:

- The path of equipment or accumulation (*sambhāra-mārga*): starting with the arising of the *bodhi-citta*, and the preliminary cultivation of the six perfections, with a mastery of mindfulness and calm.
- The path of application or preparation (*prayoga-mārga*); four stages of penetrating insight, meditatively focusing on the idea of emptiness.

[5] That is, the four phases of a great eon – see p. 33. Note that the term 'incalculable' is used both for any of these four phases and also for a much larger number.

[6] *BTTA*.129–33, 141–5; Williams, 2009: 200–8.

- The path of seeing (*darśana-mārga*): the breakthrough to the Noble level, akin to stream-entry (see pp. 84–6),[7] in a direct non-conceptual seeing of emptiness; this brings entry to the first of the ten stages of the Noble *Bodhisattva*.
- The path of development (*bhāvanā-mārga*): the remaining nine stages and the cultivation of their perfections to full strength.
- The path of the adept (*aśaikṣa-mārga*): Buddhahood.

The ten stages pertain to the Noble (*Ārya*) *Bodhisattva*, though just as the ordinary Eight-factored Path leads to the Noble Eight-factored Path, so the *Bodhisattva* practises the perfections at an ordinary level before becoming a spiritually ennobled person. The *Daśa-bhūmika Sūtra* correlates the ten stages with the ten perfections, and the *Bodhisattva-piṭaka Sūtra*, a text probably dating from the second century CE (Pagel, 1995: 2), treats the perfections in depth. The ten stages and their corresponding perfections are shown in Table 2.

The idea of 'perfections' was also found in the early schools (see pp. 99–100); the Theravāda has a list of ten perfections, which overlaps with the Mahāyāna list: giving, moral virtue, wisdom, renunciation, vigour, patience, truthfulness, determination, lovingkindness and equanimity. The Perfection of Wisdom literature recognized that only the perfections *to the highest degree* were what was needed for Buddhahood (Conze, 1973: 155), and the influential Tibetan master Tsongkh'apa (1357–1419) held that

Table 2 Bodhisattva *stages and perfections*

Stage	*Perfection*
1. Joyous (*Pramuditā*)	Generosity (*dāna*)
2. Stainless (*Vimāla*)	Moral virtue (*śīla*)
3. Luminous (*Prabhākarī*)	Endurance or patient acceptance (*kṣānti*)
4. Radiant (*Arciṣmatī*)	Vigour or energy (*vīrya*)
5. Difficult to Conquer (*Sudurjayā*)	Meditation (*dhyāna*)
6. Approaching, or Face-to-face (*Abhimukī*)	Wisdom (*prajñā*)
7. Gone Afar (*Dūraṅgamā*)	Skill in means (*upāya-kauśalya*)
8. Immovable (*Acalā*)	Vow or determination (*praṇidhāna*)
9. Good Intelligence (*Sādhumatī*)	Power (*bala*)
10. Cloud of *Dharma* (*Dharmameghā*)	Gnosis (*jñāna*)

[7] Though in the Theravāda understanding of the *Bodhisattva* path, a Buddha does not even attain stream-entry until the night of his enlightenment, when all four Noble stages are attained in one sitting. This clearly implies that the fetters normally overcome at stream-entry are still existent, though only at an extremely minimal level, just prior to Buddhahood.

'Hīnayāna' and Mahāyāna were not differentiated by their view (of emptiness), but through their *upāya*, or means that they used, which in the case of the *Bodhisattva* is based on the *bodhi-citta*. Accordingly, Mahāyānists still revered *Arhats*, some of whom where seen to remain in a suspended meditative state in remote mountain locations. Indeed Tibetan and especially Chinese Buddhism includes reverence to a set of sixteen or eighteen such great *Arhats* (Ray, 1994: 179–212).

On the Mahāyāna path, in the first stage, the Noble *Bodhisattva* is said to have psychic powers and the meditative ability to see many Buddhas from different parts of the universe, and to receive teachings from them. Such abilities are seen to strengthen through the following stages. In the first stage, the *Bodhisattva* is full of joy and faith, and concentrates on developing the perfection of generosity to a high degree. This is done by giving away wealth, teachings, life, limb and even spouse and family, for the benefit of others. The good karma generated by such acts is dedicated to the future Buddhahood of himself or herself and others (*BTTA*.128). Such transfer (*pariṇāmanā*) of karmic fruitfulness (see pp. 45–6) is seen as possible as karmic fruitfulness is 'empty' and does not inherently 'belong' to any particular 'being'. In the Mahāyāna, the aspiration is usually that karmic fruitfulness is shared with *all* beings (e.g. Tatz, 1994: 24), and typically to help them attain enlightenment. Humans should transfer it for the benefit of other humans, and beings in unfortunate rebirths. They should also transfer it to Buddhas and *Bodhisattvas* with a view to increasing their perfections and virtues (*Ss*.205–6). In turn, though, advanced *Bodhisattvas* and Buddhas are seen as transferring it to devotees who ask for such help in faith. Śāntideva praises the transfer of karmic fruitfulness in the final chapter (x) of his *Bodhicaryāvatāra*, aspiring that, by the good karma generated by his writing this poem, humans and other beings should be free from various afflictions and be endowed with morality, faith, wisdom and compassion. In verse 56 (cf. *Ss*.256–7), he even prays that the sufferings of the world should ripen in him: that he should take on the bad karma of others, not just give them his karmic fruitfulness. Likewise, there is a Tibetan practice called *tong-len* (*gtong len*), of breathing out one's positive qualities to others and breathing in their negative qualities and suffering, so as to help overcome these (Willis, 1989: 18, 137).

In the second stage, the *Bodhisattva* concentrates on the perfection of moral virtue until his conduct becomes spontaneously pure. He also urges others to avoid immorality, as it leads to unfortunate rebirths. His meditative development allows him to see and worship many more Buddhas. In the third stage, bright with wisdom, he concentrates on the perfection of patient acceptance, aided by meditations on lovingkindness and compassion. He develops great forbearance in adversity, avoids anger, and patiently perseveres in seeking to fathom the profound *Dharma*. In the fourth stage, the perfection of vigour is developed, due to increasing aspiration and compassion. Mindful alertness is emphasized, and the stage is particularly appropriate for practising the discipline of a monk or nun. In the fifth stage, which is beyond the power of Māra to conquer, the focus is on the perfection of meditation. Meditative trances are mastered, but the heavenly rebirths that they can lead to are not accepted. The four True Realities for the Spiritually Ennobled are comprehended and the ability to move between conventional and ultimate truth is developed. Abilities in such fields as maths, medicine and poetry are cultivated, as ways to help others and teach the *Dharma*.

In the sixth stage, the perfection of wisdom is attained, with full mastery of what had been initially glimpsed at the 'path of seeing'. The *Bodhisattva* gains full insight into Conditioned Arising, non-Self and emptiness and, by the perfection of wisdom, the five previously emphasized perfections become transcendent, attaining completeness and full perfection. Their most difficult acts are carried out totally free of self-consciousness or ulterior motive. For example, in giving, he does not perceive 'giver', 'gift', 'recipient' or 'result'; for all dissolve in emptiness (*BTTA*.131).

At the completion of stage six and entry into stage seven, the *Bodhisattva* reaches a level of development parallel to that of the *Arhat* (Williams and Tribe, 2000: 133–4). He or she is free of 'obscuration' (*āvaraṇa*) in the form of the 'defilements' (*kleśa*) of greed, hatred and delusion. At death, he *could* leave the round of rebirths and enter final *Nirvāṇa*,[8] but his Mahāyāna 'great compassion' prevents him from doing so. Knowing that *saṃsāra* is not ultimately different from *Nirvāṇa*, he attains 'non-abiding *Nirvāṇa*' (see p. 137), not attached to or resting in either *saṃsāra* or *Nirvāṇa*.[9] From the first stage, the *Bodhisattva* is reborn according to the force of his or her vow, rather than from his or her karma; from the third stage, rebirth is according to the *Bodhisattva*'s force of meditative concentration; from the seventh stage, rebirth is according to superhuman power; all three means are forms

[8] At least, this is a possibility according to those Mahāyāna texts, such as the *Akṣobhyavyūha Sūtra*, which support a 'three vehicle' (*tri-yāna*) rather than 'one vehicle' (*eka-yāna*) model. The first of these sees the goals of Arhatship or Pratyekabuddhahood as genuine goals, which preclude the attainment of the higher goal, perfect Buddhahood. 'One vehicle' texts, such as the *Lotus Sūtra* (see p. 111), see the first two 'goals' as not what they seem: they are really provisional way-stations towards perfect Buddhahood.

[9] The Sanskrit for 'non-abiding' is *apratiṣṭhita*, in Pali *apatiṭṭhita* (Harvey, 1995a: 217–22). At p. 76, this is translated as 'unsupported' when applied to a form of consciousness that the Pali *Suttas* imply is itself *Nirvāṇa*.

of rebirth directed by conscious purpose.[10] From the seventh stage, the *Bodhisattva* becomes a transcendent being who, by his perfection of skilful means, magically projects himself into many worlds so as to teach and help beings in appropriate ways. As the Mahāyāna developed, such beings were looked to as heavenly saviours.

As a result of the seventh stage, at the eighth stage the *Bodhisattva* has reached a non-relapsing, irreversible (*avinivartanīya*) level, such that he[11] is now certain to attain Buddhahood.[12] From this stage, his meditative insight imbues all his experience, and the many obscurations of the knowable (*jñey'āvaraṇa*) – preventing the omniscience of a Buddha – begin to be overcome. His knowledge enables him to appear anywhere in the universe at will, teaching beings while appearing just like them. He fully masters the transfer of karmic fruitfulness from his vast store, so that beings who pray to him receive it as a free spiritual uplift of grace. In the ninth stage, the *Bodhisattva* perfects his power, using his tremendous insight into beings' characters to guide and teach them in the most precisely appropriate ways.

In the tenth stage, the *Bodhisattva* dwells in the Tuṣita heaven, as does Maitreya now (see p. 15). He has a resplendent body and is surrounded by a retinue of lesser *Bodhisattvas*. In the Diamond-like meditative concentration of omniscience, he has the perfection of gnosis. Buddhas then come to consecrate him as ready for perfect Buddhahood, which he attains in the following *Tathāgata*-stage.

The attainment of Buddhahood is not seen as taking place on earth, but in the Akaniṣṭha heaven (*Lanka*.361). In early Buddhism, this was seen as the most refined of the elemental form heavens and the highest of the five 'pure abodes', where only non-returners are reborn and subsequently become *Arhats* (see p. 35). The life-span of the 'Eldest' (Pali Akaniṭṭha) gods there was seen as 16,000 eons. In some ways, the advanced level *Bodhisattvas* of the higher stages can be seen as akin to the non-returners of early teachings, as non-returners' insight was often seen as close to that of *Arhats*, but they continued in heavenly rebirths before finally attaining *Nirvāṇa* – with a non-returner who becomes an *Arahat* early in his life in the Akaniṣṭha heaven having 16,000 eons as an *Arhat* deity. The Mahāyāna would stress, however, that advanced *Bodhisattvas* and Buddhas have

[10] Nagao, 1991: 30–1, citing the *Mahāyāna-sūtrālaṃkāra* XX–XXI.8

[11] For a discussion of different Mahāyāna views on how far a person can progress up the *Bodhisattva* path while still in female form, see Harvey, 2000: 373–6. Vasubandhu held that this was up to the seventh stage. The Tiantai school holds that a Buddha could be female.

[12] On a 'one vehicle' interpretation, this must mean going beyond any notion that a lesser form of enlightenment was either desirable or possible.

greater compassion than an *Arhat* or lesser grade of saint, and that advanced *Bodhisattvas* live for far more than 16,000 eons, as *Bodhisattvas* then Buddhas.

Given the length, and stages, of the *Bodhisattva* path, it is well to note that what may apply to a *Bodhisattva* at one stage may not apply at another, though they all share the same goal, perfect Buddhahood, for the sake of helping others most effectively. A '*Bodhisattva*' may be:

1. a person who has just taken the *Bodhisattva* vows for the first time;
2. any other *Bodhisattva* at the 'ordinary' level who has not yet experienced the 'path of seeing' which marks entry to the first of the ten stages of the path of the Noble *Bodhisattva*;
3. a Noble *Bodhisattva* in one of the initial stages;
4. a Noble *Bodhisattva* of stage seven, whose insight seems akin to that of an *Arhat* and who is free of the defilements, but whose great compassion prevents him or her from leaving the round of rebirths at death;
5. a Noble *Bodhisattva* of stages eight to ten, who is now irreversibly bound for Buddhahood and who is a transcendent being that in time came to be seen as a saviour being.

It is as well to remember, then, that '*Bodhisattva*' is a path-term rather than a goal-term: it refers to the kind of being who is at one or other point along a long path. When a Mahāyāna *Sūtra* attributes some quality to 'a' or 'the' '*Bodhisattva*', it may well be describing the ideal, advanced *Bodhisattva*, what all *Bodhisattvas* should aim to be before finally becoming a Buddha. One should thus be careful of taking such passages as applicable to all *Bodhisattvas*.[13] Comparisons between 'the *Bodhisattva*' and 'the *Arhat*' are thus, strictly speaking, inappropriate. If anything, one should compare the *Bodhisattva* and the *śrāvaka* (both primarily path-terms) or the *Arhat* and the Buddha (both goal-terms), otherwise the *Bodhisattva* of a particular stage and the *Arhat*. That said, the *Bodhisattva* path is so immensely long that it, and its orientation to bring benefit to others, can be seen to have effectively become a goal, in the form of an ever-maturing mode of being. For example, the Chinese Tiantai (T'ien-t'ai) school says that the practitioner is forever 'becoming a Buddha', in an ongoing process.

At this point, it is worth taking up the issue of whether a *Bodhisattva* 'postpones' his or her *Nirvāṇa*, so as to bring all other beings to *Nirvāṇa*

[13] There is sometimes a similar lack of clarity in Mahāyāna texts in that 'disciples' (*śrāvakas*) and *Arhats* are equated. More properly, a *śrāvaka* (Pali *sāvaka*) is someone who either is an *Arhat* or aims at becoming one, and may have attained lesser grades of sanctity, so as to be a stream-enterer, once-returner or non-returner.

first, as is sometimes said in textbooks on Buddhism.[14] The path to Arhatship, along with its *Nirvāṇa*-in-life and *Nirvāṇa*-beyond-death, or final *Nirvāṇa*, is far shorter than the *Bodhisattva* path to perfect Buddhahood, so the *Bodhisattva* is indeed choosing a path in which *Nirvāṇa* will come much later rather than sooner. In any case, even when a *Bodhisattva* has developed – slowly, given all that needs to be developed along the way – to the same level of wisdom as an *Arhat*, and thus effectively has *Nirvāṇa*-in-life, he does not take the consequence of this, *Nirvāna*-beyond-death, that is, leaving the round of rebirths at the end of the life in which *Nirvāṇa*-in-life had been attained. Rather, the advanced *Bodhisattva* experiences non-abiding *Nirvāṇa* while still staying in *saṃsāra*, building up the final qualities that will bring the omniscience of a perfect Buddha, and not neglecting the suffering beings of *saṃsāra*. Once a perfect Buddha, the ex-*Bodhisattva* has both non-abiding *Nirvāṇa* and a Buddha's omniscience. In texts which include the idea of non-abiding *Nirvāṇa*, neither of these are things which a *Bodhisattva* would want to postpone – for Buddhahood is the goal of the *Bodhisattva*, providing the omniscient wisdom that informs the most effective way of compassionately helping suffering beings, and the combination of strong wisdom and compassion is what brings the *Bodhisattva* to non-abiding *Nirvāṇa*. Nevertheless, before the idea of non-abiding *Nirvāṇa* was developed, and it was still thought that a Buddha would at some time, albeit after a hugely long life, enter 'final' *Nirvāṇa*, it was believed that some *Bodhisattva*s would even hold back from Buddhahood, as this would entail them eventually leaving the world and losing contact with suffering beings, though at the level of the high-stage *Bodhisattva*, their difference from a perfect Buddha is hard to realistically specify.

MAHĀYĀNA BUDDHOLOGY: EXPANSION WITH REGARD TO THE NUMBER, LOCATION, LIFE-SPAN AND NATURE OF BUDDHAS

After the death of the historical Buddha, though his teachings remained in the world, there was still a desire for experiencing the presence of a Buddha: such direct contact was seen as spiritually very efficacious, and as conveying a potent blessing (*adhiṣṭhāna*; Hookham, 2004). Early Buddhism accepted a line of past earthly Buddhas, spread over the eons (see p. 15), though it had emphasized that a world-system can only have one Buddha, and the

[14] Williams and Tribe (2000: 103–4) and Williams (2009: 58–62, 185–6) critically examine this claim.

tradition he starts, at a time.[15] The Mahāyāna, though, emphasized that as there were countless world-systems in the universe – not itself a new idea – many of these could be the realms of present-day Buddhas, which could be contacted and bring benefit to this world (*BS1*.212–14). Indeed, Buddhas were seen as being as numerous as 'the grains of sand in the [river] Ganges' (e.g. Gómez, 1996: 149).

The belief that such Buddhas could be contacted seems to have its roots in the early Buddhist practice of 'recollection of the Buddha' (*Buddhānusmṛti*, see p. 105; Williams, 2009: 209–14). In the Theravāda version of this, recollection of the Buddha's qualities leads to the overcoming of fear, and a state in which the meditator 'comes to feel as if he were living in the Master's presence', so as to avoid doing any unwholesome act (*Vism*.213). This is said to lead to gaining a relatively deep state of meditative calm,[16] and then a heavenly rebirth. In the Mahāyāna, recollection of the Buddha became especially important. A text of particular influence in China was the *Pratyutpanna-buddha-saṃmukhāvasthita-samādhi Sūtra*: the '*Sūtra* on the Meditative Concentration of Direct Encounter with Buddhas of the Present' – the *Pratyutpanna Sūtra* for short (Harrison, 1978, 1990). This was first translated into Chinese in 179 CE, and focuses on the Buddha Amitāyus. Practising strict morality, a person meditates in seclusion, visualizing this Buddha's form and reflecting on his qualities. This is done almost continuously for seven days, after which Amitāyus is seen with the physical eyes, or in a dream. Here the 'as if' presence of the/a Buddha becomes what is seen as a real living presence, which not only can be worshipped but also can give new teachings, so as to speed progress towards enlightenment.

Pure Lands and other Buddha-fields

Each of the Buddhas throughout the universe is seen to have a 'Buddha-field' (*Buddha-kṣetra*),[17] a domain that he had previously purified by his actions from stage eight of the *Bodhisattva* path. He is said to finally attain his Buddhahood in the Akaniṣṭha heaven of one of the world-systems of his Field or Domain. Many such Fields are said to be 'pure' – called 'Pure Lands' (*jingtu* (*ching-t'u*)) in Chinese Buddhism: ideal regions created by the appropriate Buddha. Buddhism had always accepted that karma is a

[15] *M*.III.65; *Miln*.236–9 (*BS1*.211–12; *BS2*.6); *Vibh-a*.434–6.
[16] 'Access' concentration (*Vism*.111), at the brink of the first *jhāna* (see p. 329).
[17] See p. 100; Sponberg, 2007; Williams, 2009: 214–18.

dominant force in the world. Combining this with the Yogācāra notion of reality as thought-only, there developed the idea that a Buddha could draw on his immeasurable store of karmic fruitfulness, and the power of his mind, to conjure up a world for the benefit of others. While these Pure Lands are described in paradisiacal terms, they are primarily realms where it is easy to hear and practise the *Dharma*: conditions very conducive to attaining awakening. Pure Lands are outside the normal system of rebirths, including heavenly ones, according to personal karma. To be reborn in one requires not only the dedication of one's own karmic fruitfulness to this end, but also a transfer of some of the huge stock of karmic fruitfulness of a Land's presiding Buddha, stimulated by devout prayer. Once faith has led to rebirth in a Pure Land, either as a human-like being or god, a person can develop his or her wisdom and so become either an *Arhat* or a high-level *Bodhisattva.*

The notion of a realm with ideal conditions for attaining enlightenment builds on a number of concepts in earlier Buddhism on times or levels of existence with better conditions than the present human realm (see Gethin, 1997):

- *Another time:* the glorious world of the past *Cakravartin* emperor Mahāsudarśana, with trees of gold and precious stones (*D.*II.169–98 (*SB.*98–115)), or of the future one Saṅkha (*D.*III.75–7), when humans will live for 80,000 years, and the next Buddha, Maitreya, will live and teach.
- *Another level:* such as the Tuṣita heaven where Maitreya currently dwells as a *Bodhisattva*, or the 'pure abodes', where non-returners become *Arhats*.

The Mahāyāna idea of Pure Lands seems to combine and add to the marvellous qualities of the above, locating them in the present but in distant parts of the universe, each akin to a galaxy; for a Buddha-field is seen as a realm comprising a thousand million world-systems, complete with their attendant spheres of rebirth, from (empty) hells to heavens (Griffiths, 1994: 129).

The huge life-span of Buddhas

The Mahāyāna also developed a new perspective on the life-span and nature of the historical Buddha, whom it refers to as Śākyamuni. In early Buddhism, there is the idea that the Buddha could have lived for the remainder of the present eon, had he been asked to do so (*D.*II.103), and the Mahāyāna takes up this kind of idea. Its new perspective starts to be expressed by the middle of the second century CE, in the *Lokānuvartanā Sūtra*. Its most notable expression is in the *Lotus Sūtra* – whose full title is the *Saddharma-puṇḍarīka Sūtra*, or '*Sūtra* of the White Lotus of the True *Dharma*' (*Lotus*) – which reached its final form by 286 CE, when it was first translated into Chinese. In its chapter on the 'Duration of the life of the *Tathāgata*',[18] the Buddha explains that he became awakened countless eons ago: more eons ago than there are atoms in fifty million myriads of world-systems. Since that time, he has been constantly teaching in our 'Sahā world-system' and countless others. Over the ages, he had already appeared on earth in the form of past Buddhas such as Dīpaṅkara (see p. 15), and taught according to people's spiritual capacities. The idea of the earthly Buddha as the manifestation of a heavenly Buddha had already been expressed in the Lokottaravādin *Mahāvastu* (see p. 98), but the idea that the long line of past earthly Buddhas were manifestations of the same Buddha was a new one. The *Lotus Sūtra* says that all such earthly Buddhas teach those of lesser understanding that Buddhas pass into final *Nirvāṇa*, beyond contact with living beings, when they die. The *Sūtra* holds, though, that this is only a skilful means, to ensure that people do not become overly dependent on Buddhas, but actually use the spiritual medicine that Buddhas give (Pye, 2003; Williams, 2009: 151–7). In fact, the heavenly Buddha (also known as Śākyamuni), who appeared in the form of earthly Buddhas, will live on for twice the time that has passed since he became awakened; only then will he pass into final *Nirvāṇa* (*BTTA*; 135; cf. *EB*.5.1). In this world, this compassionate 'protector of all creatures' has a presence on Vultures' Peak near where the council following the Buddha's death was held. Those who are virtuous and gentle may even now, with the eye of faith, see him preaching there.

This message of light and hope, then, sees Śākyamuni as a manifestation skilfully projected into earthly life by a long-enlightened transcendent being, who is still available to teach the faithful through visionary experiences. At the popular level, the message is taken to mean that the omniscient Buddha Śākyamuni is an omnipresent, eternal being, watching over the world and supremely worthy of worship. While he is seen as having been a Buddha for a hugely long time, however, the idea is still expressed that he became a Buddha by practising the *Bodhisattva* path, starting out as an ordinary being. In the *Lotus Sūtra*, then, he is neither a recently awakened human who has passed into *Nirvāṇa*, nor an eternal monotheistic God-type figure.

The Mahāyāna has different views on the question of whether Śākyamuni Buddha, or any other perfect Buddha, will, after a hugely long

[18] No. 15 in the Sanskrit version, 16 in the Chinese.

life, eventually attain *Nirvāṇa*-beyond-death (Williams, 2009: 185–6). The earlier view, as expressed in the *Lotus Sūtra*, the *Akṣobhya-vyūha Sūtra* and in the earlier recension of the *Sukhāvatī-vyūha Sūtra*, was that he *will* eventually attain this, thus going beyond any possibility of contact with the beings of *saṃsāra*. Nevertheless, once the idea of non-abiding *Nirvāṇa* (see p. 137) had been developed in the Mahāyāna, it allowed the possibility that a perfect Buddha could continue forever, both experiencing the benefits of *Nirvāṇa*, and aiding the beings of *saṃsāra*, with no need to enter 'final' *Nirvāṇa*. Some texts therefore came to express this view, and East Asian forms of Buddhism tend to interpret the *Lotus Sūtra* in this way – alongside texts with the rather different view which talks of some *Bodhisattvas postponing* Buddhahood, as they lacked the idea of non-abiding *Nirvāṇa*. The *Gaṇḍavyūha Sūtra*, a key text of the Huayan school, ends with the 'Prayer of Samantabhadra', a 62-verse resolve of the advanced *Bodhisattva* (or Buddha?) Samantabhadra, 'Universally Good', which is often used as a basis for *Bodhisattva* vows.[19] Samantabhadra vows to remain (presumably as a *Bodhisattva* then Buddha) as long as any living being remains, helping them until the end of time or perhaps for countless eons (vv. 22, 26).

The Trikāya *doctrine*

As the above kind of ideas developed, some systematization on the nature of different aspects of Buddhahood came to be needed. By the fourth century, this was done by the Yogācārins in such texts as the *Mahāyāna-sūtrālaṃkāra* (of Maitryanātha?) and its commentary, and Asaṅga's *Mahāyāna-saṃgraha*.[20] Here one finds the *Trikāya* or 'Three-body' doctrine, a central framework of Mahāyāna belief which sees Buddhahood as having three aspects: (i) the *Nirmāṇa-kāya*, or 'Transformation-body', (ii) the *Saṃbhoga-kāya*, or 'Enjoyment-body', and (iii) the *Dharma-kāya*, or '*Dharma*-body'.

The idea of Transformation-bodies builds on the early idea that deep meditation enables a person to generate a mind-made body (*D*.I.77), and to have various psychic powers, such as the ability to multiply one's form (*D*.I.78–83).[21] The Lokottaravādins had already seen the historical Buddha as a mind-made body sent by the Buddha from the Tuṣita heaven. In the Mahāyāna, the 'Transformation-body' refers to earthly Buddhas, seen as

[19] *BT*.172–8; Cleary, 1989: 387–94; Williams, 2009: 137–8. Samantabhadra is also seen as a protector of those who chant the *Lotus Sūtra* (*EB*.5.2.3).

[20] *BT*.94–5; Dutt, 1978: 136–70; Griffiths, 1994; Williams, 2009: 176–82; Xing, 2005a.

[21] For developed Theravādin ideas on Buddha 'bodies', see Reynolds, 1977.

teaching devices compassionately projected into the world to show people the path to Buddhahood. At death, they are generally withdrawn back into the heavenly Buddha, or even advanced *Bodhisattva*, who manifested them. Besides such supreme Transformation-bodies of a Buddha, there are also other types. The term is also applied to certain religious teachers, even non-Buddhist ones, who are seen as using skilful means to draw people in a wholesome direction; D. T. Suzuki (1870–1966), who did much to make the West aware of Zen Buddhism, saw Christ in this way. Transformation-bodies may also include animals acting in compassionate ways, and even objects which mysteriously appear when they can be of great help to people.

Some texts see Transformation-body people as actual beings of flesh and blood, while others, such as the *Suvarṇa-bhāsottama Sūtra* (*Svb*.18), see them as mere appearances. Of course for the Yogācāra school, the whole world of people and things is just an appearance, as this perspective takes only direct experience as real. An 'external' physical world – depending on how one interprets what they are saying – is either denied or seen as a problematic speculative concept for which we have no reliable evidence in experience (see p. 134). While ordinary beings are seen as streams of mental processes, with an 'external' world as a projection from their direct experience, a Transformation-body is seen to be *only* an appearance in the mind-stream of others, with no mind-stream of its own other than that of the projecting 'Enjoyment-body'.

When a *Bodhisattva* attains Buddhahood, it is as an Enjoyment-body being with a refulgent subtle body of limitless form, which is the product of the karmic fruitfulness of a *Bodhisattva*'s training. It is adopted by a Buddha partly for the 'enjoyment' of Noble *Bodhisattvas* – those in this Land or those to whom he appears through visionary experiences, giving them teachings. Early Buddhism had the idea that the Buddha had a body – no doubt in the sense of a spiritual body – endowed with the thirty-two special characteristics of a Great Man (*D*.III.42–79; see pp. 105–6). In the Mahāyāna, Enjoyment-body Buddhas such as the heavenly Śākyamuni were seen to have these. The form and wondrous powers of such Buddhas vary slightly according to their past *Bodhisattva* vows and karmic fruitfulness.

Each Enjoyment-body Buddha is seen as presiding over his own Buddha-field, but besides the 'Pure' Buddha-fields, there are also 'impure' ones, normal world-systems like our own. As to why Śākyamuni Buddha's Buddha-field is not pure, different answers were given: the historical Buddha was a Transformation-body sent by another Buddha from a Pure Land; or sent by the Enjoyment-body form of Śākyamuni from the mini-Pure Land realm of Vultures' Peak in our world, as in the *Lotus Sūtra*; or

Śākyamuni is special in being able to save beings even in an impure realm, working in ways compassionately suited to beings born in such a realm, as in the *Karuṇā-puṇḍarīka Sūtra*; or this realm is really a pure one, but beings will not see this until they awaken and are without mental impurities, as in the *Vimalakīrti-nirdeśa Sūtra* (Williams, 2009: 217–18).

Before considering the third aspect of a Buddha, '*Dharma-kāya*', it is helpful to look at the history of this term, which is a compound word that can function as either a noun or an adjective. In early Buddhism, the Buddha is described as 'one who has become *Dharma*' (Pali *Dhamma-bhūta*) and 'one having *Dharma* as his body' (Pali *Dhamma-kāya*, Skt *Dharma-kāya*; *D*.III.84). The latter seems to have meant that the Buddha is spiritually 'embodied' in the *Dharma* – though one might also say that the *Dharma* is physically embodied in the Buddha. Here '*Dharma*' can mean either (a) the Buddha's teachings, or (b) the qualities of the path and its culmination that the Buddha had practised and exemplified, as suggested in a *Sutta* passage where the Buddha says 'who sees *Dhamma* sees me' (*S*. III.120). *Dharma-kāya* can also mean 'the body' or 'collection' (*kāya*) of teachings (*Miln*. 73 (*BTTA*. 119)). The Theravāda commentator Buddhaghosa explains the *Dhammakāya* as the Buddha's 'body' as referring to *Nirvāṇa* along with the four 'path' and four 'fruit' experiences that know this (*S-a*.II.314). He also says that the Buddha's *Dhamma*-body perfected the pure collections of moral virtue, meditation, wisdom, liberation and knowledge-and-vision-of-liberation (*Vism*.234). This is in line with a passage in the Pali *Apadāna* (p. 532, cf. 13, 168), where the *Arahat*-nun Mahāpajāpatī, the Buddha's step-mother, says that while she brought up the Buddha's physical body, 'My blameless *Dhamma*-body was brought up by you'. The Sarvāstivādins also speculated on the nature of the Buddha's '*Dharma*-body' (Dutt, 1978: 142–7; Xing, 2005a: 35–44). Vasubandhu explains that while Buddhas differ in the length of their lives, they have 'equally accumulated karmic fruitfulness and knowledge, in that they have realized the same *dharma-kāya*' (*AKB*.VII.34). The commentarial *Vyākhā* here explains *dharma-kāya* as 'a series of taintless *dharmas*', which are the *dharmas* that make a person a Buddha, namely the five pure collections, as at *Vism*.234 (*AKB*. IV.32). That is, the '*dharma-kāya*' is not a single entity but a collection of pure qualities of a type that are found in any Buddha.

In the *Aṣṭasāhasrikā* Perfection of Wisdom *Sūtra*, the *dharma-kāya* is what a Buddha is really about, rather than his physical body and the remaining relics of this. Paul Williams traces three linked meanings of '*dharma-kāya*' developed in various Perfection of Wisdom (*Prajñāpāramitā*) texts: 'First, the *dharmakāya* is the collection of teachings, particularly the Prajñāpāramitā itself. Second, it is the pure *dharmas* possessed by the Buddha, specifically the pure mental *dharmas* cognizing emptiness. And third, it comes to refer to emptiness itself, the true nature of things' (Williams, 2009: 177). Similarly in the *Niraupamyastava*, plausibly attributed to Nāgārjuna, *dharma-kāya* is timeless *dharma*-ness (Williams, 2009: 178).

In his 1992 'Is the *Dharma-kāya* the Real "Phantom Body" of the Buddha?', Paul Harrison examines how the term *dharma-kāya* was used in: (a) texts translated into Chinese by Lokakṣema – including the *Aṣṭasāhasrikā* – around the end of the second century CE, one of the earliest pieces of datable literary evidence for the Mahāyāna, and (b) some texts of the 'middle' Mahāyāna period, such as the *Laṅkāvatāra Sūtra*, first translated into Chinese around the middle of the fifth century CE. In the Lokakṣema corpus of texts, Harrison never finds '*dharma-kāya*' meaning 'body which is *Dharma*', that is, some kind of mysterious cosmic Buddha-body, but either 'having the *Dharma* as body' or body, that is, collection, of *dharmas*: 'qualities, principles of existence, truths or teachings' (1992: 67), as in Śrāvakayāna texts. This, then, undercuts, at least for the early Mahāyāna, the 'prevailing notion that the *dharma-kāya* is some kind of Buddhist "Godhead" or "Cosmic Body" invented by the followers of the Mahāyāna' (1992: 73–4). The *Trikāya-stava* (*EB*.4.3.4), a devotional text which was popular by the end of the fourth century, still speaks of the *dharma-kāya* as 'neither one nor many' – which is in tension with interpretations of 'it' as a single entity, and when it is said that it is 'to be realized by oneself', this makes it sound much like the *Dharma* refuge of Theravāda Buddhism, which in the highest sense is *Nirvāṇa*, but it also includes the path to this. Harrison sees early Western interpreters of Buddhism, such as Edward Conze (1904–79) and D. T. Suzuki, as having been influenced in their translations by later developments in *Trikāya* thought, and, in Suzuki's case, even by attempts to convey Buddhist ideas in ways more appealing to Christians. Later scholars, too, have 'misconstrued many key passages . . . metaphor gives way to metaphysics' (Harrison, 1992: 74). He leaves open the question of whether Yogācāra developments of the doctrine need re-examining, to see if these have also been misinterpreted.

In the developed Yogācāra idea of the *Dharma*-body, this is the shared kind of inner nature that any Buddha attains, their Buddha-ness (*buddhatā*): omniscient knowledge, and the perfect wisdom and other spiritual qualities through which a *Bodhisattva* becomes a Buddha. It is also known as the *Svābhāvika-kāya* or Intrinsic-body, as it is without any adventitious defilements in its self-contained nature. It is the other-dependent nature (see pp. 135–6) purified of the deluded subject/object distinction, pure radiant consciousness, a timeless thusness which is the real nature of things, the basis from which the ordinary worldly phenomena of the illusory constructed nature appear. These phenomena include the other two bodies, which are simply ways in which the *Dharma*-body appears to people. The *Śrīmālā-devī-siṃhanāda Sūtra* says that when obscured by defilements, it is the *Tathāgata-garbha*. It is also the *Dharma-dhātu*, or *Dharma*-realm (see pp. 141, 147): the universe as truly understood by a Buddha, for a Buddha knows that his nature exemplifies the nature of reality, has the same empty nature as other phenomena, and interpenetrates them. A Buddha's knowledge is beyond the subject/object duality, so he cannot be distinguished from the thusness which is the 'object' of his knowledge. As a Buddha's knowledge is also omniscient, he is non-different from *all* empty phenomena: he is the 'same' as everything.

In Tibet, the influential Gelugpa school, to which the Dalai Lama belongs, and which sees the Prāsaṅgika-Mādhyamika as expressing the highest truth, regards the *Dharma*-body as having two aspects: the Intrinsic-body (in their sense) and the Gnosis-body (*jñāna-kāya*).[22] The first of these is the emptiness of inherent existence in *any* phenomenon, including a Buddha's enlightened consciousness: the non-nature which is, at any time, the very nature of *dharmas*, their *dharma*-ness (*dharmatā*). As this emptiness gives the minds of being the lack of fixity that enables them to become enlightened, this is the *Tathāgata-garbha* as understood in a self-emptiness way (see p. 126). The Intrinsic-body is also something *particular* to Buddhas: their lack of defilements and obscurations to omniscience. The Gnosis-body is a Buddha's omniscient consciousness, empty of the deluded subject/object distinction, and compassionately ready to respond to the needs of beings.

The Chinese Tiantai school, which sees the *Lotus Sūtra* as expressing the highest truth in Buddhism, regards the Buddha of the *Sūtra*'s chapter on the life-span of the *Tathāgata* (see pp. 163–4) as the eternal *Dharma*-body, rather than as a particular Enjoyment-body Buddha.[23] In this aspect, he is sometimes identified as Vairocana, the 'Resplendent One' referred to in the *Avataṃsaka Sūtra*. This idea is also found in the Tendai, the Japanese form of this school, and the Nichiren school, which split off from this. Among other things, this overcomes a tension between seeing past earthly Buddhas as Transformation-bodies of an Enjoyment-body *Śākyamuni*, but the next earthly Buddha being seen as a manifestation of *Maitreya*, once he

[22] Dalai Lama, 1971: 120–5; Williams, 2009: 182–4.

[23] *Lotus Sūtra* translation by Kato *et al.*, p. 382: *trikāya* entry in glossary; Williams, 2009: 157–8, 162.

is a Buddha; and indeed the Yogācārins had criticized the idea of past earthly Buddhas as having been Transformation-bodies of one heavenly Enjoyment-body (Griffiths, 1994: 120–1).

In the Huayan and the Japanese tantric Shingon school, the *Dharma*-body is personified as the Buddha (Mahā-)Vairocana. It is regarded as having a very subtle, shining, limitless material form from which speech can come, due to the autonomous working of the *Bodhisattva* vows. In this respect, the *Dharma*-body seems to become somewhat akin to the concept of God in other religions. In the tenth century, the process of personification was carried further, in the concept of the *Ādi*, or 'Primordial', ever-awakened Buddha, named variously as Samantabhadra, Vajradhara or Vairocana. The Yogācārins resisted the idea of a first and always enlightened Buddha, though, arguing that any Buddha needs to be first inspired by a past Buddha, and needs then to develop the *Bodhisattva* perfections (Griffiths, 1994: 121).

On the ultimate level, only the *Dharma*-body in its aspect as emptiness of inherent existence or the non-dual nature of consciousness is real; the Transformation- and Enjoyment-bodies, known in the Śūnyatāvādin perspective and Tathāgata-garbha thought as 'form (*rūpa*)' bodies, are provisional ways of talking about and apprehending it. The real nature of a *Tathāgata* cannot be seen by seeing his physical form, as '*Tathāgatas* have the *Dharma* as their body' (*Asta*.513, as translated at Harrison, 1992: 52). Transformation- and Enjoyment-body Buddhas, Pure Lands, and high-level *Bodhisattvas*, then, are not truly real: any more than the book you are now reading or the eyes with which you read it! In emptiness, nothing stands out with separate reality. At the conventional level of truth, however, such Buddhas, etc. are just as real as anything else. Indeed in popular Mahāyāna practice, the Enjoyment-body Buddhas and advanced *Bodhisattvas* are treated as wholly real, and rebirth in their Pure Lands is ardently sought through faith. The rather disconcerting feeling generated by switching between ultimate and conventional truth is nicely captured in an explanation given by a Chinese recluse to John Blofeld, in which he also draws on the Chinese idea of 'One Mind' (see p. 145): 'Believe me, the *Bodhisattvas* are as real as earth and sky, and have infinite power to aid beings in distress, but they exist within our common mind, which, to speak the truth, is itself the *container* of earth and sky' (Blofeld, 1987: 151).

From the conventional perspective, the high-level *Bodhisattvas* and heavenly Buddhas are those who have heroically striven to be close to, or attained to, Buddhahood. From the ultimate perspective, they are the symbolic forms in which the 'minds' of empty 'beings' perceive the *Dharma*-body, the all-encompassing totality which is the *Dharma*-realm described in the *Avataṃsaka Sūtra*. As an analogy, the *Dharma*-body can be seen as a blinding blaze of light. Only a Buddha can see this in an unobstructed fashion. The obstructions remaining in the minds of advanced Noble *Bodhisattvas* mean that the light is filtered and they see it as Enjoyment-body Buddhas. In ordinary beings, the light is even more filtered, so that they can only see it in the form of Transformation-bodies. Those with great insight, though, can see it in the thusness of any worldly object, for as the *Avataṃsaka Sūtra* says, the whole mystery is present in a grain of dust. To non-Buddhists such as Hindus, the *Dharma*-body is known in the form of Enjoyment-bodies which take the form of the gods of their religion (*Lanka*.192–3). In Buddhist Japan, indeed, the major *kamis*, or deities, of the indigenous Shintō religion became identified with particular heavenly Buddhas or high-level *Bodhisattvas*.

Given the idea of the huge length of the *Bodhisattva* path, no one who started out on this path under the historical Buddha, roughly 2,500 years ago, will have had time to become a Buddha since then. *Bodhisattvas* who were already well advanced on their path at that time could, in principle, have become Buddhas since – but not in our world-system, as the classical Mahāyāna still had the idea that while the influence of a Buddha lasts in a world, no new Buddha will appear there (Griffiths, 1994: 119–26). As we will see below, though, the tantric path is seen to be able to speed up the *Bodhisattva* path and potentially bring Buddhahood in one lifetime. In any case, our world can still contain advanced *Bodhisattvas*, or Transformation-bodies of them (for they, like Buddhas, can have these), or of Buddhas from other Buddha-fields. Thus, in Tibetan Buddhism, there are roughly 3,000 *trulkus* (*sprul-sku*), Transformation-bodies, mostly in the form of recognized rebirths of past teachers who are seen to have the ability to choose their next rebirth (Samuel, 1993: 281–6). A few are seen as 'supreme' *trulkus* or *namtruls* (*rnam 'phrul*), emanations.[24] These are beings who are seen as re-manifested Transformation-bodies. These include the Dalai Lamas, seen as Transformation-bodies of the advanced *Bodhisattva* Avalokiteśvara, and the Panchen Lamas, seen as Transformation-bodies of Amitābha Buddha. These are typically regarded as actual forms of these beings, though another view, favoured by the present Dalai Lama – perhaps from modesty, or because he takes a more modernist view – is that they embody their virtues and have thus been specially blessed by them (Williams, 2004: 2–23).

[24] And sometimes as *trulpas* (*sprul pa*), though this can be used of emanations of beings other than Buddhas and advanced *Bodhisattvas*.

Thus the Dalai Lamas are seen to particularly express the compassion of Avalokiteśvara.

In East Asian Buddhism, the tenth-century Chan monk Budai (see p. 176) is seen to have been a manifestation of Maitreya, and is actually referred to as Milo-fo, Maitreya Buddha, and the Japanese Nichiren Shō-shū sees Nichiren (see pp. 233–4) as a Buddha (for Nichiren-shū, he is a great *Bodhisattva*). Moreover, the term 'buddha' can sometimes be used rather loosely for a person of advanced spiritual development, and there is the idea that, due to the Buddha-nature, everyone is already a buddha, even if they do not yet act like one. Furthermore there is a Japanese practice in which, around seven days after their death, people are given posthumous names and are popularly considered to become buddhas (Reader, 1991: 41, 90): the word for a departed soul, *hotuke*, also means a buddha, and the after-death rituals are seen to help the dead become both a revered ancestor and a buddha. Here Shintō influence may be at work, though there is also the Buddhist idea of going to the Pure Land and then becoming a buddha.

THE MAHĀYĀNA PANTHEON

Of the 'countless' heavenly Buddhas and advanced *Bodhisattvas*, some of the named ones became focuses of devotion as saviour beings, with specific advanced *Bodhisattvas* also symbolizing and exemplifying specific spiritual qualities.[25] In the cults of these beings, one sees the more faith-related 'religious' aspects of the Mahāyāna, as a balancing complement to its refined wisdom aspect, and with the compassion-based *Bodhisattva* path as a bridging concern. One sees a yearning for continuing contact with the Buddha(s) leading to ideas of a variety of saviour beings and ideal realms, these being located in many areas of the immense cosmos that earlier Buddhism had previously conceived of. In this process, one might say that a variety of Buddhist super-*devas*, *devas* with liberating wisdom and huge compassion, become the focus of devotion, contemplation and calls for inspiration and spiritual and practical help. Magical cosmic vistas open up, in which sources of help-from-beyond are drawn on to complement the help had from one's own inner resources, and from the Buddha's inspiration, the power of his relics, his taught and chanted *Dharma*, and the ongoing support of the monastic community. One can see this as showing a 'theistic' side to the Mahāyāna, though it is a theism that is framed by the idea that the celestial *Bodhisattvas* and Buddhas are empty of inherent existence.

[25] See Getty, 1988, and Williams, 2009: 218–43 for an overview of them.

Of the heavenly Buddhas, one of the earliest mentioned is Amitābha,[26] who became of central importance in the Pure Land schools of Eastern Buddhism, where he is known as Amituo (A-mi-t'o) (China) or Amida (Japan).[27] The name 'Amitābha', or 'Immeasurable Radiance', is an expression of light symbolism. In early Buddhism, radiance was already associated with Brahmā gods, wisdom and the 'brightly shining' level of mind (see p. 68), and of course radiance is associated with the *Tathāgata-garbha*. The alternative name of 'Amitāyus' means 'Immeasurable Life', referring to the immensely long life of this Buddha. His cult is based on three key *Sūtras*: the 'Larger' and 'Smaller' *Sukhāvatī-vyūha*, or 'Array of the Happy Land' *Sūtras*, and the *Guanwuliangshoufo Jing* (*Kuan-wu-liang-shou-fo Ching*). The last of these may have originated in Kashmir (north-west India), Central Asia or China, or evolved through all three; its title in Sanskrit would be the *Amitāyur-buddhānusmṛti Sūtra*: 'The *Sūtra* on recollection of the Buddha Amitāyus'. The 'Larger' *Sūtra* was composed by the late second century CE, and the 'Smaller' one was first translated into Chinese in 402 CE, though Japanese scholars often see it as older than the 'Larger' one.

The 'Larger' Happy Land *Sūtra* tells how, many eons ago, under a previous Buddha, the monk Dharmākara aspired to become a Buddha in a future time. After hearing of the Pure Lands of many Buddhas, he resolved that he would generate one combining the excellences of all of them. He then made forty-seven *Bodhisattva* vows,[28] describing these excellences, and affirming that he would only become a Buddha when his *Bodhisattva* course had been karmically potent enough to produce such a Pure Land, which it is seen to have been, for he became the Buddha Amitābha. In his Pure Land, called Sukhāvatī, the Happy Land, beings are seen to have, if they wish, immeasurably long lives, in which progress to Buddhahood is accelerated. Their next life will be as a Buddha, unless as advanced *Bodhisattvas* they choose to be reborn elsewhere to aid beings. Inhabitants of this realm are seen to have the highest 'perfections', memory of previous lives, and the ability to see myriads of other Buddha Lands. They immediately hear whatever *Dharma* they wish, have no idea of property, even with regard to their own bodies, and have the same happiness and meditative powers of those in deep meditative trance. Sukhāvatī is seen as a paradise full of 'jewel-trees', which stimulate calm and contemplative states of mind, a realm

[26] *BS1*.232–6; *BS2*.8; *EB*.5.4.1; Blum, 2002: Cleary, n.d.; Cowell, 1985; Gómez, 1996; Ingaki, 1995; Malalasekera *et al.*, 1964; Pas, 1995: 145–64.
[27] Or these followed by *-fo* (China) or *butsu* (Japan): Buddha.
[28] In the Sanskrit text; forty-eight in its Chinese version.

where everything is as beings wish, free from temptation and defilement. Most importantly, in line with one of Dharmākara's vows, he is seen to appear before any dying being who aspires to awakening and devoutly calls him to mind, with his *Bodhisattva* helpers conducting him or her to his Pure Land.

Amitābha's Happy Land is seen to lie far away in the 'western' region of the universe. To attain rebirth there, the 'Larger' Happy Land *Sūtra* says that a person needs to earnestly desire it, have faith in Amitābha, arouse the *bodhi-citta*, generate karmic fruitfulness, and dedicate the power of this towards such a rebirth. In the 'Smaller' *Sūtra*, there is only reference to repeating and remembering Amitābha's name for several nights before death. In the *Amitāyur-buddhānusmṛti Sūtra*, it is possible to scrape into the Happy Land on a bare minimum of personal worth, due to Amitābha's grace. Only someone who slanders or obstructs the *Dharma* cannot be reborn there. A person must nevertheless prepare himself before death by serenely reciting *Nāmo'mitābhāya Buddhāya*, 'Honour to Amitābha Buddha', ten times while continually thinking of Amitābha. In the Happy Land, however, an evil-doer will initially go through a kind of purgatory, being reborn in a 'lotus' which remains closed for many ages before he can benefit from the Pure Land. Others will be closer to awakening according to the extent of their faith, virtue, meditation and knowledge. The notion of gaining rebirth in this Happy Land has thus long provided a hope to people struggling with existence, living less than perfect lives. If currently unable to behave like true *Bodhisattvas*, the environment of the Happy Land will enable them to do so, and the immeasurably long life-span there will encompass the hugely long *Bodhisattva* path.

A heavenly Buddha whose popularity was perhaps earlier than that of Amitābha, is Akṣobhya, the 'Imperturbable'.[29] The *Akṣobhya-vyūha Sūtra* has a version that was translated into Chinese near the end of the second century CE, and may have originated in north-west India, though many images of this Buddha from north-east India show his popularity there. His Pure Land, Abhirati, is seen to lie to the east, and the *Bodhisattva* who produced it is said to have been very moral and free from anger. His realm is seen as a beautiful environment, free of inconveniences such as brambles or mountains, menstruation for women, or the need to grow food. Those there may become *Arhats* or progress towards Buddhahood. A person gains rebirth in this land by assiduous moral and spiritual practice, vowing to be reborn there, dedicating his or her karmic fruitfulness to this, and

[29] *EB*.5.4.3; Malalasekera *et al.*, 1964; Nattier, 2000.

visualizing Buddhas teaching in their Buddha-fields. Eventually, Akṣobhya will pass into final *Nirvāṇa*, though his place will later be taken by another Buddha. While not important in Chinese Buddhism, he eventually became important in Indo-Tibetan tantric Buddhism, as one of a set of five Buddhas depicted in many *maṇḍalas*, with him often as the central one (see p. 185).

Another popular heavenly Buddha is Bhaiṣajya-guru (Jap. Yakushi), the 'Master of Healing',[30] his Pure Land being in an 'eastern' region of the universe. His vows are such that faith in him and sincere repetition of his name will lead to the curing of illnesses and deformities, and give a person insight into his own bad karma, so that he will reform and aspire to Buddhahood. Calling on him at death may also enable a person to avoid an unfortunate rebirth that bad karma would otherwise lead to. Texts dedicated to him are the *Bhaiṣajya-guru Sūtra*, perhaps composed in Central Asia and first introduced into China in the fourth century, and 'The *Sūtra* on the Seven Buddhas'. His cult has been particularly important in Japan, where he has been called on to protect the state from disasters and disease. He is usually portrayed as blue in colour, and holding a bowl of medicine.

Devotion to heavenly Buddhas seems to have predated that to advanced *Bodhisattvas*. In Mahāyāna texts translated into Chinese by Lokakṣema in the late second century CE, advanced *Bodhisattvas* such as Mañjuśrī are referred to, but as wise and inspiring examples, rather than saviour beings who were focuses of cults. *Bodhisattvas* as objects of cults do not appear in Chinese translations until the second half of the third century, and there appears to have been little iconographical portrayal of them in India until the sixth century. Paul Harrison (2000) argues that, other than Maitreya, they may have originally been the products of inspired literary imagination, to provide embodiments of the ideals of the developing Mahāyāna movement. This development may also have been fed by inputs from meditative experiences: if certain qualities were being assiduously cultivated, it is natural that people would come to experience visions of beings who were particularly rich in such qualities, and then to start to give names to such beings. In time, these would then take on a life of their own in the developing movement, and would be called on for help in developing such qualities, or to bring other benefits. From this stage, they would then function as transcendent, celestial saviour beings.

[30] *EB*.5.4.2.; Malalasekera *et al.*, 1968; Birnbaum, 1980.

Of the advanced *Bodhisattva*s, the earliest one referred to is Maitreya (Pali Metteyya), 'The Kindly One', who is acknowledged even in the Theravāda and other early schools as the being who will become the next Buddha on earth (*D*.III.75–7). In the Mahāyāna, it is said that he is a tenth stage *Bodhisattva*,[31] residing – as in the earlier tradition – in the Tuṣita heaven of our world, not in a Pure Land. After attaining Buddhahood, he will descend in the form of a Transformation-body to be the next Buddha to teach on earth.[32] In Tibet and Korea, Maitreya is sometimes shown, in anticipation, as a Buddha. Maitreya is generally shown seated on a throne with lowered legs, crossed at the ankles. In China, 'Maitreya Buddha' (Milo-fo) is also often portrayed in the form of one of his recognized manifestations, the tenth-century Budai (Pu-tai). This Chan monk was a jolly, pot-bellied, wandering teacher who carried presents for children in his cloth bag (*budai*). In the West, images of Budai are often known as 'Laughing Buddhas'. In China, the cult of Maitreya was earlier than that of Amitābha, and originally a rival to it. There came to be a number of millenarian movements focused on Maitreya – nine during the fifth and sixth centuries – led by people claiming to be incarnations or prophets of Maitreya who would usher in his golden age.

Avalokiteśvara, while not the most popular of advanced *Bodhisattva*s in the early Mahāyāna, in time was to become so.[33] He is often seen as a tenth-stage *Bodhisattva* who is one of the two helpers of Amitābha, along with Mahāsthāmaprāpta ('He of Great Power'). The latter represents Amitābha's wisdom, and acts on his behalf in opening people's eyes to the need for liberation. Avalokiteśvara enacts Amitābha's compassionate concern for the world, and is in fact seen as the very embodiment of compassion, the driving force of all *Bodhisattva*s. In China, he is widely understood to now be a Buddha, working for the salvation of all beings. One text, 'The *Sūtra* of the Secret Method of Master-perceiver *Bodhisattva* with a Thousand Bright Eyes'[34] says that he became a Buddha before Śākyamuni, and taught him; others see his having become a Buddha after Śākyamuni, on his mythical mountain home of Potalaka, where he is now seen to dwell. This has been variously identified as somewhere in south India, the mountain island of Putua (P'u-t'o) off the Chinese coast (an important centre of devotion to him), or the Potala Palace of the Dalai Lama in Lhasa, the capital of Tibet.

31 *BSI*.237–42; Sponberg and Hardacre, 1988.

32 Though the Yogācāra saw the existence of a *Bodhisattva* in the Tuṣita heaven as itself a Transformation-body form (Griffiths, 1994: 91)!

33 *EB*.5.2.1. Malalasekera *et al.*, 1967; Tay, 1976–7; Blofeld, 1988.

34 Taishō 20: 1065; my thanks to Gene Reeves for this reference.

The name Avalokiteśvara means 'The Lord Who Looks Down (with compassion)', while in China he is called Guanyin (Kuan-yin), 'Cry Regarder', or Guanshiyin (Kuan-shih-yin), 'Regarder of the Cries of the World', these names being based on a Sanskrit form 'Avalokitasvara'. In Japan he is known as Kwannon or Kannon, and in Tibet as Chenrezi (sPyan ras gzigs): the 'All-Seeing'. In all Mahāyāna lands, he is the focus of devout worship, contemplation and prayers for help.

An important text on him is the chapter[35] in the *Lotus Sūtra* on the 'All-sided One' which originally circulated as a separate *Sūtra*, and is often still treated as such. It is believed that his manifestations in many worlds are in forms which may include a Transformation-body Buddha, an *Arhat*, a Hindu god, a monk, nun, layman or laywoman. He even manifests himself in hells, and in the worlds of ghosts or animals, to help such beings. In one Chinese painting, he is shown appearing in the form of a bull, in order to convert a butcher from his wrong livelihood. His various manifestations may mysteriously disappear after they have appeared to help someone, or they may live out a full life, or even a series of them, as in the case of the Dalai Lamas of Tibet (see p. 171).

Avalokiteśvara is the focus of the *Kāraṇḍavyūha Sūtra*, which even talks of him creating our world – sun, moon and earth – and the gods of Hinduism, with them then ruling with his permission (Williams, 2009: 222). He is known as Maheśvara, 'Great Lord', as is the Hindu god Śiva, is sometimes said to have a blue throat, like Śiva, and there are possible historical connections between their cults. The idea of a *Bodhisattva* creating our world, the world that the historical Buddha had said was *duḥkha*, painful, is a fascinating development, but is perhaps an understandable one in the context of rivalry between Buddhism and a resurgent Hinduism and its great creator deities. In any case, Avalokiteśvara is seen here as only creating one region of the cosmos, not the whole universe, and is not seen as creating sentient beings other than Hindu gods, or particular Transformation-bodies.

Like most other high-level *Bodhisattva*s, Avalokiteśvara is shown crowned and with royal garments, rather than the monastic robes of a Buddha. This is to show that *Bodhisattva*s are more in contact with the world than Buddhas, and more actively engaged in helping beings. In his crown, Avalokiteśvara has an image of Amitābha, the inspiration of his work. He holds a lotus bud, which symbolizes the pure beauty of his compassion, or the worldly minds of beings which he encourages in their efforts to 'bloom'

[35] No. 24 in the Sanskrit version, 25 in the Chinese.

into awakening. He is often shown with his hands cupped together around a 'wish granting jewel' (*cintā-maṇi*). Originally a pre-Buddhist amulet against evil, this became an emblem of his willingness to grant righteous wishes. Its clarity also symbolizes the natural purity, hidden by coverings of spiritual defilements, in the minds of beings. These defilements are suggested by the cupping hands, also said to be like a lotus bud.

Another important advanced *Bodhisattva* is Mañjuśrī,[36] 'Sweet Glory', who with Samantabhadra, 'Universally Good', is said to be the helper of the heavenly Buddha Śākyamuni. A tenth-stage *Bodhisattva*, he is seen as the greatest embodiment of wisdom, and has the special task of destroying ignorance and awakening spiritual knowledge. Accordingly, he is shown holding a lotus on which rests a copy of a Perfection of Wisdom *Sūtra*, and wielding a flaming sword, symbolic of the wisdom with which he cuts through delusion (see Plate 3). He is seen as the patron of scholars and a protector of *Dharma*-preachers. Those who devoutly recite his name, and meditate on his teachings and images, are said to be protected by him, to have many good rebirths, and to see him in dreams and meditative visions, in which he inspires and teaches them. He is seen to have a particular association with mount Wutai (Wu-t'ai) Shan in China. He is sometimes seen as a Buddha, and in any case can manifest himself as a Buddha or in many other forms. The *Ajātaśatru-kaukṛtya-vinodanā Sūtra*, composed by the second century CE, sees him as having inspired Śākyamuni Buddha to take up the *Bodhisattva* path (*BS*2.20; Harrison, 2000: 169–70), and a *Sūtra* cited at *Ss*.13–14 has him vowing to remain until the end of *saṃsāra* so as to help beings.

The advanced *Bodhisattva* Kṣitigarbha, or 'Earth-matrix', is also associated with Śākyamuni's Buddha-field, our world (Hua, 1974). In Japan, where he is known as Jizō, he is the second most popular *Bodhisattva.* His vows were to help humankind until the next Buddha appears on earth. He acts as a guardian of travellers, those in trouble and women and children. He is regarded as continually working for the alleviation of those reborn in hells, and to be particularly concerned about the destiny of dead children. He is shown in a monastic robe, as a genial figure holding a staff with which he opens the doors of hells. In Japan, statues of him are often found at the side of country roads and mountain paths, and they are placed in graveyards as prayer-offerings for the good rebirth of dead children and miscarried or aborted foetuses (Harvey, 2000: 333–41).

[36] Tribe, 1997; Harrison, 2000.

Plate 3: A *t'angka*, or hanging scroll, depicting the *Bodhisattva* Mañjuśrī, at a Tibetan Buddhist College in the Lake District, England.

THE TANTRIC PERSPECTIVE

In Indian Buddhism, a form of the Mahāyāna developed which in time saw itself as a new, more powerful 'vehicle' to salvation. This came to predominate in the lands of Northern Buddhism, while in Korea and Japan it exists alongside various other forms of the Mahāyāna.

The new approach was based on a large body of texts called *Tantras* – or later classified as of this type – which outline complex meditational 'systems' which incorporate ritual, magic and a rich symbolism. Texts of a tantric type began to appear from the second century CE and were being translated into Chinese in the third and fourth centuries CE. They continued being composed in India until around 1200 CE. Nevertheless, some were said to have been taught by the historical Buddha, to a select band of disciples who had then passed them on; others were seen as taught by the tantric deity Vajradhara, seen as a form in which the Buddha appeared to legendary masters of the past.

The Mantranaya and the origin of tantric Buddhism

Tantric practice centres on the ritual evocation, especially through the use of *mantras* and visualization, of deities that are seen as in some sense awakened (see pp. 185–9). Such methods were originally for worldly ends – part of the Mahāyāna aim of compassionately helping beings. In time, they became part of advanced practices for those who had prepared themselves by prior Mahāyāna training. These aimed to generate deep religious experiences which can lead to Buddhahood more quickly than the hugely long *Bodhisattva* path. The emphasis on power and efficacy can be seen as a development of the idea of meditative psychic powers (Pali *iddhi*, Skt *ṛddhi*), which was there from the beginning in Buddhism.

The early phase of tantric Buddhism called itself the '*Mantra-naya*' or 'way of *mantras*' (the term *Mantra-yāna* was a later coining), this being seen as a complement to the *Pāramitā-naya*, or 'way of the perfections', as part of Mahāyāna practice (Williams and Tribe, 2000: 141–7). From the third century, *Sūtras* contained *dhāraṇīs*, short formulas 'preserving' or 'maintaining' the *Dharma* and aiding its followers. The pre-Mahāyāna *Sūtras* also contain *parittas* (see pp. 249–50), or short protective chants. Building on such a basis, the practice of using *mantras*, or sacred words of power, was adopted from Hinduism, where they were originally used in the *Vedas*. These 'mental instruments' were used to contact gods, or as spells to gain a good harvest, health, children or even to bewitch someone. In tantric Buddhism, they also became chanted in rites to aid visualizations, in which a particular holy being is conjured up out of emptiness, as a basis for developing the spiritual qualities that the being embodies.

Each tantric deity is seen to have its *mantra*, in short and long forms, which consist of a syllable, word or string of these that are seen to express and embody its nature. The most famous *mantra* is that of Avalokiteśvara: *Oṃ maṇi padme hūṃ*, which is first found in the *Kāraṇḍavyūha Sūtra*. *Oṃ* and *hūṃ* are sacred sounds used in the *Vedas*, the first being seen as the basic sound of the universe. *Maṇi padme* literally means 'O jewelled-lotus lady'. In later exegesis, *maṇi* is seen as referring to the jewel that this *Bodhisattva* holds, while *padme* refers to his symbol, the lotus. A complex set of symbolic explanations is also given to this *mantra*. For example, its six syllables are associated with the six perfections, or the six realms of rebirth. As it is recited, rays of light may be visualized as streaming out to the beings in these realms.

The elements which led to the rise and development of tantric Buddhism, in a context where tantric methods were affecting all Indian religions, were various. Tantric forms of Indian religion were particularly strong within strands of Hinduism centred on the deity Śiva, a paradoxical figure seen to periodically re-create and later destroy the world, and an ascetic practitioner of yoga, dwelling in cremation grounds, whose symbol was the *liṅgam*, or phallus, emblem of creative power. Tantric Buddhism developed in competition with tantric Śaivism, and, borrowing from its complex symbolism and ritual techniques, adapted them in Buddhist guise, geared to Buddhist goals (Berkwitz, 2010: 125–8). In doing so, it claimed that the Śaiva texts had originally been taught by the Buddha, or that the Hindu gods associated with them were forms in which Buddhas or advanced *Bodhisattvas* compassionately appear; it also described the subjugation of Śiva by the Buddhist deity Vajrapāṇi (Williams and Tribe, 2000: 182–4). Alexis Sanderson sees Śaiva influence on all Buddhist tantric texts, this becoming more pervasive over time. For the *Yoginī Tantras* (ninth to tenth centuries), 'almost everything concrete in this system [i.e. symbols etc.] is non-Buddhist in origin even though the whole is entirely Buddhist in its function' (1994: 92).

Tantric Buddhism more broadly augmented the magical side of Buddhism with elements drawn from the beliefs and practices common in agricultural societies, in addition to *mantras*. These were seen to aid 'success' (*siddhi*) in both worldly and spiritual matters. Rituals used in the monasteries to bring aid to their supporting communities, and as a preliminary to higher practices, came in time to play an increasing role within such higher practices, aimed at soteriological goals. Further, female 'deities' and reinterpreted Hindu ones were admitted into the greatly expanded pantheon of Buddhist holy beings.

Key Mahāyāna concepts were used to give a rationale for developing new methods for attaining spiritual realization. If the world was non-different from *Nirvāṇa*, *any* object or action could potentially be used as a route to ultimate truth, if the motive and method were right, using skilful means. Rites could be used to harness the unconscious forces of passion or hatred and 'magically' transmute them into their opposites. If all was 'thought-only', complex and vivid visualizations could be developed as a new, and transforming, world of experience.

The phases of tantric texts, and the Vajrayāna

The development of Indian tantric texts, and their concerns, are summarized in Table 3 (Williams and Tribe, 2000: 151–64), at least in terms of how the developed tradition came to look back on the texts:

Table 3 *Indian tantric texts*

Tantra *type and dates*	*Texts: number in the Tibetan* Kangyur (bK'-'gyur) *or canon of scriptures, and key examples*	*Features*
Kriyā/Action. 2nd–6th centuries.	Over 450. Termed *dhāraṇī, kalpa, rājñī* or *sūtra*. *Mahā-megha Sūtra*; *Mañjuśrī-mūla-kalpa*.	Magical rituals to aid and protect. Use *mantras* and early forms of *maṇḍalas*. Both used in other classes, below.
Caryā/Practice. Early–mid 7th century.	8. *Mahā-vairocana*/*Mahā-vairocan'ābhisaṃbodhi Sūtra*.	Practices include identifying with a deity, e.g. a Buddha.
Yoga/Union. Early 8th century onwards.	15. (*Sarva-tathāgata*)-*Tattva-saṃgraha Sūtra*; *Sarva-durgati-pariśodhana Tantra*; *Vajra-śekhara Tantra*; *Nāma-saṃgīti*.	Minor sexual elements.
Mahā-yoga/Great Union or *Yogottara*/Higher Yoga. By end of 8th century.	37 'Father' *Tantras* *Guhyasamāja Tantra*; *Māyā-jāla Tantra*; *Vajra-bhairava Tantra*.	Sexual elements and forbidden/ impure substances.
Yoginī/Female *Yogin* or *Yoga-niruttara*/ *Yogānuttara*/Highest Union. 9th–10th centuries.	82 'Mother' *Tantras* *Hevajra Tantra*; *Kāla-cakra Tantra*; *Saṃvara Tantra*.	Sexual elements and forbidden/ impure substances, plus cremation-ground links from Hindu *Śaiva* Tantra. Practitioners = (*Mahā-*)*siddhas*.

In Tibetan Buddhism, the last two classes of *Tantra* are seen as *Anuttara-yoga*/Supreme Union *Tantras*: the *Mahā-yoga* ones being broadly equivalent to the 'Father' class of these and the *Yoginī* ones to the 'Mother' class of them. The Nyingmapa school uses the terms *Mahā-yoga* and *Anu-yoga*/Complementary Union for these, and adds *Ati-yoga*/Surpassing Union, also known as *Dzogch'en* (*rDzogs chen*; 'The Great Completion/Perfection'). *Kriyā, Caryā* and *Yoga Tantras* are sometimes termed 'outer *Tantras*', and the remaining ones 'inner *Tantras*'. The tantric levels vary mainly according to the type of personal relationship established with a deity: that of the *Kriyā* level is likened to the exchange of amorous glances between a man and woman, while that of the more advanced *Anuttara-yoga* level is like the bliss of sexual union. These two levels are the ones most often practised in Tibet.

The earlier texts had more of an emphasis on worldly aims (cf. *EB*.7.5.2), but over time, more supra-worldly aims, related to Buddhahood, became more important. From the time of the *Yoga Tantras*, that is, the eighth century, tantric modes of Buddhism increasingly became the dominant ones in India, and tantric Buddhism saw itself as a new and more powerful spiritual vehicle, whose means bring Buddhahood, not just worldly protection. It thus started to call itself the *Vajra-yāna*, the 'Thunderbolt' or 'Diamond' vehicle. In pre-Buddhist India, the *Vajra* was seen as the power-laden sceptre of Indra, ruler of the Vedic gods. In early Buddhism, the *Arhat* was said to have a mind like a *Vajra* (Pali *vajira*, *A*.I.124), and in the Mahāyāna a tenth-stage *Bodhisattva* is said to enter a *Vajra*-like meditative state. Tantric Buddhism saw the *Vajra* as a good symbol for its powerful methods and the awakened mind. This was because it saw it as a substance which was: as irresistible as a thunderbolt, suggesting the overwhelming power of the awakened mind to destroy spiritual obstacles; as hard as a diamond, suggesting the indestructible nature of the awakened mind; and as clear as empty space, suggesting the 'empty', void-like nature of such a mind. The *Vajra*, then, symbolized awakening, ultimate reality, and the *Dharma*-body, personified as Vajrasattva, the *Vajra*-being. The aim of the Vajrayāna adept was to become conscious of the identity between Vajra-sattva and his 'own' empty 'nature', so as to 'become' such a 'being'. To do this was to gain awakening, or *siddhi*: (spiritual) 'success'.

The *Vajra*-sceptre became a symbolic ritual implement, as did the *Vajra*-bell (see Bechert and Gombrich, 1984: 261), as held by the figure in Plate 4. These primarily symbolize skilful means and wisdom, a complementary pair whose perfect union is seen as sparking off awakening. There are many explanations of the symbolism of the parts of the implements. For example, the centre of the sceptre symbolizes emptiness, and three bulges either side

Plate 4: Vajrapāṇi holding a *Vajra* and *Vajra*-bell.

of it represent the sense-desire, elemental form, and formless worlds, which 'emerge' from emptiness. The axis and four prongs represent the five main Vajrayāna Buddhas, whose unity is suggested by the merging of the prongs at the end of the sceptre. The whole is thus a supreme image of the *Dharma*-body, from which the world and Buddhas emerge. The handle of the bell also represents the timeless *Dharma*-body, while the bell part, with its fading tone, represents the conditioned world of change. Together, they show that these two are inextricably linked.

The figure of Vajrapāṇi, or 'Vajra-in-hand', became increasingly important through the phases of tantric Buddhism. In early Buddhism, he was a minor deity (*yakṣa*, Pali *yakkha*) who threatens to use a thunderbolt to split open the heads of people when they refused to answer a crucial direct question from the Buddha (*D.*1.95; *M.*1.231). The Theravāda commentaries identify him, though, with Sakka (Skt Śakra), the key Vedic deity Indra, seen in the Theravāda as a stream-enterer follower of the Buddha. In tantric

Buddhism, he becomes at least an advanced *Bodhisattva*. Many other holy beings also have '*vajra*' added to their names, or are newly referred to beings, such as Vajradhara ('Vajra-holder') and Vajrasattva, arguably forms of Vajrapāṇi.

Tantric deities and adepts

As the *Tantras* developed, the pantheon of holy beings expanded, and new kinds were focused on. In the *Kriyā Tantras*, there were the awakened beings of the Buddha 'family', plus the unawakened peaceful deities of the *Padma* (Lotus) family and fierce ones of the *Vajra* family; these last two awaited full conversion to Buddhism, respectively by Avalokiteśvara and Vajrapāṇi. In the *Caryā Tantras*, the most important Buddha is Vairocana ('The Resplendent One') – also important in the *Avataṃsaka Sūtra*. In the *Yoga Tantras*, two further families of deities are added: the *Ratna* (Gem) and *Karma* (Action). Vairocana, of the Buddha family, remains central, but he is surrounded, in *maṇḍalas*, by the other Buddhas in their Pure Lands: Akṣobhya ('The Imperturbable'; *Vajra* family) to the East; Amitābha ('Immeasurable Radiance'; *Padma* family) to the West; Ratnasambhava ('The Jewel-born One'; *Ratna* family) to the South; Amoghasiddhi ('Infallible Success'; *Karma* family) to the North. In the *Mahā-yoga Tantras*, Akṣobhya and his *Vajra* family become central. This is also so in the *Yoginī Tantras*, which add many horrific-looking fierce and semi-fierce deities, for example Hevajra and Cakrasaṃvara, and female deities, such as Vajravārāhī, Vajrayoginī and Vajraḍākinī.

The five main Buddhas are called the five 'Conquerors (of delusion and death)' (Skt *Jina*) and the 'central' Buddha is the specific focus in the relevant text and related *maṇḍala*. All are seen as expressing aspects of the *Dharma*-body. Some systems add a sixth Buddha: Vajrasattva, Vajradhara or Samantabhadra ('Universally Good'), representing the ever-awakened *Ādi*, or primordial, Buddha, seen as unifying and manifesting the other Buddhas.

The deities belonging to each of the five families are seen to correspond to the predominant faults of particular kinds of people, who will particularly benefit from working with them (Williams and Tribe, 2000: 156–9; Berzin, 2002). Within each family, deities may be of four different types, to correspond to further variations in human character (Snellgrove, 1987). They may be male or female, and peaceful or wrathful in appearance. The male, peaceful ones are the five *Jinas* themselves and the ordinary *Bodhisattvas* of the Mahāyāna. The wrathful ones are for dealing with strongly negative emotions. The anger which the deity shows is not that of a vengeful god, but, hate-free, it aims to open up the practitioner's heart by devastating his hesitations, doubts, confusions and ignorance. The male wrathful deities are called *Heruka*s and also *Vidyā-rājā*s, 'Knowledge-kings'. Plate 5 shows a popular one called Yamāntaka, 'Conqueror of Death', the wrathful form of the *Bodhisattva* Mañjuśrī. By visualizing such a fearful form, which has the head of a raging bull, the practitioner can clearly see the danger in his own tendency to anger, and can transmute it into a wisdom. Yamāntaka is shown free and unbridled, like all wrathful deities, trampling on corpses representing the 'I am' conceit and its limiting, deadening influence. On his main head he wears as ornaments a crown of skulls, representing the five main human faults; the garland of heads hanging at his waist represents his triumph over many confused and neurotic ideas. One also finds the Vajrayāna using, as ritual implements, human skulls as drums, and human thigh-bones as a kind of trumpet. The use of such items helps impress on the mind the ever-present possibility of death, and also aids in overcoming the inability to see potential purity in everything.

Plate 5 not only shows Yamāntaka, but also a wrathful female deity. These are called *Ḍākinī*s ('sky-goers'), which are seen as playful but tricky beings, often portrayed wielding a chopper and holding a skull-cup containing poison (human faults) transformed into the nectar of Deathlessness. The *Ḍākinī*s are sometimes portrayed as the consorts of the *Heruka*s, just as female peaceful deities are sometimes seen as the consorts of the male peaceful ones. A consort is called the 'Wisdom' (Skt *Prajñā*) of her respective male partner, and represents the power which makes possible the engaged skilful means of the male. Together, the two form a wisdom-energy, often represented, as in Plate 5, as 'Father', and 'Mother' (in Tibetan, *Yab* and *Yum*), in sexual union (*BS2*.54). This form symbolizes the idea that, just as sexual union leads to great pleasure, so the union of skilful means and wisdom leads to the bliss of awakening. Such sexual symbolism is minimized in East Asian Tantric Buddhism, as it offended against Confucian propriety.

A male peaceful deity is called a *Bhagavat*, or 'Lord', while a female one is called a *Bhagavatī*, or 'Lady'. While some of the twenty-one forms of the *Bodhisattva* Tārā, the 'Saviouress', are wrathful, the peaceful 'Green' and 'White' forms are the most popular 'Ladies' (*EB*.5.2.2; see Plate 6).[37] In Tibet, these came to be among the most well-loved deities, one becoming Tibet's patron goddess. They are seen as graceful, attractive and approachable, and as ever-ready to tenderly care for those in distress. Their compassionate

[37] *BTTA*.176; Williams and Tribe, 2000: 169.

Plate 5: A Tibetan image of the *Heruka* Yamāntaka and his female consort.

nature, in responding to those who call on them, is reflected in the story that they were born from two tears shed by Avalokiteśvara when he saw the horrors of hell. Tārā is seen to have vowed to remain in female form throughout her lives as a *Bodhisattva* then Buddha. Indeed, Tibetans

Plate 6: An image of Tārā in the courtyard of a temple in Kathmandu, Nepal.

often see her as a female Buddha. Her cult seems to have developed by the seventh century. She is sometimes said to be the 'Mother of all the Buddhas', as was the earlier deity Prajñāpāramitā, 'Perfection of Wisdom' (*EB*.4.2.1).

The goal and philosophy of the Vajrayāna remained Mahāyānist, but its means were seen as far more powerful, so as to lead to Buddhahood in just *one* lifetime:[38] a kind of 'super-charged' Mahāyāna, but Mahāyāna nonetheless. It was seen to work, not so much by building up the causes of Buddhahood, but by visualizing and evoking the *result* of this path so as to make the result *part* of the path to it. In Tibet, it is often held that tantric means are needed for anyone to complete the path to Buddhahood. Here one might say that, while the classical Mahāyāna came to include celestial Buddhas and *Bodhisattva*s that were seen to help a being along the path, in the Vajrayāna, these beings are also internalized, as *inner* aids. Of course, in early Mahāyāna, part of the great compassion of the *Bodhisattva* was a willingness to take the long route to Buddhahood rather than the shorter one to becoming an *Arhat*. As *Tantra*s were seen to shorten the path to Buddhahood, this particular excellence of compassion could be seen to be reduced and, in *this* respect, the path made more akin to the pre-Mahāyāna path, though it retained the Mahāyāna strong emphasis on compassion.

One who has attained various kinds of magical accomplishment, even up to Buddhahood, by the tantric path is called a *Siddha*, or 'Accomplished One', and there are accounts of the lives of the eighty-four *Mahā-siddha*s or 'Great Accomplished Ones', who lived between the eighth and twelfth centuries.[39] They were usually long-haired laypeople, often from low castes, who lived unconventional wandering lives as crazy-sounding wizard-saints, including people who are known as the Wise Washerman, the Divine Cobbler, the Mad Princess, *Siddha* Two-teeth and the Rejected Wastrel. They were inspired and trained by *Guru*s and in turn became great *Guru*s. They sought to inject a fresh dynamic spirit into the somewhat over-systematized Mahāyāna, and re-emphasized the role of the lay practitioner, though they could also be monks. They included Tilopa (988–1069) and Nāropa (1016–1100), who were important inspirers of Tibetan Buddhism, and some are seen to have passed on teachings to Padmasambhava and Vimalamitra (both eighth century). Padmasambhava is seen as a 'second Buddha' (Samuel, 1993: 19), and also as a Transformation-body of Amitābha Buddha (Powers, 2007b: 371). Other *siddha*s spread tantric Buddhism to

38 Katz, 1982: 283–4; Samuel, 1993: 21; Williams and Tribe, 2000: 166.
39 *BTTA*.193; *EB*.5.5.7; Ray, 1989; Samuel, 1993: 419–35.

China, Indonesia and Cambodia. The tantric way fairly soon became absorbed into the mainstream of Indian Mahāyāna, being studied at monastic universities from the eighth century. Nevertheless, in the Vajrāyana phase of Mahāyāna Buddhism, differences with Śrāvakayāna-emphasizing traditions become much more marked than in earlier Mahāyāna.

Features of tantric Buddhism

Significant features which tend to be found in tantric forms of Buddhism, in various mixes (Williams and Tribe, 2000: 147–50, 175–6), are:

- The use of esoteric language, of veiled meaning, and the need for keeping aspects of the rites and their meaning secret.
- The importance of the *Guru*, a spiritual preceptor known in Tibet as *Lama* (*bla-ma*), or 'Superior One', or the *Vajrācārya* (*Vajra*-master). He (occasionally, she) is not only a spiritual teacher, but also one who gives *abhiṣeka* – 'empowerment' to use, or 'consecration' into, the various tantric practices – and is to be visualized as embodying the qualities of the Buddhas. Such a person, whether a monk, nun or advanced lay practitioner, guides a small group of initiates in the use of the potent tantric methods.
- The practitioners undertake *samayas*, tantric vows to do such things as daily recite a *sādhana*, a ritual text concerning a visualization, or to carry out certain practices, such as to pay special respect to women. These vows are in addition to ordinary lay or monastic precepts, and *Bodhisattva* vows.
- A re-evaluation of the status and role of women, so that many holy beings are seen as female, and respect for women – seen as symbolizing wisdom – is greatly praised.
- The ritual use of *maṇḍalas*, sacred 'circles' portraying the world of, and as seen by, a particular deity and his or her entourage (see pp. 349–52).
- Analogical thinking, in which correspondences are seen to exist between such things as aspects of a ritual, factors of body or mind, elements, or human faults, and particular Buddhas or kinds of wisdom – so that work on one thing links one to that which corresponds to it. The many iconographic features of tantric deities are also given precise symbolic meaning.
- A re-evaluation of the body, with it seen as the arena for sacred action, and as encompassing a mystical structure involving channels (*nāḍī*) and centres (*cakra*) through which energy (*prāṇa*) flows. Here, it should be

noted that while Buddhism up to the earlier forms of the Mahāyāna had often talked of the unlovely aspects of the body, early Buddhism had also said that *Nirvāṇa* is to be found through practice in 'this fathom-long carcase' (see p. 70).

- A re-evaluation of negative mental states, such as pride and lust (*rāga*).
- Sexual yoga.
- Antinomian acts and foul offerings.

In regard to mental states such as pride/conceit and lust, while Buddhism had always seen these as things to overcome, the Pali *Bhikkhunī Sutta* (*A*.II.145–6) says, 'based on craving, craving can be abandoned . . . based on conceit, conceit can be abandoned', in the sense that the craving to be an *Arhat* and feeling that one is oneself capable of becoming one, can be a spur to attaining this state (Webster, 2005: 129–40). Nevertheless, sexual desire can play no part in this. That said, greed (related to lust) is seen as a lesser fault than hatred and delusion, even though it, like delusion, fades slowly (*A*.I.200). In Mahāyāna Buddhism, the *Bodhisattva* is seen to remain in *saṃsāra* by retaining a sliver of the lesser of these faults in the form of holy attachment. In tantric Buddhism, there is both the idea of developing 'tantric pride' when one identifies with an awakened deity in visualizing him or her, and a praising of lust. The *Hevajra Tantra* asserts that the world is bound by passion or lust, and may also be released by it (Williams and Tribe, 2000: 150). This referred to the practice of sexual yoga, in which the power of lust is harnessed, and transmuted into a power for liberation, by means of visualizing the flow of various mystical energies within the body. The Vajrayāna also spoke of its goal in positive terms as 'great bliss' (*mahā sukha*). While this was on the analogy of sexual bliss, the term is not without precedent even in the Pali *Sutta*s, where *Nirvāṇa* is sometimes seen as the 'highest bliss' (*parama sukha*: *M*.I.508), albeit without any sexual allusions. In any case, tantric sexual yoga can be done in a visualized, rather than physical form, so that monastics can preserve their celibacy.

Taboo- and convention-breaking practices were used to overcome attachments and aid insight into seeing everything as the *Dharma*-body, beyond 'dualistic' divisions (*BTTA*.186; *EB*.5.5.1–2). At a time when vegetarianism had become widespread among Mahāyāna Buddhists and high-caste Hindus, such rites might be carried out after eating various meats and drinking wine, in a cemetery at night, the sexual partner being a low-caste girl visualized as a deity. In early Buddhism, cemeteries had often been seen as good places in which to meditate on the nature of the body and death, but they were also favoured as places to practise by Śaiva ascetics, and the bizarre-sounding tantric rites were certainly an innovation in Buddhism.

Such tantric rituals could also include the use, either as offerings, or as things to ritually consume, of foul substances such as urine and faeces, or flesh from dogs, elephants or even humans. While disgust at such things is common to most human cultures, the Brahmanical aspects of Hinduism had heightened ideas of ritual 'purity' associated with its caste system, and vegetarianism was seen as a 'pure' way of living. Śaiva *tantra* went against some of these norms to exploit the power of the forbidden, and tantric Buddhism did likewise. That said, rather tamer versions of these rites became integrated into the monastic practice and yogic training in Tibetan tantric traditions. Forms of flesh and foul 'elixirs' are still to be added to the periodic tantric feasts celebrated in monastic communities, but they are represented in various ways, such as by consecrated medicinal pills, added to alcoholic liquid, and distributed by the teaspoon.

Practice in relation to the 'foul' can also be seen to build on precedents, in the pre-Mahāyāna *Sūtras*, on transcending normal disgust and attachment. It is said that the best kind of 'success' (Pali *iddhi*, Skt *ṛddhi*) is to be able, at will, to enter a state in which one can perceive things in a variety of ways.[40] As explained in the *Paṭisambhidāmagga* (*Patis*.II.212, cf. *Vism*.382), these are: (a) 'perceiving the non-disgusting in what is disgusting (*paṭikkūle*)': by developing lovingkindness for a person with a disagreeable body, or analysing a disagreeable thing or substance into its elements; (b) 'perceiving the disgusting in what is non-disgusting': by focusing on the foul/unlovely (*asubha*) aspect of, or impermanence of, an agreeable sense-object. The final aim, is: (c), 'avoiding both the disgusting and non-disgusting, may I abide in equanimity, mindful and clearly aware'. The aim in *tantra* was also to end with the same attitude to everything, but in this case, all was to be seen as pure, so the second aspect above was not used, though of course negative attachments are seen as attacked with the help of wrathful deities.

Tantric texts also sometimes say one should 'kill' or 'lie', but such recommendations were generally interpreted symbolically, or seen as applying principles found already in earlier Mahāyāna Buddhism: that sometimes, in constrained circumstances, compassion might require one to break a precept in the course of helping someone, this being a form of 'skill in means' (Williams and Tribe, 2000: 178–80). Support for Buddhist moral norms is still generally expected. While the tantric adept Tilopa accepted a woman running a very successful liquor store as his disciple, he made her close it down as a condition of accepting her (Ray, 1980: 229–30).

[40] *D*.III.112–13 , cf. *M*.III.301, *A*.III.169–70, 430–31, *S*.V.119–20.

Tantric Buddhism is broader than the sexual and transgressive aspects which appeared in its later Indian phases, but an example of this kind of material, from the *Guhyasamāja Tantra*, a *Mahā-yoga* one, is *BTTA*.187. Here, enjoyment of all desires, not discipline, is said to be the way to Buddhahood, and sexual yoga is advocated; the *yogin* sees himself as identical with the supreme object of worship; the objects of the five senses are identified with the five main Buddhas, starting with Vairocana; of the senses, *citta*, thought or mind/heart, is the essence, and it is Samantabhadra, the hidden Lord; one should concentrate on the body, speech and mind of all Buddhas, and aspire to attain these; the recitation of *mantras* is central. One should contemplate: the Perfection of Wisdom, 'naturally translucent' (like the *Tathāgata-garbha*) and unproduced; Nirvanic 'non-production', translucent, signless and neither dual nor non-dual. One should focus on deities of the *Vajra* family of Akṣobhya Buddha, which is associated with wrath/hatred, and should worship a twelve-year-old girl. Thus will anyone attain Buddhahood.

The *Mahā-siddha* Saraha (ninth century?) developed an iconoclastic, intuitionist approach which dispensed with *mantras* and complex rites as sidetracks. In his *Dohā-kośa* (*BS1*.175–80; *BTTA*.18), he says that perfect knowledge may be developed without being a monk, but while married and enjoying sense-pleasures. He rigorously emphasizes the importance of spiritual practice, under a *Guru*, rather than dying of thirst 'in the desert of multitudinous treatises' (v. 56). Such practice involved cultivating a state free from thought, a spontaneous, natural state akin to the innocence of a child. This '*Sahaja-yāna*' way would make manifest the 'Innate' (*Sahaja*), the profound, non-dual ultimate reality which could be seen in everything (*EB*.5.5.6; *BS2*.53).

Among the latest tantric texts is the *Kāla-cakra* (*BP*.23), or 'Wheel of Time', *Tantra*, for which the present Dalai Lama often gives initiations. Dating from the eleventh century, it warns of Muslim invasions of India, and in some ways seeks to form an alliance with Hinduism against these. It looks forward to a future ideal world of peace, and the arising of a Buddhist saviour of the world from the mythical land of Śambhala. It also has teachings on manipulations of inner bodily energies, and on astrology and medicine.

CHAPTER 7

The Later History and Spread of Buddhism

INDIA AND CENTRAL ASIA

During the Hindu Gupta dynasty (320–540), which ruled much of north India, Hinduism grew stronger. Buddhism generally continued to flourish, though, with the rulers patronizing both religions. During the century from around 450 CE, the White Huns, originally from Central Asia, devastated monasteries in Afghanistan, northern Pakistan and areas of western India. By the seventh century, a slow recovery was being made in the north-west, with the Buddhism of southern Pakistan remaining strong. In western and some southern regions of India, though, it was losing out to Hinduism and Jainism. From 750 CE, the mostly Buddhist Pāla dynasty ruled in the north-east, patronizing Buddhism and supporting five monastic universities, the major one being the internationally renowned Nālandā. In the eleventh century, Pāla rule weakened, and it was followed in 1118 by the Hindu Sen dynasty. From 986 CE, the Muslim Turks started raiding north-west India from Afghanistan, plundering western India early in the eleventh century. Forced conversions to Islam were made, and Buddhist images smashed, due to the Islamic dislike of 'idolatry'. Indeed, in India, the Islamic term for an 'idol' became '*budd*'. By 1192, the Turks established rule over north India from Delhi. The north-eastern stronghold of Buddhism then fell, with the destruction of Nālandā university in 1198. In the north-east, east and Kashmir, Buddhism lingered on for another two centuries or so, with some royal patronage in the latter two areas. In Kashmir it was forcibly stamped out by the Muslims in the fifteenth century. Buddhist refugees fled to south India (where Hindu kings resisted Muslim power), South-east Asia, Nepal and Tibet. What is now known as the Theravāda school continued on the south-east coast, in Tamil Nadu, until at least the seventeenth century (Berkwitz, 2010: 142), before it withdrew from the war-torn region to the island of Ceylon. From the sixteenth century, however, it had been reintroduced from Burma to the north-eastern fringes of the Indian sub-continent.

North of Tibet, in the area known as Central Asia, was an international trade-route called the Silk Road, as silk was exported along it from China to north-west India, and even to the Mediterranean world. Among Indian merchants were many Buddhists who, often accompanied by wandering monks, helped spread the religion in Central Asia.[1] Buddhism was present in the region from the second century BCE, and in the first century CE the Sarvāstivāda fraternity flourished in several of the city states of the area, with many monks drawing on Mahāyāna ideas and practices. Central Asia remained Buddhist until the tenth or eleventh century, when the Turks brought conversions to Islam.

What factors contributed to the decline and virtual demise of Buddhism within the Indian sub-continent (excluding the Himālayan region and Ceylon)?[2] One was a dilution of the distinctiveness of Buddhism relative to the rising power of Hinduism. Mahāyāna writers were quite critical of Hinduism, but the surface similarities of Hindu and Mahāyāna devotional cults and Tantrism may have led the laity to perceive the two religions as quite similar. Hinduism also borrowed elements from Buddhism. The devotees of the god Viṣṇu came to frown on animal sacrifices and to practise vegetarianism (also influenced by Jainism), while some Śaivites (followers of the god Śiva) viewed caste-distinctions as being of little relevance to religious practice. The great theologian Śaṅkara (788–820) developed a monasticism paralleling that of the *Saṅgha*, and also used the Buddhist concept of 'two levels of truth', already borrowed by his predecessor Gauḍapāda (seventh century). Hinduism could not ignore the Buddha; so by around the sixth century, it recognized him as the ninth incarnation of Viṣṇu. In contrast, in Buddhist Ceylon, Viṣṇu came to be seen as a *Bodhisattva*, that is, one who would be a Buddha in the future.

Hindu hostility also played a part. The Buddha incarnation was seen as a way to delude demons into denying the authority of the *Vedas*, so as to lead them to hell. Śaṅkara described the Buddha as an enemy of the people, and sporadic persecution was directed at Buddhists from the sixth century. There is also evidence for social ostracism of Buddhists, probably due to their lack of enthusiasm for the caste system, which became particularly influential on society from around 600 CE. While Buddhism sought to influence society from its monastic centres, Hinduism wove itself into the fabric of society through the caste system, with Brahmin priests having a

[1] On this region, see Bechert and Gombrich, 1984: 99–107; Puri, 1987.
[2] Joshi, 1977: 379–418; Ling, 1980: 24–46.

certain authority over others within it. Unlike the more universal Buddhism, Hinduism came to be seen as the 'national' religion of India.

The Muslim invasions were the worst blow, however, for Buddhism had few royal defenders and, unlike Hinduism with its *Kṣatriya* warrior class, it lacked a soldierly spirit. The *Saṅgha*, whose survival is essential for the flourishing of Buddhism, was an easily identifiable and thus vulnerable institution. The devastation of agriculture due to the invasions also meant that the laity no longer had surpluses to support their monks. The *Saṅgha* thus died out in most areas, and could not be revived without existing monks to ordain new ones. Between the alien Muslims, with their doctrinal justification of a 'holy war' to spread the faith, and Hindus, closely identified with Indian culture and with a more entrenched social dimension, the Buddhists were squeezed out of existence. Lay Buddhists were left with a folk form of Buddhism, and gradually merged into Hinduism, or converted to Islam. Buddhism therefore died out in all but the fringes of its homeland, though it had long since spread beyond it.

LAṄKĀ[3]

The history of the island of Ceylon or Laṅkā (now known as a state as Sri Lanka) and its Buddhism is chronicled in works such as the *Dīpavaṃsa*, *Mahāvaṃsa* (*Mvm.*) and *Cūlavaṃsa*, respectively of the fourth, sixth and thirteenth to nineteenth centuries CE. The island was well connected to many areas of mainland India through sea transport. The monks of Mahinda's mission of around 250 BCE brought the Pali Canon in their memories, along with the developing commentaries. These continued to be orally transmitted until around 20 BCE, when invasion and famine meant that parts of the Canon could be lost as monks died (Berkwitz, 2010: 48–51). A council was therefore held to see to the writing down of the Canon, in Pali, and the commentaries in the local Sinhala dialect of Indo-Aryan. Mahinda established an indigenous *Saṅgha* in Laṅkā, and his sister, the nun Saṅghamittā, brought a cutting from the original *Bodhi*-tree to plant in the capital Anurādhapura. She also brought relics of the Buddha, which were enshrined in the first of the many *Dagabas* (*Stūpas*) to be built on the island.

Since then, Buddhism has been the major religion. The *Saṅgha* taught and advised the kings, and at several times in the island's history it

[3] On this, see Bechert and Gombrich, 1984: 133–46; Berkwitz, 2010: 121–5; Gombrich, 2006; Rahula, 1966.

influenced the choice of ruler. The Sinhalese have long felt that civilized life is impossible without the presence of monks in society. They required their kings to be Buddhist, and from the tenth century saw them as *Bodhisattvas*. In general, the most devout kings have been the most active in social welfare: building irrigation works, supporting medical and veterinary services, and providing homes for the incurable. Education was supported via support for the monks, who became the educators of the people.

In the fifth century, the monk Buddhaghosa came to Laṅkā, as he had heard that extensive commentaries on the scriptures existed there. He was allowed to translate these into Pali, edit them and add certain thoughts of his own. To prove his suitability for this task, he first composed the *Visuddhimagga* (*Vism.*), or 'Path of Purification', a masterly survey of meditation and doctrine which became the classic expression of Theravāda Buddhism (Berkwitz, 2010: 113–17). Laṅkā and other Theravāda lands produced a thriving Pali literature: chronicles, commentaries and sub-commentaries, and works of devotion, doctrine and *Abhidhamma*. Of particular note is Anuruddha's *Abhidhammattha-saṅgaha* (perhaps late sixth century), a systematic compendium of *Abhidhamma*.[4]

Three monastic fraternities developed, though all used the Pali Canon as scripture. The oldest was centred on the Mahāvihāra, the 'Great Monastery' established by Mahinda, which went on to become one of the major centres of the Buddhist world. Then, late in the first century BCE, King Vaṭṭagāmaṇi donated the Abhayagiri monastery to a favoured monk. As this was not given to the community as a whole, the monk was expelled from the Mahāvihāra fraternity, leading to a schism (*Mvm.*33.95ff.). Later, the Jetavana fraternity formed, again due to donation of a monastery to an individual monk, by King Mahāsena (274–301 CE; *Mvm.*37.32ff.). The monks of the Abhayagiri fraternity were more receptive to Mahāyāna ideas than the more conservative Mahāvihāra monks, while the Jetavana monks vacillated. Mahāsena supported the Mahāyāna and destroyed the Great Monastery, but his successor rebuilt it.

Terms used in Laṅkā to refer to what were probably Mahāyāna ideas were (Harvey, 2008: 118–20): 'the teaching of the great emptiness (*mahā-suññatā*)'; Vitaṇḍa-vāda – a frivolous teaching based on jugglery of words and vain arguments; Vetulya-vāda, the 'enlarged (Skt *vaitulya* or *vaipulya*) teaching', based on texts that are not the word of the Buddha, perhaps seen as rather inflated and hyped up. The closely related term *vaitulika* means

[4] Bodhi, 1993; Wijeratne and Gethin, 2002.

'magicians'. The associated texts were seen as corrupting Buddhism and over the centuries some kings came to burn them.

The Mahāvihāra fraternity was later strengthened by the work of Buddhaghosa, and continued to be resistant to Mahāyāna ideas, tenaciously preserving its traditions. Nevertheless, it did draw on various ideas and practices from north India *if* they were seen as compatible with their traditions (Cousins, 1997a: 391). Rahula (1966: 128) claims that Buddha-images were mainly popularized in Laṅkā by Mahāyānists, and then fully accepted.

In the eighth and ninth centuries, there was a period of considerable Mahāyāna and tantric influence in Laṅkā (Deegalle, 1999). In the ninth century, tantric Vājiriyavāda (Skt Vajrayāna) arrived and had influence for at least 300 years (Gombrich, 1971: 31). Gombrich claims that a tenth-century inscription saying that only *Bodhisattvas* could be kings of the island shows Mahāyāna influence (1971: 31). He describes some Kandyan statues of Metteyya (Skt Maitreya) Buddha as having a small meditating Buddha in its headgear, and as holding a lotus, both of which elements may derive from past statues of the Mahāyāna *Bodhisattva* Avalokiteśvara (1971: 92–3), and he refers to a little-worshipped deity Nātha ('Lord') as a survival of Avalokiteśvara, for whom this was an epithet (1971: 177–8).

From the late tenth century, there was a decline in Buddhism and monastic discipline due to Tamil invasions and civil wars. In the early eleventh century, the monks' ordination-line had to be reimported from Burma, where it had recently been taken, but the nuns' Order died out. King Parakkama Bahu I (1153–86) halted the decline and purified the *Saṅgha*, also unifying it on the basis of the Mahāvihāra fraternity (*Cūlavaṃsa* 78.20–3; *EB*.6.4). Around this period, Southern Buddhism entered its golden age in both Laṅkā and South-east Asia, incorporating selected Mahāyāna/Mantranaya practices and aspirations into its existing framework of *Sutta* teachings, Vibhajjavādin *Abhidhamma*, and a *Vinaya*, or monastic code, described as that of the Theriyas (Skt Sthāvira, Elders), that is, seen as going back to the Elders of the first schism. Buddhaghosa says that the monk who asked him to write the *Visuddhimagga* was 'a member of the lineage of the Mahāvihāra-vāsins, illustrious Theriyas, best of Vibhajjavādins' (*Vism*.711–12). When active in south India, the monks of the three Laṅkān fraternities had been known as of the Laṅkā (Taprobane) school: the Tāmraparṇīyas (Pali Tambapaṇṇiyas), and the equivalent terms Laṅkāvaṃsa and Sihalavaṃsa also became well known in Laṅkā and then South-east Asia. In north India, the three schools of Laṅkā and their Indian affiliates tended to be referred to collectively as the Sthāvira fraternity

(Skilling, 2009: 66–7). In time, the term 'Theriyas' and name Theravāda became preferred among well-educated monks (Cousins, 1997a: 391). Yet only from the early twentieth century was 'Theravāda' popularized as the name for the Buddhism of Laṅkā and much of South-east Asia (Skilling, 2009; Skilling *et al.*, 2012), in a wider context in which the pejorative term 'Hīnayāna' (see pp. 110, 112–13) was being applied by some to the tradition, and in a wish to differentiate themselves from 'Mahāyānists' while accepting them within 'Buddhism'. The Theravāda self-image was one of a school that has preserved the original teachings of the Buddha without distortions, or indeed, as is now sometimes said in Sri Lanka, in its 'pristine purity'.[5] Mahāyāna teachings tend to be seen either as alien corruptions, to be ignored, or simply studied as part of the history of Buddhism.

In the colonial period, Laṅkā became a prized goal for Western powers. The Catholic Portuguese (1505–1658), then the Calvinist Dutch (1658–1796) controlled certain lowland coastal regions. In the late sixteenth century, persecution by a Śaivite king led to a decline in which the ordination-line for monks (but not novices) was again lost (Gombrich, 2006: 166). Only in 1753 was it successfully reintroduced, from Siam (now called Thailand). The British finally brought an end to the highland kingdom of Kandy in 1815, so as to rule the whole island. While only the Portuguese had persecuted Buddhism, each colonial power tried to transmit its own brand of Christianity to the islanders.

SOUTH-EAST ASIA EXCLUDING VIETNAM[6]

A small Buddhist community may have existed among the Mons of southern Burma/central Thailand since the time of Asoka. In any case, a tradition using Pali was probably introduced to the Mons in the early centuries CE, perhaps from India. In northern Burma, the Sarvāstivāda fraternity and Mahāyāna forms of Buddhism, along with Hinduism, were present from the third century CE, with tantric Buddhism arriving by the ninth century. A change came about when a northern king, Anawratā (1044–77), unified the country, and then his successor Kyanzitth (1084–1113) gave great support to the Theriya tradition of the Mons, with study of a version of the Pali Canon that was brought from Laṅkā. Since that time, Theriya/Theravāda

[5] For example the Sri Lanka *Daily News* (29 Oct. 2011) quoted the prime minister of the island as saying 'Sri Lanka had been able to protect Buddhism in its pristine purity for more than 2,500 years' (www.dailynews.lk/2011/10/29/news03.asp).

[6] On this, see Bechert and Gombrich, 1984: 147–70; Hazra, 1982.

Buddhism increasingly became the main religion of the Burmese, though tantra-like elements have lingered on (*BP*.30), and the gods (*nats*) of the pre-Buddhist nature religion have a place in Buddhist cosmology (Hall, 1981: 159–63). By the fifteenth century, a Theravāda ordination-line from Laṅkā was finally established as the orthodox one.

Merchants brought Brahmanism to the Khmers of Cambodia in the first century CE, and north Indian Sanskritizing forms of Buddhism in the second century (Bechert and Gombrich, 1984: 159–70). From the sixth century, a mix of Hindu Śaivism and Mahāyāna was the religion of urban areas, though there was some royal persecution of Buddhism in the seventh century. From 802 to 1432, there was a powerful Khmer empire, with the king sometimes being seen as an incarnation of both Śiva and a great *Bodhisattva*. This culture built both the originally Hindu temple complex of Angkor Wat, dedicated to the god Viṣṇu, and the nearby Buddhist one of Angkor Thom. Tantrism also had an influence. From the twelfth century, Mon missions won over the lower classes and country folk, who seem to have preferred Theravāda to the complex religion of the court. In the fourteenth century, royalty turned to the Theravāda, and the tradition became well established in the country as a whole.

As regards the situation in the region that is now Thailand, a form of Buddhism using Pali, probably related to the Theriya tradition, seems to have been predominant from around the fifth century CE, though there were also cults to *Bodhisattvas* such as Avalokiteśvara and to Brahmanical deities such as Viṣṇu, Śiva and Sūrya. When Khmer power declined in the thirteenth century, the Tai people, who had migrated from China, were able to establish various states in the area, drawing on the Mon Theriya tradition and Brahmanical cults, with Brahmanical rituals continuing up to the present as a minor strand alongside Buddhism (Skilling, 2009: 75). Like Burma, Siam/Thailand had links with the Buddhism of Laṅkā over the centuries.

The Tai people also settled in Laos. Early in the fourteenth century, the Cambodian wife of a ruler helped convert the royal court and people to Theriya Buddhism, so that it became the official religion of Laos in around 1350. In the fifteenth century, Theriya Buddhism also spread to the Dai, another branch of the Tai people in what is now the Yunnan province of China.

Buddhism was present in the Malay peninsula from the fourth century, with a Buddhist state existing in the north in the fifth century. From this time, Śaivism and Mahāyāna Buddhism were influential in the peninsula and on the Indonesian islands of Java and Sumatra. In the seventh century, the Sarvāstivādins also became well established on Sumatra, and tantric Buddhism became popular in the region in the eighth century. In around 800, a huge *Stūpa*, still the largest monument in the southern hemisphere, was built at Borobuḍur, Java (Bechert and Gombrich, 1984: 63), depicting scenes from many texts, but especially the *Avataṃsaka Sūtra*. From the eleventh century, the dominant religion of the region increasingly became a mix of the tantric forms of Buddhism and Śaivism. In the fourteenth century, Islam was brought by merchants, and in the fifteenth century it rapidly spread to become the dominant religion. The Hindu–Buddhist syncretism still exists on the small island of Bali, however, and Buddhism is also found among the Chinese community in the region.

Yogāvacara: *esoteric Southern Buddhism*

Especially in South-east Asia, Southern Buddhism includes a strand of practice that Heinz Bechert has called 'tantric Theravāda'. This has been especially studied in Cambodia by François Bizot, but there is also evidence of it in Laos and parts of Thailand and Burma, and marginally in Laṅkā. Lance Cousins (1997b) prefers to call the tradition 'Esoteric Southern Buddhism', and Kate Crosby calls it by a term used by the tradition: the *Yogāvacara*, or 'Practitioner of Spiritual Discipline' tradition (2000: 141). As a tantra-like form of Theravāda, it is Mantranaya, rather than Vajrayāna in form. Kate Crosby's summary (2000: 141–2) of the features of this kind of tradition includes:

1. The creation of a Buddha within through the performance of ritual by placing and recognizing within one's body the qualities of the Buddha, which in turn become the Buddha.
2. The use of sacred language, combined with microcosm to macrocosm identity. Sacred syllables or phrases are used to represent a larger entity. Groups of syllables of a particular number represent other significant groups of the same number. This use of sacred language includes use of heart syllables (akin to Mahāyāna *dhāraṇī*), mantras and yantras [sacred diagrams]. . .
5. Esoteric interpretations of words, objects and myths that otherwise have a standard exoteric meaning or purpose in Theravāda Buddhism.
6. The necessity of initiation prior to the performance of a ritual or practice.

Tantra-like practices include protective chants and diagrams which are seen to symbolically surround a person with *Arahats* and protective *Suttas* (*EB*.6.6). Also, the body is visualized as the *Bodhi*-tree, and there may be visualization of a 'crystal sphere' in the body, representing one's potential for awakening or enlightenment. There is also a kind of esoteric yogic pilgrimage. One of these is called 'the Road to Laṅkā', where 'Laṅkā' symbolizes the womb of Mahāmāyā, the mother of the Buddha. Here, the initiate regresses to the womb of Mahāmāyā to be reborn as the Buddha. Short chants may be done in a revolving way, such as one whose syllables represent the names of the books of the *Abhidhamma – (Dhamma)-saṅgaṇī, Vibhaṅga, Dhātukathā, Puggalapaññatti, Kathāvatthu, Yamaka, Paṭṭhāna* – and are seen to encapsulate their wisdom:

saṃ[7] *vi dhā pu ka ya pa*
vi dhā pu ka ya pa saṃ
dhā pu ka ya pa saṃ vi
pu ka ya pa saṃ vi dhā
ka ya pa saṃ vi dhā pu
ya pa saṃ vi dhā pu ka
pa saṃ vi dhā pu ka ya
saṃ vi dhā pu ka ya pa. . . (cf. *BP*.29)

A *yantra*, known as *yan* in Thailand, consists of words and letters mindfully drawn, on paper, cloth (usually robe cloth), silver or gold foil, or as tattoos, in a flowing script to form a *maṇḍala*-like pattern (Shaw, 2009: 119–21). They are often used for magical protection, but also have meditative resonances. Their subtle linear form is used to inscribe syllables related to esoteric Buddhism, for example those of *na mo bu ddhā ya* (*namo buddhāya*: reverence to the Buddha), with each syllable corresponding to a certain element and one of the five *khandhas*.

There are various possibilities for the origin of these traditions, all of whose terms are in Pali and whose basic concepts are Theravāda: influence from the Abhayagiri fraternity, the Sarvāstivāda, or tantric Mahāyāna Buddhism or Hinduism. It may be, though, that the trend towards tantric methods in Indian religions simply produced a Theravāda Buddhist variant in South-east Asia, without this being shaped by either tantric forms of the Mahāyāna or Hinduism. Cousins has explored the possibility that it developed within the Mahāvihāra tradition in Laṅkā and beyond, as there is evidence for secret texts within this (1997b: 191–3). In Thailand, though, nineteenth-century reforms spearheaded by the new Dhammayutika Nikāya sought to move away from using such esoteric practices.

THE LANDS OF NORTHERN BUDDHISM[8]

Nepal shared in the developments of north Indian Buddhism and Hinduism, and by the thirteenth century, Hinduism had become the

[7] *Saṃ* is pronounced much as *Saṅ*.

[8] On this, see for example Batchelor, 1987; Bechert and Gombrich, 1984: 108–14 (Nepal) and 253–70 (Tibet); Berkwitz, 2010: 156–62 (Nepal); Powers, 2007b; Samuel, 1993, 2012; Snellgrove and Richardson, 1968.

dominant religion, favoured by rulers. By the fifteenth century, monks were increasingly abandoning celibacy and forming an hereditary caste, and scholarship was declining. Buddhism has been found mainly among the Newars of the Kathmandu valley. Since 1786, when the Gurkhas, from India, conquered the country, the Newars have held out against rulers' attempts to fully Hinduize this area. There are also various ethnic groups in areas bordering Tibet, influenced by its religions (*EB*.7.2); the Gurkhas also came to include some of these.

Buddhism did not reach Tibet, the heartland of Northern Buddhism, until relatively late, the country being isolated and mountainous. In time, Tibetans and their Indian teachers successfully transplanted and continued the complex and rich form of tantric Mahāyāna found in late Indian Buddhism, prior to its demise in most regions of India itself. While Tibetan thinkers often showed originality, they saw themselves as simply clarifying the ideas of Indian Buddhism.

The indigenous religion of Tibet was some form of shamanism focused on spirit-essences within a person and their close relationship to various deities (Samuel, 1993: 438–44). Divination through spirit-possession was important, and there was also a ritual cult of dead kings, presided over by court priests called *Bön-pos*. It is wrong, though, to see the whole early tradition as 'Bön' (Samuel, 1993: 10–13). While the early Bön tradition eventually faded with the coming of Buddhism, one of the same name developed from the eleventh century, and shamanism continued as a key mode of Tibetan religious life.

The first real Buddhist influence in Tibet came under King Songtsen Gampo (Song bstan sgam po;[9] 618–50 CE) who, it is said, was converted by his two wives, from Nepal and China. A minister visited India for texts and then invented the first Tibetan script, for writing down translations. After the king's death, the impetus for Buddhism ran out, though many Tibetans studied it in Nepal. In the following century, Buddhist influences came from India, China and Central Asia, and King Tr'isong Deutsen (Khr srong lde'u bstan; 740–98) tried to establish the first monastery in the country. Tradition says, however, that his efforts were frustrated by earthquakes and disease, seen as coming from the hostility of the Bön deities. The problems continued even after the Mahāyāna teacher Śāntarakṣita, of Nālandā university, was brought to bless the site. The latter advised the king that tantric Buddhism would have most appeal for the Tibetans, with their shamanistic

[9] Tibetan names and terms are given roughly as they are pronounced, followed by their full Tibetan spelling as transcribed into the Roman script according to the Wylie system.

leanings, and suggested that *Mahāsiddha* Padmasambhava be invited to Tibet. When he came, he is said to have successfully exorcized the site in around 775, and then to have converted many of the native deities (*EB*.7.1), so that they became protectors of Buddhism. He converted many people, and Buddhism was recognized as the state religion in 779. Translations were carried out in earnest, and in the period up to around 1000 CE, many Tibetans studied in India and Indian teachers visited Tibet.

Under the auspices of King Tr'isong Deutsen, there was a debate or debates in the capital, Lhasa, at the Samyé (bSam yas) monastery – in 797 if there was just one debate – between Kamalaśīla, a disciple of Śāntarakṣita, and the Chinese monk Heshang Moheyan (*EB*.7.3). These two represented, respectively, the Indian gradualist approach to awakening, in which this was the result of gradual training in morality and the other perfections, and the Chan (Chinese Zen) idea that it was attained suddenly, through going beyond conceptual thinking (Ruegg, 1989b; Williams, 2009: 191–4). The Indian approach won the day, such that the Buddhism which took root was a mixture of monastically based Indian Mahāyāna, represented by Śāntarakṣita, and tantric mysticism and ritual, represented by the revered Padmasambhava: a mix which became typical for Tibet. Of course the Vajrayāna traditions that Tibet adopted were themselves concerned with a relatively quick path, but there was more concern with systematically preparing the ground for sudden progress than Chan seemed to have. The priests of Tibetan Buddhism are generally known as *Lamas* (*bLa ma*), which corresponds to the Sanskrit word *Guru*, denoting a respected teacher who is seen as a source of liberating truth (Samuel, 1993: 280–1). *Lamas* might either be celibate monks, occasionally nuns, or non-celibate tantric ritual specialists.

The school which looks back to Padmasambhava – known as 'Guru Rinpoche', the Precious Guru[10] – as its founder is the Nyingmapa (rNying ma pa): those who (*pa*) are 'Adherents of the Old (*Tantras*)' (Powers, 2007b: 367–97). It has a strong emphasis on tantrism and magic, and emphasizes experience, not study, as the basis of learning. It has a system of nine spiritual 'vehicles' (*yāna*): those of the *Śrāvaka*, *Pratyeka-buddha* and *Bodhisattva*, which it sees as ways of 'renunciation' of defilements; those of the three 'outer *Tantras*' (see p. 183), which it sees as ways of 'purification'; and those of the three 'inner *Tantras*': *Mahā-yoga*, *Anu-yoga* and *Ati-yoga*, which it sees as ways of transformation, which transmute defilements into

[10] His consort Yeshey Tsoygal (Ye shes mtsho rgyal) is also greatly revered (*BP*.10).

forms of wisdom, rather than seeking to simply negate them. In Nyingmapa doctrine, these are all seen as appropriate for people at different levels of spiritual development. However, in practice, everyone is encouraged to practise the inner/*Anuttara-yoga Tantras*, provided that the basic refuge and *Bodhisattva* commitments and vows are also maintained. *Ati-yoga*, the highest teaching, concerns the doctrines and practices of *Dzogch'en* (*rDzogs chen*), or the 'Great Completion/Perfection' (Samuel, 1993: 463–6; see pp. 359–61). This seeks to bring the practitioner to awareness of an uncreated radiant emptiness known as *rig pa* (Skt *vidyā*, insight-knowledge). This is symbolized by Samantabhadra (Kuntu Sangpo (Kun tu bzang po)), the primordial Buddha who embodies the *Dharma-kāya* (*BP*.5), but it is also already present in all beings, as in one interpretation of the Tathāgata-garbha teachings. The aim is to let go of all mental activities and content, so as to be aware of that in which they occur. Here there are parallels to Chan ideas and practices, and other Tibetan schools saw such similarities as grounds for critical comments. Among the schools of Tibetan Buddhism, the Nyingmapa is the one which is most open to practices such as sexual *yoga*, though this can only be practised by partners who have absolute control over their bodies, and after years of training. In this, the semen, symbolizing the *bodhi-citta*, is retained, and seen to ascend through a channel in the back to the summit of the head. Some Nyingmapa non-monastic followers, and sometimes also monks who disrobe, perhaps temporarily, practise this with a partner.

Over the centuries, the Nyingmapas claim to have discovered many *termas* (*gTer ma*) or 'treasure' texts, which are attributed to Padmasambhava and seen as discovered by a *tertön* (*gTer ston*) or 'treasure-finder'. *Termas* might be physical texts or religious artefacts. In the case of 'mind *termas*', they are seen to have been buried in the unconscious mind of a disciple by Padmasambhava, then rediscovered there by a later incarnation of that disciple. The teaching-transmission by *termas*, which is seen to jump direct from a past teacher to a present recipient, is seen to complement the more usual *Kama* (*bKa'ma*; Oral Tradition) transmission, by which oral and written teachings are passed down the generations.

The Nyingmapas were influenced by indigenous shamanism, and by the eleventh century the Bön element of this had itself become much reshaped by Buddhist influence. However, Bön hostility led to King Lang Darma (gLang dar ma; 838–42) persecuting Buddhism. Though he was then assassinated by a Buddhist monk, the following period of political turmoil did not favour the spread of Buddhism. In this time, political power was held by regional kings and even some large monasteries.

The later Bönpos, or followers of Bön, came to look back to an enlightened founder of a similar nature to the Buddha as seen by the Buddhists. They denied that the Buddha was an awakened one, though, and saw their founder as predating him, having lived in western Tibet or an area further west, perhaps Iran. Like the Nyingmapas, the Bönpos have a system of nine 'vehicles' or stages of progress. While the first is unlike the Nyingmapa one, as it concerns astrology, divination and medical diagnosis (perhaps similar to *some* aspects of the Nyingmapa *Kriyā* and *Caryā* 'vehicles'), the highest stage, as in the Nyingmapa system, concerns *Dzogch'en* teachings. The Bönpos also share with the Nyingmapas the idea of *termas*, and were influenced by Buddhism to take up monasticism. As a tradition strongly influenced by Buddhism, but one seen by itself and Buddhists as not part of Buddhism, it is a kind of frowned on but tolerated minority.[11]

In the eleventh century, a renaissance of Buddhism led to its firm establishment throughout Tibet and the development of several new schools that were based on new translations of Buddhist texts, so as to be referred to as 'new translation' (*sarma* (*gsar ma*)) schools. At the invitation of a regional king, the ageing monk-professor Atiśa came from India on a missionary tour in 1042. He helped purify the *Saṅgha*, emphasizing celibacy, and improved Tibet's understanding of Buddhist doctrine, as based on a mix of Mādhyamika and the *Tantras* (*BP*.24; *EB*.7.4). His reforms led his main disciple to establish the Kadampa (bKa' gdams pa), or 'Bound by Command (of monastic discipline) School', and also influenced two other new schools of the period. The first was the Kagyüdpa (bKa' brgyud pa), the 'Whispered Transmission school' (Powers, 2007b: 399–431). Its founder was Marpa (1012–97), a married layman who had studied with tantric *Gurus* in India and translated many texts. He emphasized a complex system of yoga and secret instructions whispered from master to disciple. His chief pupil was the great poet-hermit-saint Milarepa (Mi la ras pa; 1040–1123; *EB*.7.6), whose own pupil Gampopa (sGam po pa) first established Kagyüdpa monasteries. The other new school was the Sakyapa (Sa skya pa), founded in 1073 at the Sakya monastery. It is noted for its scholarship and is close to the Kagyüdpa in most matters.

The powerful Mongols had designs on disunified Tibet and, in 1244, their ruler summoned the head Sakyapa *Lama* to his court. In return for the submission of Tibet, the *Lama* was made regent over it. He also spread (Sakyapa) Buddhism to Mongolia and regions of northern China within the Mongolian empire. His successor Pakpa ('Phags-pa; 1235–89) was the

[11] Bechert and Gombrich, 1984: 268–70; Powers 2007b: 497–513.

spiritual adviser to Khubilai Khan, who became Mongol emperor of China. Sakyapa power was resisted by the other schools and their soldiers, and came to an end in 1336. A line of kings followed from 1358 to 1635.

By the fourteenth century, the Tibetan Canon of scriptures, based on careful and often literal translations, was complete. Tibet's Buddhism is the direct heir of late north Indian Buddhism, and as the Muslims had destroyed libraries in India, the Tibetan Canon is the best, if incomplete, indication of the nature of this.

An idea which seems to have originated with the Kagyüdpas in the thirteenth century is that of recognized Transformation-bodies or *trulkus* (*sprul-sku*), of which there are now around 3,000 in Tibet (see p. 171). A *trulku* is often referred to as a 'reincarnate (*yangsid* (*yang srid*)) *Lama*'. Though in Buddhism all people are seen as the rebirths of some past being, *trulkus* are different in being the rebirth of an identified past person, who was a key *Lama*, and in some cases being also a manifestation of a celestial being. *Trulkus* are recognized as children, based on predictions of their predecessors and the child's ability to pick out the latter's possessions from similar-looking ones. This practice became the basis for a system of succession to leadership of monasteries, and the political power that sometimes attended this. A new series of *trulkus* can start at any time, while an existing one can be discontinued or become suspended. In some cases, one *trulku* is reborn as three persons – his 'body', 'speech' and 'mind' incarnations. The Nyingmapas and Kagyüdpas came to have numerous lineages of *trulkus*.

In Tibetan Buddhism, various kinds of 'lineages' are prized: monastic ordination lineages; incarnational lineages; textual transmission lineages, conventional or through discovery of *termas*; lineages of oral teachings; initiation/empowerment lineages. In their different ways, all seek authentic transmission of the *Dharma*. In reply to a question on the matter, Atiśa said that direct personal instructions from a teacher were more important than scriptural texts, as they preserved the continuity and integrity of the living tradition. Tantric initiations are preceded by a master reciting a relevant text to a pupil, which action is seen as a direct textual transmission (*lung* or *upadeśa*); this signifies formal permission to study the text and is regarded as producing capacities in the pupil to properly understand it. The different schools arose from allegiance to different lineages of practice or exegetical or philosophical traditions, or to a certain body of texts. While there have been some disagreements between them, practitioners not uncommonly draw on elements from different schools.

The last major school of Tibetan Buddhism was founded by the reformer Tsongkh'apa (Tsong kha pa; 1357–1419), on the basis of the Kadampa school and Atiśa's arrangement of teachings in a series of levels, with a purified tantrism at the top. He founded the Gelugpa (dGe lugs pa), or 'Followers of the Way of Virtue', whose monks are distinguished from others by the yellow colour of their ceremonial hats. Tsongkh'apa emphasized the study of Mādhyamika (*BS2*.24), and the following of moral and monastic discipline. He cut down on magical practices and eliminated sexual yoga for monks, other than in visualized form. In his 'Great Exposition of the Stages of the Way' (*Lamrim Ch'enmo* (*Lam rim che ba*); Cutler, 2002), he argues that one should progress from seeking a good rebirth (a worldly goal), to seeking liberation for oneself (Hīnayāna motivation), to seeking Buddhahood so as to aid the liberation of others (Mahāyāna motivation), with Vajrayāna methods then helping to more speedily attain the Mahāyāna goals. Higher levels of truth or practice are seen to build on, but not subvert, lower ones. Logical analysis prepares the way for direct, non-conceptual insight, and textual transmissions are as important as oral ones.

Near the capital, Lhasa, the three main Gelugpa monasteries, Gan den (dGa'ldan), Drepung ('Bras spungs) and Sera, were modelled on the monastic universities of India, and became great centres of Buddhist scholarship, logic and debate. Among *Tantra*s, they emphasize the *Guyhasamāja* and *Cakra-saṃvara*, and particularly the *Kāla-cakra*, or 'Wheel of Time' (see p. 193).

In the sixteenth century, the head of the Gelugpa school reintroduced Buddhism to the Mongols, who had lapsed from it. One of the Mongol rulers, Altan Khan, therefore gave him the Mongolian title of *Dalai*, 'Ocean (of Wisdom)', *Lama*. He was regarded as the second reincarnation of a former Gelugpa leader, Tsongkh'apa's nephew, so that the latter was seen, retrospectively, as the first Dalai Lama. Each Dalai Lama was seen as a *trulku* who was also a remanifested Transformation-body of Avalokiteśvara (*EB*.7.6). The other major Gelugpa *trulku* is the Panchen Lama, seen as a repeated incarnation of Amitābha Buddha.

In 1641, the Mongolians invaded Tibet and established the fifth Dalai Lama as ruler of the country. From then on, the Gelugpa school became the 'established church'. Some of the Kagyüdpa monks and *Lama*s who were unhappy with this moved to Bhutan and Sikkim, thus helping the Drukpa ('Brug pa) Kagyüdpa school to become dominant in Bhutan (Berkwitz, 2010: 163–5). The Jonangpa (Jo nang pa), which branched off from the Sakyapa, was suppressed in the seventeenth century by the fifth Dalai Lama, who had its monasteries destroyed or forced to convert to the Gelugpa outlook, and had some of its books burnt. It supported the 'other-emptiness' view, opposed to the Gelugpa 'self-emptiness' one (see pp. 126–7).

Its suppression may well have been as much for political as doctrinal reasons, as the school had been aligned with the leaders of the Karma Kagyüdpa school, who had fought against, and lost to, the fifth Dalai Lama for political control of Tibet. The fifth Dalai Lama, though, was not narrowly Gelugpa, as he also drew on some Nyingmapa teachings.

As secular kingship had broken down in Tibet, the monasteries, as key players in society and the economy, came to take on political power, aided by the Mongolian Khans. While three of the four main schools of Tibetan Buddhism vied with each other for political power, their religious differences were more of emphasis than of rival views.

Some Jonangpa monasteries survived in eastern Tibet, and though their printing blocks were locked away, access to them was regained in the nineteenth century by *Lamas* of the Ri-may (Ris med) movement (Samuel, 1993: 525–32, 535–47). Ri-may, 'Impartial', 'Non-aligned' or 'All-embracing', was a kind of universalistic eclectic movement that arose in Nyingmapa circles in eastern Tibet, and came to draw in adherents of other schools, even including some Gelugpa ones. However, the Ri-may movement was primarily a teachings-synthesis that rivalled the Gelugpa synthesis. With few exceptions, *Lamas* of the Ri-may traditions trained at Ri-may centres, and Gelugpa ones at Gelugpa centres, with only limited contact between them. The Ri-may synthesis drew together the three non-Gelugpa schools (and some of the semi-Buddhist Bön). These already had in common the existence of lay *yogins*, an interest in the old *Tantras* and *termas*, and the relatively formless *Dzogch'en* teachings/practices provided a unifying perspective.

Both the Gelugpa and Ri-may syntheses united the scholarly/monastic and yogic/shamanic/visionary elements of Tibetan Buddhism, though respectively emphasizing the first and second of these. The Gelugpa has had more of a place for monastic hierarchy, and larger monasteries, while the Ri-may has had less place for these, and has valued individual spiritual authority more. Ri-may is not a school with a definite doctrinal position; some of its proponents supported the Jonangpa other-emptiness position, and others opposed it. Its scholarly aspect has been more original and exploratory than the Gelugpa one has mainly become. It is not an organized monastic order, and its followers still belong to their school lineages. The Gelugpas have a linear, structured, single path, while Ri-may followers have a collection of alternative paths and methods as options suited for different practitioners. It thus 'helped to break down the sectarian divisions that had developed over the centuries between different traditions, each progressively entrenched within its own institutional monastic base' (Samuel, 1993: 542). Yet the Ri-may movement has not eradicated all sectarian feeling among the non-Gelugpa schools and, while the Gelugpa is relatively more sectarian, the present Dalai Lama, who belongs to this school, has a very open and non-sectarian attitude.

In Mongolia, from the sixteenth century, Buddhism became well established and popular, pacifying a once war-like people. Nevertheless, the fragmented nature of Mongolian society meant that Buddhism did not reach some parts until the nineteenth century. The indigenous religion of the Mongols was a form of shamanism, though they were influenced, through the Uighur people, by Iranian Manichaeism, a syncretistic religion which built on Zoroastrianism and in time drew on Christian and Buddhist elements (there is a Manichaean hymn to 'Jesus the Buddha'). The chief Manichaean deity was Ohrmazd or Ahura Mazdā, a god of Light. Chinese Daoism also had some influence among the Mongols, and Nestorian Christianity had a small presence. From Buddhism, the Mongols were particularly attracted to wrathful tantric deities of terrifying appearance. Tantric identification with a deity was felt to be similar to shamanic possession by a deity. It was not just such tantric aspects that were accepted, though, but also Buddhist philosophy.

In the eighteenth century, Buddhism spread northwards from Mongolia to the nomads of what are now the Buryat and Tuva Republics in the Russian Federation. A branch of the Mongolian people also migrated westwards to an area by the Caspian sea that is now the Republic of Kalmykia, also in the Russian Federation.

CHINA[12]

Early history

As the religion of foreign merchants arriving from Central Asia, Buddhism was present in China by around 50 CE. By the middle of the next century, Chinese interest led to texts being translated: first Śrāvakayāna works on meditation and *Abhidharma*, then also Perfection of Wisdom *Sūtras* and works on the Pure Lands of Amitābha and Akṣobhya. China thus came to see an influx of hundreds of Buddhist texts translated from Indic languages.

Unlike most other lands where Buddhism spread, China already had an ancient literate civilization; yet Buddhism managed to bridge the wide cultural chasm between the Indian and Chinese worlds (Zürcher, 1989), as it has been doing with the West over the last century or so. The dominant

[12] On this, see Bechert and Gombrich, 1984; Ch'en, 1964; Zürcher, 1959: 193–211.

ideology of society was Confucianism, a social philosophy going back to Kong Fuzi (Kung Fu-tzu;[13] Confucius; 551–497 BCE). Kong stressed the importance of the family and correct, harmonious social relationships, particularly filial piety, or respect for parents. This extended to respectful worship of ancestors, in line with long-standing Chinese practice. Man was seen as part of a triangle of forces: Earth, Man and an impersonally conceived Heaven (*Tian* (*T'ien*)). Kong's ideal was the scholar-gentleman, who studied the ancient classics that he had edited, and cultivated a life of human-ness and proper, respectful social relationships. In the Han dynasty (206 BCE–220 CE), such scholar-gentlemen ran the bureaucracy of the huge Chinese empire on behalf of the emperor, who was seen as the mediator of the forces of Earth, Man and Heaven, and as worthy of worship.

The other strand of Chinese thought was Daoism, a religio-philosophical system founded by the semi-mythical Laozi (La-tzu; 'Old Sage'), said to have been born in 604 BCE. The *Dao-De-Jing* (*Tao-Te-Ching*), 'The Standard Work on the Way (*Dao* (*Tao*)) and its Power', is attributed to him. This sees the mysterious, indescribable *Dao* as a force flowing through and generating all things in nature. The Daoist sage is one who tries to be like the *Dao* in acting effortlessly, spontaneously and naturally. Thus Daoism dislikes the formality engendered by Confucianism, though it shares its love of harmony. The sage should be humble, compassionate and seek to become one with the *Dao* by meditatively contemplating it. From the second century CE, a form of Daoism developed which was based on worship of many gods, and the quest for longevity, or physical 'immortality', using alchemy, diet and meditation.

In Buddhism's transmission to China, some of the problems it faced related to its monasticism. Celibacy was seen as undermining the Chinese stress on continuing the family line, so as not to deprive the ancestors of worship. The 'unfilial' monks also lived a life which was not based on home and family, the centre of Chinese life. Moreover, the Chinese expected all but the scholar-gentleman to be engaged in productive work, but the monks lived off alms. When monasteries in time became wealthy, through the donation of both land and precious metals for images, Buddhism was attacked as being an economic drain on the country. The *Saṅgha* was also regarded with some suspicion; for it was an autonomous group, which needed to be regulated before it could fit into the totalitarian structure of

[13] Romanized Chinese terms are here given in the modern Pinyin system. Where another form follows in brackets, it is the equivalent in the older Wade-Giles system, as used in many older books on Buddhism, such as the first edition of this book. This is only given where it differs from the Pinyin.

Chinese society. A symbol of this autonomy was the fact that, initially, monks would not bow in worship to the emperor; for monks should not bow to even the most senior layperson.

Though the Chinese loved foreign exotica, the nationalistic Confucian literati came to criticize the growing religion as suitable only for foreign barbarians (*BT*.125–38). Buddhist thought tended to see class differences as unimportant, while social hierarchy was important in Confucianism. The other-worldly aspects of Buddhist thought were also in tension with Chinese pragmatism and focus on this world. To Confucian rationalists, there was no evidence for rebirth, there was nothing wrong with killing animals, and the fate of individuals and kingdoms depended on the will of Heaven, not individual karma.

How was it, then, that Buddhism came to be for a long time the main religion of all classes in China, with Daoism as the second religion, and Confucianism remaining as the main influence on social ethics? A key event was the decline and break-up of the Han dynasty, which led to a crisis of values due to the apparent failure of Confucianism. In this situation of uncertainty, Buddhism stepped in to fill a vacuum and put down its roots. In some ways, this has parallels with the origins of Buddhism in India, which was also at a time of social change, anxiety and the seeking of new values.

Buddhism had *both* a developed ethic, as Confucianism had, *and* a developed philosophy, as Daoism had. It was more popularly orientated than Confucianism, and had a more systematic philosophy of human nature than Daoism. Particularly popular was the concept of all people having the Buddha-nature, an equal potential for enlightenment, which reintroduced to China the notion of the equal worth of all people. This idea had fallen out of favour since it had been expressed by Mozi (Mo-tzu (470–391 BCE)), a critic of both Confucianism and Daoism. The compassionate assistance of heavenly Buddhas and the great *Bodhisattva*s brought hope and solace in sorrow; the karma-rebirth doctrines came to be seen as a good support for morality, and the 'alien' faith proved to be adaptable and tolerant. Adaptations were facilitated by the notion of skilful means. Ancestors could be cared for by transferring karmic fruitfulness to them, so that Buddhist monks came to be much called on for rites for the dead. Dead abbots were worshipped as the 'ancestors' of a monastery, and a novice monk was expected to behave in a respectful, filial way towards the monk assigned to watch over him.[14] Moreover, schools of Buddhism

[14] Though there were precedents for filial piety in Indian Buddhism (Xing, 2005b), these were given more emphasis in China: *EB*.8.2.

developed which had a more this-worldly, pragmatic emphasis, though there were also some that expressed themselves in very abstract language.

Following the Han dynasty, China was split into a northern part, controlled by non-Chinese 'barbarians' such as the Huns, and a southern part, governed by a series of weak Chinese dynasties. In the north, missionary monks had a reputation for meditation-based psychic powers, and so were sought out by the magic-loving people to teach meditation, seen as a means of protection in the war-torn period. The rulers sought out the 'psychic' monks as advisers on political and military matters, and the monks then gradually civilized them, tempered their excesses and converted them into protectors of Buddhism: a good example of skilful means at work. As a non-Chinese religion, Buddhism found favour with the powerful rulers, and also became the religion of the people. The practical side of Buddhism was stressed, in the form of devotion, meditation and good works, with more than 30,000 temples being constructed in the north by the sixth century. Many translations were also made, especially by the large translation-bureau run by the Central Asian monk Kumārajīva (334–413) from 402 to 413 CE. Brief Daoist- and Confucian-inspired suppressions in 446–52 and 574–8 were ineffective in stemming the growth of Buddhism.

In the south, Buddhism at first allied itself with Daoism; for it was seen as a form of Daoism that Laozi had taught to foreigners to the west of China. Daoists looked to Buddhism for solutions to certain problems in Daoist philosophy and, until the fourth century, Buddhist terms were frequently translated by Daoist ones. Emphasis in the south was not on religious practice but on intellectual discussion among the nobility and literati, particularly on the Perfection of Wisdom literature. Once Buddhism began to flourish in its own right, Daoism looked on it as a rival, while being influenced by some of its forms such as a Canon of scriptures and an ecclesiastical structure. When the Sui dynasty (581–618) reunified China, Buddhism was consolidated in Chinese culture, as it was seen as a unifying force that also encouraged peace.

The schools of Chinese Buddhism

From the fifth century, a number of different schools of Buddhism emerged, each being known as a *zong* (*tsung*): a 'clan' which traced its lineage back to a certain founder or patriarch. Each school specialized in a particular aspect of Buddhist teaching or practice, and monks and nuns often studied or practised according to several of them.

Some of the schools were straight imports from India. The first was the Sanlun, or 'Three Treatise' school, which was the Chinese form of the Mādhyamika (*BT*.143–50; Williams, 2009: 81–3). This was introduced by the translator Kumārajīva, and was based on three key texts: the *Madhyamaka-kārikā*, some verses of Nāgārjuna, and a work of Āryadeva, in each case embedded in a commentary. The second was the Faxiang (Fa-hsiang), or 'Characteristics of *Dharmas*' school, a form of the Yogācāra introduced by the pilgrim-translator Xuanzang (Hsüan-tsang; 602–64; *BT*.150–5). An earlier form of the Yogācāra known as Shelun, introduced in the sixth century by the translator Paramārtha, died out. Paramārtha (499–569) also introduced the Zhushe (Chu-she), a form of the Sarvāstivāda based on the study of the *Abhidharma-kośa*. It was then organized by Xuanzang. These schools lost their separate identity after a time, but as subjects of study they influenced others. A late import, arriving in the eighth century, was the Zhenyan (Chen-yen), the '*Mantra*' or 'Efficacious Word' school. While it died out in China in a ninth-century persecution of Buddhism, this form of the Mantranaya had considerable success in Korea and Japan.

Paramārtha is also probably the author of two texts that were widely influential in Chinese Buddhism: the *Foxinglun* (*Fo hsing lun*) or 'Treatise on the Buddha-nature' (King, 1991) and *Dasheng qixinlun* (*Ta-ch'eng ch'i-hsin lun*) or 'Treatise on the Awakening of Faith in the Mahāyāna'.[15] Here one finds the *Tathāgata-garbha* being portrayed in cosmological terms as the 'One Mind' that encompasses the whole of reality, both awakened and unawakened; as a single, universal reality, rather than, as is typical in Indian Buddhism, an aspect of individual beings. This seemingly monistic doctrine is reminiscent of the Brahmanical idea that the Self (*Ātman*) is identical with *Brahman*, the sacred, and that 'everything is *Brahman*', and also with Daoist ideas of everything as the play of the *Dao* (see p. 211).

Chinese Buddhism received more or less the whole gamut of Indian Buddhist texts and ideas, as well as developing new texts that were claimed by some to be of Indian origin. While China had a much more developed historical sense than India, ironically it took seriously the claim in Mahāyāna Indian *Sūtras* that they came from the historical Buddha. It thus had to make sense of the great variety of teachings of Indian Buddhism as coming from one person. Two important schools which originated in China were ones which, stimulated by the Chinese love of harmony, produced philosophical syntheses of the teachings of different texts. They

[15] *BTTA*.209; Hakeda, 1967; Williams, 2009: 115–19.

emphasized that the Buddha taught according to skilful means, and they categorized the various Śrāvakayāna and Mahāyāna *Sūtras* as belonging to one or other of several levels of teaching, given at different periods in his life: *panjiao* (*p'an-chiao*) systems (Ch'en, 1964: 305–11, 18–19). At the highest level, the schools placed a chosen *Sūtra* as representing supreme truth. The Tiantai (T'ien-t'ai) school, founded by Zhiyi (Chih-i; 539–97; *BS*2.32), was named after Mount 'Heavenly Terrace', where its headquarters was located. It stressed both study and meditation, emphasized the notion of the Buddha-nature as present in all things, and that the world is non-different from the ultimate 'One Mind', thusness, emptiness or *Nirvāṇa*.[16] Its *panjiao* system saw the Buddha as having taught: three weeks on the *Avataṃsaka Sūtra*, which only a few understood; then twelve years on the *Āgamas*, on the True Realities for the Spiritually Ennobled and Conditioned Arising, for those of lesser understanding; then eight years on initial Mahāyāna teachings on the *Bodhisattva* ideal; then twenty-two years on Perfection of Wisdom teachings, that all distinctions, such as between *saṃsāra* and *Nirvāṇa*, are artificial products of the mind; and finally eight years teaching the *Lotus* and *Mahāparinirvāṇa Sūtras*, on the Buddha-nature in all beings, the Buddha as the saviour of all and that the 'three vehicles' are united in one (see p. 111).

The Huayan (Hua-yen) school, however, put the *Avataṃsaka Sūtra* in pride of place.[17] Founded by the meditation-master Dushun (Tushun; 557–640), it was philosophically systematized by its third patriarch Fazang (Fa-tsang; 643–712), and came to be influential on the Chan school. Both the synthesizing schools flourished in the Tang (T'ang) dynasty (618–907). Influenced by Chinese ways of thought, they emphasized ultimate reality as immanent in the world, like the *Dao*, and as fathomable by penetration into the thusness of any natural phenomenon.

In seeking to be all-inclusive, Tiantai and Huayan diffused much energy in long hours of study and a range of practices. Their ideas could also be very abstruse and difficult to pin down. The remaining schools studied only a few selected texts, and focused their energy on a limited number of practices. The smallest was the Lü, or 'Vinaya' school, introduced around 650 CE. Based on the Śrāvakayāna-emphasizing Dharmaguptaka school, it placed importance on the study of monastic discipline, and had high standards for ordination and monastic life. In these respects it influenced the practice of

[16] *BT*.155–66; Williams, 2009: 161–5; Swanson, 1989.
[17] See pp. 145–9; Cook, 1977; Cleary, 1983; Williams, 2009: 129–48.

other schools, especially Chan. The two other practice-orientated schools became the most successful: Jingtu and Chan.

The Pure Land school[18]

The Jingtu (Ching-t'u), or 'Pure Land' school became the most popular form of Buddhism in China, particularly among the laity. It is based on the three main *Sūtras* related to Amitābha (see pp. 173–4), and the *Sukhāvatī-vyūhopadeśa* ('Instruction on the Array of the Happy Land'), a work attributed to Vasubandhu[19] which systematizes the ideas of the Larger *Sukhāvatī-vyūha Sūtra*. At the start of the fifth century, Huiyuan (334–416) organized a society for meditation on Amitābha's Pure Land, but Tanluan (T'an-luan; 476–542) was the first to properly organize the school, and is regarded as its first patriarch. He was a learned former Daoist, inspired by a missionary monk to see true immortality as gaining immeasurable life in Sukhāvatī (the 'Happy Land'). While his writings drew on Mādhyamika and Yogācāra ideas, he stressed faith in the power of Amitābha's vows, which could save even an evil-doer. His ideal was establishing a pure, firm and uninterrupted faith throughout life. This would ensure the ability, as death approached, to call on Amitābha for ten consecutive moments of genuine faith: the minimum requirement for rebirth in Sukhāvatī. The main practice he advocated was one called *nianfo* (*nien-fo*, Jap. *nembutsu*), a term which translated *Buddhānusmṛti*, 'recollection of the Buddha' (see p. 162). He explained it to mean both 'recollection' and 'calling on' Amitābha, this being done by repeatedly reciting the Chinese translation of the short formula of praise to Amitābha (see pp. 174, 255).

The second patriarch, Daochuo (Tao-ch'o; 562–645), emphasized the idea that, from 549 CE, the world was in the degenerate age of the 'latter-day *Dharma*' (Ch. *mofa* (*ma-fa*), Jap. *mappō*). This was because the Chinese thought that 549 was 1,500 years after the Buddha's death, thus being the beginning of an age of decline in Buddhism and morality predicted by the *Lotus Sūtra* (cf. *BP*.20–1). In such a situation, most people could not follow the difficult 'path of the saints', based on their own virtue and meditation, but must rely on the 'easy path' of devotion to Amitābha. 'Self-power' (*zili* (*tzu-li*)) must be replaced by 'other-power' (*tali* (*t'a-li*)). The third patriarch, Shandao (Shan-tao; 613–81) gave the school its classical form and did much

[18] On this, see: *BT*.197–207; Foard, Solomon and Payne, 1996; Williams, 2009: 212–14, 243–54.

[19] It is only available in Chinese and the Sanskrit title is a reconstruction.

to popularize it. From the ninth century, the school was so widely diffused that it no longer needed special patriarchs as leaders.

The Chan school[20]

The name of the Chan (Ch'an; Jap. Zen), or 'Meditation' school is an abbreviated transliteration of the Sanskrit *dhyāna*, referring to the state of deep meditation (Pali *jhāna*). In time, Chan became the most popular school among monks, artists and intellectuals. Like Tantric Buddhism in India, it developed powerful new methods of practice. In its terminology and spontaneous style, it was influenced by Daoism, and its expression of Buddhist ideas in direct, down-to-earth form was also in keeping with the Chinese temper. Meditation (*chan*) had existed in Chinese Buddhism from its earliest days, but Chan specialized in it. Its founding genius was seen as the semi-legendary Indian monk Bodhidharma, who may have been active in China in the period 470 to 520 CE, and appears to have been a great meditation-master and champion of the *Laṅkāvatāra Sūtra*. One of the legends about him was that he spent nine years in meditation gazing at a wall, until his legs fell off! This illustrates the Chan single-minded emphasis on meditation as *the* method for attaining awakening. Another legend is that he told the pious emperor Wu that the latter had generated 'no karmic fruitfulness at all' by his many good works. This shocking saying probably meant that karmic fruitfulness, like everything else, is empty of inherent existence, and that more important than good works is insight into reality. Though good works, devotion and study play their part in Chan, they should not become hindering focuses of attachment. Chan therefore has an iconoclastic streak, such that certain accomplished masters are said to have burnt Buddha-images (Danxia (Tan-hsia), 739–834, Jap. Tanka) or torn up *Sūtras* (Huineng; see below) as a means of undercutting someone's attachment. This has sometimes been misunderstood by Western students of Chan/Zen. When one such student, after a few days in a Japanese monastery, remarked that the old masters used to burn or spit on Buddha-images, not bow to them, the master simply replied 'If you want to spit, you spit. I prefer to bow' (Kapleau, 2000: 235).

The philosophical background of Chan comes from various texts and streams of thought. One is the Perfection of Wisdom *Sūtras*, especially the *Heart* and *Diamond-cutter* and their idea of emptiness, two levels of truth,

[20] On this, see Dumoulin, 2005a.

and paradoxical modes of expression. Another is the *Laṅkāvatāra Sūtra*, a Yogācāra text which also draws on ideas of the *Tathāgata-garbha*. The Indian Yogācāra school saw human experience as a projection out of the 'storehouse consciousness', due to the maturation of karmic seeds in it. The *Laṅkāvatāra Sūtra* equated this kind of unconscious mind with the *Tathāgata-garbha* (see p. 143). Another influence came from the above two texts on the 'Buddha-nature': the 'Treatise on the Buddha-nature' and 'Treatise on the Awakening of Faith in the Mahāyāna'. As the *Dharma-kāya*, the 'One Mind' of the latter text is seen in Chan as the 'original enlightenment' of all beings (see p. 145). Moreover, discursive thought and its 'dualistic' distinctions are disparaged – unlike, for example, in the Tibetan Gelugpa school – as masking its glorious, pure, innate reality. Many of these ideas are also found in the Huayan school, with its ideas of the One Mind as the unifying principle from which everything is made (see p. 150). In many ways Huayan can be seen as the philosophical counterpart of Chan.

A saying attributed to Bodhidharma, first found in an 1108 text, is:

> A special transmission outside the scriptures;
> Without depending on words and letters;
> Pointing directly to the human mind;
> Seeing the innate nature, one becomes a Buddha.

This expresses the secondary importance of study in Chan, and the idea that insight arises by direct mind-to-mind transmission from master to pupil – an idea that in some ways parallels that of a tantric *Guru* initiating a pupil. The 'innate nature' within the mind is the Buddha-nature. Various levels of awakening (Ch. *wu*, Jap. *satori*) are attained by gaining direct insight into this. The highest realization is when this potentiality is fully actualized – or when this, as a hidden actuality, is known and expressed – and a person becomes a Buddha, one who truly knows that his mind had never been separate from Buddhahood. Other people and their teachings cannot really *make* a person see their Buddha-nature. This must come as a direct intuition, when the practitioner totally stops looking outside himself for ultimate reality. The Chan master, then, can only try to stimulate the arising of this realization from *within* his pupil.

In the eighth century, there was controversy among some groups of Chan practitioners. A Southern school emphasized that, for the wise, awakening comes suddenly, and it attributed to the flourishing Northern school the view that it is arrived at in stages, by a gradual process of purification (Dumoulin, 2005a: 107–21). The Southern school took Huineng (638–713) as the 'sixth patriarch' of Chan, while the Northern one took Shenxiu (Shen-hsiu; 600–706) as this. The bitter squabbles between the schools was due to the earnestness with which their followers sought awakening/enlightenment, and the importance which had come to be attached to the genuine 'mind-to-mind' transmission of truth. The matter was settled at a council in 796, when an emperor chose in favour of the Southern school. Subsequently, the various groups of Chan practitioners were assembled under the umbrella of this school. Its ascendancy was due to the campaigning of Shenhui (668–760; *BS2*.56; *BTTA*.212), who championed its cause by building up Huineng into a legendary figure regarded as the second founder of Chan. The tradition came to accept an account of his life and teachings given in the *Liuzi-tan-jing* (*Liu-tzu T'an-ching*), 'The *Platform Sūtra* of the Sixth Patriarch', composed around 820 CE (*Plat.*; *BT*.211–25; *EB*.8.6.1). This relates that Huineng, as an illiterate boy, had a flash of insight when he heard a monk reciting from the *Diamond-cutter* Perfection of Wisdom *Sūtra*. As a young man, he went to join the monastic community of the 'fifth patriarch', Hongren (Hungjen; 601–74), and was put to work in the kitchens, without being ordained. Eight months later, the patriarch was due to name his successor, whom everyone expected to be the community's chief monk, Shenxiu. Nevertheless, the patriarch decided to choose his successor on the basis of the insight expressed in a verse. Shenxiu wrote on the monastery wall:

> The body is the Bodhi [Awakening] tree;
> The mind is like a clear mirror.
> At all times we must strive to polish it,
> And must not let the dust collect. (*Plat.* sec. 6)

This was judged to express only partial understanding and was surpassed by two verses which Huineng had a friend write on the wall:

> Bodhi originally has no tree;
> The mirror also has no stand
> Buddha-nature is always clean and pure;
> Where is there room for dust?
>
> The mind is the Bodhi tree,
> The body is the mirror stand.
> The mirror is originally clean and pure;
> Where can it be stained by dust? (*Plat.* sec. 8)

Here, the ultimate level of truth is expressed: all phenomena, however exalted, are empty of substantial reality, and cannot stain the Buddha-nature, which is empty of any real defilements. To be like a mirror clearly reflecting reality, the mind has no need of gradual purification – it is already the pristine Buddha-nature. One does not need to purify oneself to Buddhahood, but to realize one's innate purity, which is also the *Dharma*-body or true thusness. Hongren then called Huineng to his room at midnight, deepened his wisdom by teaching the *Diamond-cutter Sūtra*, and made him the sixth patriarch. Huineng secretly left the community, lest jealousy over a mere kitchen helper becoming patriarch should cause difficulties. For sixteen years he lived in the mountains as a layman, and then in 676 he ordained and came to gather many pupils.

The methods developed by Chan were aimed at enabling a person to directly intuit his or her true nature. To do this, the mind must be free of old habits, prejudices, restrictive thought-processes, and even ordinary conceptual thought. The basis for doing this, especially in the monasteries, was a disciplined life-style, informed both by Buddhist monastic rules as well as Confucian restraint and emphasis on ritual form. These set up a moral context and limited the expression of ego-desires so that a person could cultivate a naturalness and spontaneity which came from deep within: from the pure depths of the storehouse consciousness. Hence spontaneity was set within a context of set forms of discipline, ritual and monastic hierarchy. While a layperson could practise Chan, as it did not require long hours of study, monastic life was seen as providing a more conducive atmosphere for meditation, and gave closer access to the all-important meditation-master. As he would have many pupils, private interviews (*dukan* (*tu-k'an*), Jap. *dokusan*) with him were precious and long-awaited. In such an interview, the master would diagnose the specific spiritual problem that a pupil was currently subject to, and treat it accordingly. This might be by advice or explanation, or even by provocation, sudden actions, blows or shouts: whatever was appropriate to the pupil's state of mind, so as to help trigger an awakening, dependent on the right moment, the pupil's own Buddha-nature, and the master's direct pointing at this. The fierce methods used by some are reflected by this description of the demeanour of Mazu (Ma-tsu; 709–88): 'His stride was like a bull's and his gaze like a tiger's' (Dumoulin, 2005a: 163). The master would sometimes engage his pupil in a rapid dialogue which compressed different levels of understanding, and was intended to prod the pupil into himself finding and expressing the ultimate level of truth. In this, Chan was influenced by the Perfection of Wisdom paradoxical style of dialogue, Mādhyamika dialectic, and a probing style of questioning found in the

Śūraṅgama Sūtra (*Leng Yan Jing* (*Leng Yen Ching*)), which is a text probably composed in China.

While Chan sees itself as not 'depending on words and letters', it developed its own style of rhetorical language to help spark off or express an experience of awakening. Dale Wright (1993) sees it as using four types of rhetoric:

- Of strangeness: using language in unconventional ways, not to represent facts in the world, or explain or persuade, but to challenge, and hint at true reality that is overlooked but present in everyday experiences.
- Of direct pointing: by gesture or action, to arrest the discursive mind and aid an immediate perception of thusness, the open space that is the empty groundlessness of reality.
- Of silence: to challenge ordinary forms of language, thought and awareness.
- Of disruption: to disorientate and disrupt; 'most unsettling is the realization that, not only does it [disruptive language] not make sense, but it won't make sense so long as I remain who I am, that is a subject self supported by particular conventions of placement in the world. The language of Chan throws into question the self/world relation that supports the reader's position as the one who grasps and acts in the world. (Wright, 1993: 32).

Here one can see a connection both to early Buddhist ideas on non-Self and to the Yogācāra perspective, which sees the subject/object duality as an illusion imposed on the flow of direct experience.

A simple example of a dialogue using such language is:

Monk: How can silence be expressed?
Master: I will not express it here.
Monk: Where will you express it?
Master: Last night at midnight, I lost three pennies by my bed. (*BT*.236)

Here, the 'thusness' of silence is conveyed, not by describing it, but by conjuring up the picture of groping for some coins in the darkness and silence of night.

Records of some of the question-and-answer sessions (*wen-dai* (*wen-tai*), Jap. *mondō*), and of the spontaneous acts of masters, provided important paradigms for Chan practice. Such a record was known as a *gong-an* (*kung-an*, Jap. *kōan*), or 'public record' (*EB*.9.6). These were used as themes for one type of meditation, and as discussion-points in private interviews. They were used increasingly from the eighth century, and by the twelfth century there were large anthologies of them, including the 'Blue Cliff Record' and the 'Gateless Barrier'.[21] These were used as the basis of a system in which practitioners would have to wrestle with a series of enigmatic questions, such as 'what was my original face before my mother and father were born?', that is, what is my true nature, beyond existence in time and space? This was a way to educate people the 'hard way'.

Chan is said to have originated in a supposed incident in the Buddha's life, when he held up a flower to a group of his disciples. Mahākāśyapa smiled in understanding at this silent sermon, and so received the 'seal of *Dharma*' to pass on the teaching. This story, which acts as a kind of foundation myth for Chan, seems to have originated with the Chan literati during the Song period (960–1279; Welter, 2000). Mahākāśyapa (Pali Mahākassapa) was one of the Buddha's main disciples, an *Arhat* who was a relatively ascetic figure who loved the beauty of mountains and forests, and is seen in several Buddhist texts of north-west India as the Buddha's successor (Ray, 1994: 105–18). A flower exemplifies both the beauty and impermanence of the world, and it is said that Mahākāśyapa learnt of the Buddha's death on meeting an ascetic with a flower that had been offered in devotion to the dead Buddha (*D*.II.162).

Of the five Chan lineages that developed (Dumoulin, 2005a: 211–42), two survived the vicissitudes of history, and came to dominate after the eleventh century. The first is the Linji (Lin-chi, Jap. Rinzai) school, founded by Linji (died 867). It emphasizes the use of *gong-an*s, harsh methods in interviews, and that awakenings come suddenly. The second is the Caodong (Ts'ao-tung, Jap. Sōtō) school, founded by Dongshan (Tung-shan; 807–69) and Caoshan (Ts'ao-shan; 840–901). The school's name may allude to their names. It emphasizes a form of sitting meditation, and came to see awakenings as gradually unfolding. While the Japanese forms of these two schools have remained separate, they merged in China during the Ming dynasty (1368–1644).

By the sixteenth century, the pervasive Pure Land practice of *nianfo* came to be part of the daily liturgy of Chan monasteries. In this context, however, it became more of a Chan 'self-power' exercise than a Pure Land 'other-power' one. This was because, in addition to the recitation, a common topic of meditation was 'who recites the name of the Buddha?', that is, what is one's true nature? A syncretism between Pure Land and Chan also developed, in which the Buddha-nature 'within' and Amitābha Buddha 'without' were seen as different ways of looking at the same reality.

[21] Respectively the *Biyan Lu* (*Pi-yen-lu*, Jap. *Hekiganroku*) and the *Wumenguan* (*Wu-men-kuan*, Jap. *Mumonkan*).

Later history

Buddhism flourished in the Tang (T'ang) dynasty (618–907), when monasteries were large, well-endowed institutions which fostered artistic creativity, cared for the sick, old and orphans, and ran community development projects. Buddhism's influence and the wealth accumulated by its monasteries, however, led to machinations by rival Daoists. The government was in need of money after a civil war, and looked for funds to the precious metals used in Buddhist images, temple lands and the tax exemption enjoyed by monks and the laity working in the monasteries. In 842, the emperor confiscated land belonging to lax monks and nuns, and in 845 he had all but a few temple-monasteries destroyed, laicized many monks and nuns, and took much of the *Saṅgha*'s land. The persecution was short, but it devastated Buddhist institutions throughout China. The emperor died in 846, and his policy was reversed, but most schools did not recover and went into decline. Tiantai retained some of its power, but the main surviving schools were Chan and Pure Land. Chan survived because it was less dependent on libraries and images, etc., its monks had come to grow their own food, and many of its centres were geographically isolated. Pure Land survived because it was mainly a lay movement. Buddhism in China was now past its peak.

During the Song (Sung) dynasty (960–1279), though, the entire Canon of Buddhist scriptures was printed, using over 130,000 wooden printing blocks (972–83). In time, however, Buddhism came to lose out to the rising power of Neo-Confucianism, which reached its classic form in the twelfth century. Drawing elements from Buddhist philosophy, this was an all-embracing ideology and metaphysic which became the basis of competitive civil-service exams. Under its influence, Buddhism was increasingly seen as fit only for the masses. The decline of Buddhism under this reformulated expression of indigenous Chinese beliefs is in some ways akin to its decline in India under Hinduism, a reformulated Brahmanism. In both cases, a religion or philosophy closely tied to a national culture came to overshadow a universal religion from which it borrowed. In time, however, it became quite common for people's practice to draw on Confucianism, Daoism and Buddhism.

In the Mongolian Yuan dynasty (1280–1368), state patronage increased again, though it was mainly for Northern Buddhism. Early in the Ming dynasty (1368–1644), Buddhism had a small revival due to initial state encouragement, but then the control of education by Confucian scholars, and the prevention of Buddhists being state officials, led to a decline in

Buddhist scholarship. Popular Buddhism still thrived, however, though it became increasingly mingled with Daoism and folk religion. In the Qing (Ch'ing), or Manchu dynasty (1644–1911), Buddhism continued to be criticized by Neo-Confucian propaganda, but in the seventeenth century it was spread to the island of Taiwan by Chinese immigrants.

VIETNAM AND KOREA[22]

Śrāvakayāna and Mahāyāna Buddhism had reached north Vietnam, from both China and India, by the third century CE. The Pure Land school was influential at the popular level from the ninth century, and Thien (Ch. Chan) became the most influential school in the monasteries (Thien-An, 1975). From the tenth century, Buddhism flourished among all classes of people, and state patronage began, with Thien monks being the learned cultural elite.

In the south, Hinduism and Śrāvakayāna and Mahāyāna Buddhism reached the kingdom of Champā by the third century CE. By around 900 CE, a mix of the Mahāyāna and Śaivism was patronized by the rulers. In the fifteenth century, an invasion from the north led to the subsequent dominance of the Chinese-based form of the Mahāyāna over all of Vietnam, though Theravāda continued to exist in the south near to Cambodia. A revival of Confucianism as the state ideology led to a gradual decline in Buddhism, however, and from the late sixteenth century, Catholic Christianity, spread by Spanish then French missionaries, had some success in the south. In the eighteenth century, Buddhism had something of a revival.

The indigenous religion of Korea is a form of shamanism, as in many cultures, and this continues to this day. By the late fourth century, Buddhism had reached the north and south-east, and by the sixth century it had penetrated the whole of the Korean peninsula, bringing much of Chinese culture with it. In the sixth and seventh centuries, Korean monks studying in China brought back most of the schools of Chinese Buddhism. Buddhism became the religion of the elite, with its Pure Land form having some success among the common people. Confucianism was the philosophy of the lower aristocracy, however. During the Silla period (688–935), Buddhism became a dominant force in society, with Seon (Ch. Chan) becoming a major school from the ninth century (Mu Soeng, 1987). In the Koryo period (935–1392), Buddhism was very influential, being a

[22] On these, see Bechert and Gombrich, 1984: 198–208; Chun, 1974; Thien-An, 1975.

popular as well as aristocratic religion from the twelfth century. There was considerable state patronage, and Buddhist monks succeeded, in 1036, in getting the death penalty abolished. The entire Chinese Canon was printed in the twelfth century and a new edition was printed in the thirteenth century, using 81,258 wooden printing blocks (which are still in existence). In the fourteenth century, Buddhism dominated cultural life.

The unconventional monk-cum-layman Won Hyo (617–86)[23] wrote extensive commentaries on the doctrines and *Sūtras* emphasized by all the competing schools, seeking to harmonize them around the idea of the 'One Mind'. His writings were influential in China, and in Korea he was the first to develop the syncretistic trend which was to become common. After the introduction of Seon in the ninth century, however, there was considerable rivalry between it, emphasizing mind-to-mind oral teaching, and the other, *Sūtra*-based schools, particularly Hwaom (Ch. Huayan). Seon also argued for a 'sudden' approach to realization, rather than a gradualist one. Uich'on (1055–1101) was the first to attempt a reconciliation between what he saw as one-sided approaches emphasizing study or meditation, instead of a balance of the two. His rapprochement was based on a revival of the Ch'ont'ae (Ch. Tiantai) school, but after his death this just became another contending school. The person most responsible for the harmonizing trend of Korean Buddhism was the Seon monk Chinul (1158–1210; Mu Soeng, 1987: 82–108), who also established a truly Korean form of Seon. Unusually, he used the *Sūtras* to guide his Seon practice, and so came to teach the usefulness of scriptural study. As in traditional Seon, he accepted the central importance of sudden insights into one's Buddha-nature. He also accepted, however, that many people needed to mature such insights by gradual cultivation of wholesome states, while seeing that these and defilements were empty of inherent existence (*BS*2.41). He drew on the practices of several schools in a pragmatic way, according to the needs of people of different capacities. Essentially, however, he developed a synthesis of Seon with the philosophy and practices of Hwaom. In the fourteenth century, the Linji *gong-an* method, which he had begun to experiment with, became the normative Seon method.

Buddhism suffered a reversal in the Yi dynasty (1392–1910), when Neo-Confucianism from China came to be adopted as the state ideology. In the early fifteenth century, monastery lands were confiscated, monasteries were reduced to 242, then 88, and schools were reduced to 7, then to 2 umbrella organizations. These were the Seon, or Meditation school, dominated by

[23] *BP*.44; Mu Soeng, 1987: 33–43.

Seon, but including Kyeyul (Ch. Lü), Ch'ont'ae and Milgyo (Ch. Zhenyan), and the Kyo, or Textual school, which included the remaining schools. Monks were banned from entering the capital (1623), and aristocrats' children were forbidden from ordaining. Buddhism therefore retreated to mountain monasteries, and ticked over as a religion of the masses, as in China, with a revival developing in the 1890s.

JAPAN[24]

Early history

The indigenous religious tradition of Japan is Shintō, the 'Way of the Gods', which is based on worship of a range of divine beings, each known as a *kami*. Some are seen as personalized creative forces, many as impersonal forces present in notable natural objects and animals, and some as extraordinary humans: anything awe-inspiring or mysterious can be seen as a *kami*. The tradition did not have a strong ethical dimension, but it had a developed appreciation of natural beauty, and a concern for ritual purity.

Buddhism first officially reached Japan in 538 CE, when a Korean king sent ambassadors with a Buddha-image, scriptures and a group of monks (*BP*.17). Subsequently, it brought much of Chinese civilization, including Confucianism and Daoism, to a country in the process of developing a centralized monarchy. Buddhism was at first adopted through the appeal of its art and ritual, the protective power offered by rites generating karmic fruitfulness or drawing on the power of holy beings, and the power of its ethic to encourage unity among rival clans. It is said that the pious and learned regent, Prince Shōtoku (573–622; *EB*.9.1), firmly implanted Buddhism by making it the state religion, with responsibility for the welfare of Japan, and made Confucianism the state philosophy. From this early period onwards, Buddhism had links with the power of the state.

In the Nara period (710–84), the devout emperor Shōmu ordered the building of temples throughout the land. Monks acted as scribes, thus introducing writing, and helped open up a country-wide road system. Six schools of Chinese Buddhism were introduced, the most influential being the Kegon (Ch. Huayan). In Nara, the capital, Shōmu built a temple enshrining a 16-metre tall image of Vairocana: the central, *Dharma*-body Buddha according to the Kegon school. This image represented the centre of both spiritual and temporal power in the realm. Just as Kegon saw

[24] On this, see: Bechert and Gombrich, 1984: 212–30; Kasahara, 2001; Kitagawa, 1990.

ultimate reality as interpenetrating phenomenal reality without these impeding each other, so the power of the emperor was seen as interpenetrating Japanese society. This notion fitted well with the blend of collectivism and individualism found in Japanese culture. A Nara *kami* was also recognized as a *Bodhisattva* and made the protector of the main temple.

Nara Buddhism was primarily for the elite. It attracted wealth and also politically ambitious monks, who had been ordered to ordain for the karmic benefit of the ruler. Consequently it became corrupt and politically meddlesome. The capital was therefore moved to Kyoto at the start of the Heian period (794–1185). Japanese Buddhism now came of age.

The Japanese monk Saichō (767–822) introduced the Tendai (Ch. Tiantai) school from China in 805 (*BT*.255–76; *EB*.9.4). Its head temple-monastery was set up on Mount Hiei, near Kyoto, where Saichō established a twelve-year training regime of study, meditation and monastic discipline. This became the most important temple in the land, and housed 30,000 monks in its heyday. In his wide-ranging synthesis, the *Lotus Sūtra* represented the highest truth, but elements of *chan*, Amitābha devotion and esoteric tantric practices were included.

The Japanese monk Kūkai (774–835) brought the Mantranaya Zhenyan school from China in 816.[25] In Japan it is called Shingon, and Kūkai established its central temple on Mount Kōya, 50 miles from the capital. He helped develop the present written form of Japanese, had a notable impact on the arts, and popularized many protective rites and liturgies. Shingon's colourful and complex rites came to supplant Tendai influence at the royal court, and the school also had some influence on Tendai itself. Kūkai, who is often referred to by his honorific title Kōbō Daishi ('Grand Master of the Dissemination of the *Dharma*'), is lauded as a cultural innovator, and sites believed to be associated with him are the focuses of the 88-temple pilgrimage route around the island of Shikoku (see p. 259), he being seen to spiritually accompany each pilgrim.

Shingon practitioners aim to establish contact with various holy powers, an important Shingon ritual being the *goma* (Skt *homa*) fire ceremony. This ultimately derives from the Brahmanical fire ceremony in which offerings to the gods were placed in a sacred fire. A form of this was adopted by Indian Tantric Buddhism, and found its way via China into the Shingon school, from which Tendai also adopted it. The ceremony is performed to attain some special end, such as peace or victory. For cure of an illness, offerings are often made to Yakushi (Bhaiṣajya-guru) Buddha. A monk (nowadays,

[25] See *BS2*.56, *BT*.287–313; Hakeda, 1972; Kiyota, 1978c.

married cleric) offers fragrant wood, oil and incense in a fire on an altar before an image or *mandara* (Skt *maṇḍala*), while making various *mudrās*, or symbolic hand-gestures. Shingon sees using *mudrās*, *mantras* and visualizations of symbols and images as the 'three mysteries' (*sanmitsu*). These attune body, speech and mind to Vairocana (Jap. Dainichi), the supreme Buddha, who represents the all-pervading ultimate reality, and so enable a person to know their identity with him. The '*Maṇḍala* of Two Principles' consists of the *Vajra*-realm and the *Garbha*/Womb-realm *maṇḍalas*, both with Vairocana at the centre. The first represents true reality in static form, and the timeless wisdom of Vairocana; the second represents his wisdom-imbued compassion dynamically active in the world.

In Tendai and Shingon, an important idea was *hongaku shisō*, 'original' or 'innate' awakening/enlightenment (Stone, 1999), a phrase that first occurs in the 'Awakening of Faith in the Mahāyāna' (see p. 214). This idea became of fundamental influence on Japanese Buddhism from this time, and saw all phenomena of the everyday world as somehow having the awakened nature of a Buddha.[26] Religious practice was aimed not at becoming a Buddha, but at truly knowing that one already was one.

While the Tendai and Shingon schools flourished at the court, devotion to Amitābha and Avalokiteśvara was being spread among the people. Shintō remained strong in the countryside, though it came to be synthesized with Buddhism in a form known as Ryōbu, or 'Dual aspect', Shintō (*EB*.9.2). In this, the Shingon and Tendai schools taught that major *kamis* were manifestations of heavenly Buddhas and *Bodhisattvas*, the sun-goddess Amaterasu being a form of Vairocana. In Shintō shrines, images of the corresponding Buddhist holy beings were set up, and Shintō borrowed heavily from Buddhism, as well as Confucianism and Daoism, to systematize and strengthen itself.

In late Heian times, the Tendai and Shingon schools became decadent and a period of social, political and religious chaos occurred, such that the 'period of the latter-day *Dharma*' (*mappō*) was seen to have started in 1052. During the troubled Kamakura period (1192–1333), rule was by military Shōguns and the *bushi*, or the warrior-knight class, now generally known by their later name, *samurai*. The latter helped Buddhism spread to the people, however, and thus put down deep roots. Five new schools began, which were simpler and more practical than the long, complex Tendai path, and more open than esoteric Shingon ritual. All were founded by monks who

[26] *BP*.18; Hubbard and Swanson, 1997: 4–6.

had gone through the Tendai training on Mount Hiei, but felt it to have become corrupt. In their different ways, all attached importance to the quality of faith. Moreover, Japanese Buddhist schools had harder edges than in other Buddhist lands, and became more like separate sects, with their own specific lay followers. They also tended to split into many sub-sects over time.

The Pure Land schools

Aspects of Pure Land practice existed in the Tendai synthesis (*EB*.9.5), and during the tenth century various unorthodox Tendai monks had begun to spread devotion to Amida (Skt Amitābha) among the people (*BS*2.9). The school did not take off until the Kamakura era, though, under the leadership of Hōnen (1133–1212) and Shinran (1173–1263).[27] Hōnen was a scholar-monk who, at forty-three, came to view the Tendai path as too difficult a means to awakening in the degenerate *mappō* age. He therefore humbly turned to the 'easy path' of reliance on Amida and his 'original vow' to save all (*BS*2.42). Leaving Mount Hiei, he popularized the practice of *nembutsu* (see p. 216) in Kyoto for many years, and wrote a work emphasizing a sincere and simple faith in Amida. He was disrobed and banished from Kyoto, however, as the Tendai authorities did not like him going against orthodoxy. The aged Hōnen, however, just took this as an opportunity to preach in the countryside, feeling concern lest the divine powers which he saw as protecting him would punish those opposing his message. He did not himself found a new school (*shū*), but one developed from his followers. These comprised the first Japanese Buddhist group independent of state power, uniting people of different classes. Harassment strengthened their unity, so that they eventually split off from Tendai to become the Jōdo-shū, or 'Pure Land school'.

Shinran left Mount Hiei to follow Hōnen, going into exile with him and then travelling widely to popularize Amida-devotion among the poor and the *bushi*. He felt incapable of attaining awakening by his own efforts, so his last resort was faith in Amida – though he said he did not know whether the *nembutsu* would lead to the Pure Land or hell. He felt that humans were helpless sinners, full of passion and depravity, ignorant of what is truly good or evil. His interpretation of Hōnen's message made it simpler and more extreme. People must give up any hopeless attempt at 'self-power'

[27] *BT*.314–44; *EB*.9.3; Williams, 2009: 254–66.

(Jap. *jiriki*) and should beware lest the deliberate cultivation of virtue or wisdom leads to pride and lack of faith in Amida. Hōnen taught that, as even wicked people could be reborn in Sukhāvatī, then good ones certainly could be; Shinran taught that, as even good people could be reborn there, 'wicked' ones stood an even better chance (*BT*.340): an idea paralleling the Christian concept of the 'salvation of sinners'. Salvation comes from gratefully accepting Amida's saving grace, not by any good works. Even a person's faith comes from grace (*BS2*.59), for the all-pervading power of Amida can be found within one, prompting the Buddha-nature to overcome arrogance and sin.

For Hōnen, *nembutsu* recitation was the central religious act, but worship of other Buddhas and *Bodhisattva*s was still accepted. One should seek to improve oneself and practise frequent repetitions of the *nembutsu* to make salvation more certain. Only one's attitude could make this a form of 'self-power', not the number of recitations. Shinran taught, however, that one sincere recitation – an expression of *shinjin*, self-abandoning true entrusting – was sufficient; after this, recitations should be done simply to thank Amida for already having saved one, *shinjin* being equivalent to stream-entry (see pp. 85–6). Repetition to aid salvation was a form of 'self-power'. As it is so easy to slip into the way of 'self-power', Shinran taught that 'other-power' (Jap. *tariki*) was the *difficult* path, not the 'easy path' (see p. 216). While salvation by pure grace is very unlike the early Buddhist emphasis on self-reliance, it does share with it the ideal of 'letting go'. Early Buddhism advocated letting go of all conditioned phenomena so as to undermine the 'I am' conceit, while Shinran advocated letting go of 'self-power' into the saving power of Amida. Both aim to overcome egoism, but the early Buddhists saw this as possible by cultivating inner resources through practising the *Dharma* taught by Gautama, while Shinran saw the resources as coming from Amida, or at least only Amida had the power to enable a person to access their Buddha-nature, as he was himself an embodiment of it.

While most of Hōnen's monastic followers retained celibacy, Shinran abandoned it when he dreamt that Avalokiteśvara – or, in one account, Shōtoku – told him to marry. He regarded monasticism as unnecessary for salvation, and marriage as a realistic admission of human weakness. He thus initiated a kind of married hereditary clergy, and advocated the family as the centre of religious life. Though an aristocrat by birth, he humbly described himself as an 'ignorant baldhead', addressing his followers as 'fellow believers'. In time, these formed the Jōdo-shin-shū, or 'True Pure Land school', also known as the Shin-shū.

The Zen schools[28]

Zen meditation had been included in Tendai, and Chan masters had visited from China, but Zen never caught on as a separate school until the Kamakura period. The monk Eisai (1141–1215) first introduced it from China, in its Rinzai (Ch. Linji) form. He experienced opposition from Tendai monks when he said that Zen was the best form of practice, but his adaptability ensured that Zen took root, for he also gave Tendai, Shingon and Ritsu (Ch. Lü) teachings. When it was said that Zen would have a debilitating effect on people, he argued that it would strengthen them and protect the land (*BS*2.34; *BT*.363–5). Indeed, Zen's meditational and ethical discipline, and indifference to death, appealed to the *bushi*, who were thereby better able to resist two attempted Mongolian invasions in 1274 and 1281. Eisai gained the protection of a Shōgun (military dictator) at the capital Kamakura, and established the long-lasting alliance between Rinzai and the *bushi*/samurai. This can be seen as an example of 'skilful means', in the form of an adaptation of Buddhism to the way of life of a particular group of people.

While Rinzai Zen was mainly successful among the samurai, Sōtō (Ch. Cao-dong) Zen had a more popular appeal, becoming known as 'farmers' Zen'. It was introduced by Dōgen (1200–53), perhaps the greatest figure in Japanese Buddhism (Dumoulin, 2005b: 51–119). This religious genius, admired by all Japanese, gave Zen both an identity fully separate from Tendai, and a more Japanese form. As a Tendai monk, a problem which plagued him was, if people already have the Buddha-nature, why do they need to exert themselves in religious practice to attain Buddhahood? His quest for an answer took him to a Rinzai temple, and then to China. There he met a master who sparked off an awakening in him. In 1227, he returned to Japan, and though he did not want to found a new school, his single-minded advocation of Zen meant that one formed around him. He attracted many pupils, monastic and lay, male and female, and several times had to move to a bigger temple to accommodate his community. He emphasized a strict and simple life of monastic discipline and *zazen*, or 'sitting meditation', and preferred to have a few good pupils rather than a richly patronized monastery with many sham ones.

Dōgen left many writings, the most important of which is the *Shōbōgenzō*.[29] Like Eisai and Chinul, he was critical of the late Chan neglect

[28] On these, see: *BT*.355–98; Dumoulin, 2005b.

[29] *BT*.367–73; Cleary, 2000; Masunaga, 1971; Putney, 1996; Waddell and Abe, 2002.

of the *Sūtras*, seeing these as in accord with the direct mind-to-mind transmission of truth. He was himself widely read in Śrāvakayāna and Mahāyāna *Sūtras*, and felt that study was acceptable provided it was done to support practice, and not for its own sake: 'It is you who gets lost in the *Sūtras*, not the *Sūtras* that lead you astray.'

In his reading, Dōgen was deeply impressed by the personal example of the historical Buddha, whom he saw as having lived a simple ascetic life of constant exertion for the benefit of others. For Zen, Śākyamuni became less of a glorious heavenly being, as in the previous Mahāyāna, and returned to being more of a human-like teacher and example. In line with this, both Chan and Zen have had a liking for the early *Arhat* followers of the Buddha. For Dōgen, reading the *Sūtras* was seen as leading to faith in the Buddha and ultimate reality. Such faith was also roused by experience of impermanence and suffering (cf. p. 67) – Dōgen's parents died when he was young – so that the *Dharma* was looked to as a way to transcend the pain of these. Faith should lead to respect for any Buddhist object or practice, and should lead to trust in one's Zen teacher.

Dōgen advocated *zazen*, or 'sitting meditation', as a return to the true Buddhism of the Buddha, a natural and easy method open to all and encompassing all other practices. He criticized the Rinzai reliance on the *kōan* (see pp. 221–2) as one-sidedly mental, and stressed the importance of also training the body by correctly using the 'lotus' meditation posture of the Buddhas. *Zazen* is not seen as a 'method' to 'attain' awakening, but is itself awakening, a way of simply exhibiting one's innate Buddha-nature (Cook, 1983). Thus did Dōgen resolve the problem which had set him on his spiritual quest; moreover, he came to see the whole impermanent world as *being* the Buddha-nature (see p. 145), as a kind of thusly-changing-reality-flow, whose true nature needs to be known and expressed. A person must sit in *zazen* with constant awareness, and with faith that he is already a Buddha. The process is one of self-forgetting in which the Buddha-nature gradually unfolds its infinite potential throughout one's life:

> To study the way of the Buddha is to study your own self. To study your own self is to forget yourself. To forget yourself is to have the objective world prevail in you [or: be enlightened by all things]. To have the objective world prevail in you, is to let go of your 'own' body and mind as well as the body and mind of 'others'. (*Shōbōgenzō shakui, Genjōkōan* (*BT*.371))

As an aid to this, physical, mental, moral and intellectual discipline provide a fitting framework for a life of selfless action. Dōgen was thus critical of an antinomian strand that he perceived in some forms of Chan/Zen, which he saw as the 'naturalist heresy' (*jinen gedō*): the idea that the mind as it naturally is is already identical with the awakened mind, an idea linked to what Dōgen called the 'Senika heresy' (*senni-gedō*),[30] which saw the Buddha-nature as a permanent Self residing in a being (Faure, 1991: 59–63).

The Nichiren school[31]

The Nichiren school is named after the monk Nichiren ('Sun-lotus'; 1222–82). This fisherman's son aimed to reform Tendai by a single-minded advocacy of its chief scripture, the *Lotus Sūtra*, which he regarded as expressing the essence of Buddhism. He saw himself both as the successor to the founder of the Tiantai school, and as the incarnation of a *Bodhisattva* which the *Lotus Sūtra* said would protect its teachings in the *mappō* age. He was probably influenced by a kind of Tendai meditation which involved worship and recitation of the *Lotus Sūtra*, and circumambulation of a copy of it (Stevenson, 1986: 67–72).

In 1253, he started a campaign to convert Japan to faith in the *Lotus Sūtra*. He saw a number of natural calamities as a product of national degeneracy, and predicted the attempted Mongol invasion of 1274. He was a patriot who had a mission to save Japan, saying that it would prosper when it revered true Buddhism, and would be the source from which this spread to the whole world, bringing about a golden age. He advocated a 'self-power' method that was easy for all to practise. This was to chant the formula *Namu myō-hō ren-ge-kyō*, 'Honour to the *Lotus Sūtra* of the True *Dharma*', and to contemplate a wooden plaque or scroll, known as a *gohonzon*, on which this invocation was written (see p. 257). This would activate the Buddha-nature, lead to the moral uplift of the individual and society, and to the attainment of Buddhahood, even in the age of *mappō* (*BS2*.57). Nichiren castigated all other schools as wicked ruiners of the country, and said that the state should wipe them out. This was because they all neglected the Śākyamuni of the *Lotus Sūtra* in some way. The Pure Land schools worshipped the imaginary Amida, the Zen schools revered the earthly Śākyamuni, but not the heavenly one, and the Shingon worshipped Vairocana. If Shinran wondered if the *nembutsu* recitation would lead to hell, Nichiren was sure that it would! Such virulent denunciation is most

[30] Named after an Indian, Śreṇika Vatsagotra, whose views were criticized by the Buddha: *Asta*.8–9 (and see note on p. 72 of the translation), Conze, 1975: 12–13, 101–2, and the *Mahāparinirvāṇa Sūtra*, ch. 39. He seems identical with the 'Vacchagotta' of the Pali *Suttas*, who asks the undetermined questions (*M*.1.483–9), that is, is fixated on the idea of a 'Self' (see pp. 78–9).

[31] On this, see: *BT*.345–54; Habito and Stone, 1999; Kodena, 1979; Williams, 2009: 165–71.

uncharacteristic of Buddhism, and Nichiren cuts a figure more like an Old Testament prophet than a traditional Buddhist sage. His pronouncements meant that he was nearly executed, and was twice banished. He took all such sufferings in the spirit of a martyr, seeing them as the results of his karma and as helping to purify him. Moreover, his charismatic style of fierce evangelism and personal courage attracted many, who came to form the Nichiren school.

Later history

The Ashikaga period (1333–1573) was one of almost constant turmoil, with simultaneous rule by two emperors followed by rule by rival warring Shōguns. During this time, Rinzai Zen had great influence. Zen temples were havens of peace, culture, education and art, with Rinzai fostering developments in painting, calligraphy, sculpture, printing, gardening, architecture, literature, theatre and medicine.

In the Jōdo-shū, Ryōyo (1341–1420) developed the idea that the Pure Land is in fact everywhere, and is to be entered by a changed attitude of mind during life, rather than at death. In the Jōdo-shin-shū, the 'second founder', Rennyo (1415–99), opposed a strand of thought which said that moral conduct was irrelevant to those with faith in Amida. He stressed that sincere faith implied a pure heart, and that a moral life expressed gratitude to Amida. He taught that other schools should not be criticized, but that Amida alone should be worshipped as the 'original Buddha' who includes all others. That is, Amida was the embodiment of the *Dharma*-body.

Jōdo-shin-shū became centred on fortified temples, with its armed followers acting to defend the faith. In the last century of the Ashikaga period, the sect organized and led peasant uprisings and became the ruling power in one region of Japan. Tendai and Shingon also maintained troops, some of them monks, and in the sixteenth century Nichiren Buddhists attacked the Shin and Tendai headquarters before being defeated (*BP*.19). Such un-Buddhist behaviour can perhaps be seen as the product of violent times where political power was up for grabs and ambition rose to the surface. However, the idea that violence might be used in defence of the *Dharma* – which people would not unnaturally come to see as defence of the *Dharma as understood by their sect* – had unfortunately been expressed in sections of the Mahāyāna *Mahāparinirvāṇa Sūtra*.[32]

[32] Harvey, 2000: 137–8, 265; Williams, 2009: 163–5.

Two powerful Shōguns then put an end to military monasteries, leading up to the Tokugawa era (1603–1867), when the country was unified under a military dictatorship. During this time, Japan closed its doors to all but a few traders from the outside world. In the sixteenth century, the Portuguese had brought Christianity to Japan. Some rulers had favoured it as a foil to the power of Buddhist monasteries, and had propagated it with violence. Now, it was ruthlessly persecuted as being a possible conduit of foreign influence, and struggled on as the secret religion of a few.

In 1614, Buddhism was made the established Church and arm of the state, with all people having to register and periodically attend at their nearest temple. Buddhism was not short of financial support, but became too comfortable and moribund. The code of the influential samurai contained several un-Buddhist elements, such as the obligation to revenge and a disregard for life. An increasing secularism also developed as people moved to growing cities. Nevertheless, Buddhist scholarship continued, primary schools were run, and the Rinzai master Hakuin (1685–1768) revitalized the use of the *kōan* (*EB*.9.6) and gave many popular sermons. The Zen layman Bashō (1644–94) also popularized the seventeen-syllable *haiku* poem as a religious art form (Suzuki, 1959: 215–67; see pp. 373–5). A new Zen school, Ōbaku, also developed which drew on Pure Land and tantric elements (Dumoulin, 2005b: 299–309). It arose from the influence of Chan monks fleeing political turmoil in China, and its most famous proponent was Tetsugen Dōkō (1630–82), who regarded Amida Buddha as representing the 'self-nature of the One Mind'. The school had some initial success, but did not surpass the popularity of Rinzai or Sōtō Zen, and nowadays has only a handful of operating temples.

In spite of these developments, Neo-Confucianism became increasingly influential as the state ideology in the Tokugawa era, and from the eighteenth century a new form of Shintō began to be developed as the 'true religion' of the Japanese, a pure and spontaneous expression of religiosity unlike the 'artificialities' of foreign Buddhism and Confucianism. In 1868, this culminated in a coup d'état which ended the Tokugawa Shōgunate, which supported these foreign traditions. Power was restored to the emperor, seen as a *kami* who had descended from the sun-goddess. Soon after, Japan opened its doors to Western influence.

OVERVIEW AND COMPARATIVE REFLECTIONS

While the self-power/other-power distinction arose in Eastern Buddhism, it is a useful one to apply across all forms of Buddhism. Broadly speaking, one

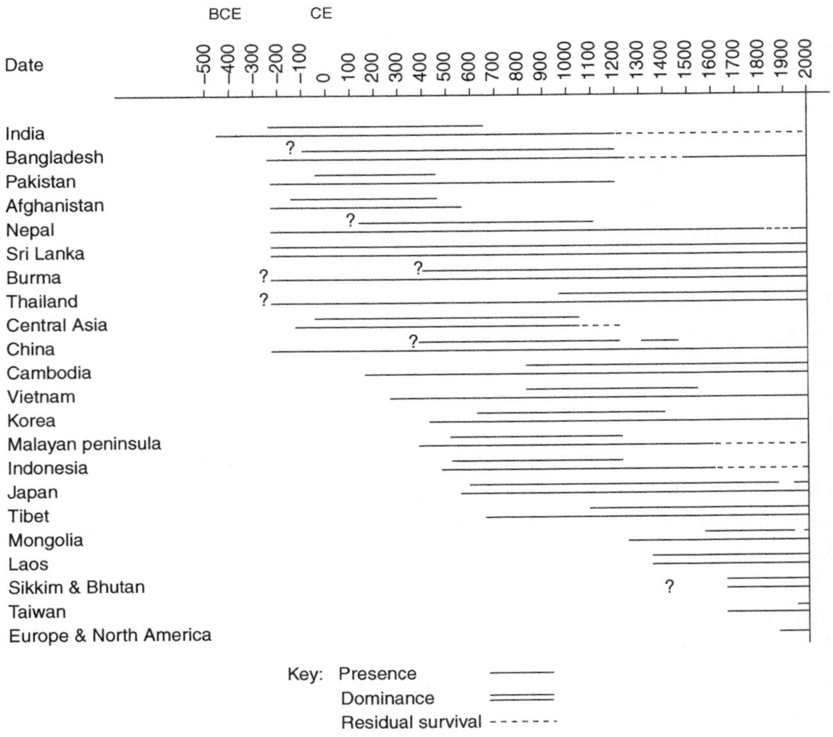

Figure 2: Chart showing the presence, dominance and residual survival of Buddhism in different lands.

can plot the traditions on a spectrum thus: *self-power end* <– 1. Chan/Zen; 2. Theravāda; 3. Tiantai/Tendai and Huayan/Kegon; 4. Tibetan Vajrayāna and Shingon; 5. Nichiren; 6. Jingtu and Jōdo; 7. Jōdo-shin –> *other-power end*. Self-power aspects include: the cultivation of morality, meditation and wisdom; being one's own refuge; basic radiance of mind; Buddha-nature; chanting practice; compassionate action. Other-power aspects include: the Buddha and *Saṅgha* members as teachers; oral and textual teachings; the power of chanted texts (e.g. *paritta* texts or the *Lotus Sūtra*); aid from celestial *Bodhisattvas* and Buddhas, and gods; visualized deities; the saving power of Amitābha Buddha. Also, pilgrimage sites and relics offer some degree of other-power (see pp. 100, 248, 258). At the popular level, in all Asian traditions, Buddhism often also draws on magical elements (e.g. *BTTA*.214) which combine power from beyond and the idea that this can be manipulated by certain means, thus combining other- and self-power elements.

CHAPTER 8

Buddhist Practice: Devotion

Most traditions of Buddhism consider *saddhā* (Skt *śraddhā*), 'trustful confidence' or 'faith', as a quality which must be balanced by wisdom, and as a preparation for, or accompaniment of, meditation.[1] Given this proviso, devotion plays an important part in the life of most Buddhists. While it can often have a meditative quality to it, it is associated with 'morality' in the triad 'morality, meditation and wisdom', and is seen as perfected at the same time as it, on reaching stream-entry (see p. 85). Among the ideas that are implicit in the devotion-related actions of most Asian Buddhists, Shenpen Hookham (2004) has identified the following:

- *Adhiṣṭhāna* (Skt, Pali *adhiṭṭhāna*): 'influence or blessing, a kind of power that passes from one person to the next like a contagious disease' (2004: 187). Monks and nuns bear this by their connection back to the Buddha's great spiritual power through their ordination-lineages, as well as through the virtue of their way of life. Such a blessing may be conveyed by a short chant, or laying hands on the head, or the passing on of a blessed object, such as a piece of script, an image, or a cord that has been connected to chanting monks.
- *Nidāna*: connection, the kind of physical proximity that allows *adhiṣṭhāna* to pass from one thing or person to another. This is especially the case when, with an open heart, a person makes offerings or shows devotion to an image, monument or person connected to the Buddha.
- *Puṇya* (Pali *puñña*, translated in this book as 'karmic fruitfulness'): the positive power or energy of goodness that can be actively accumulated and then directed to whatever goal one chooses. It is more abundant when giving to those rich in *adhiṣṭhāna*, or when giving out of compassion to those in need.
- *Praṇidhāna* (Pali *paṇidhāna*): a firm resolve, earnest wish or prayerful vow that carries with it the power to accomplish its positive purpose.

[1] Conze, 1993; *BTTA*.25–8, 170; Gethin, 2001: 106–12.

'Many Buddhist ceremonies and rituals are basically about making a connection that will cause *adhiṣṭhāna* to flow, then performing actions that will generate *puṇya* and then dedicating the *puṇya* in the form of *pranidhāṇa*s for the general good as well as for specific purposes' (2004: 196).

- *Satya-vākya* (Pali *sacca-vacana* or *sacca-kiriyā*, discussed at *Miln*.119–22): an asseveration or solemn utterance of some truth about the Buddha, *Dharma* or *Saṅgha*, or of either a genuine virtue or embarrassing failing of oneself, which is seen to release a wonder-working power-for-good, to the benefit of oneself and others (Harvey, 1993: 67–75).

The first three of these connect to the ideas emphasized in the *Avadāna* literature (see p. 100). To the above list can be added the principle that one tends naturally to become more like that which or whom one devoutly contemplates, values and/or associates with. Just as it is better to have virtuous than unvirtuous friends, as they influence one, so good qualities are nurtured by attunement to anything linked to states of high spiritual development.

FOCUSES AND LOCATIONS OF DEVOTIONAL ACTS

Devotion to Buddhas and *Bodhisattva*s is focused or channelled by the use of various artefacts such as images. At home, it can be expressed before a home shrine, which may be as simple as a high shelf and a picture in a quiet corner. In temples, there will always be some kind of shrine-room or image-hall, where large images are housed: in Theravāda temples, these are of Gotama, sometimes flanked by his two chief *Arahat* disciples; in Mahāyāna ones, there is often a group of three heavenly Buddhas, or a Buddha and two *Bodhisattvas*, perhaps with images of sixteen or eighteen chief *Arahat* disciples along the walls of the hall. There will always be accommodation for monks and/or nuns, or, as in Japan, married clerics. Thus temples are in fact temple-monasteries, Theravāda ones often being known by the Pali term for a monastery, *vihāra*. There is frequently a *Stūpa* of some kind, including the multi-roofed form, known in the West as a Pagoda, which evolved in China. Most *Stūpa*s are such that one cannot enter them, except for some in Burma and the East Asian multi-roofed form. They can be anything from a metre high, with some large ones being the major feature of a temple. The most revered *Stūpa* in Sri Lanka is the Mahāthūpa or Ruvanvelisāya Dagoba, Anurādhapurā; dating from the second century BCE, it is 103 metres tall and 287 in circumference (see Plate 7). It contains relics of the Buddha brought from India, and its relic chamber is said to centre on

Plate 7: Ruvanvelisāya Dagoba, Anurādhapura, Sri Lanka.

a 20-metre-high *Bodhi*-tree of silver with a solid gold Buddha at its base, surrounded by depictions of scenes from the Buddha's life (Strong, 2004: 160–71). In Burma, the famous gold-plated, 112-metre-high Shwe-dāgon *Stūpa*, in Rangoon, is said to contain some hairs of Gotama, and belongings of three previous Buddhas. Because of the sanctity of these, it has been encased in gold plate and gold leaf, and topped by an orb studded with diamonds. Temples may also have the following: a meeting/preaching hall; a separate meditation-hall, as in Zen temples; a *Bodhi*-tree, as at many Theravāda temples; a library and administrative buildings; and finally shrines for one or more gods or nature spirits (cf. *EB*.6.2). Most temples are free-standing, but throughout the Buddhist world there are also natural and specially excavated caves, whose cool, calm, rather awesome interiors have been used as temples.

Devotional artefacts may be paid for by a community or an individual. In either case, the community can share in its embellishment: in South-east Asia, images are often gradually gilded with individual squares of gold leaf. As giving generates karmic fruitfulness, which can be shared, artefacts may be specially donated, perhaps for the benefit of a newborn child, someone who has recently died, success in a business venture, or an end to a war. In 1961 the Burmese government organized the making of 60,000 temporary sand *Stūpas* to avert a world calamity predicted by astrologers throughout Asia (Spiro, 1971: 258–9). The motive of generating karmic fruitfulness means that temples often have more images than are 'needed', and new *Stūpas* may be built beside crumbling old ones. This is because there is generally more joy in starting something new than in repairing something. Greater joy leaves a stronger wholesome 'imprint' on the mind, and so is seen as producing better-quality karmic fruits. In Burma, '*Stūpa* Builder' is a title of respect, and karmic fruitfulness *Stūpas* are so popular that several can be seen in any landscape.

BOWING, OFFERINGS AND CHANTING[2]

Most Buddhist devotional acts are not congregational in essence, though they are frequently occasions for coming together in a shared activity and experience. In the home, they are often carried out in the morning and/or evening. Temple visits can be at any time, though they are most common at festivals, or at special 'observance days' (see p. 259). On visiting a temple, a person performs acts which amount to showing devotion to the 'three refuges'. The Buddha is represented by image, *Stūpa* and *Bodhi*-tree; the *Dhamma* is represented by a sermon, or informal teachings which the monks may give; and the *Saṅgha* is represented by the monks. Devotion at home or temple is expressed by *pūjā*: 'reverencing', or 'honouring', which involves bowing, making offerings and chanting. It does not necessarily involve the adoration that is part of 'worship', but it may sometimes do so.

In Buddhist cultures, people bow on many occasions. Children bow to parents and teachers; adults bow to monks, nuns, *Lamas* and the elderly;

[2] On these, see *EB*.5.5.3; Khantipālo, 1982; Welch, 1967: 89–104, 382–7.

and monks bow to those ordained for longer than themselves. Such lowering of the head acknowledges someone else as having more experience of life or of spiritual practice, and develops respect and humility. It is natural, then, to bow before sacred objects which point towards the highest reality, and also to locate a Buddha-image on the highest 'seat' in a room. Within a shrine-room or the compound surrounding a *Stūpa* or *Bodhi*-tree, humility is also shown by not wearing shoes; for in ancient times, wearing shoes was a sign of wealth and status, and of course they may also bring in dirt.

Bowing before sacred objects is generally done three times, so as to show respect to the 'three refuges'. A person stands or kneels with palms joined in a gesture known as *namaskāra*. They are held at the chest and forehead or, in Northern Buddhism, at the chest, lips and forehead: symbolizing respect offered by body, speech and mind. From a kneeling position, a person then places the elbows, hands and head on the ground. In Northern Buddhism, a fuller form known as a 'grand prostration' involves laying full-length on the ground. Devotion is also shown by circumambulation of *Stūpas*, *Bodhi*-trees and temples, which in Northern Buddhism may be done by repeated prostrations. In Eastern Buddhism, too, an important practice is repeated bowing before an image in a spirit of repentance.

Offerings are usually accompanied by appropriate chanted verses. Together, these aim to arouse joyful and devout contemplation of the qualities of a holy being, and aspiration for spiritual progress. Such acts consequently generate karmic fruitfulness. The most common offerings are flowers. One Theravāda flower-offering verse says, in Pali:

> This mass of flowers, fresh-hued, odorous and choice,
> I offer at the blessed lotus-like feet of the Lord of sages.
> With diverse flowers, the Buddha/*Dhamma*/*Saṅgha* I revere;
> And through this karmic fruitfulness may there be release.
> Just as this flower fades, so my body goes towards destruction.

This combines joyous reverence, aspiration and reflection on the impermanence of human life. A Zen flower-offering verse aspires that the 'flowers of the mind' should 'bloom in the springtime of enlightenment'.

The pleasant odour of smouldering incense-sticks frequently greets a person on entering a Buddhist temple. A Pali incense-offering verse refers to the Buddha as 'He of fragrant body and fragrant face, fragrant with infinite virtues'. This reflects the idea that the Buddha had an 'odour of sanctity': a certain 'air' about him suggestive of his glorious character and virtues. Incense both reminds a person of this and also creates a sense of delight, which can then be focused on the Buddha. Another common

Plate 8: A Thai Buddha-image and offerings, in the shrine-room of a meditation centre in Manchester, England.

offering is the light of small lamps or candles, a reminder of Buddhas as 'Enlightened' beings who give light to the world through their teachings. A Theravāda offering verse thus describes the Buddha as 'the lamp of the three worlds, dispeller of darkness'.

In Northern Buddhism, butter-lamps of finely wrought silver often burn perpetually before images. It is also common for seven kinds of offerings to be set before an image. Water 'for the face' and 'for the feet' symbolizes hospitality, while flowers, incense, lamps, perfume and food represent the five senses, ideally expressing a devotee's dedication of his or her whole being to spiritual development. The offerings are placed in seven bowls, or water and grain in these are visualized as being the offerings. The devotee also uses *mudrās*, ritual gestures representing offerings such as flowers, a lamp, or the whole world. He or she may additionally offer a white cotton or silk *kuttha* (Tib. *kha-btags*), generally known as a 'scarf of felicity', to an image. These are normally used as a friendship-offering to put a relationship on a good footing. Here they are used to form a bond of friendship with a holy being.

In all schools of Buddhism, chanting is very common as a vehicle for devotion or other ceremonial acts. Its use derives from early Buddhism, when Indian society made little use of writing, and a learned person was 'much-heard' rather than 'well-read'. Chanting aids accurate memory of the Buddha's teachings, as it has a rhythm which encourages the mind to flow on from word to word, and usually lacks melody, which might demand that the sound of some words be distorted. It is also a public medium, so that errors of memory could be known and corrected. After the teachings were written down, it was still thought better that they be well memorized, and chanting had also become part of devotional life.

Buddhist chanting is neither singing nor a monotonous dirge. While being deep-toned and slightly solemn, it holds the interest with its small variations of pitch and rhythm.[3] It is particularly impressive when a group of monks and/or nuns chant, for they may use different keys, all blending into a harmonious whole. The chants are usually in ancient languages, such as Pali or old Tibetan, thus giving them an added air of sanctity. This, plus their sound-quality and accompanying thoughts, generate a mixture of uplifting joy, often felt as a glow of warmth in the chest, and contemplative calm. Such states tend to arise even in those listening to a chant, if they do so with a relaxed but attentive mind. Chanting constitutes perhaps the most widely practised type of meditation in Buddhism and when monks and

[3] Examples can be heard at BuddhaNet Audio: www.buddhanet.net/audio-chant.htm.

nuns transmit something of the tranquillity of their way of life by chanting for the laity, this is a kind of broadcast meditation. All monks know the basic meaning of the chants, and can explain them to the laity. A full understanding depends on knowledge of the relevant language, which most monks train in to some extent. Vernacular chants also exist.

In all traditions, the most common chants are short verbal formulas, which may be strung together or repeated to form longer continuous chants. A very common Southern Buddhist chant, honouring Gotama Buddha, is: *Namo tassa bhagavato, arahato, sammā-sambuddhassa*, 'Honour to the Blessed One, *Arahat*, perfectly and completely Awakened One'. This is repeated three times and is usually followed by a chanted avowal of commitment to the 'three refuges' and five moral precepts.

In all traditions, rosaries can be used to count off repeated chants. In Southern Buddhism, a *mantra* may be used such as '*du sa ni ma; sa ni ma du; ni ma du sa; ma du sa ni*'. This is based on the initial letters of the words for the four True Realities for the Spiritually Ennobled: *dukkha, samudaya, nirodha, magga*. It concentrates the mind, keeps it alert and opens it to understanding. A devotional rosary-chant used in Southern Buddhism is '*Buddha, Dhamma, Saṅgha*', and a popular Tibetan one is '*oṃ maṇi padme huṃ*' (see p. 181).

THE REFUGES

The key expression of commitment to Buddhism is 'taking the refuges'.[4] The ancient formula for this, in its Pali form, begins: '*Buddhaṃ saraṇaṃ gacchāmi, Dhammaṃ saraṇaṃ gacchāmi, Saṅghaṃ saraṇaṃ gacchāmi*'. This affirms that 'I go to the Buddha as refuge, I go to the *Dhamma* as refuge, I go to the *Saṅgha* as refuge'. Each affirmation is then repeated 'for the second time . . .' (*dutiyam pi . . .*) and 'for the third time . . .' (*tatiyam pi . . .*). The threefold repetition marks off the recitation from ordinary uses of speech, and ensures that the mind dwells on the meaning of each affirmation at least once. The notion of a 'refuge', here, is not that of a place to hide, but of something the thought of which purifies, uplifts and strengthens the heart. Orientation towards these three guides to a better way of living is experienced as a joyful haven of calm, a firm 'island amidst a flood', in contrast to the troubles of life. The 'refuges' remind the Buddhist of calm, wise, spiritual people and states of mind, and so help engender these states. The value of the Buddha, *Dhamma* and *Saṅgha* is denoted by the fact that they

[4] *BS1*. 182–3; *BS2*.13 (*Khp-a*.21–2); Bodhi, 1981; Carter, 1982; Nyanaponika, 1983.

are also known as the *Tiratana* (Skt *Triratna*) or 'three jewels': spiritual treasures of supreme worth.

The meaning of each refuge varies somewhat between different traditions. The Theravāda understanding is expressed in a frequently used chant drawn from the Pali Canon (e.g. *S*.v.343). On the Buddha, it affirms: 'Thus he is the Blessed One: because he is an *Arahat*, perfectly and completely Awakened, accomplished in true knowledge and conduct, fortunate, knower of worlds, unsurpassed leader of persons to be tamed, teacher of gods and humans, Buddha, Blessed One'. The 'Buddha' referred to here is primarily Gotama, who is regarded with reverence and gratitude as the rediscoverer and exemplifier of *Dhamma*, who also showed others how to live by and experience it. These feelings naturally develop greater depth as benefits of living by *Dhamma* are experienced. One recently popularized Sinhalese liturgy, the *Buddha Pūjā* or *Bōdhi Pūjā*, states, 'Thus infinite, possessing measureless qualities, unequalled, equal to the unequalled, god to the gods, to me the Blessed One, my own Buddha mother, my own Buddha father, the orb of dawn to the darkness of delusion . . .' (Gombrich, 1981: 67). The Buddha refuge not only refers to Gotama, but also to previous and future Buddhas, and to the principle of awakening as supremely worthy of attainment. In this respect, the first refuge can also be taken as a pointer to the various spiritual qualities developing within the practitioner.

The Pali chant on *Dhamma* is: 'Well-expounded by the Blessed One is *Dhamma*, directly visible, immediate, inviting one to come and see, applicable, to be personally experienced by the wise'. This emphasizes *Dhamma* as ever available, open to experiential investigation, practical and transformatory. As refuge, *Dhamma* is explained as the Noble Eight-factored Path (*Khp-a*.19). More generally, as explained in the Pali commentaries, it refers to: (a) *pariyatti*, or the body of teachings, (b) *paṭipatti* or the 'practice' of the way, and (c) *paṭivedha*, or 'realization' of the stages of sanctity – in the highest sense, *Nirvāṇa* itself. *Dhamma*, then, is to be heard/read and understood, practised and realized. It is also the 'law-orderliness' inherent in nature, the 'Basic Pattern' in which phenomena occur according to the Conditioned Arising principle, from appropriate conditions.

The Pali chant on the *Saṅgha*, or Community is: 'The Community of the Blessed One's disciples is practising the good way, practising the straight way, practising the true way, practising the proper way; that is, the four pairs of persons, the eight types of individuals; this Community . . . is worthy of gifts, hospitality, offerings, and reverential salutation, the unsurpassed field of karmic fruitfulness for the world'. Here, the 'four pairs of persons, the eight types of individuals' are the stream-enterer, once-returner, non-returner, *Arahat*, and those well established on the paths to these spiritual 'fruits' (see pp. 85–7); that is, all who have attained *Nirvāṇa*, glimpsed it, or are on the brink of glimpsing it. This is the precious *ariya-Saṅgha* (*Vism.*218), the Community of 'Noble' persons, who may be found mainly within the monastic *Saṅgha*, its symbolic representative, but also among spiritually advanced laypeople or even gods. Being of exemplary conduct, its members are worthy of gifts and respect; the monastic *Saṅgha* seeks to emulate them in this. The concept of a 'field of karmic fruitfulness' (see p. 44) is that, just as a seed planted in better ground yields better fruit, so a gift given to a more virtuous person generates more karmic fruitfulness (*M.*III.255–7). This idea is partly based on the fact that, if one gives to someone of suspect character, one may regret the act somewhat; whereas in giving to a virtuous or holy person, one puts all one's heart into the act and can rejoice at it. Giving also sets up a bond of association (a *nidāna*; see p. 237). The Noble *Saṅgha* therefore benefits the world with the opportunity for generating abundant auspicious, purifying karmic fruitfulness.

In the Mahāyāna, the 'Three-body' doctrine means that the Buddha refuge refers not only to Gotama and other Transformation-body Buddhas, but also, and more importantly, to the heavenly Enjoyment-body Buddhas. In the Pure Land schools, emphasis is primarily or exclusively on Amitābha. In Chan/Zen, the emphasis is on the historical Buddha as a heroic, stirring example, but more particularly on the idea of the Buddha-nature within: 'take refuge in the three treasures in your own natures. The Buddha is enlightenment, the *Dharma* is truth, the *Saṅgha* is purity . . . take refuge in the Buddha within yourselves . . . If you do not rely upon your own natures, there is nothing else on which to rely' (*Plat.* sec. 23). Transformation-body Buddhas are also figuratively seen as good and wise thoughts within one's mind, and refuge is taken in 'the future perfect Enjoyment-body in my own physical body' (*Plat.* sec. 20). In the Mahāyāna, the *Dharma* refuge, in its highest sense, refers to the *Dharma*-body. Noble *Bodhisattvas* are included in the *Saṅgha* refuge, and taking refuge in them is allied to taking vows, often repeated on a daily basis, to become like them.

In the Mantranaya of Northern Buddhism, extra refuges are taken. Prior to the three usual ones, a person takes refuge in his *Lama/Guru*, the source of his deepening knowledge of the other refuges and regarded as an embodiment of their virtues (*EB.*5.5.5). After the usual refuges, an individual may then take refuge in his *yidam*, a holy being which is his tutelary deity (see p. 349). An adept preparing for training in meditative visualizations must also complete preliminary practices of a devotional and purificatory nature. Five or six such practices are generally given, each of which must be done

100,000 times. One is the 'grand prostration', which is done while holding wooden blocks, to prevent the hands being blistered by repeatedly sliding along the floor (or a special wooden board) to the fully prostrate position, while dedicating oneself to one's *Guru* (Blofeld, 1987: 151). After a period of struggle and pain, the practice is said to induce great joy. It also conduces to a balance of 'self-power' and 'other-power': relying on oneself and on the power of holy beings.

A related foundational practice is that of *Guru-yoga*, in which a practitioner visualizes, either in front of him or above his head, the *yidam* and the lineage of *Gurus/Lamas*, including the practitioner's own *Lama*, who have passed on teachings on these. These are all asked for inspiration and blessings, and are seen to merge and flow as light through the crown of the practitioner's head into his or her heart. As the Gelugpa Lama Yeshe puts it:

> We then meditate upon the feeling that our guru, who in essence is identical with the deity, and our own subtle consciousness have become indistinguishably one. The essence of the guru is wisdom, the perfectly clear and radiant state of mind in which bliss and the realization of emptiness are inseparably unified . . . By visualizing in this way and thinking of the personal kindness shown to you by your guru, a powerful connection is established . . . The purpose of seeing the guru in an exalted aspect . . . is solely to speed your own spiritual evolution. (*MW*.188–9)

As expressed by Sarah Harding, 'All buddha qualities are projected and identified with the guru' (Kongtrul, 2002: 11–12). Yet while one looks on one's *Guru as if* he were perfect, there should not be blind faith or taking a *Guru*'s quirks and faults as if they were virtues (Kongtrul, 2002: 92). The point is to focus on the deeper and exemplary aspects of one's *Guru*, and the *Dharma* he teaches.

ATTITUDES TO IMAGES

Images always function as reminders of the spiritual qualities of holy beings, if in no other way. When a Theravādin, for example, expresses devotion before an image of Gotama Buddha, he is reminded of his struggle for awakening, his perfections, his teachings and the ideal he represents. He joyfully recollects the Buddha, developing a warm heart and a pure mind. The spiritual qualities expressed by the form of a good image also help to stimulate the arising of such qualities in one who contemplates it.

In Northern and Eastern Buddhism, except perhaps in Chan/Zen, images function as more than reminders. Especially in Mantranaya schools, they are seen as infused with the spirit and power of the being they represent. Moreover, as image and being 'meet' in both being empty of inherent existence and 'mind-only', the image comes to be seen as an actual form of the being. For this, it must have the traditional form and symbolism and be consecrated (*BS2*.23). This is done by chanting prayers and *mantras* over it; by placing in it scriptures or relics, and even internal organs of clay, and by completing and wetting the eyes. This associates it with holy sounds and objects, giving it a power-for-good, and animates it, the wet eyes suggesting the response of a living gaze. Accordingly, in Japan, some images, known as *hibutsu*, 'Secret Buddhas', are only rarely shown to the public, so as not to 'disturb' them in their sanctuary; their beneficent presence can, however, still be drawn on from outside.

Even in Southern Buddhism, a temple image seems to act as more than a reminder; for it is generally thought that it must be consecrated before it can function as a focus for devotion.[5] Consecration involves the placing of relics in the image, and a monk reciting some Pali verses over it. In Sri Lanka, these verses are the ones said to have been spoken by the Buddha immediately after his awakening. This harmonizes with the fact that the eyes are often completed at around 5 a.m., seen as the time at which Gotama became fully awakened. These two aspects seem to suggest that the consecrated image is seen as a representative of, rather than just a representation of, the Buddha. Other aspects of consecration reinforce this idea. In Sri Lanka, the lay craftsmen completing the eyes act as if this were connecting the image to a source of power which, like electricity, is dangerous if handled carelessly. They ritually prepare themselves for hours, and then only look at the eyes in a mirror while painting them in; until completed, their direct gaze is considered harmful. Some modernist monks deny that there is any need to consecrate images.

In fact, in Southern Buddhism there is a widely held belief in a kind of 'Buddha-force' which will remain in the world for as long as Buddhism is practised (see p. 80). Indeed, a booklet produced by a Thai temple in London says of the Buddha: 'Although now his physical form no longer exists, his spiritual form, that is his benevolence and great compassion remains in the world'. This attitude is reflected in the way that Southern Buddhists regard relics and *Bodhi*-trees as having a protective power-for-good.[6] The 'Buddha-force' which many believe in is particularly associated with images, especially ones used in devotion for centuries, suggesting that

[5] *BP*.2; Gombrich, 1966 and 1971: 113–14, 138–40.

[6] On relic-related devotion, see *EB*.6.1.2 and 6.5.2 for South-east Asia and *BP*.3 and *BS2*.22 on China, plus Harvey, 2007d: 133a–137b, and Strong, 2004.

these are seen as having been thus 'charged up' with the Buddha's power (*adhiṣṭhāna*). Less-educated Southern Buddhists sometimes go so far as to regard the Buddha as still alive as an individual, and as somehow present in consecrated images of himself.

PROTECTIVE CHANTING

In all schools of Buddhism, chanting, or listening to it, is often used as a form of protection. In Southern Buddhism, chanted passages called *parittas*, or 'safety-runes' are used.[7] Most are excerpts from the Pali scriptures, the most common one being that on the qualities of the three refuges, as translated above. Other popular ones include: the *Karaṇīya-metta Sutta* (see p. 279), which radiates feelings of lovingkindness to all living beings; the *Maṅgala Sutta* (*BP*.35), which describes such 'blessings' as a good education, generosity, hearing the *Dhamma* and attaining *Nirvāṇa*; and the *Ratana Sutta*, which calls down the protection of the gods and praises the 'three jewels' (see *Khp*.2–6 and 8–9). While most *parittas* are used as a general protection, some are used against particular dangers, such as one against death from snakebite, said in the *Suttas* to have been given by the Buddha specifically as a '*paritta*' (*Khandha paritta*: *A*.II. 72). *Parittas* are used, for example, for warding off wild animals, human attackers or ghosts, exorcizing people, curing illnesses and averting dangers from accidents or natural disasters. They are also used to gain a good harvest, to help pass an exam, to bless a new building or simply to generate karmic fruitfulness. There are limits to their power, though. They are said to work only for a virtuous person with confidence in the 'three refuges', and cannot, for example, cure a person of an illness if it is due to his past karma (*Miln*.150–4). Within these limits, the working of *parittas* is seen as involving a number of factors.

First, to chant or listen to a *paritta* is soothing and leads to self-confidence and a calm, pure mind, due to both its sound-quality and meaning. As the mind is in a healthier state, this may cure psychosomatic illnesses, or make a person more alert and better at avoiding the dangers of life. Secondly, chanting a *paritta*, especially one which expresses lovingkindness to all beings, is thought to calm down a hostile person, animal or ghost, making them more well-disposed towards the chanter and listeners. Thirdly, as well as generating new karmic fruitfulness, *paritta*-chanting is thought to stimulate past karmic fruitfulness into bringing some of its fruits immediately. Fourthly, chanting or listening to a *paritta* is thought to please those gods who are devotees of the

[7] Known in Sri Lanka as *pirit*. See *EB*.6.5.3; Gombrich, 1971: 201–6; Harvey, 1993; Piyadassi, 1999.

Buddha, so that they offer what protection and assistance it is in their power to give. Finally, the spiritual power of the Buddha, the 'greatly compassionate protector' (*Mahājayamaṅgala Gāthā paritta*), and of the truth he expressed, is seen as continuing in his words, with its beneficial influence being liberated when these are devoutly chanted. This partly relates to the above concept of the 'asseveration of truth' (see p. 238). Accordingly, a *Ratana Sutta* refrain, 'by this truth, may there be well-being!', is repeated after various excellences of the 'three jewels' have been enumerated.

While an ordinary layperson or specialist chanter can activate the power of the Buddha's words by chanting, it is more efficacious for monastics to do so. This is because they try to live fully the way of life taught by the Buddha. When members of the monastic *Saṅgha* chant the *Dhamma*, as taught by the Buddha, there is a powerful combination, of benefit to listening laypeople. To symbolize the protective power passing from the monks (*adhiṣṭhāna*; see p. 237), they hold a cord while chanting *paritta*. This is also tied to a Buddha-image, suggesting that the image is being impregnated with the *paritta*'s power, or, equally, that it is discharging some of its previously accumulated power to add to that of the *paritta*. Afterwards, pieces of the '*paritta*-cord' are tied to the laypeople's wrists as a reminder of, and a 'store' of, the *paritta*'s protective power. When the cord is tied on, a Pali verse is uttered which means: 'By the majesty of the power attained by all Buddhas, Solitary Buddhas and *Arahats*, I tie on a complete protection'.

In Eastern and Northern traditions, including Chan/Zen, chanted formulas used in a similar way to *parittas* are *dhāraṇīs*, utterances 'preserving' Buddhism and its followers (*BS2*.46, 47). These are strings of Sanskrit words and syllables, which may either be devotional in nature or be mnemonic formulas summarizing a *Sūtra* or teaching, which may be unintelligible without explanation. A short example from the *Lotus Sūtra* is: '*Aṭṭe taṭṭe naṭṭe vanaṭṭe anaḍe nāḍi kunaḍi svāhā*'. Their recitation is seen to both preserve memory of the *Dharma* and preserve the chanter, through the truth-power of the *Dharma*. The Southern '*du, sa, ni, ma* . . .' rosary-chant quoted above is akin to these.

SOME MAHĀYĀNA FOCUSES OF DEVOTION

Avalokiteśvara

Devotion to Avalokiteśvara pervades Eastern and Northern Buddhism.[8] A text much used in liturgies is the verse section of the *Avalokiteśvara Sūtra*,

[8] Tay, 1976–77; Blofeld, 1988; Samuel, 1993: 482–5; Williams 2009: 221–5.

an extract from the *Lotus Sūtra*. Expressing profound devotion, this speaks of:

> True regard, serene regard, far-reaching wise regard, regard of pity, compassionate regard, ever longed for, ever looked for! Pure and serene in radiance, wisdom's sun destroying darkness . . . law of pity, thunder quivering, compassion wondrous as a great cloud, pouring spiritual rain like nectar, quenching the flames of distress![9]

Statues and paintings of Avalokiteśvara are found in abundance, depicting him in around 130 different ways, each aiming to express some aspect of his nature. In China, as Guanyin (Kuan-yin), 'he' gradually came to be portrayed as female, this development perhaps beginning in the tenth century, and culminating in the sixteenth. This may have been because the Chinese saw his compassion as a female quality; it may also have been partly due to the female reference in his *mantra* (see p. 181). Moreover, from the fifth century, some of 'his' popular incarnations were female (*EB*.8.7.2), and 'he' may also have merged with a pre-Buddhist goddess thought to care for mariners. Guanyin thus became an all-compassionate 'mother goddess', the most popular deity in all of China, being portrayed as a graceful, lotus-holding figure in a white robe (see Plate 9; *BP*.13).

Another artistic form found in Tibet and Japan shows Avalokiteśvara with 'a thousand' arms (fewer, for practical reasons, in statues) and eleven heads (see Plate 10), as described in the *Kāraṇḍavyūha Sūtra*. In the statue shown, most of the hands hold objects symbolizing the many ways in which this *Bodhisattva* helps beings, using his skilful means. There is also an eye on each palm, representing his ever-watchful nature, ready to rush to the aid of beings. His eleven heads are explained by a story that, on seeing so many beings suffering in the hells, his horror and tears caused him momentarily to despair of fulfilling his vow to save all. His head then split into ten pieces, as he said it would if he ever abandoned his resolve. Amitābha Buddha then brought him back to life to renew his vow. Making each of the head-fragments into a new head, he assembled them on Avalokiteśvara's shoulders, and surmounted them with a replica of his own head, symbolizing that he would continue to inspire the *Bodhisattva* in his work. With eleven heads, Avalokiteśvara was now even better equipped to look for beings in need! From Avalokiteśvara's tears, moreover, two forms of Tārā had been born (see pp. 186–9; Williams, 2009: 225).

The *Avalokiteśvara Sutrā* says that Avalokiteśvara will instantly respond to those who 'with all their mind call upon his name'. 'By virtue of the

[9] *Lotus Sūtra*, Kato translation, p. 326; cf. *BTTA*.175.

Plate 9: A modern porcelain figure of Guanyin.

Plate 10: Senju (1,000-armed) Kannon Bosatsu, at pilgrimage temple no. 58, Senyū-ji, Shikoku, Japan.

power of that *Bodhisattva*'s majesty' (Kato transl., p. 319), they will be unburnt by a fire; saved at sea in a storm; the hearts of murdering foes will turn to kindness; as prisoners, guilty or innocent, they will be set free from their chains; merchants will be freed from the dangers of robbers; threatening wild beasts will flee; success will be attained in a court of law or battle; and a woman will have a virtuous child, of the sex of her choice. Devotees will also be freed from attachment, hatred and delusion by 'keeping in mind and remembering' Avalokiteśvara. Much of this is comparable to the power attributed to *paritta*-chanting. The wondrous help of Avalokiteśvara is understood both as a literal intervention in the world, perhaps through the aid of a mysterious stranger, or a vision guiding someone through mists on a dangerous mountain (Blofeld, 1988: 30–3), and as coming from the power of a devotee's faith. In the *Śūraṅgama Sūtra*, it is said that Avalokiteśvara aids beings by awakening them to their compassionate Buddha-nature, and in accordance with this, any act of great kindness may be seen as the 'help' of Avalokiteśvara.

Chan/Zen, for which 'To be compassionate is Guanyin' (*Plat.* sec. 35), generally understands his/her aid in purely internal spiritual terms: for a 'storm' is anger, 'fire' is desire, 'chains' are simply those of fear, a sense of oppression comes from lack of patience, and animals only threaten one who has ill-will. Accordingly, Chan/Zen devotion to Guanyin is thought of primarily in terms of 'developing the heart of Guanyin': growing the seed of great compassion so that one becomes ever-ready to help others.

In Northern Buddhism, the *Maṇi mantra* (see p. 181) is very popular in invoking the help of Avalokiteśvara (Tib. Chenresig (Spyan ras gzigs)) and in developing compassion.[10] Accompanied by the click of rosaries, it is frequently heard on the lips of all who have any degree of devotion to Buddhism. It may be uttered as a person goes about his or her business, either under the breath or as an audible rhythmic murmur called 'purring' by the Tibetans. The Tibetans also activate the power of this *mantra*, and generate karmic fruitfulness, by use of the '*Maṇi* religion wheel', known in the West as a 'prayer wheel'. The formula is carved or painted on the outside of a cylinder, and is written many times on a tightly rolled piece of paper inside. Each revolution of the cylinder is held to be equivalent to the repetition of all the formulas written on and in it, an idea related to that of the Buddha's first sermon as the 'Setting in motion of the *Dharma*-wheel'. '*Maṇi* religion wheels' are of various types. Hand-held ones have cylinders about 7 centimetres long, mounted on handles about 12 centimetres long; a small weight attached to the cylinder on a chain enables it to be spun on a spindle fixed in the handle. Wheels around 25 centimetres high are also fixed in rows along the sides of *Stūpa*s or monasteries, so that people can turn them as they circumambulate these. The largest wheels, found at the entrance to temples, may be 4 metres high and 2 metres in diameter, and contain thousands of *Maṇi* formulas, along with scriptures and images. There are also wheels driven by streams or chimney smoke. The *Maṇi mantra* is also carved on stones deposited on hill-top cairns, on rock-faces by the side of paths, on long walls specially built at the approaches to towns, and is printed on 'prayer flags'. Karmic fruitfulness accrues to those who pay for any of these or produce them, to all who glance at them, thinking of Avalokiteśvara and his compassion, and even insects who come into contact with them.

In predominantly Theravāda Thailand, devotion to Avalokiteśvara is found among the Chinese minority, and one sometimes finds small statues of him/her in the precincts of Theravāda temples.

[10] See Ekvall, 1964: 115–18, 129–30, 239; Powers, 2007b: 22–5; Samuel, 2012.

Amitābha[11]

Devotion to Amitābha Buddha is found within most schools of the Mahāyāna, but is the essence of Pure Land practice, which centres on the 'Buddha invocation' (Ch. *nianfo* (*nien-fo*), Jap. *nembutsu*). This is the repetition of '*Nan-mo A-mi-tuo Fo*' (*Nan-mo A-mi-t'o Fo*) in Chinese or '*Namu Amida Butsu*' in Japanese: equivalents of the Sanskrit '*Namo'mitābhāya Buddhāya*', meaning 'Hail to Amitābha Buddha'. In China, recitation is done in tune with the steady and natural breath, and may be repeated many times a day, as the practitioner never knows when he has done it the minimum necessary 'ten times' with 'unwavering concentration'. A by-product of concentration, focused on Amitābha and the awakening attainable in his Pure Land, is that the mind is purified of distracting passions. The *nembutsu* also has a certain *mantra*-like quality, in that it is seen as opening up a channel between a holy being and a devotee: in this case, the channel of grace. Furthermore, when the practice is done wholeheartedly, it becomes spontaneous, and can be seen as reciting itself in a mental space in which the ego has temporarily dissolved. Through association with *nembutsu*-practice, a person's rosary often comes to be a revered object; touching it may immediately start the recitation revolving in the mind, and bring on the associated mental states.

In China, Shandao (613–81) came to emphasize the invocation as the 'primary' Pure Land practice. 'Secondary' ones included: chanting the Pure Land *Sūtras*; visualization of Amitābha and his Pure Land; worship of various Buddhas; singing hymns of praise to Amitābha; resolving to be reborn in his land, and developing generosity and compassion by helping the needy, and through vegetarianism. In Japan, the Jōdo-shin school came to put single-minded emphasis on Amitābha Buddha, and on the *nembutsu* as including all other practices, though the secondary practices could be done as expressions of gratitude for salvation. The sole aim of the *nembutsu* is to facilitate the awakening of faith; the moment when this truly occurs is seen as a transcendental, atemporal experience in which the devotee is at one with Amitābha in the form of the numinous *nembutsu*, in an experience akin to stream-entry.[12] After faith has arisen, any recitation is done solely as an expression of gratitude, often shown by merely wearing a rosary wrapped

11 See *BP*.31; Corless, 1979.

12 See p. 230; note that in early Buddhism, one route to stream-entry was by being a 'faith follower'.

Plate 11: A small Japanese shrine depicting Amitābha and his two *Bodhisattva* helpers. Lacquered wood, with sandalwood figures.

around the hand. This is also a reminder that 'sinful humans' are but a bundle of passions compared to Amitābha. Devotees express joyful adoration of Amitābha, and liken him to father and mother, so that he is commonly called *Oyasama*, 'The Parent'. Shinran talks of him as an inexpressibly 'pure light' that 'destroys karmic bondage', an ultimate haven full of love that gives comfort (Burtt, 1987: 218–22).

Plate 11 shows a small Japanese shrine which opens out to show Amitābha in meditation, with the meeting of his index fingers and thumbs indicating that devotees should give up 'self-power' and rely on 'other-power' for salvation. Amitābha appears as a serene and gentle being, who draws the devotee to him by his compassion. His radiant form, floating on a lotus, is flanked by his two *Bodhisattva* helpers: Avalokiteśvara (offering three wish-granting jewels on a lotus) to his left, and Mahāsthāmaprāpta to his right. The whole seeks to depict the central focus of Sukhāvatī, and to stimulate an uplifting spiritual experience, deepening the aspiration to be reborn in this Pure Land. Indeed, much Mahāyāna art has been inspired by visionary experiences and has helped to inspire further experiences of a similar kind.

Bhaiṣajya-Guru

Devotion to Bhaiṣajya-guru Buddha (Jap. Yakushi Nyorai), the 'Master of Healing', is important in both Northern and Eastern Buddhism (Birnbaum, 1980). In Chinese temples, image-halls most commonly have images of him and Amitābha flanking one of Śākyamuni. He generally holds a bowl said to be made of beryl, a translucent crystalline substance thought to have healing properties. His body is also said to be like beryl, and to blaze with light. In one Chinese healing rite, a person keeps eight vows for seven days, makes offerings to monks, worships Bhaiṣajya-guru, recites his *Sūtra* forty-nine times, makes seven images of him, and then contemplates his image so that it comes alive with his spiritual force and healing energy. Tuning in to this, the devotee then mentally merges with him.

The Lotus Sūtra

Within the Japanese Nichiren schools, the symbolically rich title of the '*Lotus Sūtra* of the True *Dharma*', *Myōhō-renge-kyō*, is a revered focus of devotion. This is known as the *daimoku*, and is seen to represent ultimate reality in its intrinsic purity. It is contained in the seven-syllable invocatory formula, '*Na-mu myō-hō ren-ge-kyō*', whose repetition, accompanied by drums, is the central practice. Chanting this with sincere faith in the power of the truths of the *Sūtra* is held to purify the mind, protect and benefit the chanter, and develop the *Bodhisattva* perfections. The title is also written or carved on a scroll or plaque known as the *gohonzon*, or 'main object of worship'.[13] Down the centre of this is the invocation in bold Japanese characters; above, left and right are the names of Prabhūtaratna Buddha – a past Buddha who remanifests himself in an incident in the *Lotus Sūtra* (ch. 11), – and Śākyamuni; at its sides are the names of the 'four great kings', guardian deities who live in the lowest heaven described in ancient Buddhist cosmology; in the remaining space are names of various holy beings mentioned in the *Sūtra* – including the *Bodhisattva*[14] of whom Nichiren said he was an incarnation – and of certain Shintō *kamis*. The *gohonzon* is seen as representing the final truth, as revealed in the *Sūtra*, emphasizing Śākyamuni Buddha as all-pervading reality and universal power. The *gohonzon* is thus the primary focus of worship and object of contemplation, prominently displayed in Nichiren temples between images

[13] For an example, see Bechert and Gombrich, 1984: 226. The main image in a Buddhist temple is a *honzon*. For Chinese tales of the power of devotion to the *Lotus Sūtra*, see *BP*.36.

[14] Viśiṣṭacāritra (Jap. Jogyō), mentioned in chs. 15 and 21 of the Chinese version of the *Lotus Sūtra*.

of Śākyamuni and Prabhūtaratna. The sub-sect known as the Nichiren Shō-shū, however, has an image of Nichiren himself in a central position, as they see him as a Buddha. A secondary Nichiren practice is to chant the sections of the *Lotus Sūtra* on skilful means and the 'eternal' life-span of Śākyamuni.

PILGRIMAGE

Pilgrimage is a fairly common practice in Buddhism, and may be done for a variety of reasons: to bring alive events from the life of holy beings and so strengthen spiritual aspirations; to generate karmic fruitfulness; to be suffused by the beneficial influence (see p. 237) of relics and *Bodhi*-trees; to receive protection from deities at the sites; or to fulfil a vow that pilgrimage would be made if aid were received from a certain *Bodhisattva*. The most ancient sites are those of the Buddha's birth, first sermon, awakening and *parinirvāṇa*. The Buddha said these should be visited with thoughts of reverence, such that anyone dying on the journey would be reborn in a heaven (*D*.II. 140–1). The most important is Bodh-Gayā, whose focus is an ancient *Bodhi*-tree directly descended from the one under which Gotama attained awakening. Its sagging boughs are reverently propped up, prayer flags flutter from its branches, and pilgrims treasure any leaves which fall from it.

In Sri Lanka, a cutting from the original *Bodhi*-tree grows at the ancient capital, Anurādhapura, and is a favourite pilgrimage site. Another is in Kandy, where the 'Temple of the Tooth' houses a tooth-relic of the Buddha. Pilgrims also visit Mount Siripāda, known in English as 'Adam's Peak', the most spectacular mountain in Sri Lanka. On its summit is a 1.7-metre-long depression in the rock, held to be a footprint left by the Buddha when he used his meditative powers to fly to the island on a teaching trip. Such 'footprints' exist elsewhere in the Buddhist world, and are greatly valued as objects associated with Gotama. On Siripāda, devotion is expressed both at the 'footprint' and at the shrine of Saman, the stream-enterer god seen as guarding the peak. In a remarkably ecumenical spirit, Hindus revere the footprint as that of Śiva, and Muslims revere it as Adam's.

In South-east Asia, pilgrimage sites such as the Shwe-dāgon *Stūpa* are revered for their relics, or as the site of a claimed visit by Gotama in his final or previous lives. An important Tibetan site is in its capital, Lhasa: the Potala Palace, traditional home of the Dalai Lamas. Another is Mount Kailāsa (*EB*.7.5.1), identified with Mount Meru, the central mountain of the world, and associated with Milarepa (see p. 206). In China, pilgrims visit four sacred mountains (*Shan*) seen as this-worldly 'residences' of certain great *Bodhisattvas*: Putuo (P'ut'o) for Avalokiteśvara, Wutai (Wut'ai) for Mañjuśrī (*BS2*. 11), Emei (O-mei) for Samantabhadra, and Jiuhua (Chiuhua) for Kṣitigarbha. In Japan, Avalokiteśvara is said to have manifested himself in one or other of his guises at thirty-three sites in the environs of the ancient capitals Nara and Kyoto, which are now the focus of the 746-miles-long Saikoku pilgrimage route. The longer Shikoku pilgrimage, stretching for 886 miles around Shikoku island, links 88 temples associated with Kōbō Daishi, founder of the Shingon school (see p. 227), its temples dedicated to a variety of holy beings, but especially Bhaiṣajyaguru and Avalokiteśvara (Reader, 2006). Each such site has a temple or shrine, where *Sūtras* are chanted and pilgrims get stamps put in their special books or on scrolls, which are treasured as reminders of the pilgrimage and the devotion it expressed and aroused. The especially devout pilgrim may perform ascetic practices, such as bathing in a freezing cold waterfall or praying all night. Typical motives for doing such pilgrimages, in Japan, are to help the health of the pilgrim or a family member, to make good karma to transfer to an ancestor, to bring harmony and/or prosperity to one's family and, nowadays, to avoid traffic accidents, and to enjoy nature or visit places of traditional Japanese culture.

FESTIVALS

Buddhists enjoy and appreciate festivals as times for reaffirming devotion and commitment, generating karmic fruitfulness for the individual and community, strengthening community ties and values, and merry-making (Gombrich, 1986). The Southern, Northern and Eastern traditions each have their major festivals, and there are also national variations on these, as well as local festivals, for example on the anniversary of the founding of a temple. Some festivals which Buddhists celebrate are not Buddhist, as such, but pertain to the agricultural cycle, national deities, or traditions such as Confucianism.

In Southern Buddhism, most major festivals occur at the time of a full moon. As in Northern Buddhism, the lunar cycle also marks off the sabbath-like *uposatha*s (Skt *poṣadha*), or 'observance days', at the full moon, new moon and, less importantly, two half-moon days. Except at times of major festivals, observance days are attended only by the more devout, who spend a day and night at their local monastery. The monks are solemnly offered food, commitment to certain ethical precepts is made, the monks chant for the laity, and sometimes a sermon is given: features also occurring at all Southern Buddhist festivals. The rest of the time is spent in expressing devotion, reading, talking to the monks and perhaps in some meditation.

In the lands of Southern Buddhism, the festival year starts at the traditional New Year, celebrated at various times, for up to four days, in mid-April. On the first day, houses are thoroughly cleaned of the dirt of the old year. Water, sometimes scented, is ceremonially poured over Buddha-images and the hands of monks and elderly relatives, as a mark of respect. In South-east Asia, this is frequently followed by a good-humoured period when the laity throw water at all and sundry. On the second day, in Thailand, Cambodia and Laos, sand *Stūpa*s are built in temple-compounds or on river banks. When the new year starts on the next day, the sand is spread out to form a new compound floor, or is washed away by the river. Its dispersal is seen as symbolically 'cleansing' a person of the past year's bad deeds, represented by the grains of sand. Reflecting on past misdeeds, people thus rededicate themselves to Buddhist values. Accordingly, the New Year is also a time for aiding living beings by releasing caged birds and rescuing fish from drying-out ponds and streams. Accompanying festivities may include boat races, kite fights, music, traditional dancing and plays.

At the full moon in the lunar month of Vesākha, usually in May, comes *Vesākha Pūjā*, celebrating the Buddha's birth, awakening and *parinirvāṇa*. In Sri Lanka, this is the most important festival, when houses are decorated with garlands and paper lanterns, and driveways and temple courtyards are illuminated. People wander between pavement pantomimes and pavilions displaying paintings of the Buddha's life, and food is given out from road-side alms-stalls. In Burma, *Bodhi*-trees are watered with scented water, while in Thailand, Cambodia and Laos, the monks lead the laity in a threefold circumambulation of a temple, *Stūpa* or Buddha-image. The sermon which follows, on the Buddha's life, sometimes lasts all night.

In Sri Lanka, the next full moon day marks the *Poson* festival, celebrating the spreading of Buddhism to the island by Mahinda. Paintings of him are paraded through the streets to the sound of drumming, and pilgrimages are made to Anurādhapura and nearby Mihintale, where he met and converted the king. The next full moon marks *Āsāḷha Pūjā*, celebrating the Buddha's renunciation and first sermon, and marking the start of the three-month period of *Vassa* (the 'Rains'). During this, monks stay at their home monasteries, except for short absences, for concentration on study and meditation, and many young men in South-east Asia temporarily ordain. The laity also deepen their religious commitment. They tend to avoid festivities, especially secular ones such as marriages, and more people than usual observe *uposatha*s at their local monasteries. Most ordinations take place in the time leading up to *Āsāḷha Pūjā*, with their karmic fruitfulness seen as contributing to the timely start of the rains.

At the full moon marking the end of *Vassa*, the monks hold the ceremony of *Pavāraṇā*. When they chant and meditate, wax drips into a bowl of water from a burning candle, and it is thought that something of the monks' karmic fruitfulness, built up during *Vassa*, suffuses and sacralizes the water. This is then sprinkled on the laity as a blessing. In South-east Asia, especially Burma, the following day is the *Tāvatiṃsa* festival, celebrating the time when the Buddha, after spending *Vassa* in the Tāvatiṃsa heaven teaching his mother, descended to earth. As the 'light' of the world was then accessible again, this is a festival of lights, which illuminate houses, monasteries and *Stūpa*s, and may be floated on rivers in small leaf-boats. A special food-offering is also made to a procession of monks, headed by a layman holding a Buddha-image and alms-bowl, symbolizing the returning Buddha.

The following month is the season for *Kaṭhina* celebrations, at which new robes, useful goods and money are given to the monasteries. The focal act is the donation of patches of cloth which the monks dye and make into a special robe, during the same day, commemorating the robes made from sewn-together rags in early Buddhism. These highly auspicious ceremonies, held at most local *vihāra*s, complete the annual round of the more important festivals in Southern Buddhism.

Other than in Nepal, several festivals in Northern Buddhism more or less coincide with corresponding Southern ones: the celebration of the awakening and *parinirvāṇa* of the Buddha (his birth being celebrated eight days earlier), the first sermon and the descent from a heaven (here seen as the Tuṣita heaven). The different schools also have festivals relating to their founders, with the death of Tsongkh'apa (in November) being of general importance; monasteries also have festivals relating to their specific tutelary deity. An important and characteristic festival centres on the Tibetan New Year, in February. In the preceding two weeks, monks dressed in masks and brightly coloured robes perform impressive ritual dances before a large lay audience.[15] Accompanied by booming alpine horns, drums, shrilling oboes and clashing cymbals, they act out a series of solemn but impressive movements, lasting several hours. These are seen as driving away evil powers, while other rituals seek to help beings to progress towards awakening. From the fourth to the twenty-fifth day of the first month, monks perform the

[15] Bechert and Gombrich, 1984: 242–3 show such dances at the 1974 coronation of the king of Bhutan.

ceremonies of *Monlam* (*sMon lam*), the 'Great Vow', centred on a five-day celebration of the Buddha's 'marvel of the pairs' at Śrāvasti (Pali Sāvatthī; see p. 26). As an event in which rival teachers were confounded, this became an appropriate symbol for the overcoming of evil forces, and of Buddhism's past victory over Bön. On the thirteenth day, dances portray Tibetan Buddhism's fierce protector-deities in their struggle against demons and spiritual ignorance. These are represented by a small human effigy which is ritually killed, symbolizing victory over evil and the securing of a safe and prosperous new year. To raise people's energy levels for the new year, horse races and archery competitions are held around this period.

In the lands of Eastern Buddhism, the annual round of festivals has fewer Buddhist elements, and more from Confucianism, Shintō and folk traditions. In Communist China, festivals were for a time largely secularized and politicized, though they have continued much as before in Taiwan and among expatriate Chinese. Among the Chinese, who determine festivals by a lunar calendar, the birth of the Buddha is celebrated in May, as in Korea, while in Japan it is celebrated on 8 April. The principal rite recalls the story that the newborn Śākyamuni stood and was bathed by water sent down by gods: small standing images of the child are placed in bowls and scented water or tea is ladled over them. For Chinese Buddhists, the festival is also a popular time for the release of living beings into the water or air. In Korea, it is a time for illuminating temples with paper lanterns. In Japan the festival is known as *Hana matsuri*, the 'Flower Festival', and retains elements of a pre-Buddhist festival involving the gathering of wild mountain flowers so as to bring home deities to protect the rice-fields. The Buddhist connection is that Śākyamuni was born in a flower-laden grove, so that the infant-Buddha images are housed in floral shrines.

The other important Chinese Buddhist festivals are those of the 'birth', 'awakening' and 'death' of Guanyin, and especially *Ullambana*, which is also celebrated by non-Buddhists. This 'Festival of Hungry Ghosts', in August/September, is when ancestors reborn as ghosts are said to wander in the human world, as a potential source of danger. At the full moon, which ends the three-month 'Summer Retreat', monks transfer karmic fruitfulness, put out food and chant *Sūtra*s for them, so as to help them to better rebirths. The laity sponsor the rites and participate by burning large paper boats which will help 'ferry across' hungry ghosts to a better world, thus showing filial regard for ancestors. A favourite story told at this time is that of Mu-lian (Mu-lien),[16] a key *Arhat* disciple of the Buddha who

[16] Skt Maudgalyāyana, Pali Moggallāna.

discovered that his mother was reborn as a hungry ghost or in a hell (there are two versions of the story). On the advice of the Buddha, he then helped her attain a better rebirth by transferring karmic fruitfulness to her (*BS2*.35 and 46; *EB*.2.5.4). In Japan, *Ullambana* became *O-bon*, the 'Feast for the Dead', celebrated from 13 to 15 July. Graves are washed and tended, and an altar is set up in or near the home for offerings of fresh herbs and flowers. A fire and candles are lit to welcome ancestral spirits to partake of the offerings, and a Buddhist priest is invited to chant a *Sūtra* in each home in his parish.

CHAPTER 9

Buddhist Practice: Ethics[1]

THE ROLE AND BASIS OF ETHICS IN BUDDHISM

In Buddhism, moral virtue (Pali *sīla*, Skt *śīla*) is the foundation of the spiritual path, though a fixed clinging to rules and observances as if they alone were the whole of the path is seen as a hindering 'fetter' (see p. 85). Virtue is seen to generate freedom from remorse, and this helps a person to develop on through gladness and joy to meditative calm, insight and liberation (*A*.v.2). While this model of ethics as part of a 'path' predominates, it is modified in some Mahāyāna schools, particularly in Japan. Here, Sōtō Zen sees morality as the making manifest of one's innate Buddha-nature, while Jōdo-shin sees it as simply expressing gratitude to Amitābha for having saved one.

The overcoming of *dukkha*, both in oneself and in others, is Buddhism's central preoccupation, towards which ethical action contributes. It is seen as in the nature of things that behaving ethically reduces suffering and increases happiness, for oneself and those one interacts with. A moral life is not a burdensome duty or set of bare 'oughts' but an uplifting source of happiness, in which the sacrifice of lesser pleasures facilitates the experiencing of more enriching and satisfying ones. Accordingly, Buddhism says that, if one wants to attain prosperity, amicable social relationships or a good reputation, self-confidence or calm and joy, a good rebirth or progress towards *Nirvāṇa*, then act in such and such a way: for this is how such things are fostered (*BS1*.83–6). If one behaves otherwise, then one will suffer in this and subsequent lives, as a natural (karmic) result of unwholesome actions. It is not, though, that the reason something *is* a good action is that it brings pleasant karmic fruits to the person who does the action. Rather,

[1] The subject of this chapter has been treated in depth in Harvey, 2000; Harvey 2009b: 375–87 cites some key texts; Keown, 2000 is a useful collection on Buddhist ethics, and Saddhatissa, 1970, a classic study of Theravāda ethics. Also, the open-access web-journal *Journal of Buddhist Ethics* has many excellent articles on the topic.

such fruits come *because* an action is *itself* a blameless one which is *kusala* (Skt *kuśala*): 'wholesome' – coming from a morally healthy state of mind, and nurturing this – and 'skilful' – informed by wisdom (Cousins, 1996b; Harvey 2009b: 381–2). That said, the karmic benefits of virtuous actions often become part of the motivation for doing them, though a higher motive is to do it for the goodness of the action itself.

Bad actions are *akusala* – unwholesome, unskilful – and the *Suttas* and *Vinaya* say in relation to such actions that (Harvey, 2011):

1. unwise attention (*A*.I.199–201) feeds greed, hatred and delusion, which are 'the unwholesome' (*A*.I.197) and the roots (*M*.I.46–7, *A*.I.263) which sustain
2. 'the unwholesome': specified unwholesome actions of body, speech or mind (*M*.I.46–7; *A*.V.292–97),
3. which are intentional (*Vin*.IV.124–5), of unwholesome volition,
4. corrupt (*A*.V.292–7), dark (*M*.I.389–91), with fault/blameable (by the wise) (*D*.III.157, *A*.I.263), criticized by the wise, not to be done (*M*.II.114–15, *A*.I. 188–93),
5. as they bring pain and injury to oneself or to others (*M*.I.415–19, *M*.II.114–15; *A*.I.201–5) in a way that is anticipated by correct perception of the immediate facts of the situation (*Vin*.IV.124–25), such that one should not inflict on another what one would not like inflicted on oneself (S.V.353–6),
6. and that, as a karmic result, bring dark harm and pain in this and later lives to the agent (*M*.II.114–15; *A*.I.201–5, *A*.V.292–7), as well as
7. unwholesome character tendencies (*M*.II.114–15), obscuring wisdom and moving one away from *Nirvāṇa* (*M*.I.115–16).

Wholesome actions have the opposite qualities.

Buddhist ethics sees the goodness or badness of an action as residing in a combination of: (a) the mental state, including will, that it springs from, as in Western Kantian ethics; (b) the (immediate predicable) effects on those to whom the action is directed, as in Utilitarianism; and (c) the virtues or vices that it expresses and helps to cultivate – so as to move towards the perfection of enlightenment – as in virtue ethics.[2] Buddhist ethics also has levels of practice suiting different levels of commitment, rather than one set of universal obligations. Most importantly, monks and nuns make

[2] Keown, 1992 and 2000: 17–38 emphasize the 'virtue ethics' aspect of Buddhist ethics, as opposed to a previously often Utilitarian reading. Harvey, 2000: 49–51 assesses some of this and Harvey, 2011 develops this further.

undertakings ruling out actions, such as sexual intercourse, which are acceptable for a layperson.

As a Buddhist comes to understand the extent of *dukkha* in his or her own life, a natural development is concern about others' suffering, and a deepening compassion. Indeed, the importance of 'comparing oneself with others' is stressed: 'Since the self of others is dear to each one, let him who loves himself not harm another' (*Ud*.47). The key basis for ethical action is the reflection that it is inappropriate to inflict on other beings what one oneself finds unpleasant (*S*.v.353–4). Others are just like oneself in desiring happiness and disliking pain, so there is no good reason to add to the common lot of suffering. Moreover, the benefit of self and others are intertwined, so that concern to lessen one's own suffering goes hand-in-hand with lessening that of others. Helping others helps oneself (through karmic results and developing good qualities of mind), and helping oneself (by purifying one's character) enables one to help others better. This is compared to the way that two acrobats, working together and relying on each other, contribute to looking after their partner by mindfully looking after themselves (*S*.v.168–9). Hence mindful attention to one's own mental states and actions protects oneself and hence protects others, and protecting others through patience, harmlessness, lovingkindness and sympathy protects oneself.

One implication of 'impermanence' is that people should always be respected as capable of change-for-the-better. The *Suttas* contain a famous example of this, when the Buddha visited the haunt of the murderous bandit Aṅgulimāla, seeing that he needed only a little exhortation to change his ways: the latter became a monk and soon attained *Nirvāṇa* (*M*.II.97–105 (*BS2*.97)). Whatever a person is like on the surface, the depths of his mind are seen as 'brightly shining' and free from active defilements (see p. 68). This depth-purity, known in the Mahāyāna as the *Tathāgata-garbha* or the Buddha-nature, represents the potential for ultimate transformation, and as such is a basis for respecting all beings.

The changes involved in the round of rebirths are also ethically relevant. Any suffering one now witnesses will have been undergone by oneself in one of one's countless past lives (*S*.II.186), and all beings will have been good to one at some time, as close relatives or friends (*S*.II.189–90). Such considerations stimulate compassion, and positive regard for others, irrespective of their present roles, character or species. Compassion is also appropriate towards someone who, being so evil as to have no apparent good points, will in future lives undergo great suffering as a karmic result of their actions (*Vism*.340).

The teaching on non-Self, entailing that no permanent self or I exists within a person, does not itself support a positive regard for persons as unique entities, as do Christian teachings.[3] Rather, it supports ethics by undermining the very source of lack of respect, self-ishness. This is done by undercutting the notion that 'I' am a substantial, self-identical entity, one that should be gratified and be able to brush aside others if they get in 'my' way. It does not deny that each person has an individual history and character, but it emphasizes that these are compounds of universal factors. In particular, it means that 'your' suffering and 'my' suffering are not inherently different (*Bca.*VIII). They are just suffering, so the barrier which generally keeps us within our own 'self-interest' should be dissolved, or widened in its scope until it includes all beings. The non-Self teaching also emphasizes that we are not as in control of ourselves as we would like to think: this adds a leavening of humility and a sense of humour to our attitude to the weaknesses of ourselves and others. Besides such arguments for ethical action, Buddhism also encourages it through the popular *Jātaka* stories, on former lives and actions of Gotama (e.g. *BTTA*.73, Appleton, 2010, and see *Jat.* in abbreviations).

GIVING[4]

The primary ethical activity which a Buddhist learns to develop is giving, *dāna*, which forms a basis for further moral and spiritual development. In Southern Buddhism, it is the first of the ten 'bases for effecting karmic fruitfulness' (see p. 44). The key focus of giving is the monastic *Saṅgha*, which depends on the laity for such items as alms-food, robes, medicine and accommodation. The monks and nuns, by teaching and example, return a greater gift, for 'The gift of *Dhamma* excels all gifts' (*Dhp*.354). Such acts of mutual giving thus form a key feature of the lay–monastic relationship: 'Thus, monks, this holy life is lived in mutual dependence, for ferrying across the flood [of *saṃsāra*], for the utter ending of *dukkha*' (*It*.111). The *Saṅgha*, moreover, is a potent 'field of karmic fruitfulness' (*S*.v.343), so gifts 'planted' in it are seen as providing a good harvest of karmic fruitfulness for the donors. As alms bestow long life, good appearance, happiness and strength on the recipient, then these, in a human or heavenly rebirth, are said to be the karmic results of alms-giving (*A*.IV.57). On the other hand, being stingy is said to lead to being poor

[3] On Buddhism and human rights, see Keown, 2000: 57–80.
[4] On this, see for example *BW*.169–72; *EB*.1.4.2; Bodhi, 2003; Harvey, 2000: 61–6.

(*M*.III.205[5]). Generosity is not only practised towards the *Saṅgha*, but is a pervading value of Buddhist societies. Fielding Hall, a British official in nineteenth-century Burma, describes how people happily used their funds to build resthouses for travellers, monastery schools, bridges and wells (1902: 106–15).

One fairly common practice is granting freedom to birds or fish (*BS*2.44; *EB*.9.5; Tucker and Williams, 1997: 149–65). Another is to contribute to the costs of printing Buddhist books for free distribution, and in recent years, many excellent websites have also developed, such as Access to Insight (www.accesstoinsight.org), which make much material freely available. Buddhists are also keen to give their assistance, goods and money at an ordination, funeral or festival or when someone is ill, so as to generate karmic fruitfulness, and share it with others. Communities are bound together in communal karmically fruitful deeds, and obligations are fulfilled by contributing to a ceremony sponsored by someone who has previously helped one in this way. Some ceremonies can be expensive, and so a rich person may also help sponsor the ordination of a poorer person's son.

While any act of giving is seen as generating karmic fruitfulness, this becomes more abundant as the motive becomes purer (*A*.IV.60–3; Harvey, 2000: 19–21). Giving may initially be performed for the sake of material karmic results, but the joy and contentment that giving brings are then likely to provide the motive. The constant practice of giving also aids spiritual development by reducing possessiveness, cultivating an open-hearted and sensitive attitude towards others, and expressing non-attachment and renunciation, reflected in the practice of 'giving up' home and family life to become a monk or nun. Giving is also the first of the *Bodhisattva* 'perfections' (p. 156), according to all traditions. It gives a basis for moral restraint, which is seen as even more karmically fruitful (A.IV.393–6 (*BW*.178–9)).

KEEPING THE PRECEPTS[6]

On a basis of developing *dāna*, the Buddhist cultivates moral virtue by observing ethical precepts, the most common of which are the 'five virtues' (*pañca-sīlāni*; *BW*.172–4). The avowal of each of these begins 'I undertake

[5] Nevertheless, not all unhappiness is seen as due to past karma; other causes are at work too (see p. 41).

[6] On this, see Bodhi, 1981; Harvey, 2000: 66–88. *BS1*.70–3 quotes Buddhaghosa on the first four precepts. The precepts are also discussed by Buddhaghosa at *Khp-a*.23–37, and Heng-ching Shih, 1994 is a Mahāyāna text on the precepts.

the rule of training to abstain from. . .'. The five abstentions are from: (i) 'onslaught on [i.e. killing] living beings', (ii) 'taking what is not given', (iii) 'misconduct concerning sense-pleasures', (iv) 'false speech', and (v) 'alcoholic drink or drugs that are an opportunity for heedlessness'. Each precept is a 'rule of training' – as is each item of the monastic code – which is a promise or vow to oneself. They are not 'commandments' from without, though their difference from these, in practice, can be exaggerated. In societies where Buddhism is the dominant religion, they become broadly expected norms for people to seek to live by. Moreover, while the 'taking' of the precepts, by ritually chanting them, can be done by a layperson at any time, they are frequently 'taken' by chanting them after a monk, who fulfils the role of 'administering' them. In such a context, the resolve to keep the precepts has a greater psychological impact, and thus generates more karmic fruitfulness.

In Southern Buddhism, the five precepts are chanted at most ceremonies, and often on a daily basis. People try to live up to them as best they can, according to their commitment and circumstances, but with particular care on observance or festival days. In East Asia, where Buddhism is only one ingredient in the religious situation, the precepts are only taken by those with a fairly strong commitment to Buddhism. In China, they are first taken, perhaps during a stay at a monastery, at a 'lay ordination' ceremony, which makes a person a recognized layman (*upāsaka*) or laywoman (*upāsikā*) (Welch, 1967: 361–5). The precepts are then regarded as quite weighty vows, so that a person may omit one if he feels he cannot yet live up to it (the first is never omitted, though). In Sōtō Zen, devout laypeople take the precepts at *Jūkai*, a week-long set of ceremonies held every spring while staying at a temple. First-timers also have a lay ordination ceremony. The precepts taken consist of commitment to the three refuges, the 'three pure precepts' – 'Cease from evil, do only good, do good for others' – and 'ten great precepts' that begin the fifty-eight *Bodhisattva* precepts from the *Brahmajāla Sūtra* (see p. 294): equivalent to the first four of the five precepts, plus: (v) not taking or selling drugs or alcohol, (vi) not speaking against others, (vii) not praising oneself and abusing others, (viii) not being mean in giving *Dharma* or wealth, (ix) not being angry, and (x) not defaming the 'three jewels'. In Zen, the precepts are seen both to have a literal meaning, and also to remind the practitioner that all is one in the Buddha-nature.[7]

Closely related to keeping the precepts is 'right livelihood (*BW*.124–8). This is making one's living in a way that does not involve the habitual

[7] *BS*2.60; Aitken, 1984: 4–104; Harvey, 2000: 14–15; Jiyu-Kennett, 1999: 213–14.

breaking of the precepts by bringing harm to other beings, but which hopefully aids others and helps cultivate one's faculties and abilities (see p. 83).

Emphasis is sometimes laid on the need for a 'middle way' in keeping the precepts, avoiding the extremes of laxity and rigidity. In any case, Buddhism does not encourage the developing of strong guilt feelings if a precept is broken. Guilt is seen as part of the natural karmic result of unskilful action, and may therefore act as a deterrent. It should not be further indulged in, though, to produce self-dislike and mental turbulence, a spiritual hindrance. Regretting misdeeds is skilful – the acknowledgement of faults is an important part of monastic training – but only if this does not unnecessarily harp on past failings. All traditions see sincere regret as at least lessening the bad karma of actions, and counteractive good actions as able to dilute the effects of bad actions. Nevertheless, Buddhism emphasizes a forward-looking morality of always seeking to do better in the future: taking the precepts as ideals to live up to in an increasingly complete way. The Mahāyāna, though, has confessions of misdeeds as part of some liturgies (*BP*.14 (p. 187)); for example in the Chinese Tiantai school, there are elaborate monastic 'repentance' (*chan-hui* (*ch'an-hui*)) ceremonies (Stevenson, 1986: 61–9), perhaps influenced by the importance attached by Confucianism to ritualized propriety in social relations. The ceremonies involve shame at failings and vows to reform. The 'repentance' is not just for remembered misdeeds, but for the misdeeds of past lives – and for the deeds of oneself *and* all beings: repentance for the actions, attitudes and ways of thinking that have sustained *saṃsāra* for oneself and others. The rituals include chanted *dhāraṇīs* seen as able to remove past bad karma and aid spiritual progress. Monastics sometimes lead laypeople in 'repentance' rituals, though laypeople also sponsor monastics to do them on their behalf.

The role of 'conscience' is performed by mindfulness, which makes one aware of one's actions and motives, along with *hiri* (Skt *hirī*) and *ottappa* (Skt *apatrapya*): the two 'bright states which guard the world' (*A*.I.51) and the immediate causes of virtue. *Hiri* is 'self-respect', which causes one to seek to avoid any action which one feels is not worthy of oneself and lowers one's moral integrity. *Ottappa* is 'regard for consequences', being stimulated by concern over reproach and blame (whether from oneself or others), embarrassment before others (especially those one respects) legal punishment, or the karmic results of an action (*Asl*.124–7).

For an action to break a precept and so be karmically harmful, it must be done with intention; this is not the case, for example, if one accidentally treads on an insect (*EB*.2.3.2). To tell someone else to do a precept-breaking action on one's behalf, though, is still a breach of the precept, for oneself and them (Harvey, 1999: 280). Worse bad karma accrues, moreover, as the force of will behind an action increases; for this leaves a greater karmic 'trace' on the mind. Several things follow from this (Harvey, 2000: 52–8). First, a state of diminished responsibility, due to madness or inflamed passion, reduces the karmic seriousness of an unwholesome action (*Miln*.221). Secondly, it is worse to premeditate an action. Thirdly, it is worse to do a wrong action if one does not regard it as wrong; for then it will be done in a deluded state without restraint or hesitation (*Miln*.84) – as seen in the twentieth century, with ideologies such as those of Hitler, Stalin and the Khmer Rouge 'justifying' the killing of many. Thus killing a human or animal without compunction is worse than doing so with trepidation. Finally, it is worse to kill a large animal than a small one, for the former involves a more sustained effort (*BS1*.70–1). The gravity of an action also depends on the perversity of the intention. To harm a virtuous person, or a respect-worthy one such as a parent, is worse than harming others. Similarly, it is worse to harm a more highly developed form of life. While humans are seen as superior to animals, this is only a matter of degree; humans should show their superiority by using their freedom of choice to treat animals well, not by maltreating them.

The Mahāyāna emphasis on 'skilful means' (see pp. 111, 192) entails that this tradition has a greater tendency than Theravāda to flexibly adapt the precepts to circumstances (Harvey, 2000: 134–40). Asaṅga's *Bodhisattva-bhūmi* (Tatz, 1986: 70–1) says that an (advanced) *Bodhisattva* may kill a person about to kill many people – so that he saves them and the assailant avoids the evil karma of killing – provided that this is done out of genuine compassion, and with a willingness to suffer the karmic consequences of killing; however, if this is sincere, such consequences will be lighter than normal. He may also lie to save others, and steal the booty of thieves and unjust rulers, so that they are hindered in their evil ways.

The first precept

The first precept, regarded as the most important, is the resolution not to intentionally kill any human, animal, bird, fish or insect: the word for 'living being' (Pali *pāṇa*, Skt *prāṇa*) in the precept literally means a 'breather'. While this has not meant that most Buddhists have been pacifists, pacifism has been the ideal (Harris, 1994; Harvey, 2000: 239–85). While the 'wrong livelihood' of 'trade in arms' refers to the arms-salesman and not the soldier, a person who makes his living as a soldier and who dies in battle is said to be reborn in a hell or as an animal (*S*.IV.308–9).

It is emphasized that war is inconclusive and futile: 'Victory breeds enmity; the defeated one sleeps badly. The peaceful one sleeps at ease, having abandoned victory and defeat' (*Dhp*.201; *S*.I.83); 'The slayer gets a slayer in his turn, the conqueror gets one who conquers him' (*S*.I.85). Accordingly, Buddhism contributed to ending Asoka's violent expansion of his empire (see p. 101) and tamed the war-like Tibetans and Mongolians; Chinese Buddhists were noted for 'shirking their military duties', and an early president of the United Nations was the devout Burmese Buddhist U Thant. Most lay Buddhists have been prepared to break the first precept in self-defence, though, and many have helped defend the community. In Thailand, the army is well respected for its role in serving and helping to run the country. The history of Buddhist countries has not been free of wars, and sometimes Buddhist sects have fought each other, as seen in Chapter 7. The communal strife which erupted in Sri Lanka in 1983, pitting sections of the minority Tamil (mainly Hindu) and Sinhalese (mainly Buddhist) populations against each other, and leading to armed conflict lasting until 2009 (see pp. 382–3), unfortunately shows that Buddhists are not immune from letting communalism make them forget some of their principles (Harvey, 2000: 255–60).

While Buddhism has no real objection to contraception, abortion is seen as breaking the first precept, as it cuts off a 'precious human rebirth', seen as beginning at conception.[8] The bad karma from an abortion is often seen to vary according to the age of the foetus, as it involves killing a being with whom the mother has a more developed relationship, and requires more forceful means, but most Buddhists would accept abortion to save the mother's life. In secularizing, post-war Japan, abortion has been quite common, but many women have felt the need to atone for their deed by caring for the spirit of their aborted child through the cult of the *Bodhisattva* Jizō in the ritual known as *mizuko kuyō*.[9] Suicide again wastes a 'precious human rebirth', and the suffering instigating it is seen as probably set to continue unabated and intensified into the next, perhaps sub-human, rebirth (Harvey, 2000: 286–310). The case of someone compassionately 'giving' his life to help others is different, though. The *Jātaka* stories contain a number of examples of the *Bodhisattva* giving up his life or a body part to save or help another being (*BS1*.24–6; *BS2*.18 and 19), and there is a small tradition in Eastern Buddhism of 'religious suicides', as self-offerings to the

[8] *D*.II.62–3; *Vin*.I.93. On the topic of abortion, see: Keown, 1995, 1998, 2000: 136–68; Harvey, 2000: 311–52, 2001.

[9] LaFleur, 1992; Cabezón, 1992: 65–89.

Buddhas (Benn, 2007). During the Vietnam war, a number of Buddhists burnt themselves to death to bring the world's attention to the plight of the South Vietnamese people under the Diem regime, their hope being that the karmic fruitfulness of the act of self-giving would help sustain Buddhism, and bring peace to Vietnam and the world.

While it is relatively easy to avoid killing humans, other forms of life can cause more problems in practice.[10] There is generally a preference for removing pests to a safe distance and releasing them, though certain deadly and vicious snakes would be killed without hesitation. When Buddhists do kill pests, they may try to counteract the bad karmic results of doing so. In Burma, farmers might only countenance the killing of a plague of crop-eating rats by arguing that some of the money thus saved can be used for karmically fruitful deeds. In Zen monasteries, rites are carried out to aid the destiny of vermin which have been killed.

Emperor Asoka (see p. 101) made laws against killing animals on observance days, the castrating or branding of cattle, and indiscriminate burning of forests; some Theravāda kings have also prohibited or limited the slaughter of animals. Nevertheless, the first precept does not mean that most Buddhists are vegetarian, and the Buddha himself seems to have accepted meat in his alms-bowl (Harvey, 2000: 159–63). His emphasis was on avoiding intentional killing, so that it was worse to swat a fly than to eat a dead animal. He allowed a monk to eat flesh if he had not seen, heard or suspected that the creature had been killed specifically for him, such food then being 'blameless'.[11] As monks lived off alms, they should not pick and choose what food was acceptable, or deprive a donor of the opportunity to do a karmically fruitful act by refusing 'blameless' food. As regards laypeople, even killing so as to give meat as alms generates bad karmic results, due to the distress felt by the animals while being brought to slaughter, and the pain when killed (*M.*I.371).

'Right livelihood' rules out 'trade in flesh', seen as including the butcher, hunter and fisherman: jobs which no committed Buddhist would carry out. In Buddhist societies, butchers are usually non-Buddhists, for example Muslims, and are seen as depraved or as outcastes. The position that meat is acceptable if someone else kills the animal is not necessarily an easy get-out clause. Buddhist countries lack the mass slaughter-houses of the West – which would be seen as hells on earth – so to get meat is more likely to

[10] On Buddhism, animals and the environment, see Batchelor and Brown, 1992; Harvey, 2000: 150–86, 2007b; Keown, 2000: 81–135; Tucker and Williams, 1997.

[11] *M.*II.368–71 and *Vin.*I.236–8 (*BTTA*.2).

involve *asking* a butcher to kill an animal, or killing it oneself. Indeed raising livestock for slaughter is generally seen as a breach of 'right livelihood' which Buddhists tend to steer clear of.

In Southern Buddhism, while only a few are vegetarian, this is universally admired, and most people have an uneasy conscience when they *think* about meat-eating (Gombrich, 1971: 260–2). Some abstain on observance days, when they may also avoid farming, as it might harm worms and insects. A few monks are vegetarian and occasionally monks organize boycotts of butchers' shops in remote villages. In general, it is seen as worse to eat the flesh of an animal at a higher level of existence: it is worst to eat beef (in Burma, it was once a crime to kill a cow), less bad to eat goats or fowl, less bad again to eat eggs (usually seen as being fertilized), and least bad to eat fish, the most common form of flesh eaten. Many people catch their own fish, but those who make a living by fishing are looked down on in society.

In the Mahāyāna, the *Laṅkāvatāra Sūtra*[12] denies that the Buddha allowed 'blameless' meat for monks, and argues against meat-eating: all beings have been relatives in a past life; meat stinks; eating it hinders meditation and leads to bad health, arrogance and rebirth as a carnivorous animal or low-class human; if no meat is eaten, killing for consumption will cease. In China, the *Bodhisattva* precepts in the *Brahmajāla Sūtra*, used as a supplementary monastic code and also influential on pious laypeople, requires vegetarianism, and vegetarian feasts have been common at Buddhist celebrations (*BS*2.45). In Japanese tradition, no beef was eaten and vegetarianism was required of monastics, though in 1872, as part of the modernization of Japan and its drive to learn from Western culture, the formal ban on meat-eating in the monasteries was lifted by the government (Jaffe, 2001: 26–33). The Japanese preference for all kinds of food from the sea is probably due to Buddhist influence (fish are a low form of life), as well as the fact that Japan is an island. Unfortunately, whales also live in the sea, and more powerful boats and an increasing secularism means that Japan now catches many of these (though the public's taste for whale-meat is in decline).

Most lands of Northern Buddhism have a harsh, cold climate, so that vegetarianism is seen as impractical. Nevertheless, among nomadic herdsmen, older, more pious members of families generally avoid killing livestock, and those who work as professional butchers are despised. In general, large animals are killed for food, in preference to killing many small ones for the same amount of meat. Nevertheless, Tibetans are noted for their

[12] *Lanka*.244–59, as at *BT*.91–2. See also Harvey, 2000: 163–5.

kindness to animals; scruples are had even about eating wild honey, for this is seen as entailing both theft from and murder of bees.

The other precepts

The second precept is seen as ruling out any act of theft, but also fraud, cheating, borrowing without the intention to return, and taking more than is one's due. Often, gambling is also included. The precept clearly has relevance for the production and use of wealth (Harvey, 2000: 187–238). The ideal here is that one's wealth should be made in a moral way, which does not cheat or harm others; it should be used to give ease and pleasure to oneself and one's family, to share with others and to generate karmic fruitfulness; and it should not be the object of one's greed and longing (*S.*IV.331–7). Miserliness and over-spending are both extremes to be avoided. If someone is well-off, this is generally seen as being aided by past karmic fruitfulness, and the rich person is seen as having a greater opportunity to generate karmic fruitfulness by giving liberally to the *Saṅgha* and the community. Combined with the idea that poverty tends to encourage theft and civil discontent (*D.*III.64–9 and *D.*I.135 (*BW.*139–41)), this means that the Buddhist ideal is a society free from an imbalance of poverty and riches.

Buddhist countries are found at many different levels of economic development. At one extreme is Bhutan, now gradually emerging from a medieval life-style into the modern world. Here the people are poor, but seem generally contented, and the king has said that he is more interested in the 'Gross National Happiness' than the 'Gross National Product'. At the other extreme is Japan. Its rapid modernization has been aided by an emphasis on serving the group (rooted in traditional methods of agriculture, but reinforced by Confucianism), the samurai ethic of loyal service to feudal lord and state, and the Buddhist emphasis on selfless detachment, here in an active engaged mode (King, 1981). While the modern Japanese seem to have become attached to work almost for its own sake, recently some have become concerned that too little time is being left for relaxation and spiritual matters.

The third precept primarily concerns avoiding causing suffering by one's sexual behaviour. This includes adultery, incest, any enforced intercourse, and intercourse with those married or engaged to another or under the protection of relatives. What counts as 'adultery' varies according to the marriage patterns of different cultures, and Buddhism has been flexible in adapting to these. While monogamy is the preferred, and predominant pattern, it has also tolerated polygamy, and sometimes polyandry. Premarital sex has been regarded as a breach of the precept in some cultures, but not in others; flirting with a married woman may also be seen as a breach. Homosexual activity is rarely specified among activities breaking the lay precepts,[13] though a kind of person known as a *paṇḍaka*, which seems to mean one born as a non-normative male, especially a passive homosexual, is seen as unable to experience certain deep meditative states (Harvey, 2000: 411–34). Other socially taboo forms of sexuality have been seen as breaking the precept, doubtless due to the guilt feelings that they entail. Obsessive sexual activities also come within the precept, as do other sense-indulgences such as gorging oneself with food.

The first three precepts concern physical actions, and keeping them is the 'right action' factor of the Eight-factored Path. The fourth precept, while it only specifically refers to 'false speech', is equivalent to all four aspects of the Path-factor of 'right speech' (see p. 83). This precept is generally seen as the second most important one; for it is said that a person who has no shame at intentional lying is capable of any evil action (*M*.I.415). Moreover, in the Theravādin collection of *Jātaka* stories, though Gotama breaks several of the precepts in his past lives as a *Bodhisattva*, he is said to have never lied (*Jat.* III.499). Any form of lying or deception, either for one's own benefit or that of another, is seen as a breach of the precept, though a small 'white lie' is, for example, much less serious than lying in a court of law (*Miln*.193). Lying is to be avoided not only because it often harms others, but because it goes against the Buddhist value of seeking the truth and seeing things 'as they really are'. The more a person deceives others, the more he is likely to deceive himself; thus his delusion and spiritual ignorance increase. Lying also makes for a more complicated life: the truth is easier to remember than a network of lies.

The other forms of 'right speech' are intended to further moderate speech-actions, so as to decrease unskilful mental states and increase skilful ones. They concern avoiding: divisive words causing a listener to think less of some third party; harsh or angry words; and idle chatter. Right speech delights in speaking of people's *good* points, so as to spread harmony rather than discord; it is 'gentle, pleasing to the ear, affectionate, going to the heart, courteous'; it is spoken 'at the right time, in accordance with fact, about the goal, about *Dhamma*, about moral discipline', so as to be 'worth treasuring' (*M*.III.49).

[13] At *BSI*.71, Conze mistranslates Buddhaghosa, who does not say that there should be no sexual penetration of men, but that 'for men', those who should not be penetrated are women in various kinds of committed relationships, or under various kinds of protection.

This description clearly shows a very comprehensive concern with verbal behaviour (the same now applies to e.g. emailing). The final item, dealing with chatter, is more emphasized in a meditative setting, but in general stresses the need to use one's words wisely: to inform, aid or express kindness to others, and not just for the sake of opening one's mouth. A list of 'ten skilful actions', comprised of the seven factors of right action and speech, plus avoiding covetousness, ill-will and wrong views (*M*.III.45–50; M.I.286–90 (*BW*.156–61)), seems to be the basis of Zen's 'ten great precepts'.

The fifth precept is not listed under the Path-factors of right action or right speech, but keeping it aids 'right mindfulness'. In intoxicated states lacking mental clarity or calm, one is also more likely to break all the other precepts. Certainly the wish to avoid life's sufferings by indulging in a false happiness is best avoided. In following this precept, some seek to avoid any intoxicating, or mind-altering substances, while others regard intoxication, and not the taking of a little drink, as a breach of the precept. Buddhism is not puritanical in such matters, and unlike some Muslim countries, no Buddhist country bans the sale or consumption of alcohol. Nevertheless, making a living by its sale is a 'wrong livelihood' (*A*.III.208).

The positive implications of the precepts

While each precept is expressed in negative wording, as an abstention, one who keeps these 'rules of training' increasingly comes to express positive virtues. As the roots of unskilful action are weakened, the natural depth-purity of the mind can manifest itself. Each precept thus has a positive counterpart, respectively: (i) kindness and compassion, 'gentle and kindly, he abided compassionate to all living beings' (*M*.I.345); (ii) generosity and renunciation; (iii) 'joyous satisfaction with one's own wife' (*A*.V.138; cf. *Sn*.108), contentment and fewness-of-wishes; (iv) loving truth by searching it out, recognizing falsity and attaining precision of thought; and (v) mindfulness and clear awareness. Contentment is seen as the 'greatest of wealths' (*Dhp*.204), and the height of this virtue is shown by a remark of the eleventh-century Tibetan saint Milarepa, who, living in threadbare cotton robes in a freezing Himālayan cave, said, 'to me, everything is comfortable' (Evans-Wentz, 1951: 201)!

Taking extra precepts

Within Southern (and also Northern) Buddhism, a set of eight precepts may be taken by devout laypeople on 'observance' days (*BW*.174–6). By taking extra precepts, they undertake a discipline which reduces stimulating sense-inputs that disturb calm and concentration, so that their conduct temporarily resembles that of monks. Regular attendees at observance days, who are usually aged over forty, are therefore known by the term for a devout male or female lay disciple, *upāsaka* and *upāsikā*. In daily life, these also observe the five precepts more faithfully than other people. The Northern and Eastern traditions continue the older practice of using the terms *upāsaka* or *upāsikā* (in translation) for anyone who observes the five precepts and takes the three refuges.

The difference between the eight and five precepts is first that the third precept is replaced by one on avoiding 'non-celibate conduct (*abrahmacariya*)': all sexual activity. After the usual fifth precept, three more are then taken, concerning abstention from: (vi) 'eating at an unseasonable time', (vii) 'dancing, singing, music and visiting shows; wearing garlands, perfumes and unguents, finery and adornment', and (viii) 'high or luxurious beds'. The sixth precept entails not eating any solid food after noon. The seventh means avoiding, or keeping one's distance from, entertainments, and avoiding make-up, perfume, jewellery and clothes other than plain white ones: disciplines also followed by those attending the Zen *Jūkai* festival. The eighth is intended to diminish slothfulness or feelings of grandeur, and entails sleeping and sitting on mats. In practice, however, this is how most Asian laypeople have traditionally slept anyway.

There is also a set of ten precepts, the same as those observed by novice monks (*Khp-a*.22–37; *EB*.3.5.1). Here, the seventh precept is split into two, and there is an additional undertaking to 'abstain from accepting gold and silver', precluding the handling of money. Unlike the eight precepts, the ten are only taken on a long-term basis. A few Theravāda men, usually elderly, permanently follow them and wear white or brown. A greater number of women do so. This is because, in the Southern tradition, the full order of nuns died out, and the greatest number of precepts that a woman could formally take, until a recent revival of the nuns' order in Sri Lanka (see pp. 301–2), has been ten. More women than men also observe the eight precepts on observance days.

LOVINGKINDNESS AND COMPASSION

Lovingkindness (Pali *mettā*, Skt *maitrī*) and compassion (*karuṇā*) are seen as part of the Path-factor of 'right resolve', and as outgrowths from generosity, aids to deepening virtue and factors undercutting the attachment to 'I'. They are also the first two of the four 'immeasurables' or 'divine abidings' (*brahma-vihāra*): qualities which, when developed to a high degree in meditation, are said to make the mind 'immeasurable' and like the mind of the loving *brahmā* gods (*BW*.176–8; *Vism*.IX). Lovingkindness is the heartfelt aspiration for the happiness of beings, and is the antidote to hatred and fear. Compassion is the aspiration that beings be free from suffering, and is the antidote to cruelty. Empathetic joy (*muditā*) is joy at the joy of others, and is the antidote to jealousy and discontent. Equanimity (Pali *upekkhā*, Skt *upekṣā*) is an even-minded, unruffled serenity in the face of the ups and downs of life – one's own and that of others – which balances concern for others with a realization that suffering is an inevitable part of being alive. It is the antidote to partiality and attachment.

Lovingkindness is stressed in such verses as, 'Conquer anger by kindness; conquer evil by good; conquer the stingy by giving; conquer the liar by truth' (*Dhp*.223). Such benevolence and true friendliness is also the theme of the *Karaṇīya-metta Sutta*, a very popular *paritta* chant:

> He who is skilled in good, and who wishes to attain that State of Peace [*Nirvāṇa*] should act thus: he should be able, upright, perfectly upright, of pleasant speech, gentle and humble, contented, easy to support [as a monk], unbusy, with sense controlled, discreet, modest, not greedily attached to families [for alms]. He should not commit any slight wrong on account of which other wise men might censure him. [Then he would think]: 'May all beings be happy and secure, may they be happy-minded! Whatever living beings there are – feeble or strong, long, stout or medium, short, small or large, seen or unseen [i.e. ghosts, gods and hell-beings], those dwelling far or near, those who are born or those who await rebirth – may all beings, without exception, be happy-minded! Let none deceive another nor despise any person whatever in any place; in anger or ill-will let them not wish any suffering to each other. Just as a mother would protect her only child at the risk of her own life, even so, let him cultivate a boundless heart towards all beings. Let his thoughts of boundless lovingkindness pervade the whole world: above, below and across, without obstruction, without any hatred, without any enmity. Whether he stands, walks, sits or lies down, as long as he is awake, he should develop this mindfulness. This, they say, is divine abiding here. Not falling into wrong views, virtuous and endowed with insight, he gives up attachment for sense-desires. He will surely not come again to any womb [rebirth in the sense-desire realm]. (*Khp*.8–9; *Sn*.143–52)

Thus lovingkindness is ideally to be radiated to all beings, in the same strength as a mother's love for her child; though without the sentimentality and possessiveness that this may include. The height of this ideal is expressed thus: 'Monks, as low-down thieves might carve one limb from limb with a two-handled saw, yet even then whoever entertained hate in his heart would on that account not be one who carried out my teaching' (*M*.I.129 (*BW*.278–9)). Lovingkindness can be practised in daily life by kindly actions, and chanting the above *Sutta* with full awareness of its meaning is one of the most common forms of meditation in Southern Buddhism. A more sustained meditation on lovingkindness is also practised (see Chapter 11).

To help overcome ill-will for someone, a person developing lovingkindness may reflect that more harm comes to one from a mind badly directed by ill-will than from the actions of an adversary (*Dhp*.42). Getting angry at provocation is actually to co-operate in making oneself suffer (*Vism*.300). Other recommendations are to remember that all beings have been good to one in some past life, or to reflect that the mind is ever-changing, so that 'the person who annoyed me' is no longer precisely the same person (*Vism*.301).

Compassion, as the root-motivation of the *Bodhisattva*, is much emphasized (*EB*.4.4.1). In Eastern and Northern Buddhism, the taking of the *Bodhisattva* vows, often done after taking the precepts, is a solemn commitment which expresses the compassionate urge to aid all beings. This is to be done by constant practice of the six 'perfections' (Skt *pāramitā*): generosity, virtue, patience, vigour, meditation and wisdom (Pagel, 1995; Skorupski, 2002). In Southern Buddhism, there is a set of ten perfections (Pali *pārami*), seen as noble qualities of aid in compassionately benefiting others: generosity, virtue, non-sensuality, wisdom, vigour, patience, truthfulness, determination, lovingkindness and equanimity (Bodhi, 1996). Though a *Bodhisattva* develops these to the highest degree, they are also seen as appropriate for all aspiring for *Nirvāṇa*.

The Buddha taught that 'whoever wishes to take care of me should take care of the sick' (*Vin*.1.301–2), and in his 'Precious Garland of Advice for the King' (Hopkins and Lati Rinpoche, 1975: v. 320), Nāgārjuna advised, 'Cause the blind, the sick, the lowly, the protectorless, the wretched and the crippled equally to attain food and drink without interruption'. A good example of this compassionate ideal at work was in Tang China (618–907), where Buddhist monasteries, and lay religious societies set up by monks, ran hospitals, dispensaries, orphanages, homes for the elderly and resthouses for pilgrims; they fed beggars, did famine relief work, built roads and bridges and sank wells. In the lands of Southern Buddhism, charitable works other than running orphanages have usually been left in the hands of wealthy laymen or rulers. Monasteries have, however, informally carried out a number of welfare roles. Today, lay Buddhist welfare work includes famine relief work, running organ-banks, and the Gandhian-influenced 'Sarvodaya Śramadāna' rural development movement in Sri Lanka.[14] The latter is part

[14] www.sarvodaya.org; Harvey, 2000: 225–34; and see pp. 380–1.

of what is now called 'Engaged Buddhism',[15] another example of which is the Taiwanese Tzu Chi Foundation (www.tzuchi.org), which runs hospitals and engages in disaster relief work.

The ideal of caring for animals (Harvey, 2000: 170–4) is nicely expressed in a *Jātaka* story (no. 124), which tells of the *Bodhisattva* as a hermit who brought water to wild animals during a drought; as he was so intent on doing this, he had no time to get himself food, but the animals gathered it for him. In accord with this ideal, large Chinese monasteries have had a pool for fish rescued from the fishmonger, and livestock were released into their care, perhaps with contributions for their upkeep. Burma has 'retirement homes' for cows. Buddhism also has a tradition of providing veterinary care; in this, a badly afflicted animal would not normally be 'put out of its misery', but be cared for. Killing it would be seen as not much different from killing an afflicted human.

CARE FOR THE DYING AND THE DEAD

Compassionate help for others is no less important in death than in life, according to Buddhism (Williams and Ladwig, 2012). As death approaches, it is the duty of relatives and friends to help a person have a 'good death'; for in a rebirth perspective, death is the most important and problematic 'life-crisis'. The ideal is to die in a calm, aware state, joyfully recollecting previous good deeds, rather than regretting them (e.g., as 'too generous'), so that the best possible rebirth is obtained, within the limits set by previous karma (*M*.III.214). Active or passive euthanasia is not supported, though it is acceptable for a person to refuse treatment when it becomes too oppressive.[16]

In Southern Buddhism, monks are fed on behalf of a dying person, who is also calmed by the monks' chanting, and reminded of his good deeds. Funerals (by cremation) may have an almost festival atmosphere, and grief is seldom shown unless the death was especially untimely or tragic. Karmic fruitfulness is shared with the deceased, as it is at subsequent memorial services. At these, water is poured into a bowl until it overflows, and monks chant a verse which says that, just as water flows downwards, 'so may what is given here reach the departed' (*Khp*.6).

In Northern Buddhism, a dying or recently dead person will have the *Bardo Thodol* (*Bar-do Thos-grol*), commonly known as 'The Tibetan Book

[15] Jones, 1981; Harvey, 2000: 112–13; Queen and King, 1996; Socially Engaged Buddhism resources website: www.dharmanet.org/lcengaged.htm.

[16] See Keown, 1995, 2000: 169–82; Harvey, 2000: 292–310, 2001.

of the Dead', read to him.[17] This is to guide him through the experiences of the forty-nine days between lives, to help overcome lingering attachment to his body and family, or even gain liberating insight. At the time of death, all are said to experience the radiant *Tathāgata-garbha* (see p. 139), the ground state of awareness which is empty of defilements and attuned to the nature of reality. All but the advanced *yogin* turn away from this in incomprehension, and then undergo the normal intermediate existence (see p. 71). During this, Yama, god of the dead, holds up the 'mirror of karma': this and conscience makes a person face the details of his past life's actions (Dorje, 2005: 279–80). Visions of the various rebirth realms, and of heavenly Buddhas and *Bodhisattvas* ensue. One who does not understand the nature of these visions is drawn towards a new rebirth, according to his karma. One with understanding, however, may accelerate his development on the *Bodhisattva* path, or be able to gain rebirth in a Pure Land. After a death, the corpse is usually cremated. Sometimes, though, it is dismembered so that vultures can benefit by eating it.

In Eastern Buddhism, a dying person may hold strings attached to the hands in a painting of Amitābha. This is to help him to die peacefully, with the thought of being drawn to Amitābha's Pure Land (*BP*.48). Chinese Buddhists have monks carry out rites for the dead a number of times during the forty-nine days between lives period, and memorial rites are subsequently performed. The monks chant the name of a Buddha, or *Sūtras* to instruct the dead, and the karmic fruitfulness of the chanting and donations is transferred to them; requests are also made for the heavenly *Bodhisattvas* and Buddhas to transfer karmic fruitfulness to the dead.

THE ETHICS OF SOCIAL RELATIONSHIPS

Buddhist ethics also include guidelines for good social relationships, though how these have been adopted in practice varies considerably from culture to culture. An important basic text in this area is the *Sigālovāda Sutta*,[18] described by Asoka as the code of discipline (*Vinaya*) for the laity, paralleling that for monks and nuns. In it, the Buddha comes across Sigāla, worshipping the six directions in accordance with his father's dying wish. He advises that there is a better way to serve the 'six directions': by proper actions towards six types of persons, so as to produce harmony in the web of

[17] *BS1*.227–32; *BS2*.48. Dorje, 2005 is the most recent translation. Sogyal Rinpoche, 1992 is a recent influential book on the care of the dying that draws on ideas of the *Bardo Thodol*.

[18] *D*.III.180–93, as at *BT*.39–44, *SB*.129–38 and *BW*.116–18 (in part); Harvey, 2000: 98–100.

relationships centred on an individual. A person should 'minister' to his parents as the 'eastern quarter' (where the sun rises), his teachers to the 'south', his spouse to the 'west', his friends to the 'north', servants and employees 'below', and renunciants (monks) and Brahmins (priests) 'above'. Reciprocating, each of these should 'act in sympathy with' the person in various ways.

Regarding his parents, a person should think, 'Once supported by them, I will now be their support; I will perform duties incumbent on them, keep up the lineage and tradition of my family, make myself worthy of my heritage, and give alms on their behalf when they are dead'. On their part, his parents 'restrain him from vice, exhort him to virtue, train him to a profession, contract a suitable marriage for him, and in due time they hand over his inheritance'. Elsewhere, it is said that 'Aid for mother and father, and support for wife and children; spheres of work that bring no conflict: this is a supreme blessing' (*Khp*.3). The *Sigālovāda Sutta* says that parents only win the honour and respect of children by their kindly help to them. What parents a child gets and what child parents get is the outcome of past karma, but how the relationship is negotiated is a matter of new, chosen action. Some people have 'bad' parents, but it is said that the only way to repay the debt owed to parents for their care during childhood, is to establish them in trustful confidence, virtue, generosity or wisdom (*A*.I.61 (*BW*.118–19; *SB*.251)). The *Sigālovāda Sutta* – except in one Chinese translation – does not give obedience to parents as a duty, though this is praised in several of Asoka's edicts. Another teaching on family life is that family harmony and unity give strength, just as a tree can resist a gale better if it is part of a forest, not alone (*Jat*.I.329).

Other relationships are dealt with in the *Sigālovāda Sutta* as follows. The pupil should minister to his teachers, 'By rising [from his seat in salutation], waiting upon them, eagerness to learn, personal service, and by attention when receiving their teaching'. On their part, his teachers 'train him well, cause him to learn well, thoroughly instruct him in the lore of every art, speak well of him among friends and companions, and provide for his safety in every quarter'. The husband should minister to his wife, 'By respect, courtesy, faithfulness, handing over authority to her [in the home], and providing her with adornment'. On her part, she 'performs her duties well, shows hospitality to kin of both, is faithful, watches over the goods he brings, and shows skill and artistry in discharging all her business' (cf. *BW*.128–30). A friend should minister to friends, 'By generosity, courtesy and benevolence, treating them as one treats oneself, and by being as good as one's word'. On their part, they 'protect one when one is off one's guard, and on such occasions guard one's property; they become a refuge in danger, do not forsake one in times of trouble, and show consideration for one's family'. An employer should minister to servants and other employees, 'By assigning them work according to their strength; by supplying them with food and wages, tending them in sickness, sharing with them unusual delicacies, and granting them leave at all appropriate times'. On their part, they 'rise before him, lie down to rest after him, are content with what is given to them, do their work well, and carry about his praise and good reputation'. Lastly, a householder should minister to monks and priests, 'By lovingkindness in acts of body, speech and mind, by keeping open house to them, and supplying their temporal needs'. On their part, they 'restrain him from evil, exhort him to good, love him with kindly good thoughts, teach him what he has not heard, and correct and purify what he has heard'. Each party to these six relationships has five modes of conduct appropriate for mutual enrichment, but the monks also have an extra one: showing the layperson 'the way to a heavenly rebirth'.

As regards marriage (Harvey, 2000: 101–3), Buddhism's monastic emphasis means that it does not regard this as 'sacred', but as a contract of partnership. Nevertheless, while there is no objection in principle to divorce, social pressures mean that this is not common among Buddhists. Marriage services are not conducted by monks, though these may be asked to bless a couple at or after their marriage. In Sri Lanka, though, in response to the Christian model experienced under colonialism, some more Buddhist elements have been introduced into marriage ceremonies (Gombrich and Obeyesekere, 1988: 255–73). A Japanese Buddhist is married by Shintō rites, while a Thai one is married perhaps by a simple household ceremony in which the family ancestors are informed that the couple are married, so as not to become offended when they have intercourse (Swearer, 1995: 52–6). At the start of a more elaborate Thai ceremony, the couple are the first to offer food to monks, using a single spoon. In this way they share in an act of karmic fruitfulness, so as to link some of their future moments of happiness. In connection with this, it is said that a husband and wife, if matched in trustful confidence, virtue, generosity and wisdom, will be reborn together if they wish (*A*.II.61–2 (*BW*.119–24)).

Unlike some societies, ones whose social ethics have been Buddhist have regarded the role of the single woman (spinster, divorced or widowed) as a respected one (Nash and Nash, 1963). In Southern and Northern Buddhism, laws relating to the grounds for divorce and the division of property and children have been relatively equal with regard to the husband and wife. Writing in 1902, Fielding Hall also said that he found Burmese women to be very free compared with Western women of his day (1902: 169–86). In the lands of Eastern Buddhism, however, the Confucian social ethic has placed the wife in a clearly inferior position to the husband.

In Thailand, women have traditionally had an influential role outside the home in both small and large trading.[19] In agriculture, there is little differentiation of jobs along sexual lines, though men tend to do the heavier work and to take the more important decisions. No attention is paid if a man does a 'woman's' job, or vice versa: a woman may plough and a man be a midwife. In Southern Buddhist lands, women were traditionally found in law and medicine, and the royal harem had a major political role. In Sri Lanka, Mrs Bandaranayake was the first woman prime minister in the world (in 1960). In Northern Buddhism, women have enjoyed considerable equality regarding sexual freedom, property rights and acting on their own behalf. They often head a household, and are active in trade, if less directly active in politics. Nevertheless, today there are many women in positions of high authority among Tibetan exiles. There have also been a number of important female *Lamas*. In East Asia, where the discriminatory Confucian ethic prevailed, the Chan/Zen school in particular emphasized sexual equality, based on the idea of all having the Buddha-nature (*BP*.40).

While Buddhism sees all people as having had past lives as males and as females, and any human rebirth as the product of good karma, rebirth as a woman is seen as to some extent less favourable than as a man (Harvey, 2000: 368–76). This is because a woman undergoes certain sufferings that a man is free from: having to leave her family for her husband's; menstruation; pregnancy; childbirth; and having to wait upon a man (*S*.IV.239). The first and last points are not prescriptive, but just describe practice current in ancient India. While men and women are seen as having equal potential for virtue and for Arahatship, it is said to be impossible for a female (while being a female) to be either a Buddha or a Māra tempter-deity (*M*.III.65–6). The Buddha's equal concern for both sexes, though, is made clear in a passage where he says that he would not die until the monks and nuns, laymen and laywomen were well trained (*D*.II.104–5). The early texts refer to many *Arahat*-nuns ('far more' than 500, at *M*.I.490), a number of whom gave important teachings.[20] The *Therīgāthā* ('Verses of the Elder Nuns' (*Thig*.)) records teachings and experiences of over a hundred. The Mahāyāna gradually came to emphasize sexual equality, partly through saying

[19] On issues of the status of women in Buddhism, see Cabezón, 1992; Dewaraja, 1994; Faure, 2003; Gross, 1993; Harvey, 2000: 353–410; Horner, 1982, 1999; Paul, 1979; Samuel, 2012: 203–19.

[20] *M*.I.299–305; *S*.I.128–35 (in part in *BS2*.50); *S*.IV.374–8; Krey, 2010.

that 'maleness' and 'femaleness' are 'empty' of inherent nature (Schuster, 1981; Harvey, 2000: 371–6). While the Theravāda sees the *Bodhisattva* path as only for rare and heroic men, the Mahāyāna, for whom this path is central, sees women as able to advance far along it. The 'Perfection of Wisdom' was personified as a female *Bodhisattva* and, figuratively, as 'the mother of all the Buddhas', and Tantric Buddhism also introduced many female holy beings associated with wisdom. While the Mahāyāna still sees most Buddhas as male, the Chinese Tiantai school teaches that a Buddha can be female, and in Tibet, Tārā, Vajra-yoginī and Sarasvatī have come to be seen as fully fledged female Buddhas (Tsomo, 1988: 84).

CHAPTER 10

Buddhist Practice: The Saṅgha

The Buddha is said to have affirmed that he would not die until he had disciples who were monks and nuns, laymen and laywomen (*upāsaka* and *upāsikā*) who could teach *Dhamma* and 'establish it, expound it, analyse it, make it clear' (*D*.II.104–5). These groups are known as the four 'assemblies' (Pali *parisā*, Skt *pariṣat*; *Jat*.I.148). The term *Saṅgha* (Skt *Saṃgha*) or 'Community' refers in its highest sense to the 'Noble' *Saṅgha* of those, monastic or lay, who are fully or partially enlightened. Most typically, though, it refers to the community of monks and/or nuns, and this chapter deals with this as well as certain types of married clerics. '*Saṅgha*' in its widest sense was also occasionally used of all the four 'assemblies' (*A*.II.8) – a sense which became not uncommon in Mahāyāna circles (Prebish, 1999: 203–5).

The terms for monks and nuns are respectively *bhikkhu* (Skt *bhikṣu*) and *bhikkhunī* (Skt *bhikṣuṇī*), which literally mean 'almsman' and 'almswoman'. The original mendicancy of these, still current to varying extents, symbolized renunciation of normal worldly activities and involvements. While this was an aid to humility, it actually also ensured against becoming isolated from the laity. The often close lay–monastic relationship makes *bhikkhus* unlike most Christian 'monks'. They also differ from these in that their undertakings are not always for life, and in that they take no vow of obedience. The Buddha valued self-reliance, and left the monastic *Saṅgha* as a community of individuals sharing a life under the guidance of *Dhamma* and *Vinaya*. The job of its members is to strive for their own spiritual development, and use their knowledge and experience of *Dhamma* to guide others, when asked: not to act as an intermediary between God and humankind, or officiate at life-cycle rites. Nevertheless, in practice they have come to serve the laity in several priest-like ways.

THE ROLE OF MONASTICISM

Members of the monastic *Saṅgha* have probably constituted the most numerous clergy in the world. Though the hostility of Communist governments reduced their number from well over a million in the middle of the twentieth century,[1] a good proportion of this remains. Their life is not an 'escapist' or 'selfish' one, as is sometimes thought. A layperson can distract himself from the realities of life and personal weaknesses with such things as entertainments, pastimes, drink and sex. The simple monastic life, however, is designed to have few distractions, so that there is less opportunity to ignore greed, hatred and delusion, and thus more opportunity to work at diminishing them and to guide others in doing so. Most monks and nuns seek to do this, though a few do take to monastic life as a lazy way of making a living. As regards being 'selfish', the whole aim of monastic life is to help diminish attachment to self and its consequent desires and aversions.

The Buddha felt that the life of a householder was somewhat spiritually cramping, such that it was difficult for a layperson to perfect the 'holy life' (see p. 17). As the monastic life of one 'gone forth from home into homelessness' lacks many of the attachments and limiting involvements found in lay life, it is seen as having fewer obstacles to, and more opportunities for, persistent and consistent spiritual practice. The early texts do refer to many lay stream-enterers, and more than 1,000 eight-precept lay non-returners (*M*.I.490–1 (*BW*.386–90)). Indeed, while the conditions of lay life pose more obstacles, those who make the effort in spite of them can attain good spiritual progress (*BS2*.49; Bluck, 2002). Nevertheless, most Buddhist schools see monasticism as a superior way of life, one that all should respect and aspire to join in this or some future life (*BS1*.93–6; *EB*.2.5.1). In the Theravāda, it is said that a lay stream-enterer should even bow to a monk of lesser attainment, as a way of showing respect to his way of life (*Miln*.162–4). Such respect is reflected in the special honorific terms used to address monks, and in the fact that in South-east Asia, a monk does not 'eat food', but 'glorifies alms-food'. While the early texts refer to a few laypersons who attain Arahatship, they either immediately ordain (*Vin*.I.17) or are close to death (*S*.V.408–10). Thus it is said (*Miln*.264–6) that a lay *Arahat* must ordain on the day of his realization if he is not to pass away, as the lofty nature of this state cannot be expressed in a lay context.

[1] Cousins, 1997a: 377. For example, Lester (1973: 87–8, 175–6) reports that in 1967, during the rainy season when temporary ordinations swell numbers, there were 620,000 monks and novices in Theravāda South-east Asia.

As seen below, while there is a very clear monastic/lay division in Theravāda Buddhism, temporary ordination has developed in several countries, and sometimes ex-monks become specialists in certain rituals. Monasticism remains important in Mahāyāna lands except Nepal and Japan, as discussed below.

THE MONASTIC CODE OF DISCIPLINE

Saṅgha life is regulated by the *Vinaya*, meaning 'that by which one is led out [from suffering]'. The main components of this section of scriptures are a code of training-rules (*sikkhāpada*, Skt *śikṣāpada*) for *bhikkhus*, one for *bhikkhunī*s, and ordinances for the smooth running of communal life and ceremonies. Each code is known as a *pāṭimokkha* (Skt *prātimokṣa*), and is contained in the *Sutta-vibhaṅga* (Skt *Sūtra-vibhaṅga*). This also describes the supposed situation which led the Buddha to promulgate each rule, and mitigating circumstances which nullify or reduce the usual consequences of digression from it. The regulations for communal life, known as *kamma-vācanā*s (Skt *karma-vācanā*), are contained in the *Khandhaka* (Skt *Skandhaka*).

The *pāṭimokkha* gradually evolved during the Buddha's life, and for perhaps a century after. According to one etymology, '*pāṭimokkha*' means a 'bond': something which is 'against scattering' of spiritual states and the purity of the *Saṅgha*. In some ways, the code can be likened both to one of professional conduct and one of sports training. As an elaboration of the ten precepts, it drastically limits the indulgence of desires, and promotes a very self-controlled, calm way of life, of benefit to the monks and nuns themselves and an example which 'inspires confidence' among the laity (*Vism*.19). The rules are not so much prohibitions as aids to spiritual training that require those observing them to be ever mindful. By constantly coming up against limiting boundaries, they are made more aware of their 'greed, hatred and delusion', and so are better able to deal with them.

The *pāṭimokkha* is chanted at the observance days at the full and new moons. Originally, this ceremony was for open acknowledgement, before the community of monks or nuns, of any digression from a rule, but this soon came to be made privately by one renunciant to another prior to the ceremony. At this, the code is chanted by a leading monastic, often now in an abbreviated form, and the silence of the others is taken as a sign that their conduct is pure, with any digressions acknowledged. In this way the ceremony serves as a vital liturgical expression of the communal purity of a particular local *Saṅgha*. Accordingly, every monk present within the formally established boundary (*sīmā*) of a monastery must attend each such ceremony, unless he is ill, when he must send notice of his purity. The same applies for nuns.

The early monastic fraternities developed different versions of the original *pāṭimokkha* of perhaps 150 rules, though these codes agreed in substance and most of the details (Berkwitz, 2010: 35–8). Three are still in use, all dating from the pre-Mahāyāna period and from the Sthavira side of the first schism (see p. 90). The Theravādin code of 227 rules for monks (311 for nuns) is the one used in Southern Buddhism, the Mūla-Sarvāstivādin code of 258 rules for monks (366 for nuns) is used in Northern Buddhism, while the Dharmaguptaka code of 250 rules for monks (348 for nuns) is used in Eastern Buddhism.

The importance of celibacy – in the sense of total avoidance of sexual intercourse – is that sexual activity expresses quite strong attachment, uses energy which could otherwise be used more fruitfully, and generally leads to family responsibilities which leave less time for spiritual practice. Among the various Buddhist lists of states to be overcome on the spiritual path, desire for 'sense-pleasures' (*kāma*) is prominent: it is the first of the five hindrances to meditative calming, and in lists of the three kinds of craving, the four sorts of grasping, and the four deep-seated 'taints' affecting the mind, the first item always has sense-pleasures as its focus. The three 'roots of unwholesome action', to be gradually weakened before *Nirvāṇa* brings their destruction, are greed, hatred and delusion. The practice of the five lay precepts and lovingkindness enables a layperson to minimize hatred, and the practice of the precepts and generosity may reduce greed, but the monastic life with its fewer attachments has clear advantages here. As a form of greed, attachment to sensual pleasures is a lesser fault than hatred or ill-will, but it is seen as taking a long time to uproot (*A*.I.200), and monastic life is seen as a powerful means to aid this. Karma Lekshe Tsomo, a Western nun in the Tibetan tradition, sees celibacy as avoiding the cycle of 'clinging, unfulfilled expectation, the pain of separation' found in normal relationships, where: 'often, the longing for a companion is a wish to complement one's missing or underdeveloped qualities . . . Celibacy, on the other hand, represents a decision to rely on one's own inner authority' (1988: 55). Thus one is 'free to experience life directly, participating wholeheartedly with undivided attention', and it is also harder to blame one's problems on other people (Tsomo, 1988: 57). Celibacy has to be practised in the right way, though. The Zen monk Rōshi Kyogen Carlson notes that it is 'an extremely powerful method for developing the will. Celibacy has to be undertaken with a gentle heart and compassion, otherwise it can lead to a certain coldness, and can be misused to develop personal power' (1982: 38). Alan James, who spent time as a Theravāda monk, comments that a 'wrong' form of celibacy makes a person 'wizened and dried out . . . bitter . . . sexless', but in a 'right' form, a person's gendered nature shows an 'open . . . full face which is happy and very definitely male or female' (James and James, 1987: 40).

The rules are arranged in categories according to degrees of gravity (Ṭhānissaro, 2007). The first relates to *pārājika* actions, which 'entail defeat' in monastic life and permanent dismissal.[2] For monks, these are strong breaches of four of the ten precepts (see p. 278): intentional sexual intercourse of any kind (Wijayaratna, 1990: 89–108); theft of an object having some value; murder of a human being; and false claims, made to the laity, of having attained states such as *jhāna* or stream-entry (a possible way of attracting more alms). As serious karmic consequences are seen to follow from a monk breaking these rules, it is held to be better to become a layperson, who can at least indulge in sexual intercourse, than live as a monk who is in danger of breaking the rule against this. For nuns, there are four extra *pārājika* offences (*Vin*.IV.211–22): (with sensual intent) touching a man, or going to a rendezvous with him; not making known that another nun has broken a *pārājika* rule; and persistently imitating a monk suspended for bad behaviour. The remaining rules explained here are those of the Theravāda monks' *pāṭimokkha*.

The second category of rules, the *saṅghādisesa* ones, covers those requiring a formal meeting of the *Saṅgha* to deal with digressions from them (*Vin*.I.110–86). A digresser is put on probation, being treated as the most junior monk and excluded from official *Saṅgha* affairs for as many days as he has concealed the digression, plus six more. There are thirteen such rules for monks. Five concern actions of a sensual nature other than intercourse. Two relate to monastic residences, which should not be too large, nor should building them involve clearing away trees, which would harm living beings. Two deal with false accusations of an offence involving 'defeat'; two with causing or supporting a schism in the *Saṅgha*; one with a monk who is persistently difficult to admonish about his misdeeds (cf. M.I.27–30 (*EB*.2.3.3)); and the final one deals with a monk who 'corrupts families' by giving small gifts in the hope of receiving abundant alms in return.

The third category (*aniyata*) includes two rules excluding a monk from sitting alone with a woman in certain secluded places. This was both to protect the *Saṅgha*'s reputation, and to avoid unnecessary temptation for

[2] *Vin*.I.1–109; *BS*I.73–7; *EB*.2.3.1, which includes the extra *pārājika* rules for nuns.

monks. The fourth category (*nissaggiya*), of thirty rules, deals with actions requiring expiation (by acknowledgement) and forfeiture of an article. Allowable possessions should only be kept in a certain small quantity, except for a short period, and should not be exchanged unless worn out. While money can be accepted and used by a monastery's lay stewards, it should not be received, handled or used in transactions by monks, though in practice this not infrequently happens (*EB*.6.8.1).

Digressions from the fifth category of rules (*pācittiya*) require only expiation. The ninety-two rules included here (ninety for the Northern and Eastern codes) deal with such matters as: (i) harming living beings by directly killing them, digging the ground or destroying plants or trees; (ii) sleeping in the same dwelling as a woman, or sitting in a private place with one; (iii) various forms of wrong speech, unfriendly behaviour towards a fellow monk, and true claims to the laity of having attained higher states; (iv) eating after noon, drinking alcohol and consuming food or drink (except water) that has not been formally offered; (v) unseemly, frivolous behaviour, and going to see an army fighting or on parade; (vi) sleeping in the same place as a layman for more than three nights, or using a high, luxurious bed; (vii) disparaging the lesser rules as vexing, pretended ignorance of a rule, or knowingly concealing a monk's digression from one of the first seventeen rules.

The sixth category of rules (*pāṭidesanīya*) requires only acknowledgement for digressions. Four rules are found here, such as that a monk should not accept food from a nun who is not a relation (as nuns found it more difficult to get alms, and so should not be expected to share their food with monks). The seventh category of rules, the *sekhiya* ones, 'connected to training', are also followed by novices, and have no penalty attached to them. These guidelines – seventy-five in the Theravādin code – seek to ensure that the monks are graceful and dignified in the way that they wear their robes, walk, move and collect and eat alms-food. Such a calm deportment is much valued by the laity.

The final set of seven rules (*adhikaraṇa-samatha*) outline procedures for resolving legal questions on digressions. They mainly outline types of verdict, such as innocent, non-culpable due to insanity, and a majority verdict. After the *pāṭimokkha* code was closed, sub-categories of the rules were developed to cover acts not quite amounting to full digressions, but counted, in decreasing order of gravity, as 'grave digressions', 'digressions of wrongdoing' or as 'digressions of improper speech'.

Besides the penalties referred to above, a monastic community can impose ones such as censuring or suspension. Suspension is imposed for not accepting that a digression has been made, not making amends for it or not giving up the wrong view that sensual behaviour is not an obstacle to be overcome (*Vin*.IV.133–6). It goes beyond probation in that, for example, other monks should not speak to the monk.

The extent to which the *pāṭimokkha* is followed varies somewhat in practice. In Southern Buddhism, while there is generally a high level of adherence, many adaptations to circumstances have been accepted, and different monastic fraternities or lines of pupillary succession differ in interpretation of *Vinaya*. In Thailand, for example, while most monks belong to the Mahā Nikāya, the 'Great Fraternity', a prestigious minority belong to the Dhammayuttika Nikāya, a reformist tradition founded in the nineteenth century. Besides stressing stricter adherence to *Vinaya*, this also puts more emphasis on textual understanding and meditation, and less on pastoral work among the laity, than the Mahā Nikāya.

In Sri Lanka, the fraternities differ primarily in the castes that they recruit from (Gombrich, 1971: 294–317). This is unfortunate, as the Buddha emphasized that social differences were irrelevant within the *Saṅgha*. The caste system developed among Buddhists in Sri Lanka due to the proximity of India, and the presence of a sizable Hindu minority. In India there are the four major classes, plus the 'untouchables' and approximately 3,000 castes arranged within these classes. In Sri Lanka, though, there are only about two dozen castes; most people belong to the highest one (the rice-cultivating *goyigama*), and there is only one small group akin to 'untouchables'. People mostly marry within their caste, and while the different castes mix socially to some extent, a lower-caste person must act respectfully towards one of a higher caste, and the latter will not accept most food and drink from a lower-caste person. Since a royal decree of 1765, which referred to unworthy people being ordained, only *goyigama* men have been allowed to ordain in the Siyam Nikāya, which is based on the ordination-line that had been reintroduced in 1753 from Thailand (then known as Siam). Ordination-lines were then introduced from Burma: in 1803, to form the lower-caste Amarapura Nikāya (which came to have three sub-divisions), and in 1865, to form the reformist Rāmañña Nikāya, which is officially casteless but tends to recruit from the mid-range castes. Laymen are reluctant to pay respects to a lower-caste monk, but many of the monks are ashamed of the existence of caste in the *Saṅgha*, and modernist ones openly criticize it.

In areas of Tibetan culture, the Gelugpa school is generally stricter in adherence to *Vinaya* than the others. Due to the central role that monasteries have played in society, though, even ex-monks find a place in them. While they cannot take part in monastic services, they often still wear monastic robes, and live within the monastic complex, perhaps holding a post in the monastery's administration. Moreover, a good proportion of the monks (and all the nuns, until recently), do not take higher ordination, but follow the precepts of a novice: the ten of a Theravāda novice (see p. 278), plus twenty-six more.

In Eastern Buddhism, the small Lü (Ch.) or Ritsu (Jap.) school specializes in strict *Vinaya* observance, and has helped to improve the standards of other schools. In Chan, blows and fines were added to previous penalties. Chinese monks also followed a supplementary 'Mahāyāna' code consisting of the 'three pure precepts' (see p. 269), and a set of *Bodhisattva* precepts outlined in the *Brahmajāla Sūtra*.[3] The rules cover both lay and monastic practice, sometimes differentiating between how a rule applies to a layperson and a monastic. Celibacy is still required for the latter. They consist of the 'ten great precepts' (see p. 269) and forty-eight minor ones. Some of these are also found in the *prātimokṣa* code, but others have a more compassion-orientated flavour, requiring vegetarianism, preaching, caring for the sick and exhorting others to give up immoral behaviour. In Japan, Indian *Vinaya* codes are not followed as they were replaced by others (see below).

PATTERNS AND TYPES OF ORDINATION

Entry into the monastic *Saṅgha* is by two stages. From the age of seven or eight, a child can take the lower ordination, or 'going forth' (Pali *pabbajjā*, Skt *pravrajyā*), so as to become a *sāmaṇera* (Skt *śrāmaneraka*; female, *sāmaṇerikā*, Skt *śramaṇerī*): a 'little *samaṇa*' or novice (*EB*.2.2.2). These undertake the ten precepts (see p. 278). When aged twenty (from conception), a person can take higher ordination or 'admission' (Pali *upasampadā*, Skt *upasapadā*) as a *bhikkhu* or *bhikkhunī*. Once ordained, even as a novice, head hair is shaved off, as a sign of renunciation of vanity. Chinese monks and nuns are also identified by small scars made by burning incense cones on the scalp as an offering to the Buddha. Monastic robes are also worn: orange, yellow or orangey-brown in Southern Buddhism; russet-red in Northern Buddhism; usually grey in China and Korea; and generally black in Japan. In Northern and Eastern Buddhism, additional robes of the original orange may be used during rituals and ceremonies, while in Japan, high-ranking monks (and priests) sometimes wear elaborate silk-brocade

[3] See *EB*.8.4, and Buddhist Text Translation Society (no date), *The Brahma Net Sutra*.

robes. Another outward sign of the monk, nun or novice is the alms-bowl, which is generally a deep rounded container with a cover. Monks and nuns also take religious names, such as Ānanda (name of the Buddha's attendant monk) Metteyya (Pali for 'friendly one', and name of the next Buddha), or Ñāṇavira ('Heroic knowledge').[4]

A new novice or monk generally acts as attendant to a senior monk, his teacher and companion in the monastic life, in a relationship explicitly modelled on that of father and son (*Vin*.I.45). In South-east Asia, short-term noviciates, lasting at least a few days or weeks, are quite common. These are to generate karmic fruitfulness for a parent or dead relative, or, in Burma, as a kind of *rite de passage* for boys near puberty. Some novices, of course, stay on until they become monks. In Tibetan, Korean and to a lesser extent in Chinese tradition, people often join the monastery as children; in China, while youths from around sixteen become *de facto* novices, formal novice ordination is delayed so as to be a prelude to ordination as a full monk at twenty or more (Welch, 1967: 247, 275, 290).

Candidates for higher ordination should be free of impediments such as contagious disease, debt or recent crime, and have the permission of parents, if under twenty, and usually of a spouse, if married.[5] They may also need to be able to read, write and chant a few simple texts. To ordain a monk, a quorum of five[6] validly ordained monks is required, whose authority to ordain is seen as flowing through the unbroken monastic tradition from the Buddha. At ordination, the candidate takes the lower ordination, if he has not already done so, and then commits himself to over 200 training rules; in the Northern and Eastern traditions, he also takes the *Bodhisattva* vows.

The Buddha discouraged monks from disrobing, and originally ordination was taken with the intention that it would be for life. However, the monastic status has never been irrevocable. In most Buddhist lands, a person is expected to be a monk/priest or nun for life, but a system of temporary ordination has evolved in the Theravāda lands of South-east Asia (*EB*.6.8.2; Swearer, 1995: 46–52). Here, the tradition is that every male Buddhist should join the *Saṅgha* at some time for a limited period, usually a

[4] But 'Bhikkhu' is not a name as it just means 'Monk'; in Korea 'Sunim' is used as a title for a monk or nun, and in China, 'Shih' ('Teacher'); in Vietnam, a monk's title is 'Thich' and a nun's 'Thich Nū'; in Thailand, monks are also often addressed as 'Ajahn' ('Teacher'). In Sri Lanka, a monk ordained for ten years has the title 'Thera' ('Elder') and when ordained twenty years, 'Mahā-thera' ('Great Elder'). In Burma, 'Sayadaw' (literally 'Royal Teacher') is a title for a senior monk or abbot. In Tibet, 'Rinpoche' (also spelt Rimpoche), or 'Precious One' is a title given to *trulkus* and other very respected *Lamas*.

[5] *Vin*.I.73–6, 83; *BS*2.26; Ṭhānissaro, 2007: II, ch. 14; Wijayaratna, 1990: 117–21.

[6] In the middle Ganges valley, where Buddhism originated, ten (*BS*2.25).

Vassa (Skt *Varṣa*, the 'rains' retreat period: see pp. 88, 260). In practice around half join (Bunnag, 1973: 37) often several times during life. While the continuity of monastic life is kept up by a core of permanent monks, the system makes for a close lay–monastic relationship and a good level of lay religious knowledge and experience. Temporary monkhood is often seen as 'maturing' a young man prior to marriage, and as a way for old people to generate karmic fruitfulness for the next life. Particularly in Thailand, monastic life can provide a good education, both religious and secular, so that if a monk disrobes, his position in lay society is higher than it previously was, and he is also respected as an ex-monk. In Sri Lanka, however, an ex-monk has some stigma attached to him, and there has even been controversy over a two-week adult noviciate that one Colombo monk introduced in 1982.

In the predominantly Mantranaya tradition of Northern Buddhism, a *Lama* (*bLa ma*, Skt *Guru*) is generally a monk or nun of long standing or special charisma, but a layperson accomplished in meditation or tantric rituals may also be such a revered teacher. In the Nyingmapa school, lay *Lamas* are particularly common; they live apart from their local temple, but gather there for certain rituals. Schools other than the Gelugpa sometimes also allow experienced monks to temporarily suspend their undertaking of sexual abstinence to perform tantric rites involving sexual yoga.[7] Lay *Lamas* are broadly considered to belong to the monastic *Saṅgha*, as are other figures such as non-ordained meditator-hermits or professional scripture readers. Thus Tibetan Buddhism has a particularly rich range of religious personnel, who may be:

- *gelong* (*dge slong*): a monk who has the full *bhikṣu* ordination; some are great scholars,
- *gets'ul* (*dge tshul*) and *gets'ulma* (*dge tshul ma*): a monk or nun who follows the lower, novice ordination of thirty-six precepts; terms which cover both of the first categories are *trapa* (*grwa pa*) and *ani* (*a ni*) – roughly 'monk' and 'nun',
- a monastic or lay *Lama*, some of whom are seen as *trulkus* (see p. 171),
- *genyen* and *genyenma*: a man or woman who has taken the lay precepts so as to be an *upāsaka* or *upāsikā* and who lives in a monastery,
- non-ordained ascetic *yogins* and *yoginīs*,
- village tantric priests,
- scripture readers.[8]

[7] See Samuel, 1993: 206–7, 240–1, 275–6, 519–20, 2012: 129–64.
[8] *EB*.7.8.3; Samuel, 1993: 206, 274–81, 286–7; see Bechert and Gombrich 1984: 246–7 for some pictures.

In Nepal, centuries of Hindu influence led to the extinction of a celibate *Saṅgha* among the Newari Buddhists (though it continues among minorities of Tibetan culture, and has been revived among recent Newari Theravāda converts: LeVine and Gellner 2005). The tantric priests who remain are the descendants of monks, and form a distinct caste in society (Bechert and Gombrich, 1984: 110–11). Most are called *bhikṣus*, 'monks', while the elite are called *vajrācāryas*, '*vajra*-masters'. Both live with their families in or around their 'monasteries' and the *bhikṣus* are frequently workers in precious metals. They are 'ordained' as novices some time before they are seven, and beg for alms for four days before being released from their vows, now seen as being too difficult to follow. This ritual serves as an initiation. The *bhikṣus* also don monastic garb when performing religious duties, these being of a more limited nature than those of the *vajrācāryas*, who receive a higher initiation, are specialists in various rituals and keep alive knowledge of the scriptures.

In Japan, the lay/monastic distinction gradually diminished in importance. In the ninth century, Saichō (767–822), founder of the Tendai school, set aside the traditional *Vinaya* as not 'Mahāyāna' but 'Hīnayāna' in nature, keeping only the supplementary *Brahmajāla Sūtra* code of fifty-eight *Bodhisattva* precepts (see p. 294) for Tendai monks (*EB*.9.4), and specifying a range of required practices for those doing the twelve-year training at the Tendai head monastery (*BT*.283–6). Dōgen (1200–53), founder of Sōtō Zen, stressed a simple but rigorous life-style. He emphasized the 'three pure' and 'ten great' precepts, but also developed a meticulously detailed code for *unsui*, or trainee monks (Satō, 1973), drawing on earlier detailed Chan monastic rules (*BP*.37). This outlines how juniors should behave respectfully in the presence of seniors (sixty-two rules), how trainees should behave when relaxing or studying together, how they should behave when eating, and even how they should wash and clean their teeth (Jiyu-Kennett, 1999: 131–45). Unconventional holy men known as *hijiri* had started to leave off their monastic robes and ignore rules against meat-eating while spreading Buddhism among the common people, and in the thirteenth century, Shinran (1173–1262) introduced a married priesthood to the Jōdo-shin school (see p. 230), setting a precedent that monks of other schools sometimes followed (Jaffe, 2001: 49–51).

From this period, Japanese Buddhism also came to develop a more this-worldly orientation, which generally saw ultimate reality as pervading everyday activities. It was to be known by living within the secular world with the right attitude, be this a devout faith in Amitābha, a Nichiren-inspired urge to purify society, or a Zen approach of giving oneself wholly over to the task at hand. The role of the monk or nun thus became less central, with less charisma, and Buddhism became more lay-orientated, with devotion mainly focused before a home altar, rather than at a temple. As part of its modernization of Japan, the Meiji government in 1872 decreed that monks of all schools could marry (Jaffe, 2001), and this has been taken up to such an extent that true (celibate) monks are now mostly young men in training. The nuns remain celibate. The 1872 decree also allowed monks to eat meat, and while Zen trainees and priests remain mostly vegetarian, those of other Japanese schools are now known both to eat meat and drink alcohol. Monastic training is now seen as a preparation for the role of the priest, who performs rituals such as funerals for the laity, and generally hands on his temple to a son (Reader, 1991: 88). In the post-war period, priests' wives have been allowed to take on some priestly roles, but popular urban lay movements known as 'New Religions' have little need for priests or monks. In 1872, the number of monks and nuns in Japan was 122,882 (40% nuns; Jaffe, 2001: 85–6): 0.35 per cent of the population. In 2003, the number of traditional temple priests was 133,000 – 0.1 per cent of the population – complemented by around 140,000 lay instructors in new Buddhist movements (Horii, 2006: 11).

In Korea also, some 'monks' were married, but this trend increased rapidly during the Japanese occupation (1904–45), due to attempts to Japanize Korean life (*EB*.9.8.2). Since then, anti-Japanese feeling led to a move to re-establish celibacy for all clerics; non-celibates have now lost control of the majority of temples and are few in number (Jaffe, 2001: 3).

NUNS[9]

In Indian society of the Buddha's day, there were a few women ascetics and freelance debaters, but the ordination of women was a relative innovation. Indeed the Buddha had reservations on this, probably due to social pressures against putting women in a respected position, the potential vulnerability of women following a wandering life, and the possibility of accusations of sexual relationships between monks and nuns. However, it is said that he agreed to the repeated requests for ordination of his widowed step-mother, Mahāpajāpatī (Skt Mahāprajāpatī), when his faithful attendant monk Ānanda asked him if women were capable of becoming

[9] On these, see Harvey, 2000: 392–400; Khantipālo, 1979: 128–65; Tsomo, 1988. The Sakyadhītā website in May 2010 reported that there are more than 130,000 Buddhist nuns in the world.

stream-enterers up to *Arahats*.[10] On agreeing that they were, he instituted the *Bhikkhunī Saṅgha*. This, though, was on condition that the nuns observed eight special rules (*garu-dhamma*), such as that a nun should always respectfully bow to a monk, however junior he may be. As a junior monk who is an *Arahat* should bow to a senior one who is not, order of bowing does not indicate intrinsic worth; it does, though, provide a clear structure for who bows to whom in a monastic context, with the monks' order being older and hence senior. Other rules made the nuns dependent on the monks for many of their ceremonies, including ordination, to ensure that their *Saṅgha* would develop as a sound spiritual community fully independent of lay society. To be a spiritual adviser to nuns, a monk had to be a wise senior of good character and reputation, and also a good speaker (*A*.IV.279–80). That said, doubt has been cast on the historicity of the above account. One *Sutta* (*M*.III.253–7) seems to refer to the nuns' order existing while Mahāpajāpatī was still a layperson (Williams, 2000), and it has been suggested that the eight special rules emerged in the early *Saṅgha* as a result of debate between those supportive of female ordination, and those somewhat resistant to it.[11] The *Bhikkhunī Saṅgha* survived into the modern era only in Eastern Buddhism: in 1930, China had 225,200 nuns and 513,000 monks (Welch, 1967: 412–14)[12]. Its success there has been partly due to its having provided a respite from the low status of women in society at large; in China, nuns usually lived in inaccessible nunneries, due to Confucian strictures on the behaviour of women. In Korea, Confucian influence for a long time discouraged many women from becoming nuns, but this has changed since the 1920s, and South Korea now has around 15,000 nuns to its 8,000 monks (excluding male married clerics). Korean nuns have both a stronger emphasis on the *Vinaya* than monks, and are more accessible to the laity: the services and chanting that they do means that they are the mainstay of day-to-day Buddhism. In Taiwan, also, nuns outnumber monks 6,500 to 3,500 (Tsomo, 1988: 120–2). In Japan, where nuns number around 2,000 (Tsomo, 1988: 124), they have had a low status, having been unable to live in proper temples (only hermitages), to conduct funerals in their own right, or be recognized as Zen masters (Uchino, 1986). These restrictions have been changed in the more liberal climate since 1945.

[10] *Vin*.II.254–5 (*BTTA*.3); *EB*.2.1.4 for a parallel version.

[11] Hüsken, 2000; Nattier, 1991; Sponberg, 1992: 13–16.

[12] On nuns in Eastern Buddhism, see *BS2*.31; Tsai, 1994; Tsomo, 1988: 112–37, 154–9.

In Tibet, the nuns' ordination-line was not introduced from India, though monks ordained nuns themselves from the twelfth century.[13] An influential body of opinion, however, did not accept this as a valid form of ordination, so that nuns now follow the ten precepts of a novice, plus twenty-six more, though most Tibetan monks also only follow these. There were 12,398 nuns in Tibet in 1959, perhaps 2,000 now, and there are around 840 in northern India, 500 in Nepal (Tsomo, 1988: 151–2), and a few thousand in Bhutan; overall around 5,000 (LeVine and Gellner, 2005: 327). In recent years, the Dalai Lama has supported the move for some nuns to become full *bhikṣuṇīs*, with the help of nuns from the Chinese tradition. This move follows the impetus set up by Sakyadhītā, the International Association of Buddhist Women, founded in 1987.[14]

In Southern Buddhism, the *bhikkhunī* ordination-line once flourished, according to the two religious chronicles of Sri Lanka, the *Dīpavaṃsa* (late fourth century CE, perhaps composed by nuns) and *Mahāvaṃsa* (early sixth century). The *Dīpavaṃsa* (18.9–44) refers to *Arahat*-nuns of both ancient India as well as Sri Lanka who were great teachers and who were renowned as scholars, honoured by kings. The *Mahāvaṃsa* (34.7–8) refers to a royal donation to 60,000 monks and 30,000 *bhikkhunīs* in the first century BCE. However, the female ordination-line died out in 1017 in Laṅkā after a disastrous invasion; in Burma, it existed until at least 1279 (Carrithers, 1983: 223; Kawanami, 2007: 229), probably ending there due to Mongol attacks on the region. Until a recent revival of the *bhikkhunī* lineage in Sri Lanka, a Theravāda 'nun' has been a woman who permanently keeps the eight or ten precepts, being known as a *sil māṇiyō* (Sri Lanka), *thela-shin* (Burma), *mae chi* (Thailand), *donchee* (Cambodia) or *maekhao* (Laos). As with a monk, the head is shaved, a Pali name is taken, and a robe is worn: white, brown, pinkish-brown or yellow. However, these nuns have tended to be seen as very devout laypeople more than as full members of the monastic *Saṅgha*. Ordination is usually permanent, though in Burma many young girls ordain for a few weeks prior to puberty. The number of Theravādin nuns gradually increased during the twentieth century. Numbers are now around 45,760: 25,000 in Burma, 10,000 in Thailand, 7,000 in Cambodia, 3,000 in Sri Lanka, 700 in Laos, and 60 in Nepal 60.[15]

[13] On Tibetan nuns, see: *EB*.7.7; Havenick, 1991; Miller, 1980; Samuel, 2012: 11–16; Tsomo, 1988: 150–3; Willis 1989: 96–134.

[14] www.sakyadhita.org; LeVine and Gellner, 2005: 117–207; Tsomo, 1988.

[15] Harvey, 2000: 306; Kabilsingh, 1991: 39; Tsomo, 1988: 109, 139, 147; Tsomo, 2010, 87; www.budhapia.com/files/files_etc/20050118/S_02_H1_W.doc.

In Thailand, *mae chis* tend to do domestic chores around the monastery, with less time than monks for study. Their upkeep comes from some family help, savings, food grown by themselves and perhaps surplus alms and support from a lay donor. In a few country areas they themselves go on an alms-round. While they do not have the social prestige accorded to monks, the work of The Foundation of Thai Nuns, established in 1969, has helped to heighten people's regard for them. Nuns are now increasingly studying *Dhamma* and Pali, and are also teaching in schools attached to monasteries, helping in hospitals or working with delinquent girls. In the countryside, some gifted nuns have set up independent nunneries, and teach meditation to other nuns and visiting laywomen. In Burma, most nuns live in independent nunneries; they are often supported by lay donations, especially in the larger nunneries, and also receive food on alms-rounds. They spend several hours a day in study, and some are very experienced meditators. In Sri Lanka, traditionally the only permanent nuns were old women who kept the eight precepts and lived by begging or charity. In 1907, the institution of the ten-precept nun spread from Burma, and gradually came to attract young women. Since around 1945, these nuns have increased their activity, giving public sermons and developing an organization increasingly like that of the monks. Their time is spent in study and meditation, and in serving the laity by conducting rituals and teaching *Dhamma* to adults and children. In return, the laity support them with alms, etc. Due to their simple life-style and practice of meditation, the laity often see them as living a more virtuous life than that of the city and village monks.[16]

In the 1990s the movement to re-establish a Theravāda *bhikkhunī Saṅgha* bore fruit, though it will take time to be fully accepted by the senior monks in all the Theravādin countries. Also, many nuns prefer their present status, in which they are more independent of monks than they would be as *bhikkhunī*s. *Bhikkhunī* ordination requires a group of properly ordained *bhikkhunī*s as well as a group of monks, so it has been necessary to find a community of Mahāyāna *bhikṣuṇī*s who come up to Theravādin standards as regards ordination-line and discipline. The Chinese Dharmaguptaka ordination-line for nuns, also followed in Taiwan, South Korea and Vietnam, partly derives from fifth-century CE Sri Lanka (*BTTA*.210;

[16] On contemporary Theravāda nuns, see: Khantipālo, 1979: 153–63; Tsomo, 1988: 109–11, 138–49, 229–32, 262–6. On specific countries: Sri Lanka – Bartholomeusz, 1992 and 1994; Bloss, 1987; Gombrich and Obeyesekere, 1988: 274–95: Sasson, 2010; Thailand – Kabilsingh, 1991: 36–66, 87–93; Burma – Kawanami 1997, 2007; Laos – Tsomo, 2010.

EB.8.7.1; Heirman, 2010) and so has been looked to as the medium for the re-establishment. Twelve Theravāda nuns were ordained as *bhikkhunī*s in America in 1988, then in December 1996, eleven experienced Sri Lankan nuns were ordained as *bhikkhunī*s in Sārnāth, India, by Korean nuns and Theravāda monks. Ordinations in Sri Lanka followed in 1998 (Berkwitz, 2010: 185–90; Weeraratne, n.d.), and by 2007 there were almost 500 *bhikkhunī*s there (Kawanami, 2007: 227). Most of these are graduates, which will help the new order develop well and gain respect. At a 1998 ordination ceremony in Bodh-Gayā, 134 women from twenty-three countries were ordained as *bhikkhunī*s, including thirteen from Burma (Kawanami, 2007: 227) and fourteen from Nepal, where the *bhikkhunī* ordination is now taking off among the nuns of the new Theravāda movement (Berkwitz, 2010: 190–2; LeVine and Gellner, 2005: 189–95). Thailand seems never to have had *bhikkhunī*s, hence resistance to the (re)-establishment is stronger there (*EB*.6.7; Seeger, 2006). Nevertheless, Dr Chatsumarn Kabilsingh ordained as a novice in Sri Lanka in February 2001, and later as a *bhikkhunī*, Dhammānandā. The Thai government said that they would not recognize her as a *bhikkhunī*, but nor would they take any action against her, and she is starting to earn respect, in part due to her meticulous concern for *Vinaya*. In February 2002, a Theravādin *bhikkhunī* was ordained in Thailand itself, and by March 2010, there were around fifty *bhikkhunī*s or novices preparing to become *bhikkhunī*s.

THE ECONOMIC BASE OF THE MONASTIC LIFE[17]

The original ideal of the *bhikkhu* and *bhikkhunī* was that of a person with a minimum of possessions living a simple life-style, supported by lay donations rather than by any gainful occupation. The formal list of a monk's personal 'requisites', treated as his property, comprises an upper-, lower- and over-robe, a belt, a bowl, a razor, a needle, a water-strainer, a staff and a toothpick. In practice, a monk also has such articles as sandals, a towel, extra work robes, a shoulder bag, an umbrella, books, writing materials, a clock and a picture of his teacher. In Southern and Northern Buddhism, there is a structural tension between the ascetic tendencies of the *Saṅgha* and the laity's desire to generate more abundant karmic fruitfulness by giving to more abstemious and ascetic monks. Thus a town monk with a good reputation may be given a fridge or even the use of a car. If he lives up to

[17] A good overview of this is Ornatowski, 1996; see also Harvey, 2000: 203–6.

his reputation, though, he will use these with detachment (he cannot drive himself), and let other monks benefit from them.

The *piṇḍapāta*, or alms-round is the archetypal symbol for the dependence of monks and nuns on the laity, though the extent of its practice came to vary considerably. Today, while the morning alms-round is infrequent in Sri Lanka, it is still the norm in Theravāda South-east Asia. The giving is a calm, dignified affair, in which monks and novices silently file into a town or village, are met by women and a few men outside their homes, and open their bowls for the offering. No thanks are given for the food, as the donors are doing a karmically fruitful act, but a response such as 'may you be happy' might be given. In Southern Buddhism, other means of giving alms are: inviting monks for a meal; bringing food to, or cooking it at a monastery, and establishing a fund to buy food, which is cooked by novices or boys living at a monastery. In Northern Buddhism, monks and nuns are rarely supported by alms, except if they are on pilgrimage; though at certain festivals the laity may pay for the food of a monastery for several days. It is usual for a family to give at least one son or daughter to the monastic life, after which they often help support them by produce and income from a plot of land set aside for this purpose.

The laity also donate other goods, and their labour: for example helping to build or repair a temple. Lay stewards usually deal with cash donations. In Southern Buddhism, temple boys also deal with financial transactions if a monk is travelling or buying food at a market. In Sri Lanka, however, a small number of monks receive a salary, as school or college teachers, but this is clearly against the *Vinaya* and is not well thought of. Tibetan monks are also paid for their ritual services by the laity. State patronage has been a source of support for large temples in many countries, but this is now much rarer.

In Eastern Buddhism monks on alms-round are a rare sight, except in the case of Zen trainees. In contemporary Japan, the primary function of most Buddhist temples is to perform memorial services for the dead for households assigned an affiliation to a particular temple in a kind of formally recognized parish system. Around 75 per cent of a temple's income comes from fees for funerals and memorial services (Horii, 2006: 14), and a percentage of this income must go to sect headquarters to support its administrative activities, publications, social welfare activities and sustaining meditation institutions (Reader, 1991: 88). Most priests also have to have an extra job to support themselves and their family.

Land has been given to the *Saṅgha* since the time of the Buddha, with simple monastic dwellings then being built on it (*Vin*.II.154–9 (*BTTA*.I)).

Vinaya rules forbidding monks to dig the earth were partly intended to prevent them from becoming self-supporting, and thus isolated from the laity. In time, accumulated land-donations meant that temples became landlords in a number of countries, especially where governments granted land. Monastic landlordism developed to a notable extent in Sri Lanka, where, between the ninth and twelfth centuries, large temples owned vast estates, which included plantations, complex irrigation schemes, the villages that depended on them, and rights over some of the labour of the villagers. Nowadays, some temples in Sri Lanka might still, for example, receive half the rice grown on its land by tenant farmers. In general, the twentieth century saw a considerable reduction in monastic land-ownership, due to confiscations by Communist governments or land reforms.

In China, an additional code for Chan monasteries became in practice more important than the *prātimokṣa* and *Brahmajāla* codes: the *Bai-zhang qing-guei* (*Pai-chang ch'ing-kuei*), attributed to master Baizhang (Pai-chang; 749–814).[18] It was influenced by Confucian ideas on deportment and etiquette, but also required monks to do daily manual labour, not only around the monastery, but also in the fields and gardens: 'one day no work, one day no food'. This was partly to counter Confucian accusations that monks were social 'parasites'. Digging the earth, as a breach of traditional *Vinaya*, was seen as acceptable if done to benefit the 'three treasures', and not for personal gain. Moreover, it was more than a means of support: its physical exercise was a good complement to long hours of seated meditation; if done with awareness, it could itself be a meditation, and it helped to develop a spirit of working together on an equal basis. In later times, though, daily manual labour came to be somewhat neglected.

Large monasteries have also engaged in commercial activities. In Laṅkā, they bought land, sold produce and invested in merchants' guilds. In Tang China (618–907), they acted as pawnbrokers and lenders of grain and cloth, owned grain-mills and oil-presses and ran large markets, which started as fairs selling incense and images.[19] In Japan, Rinzai Zen temples ran fleets of trading ships to China. In Northern Buddhism, the *Vinaya* specifically allows the use of surplus donations for lending at interest, if this is of benefit to the *Dharma* and *Saṅgha*. In pre-Communist Tibet, the monasteries were key economic institutions at the centre of a web of trading and donation relationships with the two other main sectors of Tibetan society: nomadic herdsmen and agriculturalists. Individual monks invested in such things as

[18] Cf. *BS2.30* for an additional code for the Tiantai school.

[19] Ch'en 1973: 125–78, 1976; for the modern period: Welch, 1967: 199–202 (*EB*.8.8).

herds and seed-grain, but most capital was received and administered at the level of the 'college', a sub-division of the monastery which inherited the possessions of its members (*EB*.7.8.2). Its superintendent, monastic or lay, ensured its support by getting a good return from land worked by lease-holders or peasants attached to the monastery, from grazing, forest and water rights, college herds, trade with China and India, bartering with herdsmen, and from loans and investments.

STUDY AND MEDITATION

Monastic life can be broadly divided into personal, communal and pastoral activities. The first includes observing the monastic code, meditation and study, all as means to spiritual development and the preservation of the *Dhamma* for the benefit of all. In practice, monks and nuns have tended to emphasize either study or meditation. Such specialization seems to have existed to some extent even in early Buddhism (*A*.III.355–6 (*SB*.260–1)).

In Southern Buddhism, a distinction developed, early in the Christian era, between 'book-duty' (*gantha-dhura*) monks, with the duty of study and teaching, and 'insight-duty' (*vipassanā-dhura*) ones, with the duty of meditation.[20] The former tend to dwell in villages, towns and cities, studying and ministering to the laity, while the latter tend to live a more secluded, ascetic life-style in the forest. Some 'forest-dwelling' monks, however, simply belong to a section of the *Saṅgha* that once lived in the forest. When the teachings were first written down in first-century BCE Laṅkā, it was decided that learning was more important than meditation, which would not be possible if the teachings were lost. In Laṅkā, therefore, many more monks have specialized in study than in meditation, a situation strengthened in recent centuries by the common belief that it is no longer possible to attain Arahatship. In the 1940s and 1950s, however, reform movements revived the forest meditation tradition, so that now, at least 3 per cent of the island's monks are genuine forest dwellers, and in 1968 a new *nikāya* for them was recognized (Carrithers, 1983). In South-east Asia, a larger proportion, though still a minority, of monks have specialized in meditation. Theravāda nuns generally practise meditation (often, but not always, of a devotional nature) more than monks, though they study less. Specialization is not always a permanent thing, for a monk might study and then turn to meditation to experientially explore what he has learnt, or return from a forest monastery to a busier town monastery. In any case, a

[20] *EB*.6.3.1; Gombrich, 1971: 270, 2006: 152.

'study' monk meditating for an hour a day may have fewer expectations and not try to force results, and thus achieve better meditation levels than many forest monks. Quality, not quantity, counts. Some monks meditate or study little, though, and are more involved in running a monastery or pastoral activities. All monks chant, however, and this has a meditative quality, sometimes powerfully so.

In Northern Buddhism, the Gelugpa school is noted for its emphasis on study, while others such as the Kagyüdpa emphasize meditation more. Full monks (*gelong*) of all schools, though, usually start by spending five years in study. This is followed by further study, by learning meditation and practising it in a hermitage, or simply by helping around the monastery. The majority of monastics, who follow only thirty-six precepts, study much less than the *gelongs*.

In Eastern Buddhism, Huayan/Kegon has a scholarly emphasis, Tiantai emphasizes both study and meditation (*BS2*.40), Pure Land emphasizes devotion, and Chan/Zen emphasizes meditation. Relative specialization of focuses of study or practice meant that Chinese monks sometimes developed different aspects of their personal cultivation by moving between different schools. Few have been proficient scholars, though, due to the difficulty of mastering written Chinese. Scholar-monks tended to reside in larger monasteries, from which they would go on lecture-tours, while the majority were semi-literate and lived in small temples ministering to the laity. In Korea, a novice monk or nun chooses to study (for about six years) or train in meditation. In recent times, the trend has been to study then meditate.

Study

The extensive scriptures have been lovingly studied by generations of monks and nuns, who have produced many commentaries and treatises based on them (Pagel, 2001). The need to preserve and disseminate the teachings has spread literate culture to many lands, ensured a generally high degree of literacy among Buddhists, and been responsible for the invention of printing and several written scripts. Buddhist monks and nuns have often been among the intellectual, cultural and artistic elite of their societies.

In Southern Buddhism, monks and novices begin by studying *Vinaya*, basic doctrines, *Jātaka* tales for use in sermons; and common chants. Some go further at monastic schools, colleges and universities. The basis of study beyond the preliminary level is a knowledge of Pali. Some Sanskrit may also be studied, as a key to knowledge of certain non-Theravādin texts. National languages have been used for many treatises and translations of key texts. Traditionally, the texts were inscribed on collections of oblong strips of dried palm-leaves, which are more long-lasting than paper in tropical climates. The first complete *printing* of the Pali Canon was in 1893, under King Chulalongkorn of Thailand, though the version printed in Roman characters by the Pali Text Society of London, since 1881, has become a widely used printed version. The 'Sixth Council', held in Burma from 1954 to 1956, cross-checked and revised the manuscript tradition and produced a printed Canon known as the *Chaṭṭha Saṅgāyana* (Sixth Council) version, now available on a CD-ROM from the Vipassana Research Institute (www.vridhamma.org). Monks also keep alive the oral tradition, with some memorizing large sections of texts – a few even know the whole Canon. In Thailand, the institution of graded examination systems in Pali, Buddhism and some secular subjects has both improved the general level of monastic education and produced a tendency to a stereotyped interpretation of scriptures. The study of subjects such as psychology, philosophy and basic science is seen by traditionalists as leading monks to be worldly and more prone to disrobe, while modernists hold that monks need knowledge of them to be efficient communicators of Buddhism to an increasingly well-educated laity.

In China, Buddhism met a well-developed literate culture, so the entire corpus of available texts in Sanskrit and other Indian and Central Asian languages was gradually translated: a vast task which is probably the greatest translation-project the world has seen. The Chinese Canon was also used in Korea, Vietnam and Japan, and was only translated into Japanese early in the twentieth century. Besides translating genuine *Sūtras* from their Sanskrit originals, the Chinese also composed many themselves, listed as 'spurious *Sūtras*' in their *Sūtra* catalogues. These included texts arising from creative inspiration, but also simplified abbreviations of *Sūtras*, and attempts to palm off folk beliefs as Buddhism, or to take advantage of it for some purpose. The value attached to the *Platform Sūtra* (see p. 219), however, meant that this Chinese text was counted as a 'genuine' *Sūtra* (*Jing*). The Chinese invented printing in the seventh century, using carved wooden blocks to reproduce Buddhist images and short *dhāraṇī* chants; one of the latter survives from around 660 CE. Soon after, texts were printed. The world's oldest extant printed book is in fact a copy of the 'Diamond-cutter' Perfection of Wisdom *Sūtra*, printed in 868 CE. The entire Canon was printed from 972 to 983, while the eleventh century saw the invention of movable wooden type. The largest and most definitive edition of the Chinese Canon is now the *Taishō Daizōkyō*, produced from 1924 to 1934 in Japan.

In Northern Buddhism, texts are collections of oblong strips of paper printed by wood-blocks. Traditional study was based on daily lectures on selected texts, followed by memorization and study of them. After the minimum five years, some monks would then spend at least seven years in a Tantric college in which mystical tantric texts would be studied and then used as a basis for meditations. The Gelugpas have emphasized logic as a basic formative discipline, a student's doctrinal understanding being tested by public dialectical debates. Their full course of study could last up to twenty-five years, leading to the title of first or second class *geshé* (*dge bshes*), a kind of Doctor of Buddhology. Traditional study also included medicine, astrology, astronomy, grammar, calligraphy and religious painting. Since the destruction of many monasteries in Tibet by the Communist Chinese, traditional monastic learning has been continued by refugee monks in India and elsewhere.

The meditative life

In Southern Buddhism, a forest monastery usually consists of a simple wooden meeting-hall/shrine-room and *kuti*s (huts) or even caves as dwellings. It is usual for monks specializing in meditation to adhere to *Vinaya* more strictly, and they may also undertake, at least temporarily, some of the thirteen *dhutaṅga*s, or 'austere practices', intended to cultivate non-attachment and vigour.[21] Those more commonly practised include: living only off alms-food; eating only one meal a day, at around 10 a.m.; eating food only from the alms-bowl; and living at least half a mile from a village. The more hardy might undertake to live at the foot of a tree, or sleep in the sitting position. In Thailand, the *dhutaṅga*s are often practised by monks walking on pilgrimage, sleeping under large umbrellas equipped with mosquito-nets. Paradoxically, while such wandering monks are conventionally admired, as approximating to the wandering life of the early *Saṅgha*, Thais have an ambivalent attitude towards them, as they are not properly integrated within the institutionalized monastic community.[22] That said, the most respected monks in the country have included forest monks, such as the reputed *Arahat* Ajahn Mun Buridatta (1870–1949) and some of his disciples, such as Ajahn Chah (1918–92).[23]

[21] *Vin*.III.171–2; *Vism*.II; Khantipālo, 1979: 110–13; Ray, 1994: 293–323; Tambiah, 1984: 137, 175–6.

[22] Ray, 1994 traces a line of forest ascetics and saints from early Buddhism through to the Mahāyāna, arguing that they represented a persistent model of *Saṅgha* life that contrasted with that of institutionalized monasticism, with its emphasis on study and group living.

[23] Mahā Boowa, 2005; Tambiah, 1984: 81–110; Ṭhānissaro, 1999b.

In Northern Buddhism, many monasteries have caves or huts for intensive meditation or scholarship. Seclusion in such hermitages might be for a short period or, in the Kagyüdpa and Nyingmapa schools, for perhaps three years, three months and three days. During this time the meditator is alone, with food and water being silently passed in through a small opening. Such seclusion is, of course, voluntary, and is only entered after an exhaustive preparation. It is used as a time to wholeheartedly develop meditation by drawing on both previous practice and innate mental resources.

In Eastern Buddhism, isolated retreats have also been practised, but the Chan/Zen school developed the institution of the 'meditation-hall' (Jap. *zendō*) as the focus of life in larger, well-run monasteries, with the *sesshin* as a period of intense meditation practice in this.[24] On a raised platform at the edge of the hall, the monks and nuns or trainees meditate, sleep and (in Japan) eat, with their few possessions neatly packed in a small box above or behind them. During meditation periods, a wakefulness-aider (*jikodō*) patrols with a flat stick with which to compassionately rouse any who are sleepy by hitting them on the shoulder. Energy is also roused by alternating periods of sitting and walking meditation, done in a circle in a slow, dignified yet powerful way, sometimes said to be like the majestic advance of a tiger; this suddenly stops when a signal is given. In Chinese tradition, monks sign up for six-month periods in the meditation-hall, while others perform devotions, study, run the monastery and come to the hall for evening meditation. In Japan, a trainee's day includes both meditation and manual labour.

A striking form of ascetic practice is found in the Japanese Tendai school: the *sennichi kaihōgyō*, or mountain-circumambulating austerity, done around the Tendai head temple on Mount Hiei. Each year, several priests perform the 100-day version of this, so as to be able to become head priests in the temple-complex. Once a decade, on average, a priest performs the awesome 1,000-day version. For the latter, he must be single, have the permission of the Tendai authorities, and have completed the twelve-year training period on the mountain. The 1,000 days are spread over seven years. They involve quickly walking a 22-mile route round the mountain, in socks and straw sandals, starting at midnight after around three hours' sleep, standing under freezing waterfalls, living on a meagre amount of food, and, at the 700-day mark, going without food, water, sleep or lying down for nine days, while continuing to walk. The person doing this, once he has started, should be prepared to kill himself rather than give up. Completing

[24] Maezumi and Glassman, 2002: 43–51; Suzuki, 1970a: 314–62.

the 1,000 days is seen to lead to buddhahood. The context for this practice is that Japan has a tradition of mountain ascetics, whose fasting etc. is seen to reverse normal human activities and so acquire power, which is then used for the benefit of the community. The chanting of *mantras*, texts such as the *Heart Sūtra* and invocations from the *Lotus Sūtra* accompany such austerities, which

> have a strongly purificatory and exorcistic dimension: the crushing or punishing of the body . . . works to drive or wash out the impurities of the mind, removing . . . all the barriers, physical or mental, that might prevent the practitioner from achieving higher consciousness and powers. (Reader, 1991: 121)

While the Buddha had a strongly ascetic phase prior to his enlightenment (see p. 19), he then saw this as an extreme to be avoided. The above kind of practice, though, seems to express the view that his asceticism was a necessary preparation for his Buddhahood.

COMMUNAL LIFE

While monks and nuns may spend some time in solitary meditation, the monastic life is nurtured and supported by a communal life-style. In having shared values and ideals, the *Saṅgha* supports the spiritual development of its members by solidarity, example, teaching, mutual acknowledgement of digressions, an ordered life-style, communal discipline and minimal privacy. The ideal is that possessions should be shared, even down to the contents of an alms-bowl (*M*.II.251). Dōgen, the founder of Sōtō Zen, held that most actions of monks should be done in an identical manner, the correct ordering of daily life being the heart of Buddhism.

The section of *Vinaya* called the *Khandhaka* (see p. 289) can be seen as the *Saṅgha*'s constitution. It regulates communal life according to the legal devices set out in the *kamma-vācanās*, or 'announcements of action', which are dealt with by a quorum of monks democratically reaching a consensus on a proposal. This then becomes a valid 'action of the *Saṅgha*'. The *Khandhaka* deals with both procedures and rules. The procedures regulate such matters as the *Vassa* rains retreat, ordination, the *pāṭimokkha* ceremony, disciplinary issues, disputes and schisms. The specific discipline of *Vassa* is generally observed quite well in Southern Buddhism, less so in Northern Buddhism, and not much in Eastern Buddhism, where it is known as the 'Summer Retreat'. The *Khandhaka* rules regulate, for example, the use of leather objects, the size and type of robes, and foods, drinks and medicines allowable to monks, especially after the last meal at noon.

Within the original *Saṅgha*, there was an order of precedence according to length of time as a monk, apportioning of duties to officials according to their abilities (which gave them no authority over others), equality in decision-making, and no hierarchy. The extent to which these features survive varies, but the basic equality of the monks has been preserved in all places except perhaps Japan. Mild hierarchies exist within each monastic fraternity in Sri Lanka, while in Thailand the government developed a strong national administrative hierarchy in the twentieth century. Headed by a '*Saṅgha-rājā*' (appointed by the king) and a monastic council, it deals with such matters as discipline, supervision of *Saṅgha* property, registration of monks, and organization of ecclesiastical examinations. National hierarchies once existed in Sri Lanka, Burma, Cambodia and Laos, but lapsed when colonization or Communist governments brought an end to the monarchies on which they depended. In Burma, each monastery or small group of them thus became an independent unit, though the government reinstituted a national hierarchy in 1980. Theravāda abbots are usually appointed with the consent of other monks and leading laity, though in Sri Lanka they are either the eldest disciple of the previous abbot or his nephew. Their responsibilities are mainly administrative and their individual power is that of their charisma, if any, and their 'inviting' monks to do certain things (though it would be bad form to refuse).

In Chinese Buddhism, there has been no national hierarchy in recent centuries, though the nationwide Chinese Buddhist Association was formed in 1929 as part of a revival of Buddhism. Before the Communist era, most monasteries were independent institutions, except in the case of some which were branch monasteries of larger ones. There were around 100,000 small 'hereditary temples', each owned by the monks who lived there, and passed on to those who lived as novices there, so as to become the monastic 'sons' of the head monk (Welch, 1967: 247–303). Ordination as full monks or nuns was only conferred at around 300 large 'public monasteries' (*EB*.8.5), which avoided having novices living there so as not to become 'hereditary' in this sense. The population of hereditary temples was small, from one to thirty monks and novices, though 95 per cent of monks lived in them. Public monasteries had from twenty up to a thousand residents. Public monasteries were often located in inaccessible places, especially near to or on mountains, and were dedicated to meditation, devotion, study and strict discipline. Their size necessitated efficient organization, headed by an abbot. Under him would come a variety of officials who were appointed every six months, being chosen from monks of the appropriate level of seniority, of which there were a number of ranks.

South Korea now has a national hierarchy, headed by monks and nuns but also including married clerics. In Japan, though, each sub-sect has had its own hierarchy. In 1970, there were 162 sub-sects: 48 Shingon, 37 Nichiren, 25 Pure Land, 23 Zen, 20 Tendai, 7 Nara (e.g. Kegon) and 2 'other'.

In Tibetan Buddhism, each of the schools has its hierarchy, with key positions being taken by *trulku Lamas* (see p. 207). Traditionally, each large monastery had its own resident *trulku* (sometimes, but not always, the abbot), who was the focus of much of its ritual life. In key Gelugpa monasteries, the abbots were usually eminent *geshés*. In Tibet, as in Sri Lanka, some monasteries stayed under the control of one family by the abbotship going from uncle to nephew. Within the monasteries, there were a variety of officials in charge of such matters as property, revenue, discipline, tantric initiations, music and chanting. Offices were usually held for a specific term, and candidates for them were short-listed by the community before being selected by the school's hierarchy.

As in all traditions, the monastic day in Southern Buddhism starts early, around 5 a.m. A typical routine in a Thai town or village monastery (Khantipālo, 1979: 91–127) begins with study or meditation, with breakfast being taken at around 7 a.m., after the alms-round. Communal chanting then follows for about an hour, though some senior monks might chant at the house of a layperson who has invited them for their meal. From around 9 to 10.30 a.m., seniors teach juniors and novices; the last meal of the day is then eaten so as to finish before noon. After a siesta, classes continue from 1.30 to 5 p.m. Alternatively, there might be an ordination, *pāṭimokkha* ceremony or chanting at the laity's request. Around 5 p.m., cool fruit drinks, or milkless tea or coffee are served. After chores or free time, chanting takes place from around 7 to 8 p.m. The evening is then spent in administrative work, seeing lay visitors, study and some meditation or chanting. In Thai forest monasteries, morning and sometimes evening chanting is omitted, and monks usually eat only morning alms-food. The siesta lasts from around 10 a.m. to 3 p.m., to recoup energy after meditating for much of the night. There is little if any study, this generally being replaced by work. In the evening the abbot may give a long experience-based discourse, then personal meditation guidance.

In Northern Buddhism, monastic life is regulated by obligatory attendance at daily and periodic rituals. These include *Sūtra*-recitation, worship and visualization of holy beings, exorcizing of evil powers, and generating karmic fruitfulness for self, the dead, evil-doers and the monastic and lay communities. In these complex rituals, the monks may wear special hats symbolizing the holy beings they are seeking to invoke, and accompany their deep-throated liturgy with ritual hand-gestures, the manipulation of ritual instruments, and the sounds of drums and horns. Communal rituals in the early morning and evening may last for around two hours. The first and last hours of the day might be spent in private meditation. In larger monasteries, student monks receive a sermon and learned discussion of a text in the morning and spend from 2 to 4 p.m. and 6 to 10 p.m. in private study. The duty of a few monks is to worship the monastery's specific protector 'Lord' for twenty hours a day in the most sacred shrine in the monastery. As in Eastern Buddhism, the rule against meals after noon is not generally observed, though these are referred to as 'medicine'.

In Chinese Buddhism, while life in hereditary temples is a fairly relaxed one of devotion, some study and rituals for the laity, the regime of public monasteries is usually rigorous and closely regulated. The monastery buildings such as meditation-hall, Buddha-recitation hall, shrine-hall, *Dharma* hall, wandering monks' hall, ancestors' hall, refectory and business office are all laid out in a very orderly fashion within a wall-enclosed rectangle. The key building is the meditation-hall, or sometimes the Buddha-recitation hall, where invocation of Amitābha and *Sūtra*-recitations are performed. The schedule of meditation, meals, devotion, etc., and the series of phases within these, is mostly regulated by a signal-system of bells, drums and sounding boards. For those signed up in the meditation-hall, around nine hours per day are spent there, alternating between meditation and circumambulation of an image. In weeks of intensive practice, this can rise to fourteen hours. Much of this discipline is also found in South Korea, Taiwan and the Japanese Zen training temple. The Zen trainees sometimes rise as early as 3 a.m. for meditation. Verses are recited before or after shaving, cleaning the teeth, using the lavatory and bathing. One mealtime verse includes, 'The first bite is to discard evil; the second bite is so that we may train in perfection; the third bite is to help all beings; we pray that all may be enlightened. We must think deeply of the ways and means by which this food has come' (Jiyu-Kennett, 1999: 122–3). Before eating, some grains of rice are set aside for the 'hungry ghosts'.

While monks are often assisted by novices, lay administrators and workers and, in Southern Buddhism, boys serving at the monastery in return for their keep, they also have work to do, especially the more junior ones. In all traditions, work includes such tasks as washing and mending robes, repairing or erecting buildings, fuel-gathering, preparing articles for ritual use, and keeping the monastery tidy. Common to most traditions is the careful sweeping of paths and courtyards. This is not only for cleanliness and exercise, but is also praised by the *Vinaya* as an opportunity for calm, mindful action and serving others (*Vin*.VI.129–30). In Southern Buddhism, the forest monks particularly value work due to its developing vigour, a good complement to the calm of meditation. In Eastern Buddhism, the Chan/Zen tradition praises work and extends it to include gardening, food-growing and cooking. The positions of head cook and head gardener are indeed important ones in Zen temples. The Chan/Zen attitude that awakening can be discovered in ordinary everyday activities, done with full presence of mind, is well expressed in a saying of the lay Chan master Pang Jushi (P'ang Chü-shih; 740–808): 'How wondrous this, how mysterious! I carry fuel, I draw water' (Suzuki, 1959: 16). In all Buddhist traditions, monks may also be involved in producing religious art.

RELATIONS WITH THE LAITY

Over the centuries, and in many lands, Buddhist monks and nuns have acted as 'good friends' (*kalyāṇa-mitta*, Skt *kalyāṇa-mitra*) to the laity in a variety of ways, starting with being good examples and thus fertile 'fields of karmic fruitfulness'. The ethos of the *Saṅgha* has thus been radiated out into society, and the lay world has received various benefits from the 'world-renouncing' *Saṅgha* that it supports.

In many lands in the twentieth century, the actions of unsympathetic Communist governments, or increasing secularization, reduced the role of the *Saṅgha* in people's lives. In any case, this role had been reduced in East Asia, due to the influence of Confucianism, or, as in Japan, the existence of a more lay-centred tradition. It is thus in the non-Communist lands of Southern Buddhism that the widest spectrum of lay–monastic relationships has continued into, and developed within, the modern world. Here, each village has at least one monastery which, though it is physically outside it, for quietness, is the focus of its life. The abbot is usually the most respected and influential man in the village and is sought out for advice on many matters, such as the arbitration of disputes, so as to act somewhat like a village parson (Lester, 1973: 109–29). In South-east Asia, the monastery has offered a number of public services, such as free accommodation. The old may use it as a retirement home by becoming monks or nuns; the homeless or chronically sick may be offered its shelter; temple boys from poor families are supported by it in return for their help with chores; boys studying away from home in a town may use it as a hostel; and travellers may use it as a resthouse. The monastery houses the village library, was the centre from which news from beyond the village traditionally radiated, and is the place where most gatherings of any size take place. It also serves in a limited way as a redistributor of property, for land donated by a wealthy patron may be let out for a nominal rent to farmers. Surplus donations of money may also be used by an abbot to help fund the building of a new school (Bunnag, 1973: 199).

In Southern Buddhism, monks give sermons to the laity within the monastery, at funerals, at memorial services in the home, and at blessing ceremonies for some new venture. The themes are most frequently ethical, and often draw on the *Jātaka* stories. Teaching of a less formal nature is given to those who come to ask for advice on personal problems and with questions on *Dhamma*: visitors are always welcome.[25] In the twentieth century, teaching meditation to the laity increased in South-east Asia, and was revived in Sri Lanka. In Northern Buddhism, one way in which the monks have communicated with the laity is through the performance of open-air mystery plays at certain festivals. In Chinese Buddhism, while the more learned laity might attend scholarly expositions of *Sūtra*s at monasteries, traditionally the *Dharma* was spread among the often illiterate masses by peripatetic preachers, who held their audiences' attention with amusing and entertaining stories, and dramatic elaborations of episodes from *Sūtra*s.

The *Saṅgha* has also been active in education. In the lands of Southern and Northern Buddhism, monasteries were the major, or sole, source of education until modern times. This is reflected in the fact that the most common Burmese term for a monastery, *kyaung*, means 'school'. The education offered by monasteries was of an elementary nature, covering such matters as reading, writing, basic religious knowledge, arithmetic and cultural traditions. It ensured, though, that the literacy rate in these lands has been high by Asian standards. In Southern Buddhism, it was mainly boys who were educated at the monastery schools, but they passed on something of their education to their sisters and wives, and there were also some purely lay schools organized for girls. In Tibet, the Communist Chinese ended the educational role of the monastery, and modernization has also meant that education in Sri Lanka, Burma and Thailand is now primarily in state schools, so that the monks have mostly lost their traditional role as schoolteachers. Some monastery schools are recognized and supported by the state as primary schools, however, and some monks with modern educational qualifications also function in the state system as teachers and lecturers. This has generated much criticism, though, for many see it as depriving the monk of any specifically religious role.

[25] See *EB*.9.8.1 for pastoral advice given by an eleventh-century monk in Japan.

The *Vinaya* does not allow a monk to make a living from any profession, including being a doctor, and the Buddha advised monks to use any medical knowledge they had to help only other monks/nuns or close relatives, so as to avoid accusations if the medicines did not work. Nevertheless, it was inevitable that, in societies where monks were the literate elite, they should come to respond to lay requests for medical help. In Southern Buddhism, some are noted for expertise with herbal cures (e.g. of drug addicts), massage or therapy using coloured lights. In Northern Buddhism, some study in the monasteries to be doctors; in Eastern Buddhism, monks have also practised medicine to some extent. The *Saṅgha* has also served the laity in the area of social welfare and community development. Modern developments in this area will also be discussed in Chapter 12.

While Buddhist monks were originally wandering world-renouncers, they came in time to serve as literate ceremonial specialists to the laity, particularly at funerals. A key ritual function has been to act as the conveyers of blessings and protections. In Southern Buddhism, monks might be invited to chant *paritta* (see p. 249–50) at the opening of a new house or public building, the start of a new business venture, before or after a wedding, to aid an ill or disturbed person, or at a funeral. In Northern Buddhism, people have sought the services of monks, *Lama*s and lay ritual specialists at times of birth, illness, danger and death. The safety and health of the whole community has been seen as being ensured by the virtuous living and rituals of the *Saṅgha*. In Eastern Buddhism, monks have chanted *Sūtra*s or invocations of Amitābha Buddha for the benefit of ill or deceased persons. In periods when Buddhism played a central role in national life, as in Tang China (618–907), 'national monasteries' were supported by the state so as to promote the welfare of China and its emperor. In Southern, Northern and Eastern Buddhism, monks have also responded to lay requests for the blessing of protective amulets, such as small Buddha-images.

In both the Southern and Northern traditions, some monks use their knowledge of astrology to analyse people's characters and guide them through the ups and downs that their karma has in store for them. In Eastern Buddhism, popular demand led temples to dispense divination slips: small pieces of bamboo or paper on which is written some prediction. Nowadays, in several countries, lay people may even look to monks for hints at what lottery numbers may come up.

Monastic involvement in politics is a type of interaction with the lay world perhaps most at odds with the archetype of the monk as a non-involved world-renouncer. Nevertheless, as Buddhism spread literate culture into many societies in the process of political unification and organization, it is not surprising that the *Saṅgha* came to wield political influence, or even political power, in a number of countries. The political power of the *Saṅgha* reached its height in pre-Communist Tibet, whose ruler was the then Dalai Lama. At times of its ascendancy in China, Buddhism had considerable influence over the ruling secular elite, and Japan has had a long history of close contacts between *Saṅgha* and state. In the lands of Southern Buddhism, also, monks could have considerable political influence, and they have been politically active in Sri Lanka and Burma to varying extents since the 1930s (see pp. 379, 395 and 396).[26] In 2007, for example, Burmese monks were the vanguard of popular protest against the country's oppressive military regime.

[26] Swearer, 1995: 110–15; *EB*.6.8.3 gives a justification of this by Walpola Rāhula.

CHAPTER 11

Buddhist Practice: Meditation and Cultivation of Experience-Based Wisdom[1]

On the Buddhist path, a key quality to develop is that of *paññā* (Skt *prajñā*), understanding or wisdom. This is of three kinds, nurtured by: (i) hearing or reading teachings from scriptures and living spiritual teachers; (ii) reflection on these; and (iii) meditative 'development' or 'cultivation' (*bhāvanā*) of the *citta* (heart/mind) and the factors of the Path.[2] The third aspect is what matures true wisdom, which directly sees things 'as they really are', hence cutting through spiritual ignorance: the key aspect of awakening/enlightenment. In their different ways, the various methods of Buddhist meditation entail stepping back from involvement in the everyday flow of the mind, so as to pause and contemplatively observe. From this stance, there can then be a deep calming down, a stilling and a transformative waking up.

For all schools, there are meditative aspects to the devotional practices carried out by most laypeople, indeed chanting is perhaps the most prevalent form of Buddhist meditative cultivation. Chanting (see pp. 243–4), when done well, requires appropriate mental application, focus and mindful awareness, and helps generate energy, joy and calm, so that the mind is little affected by hindrances to meditative concentration. It thus contributes to the systematic nurturing and growing of good qualities, and undermining negative traits which hinder this process. Buddhaghosa, in his classical meditation manual the *Visuddhimagga* (Path of Purification), includes as meditation topics mindful recollection (*anussati*) of the special qualities of the Buddha, *Dhamma, Saṅgha*, using formulas that are identical to, or close to, the wording of common Pali chants (*A*.III.284–8 (*BW*.279–81)). Moreover, chanting the *Karaṇīya-metta Sutta* (see p. 279)

[1] A good overview of meditation in the different Buddhist traditions is Shaw, 2009, and a good anthology of texts on meditation is *MW*. *BM*. is an anthology of texts on meditation from the Pali Canon.

[2] *D*.III.219; *Vism*.439; *AKB*.VI.5c–d; Gethin, 2001: 222–3; cf. *BW*.321–3.

may be the most common way of practising *mettā-bhāvanā*, the cultivation of lovingkindness. When monks chant for the laity, it can also be seen as a form of 'broadcast meditation', whose effect on the laity will depend on the quality of attention in both themselves and the chanters.

Wherever Buddhism has been healthy, those who have practised formal meditation (other than chanting) have been not only the ordained, but also the more committed laypeople (*BM*.12–15). In Southern Buddhism, the most assiduous meditators are members of the *Saṅgha* in the 'forest' tradition. For many centuries, lay meditation seems to have been done mainly by those who took the 'eight precepts' temporarily or permanently. It was also done by those undergoing temporary periods in the *Saṅgha*. In the twentieth century, a revival of lay meditation began in Burma and then spread to other Theravāda lands. In Northern Buddhism, those who specialize in meditation are found among both monastics and non-ordained *yogins*. In Eastern Buddhism, devotional chanting of the Pure Land type has been most common among the laity, but Zen meditation has been practised by some laypeople as well as the ordained. In post-war Japan, some employers have even encouraged their employees to practise it. In the West, one or other of the many forms of Buddhist meditation now available is practised by a relatively high proportion of those who have turned to Buddhism.

THE APPROACH TO MEDITATION

Most types of meditation are done under the guidance of a meditation teacher. In Southern Buddhism, such a person is an advising 'good friend' (*kalyāṇa-mitta*; *BM*.10–12); Northern Buddhism has the tantric *Lama/Guru*, and Eastern Buddhism has for example the Zen *Rōshi*. The Buddha saw having such a teacher as the most powerful external factor in aiding purification of the heart (*A*.I.14), and as the 'whole of the holy life', rather than merely half of it (*S*.v.2 (*BW*.240–1)). Meditation requires personal guidance, as it is a subtle skill which cannot be properly conveyed by standardized written teachings. The teacher gets to know his pupil, guides him or her through difficulties as they occur, and guards against inept or inappropriate use of the powerful means of self-change that meditation provides (*Vism*.97–110). In return, the pupil must apply himself well to the practice and be open to where it leads.

Training the mind is a gradual process that requires patient persistence (*BW*.241–50, 267; Khantipālo, 1986). One needs to believe that it is possible and worthwhile to change oneself, and that one can do it oneself, through a process of gradual application and cultivation. Learning meditation is a skill akin to learning to play a musical instrument: it is learning how to 'tune' and 'play' the mind, and regular, patient practice is the means to this. Moreover, just as a well-tuned stringed instrument has strings neither too slack nor too tight, so in meditation the effort must be just right. Here the classical idea of the path as a 'middle way' is relevant. Meditation practice is also like gardening: one cannot force plants to grow, but one can assiduously provide them with the right conditions, so that they develop naturally. For meditation, the 'right conditions' are the appropriate application of mind and of the specific technique being used.

Most meditations are done seated on a cushion with the legs crossed with one foot on the opposite calf muscle or thigh, or both feet thus, with the hands together in the lap, and the back straight but not stiff; or with one foot on the floor in front of the crossed legs, or kneeling (*BM*.15–18; Shaw, 2009: 22–3). Once a person is accustomed to this kind of position, it is a stable one which can be used as a good basis for stilling the mind. The body remains still, with the extremities folded in, just as the attention is being centred. The general effects of meditation are a gradual increase in calm and awareness. A person becomes more patient, better able to deal with the ups and downs of life, clearer headed and more energetic. He or she becomes both more open in dealings with others, and more self-confident and able to stand his or her own ground. These effects are sometimes quite well established after about nine months of practice. The long-term effects go deeper, and are indicated below.

To develop a good basis for meditation, preliminary bowing, chanting and motivating reflections may be done. In the Northern tradition, a preparatory visualization may be done to breathe out negative qualities, seen as like black smoke, and breathe in positive qualities, seen as like radiant light (*MW*.166–8). There is also a sequence of reflections, on: the rarity and opportunity of having attained a 'precious human rebirth'; the uncertainty of when this human life will end; the fact that one will then be reborn according to one's karma; that suffering is involved in every realm of rebirth; that such suffering can only be transcended by attaining *Nirvāṇa*; and finally that one needs a spiritual guide to aid one on the path to this. This method rouses motivation for a Śrāvakayāna level of practice (see p. 110), as it concerns one's own needs. Next, there are reflections concerning the needs of others, so as to develop the Mahāyāna motivation.[3] This is done by developing the four 'divine abiding' meditations, as in the

[3] *MW*.168–71; Kongtrul, 2002: 29–33, 87; Samuel, 1993: 200; Wayman, 1991: 46–50; Williams, 2009: 196–7.

cultivation of the *bodhi-citta* (see pp. 153–4). All Mahāyāna practice presupposes this *Bodhisattva* motivation.

QUALITIES TO BE DEVELOPED BY MEDITATION

An early and influential summary of the qualities to develop on the path, many of which are strongly related to meditation, are the thirty-seven 'qualities that contribute to awakening'.[4] These consist of seven sets of qualities (Gethin, 2001):

- The four applications/establishments/presencings, or perhaps foundations of mindfulness (Pali *satipaṭṭhāna*, Skt *smṛtyupasthāna*): to be 'diligent, clearly knowing and mindful, free from desires and discontent in regard to the world' when contemplating the body, feeling-tones, states of mind, and significant basic patterns in experience (*dhammas*).
- The four right endeavours (*sammā-ppadhāna/samyak-pradhāna*): to direct desire-to-act (*chanda*), effort and energy to: avoiding the arising of unwholesome/unskilful states of mind; abandoning those that have arisen; arousing wholesome/skilful states; and sustaining and further developing these.
- The four bases of accomplishment (*iddhi-pāda/ṛddhi-pāda*): to supplement the forces of endeavour with concentration gained by desire-to-act, energy/vigour/courageous engagement (*viriya/vīrya*), inclination of mind (*citta*), or investigation.
- The five faculties (*indriya*): trustful confidence/faith (*saddhā/śraddhā*), energy, mindfulness, concentration and understanding/wisdom.
- The five powers (*bala*): the faculties when at the level of being unshakeably established.
- The seven factors of awakening (*bojjhaṅga/bodhyaṅga*): mindfulness, discrimination/analysis of *dhammas*, energy, joy, tranquillity, concentration, equanimity.
- The Noble Eight-factored Path.

These qualities or mental skills have been important both in pre-Mahāyāna[5] and Mahāyāna[6] traditions. The seven sets are groups of skills that can be combined in different ways. Several qualities recur under the same or similar names, being like notes that can appear in different chords. While the last

[4] Pali *bodhi-pakkhiyā dhammā*, Skt *bodhi-pakṣā dharmā*; *D*.II.120, III.102, 127–8; *M*.III.81.

[5] *S*.IV.360–8; *S*.V.1–293 (selection in *SB*.228–42); *Vism*.678–9; Gethin, 2001; Piyadassi, 1980; Ṭhānissaro, 1996.

[6] Dayal, 1932: 80–164; Pagel, 1995: 381–401.

set is the culminating one, the five faculties are perhaps the set that brings together the most recurrent factors (*BTTA*.23–38; Conze, 1993). Faith, and associated moral virtue, gives a good-hearted foundation that naturally leads on to the engagement of energy in practice, and hence the application of mindful awareness; this in turn helps the mind to become unified, concentrated, calm, which in turn aids the arising of understanding and wisdom from a clear mind.

Energy/courageous engagement, equivalent to right endeavour or right effort, is the expression of 'go to it and keep at it'. It serves to enable the meditator to develop and sustain the specific kind of activity that meditation is; for it is not a passive thing. It also serves to undermine unskilful states of mind which intrude on the process of meditation. To prevent such states arising, the meditator practises 'guarding the sense-doors': being circumspect about how he or she relates to sense-objects, so that they do not trigger habitual responses of attachment, aversion or confusion (*BSI*.103–5).

Mindfulness (Pali *sati*, Skt *smṛti*) is the process of bearing something in mind, be it remembered or present before the senses or mind, with clear awareness; it keeps one connected to what is actual, and reminds one of what is skilful (Gethin, 2001: 36–44). It came to be defined in the Theravāda as 'not floating away' (*Asl*.121), that is, an awareness which does not drift along the surface of things, but is a thorough and undistorted observation. Mindfulness involves 'standing back' from the processes of body and mind and calmly observing them, with full presence of mind, alert attention, mental clarity, being wide awake, fully with-it, vigilant, not on 'autopilot'. Tse-fu Kuan (2008: 41–57) has shown that it has four aspects:

- 'Simple awareness . . . conscious registering of the presence of objects . . . non-judgemental observation and recognition' (2008: 41–2), such as knowing one is breathing in, or being aware of the passing sensations arising when lifting an arm, or changing feelings. It observes without preferences, without habitual reaction, but clearly acknowledging what is actually there in the flow of experience, noting its nature. It has been described as a kind of 'bare attention' which sees things as if for the first time (Anālayo, 2003: 57–60; Nyanaponika, 1997).
- 'Protective awareness', which adds a presence of mind that naturally brings restraint of unskilful reactions to sense-objects.
- 'Introspective awareness', which identifies unskilful states that may nevertheless have arisen, and calls to mind, and thus calls into play, counteractive qualities.[7]

[7] As in the *Sutta* on the removal of distracting thoughts: *M*.I.118–22 (*BW*.275–8; *SB*.152–5; Soma, 1981).

- 'Deliberately forming conceptions', which recollects and notes such things as the qualities of the Buddha, *Dhamma* or *Saṅgha*, or of loving-kindness, or the ingredients of the body, its stages of decomposition, and the inevitability of death, all of which help to undermine unskilful states and cultivate skilful ones.

Of these aspects, the first is the basis of the rest. Mindfulness is crucial to the process of meditation because without its careful observation one cannot see things 'as they really are'.

People's normal experience of 'concentration' usually varies from a half-hearted paying attention, to becoming absorbed in a good book, when most extraneous mental chatter subsides. Buddhist meditation, in common with many other forms of meditation such as Hindu yoga, aims to cultivate the power of concentration until it can become truly 'one-pointed', with 100 per cent of the attention focused on a chosen calming object. In such a state, the mind becomes free from all distraction and wavering, in a unified state of inner stillness: mental unification. This is what is meant by meditative 'concentration' (*samādhi*) – that is, the state of being concentrat*ed*. The process of concentrat*ing*, however, is an aspect of engagement or effort.

In order for meditation to develop appropriately, the tools must be used in the right way. If a person attempted to become strongly concentrated on an object, but with insufficient energy, he would become sleepy; but too much energy and too little mental unification can lead to restless excitement (*Vism*.129–30). If he vigorously developed a concentrated state without also using mindfulness of the object, he could become obsessed or fixated on the object, this being 'wrong concentration'. Concentration, then, if developed on the basis of right effort, in unison with right mindfulness, is 'right concentration'.

The four applications of mindfulness (Anālayo, 2003; Gethin, 2001: 29–68) are listed first in the above seven sets, which emphasizes their foundational role in the cultivation of all the qualities. The practice of applying mindfulness, making it present, to four aspects of experience is detailed in the *Satipaṭṭhāna Sutta* (*M*.I.55–63[8]) and *Mahā-satipaṭṭhāna Sutta* (*D*.II.290–315), its expanded version. These texts contain what can be seen as the earliest summary of appropriate focuses of Buddhist meditation, and associated meditation methods. Under mindful contemplation of the body (*kāya*) are mindfulness of:

[8] = *BS2*.37; *BTTA*.32; *BM*.76–85; *BW*.281–90; *EB*.3.5.4; *MW*.19–25; *SB*.141–51 (cf. 232–4); Anālayo, 2003: 3–13. Anālayo, 2003 is a detailed analysis of the *Sutta*; Soma, 1998 includes a translation of the Theravādin commentary, though it wrongly translates the *Sutta* as saying that *satipaṭṭhāna* practice is the 'only way' to *Nirvāṇa*, rather than the 'direct way'.

- what sustains it: breathing in and out,
- what it does: postures (walking, standing, sitting and lying down), and various bodily movements,
- what it is composed of: its various solid and liquid components, and the four elements (earth/solidity, water/cohesion, fire/heat and wind/motion),
- its stages of decomposition after death.

Beyond the body, mindfulness observes:

- Feeling (*vedanā*): the pleasant, unpleasant and neutral feeling-tones that arise, whether from body or mind, or from ordinary worldly causes or spiritual ones, such as the joy that may arise in meditation.
- Mind-states (*citta*): the presence or absence of unwholesome states of mind, and of one's degree of mental development and concentration.
- Reality-patterns (*dhammas*) as delineated in the Buddha's *Dhamma*: the five hindrances to meditative calming (see below, pp. 328–9); the five bundles (*khandha*; see pp. 56–7); the senses and their objects and how, between them, fettering attachments can arise or be avoided; the seven factors of awakening, and how to perfect them; the four True Realities for the Spiritually Ennobled.

Samatha *and* vipassanā

Perhaps the most succinct way of summarizing the qualities needed for awakening/enlightenment is as: *samatha* (Skt *śamatha*) – calm, peace, tranquillity – and *vipassanā* (Skt *vipaśyanā*) – insight (*S.*IV.360). It is said that both *samatha* and *vipassanā* are aspects of liberating knowledge: if *samatha* is cultivated, the heart/mind (*citta*) is developed, which leads to the abandonment of attachment/lusting after (*rāga*); if *vipassanā* is cultivated, wisdom (*paññā*) is developed, which leads to abandonment of spiritual ignorance (*avijjā*, Skt *avidyā*).[9] Here one sees that the spiritual path involves work on both affective and cognitive aspects of the mind: attachment-rooted emotional reactions for and against things, and how one sees and understands things. These are interrelated, for emotional turbulence makes it difficult to see clearly, and confusion and misperception feed emotional turbulence. Working together, *samatha* and *vipassanā* bring about a state in which direct knowledge can arise in a calm, clear, peaceful mind.

[9] *A.*I.61 (*BW.*267–8); cf. *A.*II.93–5 (*BW.*269–70).

Samatha and *vipassanā* are needed for the arising of the Noble Eight-factored Path that immediately leads up to stream-entry (see p. 84), the first crucial spiritual breakthrough. Hence it is said (*A*.II.156–8 (*BW*.268–9)) that one can go on to become an *Arahat* once the Path arises from one of: (i) *vipassanā* preceded by *samatha*; (ii) *samatha* preceded by *vipassanā*; (iii) *samatha* and *vipassanā* yoked together; (iv) the mind being 'gripped by *Dhamma* excitement' but then settling down and attaining concentration. As *samatha* and *vipassanā* naturally became terms for the methods which respectively cultivated these qualities, the above four approaches came to be seen as different sequences in which such methods might be practised (Cousins, 1984). As understood in Southern Buddhism: (i) is the 'vehicle' *(-yāna)* of *samatha*, which develops deep calm, then adds insight; (ii) is the vehicle of *vipassanā* which, on the basis of preliminary calm, develops insight then deeper calm (full '*samatha*'); and (iii) is the 'yoked' method, which has alternating phases of progressively deeper levels of calm and insight; (iv) seems to have referred to insight leading to the arising of various pleasant experiences to which there is excited attachment – later called the 'defilements of insight' (*Vism*.633–8) – then a return to composure and concentration (*Patis*.II.100–1). In time it came to be seen as the way of the 'dry/bare (*sukkha*) insight worker (*vipassaka*)' (*Vism*. 666, 702): insight without the explicit need for the cultivation of *samatha*.

APPROACHES BEGINNING WITH *SAMATHA* IN SOUTHERN BUDDHISM

The most common way of developing meditation has been to practise the *samatha-yāna*, as described in such *Sutta*s as the *Sāmaññaphala*.[10] In the *samatha* aspect of this, an object is chosen, mindfulness is applied to it, and concentration is developed focused on specific aspects of the object. As concentration strengthens, mindfulness is further developed as an adjunct which is increasingly aware of the subtle states of mind which arise from deep concentration. Thus arises a state of tranquil, focused alertness, with concentration and mindfulness developed to high degrees, in lucid trances known as *jhāna*s (Skt *dhyāna*), after the 'access concentration' (*upacāra-samādhi*) that is on the brink of attaining the first of these.

In the 'vehicle of *samatha*', deeper levels of *jhāna* are developed before *vipassanā* is developed in earnest. In the method of '*samatha* and *vipassanā* yoked together', one level of *jhāna* is developed, then its impermanent and

[10] *D*.I.47–85 (*BM*.59–75; *MW*.30–7; *SB*.5–36).

unsatisfactory nature is examined with *vipassanā*, then a deeper level of *jhāna* is developed, then seen with *vipassanā*, etc. Moreover, at the time of stream-entry, when the mind gains its first glimpse of *Nirvāṇa*, there is a brief or sustained experience of a 'transcendent' (*lokuttara*) level of *jhāna*, rather than one with a conditioned object (see p. 49). For those starting with a more *vipassanā* approach, this may be the first, and perhaps only, experience of *jhāna*.

Buddhaghosa's *Visuddhimagga* describes in detail forty possible objects of meditation,[11] which primarily, but not exclusively, pertain to *samatha*. They can lead to different levels of *samatha*, and are especially helpful for different personality types, who may be more affected by greed, by hatred or delusion, or, more skilfully, by faith, intelligence or discursiveness (*Vism*.101–10 (*BS1*.116–21)):

- Mindfulness of breathing; which best suits the 'delusion' and 'discursive' types; –> any of the four *jhānas*.
- The four divine abidings: lovingkindness, compassion, empathetic joy and equanimity; for the hate type; –> third *jhāna*, or fourth by equanimity.
- The ten *kasiṇas* or 'universals': prepared examples of things which represent the elements (earth, water, fire, wind), light, or limited space – all of which suit all types; or colours, for the 'hate' type: blue, yellow, red, white; these –> any of the four *jhānas*. A *kasiṇa-maṇḍala*, or 'universal-circle', such as a blue disc, a circle of earth, or a bowl of water is focused on until it can be seen clearly in the mind's eye as a mental image, representing such a 'universal' quality as blueness, the solidity of earth or the cohesion of water (*Vism*.123–5, 170–77; *MW*.43–9).
- The four formless states: four subtle levels of existence, known from the fourth *jhāna*, and suitable for all types.
- The ten kinds of unloveliness or foulness (*asubha*, Skt *aśubha*): ten stages of the decomposition of a corpse; for the 'greed' type, to counteract lust; –> first *jhāna*.
- Mindfulness of the parts of the body; for the intelligent type; –> first *jhāna*.
- Mindfulness of the inevitability of death, recollection of the peaceful qualities of *Nirvāṇa*, perception of the repulsiveness of food or reflection on the four elements composing the body; for the intelligent type; –> access concentration.

[11] Listed at *Vism*.110–11, detailed in *Vism*. IV–X. Conze, 1972 has many selections from *Vism*.; *BM*.86–194 translates canonical texts that Buddhaghosa draws on.

- Recollections of the qualities of the Buddha, *Dhamma* or *Saṅgha*, the benefits of moral virtue or generosity, or of the various types of *devas* (see pp. 34–6); for the faith type; –> access concentration.[12]

Of these, meditation on lovingkindness and breathing, which with devotional chanting are perhaps the most common, will be described below.

Lovingkindness meditation

Lovingkindness (Pali *mettā*, Skt *maitrī*; see pp. 278–80) is seen as a 'divine abiding' (*brahma-vihāra*) or 'immeasurable' (Pali *appamāṇa*, Skt *apramāṇa*) which, when fully developed, expands the mind into an immeasurable field of benevolent concern.[13] While it can thus be used to develop the deep calm of *jhāna* (*BTTA*.34), it is generally used as a counteractive to ill-will. The practice consists of developing a friendliness which is warm, accepting, patient and unsentimental. In Southern Buddhism, one begins by focusing this on oneself,[14] to help to get to know, and come to terms with, all aspects of oneself, 'warts and all'. Once these are accepted – not in a complacent way – then other people, with their real or imagined faults, can become the objects of genuine lovingkindness: 'loving your neighbour as yourself', to use a Christian phrase, will then be welcoming and sincere.

The meditator starts by saying to himself, for example, 'may I be well and happy, may I be free from difficulties and troubles', and tries to *feel* what these words express so as to generate a joyful and warm heart. After reviewing 'unlikable' aspects of himself, he then goes on to focus lovingkindness on others. A common method (see *Vism*.IX) is for the meditator to progressively focus on a person he has respect and gratitude for, a friend, a person he is indifferent to, and a person he has some hostility towards (provided none of these is a possible object of sexual interest). Thus his mind becomes accustomed to spreading its circle of lovingkindness into increasingly difficult territory. If this is successful, he may then radiate lovingkindness to all sentient beings without exception, in all directions. The aim is to break down the barriers which make the mind friendly towards only a limited selection of beings; to cultivate an all-pervading kindness.

[12] For a modern example of *samatha* developed by recollecting qualities of the Buddha, see *BP*.16.

[13] Buddharakkhita, 1989; Nyanaponika and Ñāṇamoli, 1998; Salzberg, 1995.

[14] In Northern Buddhism, the first focus is on one's mother, as one for whom one cares dearly.

Mindfulness of breathing

Mindfulness of breathing in and out, *ānāpāna-sati*, is described in the *Ānāpāna-sati Sutta*,[15] which explains that its practice cultivates all four applications of mindfulness, which in turn develop the seven factors of awakening, and hence lead to direct knowledge and liberation. The practice has aspects that emphasize either *samatha* or *vipassanā* (*Vism*.266–93). Its popularity arises because the breath is always present, and because it becomes more subtle, and thus more calming, as a person becomes calmer; its constantly changing nature is also a good example of impermanence.

Breathing meditation to induce *samatha* is done with the eyes closed. It begins by some method of counting the in and out movements of slow, gentle breathing, so as to help the mind become accustomed to staying on the breath. Different breath-lengths may be used, or the naturally varying length of the breaths may simply be noted. With more experience, the counting is dropped after a certain time in a sitting, and the flowing sensations arising from the breath are more carefully followed; then the attention is focused on the sensations in one nostril. When a person begins meditation, the attention keeps wandering from the breath, but the method is to keep gently bringing it back to it. At first, it seems that the mind wanders more in meditation than at other times, but this is just due to a greater awareness of the fickle, shifting nature of attention. After some practice, the mind can remain on the breath for longer periods. At a certain stage, there arises a mental image, or 'sign' (*nimitta*), known as the 'acquired (*uggaha*) sign' (*MW*.44). This mental impression of the breath can take various forms, such as a patch or circle of light or a puff of smoke (*Vism*.285). It arises from there being good concentration and mindfulness focused on the breath, just as attention to a 'universal-circle' leads to a mental image of it. Once the image has arisen, in a state of deepening inner stillness, it becomes the focus of attention so as to stabilize it.

The five hindrances and access concentration

As the meditator learns to work with the mental image, he or she has to gradually suspend the 'five hindrances' which obstruct further progress.[16] Each is a mental reaction to the process of developing sustained application to any task. The first is sensual desire, where the mind reaches out for

[15] *M*.III.78–88 (*BM*.146–58; in part: *BW*.290–5; *MW*.26–8); Brahm, 2006.

[16] *D*.I.71–3 (*SB*.26–8); *S*.V.121–6 (*BW*.270–7); *EB*.3.5.5; Brahm, 2006: 29–52; Gunaratana, 1985: 28–48; Nyanaponika, 1993; Shaw, 2009: 43–8.

something more alluring and interesting than the given object. The second is ill-will, where there is a reaction of aversion to the task at hand, or to one's mental wandering or the source of distracting sounds. The third is dullness and lethargy, where there is drowsiness, mental passivity and sloth. The fourth is restlessness and worry, where the mind alternates between over-sensitized excitement at some success with the task, and unease over difficulties with it. The final hindrance is vacillation or fear of commitment, where the mind wavers back and forth, saying that the task is not worth performing. Overcoming the hindrances is likened both to the purification of gold-ore, with pure gold standing for the mind's uncovered potential (*S*.v.92), and to the training of a restless animal until it becomes still and tractable.

The hindrances may also be suspended when intently listening to a *Dhamma*-teaching. In the *Suttas*, they are often said to be suspended from the Buddha's teaching of someone about the benefits of giving, moral virtue, the heavenly rebirths these lead to and the advantages of renouncing attachment to sense-pleasures, with the listener then ready to hear and develop insight into the True Realities for the Spiritually Ennobled (*M*.1.379–80).

In *samatha* meditation, once the hindrances are suspended, the *nimitta* becomes the 'counterpart (*paṭibhāga*) sign', which has a much brighter, clearer and subtler form. This is the stage of 'access concentration' (*upacāra-samādhi*), for it is the point of access to the full concentration of *jhāna* (*Vism*.125–37). Working with this sign builds up the 'five factors of *jhāna*', which have been gradually developing all along, counteracting the hindrances (Gethin, 1998: 180–4). The first factor is 'mental application' (Pali *vitakka*, Skt *vitarka*), the process of applying the mind to the object. The second is 'examination' (*vicāra*), which leads to the mind remaining on the object. The third is 'joy' (Pali *pīti*, Skt *prīti*), which starts in the form of warm tingles and culminates in a feeling of bliss pervading the entire body. This arises as other factors become developed in a balanced way. The fourth factor is 'happiness' (*sukha*), a feeling of deep contentment which is more tranquil than joy, and which arises as the mind becomes harmonized and unagitated. The fifth *jhāna*-factor is 'one-pointedness of mind' (Pali *cittass'ekaggatā*, Skt *cittaikagratā*), that is, the mind wholly unified on the object. This arises once there is 'happiness', and the mind can contentedly stay with the object.

The jhānas *and formless attainments*

In access concentration, the *jhāna*-factors are still weak, like the legs of a toddler learning to walk. Once they are strong, the mind may briefly dip into or remain in a state of 'absorption (*appanā*)-concentration', when *jhāna* (Skt *dhyāna*), 'meditation' proper, is attained.[17] Here, the mind is blissfully absorbed in rapt concentration on the object, and is insensitive to sense-stimuli, so that *jhāna* can be seen as a sort of trance. This is not in the sense of a dull stupor with subsequent loss of memory of the state: due to the presence of a high degree of mindfulness, it is a lucid trance, and one in which wisdom is also present (*Dhs.* sec. 162). It has a peaceful calm deeper than that of sound sleep, but with greater awareness than in waking consciousness. The mind has great clarity and tranquillity, so as to be like an unruffled, pellucid lake. Due to the radically different nature of this altered state of consciousness, 'secluded from [the realm of] sense-desires, secluded from unskilful states' (*D.*I.73), it is classified as belonging to the realm of elemental form, a level of existence in which the gods of the world of elemental form also live (see pp. 35–6): it is a qualitatively different 'world' of experience. On emergence from it, there is a purifying afterglow, in which the compulsion to think is absent, and the urges to eat or sleep are weakened.

The state described above is the first of a set of four *jhānas*.[18] Once it has been fully mastered, the meditator develops the others, progressively dropping certain *jhāna*-factors as relatively gross, cultivating deeper and more subtle degrees of calm, and channelling more and more energy into one-pointedness. The fourth *jhāna* is a state of profound stillness and peace, in which the mind rests with unshakeable one-pointedness and equanimity, and breathing has calmed to the point of stopping (*S.*IV.217; *Vism.*275). The mind has a radiant purity, due to its 'brightly shining' depths having been fully uncovered and made manifest at the surface level. It is very workable like refined gold, which can be used to make all manner of precious and wonderful things (*A.*I.253–5): 'With mind concentrated, purified and cleansed, unblemished, free from defilements, malleable, workable, firm, and having gained imperturbability' (*D.*I.76). It is thus an ideal take-off point for various further developments. Indeed, it seems to have been the state from which the Buddha went on to attain awakening (*M.*I.247–9).

One possibility is simply to further deepen the process of calming by developing the four 'formless attainments' (Pali *arūpa-samāpatti*, Skt *ārūpya-samāpatti*; *Vism.*X), levels of mystical trance paralleling the 'formless' realms of rebirth (see Table 4). They are 'formless' as they have no shape or form as object, even the mental image that is the focus of the *jhānas*. In the first, the

[17] *Vism.*137–69; Cousins, 1973; Gunaratana, 1980, 1985, 2006.
[18] *BTTA.*33; *BW.*296–8; *MW.*29; *SB.*242–3.

Table 4 *States developed on the basis of* samatha *meditation*

States arising from samatha *alone*	*States present*	*When combined with* vipassanā
THE FORMLESS REALM		
States present: one-pointedness, equanimity		
8 The sphere of neither-perception-nor-non-perception		→ATTAINMENT OF CESSATION
7 The sphere of nothingness		
6 The sphere of infinite consciousness		
5 The sphere of infinite space		
THE REALM OF ELEMENTAL FORM		
4 Fourth *jhāna*–	One-pointedness equanimity	→THE SIX HIGHER KNOWLEDGES: (vi) *Nirvāṇa*, (v) seeing how beings are reborn according to their karma, (iv) memory of previous lives, (iii) mind-reading, (ii) clairaudience, (i) psychic powers
3 Third *jhāna*–	One-pointedness, happiness, equanimity	
2 Second *jhāna*–	One-pointedness, happiness, joy	
1 First *jhāna*–	One-pointedness, happiness, joy, examination, mental application	
THE SENSE-DESIRE REALM		
iii Access concentration, based on 'counterpart sign'		
ii Work on 'acquired sign', so as to suspend the hindrances		
i Work on 'preliminary sign' (e.g. the breath or a *kasiṇa-maṇḍala*)		

meditator expands the previous object, then focuses on the infinite space it then 'occupies'. Next, he focuses on the 'infinite consciousness' which had been aware of this space. Transcending this, he then focuses on the apparent nothingness that remains. Finally, even the extremely attenuated perception which had been focused on nothingness becomes the object of attention.

Cessation and the higher knowledges

The remaining states which can be developed on the basis of profound *samatha* require the addition of *vipassanā*, insight into the nature of things. It is said that one can become an *Arahat* or non-returner for example by developing any of the four *jhāna*s, or the first three formless states, then developing insight into the impermanent nature of the qualities in these refined states, so as to overcome any attachment to them (*M*.I.350–3; *A*.V.343–7; *A*.IV.422). Another possibility is, via the fourth formless state, to attain the 'cessation of perception and feeling', also known as the 'attainment of cessation' (*nirodha-samāpatti*): on emerging from this, deep wisdom arises and a person becomes an *Arahat* or non-returner (*A*.III.194, *M*.I.175, *EB*.3.5.7). Cessation is an anomalous state in which the mind totally shuts down, devoid of even subtle perception or feeling, due to turning away from even the very refined peace of the formless level. In this state, the heart stops, but a residual metabolism keeps the body alive for up to seven days (*M*.I.296, *Vism*.702–9; Griffiths, 1987). Here a person gains a sort of unconscious meeting with *Nirvāṇa*, for they are said to 'touch *Nirvāṇa* with their body'. Only someone with a mastery of the formless states who is a non-returner or *Arahat*, or on the brink of attaining these states, can attain this state.

From fourth *jhāna*, the six 'higher knowledges' (Pali *abhiññā*, Skt *abhijñā*) can also be fully developed.[19] The first three consist of various paranormal abilities. The first is a group of '(psychic) accomplishments' (Pali *iddhi*, Skt *ṛddhi*): psychokinetic abilities such as walking on water, flying, diving into the earth, and being in several places at once (*D*.I.77–8 (*EB*.3.5.6)). These are said to be developed by meditating on the elements of matter to gain control of them. The second 'higher knowledge' is clair-audience: the ability to hear sounds at great distance, including the speech of the gods. The third knowledge is that of reading the mental states of other people. The last three of these comprise the 'threefold knowledge' (Pali *tevijjā*, Skt *traividyā*): memory of past lives, seeing how beings are reborn according to their karma, and the (conscious) attainment of *Nirvāṇa*. Thus, based on the power and purity of the fourth *jhāna*, many barriers can be overcome by these knowledges, respectively those of physical laws, distance, the minds of others, time, death and, highest of all, the barrier of conditioned existence as such.

THE CONTRIBUTIONS OF *SAMATHA* AND *VIPASSANĀ* MEDITATION IN SOUTHERN BUDDHISM

Both *samatha* and *vipassanā* draw on the principle of Conditioned Arising: that everything, mental and physical, arises according to nurturing conditions, and ceases when these cease. In *samatha*, the emphasis is on

[19] *Vism*.XII–XIII; *BSI*.121–33; *BW*.273–5, 65–7, 252–3.

reconditioning the way the mind/heart works; in *vipassanā*, the emphasis is on seeing the limitations of anything that is conditioned. *Samatha* seeks to gather in energies, and integrate wholesome mental factors so as to grow a strong, kindly centre of calm and awareness, so that one is more centred, 'one's own person', more in charge of oneself, more 'together', less perturbed by external events and one's emotions; yet also more open-hearted and sensitive to the needs of others, especially through developing loving-kindness, which particularly works on the heart level.

In practising *samatha*, a person is learning to let go of objects of attachment, and discipline the mind's restless wanting, its driven-ness. This driven-ness can be observed in the way that the mind is always on the lookout for another distraction to latch on to. Even when the mind becomes quite calm, it will not necessarily stay calm unless gentle discipline is still applied. The constant hum of 'I want', 'I want more', 'I want different' has a tendency to flow on, even when slowed. And if the meditation becomes very pleasurable, then wanting can focus on this, grasping hold of it and so undermining the skilful qualities which led to it. In *samatha*, this tendency is gradually stilled. Moreover, in the deep calm it induces, the mind experiences something which is very different from normal consciousness. This gives a person a perspective from which the limitations and lack of subtlety of normal conscious experience can be directly seen. It also produces very valuable changes in a person, such as a deepening of morality.

Samatha meditation alone, however, cannot bring an experience of *Nirvāṇa*, for while it can temporarily suspend, and thus weaken, attachment, hatred and delusion, it cannot destroy them, so as to not just quieten craving, but completely uproot it from the psyche. For this, *vipassanā* is needed. *Samatha* is an ideal preparation for this, though (Gethin 1998: 198–201). It weakens the obscuring hindrances and so gives the mind the clarity in which things can be seen 'as they really are'; it strengthens positive qualities such as faith and the other faculties, so as to develop the ability to concentrate on an object for long enough to investigate it properly; it schools the mind in 'letting go'; and it makes the mind stable and strong, so that it is not agitated by the potentially disturbing insights into such matters as non-Self. In these ways, *samatha* 'tunes' the mind, calming and refining it, so as to make it more subtle, sensitive, open to new possibilities, and thus a more adequate instrument for knowledge and insight. It also loosens the hold of the defilements, which can then be destroyed by *vipassanā*, rather like first soaking dirty dishes in warm water makes it easier to get them fully clean once a cleansing agent is added.

Defilements such as greed, hatred and delusion are expressed at three levels: in overt actions of body and speech, as conscious thoughts and emotions, and deep-rooted latent tendencies in the mind. Overt defilements are restrained by moral virtue (Pali *sīla*, Skt *śīla*); conscious defilements are stilled by the *samādhi*, meditative concentration induced by *samatha* meditation; latent defilements lurking in the unconscious are dissolved by wisdom, *paññā*, induced especially by *vipassanā* meditation.

In the list of five faculties, wisdom comes after concentration, represented by *jhāna*; and right concentration is said to lead on to right knowledge (*M*.III.76). On the other hand, all factors of the Eight-factored Path, of which right concentration is the last, follow on from right view (*M*.III.71; *S*.V.2), a form of wisdom (*M*.I.301). Hence *jhāna* and wisdom aid each other: 'There is no *jhāna* for him who lacks wisdom, and no wisdom for him who lacks *jhāna*. He in whom are found both *jhāna* and wisdom, indeed, is close to *Nirvāṇa*' (*Dhp*.372).

APPROACHES BEGINNING WITH *VIPASSANĀ* IN SOUTHERN BUDDHISM

The way of *vipassanā* then *samatha* became popular in Burma in the twentieth century, and from there spread elsewhere (Cousins, 1996a; King, 1980: 116–24). The same applies for the way of 'dry *vipassanā*', which sees the deliberate cultivation of *jhāna* and even access concentration as unnecessary for awakening, momentary concentration being sufficient – though Buddhaghosa saw concentration as briefly at the level of first *jhāna* at the time of stream-entry (*Vism*.666). *Vipassanā* meditation uses a high degree of mindfulness, plus right effort and a degree of concentration: how much depends on the teacher. Typically, the breath is used as a home-base for the attention to keep returning to, so as to keep the mind calm and uncaptured by distractions. The insight that develops also naturally brings about deeper stillness and calm due to strong momentary concentration and the detachment which insight brings.

The practice of the four applications of mindfulness (*satipaṭṭhāna*s; see pp. 323–4) is the key basis of *vipassanā* meditation. Indeed the *satipaṭṭhāna*s have sometimes been presented as a uniquely *vipassanā* method, which is incorrect (Anālayo, 2003: 67–91). In *vipassanā* meditation, rather than focusing on one chosen object, as in *samatha*, the attention is opened out so that mindfulness calmly observes each passing sensory or mental object, to systematically notice certain pervasive characteristics of experience. The conditioned states that make up body and mind, of 'oneself' or 'others', are seen to constantly arise and pass away, and be unsatisfactory and impersonal processes to which it is inappropriate to become attached. When not doing sitting meditation, the meditator may carefully observe the sensations involved in movements, such as bending and stretching the arms, eating, washing and going to the toilet. 'Mindfulness of walking' is a specific kind of practice, also used by *samatha* practitioners to strengthen their mindfulness. In this, a person walks back and forth along a path with the mind focused on the sensations in the feet and calf muscles, and the various phases of walking may be mentally noted with such terms as 'lifting', 'moving' and 'putting'. This develops a light, open feeling of spaciousness, and may even lead to the 'foot' disappearing into a flow of sensations.

During seated meditation, the breath is usually investigated, for it is through this rising and falling process that the body is kept alive. *Vipassanā* meditation is more analytical and probing than *samatha* meditation, though, as it aims to investigate the nature of reality, rather than remaining focused on one relatively stable object. So what might become a distraction within *samatha* meditation can become an object for *vipassanā*. Thus the mind does not remain solely on the breath, but also observes various physical sensations as they occur, such as itches and the release of previously unnoticed tensions. As the body is more easily perceived, mindfulness takes this as its object first, so as to build up its power before observing the more fleeting and subtle mental processes, starting with feelings. These are observed as they arise and pass away, noting simply whether they are pleasant, unpleasant or neutral, born of the body or of the mind, ordinary or more spiritual. No 'significance' is attached to them, however: they are viewed simply as passing phenomena. Mindfulness then moves on to states of mind, noting moods and emotions as they arise and are allowed to pass. Finally, mindfulness investigates *dhammas*, significant reality-patterns (see p. 324), up to and including the True Realities of the Spiritually Ennobled, noting when they are present, when they are absent, how they come to arise, and how they come to cease.

Investigation of the 'three marks'

While investigating the processes described above, the aim is to experientially recognize their shared features: the 'three marks' (see pp. 57–8). Their constant arising and ceasing demonstrates that they are impermanent (*anicca*, Skt *anitya*). That they are ephemeral, unstable and limited, not the kind of thing that one can rely on, shows that they are unsatisfactory, obviously or subtly painful (*dukkha*, Skt *duḥkha*). That they rise according to conditions, cannot be controlled at will, and thus do not truly 'belong' to anyone, shows that they are non-Self (*anattā*, Skt *anātman*), 'empty of Self or what belongs to Self'. Investigation shows that the appearance of 'oneself' and external 'things' as substantial self-identical entities is a misperception. These insights are not of a conceptual, intellectual nature, but arise as flashes of penetrative understanding, or wisdom. Once these have occurred during meditation, they may also arise in the course of the day, as things are observed with mindfulness. This process, then, combines gradual cultivation and progressively deeper, and sudden, flashes of insight.

When the whole panorama of experience is seen to be made up of processes – mental or physical, internal or external, past, present or future, subtle or gross – that are non-lasting, unreliable and insubstantial, then there can be a disenchantment (Pali *nibbidā*, Skt *nirvidā*) with, a letting go of, these processes. As a person thus comes to recognize all that he or she has fondly identified with as 'I' or 'mine' as actually changing, conditioned and subtly unsatisfactory, it is directly known that these cannot be truly 'possessed' as 'mine', or be a true identity as 'I', an essence, 'my Self'. As each thing is seen in this way, this allows a relinquishing of any attachment to or identification with it, which leads to a sense of lightness, a spacious accommodation of whatever happens to arise, and joy. This will be the more complete, the more it is realized that *everything* is non-Self; that 'Self' is an empty concept. Not only an empty concept, but a harmful one: for taking something changeable as a permanent 'I' can only lead to suffering when that thing changes. And to protect 'I', we often cause suffering to others. Thus *vipassanā* comes to lead the meditator beyond the limiting habit-conditions that are rooted in I-centred-ness, hence strengthening compassion. Ultimately, it allows a glimpse of that which is totally *un*conditioned – *Nirvāṇa* – beyond change, limitation and suffering: deathless, unborn, beyond all thought of 'I'.

Vipassanā meditation thus aims to dissolve the kind of views that nourish the defilements. If body and mind are simply changing, impermanent, *dukkha*, conditioned processes, which cannot be adequately controlled by 'me', and are insubstantial products of other such processes, mental or physical, then: Why crave or be greedy for them? Why hate others, for we are all equally tied up with *dukkha*? Why continue with the delusion of protecting an essential 'me' that cannot be found? Why build up I-centred conceits ('*I* am superior', '*I* am inferior' or '*I* am just as good/bad as anyone else') around physical and mental processes which are subject to moment-to-moment change? Why be tied by any fixed view that identifies with things as 'me' or 'mine', or viewing them as 'my real Self', as substantial, solid? Let go, and be free.

Some recent methods of vipassanā *practice*

Twentieth-century Burmese methods have included the following. U Ba Khin (1899–1971[20]) taught a method that emphasizes awareness, from a concentrated mind, of the impermanence of mental and physical phenomena, particularly by attention to feelings arising from the sense of touch. Attention is given to atom-like 'clusters' (*kālapa*) of examples of the four material elements, plus of colour, odour, taste and nutritive essence, seen to be basic constituent elements of material form. Mindful awareness of the jingling buzz of the *kalāpas* is seen to bring insight into all of the 'three marks'. One gains enough concentration from mindfulness of breathing to perhaps gain a *nimitta*, then works on mindfulness of impermanent and *dukkha* feelings in different parts of the body, so that these feelings build up. The aim is for the mind to calmly observe these and let them, and incipient reactions, fade away, leaving a peaceful space in which ingrained mental habit-patterns have been dissolved. S. N. Goenka (1924–), an Indian raised in Burma, teaches U Ba Khin *vipassanā* at many centres around the world (www.dhamma.org).

Like the approach of U Ba Khin, that of Mahāsī Sayadaw (1904–82; Keown and Prebish, 2007: 677–8) is one in which *vipassanā* in time leads to deep *samatha* with *Nirvāṇa* as its object, though the former seems to put more overt emphasis on an initial phase of *samatha* as a platform for *vipassanā*, and the Mahāsī method is sometimes presented as one of 'dry *vipassanā*' (Anālayo, 2003: 64–5). The Mahāsī method emphasizes constantly observing and analysing the flow of experience, bodily and mental, aided by labelling what is perceived, starting with the 'arising' and 'falling' of the abdomen as one breathes.[21] The method is perhaps akin to slowing down a film to gain awareness of each frame, by a process of incessantly cutting up experience into segments and labelling them in an impersonal way.

A more clearly 'dry *vipassanā*' method is that of Sunlun Sayadaw (1878–1952[22]). He had a rather forceful approach that was critical of both

[20] Ba Khin, 1981; King, 1980: 125–32; Kornfield, 1995: 235–56.

[21] *MW*.113–22; King, 1980: 132–7; Kornfield, 1995: 51–82; Mahāsī Sayadaw, 1990, 1994; Nyanaponika, 1996: 85–113.

[22] King, 1980: 137–52; Kornfield, 1995: 83–116; www.sunlun.com.

conceptual thought, which he saw as used in the labelling of the Mahāsī method, and the deliberate cultivation of *samatha*. He taught a method using rough breathing to rouse energy, and sitting for long periods, which would lead to bodily pain, which should just be non-conceptually observed.

In Thailand, several teachers are associated with the austere 'forest' tradition (Tambiah, 1984). The approach of the reputed *Arahat* Ajahn Mun Bhuridatta (1870–1949) used warrior language and emphasized mindfulness of the unattractive parts and the elements of the body. It entailed taking the mind to at least access concentration focused on a body part or bodily element, but also investigation to develop *vipassanā* rather than just remaining in a peaceful *samatha* state (Mun, 1995).

Ajahn Chah (1918–92) practised meditation under a number of masters, including Ajahn Mun. The essence of his teaching was rather simple: be mindful in all activities, do not hang on to anything, let go and surrender to the way things are. In sitting meditation, one should know if the breath is coming in or out, aiding concentration on it by use of the two halves of the word *bud-dho* in tune with the in and out breath. One should let the mind naturally become peaceful, and endure any pain that may arise from the body, observing it and letting it naturally pass.[23] Once the mind has calmed, one should turn the attention outwards to investigate sense-objects and the mind's response to them, with a non-involved observation that notes the three marks in experience. If *nimitta*s or more complex visions arise, one should just contemplate them as also subject to the three marks, and let go of them. They can be of use for one who knows how to work with them, but the *jhāna*s they lead to should not be deliberately sought. The aim is to let the mind, as 'that which knows', simply witness what arises, without getting attached to pleasant states arising from either *samatha* or *vipassanā*. This leads to an experience of the mind in its 'natural' state, clear and bright. Ajahn Chah's simple yet direct teaching style, humorous yet acerbic, has had a special appeal to Westerners. In 1975 he established Wat Pah Nanachat, a special training monastery for the growing number of Westerners who sought to practise with him (www.forestsangha.org), and one American disciple, Ajhan Sumedho (1934–), has been active in spreading his tradition in the United Kingdom (see p. 443).

Buddhadāsa Bhikkhu (1906–93) was an influential intellectual as well as meditation teacher. He saw deep concentration as of some benefit, but held that while in it, *vipassanā* was not possible (*MW*.106–12, Kornfield, 1995: 117–30). He thus taught a more direct path to insight, using the

[23] *MW*.97–105; Chah, 1997; Kornfield, 1995: 33–50.

'natural' concentration of a mind calmly focused on an object of investigation.

While the above examples show a common emphasis on direct mindfulness of experience, especially of the body and feelings that are associated with it, particularly pain, one sees a range of approaches: 'natural' or forceful; using conceptual labels or anti-conceptual; structured or unstructured; drawing on *samatha* methods or dispensing with them; and taught by laypeople or monastics.

Besides the above teachers, the tradition of deep *samatha*, then *vipassanā*, continues. For example, in Burma, Pa-Auk Sayadaw (1935–) teaches both *samatha* then *vipassanā*, and 'dry' *vipassanā* (2003). In Thailand, Ajahn Lee Dhammadharo (1907–61), a disciple of Ajahn Mun, taught *samatha*, then *vipassanā* (Dhammadharo, 1994; Kornfield, 1995: 257–72), and the one-time monk Boonman Poonyathiro (1932–) has taught a *samatha*-based approach to followers in the UK, who formed the Samatha Trust.

The seven stages of purification

The stages in the development of *vipassanā* are outlined in detail in the *Visuddhimagga*, which is structured round a scheme of seven purifications found at *M*.I.145–51: two relating to morality ((1) 'purification of conduct') and *samatha* ((2) 'purification of mind'), and five relating to *vipassanā* (Gethin, 1998: 188–94). In 'purification of view' (3), no 'person' or 'being' is seen apart from changing mental and physical phenomena. In 'purification by crossing over doubt' (4), insight into Conditioned Arising starts to develop, so that the tendency to think of a self-identical 'I' continuing over time starts to wane. Reality is seen to be rapidly renewed every moment as a stream of fluxing, unsatisfactory *dhammas*. Strong confidence in the three refuges now develops. In 'purification by knowing and seeing what is the path and what is not the path' (5), clearer insight leads to the arising of ten 'defilements of insight', such as flashes of light and knowledge, great joy and a subtle delighting attachment to these phenomena. These can lead the meditator to think, wrongly, that he or she has attained *Nirvāṇa*. Once this 'pseudo-*Nirvāṇa*' is recognized, the ten states can themselves be contemplated as having the three marks, so that attachment to them gradually passes.

In the 'purification by knowing and seeing the way' (6), a series of direct knowledges develops. These start by focusing on the cessation of each passing phenomenon, such that the world comes to be seen as constantly dissolving away, a terror-inspiring phantasmagoria which is unreliable and dangerous. A strong desire for deliverance from such worthless conditioned phenomena arises. They are seen as crumbling away, oppressive and ownerless; then dread passes and sublime equanimity, clarity of mind and detachment arise. The conditioned world is simply observed as an empty and unsatisfactory flux which is not worth bothering with. Reviewing these insights, the meditator is endowed with intense faith, energy and mindfulness.

In the 'purification by knowing and seeing' (7), the mind finally lets go of conditioned phenomena so that a moment of 'Path-consciousness' (*magga-citta*) occurs, which 'sees' the unconditioned, *Nirvāṇa*. This is perceived either as: 'the signless' (Pali *animitta*, Skt *ānimitta*) – devoid of signs indicative of anything graspable; 'the aim-free' (Pali *appaṇihita*, Skt *apraṇihita*) – that which lies beyond goal-directedness concerning worthless phenomena; or as 'the empty' (Pali *suññata*) or 'emptiness' (Pali *suññatā*, Skt *śūnyatā*) – void of any grounds for ego-feeling and incapable of being conceptualized in views (see pp. 96–7; Conze, 1967: 59–69; Harvey 1986). A few moments of blissful 'Fruition-consciousness' (*phala-citta*) immediately follow, also with *Nirvāṇa* as their object (*Vism*.672–6). The first time these events take place, a person becomes a 'stream-enterer' (see pp. 84–5). The same path of seven purifications may subsequently be used to attain the three higher stages of sanctity, culminating in Arahatship, full liberation. Each attainment of 'Path-consciousness' is a profound cognitive shock, which destroys some of the hindrances and fetters and leads to great psychological and behavioural changes, so as to purify and perfect the practitioner.

While the developed Theravāda tradition does not see the truly *Noble* Path as experienced until the momentary and transcendent 'Path-consciousness' occurs, in the *Sutta*s, the Noble Path, of one 'practising for the realization of the fruit that is stream-entry', begins at the stage that seems to equate to what the developed tradition calls that of the 'lesser stream-enterer' (*Vism*.605), at the end of the fourth purification, with 'Path-consciousness' as the moment the Noble Path is then perfected. Hence the Noble Path was not originally seen as momentary (*S*.III.225, Harvey, 2014).

THE CLASSICAL PATH OF *ŚAMATHA* AND *VIPAŚYANĀ* IN NORTHERN AND EASTERN BUDDHISM

In Northern and Eastern Buddhism, calm and insight (Skt *śamatha* and *vipaśyanā*) became modified by the Mahāyāna framework of belief and motivation. An existing framework that was built on, though, was that of the five paths (Skt *mārga*), as classically expressed by Vasubandhu in his *Abhidharma-kośa*, a work of the Sarvāstivāda school:[24]

- The path of equipment or accumulation (*sambhāra-mārga*): faith, giving, moral virtue, and preliminary *śamatha* and *vipaśyanā*, culminating in gaining *samādhi*, of 'access' level or perhaps *dhyāna* (Pali *jhāna*), then practising the four applications of mindfulness (Skt *smṛtyupasthāna*).
- The path of application or preparation (*prayoga-mārga*): further development of *śamatha* and *vipaśyanā*, especially the latter, in the four 'stages of penetrating insight' (Skt *nirvedha-bhāgīya*[25]): 'glowing' (*uṣmagata*), the 'summit' (*mūrdhan*), 'acceptance' (*kṣānti*) and 'the highest ordinary state' (*laukikāgra-dharma*). In these, the mind concentrates on and gains deeper insight into and emotional acceptance of the four True Realities for the Spiritually Ennobled.
- The path of seeing (*darśana-mārga*): direct seeing of the True Realities for the Spiritually Ennobled, including *Nirvāṇa*, as at the arising of the *Dharma*-eye (see pp. 85–6) and much as in Buddhaghosa's seventh purification. This path is seen to last for fifteen moments, which rapidly accept then know each of the True Realities as applying to the sense-desire realm then the two remaining realms (*AKB*.VI.26b–d). A sixteenth moment completes this and is a 'fruit' moment, which is the first of the next path. In the path of seeing, one who has already mastered *dhyāna* becomes a once-returner or non-returner (see p. 86), and one who has still to develop it becomes a stream-enterer.
- The path of development (*bhāvanā-mārga*): further cultivation of the deep states of *śamatha*, if needed, and overcoming attachment to them. For the Mahāyāna, the development of the *Bodhisattva* perfections.
- The path of the adept (*aśaikṣa-mārga*): becoming an *Arhat*, or a Buddha.

In the Mahāyāna use of this scheme (see pp. 155–6), a person becomes a *Bodhisattva* prior to the path of equipment, and a Noble *Bodhisattva* at the path of seeing (Lodrö, 1998: 156–7).

In Northern Buddhism, the classical practice of *śamatha* and *vipaśyanā* is based on works by the eighth-century Indian teacher Kamalaśīla: the three *Bhāvanā-kramas*, or 'Stages of Meditation' (*BS*2.39, Adam, 2006). It received perhaps its most thorough formulation in the *Lamrim Ch'enmo* (*Lam rim che ba*; Cutler, 2002), or 'Graduated Path to Enlightenment' of

[24] Gethin, 1998: 194–8; Pruden's forward to Vol. III of *AKB.* translation, xiv–xxii; Williams, 2009: 200–1.

[25] *AKB*.VI.16–25b. The phrase itself occurs at *A*.II.167, and *S*.V.87–8, the latter seeing them as involving the seven factors of awakening.

Tsongkh'apa (Tsong kha pa; 1357–1419; see pp. 207–8), founder of the Gelugpa school.

In the Northern tradition (Lodrö, 1998; Sopa, 1978), meditators begin with some combination of traditional *śamatha* practices and the applications of mindfulness, so as to attain the state of *anāgamya*, 'not-(yet-)arrived' or 'the potential', equivalent to 'access' concentration, and perhaps full *dhyāna* (Pali *jhāna*). Insight into the 'three marks' may then be cultivated. This tradition preserves the term *śamatha* or 'calm abiding' (Tib. *shiné* (*zhi gnas*)) for states of concentration of at least the level of 'the potential'. The meditation method which leads to this is known as 'stabilization meditation' (*jokgom* (*'jogs sgom*); Lodrö, 1998: 96–122). It likewise preserves the term *vipaśyanā* (*lhagt'ong* (*lhag mthong*)) or 'special insight' for high levels of insight, these being developed by 'analytic meditation' (*chegom* (*dpyad sgom*)). There are seen to be nine stages of stabilization leading up to 'the potential':

- 1. stabilizing the mind; 2. continuous stabilizing: listening and reflection inspires motivation to begin focusing on the object, such as a Buddha-image, unpleasant aspects of existence, lovingkindness, the breath or the conditioned nature of things (Lodrö, 1998: 34–68);
- 3. habitual stabilization; 4. near stabilization: concentration becomes more persistent as the mind becomes non-discursive;
- 5. habituation; 6. pacifying: mindfulness reduces remaining mental wavering;
- 7. thorough pacification; 8. one-pointedness of mind: appropriate effort leads to mental pliancy and uninterrupted concentration;
- 9. *samādhi*: the mind is fully settled in 'the potential' state.[26]

In these, mental scattering/excitement and laxity are seen as the two key faults to overcome.[27] In 'the potential' state, if the meditation object were a Buddha-image, this could be vividly seen in the mind's eye, as with a Theravāda *samatha nimitta*, as if the Buddha himself were present (Cutler, 2002: 43).

While in a state of *śamatha*, the meditator then does analytic meditations, investigating the nature of the object of concentration and of the calm mind, using the four applications of mindfulness (*MW*.5–4; Lodrö, 1998: 236–46). Here, the aim is to gain a conceptual understanding of phenomena as empty of inherent nature/existence, as a preparation for a direct non-conceptual insight into emptiness (Williams, 2009: 79–81). In the Gelugpa

[26] Dharma Fellowship, n.d.; Lodrö, 1998: 68–95; Sopa, 1978: 48–56.

[27] *MW*.69–77; Lodrö, 1998: 35. Cf. *S*.v.279 and Anālayo, 2003: 178.

tradition, even the object of *śamatha* is sometimes the idea of emptiness, as nurtured by analytic reflections.[28]

In Eastern Buddhism, classical *śamatha* and *vipaśyanā* received their most systematic working out by Zhiyi (Chih-i; 539–97), founder of Tiantai school, in his *Mo-ho Zhi-Guan* (*Mo-ho Chih-Kuan*), 'The Great Stopping/Calm (*Zhi*) and Clear Observation/Insight (*Guan*)' (Cleary, 1997). The influential 'Awakening of Faith in the Mahāyāna' (see p. 214) also has a section (Part 4) devoted to *śamatha* and *vipaśyanā* (Hakeda, 1967).

The meditative disciplines advocated by Zhiyi were various, to appeal to different kinds of practitioners. They often involved prolonged retreat in a monastic context. The initial development of *śamatha* is not unlike that in the Northern tradition. Once *dhyāna* is attained, the meditator goes on to develop *guan/vipaśyanā* by developing the four applications of mindfulness, observing the very subtle breath, the thirty-two parts of the body, and the arising and ceasing of conditioned *dharmas*, so as to gain insight into impermanence, unsatisfactoriness and the non-Selfness of persons (*MW*.55–63). Next, *zhi/śamatha* becomes emphasized again so as to bring it to perfection, in 'returning practice', which brings the mind back to abiding naturally and spontaneously in its 'original state'. The 'Awakening of Faith in the Mahāyāna' seems to be describing this level of *śamatha* practice when it says that in *śamatha*, no sense-object should be taken as object, not even the breath; rather, all thoughts should be discarded as they arise, including the thought of discarding them. Both the 'Awakening of Faith' and the Tiantai tradition say that the wandering of thoughts is gradually controlled and then arrested by the reflection that all that is turned towards is thought-only, thusness, the *Dharma*-body.

Advanced *śamatha* may be practised by special techniques in which the meditator seeks to become fully absorbed in such things as ritual preparation and purification of a meditation-hall, bowing, circumambulation of images or a copy of the *Lotus Sūtra*, repentance (see p. 270), vows, recitation of *dhāraṇīs*, invocations of Amitābha's or another Buddha's name, and visualizations of the thirty-two characteristics of a Buddha.[29] *Samādhi* (*san-mei*) is cultivated either through constant sitting, constant circumambulation of an altar dedicated to Amitābha Buddha,[30] a mix of walking and sitting, or cultivation 'wherever one's mind happens to be directed at

[28] *MW*.160–3; Lodrö, 1998: 56–8; Powers, 2007b: 489–92.

[29] Stevenson, 1986, an extract from which is *EB*.8.6.2.

[30] Constant walking is also a feature of the Tendai mountain circumambulating austerity described on pp. 309–10.

the moment'. The meditator then investigates the nature of the component phenomena of these rites, and of his mind. Alternatively, the mind may be the object of attention from the start. As in the Northern 'Graduated Path', phenomena are examined so as to see them as empty and thought-only. This leads up to the transcending of the subject/object duality, as in Yogācāra accounts of the path (see p. 136). Full realization only comes, however, when even knowledge of non-duality is seen as empty, and there is a liberating insight into emptiness of inherent nature/existence, at the 'path of seeing'. The meditator must then integrate the vision of emptiness into his life, ensuring that it does not cause him to turn away from the suffering beings of the illusion-imbued conventional level of reality. According to Tiantai tradition, his *śamatha* (of a transcendent level) enables him to constantly know emptiness, hence *Nirvāṇa*, but his *vipaśyanā* enables him to know that this is no different from the world of 'suffering beings' (*BT*.160–2).

The Mahāyāna version of the classical path of *śamatha* and *vipaśyanā* was seen as a way of cultivating the *Bodhisattva* path over many lives. To accelerate progress in this, other techniques were also developed, cultivating *śamatha* and *vipaśyanā* in relatively new ways which were seen as more powerful. These primarily involved either (i) techniques of visualization (related to the early *kasiṇa-maṇḍala* method), or (ii) cultivating spontaneous insight.

PURE LAND VISUALIZATIONS

While the emphasis in Pure Land practice is on devotion, it is not without its contemplative side (*BP*.31). Pure Land chanting (see p. 255) can lead to single-minded concentration with the mind joyfully contemplating Amitābha Buddha and his qualities. As practised among Chinese people, this involves: (i) the use of a rosary with the chant, whether this chant is *Nan-mo A-mi-tuo Fo* or *A-mi-tuo*; (ii) loud chanting when the mind is sluggish, affected by 'fading'; (iii) soft chanting when the mind is scattered and in need of settling; (iv) 'diamond recitation', when the lips move soundlessly, if the mind is agitated and the breath uneven; (v) purely mental recitation, an advanced form of practice, which cultivates awareness of all as thought-only; (vi) silently doing the chant once with each in- or out-breath, breathing neither slowly nor quickly, as with the practice of counting the breath in mindfulness of breathing; (vii) reciting while walking if the mind is drowsy; practising while sitting if the mind is scattered. The practice can be done in any posture, though, and anywhere (Wei-an, 2000: 18, 19, 20, 21, 22, 23, 24–5).

There are also Pure Land visualization practices. The *Sukhāvatī-vyūhopadeśa* (see p. 216) outlines five kinds of mindful 'recollection' (*anusmṛti*) which are used to awaken absolute faith in Amitābha Buddha (*BT*.199–201; Kiyota 1978b). The first three are counted as forms of purifying *śamatha*, due to the concentration with which they are done, and the aspiration and faith which they arouse. They use, respectively, actions of body, speech and mind: bowing to Amitābha while reflecting on his wondrous powers; praising him with the invocatory formula (see p. 255) while contemplating the meaning of his name; and arousing a single-minded determination to be reborn in his Pure Land.

The fourth recollection is a visualization. In a simple form, it can be done by contemplating an image of Amitābha until it can be seen in great detail with the eyes closed. The most elaborate method, however, is outlined in the *Amitāyur-buddhānusmṛti Sūtra* (see p. 174), which describes a way of attaining *dhyāna* (accompanied by *vipaśyanā*) involving a series of sixteen meditations. Practitioners may memorize every detail of this text (forty pages in its Chinese form) as an aid to doing the visualizations it describes. The prerequisites for such practice include such things as keeping the precepts, practising compassion and arousing the *bodhi-citta* (Williams, 2009: 242–3).

The first meditation is performed by the practitioner contemplating the setting sun (symbolic of the Buddha 'Immeasurable Radiance') until its image can be held clearly before the mind's eye. The next meditations begin by developing a mental image of water; this is then seen to turn to ice, and then into shimmering, translucent beryl surrounded by hundreds of shining jewels. From their light, a jewelled tower of ten million storeys (the Pure Land) is seen to form in the sky. This vision is then firmly established, until it remains throughout the day, with the eyes open or shut. Next, visualizations of the details of the Pure Land are built up, for example jewel-trees 800 leagues high, and water in the form of soft jewels lapping over diamond sands. Next, the throne of Amitāyus/Amitābha is visualized as a huge iridescent lotus with 84,000 petals, each of which has 84,000 veins, from each of which come 84,000 rays of light, each of which is seen as clearly as one's face in a mirror! Amitāyus himself is then visualized, so that the mind, in contemplating the form in which the *Dharma*-body appears, has its own intrinsic Buddha-nature activated. Amitāyus's two *Bodhisattva* helpers are then visualized: Avalokiteśvara (Guanyin), representing Amitābha's compassion, and Mahāsthāmaprāpta ('He of Great Power'), representing his wisdom. All three give out rays of light which transmit their images throughout the jewels of the Pure Land, and the sound of *Dharma* being taught comes from light, streams and birds. Moving on, the details of the Buddha's huge body are visualized, for example an immeasurable radiance is emitted from his skin-pores, and in a halo as large as a hundred million universes are innumerable Buddhas. The attendant *Bodhisattvas* are then visualized in great detail. Next, the practitioner visualizes himself born in the Pure Land on a lotus, and then visualizes the Buddha and two *Bodhisattvas* together. The remaining meditations are on the way in which people of high, middling and low spiritual and moral abilities will be born in the Land, if they have faith.

Thus, through a series of visualizations of a radiant world, the practitioner attains a foretaste of the Pure Land, thereby transforming his perception of the ordinary world by infusing it with his vision. He attains serene certainty of birth in Sukhāvatī, and reduction of the time he will be there before his 'lotus' opens and he can behold its glories. The *Sukhāvatī-vyūhopadeśa* sees visualization, in full mind-blowing detail, as a means to gaining an insight into the 'unthinkable' (cf. p. 147), the *Dharma*-body or pure Mind (see p. 142) which lies beyond conceptual thought. It is thus counted as a form of *vipaśyanā*-developing practice. The centre of the Pure Land, Amitābha's lotus throne, is the point at which the *Dharma*-body, the essence of all Buddhas, is manifested. The Pure Land, Amitābha and the *Bodhisattvas* are said to form one organic entity, one *Dharma* which is the true object of Pure Land faith.

The *Sukhāvatī-vyūhopadeśa* regards the fifth 'recollection' as the activity of skilful means, which compassionately transfers the karmic fruitfulness of the previous practices to help all beings gain rebirth in the Pure Land.

The above contemplation of the sun and water leading to vividly visualized mental images parallels the way in which Theravāda *kasiṇa* practice, which includes contemplations of light and of water, leads to vivid *nimittas*. That the name of the presiding Buddha of the *Sukhāvatī* Pure Land means 'Immeasurable Radiance' links to the fact that many of the *brahmā-devas* of the elemental form level, which *śamatha* focusing on *nimittas* leads to experiencing, have names suggesting light and radiance, for example the Ābhassara or Streaming Radiance *devas* (see p. 36). The practice thus has elements which parallel, but go beyond, Theravāda practices of recollecting the qualities of the Buddha, or of *devas*. The imagery used in portraying the Pure Land also has some continuity with a description of the land of a past *Cakravartin* (Pali *Cakkavattin*) emperor, which had walls and trees made of such things as gold, silver, beryl, crystal, ruby and emerald (*D*.II.170–2 (*SB*.100–01); Gethin, 1997).

There are also parallels to the world as seen in the *Gaṇḍavyūha Sūtra* (see pp. 146–7), and the mind-blowing complexity of the visualization could be seen as a visual parallel to the Zen *kōan*: in order to engage in it, the practitioner must transcend his/her normal conceptual mind and go into a different mental gear. The practice of visualization also clearly has parallels to tantric practice, but Pure Land visualization does not have a range of holy beings to select from as its focus, has no sexual elements, does not include the manipulation of psycho-physical energies, and in general does not seek to realize identity with the object of visualization (though not all levels of tantric visualizations do this). While it puts more emphasis on 'other-power' than tantric practice, it does not have *Guru*-devotion, but only devotion to Amitābha and his *Bodhisattva* helpers.

TANTRIC VISUALIZATIONS

Visualizations are a central feature of tantric meditation in Northern Buddhism, and in Milgyo and Shingon, the Korean and Japanese forms of tantric Buddhism. Complex and vivid visualization practices are used to take the mind to states of deep calm, to focus on and identify with imagery that is seen as an expression of the mind's basic purity, and then to let go of the imagery so as to develop insight into the nature of mind.[31] This can be seen as *śamatha* and *vipaśyanā* developed through the generation and manipulation of mental images, which build on elements of the mind's functioning that are also found, in a simpler form, in Theravāda work on meditative *nimittas*. Undergirding the approach are elements of various Mahāyāna philosophical perspectives:

- The world is thought-only: so why not self-consciously visualize a different reality-world, in a way that transforms one's vision of the ordinary world?
- The root of the mind as the pure Buddha-nature.
- All forms as empty of inherent nature/existence.

In order to be guided through the complex and powerful meditations, a tantric practitioner must find a suitable *Lama/Guru* to act as his or her spiritual preceptor. Once he has found one with whom he has a personal affinity, he must prove his sincerity, purity and detachment before he will be accepted as a disciple; for his spiritual welfare will then be the responsibility of the *Lama*.[32] In return, the disciple should implicitly obey all his *Lama*'s instructions as a patient obeys the instructions of his doctor. He should also serve and have great devotion for his *Lama*, in the practice of *Guru-yoga* (see p. 247).

[31] *BP*.27; *MW*.163–6, 175–84; Conze, 1972: 133–9.
[32] *EB*.7.6 gives the story of Milarepa's struggles with his *Guru*, Marpa (see p. 206).

After the practitioner has carried out a number of arduous preliminaries, to purify himself (see pp. 246–7), his *Lama* will initiate him into the Mantranaya, as he will also do to each new level of practice within it. An initiation (Skt *abhiṣeka*) is regarded as having several functions (Williams and Tribe, 2000: 175–8). First, it helps remove spiritual obstructions in the practitioner. Secondly, it transmits a spiritual power from the *Lama*, seen as an 'empowerment' to practise in a certain way. Thirdly, it permits access to a body of written teachings and the oral instructions needed to understand and practise them properly. Lastly, it authorizes the practitioner to address himself in a particular way to a certain holy being or deity. At the initiation, the *Lama* selects a *mantra* and 'chosen deity' (Tib. *yidam* (*yi-dam*), Skt *iṣṭā-devatā*) appropriate to the practitioner's character type, and introduces him to the *maṇḍala*, or sacred diagram, of the *yidam*. The nature and role of *mantra, yidam* and *maṇḍala* are as follows.

Mantra*s,* mudrā*s and the* yidam

Mantras are sacred words of power, mostly unintelligible syllables or strings of syllables, which give an arrangement of sound of great potency (see pp. 180–1). When pronounced in the right way, with the right attitude of mind, the sound-arrangement of a *mantra* is seen as 'tuning in' the practitioner's mind to a being he wishes to visualize. This may perhaps be compared to the way in which certain musical chords naturally tend to evoke certain moods. In the Yogācāra 'thought-only' perspective, the holy beings invoked can be seen as not 'external' to him, but as psychic forces or levels of consciousness latent within the practitioner's own mind. A *mantra* is seen as acting like a psychic key which enables a person either to have power over 'physical' things, or to visualize and communicate with a being/force whose *mantra* it is (Evans-Wentz, 1954: 141). Each holy being has its own *mantra,* which is seen to express its particular nature. For example that of the 'Saviouress' Tārā is *oṃ tāre, tuttāre ture svāha*. Each holy being also has a short 'seed' (Skt *bīja*) *mantra*: *trāṃ* in the case of the Buddha Ratnasambhava. In Shingon, a simple visualization is focused on the seed-syllable of Vairocana, the letter '*a*', regarded as the basic sound of all language and the primordial vibration of the universe. This is visualized surrounded by a halo as it stands atop a *vajra*.

Tantric rites may involve the use of ritual gestures which, like the gestures made by the hands of Buddha-images, are known as *mudrās* or 'signs'. As has been seen, these are also used in devotion (see p. 243). On Buddha-images, they are the 'signs' which characterize particular heavenly Buddhas, for example Akṣobhya is generally shown making the 'earth-witness' gesture (as with the right hand in Plate 1). The much wider range of *mudrās* used in tantric ritual are seen as the 'signs' – and causes – of particular states of mind. What lies behind this idea is the observation that states of mind generally express themselves in a person's stance and gesture. Clenching a fist expresses anger, while holding up an open palm expresses the wish to calm down an argument. Ritual *mudrās* are seen as working on the reverse of this principle: by making various gestures, certain states of mind may be stimulated or enhanced.[33] Thus the *mudrās* are used to amplify the efficacy of the *mantras* in evoking psychic forces and higher states of consciousness. These *mudrās* are often conjoined with the use of the *Vajra*-sceptre and *Vajra*-bell in certain rituals (see pp. 183–4). The use of these implements symbolizes that the adept must come to develop both his/her 'male' skilful means (sceptre), and 'female' wisdom (bell).

A *yidam* is a particular holy being who is in harmony with the practitioner's nature, and who will act as his tutelary deity (Samuel, 1993: 163–6). A *yidam* is selected from the tantric pantheon outlined in Chapter 6 (pp. 185–9). By identifying with his *yidam*, a practitioner identifies with his own basic nature purged of faults. The *yidam* also reveals aspects of his character which he persists in overlooking, for it visually represents them. Acting as a guide for his practice, the *yidam* enables the practitioner to magically transmute the energy of his characteristic fault into a parallel kind of wisdom, embodied by the *yidam*. For example, if Akṣobhya Buddha is taken as the *yidam*, the brilliance and raw energy of hate and anger becomes '*vajra*-wrath', which can be directed in a controlled violent 'attack' on hatred and the other defilements/obstacles. One central ritual for *vajra*-wrath is the stabbing and sometimes dismemberment of an effigy symbolizing the defilements. The energy of anger may also be transmuted into the openness and precision of 'mirror-like knowledge' (*ādarśa-jñāna*),[34] which takes in all the information of the field of awareness, in an overview without any preferences.

Maṇḍalas[35]

A *maṇḍala* or '(sacred) circle' is a device developed in India between the seventh and twelfth centuries, possibly being derived from the *kasiṇa-maṇḍala*. Its

[33] This principle can also be seen to apply to the manner of breathing.
[34] According to the Karma Kagyüdpa system.
[35] *BTTA*.189–90; Berzin, 2003; Cornell University, n.d.; Rossi Collection, n.d.; Snellgrove, 1987: 136–41; Strong, 1996; Williams and Tribe, 2000: 158, 171–3.

basic function is to portray the luminous world, or Pure Land, of a specific holy being, with other holy beings particularly associated with it arrayed about it. Here an analogy is perhaps the 'circle' of a prime minister or president and their key ministers. The complex symbolism used has various roots in Buddhism, including the multivalent symbolism of *Stūpas*. The pattern of a *maṇḍala* is based on that of a circular *Stūpa* with a square base orientated to the four directions. It can, in fact, be seen as a two-dimensional *Stūpa*-temple, regarded as containing the actual manifestations of the deities represented within it. Its form can also be related to the common belief in the magical efficacy of circles, and the Indian idea of each physical world as being a circular disc with a huge mountain (Sumeru, Pali Meru), home of many gods, at its centre. The great complexity of the symbolism in some ways parallels the complexity and exactness of *Abhidharma*. Both map mind-states, but *maṇḍalas* do so in vivid visual ways, and utilize some different principles.

A *maṇḍala* may be temporarily constructed, for a particular rite, out of coloured sands or dough and fragrant powders (Bechert and Gombrich, 1984: 237), using a raised horizontal platform as a base. In a more permanent form, it may be painted on a hanging scroll, or *t'angka* (*thang-ka*), as in Plate 12. Depending on the rite the *maṇḍala* is used in, the deities in it will vary, though the one portraying the five *Jinas* (i.e. principal Buddhas; see p. 185) is the most important. By being introduced to his *yidam*'s *maṇḍala*, a practitioner can familiarize himself with the deity's world and the holy beings associated with him or her. By vivid visualization of the deity and his or her world, he may master and integrate the psychic forces they represent, so as to be able to wisely use all aspects of his being in a spiritually skilful way.

Aspects of early Buddhist thought and practice relevant to the *maṇḍala* are:

- The close relationship between cosmology and psychology, in that heavenly rebirth realms are aligned to particular meditative levels, so that a particular *jhāna/dhyāna* will lead to rebirth in one of a small group of heaven realms, if no further spiritual progress is made.
- The idea that the 'world', in the sense of the lived world of experience, is 'in this fathom-long carcass, with its mind and perception' (*S*.I.62).
- A passage which compares the make-up of a person to a walled city with six gates (the senses; *S*.IV.194–5), and one which sees a person as made up of six elements: four physical ones, plus space and consciousness (*A*.I.176).
- The fact that *samatha kasiṇa* meditations focus on colours (blue, yellow, red, white) and elements (earth, water, fire, wind and space, plus either light or consciousness), which aspects crop up in later *maṇḍala* symbolism.

Plate 12: A *t'angka* showing a *maṇḍala* surrounded by a number of Vajrayāna deities and spiritually realized beings.

Mahāyāna background ideas of course include:

- Yogācāra philosophy, in which reality (or at least all experienced reality) is 'thought-only': the flow of experience interpreted and misinterpreted.
- The *Trikāya*, or 'Three-body' doctrine on the nature of Buddhas.
- The idea of Buddhas dwelling in Pure Lands.

There are also relevant background ideas from Brahmanism that resurfaced in both Buddhist and Hindu *Tantras*:

- The importance of correspondences between various aspects of the human personality and the cosmos – microcosm and macrocosm – and also between these and *mantras*.
- The Vedic altar as a place where the presence of the *devas* was invoked: the *maṇḍala* is likewise a site for invoking divine presences.

Depending on the materials of the *maṇḍala*, the deities may be represented by metal statues, painted images or seed-*mantras*. The bands encircling the *maṇḍala* mark off its pure, sacred area from the profane area beyond, and also suggest the unfolding of spiritual vision gained by a practitioner when he visualizes himself entering the *maṇḍala*. Having crossed the threshold, he comes to the central citadel, representing the temple of his own heart. He enters by one of the four doors, over which there is a *Dharma*-wheel and two deer, representing the teachings of Buddhism. Passing one of the 'four great kings' – guardian gods accepted by all schools of Buddhism – he comes to the main *maṇḍala* deities. In the *maṇḍala* shown in Plate 12, the central deity is Akṣobhya Buddha, with Vairocana taking Akṣobhya's usual place to the east (bottom); also shown are four *Bodhisattvas*.

Visualizations

Having been given a *yidam*, *mantra* and *maṇḍala*, the tantric practitioner can then go on to perform various meditations in the form of *sādhanas*, or 'accomplishings'. *Sādhanas* involve the mind in vivid visualizations,[36] the speech in chanting *mantras* and descriptions of holy beings, and the body in the use of *mudrās*. The vivid vision comes to be seen as at least as real as 'external' physical objects, and so generation and reflection on it is a way of realizing that everything is 'thought-only', no more (or less) real than the vision. The method focuses resolutely on the idea of the mind's basic purity, and clothes this in vivid forms that are used to tune the mind out of its normal ruts by lifting it to more sublime levels. Yet this is done in a way that uses the mind's appetite for gripping forms – and then transforms this appetite. This can be seen as a classical example of the use of 'skilful means'.

One striking Tibetan tantric practice is that of *chöd* (*gCod*), literally 'cut off', championed by Machig Labdrön (Ma-gcig lab-sgron-ma, 1055–1145), a

[36] *MW*.163–6; Williams and Tribe, 2000: 169–70, 173–5.

woman seen as a *ḍākinī* (see p. 186). This practice involves meditating in wild and fearsome places, invoking wrathful demoniac powers, seeking to control these, then visualizing the cutting up of one's body, feeding the pieces to these beings, then reabsorbing all the visualized beings within oneself. The ultimate aim is insight into the illusory nature of all phenomena, especially what is seen as 'self' (Powers, 2007b: 424–8).

In general, the practice of a *sādhana* is performed in two stages (Kongtrul, 2002: 13–20). The first is that of Generation or Creation (Skt *Utpanna-krama*), which is the process of building up the visualization. The adept first familiarizes himself with the paintings and detailed textual description of the deity and his *maṇḍala*-world. He then gradually learns to build up a mental image of the deity until it is seen in full 'Technicolor' reality as a living, moving being. When the visualization is fully established, the stage of Completion (Skt *Sampanna-krama*) is entered, where the adept draws on the energies and spiritual qualities of the archetypal visualized form. The Generation and Completion phases can be seen, respectively, to carry out the same functions as *śamatha* – due to the one-pointed concentration on a mental image, and *vipaśyanā* (Kongtrul, 2002: 120–2, 141).

In the *Kriyā Tantras* (see pp. 182–3), a deity is visualized and worshipped with praises and visualized offerings, and then his or her characteristic spiritual quality is contemplated, be this the compassion of Avalokiteśvara (Samuel, 1993: 233–65) or the purity of Vajrasattva. Blessings are then seen to stream from the being in the form of light, before he or she dissolves into light and is absorbed by the adept, thus bringing about a gradual purification of the defilements. Besides the visualizations, ritual practices directed at the deity also play a key part in *Kriyā Tantras*.

The cakras *and The 'Six Yogas of Nāropa'*

The most powerful way of drawing on the powers of a visualized being is in tantric practice of the 'Supreme Union' (Skt *Anuttara-yoga*) level (see pp. 182–3). Having set aside all usual images of himself and the world by regarding them as empty of essence, the adept visualizes the seed-syllable of his *yidam*, and from this comes to build up a visualization of himself as the *yidam*. In *Anuttara-yoga*, this may typically be: Yamāntaka, a wrathful form of Mañjuśrī; Mahākāla, a wrathful form of Avalokiteśvara; Vajrayoginī, a *ḍākinī*; or a wrathful form of the Buddha Cakrasaṃvara (*EB*.5.5.4). The adept fully identifies himself with the *yidam*, thus overcoming all seeming duality between 'two' beings that are seen as equally manifestations of the empty, radiant mind/*Dharma*-body. This also has the effect of showing the arbitrary nature of ego-identification. The meditator develops 'divine pride': the pride of actually being the deity (Kongtrul, 2002: 16; Mullin, 1996: 123–6). He visualizes himself as the *yidam*, as regards both his external appearance and the inner make-up of his mystical 'physiology', a subtle body based on five psycho-physical centres known as *cakras* (*MW*.189–91; Samuel, 1993: 236–9). The *cakras* are seen as located at or near the crown of the head, the bottom of the throat, the heart, the navel, the perineum. They are visualized as like open lotus blossoms, and are seen as the centres, respectively, of thought-energy, speech-energy, emotional energy, physical energy and sexual energy. They are seen as linked by three channels (*nāḍī*) running down the spine, through which *prāṇa*, or vital energy, flows.

The meditator then sees around him the *maṇḍala* of the *yidam*, representing his Pure Land. By visualizing himself as the deity, the adept takes on some of its powers and virtues, which are symbolically expressed in many details of its appearance. Finally, the whole visualization is gradually dissolved into empty essencelessness, so as to overcome any attachment to it. Visualizations and dissolutions are then repeated until mastery of the visualized world is attained.

The Completion stage is then entered, where there is visualization and manipulation of the meditator/*yidam*'s energies and qualities. This takes great discipline and application, and is best done in a retreat setting. Here, the meditator draws on methods such as the 'Six yogas of Nāropa',[37] which were developed by the Kagyüdpas, but are also used in other schools. These are the yogas of: (i) heat (Tib. *tummo* (*gtum mo*)); (ii) illusory body; (iii) dream; (iv) clear light (Skt *prabhāsvara*; Tib. *ösel* (*'od gsal*)); (v) intermediate state (Skt *antarā-bhava*; Tib. *bardo* (*bar do*)); (vi) transference of consciousness (Tib. *phowa* (*'pho ba*)).

The yogas work with the energies of the subtle body, seen as corresponding to the subtle level of mind, dreaming consciousness. At this level, consciousness and vital energy are seen as very closely related, this idea being based on the correlation between states of mind and manner of breathing. As each *cakra* is focused on, the energy-mind is seen to gather there. The 'extremely subtle' level of consciousness is that found in the dreamless state. It is seen to correspond to and actually be non-differentiated from the extremely subtle level of the body: an indestructible translucent white 'drop' (Skt *bindu*, Tib. *tig le* (*thig le*)) of energy which travels up and down the central channel and rests in the heart *cakra*. This *bindu* is seen as the source of all physical energy.

[37] Guenther, 1963; Mullin, 1996; Powers, 2007b: 405–15. Variant listings of the 'six yogas' exist (Mullin, 1996: 29–33, 87–9, 217–18).

It is sometimes referred to in tantric texts as '*bodhi-citta*', the aspiration for awakening, as it provides the energy for attaining enlightenment when properly stimulated and transformed.

In the Kagyüdpa form of 'heat' yoga,[38] the *yogin*, having visualized his body as hollow and then visualized the components of the subtle body, then performs various breathing rhythms, including retention of the breath for up to six minutes, while following the circulation of the vital energy derived from breath as it moves through the various 'channels'. Intense concentration is then focused on the source of *tummo* heat, a spot below the navel. Using controlled breathing, a visualized almond-shaped flame is made to blaze up into the body so as to heat it up. So far is the Generation stage. The Completion stage is reached when, at a certain point, the heat is seen to melt the *bindu* as it is located between the eyebrows, leading to a 'great bliss' (Skt *mahā-sukha*) permeating the entire body. Once the great bliss is experienced, it is seen as empty of subject/object duality in the 'emptiness-bliss *samādhi*' in which all the body is seen to dissolve until only the *bindu* exists. Observing the play of thoughts in this emptiness by alternately cutting them off, then letting them flow unimpeded (as in *Mahāmudrā* practice – see p. 359), non-dual wisdom knows the 'mind-essence' as a shining emptiness, a clear light beyond conceptualizations. If this yoga is partially developed, using the Generation stage, it may be used as the basis for those that follow, for it is seen to loosen deep-rooted 'knots' in the nerve-channels, integrate psycho-physical energies, and generate the heat-energy which provides the drive for enlightenment. If it is fully developed, using the Completion stage, it is seen as a powerful means for attaining rapid spiritual progress along the *Bodhisattva* path.

In 'illusory body' yoga, the meditator contemplates his reflection in a mirror, as an aid to seeing his perceived body and the world as illusory, thought-only, yet also the *maṇḍala* of the *yidam*. In 'dream' yoga, the adept alternates short periods of sleep and meditation, to establish awareness while dreaming and gain full control of the dream-events. By waking from dreaming with no break in consciousness, the illusory nature of waking experiences as well as of dreams is recognized. In 'clear light' yoga, the *yogin* falls asleep while visualizing the five syllables of a *mantra*, so as to retain awareness even in dreamless sleep and, further, experiences the blissful brightly shining clear light of the pure mind,[39] emptiness, thusness.

[38] *MW*.171–4 for its Gelugpa form.

[39] Note that in Theravāda theory, dreamless sleep is said to consist of *bhavaṅga*, the radiant ground state of consciousness (see p. 92).

'Intermediate state' yoga prepares a person for making best spiritual use of the between lives period (see pp. 71, 281–2). Death is seen to occur when the vital energies dissolve in the *bindu* in the heart *cakra*, and only the extremely subtle level of body and mind exist. Death is seen to correspond to dreamless sleep, as the intermediate state does to dreaming, and rebirth to waking. At the time of death, all people are said to experience the 'clear light' (cf. reports of 'near-death experiences'; Sogyal Rinpoche, 1992: 316–39). Most people are said to flinch away from it in fear and incomprehension, but an advanced *yogin*, practised in clear light yoga, may be able to attain the *Dharma*-body at this time; he is seen to then go on to develop the Enjoyment-body in the intermediate existence, and the Transformation-body at rebirth. It is held that only a very few can do this, however. Others may be able to accelerate their development on the *Bodhisattva* stages, or gain rebirth in the Pure Land of their *yidam*. 'Consciousness-transference' yoga is for those who are unlikely to be able to master the previous yoga, but who have developed visualization abilities. As death approaches, it is used to direct consciousness towards a good rebirth, hopefully in a Pure Land, especially that of Amitābha Buddha.

Sexual yoga

Nyingma practice at the *Anuttara-yoga Tantra* level consists of the *Mahā-*, *Anu-* and *Ati-yogas*; *Ati-yoga* is equivalent to *Dzogch'en*, and will be discussed below. *Mahā-yoga* consists of the above work with the *yidam*, subtle body and yogas of Nāropa. *Anu-yoga* is seen as particularly appropriate for those with strong desire, provided they are not under monastic vows of celibacy; though at an advanced stage of practice, anyone might receive some *Anu-yoga* teachings. While visualizing the energy in the nerve-channels, and reciting and visualizing *mantra*s, sexual yoga is performed, with the man visualized as a male *yidam* and his partner being visualized as the *yidam*'s consort. These two are seen to represent the pair, skilful means and wisdom, with the penis being referred to, in the esoteric 'twilight speech' of the *Tantra*s, as a *vajra*, and the vagina as a lotus. At climax, the semen and its psychic energy are retained, and visualized as ascending the central nerve-channel until reaching the crown *cakra*, so as to produce a great bliss, a state of non-dual radiant clarity in which skilful means and wisdom are united, all concepts and images drop away and there is said to be a direct knowledge of emptiness. This yoga, sexual though it is, is carried out with great calm, so that lust is directly confronted, redirected and then crushed by transmuting its own energy into wisdom. All such practices are only suitable for those who have the right mental discipline and preparation.

TANTRIC TECHNIQUES OF SPONTANEITY

Two types of practice that relate to *Anuttara-yoga Tantras* and completion stage practice are:

- *Mahāmudrā*, which originated as a Kagyüdpa practice, but which has also been adopted and adapted by the Gelugpas and Sakyapas.
- *Ati-yoga*, also known as *Dzogch'en* (*rDzogs chen*; 'The Great Completion/ Perfection'; see p. 205) – a Nyingma practice, but also found in the Buddhist-influenced Bön tradition.

In both kinds of practice, tantric elements such as visualizations are minimal or only preparatory. The emphasis is on an open and direct apprehension of the nature of mind, with some basic similarities to Zen and also Theravāda practice of the four applications of mindfulness. There are seen to be subtle differences between *Mahāmudrā* and *Dzogch'en*, though Mahāyāna concepts of emptiness, thought-only and the *Tathāgata-garbha* are central in both, with the idea that, as beings already have the Buddha-nature, it must simply be allowed to manifest itself.

Both practices are relatively unstructured and direct; at a certain stage they dispense with effort so as to allow a spontaneous state of freedom to be experienced: one should let the mind reach a state of natural relaxation and openness, observe the nature of mind in that state, and so see the ultimate. They are simpler than complex visualizations, though they lack the power that these can have, are not any easier to do, and their relative simplicity means that there can be errors in assessing the level of progress made.

The 'Innate Vehicle' of Saraha (see p. 193) conveys something of the spirit of these approaches, though it is most explicitly linked with *Mahāmudrā*. Saraha's *Dohā-kośa* says:

> 20. If it's already manifest, what's the use of meditation?
> And if it's hidden, one is measuring darkness . . .
> 28. Whatever you see, that is it,
> In front, behind, in all ten directions . . .
> 106. Everything is Buddha without exception . . .
> 55. Look, listen, touch and eat
> Smell, wander, sit and stand,
> Renounce the vanity of discussion,
> Abandon thoughts and be not moved from singleness.
> 71. Do not get caught by attachment to the senses . . .

103. Do not sit at home, do not go to the forest,
But recognize mind wherever you are.
When one abides in complete and perfect enlightenment,
Where is *saṃsāra* and where is *Nirvāṇa*?
96. It is profound, it is vast,
It is neither self nor other . . . (*BTTA*.188)

Mahāmudrā

The term *mudrā* means a seal, stamp, impression or sign, and *Mahāmudrā* means 'Great Seal' or 'Great Sign'. Its aim is to see the stamp of the true nature of reality on all phenomena, and the term *mahāmudrā* is applied both to the method and to the final state of realization it leads to. This is because the way of practice is itself seen as an expression of the reality it leads to. The technique involves cultivating *śamatha*, then deepening this by a practice akin to developing the 'applications of mindfulness', then developing *vipaśyanā* into this state.[40]

When not seated in meditation, the adept should keep his body loose and gentle by doing all activities in a smooth, relaxed and spontaneous way. He cultivates simplicity and directness of thought to facilitate carrying the awareness developed in meditation into his daily life. To develop *śamatha*, the practitioner successively concentrates on a pebble, a vision of his *Lama* above his head, a Buddha-image, the seed-*mantra hūṃ*, and a shining dot.[41] Breathing then becomes the focus of attention, in a series of phases culminating in holding the breath as an aid to stilling thoughts.

Thoughts still arise, however, and they themselves now become the object of mindfulness. They are seen to chase after various objects, taking them as real, so mindfulness is used to cut off each train of thought as it arises. When the ability to do this is well established, a stage of calm is reached where the fluxing stream of innumerable thought-moments is noticed to be like a tumbling waterfall, and is recognized as that which is to be transcended. Next, the mind is allowed to remain loose and natural, so that trains of thought are allowed to arise as they will. Observing them with equanimity, however, the meditator is unaffected by the thoughts. By this technique, the flow of thought-trains slows down, the state of calm deepens, and the mind becomes like a gently flowing river from which the 'sediments' of the defilements begin to settle out. Next, the mind is kept in

[40] Kongtrul, 2002: 71–3, 142–3, 147; Powers, 2007b: 416–24; Trungpa, 1994a.
[41] Beyer, 1974: 154–61, which translates a text of Pema Karpo (Pad-ma Dkar-po, 1527–92), 'Manual on the Spontaneous Great Symbol'.

an even tension by means of alternating tensing – cutting off thought-trains as they occur – and relaxation – allowing them to develop as they will. Next, even the thought of abandoning thoughts, and all effort and mindfulness in that direction, is left behind, so that the mind flows naturally and spontaneously. In this state, without thought-trains and with no feeling of the body, various visions arise, but these and the bliss or fear which accompany them are just allowed to pass by without attachment or rejection. In this state, the mind is firm and mindfulness occurs spontaneously. Thoughts arise, but are not seen as signifying any realities, they simply come and go without effect, like a pin pricking an elephant. There is awareness that the calm mind flickers, but in a way that does not disturb its steadiness.

Having reached and established this stage, *vipaśyanā* into it is then developed. By investigating both the steadiness and flickering of the mind, the meditator comes to see that they cannot be separated, and thus have no inherent nature of their own. Likewise, it comes to be seen that the awareness which watches all this is not separate from what it watches, thus overcoming the subject/object duality. This then allows full realization to be attained, when thought-moments are observed as an empty thusness, thereby transcending their delusion-making quality.

After this state, the adept is ever in a state of meditationless meditation, where there is a natural recognition of every event as empty and unproduced, a spontaneous expression of the innate *Dharma*-body, the crystal-clear, shining, blissful true nature of mind. He lives in a spontaneous way, free from constructing thought, letting his natural 'ordinary mind' take its course, his actions being totally genuine, imbued with compassion for deluded beings.

Dzogch'en

Dzogch'en is based on the notion of the *Tathāgata-garbha* within all, seen as pure awareness (*rig pa*) – which is different from the content-laden and reactive ordinary mind (Skt *citta*, Tib. *sem* (*sems*)). *Rig pa* is regarded as thusness empty of constructing 'objects', motionless (Norbu, 2000: 32–3, 89–93; Samuel, 1993: 534–5). The aim is to directly see that: 'The empty essence of the mind is the *Dharma*-body, the radiant clear nature of the mind is the Enjoyment-body and the unimpeded universal compassion of the mind is the Transformation-body' (Ling-pa, 1982: 96).

Dzogch'en includes the possibility of recognizing *rig pa* – gaining 'the view' – from the start of practice, with the aid of a guiding *Lama*. The practitioner then rests in and cultivates *rig pa*. If this initial recognition – the way of 'uncommon' *Dzogch'en* – is not attained, then initial *śamatha* is needed, to aid it – the 'common' *Dzogch'en* approach, which is very similar to *Mahāmudrā* (Kongtrul, 2002: 137–8, 141–6). The 'common' form of *Dzogch'en* uses tantric preparations, while the 'uncommon' one is not really tantric at all, being seen as beyond the tantric approach of 'transformation' of defilements, and even beyond *Mahāmudrā* practice. In this form, it is seen by its adepts as a wholly self-sufficient path which is a 'spontaneously perfect' way encompassing all the previous 'vehicles'. Either form is seen as leading to a sudden realization of one's primordial perfection and wisdom.

For people of different mental capacities, three possible ways of developing awareness of primordial *rig pa* are provided, in three series of *Dzogch'en* teachings.[42] These are: the 'essential esoteric instruction', that is, the 'uncommon' one; the 'space' series', which uses symbolic means and emphasizes one's identity with the encompassing space that is the *Dharma*-body; and the 'nature of mind' series, in which one comes to see all appearances as the play of the mind (*sem*), so as to overcome subject/object duality and experience 'self-perfection'.

The key practice is seen not so much as a form of meditation as simply allowing radiant clarity, the true nature of mind, to manifest itself. This involves allowing thoughts to come and go as they will, without attachment or rejection concerning them or their objects, so as to be able to focus on the radiance in the thought-flow itself, apart from its content. By such a practice, the adept develops the ability to let his flow of thought-trains gradually and naturally slow down. Hence *Dzogch'en* practice is seen as a form of meditationless meditation, its 'method' being akin to the phase of *Mahāmudrā* practice which uses mindfulness to still thoughts. As described by Jigme Lingpa ('Jigs med gling pa, 1730–98; Trungpa, 1994b), one needs a *Lama* to guide one to the simplicity of clear-cut nowness. Having tasted this, one does not need to 'meditate' or philosophize, but just observe thoughts in a spacious manner. One needs to work with both thoughts and absence of thoughts, and recognize the limitations of even the *sem* which notes these. When thoughts have been allowed to naturally die away, one should be aware of the natural clarity of mind, and see the combination of stillness and activity in the mind (as in *Mahāmudrā* practice at the stage just before *vipaśyanā* aspects come into play). One should neither *think* of things as empty, nor try to control the mind, but be open to tasting the nowness of direct experience, without getting distracted by its contents. This leads to the distinction between meditation and non-meditation dropping away. One does not need to meditate in solitude, but simply

[42] Kongtrul, 2002: 144; Norbu, 2000: 43–4, 176–9; Powers, 2007b: 383–98.

work with whatever occurs in life, observing it 'like an old man watching a child at play' (Trungpa, 1994b: 288). One should not deliberately try to attain such a state, or look for Buddha-nature/*Dharma-kāya* outside immediate experience, or try to overcome certain thoughts, but let them naturally pass away by seeing the nowness in them.

At a certain point in this development, the flow suddenly stops, as true non-attraction and non-aversion to thought arises in a spontaneous instant, with the mind resting in its primordial state of *rig pa*. This is seen as the sudden attainment of enlightenment, and the unproduced spontaneous perfection of the primordial Buddha Samantabhadra, personification of the *Dharma*-body – or at least a foretaste of this.

ZEN MEDITATION[43]

Though *chan* (Jap. *zen*) is an abbreviated transliteration of the Sanskrit *dhyāna* (Pali *jhāna*), Chan or Zen meditation is not only concerned with such lucid trances, but also with 'meditation' in a broad sense. Its techniques are primarily those of developing high states of awareness, and wrestling with enigmatic *kōans*. These techniques are emphasized, respectively, by the Japanese Sōtō (Ch. Cao-dong) and Rinzai (Ch. Linji) schools (see pp. 222, 231). They are regarded as 'patriarchal' meditation, based on direct mind-to-mind transmission, in contrast to the traditional way of *śamatha* and *vipaśyanā*, in harmony with the *Sūtras*, known as '*Tathāgata*' meditation (Dumoulin, 2005a: 155–6). As will be seen, however, Sōtō practice is somewhat akin to the Theravāda way of *samatha* then *vipassanā*, and Rinzai practice to the method which yokes *samatha* and *vipassanā* together (see p. 325).

The most intense Zen practice is done during *sesshins*: prolonged periods in the meditation-hall (see p. 309). *Zazen*, or 'sitting meditation', is used as the main basis for both awareness and *kōan* meditations, though the meditator is also encouraged to develop awareness, and work with his *kōan*, while walking, and indeed in any posture. Zen, particularly in its Sōtō form, attaches great importance to establishing correct posture in sitting meditation.[44] This clearly implies a very close relationship of mind

[43] A classic Zen text is the *Platform Sūtra*, attributed to Huineng (*Plat.*; see p. 219), extracts of which are *BT*.217–25 and *EB*.8.6.1. A clear, practical, modern guide to Sōtō Zen practice is Suzuki, 1999. Maezumi and Glassman, 2002 is primarily Sōtō in orientation and Sekida, 1975 is mainly Rinzai. While much is written on Japanese Zen, for the Chinese form, Chan, see for example Chang, 1970, or Gregory, 1986: 99–128; for its Korean form, Soen, see Gregory, 1986: 199–42, or Mu Soeng, 1987; for its Vietnamese form, Thien, see Thien-An, 1975.

[44] For Dōgen's instructions, see *MW*.64–5 and Maezumi and Glassman, 2002: 13–15; see also *MW*.146–8; Maezumi and Glassman, 2002: 59–62; Sekida, 1975: 38–46.

and body. Of course in a tradition influenced by thought-only ideas, the position of the body *is* itself a mental phenomenon, so one would expect this! The lower spine should curve inwards, with the rest of the back straight and the abdomen completely relaxed. The area just below the navel, known as the *tanden* (Jap.), becomes a focus of attention in much Zen meditation (Sekida, 1975: 83–90). From here, an energy develops that radiates throughout the body, which seems to parallel the importance of the navel *cakra* in some tantric practices.

The initial task of the meditator is to learn to dampen down wandering thoughts by counting and following the breath.[45] The eyes are lowered and are kept in focus, on the wall or floor 1 to 3 metres away, but the meditator does not look at anything in particular. If any mental images (Jap. *makyō*) arise, such as glimmers of light or even visions of *Bodhisattvas*, these are dismissed as obstructing hallucinations, and dispelled by blinking. Of course in Theravāda *samatha* meditation focused on such objects as the breath, while stray mental images may initially arise due to wandering thoughts, as the mind settles into one-pointedness, mental images (*nimitta*) related to the meditation object in time naturally arise, and then become the object of attention so as to take the mind to *jhāna*. Zen may avoid working with these because its attention to the breath is mainly a preliminary to mindful attention to sitting, or work on a *kōan*, neither of which involves *nimittas*.

Just Sitting

Once the meditator has learnt how to control his or her wandering thoughts to some extent, he may go on to develop high degrees of awareness while sitting, known as 'Just Sitting' (Jap. *Shikantaza*[46]): the approach of 'silent illumination' or 'serene observation' (Jap. *moku shō*).[47] Here, the meditator cultivates *nothing but* sitting, in full awareness of the here-and-now of sitting, so as to be akin to Theravāda 'applications of mindfulness' focused on the body, specifically the sitting posture.[48]

The attention in Just Sitting tends to rest on the movement of the respiratory muscles in the *tanden* area, but is not restricted to this. The

[45] Maezumi and Glassman, 2002: 41–2; Sekida, 1975: 53–65.

[46] Meaning: *shi* = just; *kan* = paying attention to; *ta* =precisely; *za* = sitting (Ch. *zhi-guan-da-zuo* (*chih-kuan-ta-tso*)). One might perhaps think that as *shi/zhi* = *śamatha* (calm), *kan/guan* = *vipaśyanā* (insight), the term might mean 'Calm and Insight in Just Sitting'. However, the *zhi* and *guan* Chinese characters are different ones from those meaning 'calm' and 'insight'. That said, the coincidence is remarkable, and I suspect that it is deliberate, perhaps a kind of pun.

[47] *MW*.146–58; Dumoulin, 2005a: 256–61.

[48] Cf. *MW*.219–27 and Nhat Hanh, 2008.

meditator sets out to be in a state in which he is not trying to think, nor trying not to think; he just sits with no deliberate thought. When thoughts nevertheless arise, he just lets them pass by without comment, like watching traffic going over a bridge. He hears sounds, and notices any changes in his visual field, but does not react for or against them. If his mind begins 'mental chatter' on such a matter, he simply brings it back to sitting, as a Theravāda *samatha* practitioner might bring his mind back to the breath. The emphasis is on letting the mind be uncomplicated, natural, simple, straightforward and open, yet with a bright, positive attitude, in full awareness of the body sitting and the flow of passing thoughts. Ideally, the meditator should be like both an unpretentious frog (*MW*.158) and an alert swordsman faced with potential death in a sudden duel.

To practise in this way, the meditator must keep his mind fully in the present, without any thought of what the practice might 'achieve'. Dōgen, the founder of Japanese Sōtō Zen, emphasized that one should not think that meditation is a way of *becoming* a Buddha, as this is like trying to polish a brick until it becomes a mirror. He emphasized that meditative training is not a means to an end, as in some other Buddhist meditation traditions, but is to be done for its own sake, for training and awakening are one: just sitting exhibits and gradually unfolds the innate Buddha-nature that one simply needs to *allow* to become manifest. As expressed by the *Platform Sūtra*, 'The very practice of Buddha, this is Buddha' (*Plat.* sec. 42 (*BT*.225)). The meditator should sit with great energy but in a purposeless, desireless stance, with deep faith in his pure Buddha-nature within: his original Buddhahood. Here, the importance of precisely the right posture for Dōgen is relevant. While a tantric practitioner may identify himself with a visualized Buddha, one who practices Just Sitting takes up the form of a sitting Buddha – which might be seen as a kind of whole-body *mudrā* – as a way of manifesting his Buddha-nature. As the precise details of a visualized tantric form are seen as important, so are those of how to sit in meditation.

Zen 'purposelessness' parallels *Mahāmudrā* and *Dzogch'en* ideas of 'meditationless meditation', and echoes the early idea that one of the 'gateways to liberation', along with 'emptiness' and the 'signless' (see pp. 96, 340), is to see *Nirvāṇa* as the 'aim-free' (Pali *appaṇihita*, Skt *apraṇihita*) as it lies beyond goal-directedness concerning conditioned phenomena (Conze, 1967: 67–9). The emphasis on 'purposelessly', though, was perhaps particularly appropriate guidance in a Japanese context, where the development of the will is otherwise emphasized; as, for example, in the ascetic practice of sitting under a freezing waterfall (see pp. 259, 310).

Just Sitting is a radically simple, yet difficult, meditation practice that retains a classic Buddhist form of sitting in great awareness, with the breath as a key object. It emphasizes an abandoning and short-circuiting of the conceptual mind and a letting go in nowness, to stop the mind settling anywhere, and stop conceptualizing getting a grip on anything. Yet it also requires a faith in and, it seems, a belief in what looks like a subtle metaphysical doctrine: the all-encompassing 'Buddha nature' that is sometimes talked of as one's 'true self' (Maezumi and Glassman, 2002: 19, 90). While Dōgen was critical of the view that saw the Buddha-nature as a pre-existent fixed Self (see p. 233), he saw it as the true nature of oneself and everything else, but as an ever-changing, free-flowing dance of processes that had inherent in it a bright and awakened aspect.

The practice of Just Sitting leads to an effortless watching, and the natural development of a strong one-pointed concentration. This can be seen to develop *śamatha*, in the state of 'self-mastery *samādhi*' (Jap. *Jishu-zammai*; Sekida, 1975: 94–7), which seems equivalent to 'access' or 'the potential' concentration (see pp. 329, 342). The meditator's body is so relaxed that he loses awareness of its position. As the mind becomes quieter, a deeper *samādhi* is then reached, where the mind is like the unruffled surface of a clear lake. Here 'body and mind are fallen off' (Maezumi and Glassman, 2002: 27) in an experience of self-transcendence known as the 'great death'. The breath is so subtle that it seems not to exist; the meditator is unaware of time or space, but is in a condition of extreme wakefulness, a clear awareness in the tranquillity of a state where thought has stopped. It is seen in Zen as the natural purity and calm of man's 'original nature' (*Plat.* sec. 19). These descriptions would seem to indicate a state akin to at least second *dhyāna*, which is free of the activities of thought. Accordingly, 'Just Sitting' practice seems akin to the Theravāda *samatha-yāna*, which develops deep calm before developing insight (cf. Sekida, 1975: 62), as described below.

No-thought

The idea of transcending thought is much emphasized in Zen (*Plat.* sec. 17; *BP*.15; *BS2*.57). The state in which this is attained is known in Japanese as *mu-nen* or *mu-shin*.[49] *Mu-nen* (Ch. *wu-nian* (*wu-nien*)) is equivalent to Sanskrit *an-anusmṛti*, 'no-recollection', and is generally translated as 'no-thought', while *mu-shin* (Ch. *wu-xin* (*wu-hsin*)) is equivalent to *a-citta*,

[49] Discussed in Suzuki, 1969, and also in Kasulis, 1981: 39–54, who sees it as pre-reflective awareness; but it is surely this only once it has in some sense been recognized.

'no-mind' (cf. p. 143). The state referred to seems the same as the stage of *Mahāmudrā* meditation where even the effort to abandon thought-trains, and mindfulness so directed, is dropped. Such a state can be related to the Perfection of Wisdom literature's description of the 'perfection' of giving, where a gift is given with no thought of the gift, the giver or the receiver (*BTTA*.131). In Zen practice, when mindfulness reaches high intensity, it is seen as so taken up with its objects that it is not aware of itself, and bears nothing else in mind, so it is 'no-recollection'. There is no separation of subject and object, and there is no awareness of the immediately prior moment of consciousness. In the state of no-thought, the mind does not try to cloud over reality by conceptualizing it. As Seng Can's (Seng Ts'an, d. 606) popular Zen poem says: 'The more you talk about It, the more you think about It, the further from It you go;/stop talking, stop thinking, and there is nothing you will not understand' (*BTTA*.211). Such a state, at a certain level, may occasionally be experienced, for example, by a musician who is so absorbed in playing his instrument that he has no awareness of 'himself', his 'fingers', or the 'instrument': what is now sometimes referred to as a state of 'flow'.

The experience of no-thought is not confined to the quiet of sitting meditation, but can be attained in the midst of daily activities. When the meditator is digging, he is *just* digging, not thinking; when walking, he is *just* walking; when he is thinking of something, he is fully thinking of that, and not of other things (cf. *Plat.* sec. 17). 'No-thought', then, is not a state of dull thoughtlessness. When a person is in such a state, he is aware of his surroundings in a total, all-round way, without getting caught up and fixed on any particular. The mind does not pick and choose or reflect on itself, but is serenely free-flowing, innocent and direct, not encumbered with thought-forms. When the need arises, the 'mind of no-mind' can instantly react in an appropriate way.

Spontaneity and discipline

Partly influenced by the Daoist praise of natural and spontaneous action, Zen has valued this as a way of facilitating the attainment of free-flowing no-thought. Paradoxically, great discipline is necessary in cultivating spontaneity. Meditative discipline teaches a person how to go beyond the constraints of habitual, ego-centred thoughts and actions and thus allow spontaneous intuition to arise. In temporarily going beyond this feeling of 'I', a person's normal regulative, judging mind – the *manas* referred to by the Yogācāra school – is inactive, so that the underlying 'Buddha Mind' can act. The meditator allows his innate nature, the 'original mind', to function naturally and spontaneously in all activities.

The meditator seeks to bring an inner stillness to all activities, performing them with mindfulness, perhaps to the point of no-thought. Thus the daily tasks of sweeping, polishing, cooking or digging are to be done with a beauty of spirit and a consideration for others which is expressed in little things like leaving slippers neat and tidy.

Kōan *meditation*[50]

East Asian cultures have an emphasis on being attuned to context and focusing on relationships, not things. Accordingly, *kōans* have been influenced by certain Chinese literary and poetic conventions, delighting in literary allusions and metaphorical language (Wright, 1993, and see pp. 221–2). John Strong (*EB*.327) points out that:

> For years, the study of kōans in the West ... tended to focus on their mystical side ... Today, it is more commonly realized that there are many types of kōans and our study of them needs to be grounded in their literary, social, historical, ritual and even folkloric contexts. To be sure, some kōans seem to revel in absurdity intended to put the meditator in a logical double bind. But it is probably better to think of most kōans as focal points of concentration rather than as conundrums to be solved. In this context, kōans are no more illogical than classic objects of mindfulness such as one's breath.

The Western Zen teacher Robert Aitken has defined *kōans* as 'metaphorical narratives that particularize essential nature'.[51] Thomas Cleary adds that *kōans* 'contain patterns, like blueprints, for various inner exercises in attention, mental posture, and higher perception'.[52]

The practice of *kōan* meditation (Sekida, 1975: 98–107) is known in Japanese as *kanna* (Ch. *kan-hua* (*k'an-hua*)), 'seeing into the topic'. In this, the meditator contemplates the critical word or point in a *kōan* story,[53] known in Japanese as *watō* (Ch. *hua-tou* (*hua-t'ou*)). In China, the most popular *kōan* centres on the question 'Who is it that recites the name of the Buddha?', that is, who recites the invocation to Amitābha Buddha in the daily devotional practice?: 'Who am I?' Here, the meditation focuses on the question 'Who?' By focusing on one thing, the practice thus

[50] On this, see *BT*.231–40; Ciolek, 2005; Maezumi and Glassman, 2002: 83–129; Sekida, 1975: 98–107.

[51] Foreword to Cleary, 1990: ix. [52] Cleary, 1994: xv.

[53] Or perhaps something from a scripture or Buddhist practice where puzzlement is generated.

begins by developing calm concentration. To 'answer' the question, though, insight must then be developed, followed by deeper calm. Thus Rinzai *kōan* meditation can be seen as a kind of *śamatha*-and-*vipaśyanā*-yoked-together practice.

At first the meditator simply concentrates on the internally vocalized *watō*, harmonizing this with watching the breath at the *tanden*. This dampens down wandering thoughts, and may be taken all the way to a serene state of *dhyāna*. The Rinzai tradition, however, says that the meditator will lose interest in 'solving' the *kōan* if he enters this state too soon, so he should not let his mind become quite so still, but keep it in a kind of active *samādhi* (close to 'access' concentration; Sekida, 1975: 62, 95–6) where he slowly recites the *watō* and watches it as a cat watches a mouse, trying to bore deeper and deeper into it, until he reaches the point from which it comes, from which all thoughts, and questionings arise and disappear, and intuits its meaning.

In China, other than the above *kōan* and that on one's 'original face' (see p. 222), only one other is commonly used. This centres on the reply of Zhao Zhou (Chao Chou; Jap. Jōshu, 778–897) when asked if a dog had the Buddha-nature. While, at the conventional level of truth, all beings have the Buddha-nature, his reply was '*Wu*' (Jap. *Mu*) meaning 'no', 'nothing'.[54] This seems to allude to the 'emptiness' of everything and the aim seems to be to intuit the root power of the attitude of 'non-', 'not . . .': a kind of holding back, not picking or choosing, which allows complete openness. This, though, must be *felt*, *tasted*, not thought, as thought introduces concepts and preferences. '*Mu*' is not intended as a verbal answer to the question 'does a dog have the Buddha nature?', but as a device for helping to take the meditator to a place where he can see the Buddha-nature. In this place, he or she must negate both 'yes' and 'no', and stand on the sword edge of wisdom between them.

In Japanese Rinzai, the first *kōan* posed is either '*Mu*', or Hakuin's 'what is the sound of one hand clapping?' – perhaps an allusion to the Zen idea of everything as a oneness, the Buddha-nature. If this is so, how is it that differentiation, two-ness, as in two hands, also exists? How is one to state how differentiation exists within oneness? The meditator is then set to progress through a series of fifty or more *kōans*, drawn from 1,800 in five levels, with ones of an appropriate level being selected by the *Rōshi*, or Zen Master, according to a person's character, situation and level of understanding. By progressing through *kōans* over many years, the best pupils

[54] *EB*.9.6; *MW*.66–8; Maezumi and Glassman, 2002: 101–7; Sekida, 1975: 66–82.

then become *Rōshi*s themselves. This system was devised by Hakuin (1685–1768; *BT*.381–8), and the *kōans* are drawn from collections such as the 'Blue Cliff Records' and 'Gateless Barrier', both compiled in China (see p. 222). Aitken explains:

Each koan is a window that shows the whole truth but just from a single vantage. It is limited in perspective. One hundred koans give one hundred vantages. When they are enriched with insightful comments and poems, then you have ten thousand vantages. There is no end to this process of enrichment.[55]

While working on a *koān*, the meditator consults with the *Rōshi* at least twice a day in a '*sanzen*' interview, to offer responses to the *kōan*'s question, to show appropriate understanding has been gained. At first, he attempts intellectual answers, based on what he has read or heard, but these may be useless and be rejected with shouts or blows. The meditator may further try to give 'Zennish' answers by bringing objects to the *Rōshi* or doing some absurd action. These may also be rejected, thus driving the student into a state of baffled perplexity, where the habit-structures and constructs of his mind are starting to be undermined (Dumoulin, 2005a: 219–22). Attempts to 'understand' the *kōan* by fitting it into a meditator's existing 'map' of reality are cut away, to leave him or her in a not-knowing state that is open to transformation and seeing a new 'topography' of reality.

One record of a Zen interview with Master Ts'ao-shan (840–901), itself used as a *kōan*, goes:

Someone asked, 'With what sort of understanding should one be equipped to satisfactorily cope with the cross-examination of others?' The Master said, 'Don't use words and phrases'. 'Then what are you going to cross-examine about?' The Master said, 'Even the sword and the axe cannot pierce it through!' He said, 'What a fine cross-examination! But aren't there people who don't agree?' The Master said, 'There are'. 'Who?' he asked. The Master said, 'Me'. (*BT*.235)

The meditator must 'resolve' each puzzling focus by himself. Some *kōans* may be solved by relatively simple intuitions. Others require the meditator to struggle on with the question until he reaches the end of his tether. In a profound state of perplexity, he meets the 'doubt-sensation': a pure, contentless, existential 'great doubt' that affects him not just when on the meditation cushion. The mind attains one-pointed concentration on this, with no distinction between doubter and doubt. The meditator is then in a stupefied, strangely ecstatic state, where he feels as if he is walking on air, not knowing if he is standing or walking. Nothing is what it seems to be, yet all

[55] Foreword to Cleary, 1990: ix.

is bright and suddenly complete. Hence the meditator is in the 'mountains are not mountains' stage of:

> Before I had studied Zen for thirty years, I saw mountains as mountains and waters as waters. When I arrived at a more intimate knowledge, I came to the point where I saw that mountains are not mountains, and waters are not waters. But now that I have got its very substance I am at rest. For it's just that I see mountains once again as mountains, and waters once again as waters.[56]

In this condition, the meditator is said to be prone to a number of 'Zen sicknesses', whereby he will cling to some aspect of his experience, or take the lights or visions he may have as signs of revelation. These features seem akin to those of the 'pseudo-*Nirvāṇa*' on the Theravāda path (see p. 339). After the *Rōshi* helps 'cure' him, the meditator can progress. Only when he pushes on and on, throwing himself into the abyss of doubt, will an 'answer' spontaneously arise from the depths of his mind. The bigger the engulfing 'doubt-mass', the greater the realization when it collapses, just as more water comes from the melting of a larger block of ice. The deeper he goes into the doubt, not dropping it after gaining a little understanding, the more thorough will be the 'great death' – the death of aspects of ego.

The breakthrough comes suddenly, perhaps after months of struggling. The stimulus may be a stone hitting a bamboo while the meditator is sweeping, or a timely prod from his *Rōshi*. The conceptual, reasoning mind has reached its absolute dead-end, and the 'bottom' of the mind is broken through, so that the flow of thoughts suddenly stops, in a state of no-thought, and realization erupts from the depths – reminiscent of the Yogācāra 'reversal of the basis' (see p. 137). There is no longer anyone to ask or answer the question, but only a blissful, radiant emptiness beyond self and other, words or concepts. In this state of *dhyāna*, insight of various levels can be present.

Kenshō

The attainment of such a breakthrough is known in Chinese as *wu*, 'realization' and in Japanese as *satori*, 'catching on', or *kenshō*, 'seeing one's nature' (Sekida, 1975: 193–206). It is a blissful realization where a person's inner nature, the originally pure mind, is directly known in a sudden reordering of his or her perception of the world. All appears

[56] Watts, 1962: 146, attributed to the ninth-century Chan teacher Qingyuan Weixin (Ch'ingyüan Wei-hsin), known in Japan as Seigen Ishin.

vividly; each thing retaining its individuality, yet empty of separateness, so being unified with all else, including the meditator. There is just an indescribable thusness, beyond the duality of subject and object; a thusness which is dynamic and immanent in the world. This vision of unity was hinted at by the Chinese monk Sengzhao (Sêng-chao; 384–414): 'Heaven and earth and I are of the same root. The ten thousand things and I are of one substance'.[57] When a *kenshō* passes, the meditator finds the conventional world is as it was, and yet somehow different: 'mountains are once again mountains'.

Kenshōs may also be attained by an experienced practitioner of 'Just Sitting' when he emerges from deep inner stillness of the *samādhi* of no-thought, and starts to turn his mind outwards. This feature aligns with the idea that the 'Just Sitting' approach is akin to the Theravāda *samatha-yāna*, in which insight arises after deep calm. In Zen *samādhi*, there is an experience of the originally pure and shining mind uncovered by defilements. It is seen as a state where the *Dharma*-body, thusness or the Buddha-nature is experienced but there is not necessarily any recognition of it. When the mind emerges from its deep stillness, however, it is extremely alert and sensitive, and may be triggered into a *kenshō* experience, where it now sees the 'original face'.

Kenshō is not a single experience, but refers to a whole series of realizations from a beginner's shallow glimpse of the nature of mind, up to a vision of emptiness equivalent to the 'path of seeing' (see p. 156), or to Buddhahood itself. In all of these, the same 'thing' is known, but in different degrees of clarity and profundity.

Sudden awakenings

While 'sudden awakenings' are usually associated with Zen, they are also referred to in other traditions. For example the Theravāda cites the cases of a nun who suddenly attained Arahatship when she extinguished a lamp (*Thig*.112–16, cf. *Thag*.169–70), and Ānanda attaining Arahatship when in the process of lying down to sleep after intent meditation that had failed to attain this (*Vin*.II.286). In the Samye debate in Tibet (see p. 204), the gradual approach to awakening or enlightenment was favoured over a Chan-informed 'sudden' one. Yet all schools actually see key breakthroughs such as stream-entry or Arahatship as sudden transitions; so the real difference is over whether much emphasis is placed on a need for a gradual

[57] Sekida, 1975: 173–4; Suzuki, 1959: 353.

preparation for the first crucial breakthrough, as in the Theravāda and, for example, the Gelugpa schools.

While Rinzai Zen emphasizes that *kenshōs* are sudden, it holds that to become attached to these as great attainments is to have the 'stink of Zen'. It also recognizes that they can only be attained after some degree of gradual practice. Moreover, their insights need to be gradually absorbed by the meditator if they are not to be lost. In this process of maturation, what has been realized, the *Dharma*-body, is increasingly identified with what is encountered in daily life (Wright, 1998: 194–7).

In the Sōtō school, the meditator is discouraged from trying to achieve sudden *kenshōs*. Simply by 'Just Sitting', he authenticates and manifests his innate dignity and perfection, the Buddha-nature (*BT*.371–3). The point of sitting in meditation is simply to develop the skill of showing one's original awakening. Even the beginner in meditation can do this, but such a showing needs to be endlessly repeated so as to permeate more and more of life's activities. Sōtō practice is often seen as a gradualist path, in contrast to the 'sudden' Rinzai practice; in fact, it is better seen as a series of sudden actualizations of the Buddha-nature, in contrast to Rinzai's sudden *seeings* of the Buddha-nature. In Sōtō, *kenshōs* are allowed to occur naturally, as a by-product of practice, or meditative training is seen as the unfolding of one great '*kenshō*' (Maezumi and Glassman, 2002: 79–81).

Zen in action: straightforward mind at all times

The highest aim of Zen is to act in the world in a way which manifests the Buddha-nature and any measure of realization of it that the meditator has had. The highest peak of such a way of acting is expressed in a saying of the Chinese layman Bang Wen (Pang Wen, 740–808): 'Carrying wood and fetching water are miraculous performances; and I and all the Buddhas in the three times breathe through one nostril' (Chang, 1970: 54). Such a way of acting is seen in the *Platform Sūtra* as having 'straightforward mind at all times': having, in all one's activities, an uncomplicated mind free from attachments (*Plat*. sec. 14 (*BT*.218–19)). Zen emphasizes that it teaches nothing special (cf. the Perfection of Wisdom teachings; see p. 124): there is nothing to do or gain. Thus, according to a Zen saying, one who has perfected the Zen way lives as follows: 'A mountain is a mountain, water is water, when hungry I eat, when drowsy I sleep; I do not look for the Buddha, or look for the Dharma, yet I always make obeisance to the Buddha' (Chang, 1970: 182). Such a person does not eat or sleep simply because it 'is time' to do so; he eats in full awareness of eating, rather than thinking of other things. When he is ready to sleep, he does not moan about being tired, but just sleeps. He no longer thinks of Zen or Buddhism, but simply acts in a harmonious and mellow way, dwelling in the world unobtrusively but spontaneously acting so as to help all along the path to enlightenment.

The meditative arts of Zen[58]

The Zen emphasis on naturalness, spontaneity and manifesting the Buddha-nature in daily activities has meant that a whole variety of art forms came to be infused with the spirit of Zen, particularly in Japan. These include ink paintings (Jap. *Sumi-e*) of Zen Masters, whether with challengingly fierce, glaring eyes, or doing some everyday task such as chopping bamboo, or rippling with spontaneous mirth. They also include ink paintings of landscapes, plus calligraphy, poetry, *Nō* theatre, landscape gardening, *Ikebana* flower arrangement and various activities not usually considered 'arts': archery, swordsmanship and the 'Way of tea' (*Cha-no-yu*), generally known in the West as the 'Tea ceremony'.[59]

Zen arts seek to express the true 'thusness' or 'suchness' of a phenomenon or situation, its mysterious living 'spirit' as it is found as part of the ever-changing fabric of existence (Earhart, 1974: 138–9). This requires a free-flowing intuition arising from the state of no-thought. To accomplish the expression of thusness, the aspiring Zen artist must first have a long training to develop a perfect grasp of the technical skills of his or her art. He then calms his mind by giving attention to the breath, and seeks to develop intense concentration on what he wishes to portray, ideally attaining the state of no-thought. He can then overcome any duality between 'himself' and his 'subject', so that he 'becomes' it, and can directly and spontaneously express it through the instruments of his art. Inspiration arises from deep within, from the Buddha-nature which is seen as the inner nature of both himself and his subject, and he expresses its thusness from 'within' it, so to speak (Earhart, 1974: 139; Suzuki, 1959: 31). 'Becoming' an object is also found in tantric visualizations, but while the related tantric art emphasizes the hidden richness and power of the radiant nature of mind, Zen art emphasizes its participation in the simple things of ordinary life: in a stalk of bamboo rather than in a visualized *Bodhisattva*. When true Zen art is produced, it is seen as not so much a human artifice as nature spontaneously

[58] On this, see Dumoulin, 2005b: 221–56; Suzuki, 1959; Watts, 1962: 193–220.

[59] *BT*.376–80, 393–98; Shaw, 2009: 250–3; Suzuki, 1959: 269–314.

expressing itself through the artist. In Zen archery, for example, the release of the arrow should be like a ripe plum dropping from a tree, at a time when the archer has 'become' the target (Herrigel, 2004; Watts, 1962: 214).

Sumi-e painting (Brinker, 1987) is done on fragile absorbent rice paper, or on equally absorbent silk, so that the brush must dance swiftly over the material to avoid tearing it or producing blotches. No erasing, building up or remodelling is possible. After spiritually preparing himself, the artist must strike boldly, letting his brush simply move in response to his spontaneous inspiration: any deliberation will produce an artificial, un-Zen painting. The paintings are done with splashed ink or jagged brush strokes, and often take landscapes as their subjects. Black ink is used, its varying concentrations producing different tones. Colour is avoided, for the aim is to see past the details of surface appearance to capture the thusness of his subject: to re-create on paper its 'life's motion', its purposeless, free-flowing 'spirit'. An example is shown in Plate 13. Human life is shown harmoniously blending in with nature and its rhythms, in accordance with the Zen ideal. In the foreground, the asymmetric ruggedness of trees and rocks emphasizes naturalness, while in the mid-ground there is much empty space, suggesting the open, fluid and mysterious nature of reality.

Another example of a Zen art is the *haiku*, a seventeen-syllable poem form popularized as a vehicle for Zen by the layman Matsuo Bashō (1644–94), Japan's most famous poet.[60] He wandered extensively as the spirit took him, with few possessions, so as to be open to the simple yet profound aspects of ordinary things, which he then expressed in his poems in non-highbrow language. His first real Zen *haiku* (Suzuki, 1959: 238–40) occurred when talking to his meditation Master in a quiet garden. The Master asked him what reality was 'prior to the greenness of moss', that is, the underlying principle beyond yet within the world of particulars. Hearing a noise, Bashō directly answered by expressing its thusness: 'A frog jumps in: water's sound'. As a poet, he then made this into a *haiku*:

An old pond, ah!
A frog jumps in:
The water's sound.

This expresses a moment in which Bashō was the sound, and the sound was no longer a 'sound', but an indescribable expression of ultimate reality. A Zen *haiku* seeks to *show*, rather than to describe such reality. Its form is brief, so as not to get in the way, and it simply evokes the thusness of a living

60 Basho and Stryk, 2003; Dumoulin, 2005b: 348–54; Suzuki, 1959: 215–68.

Plate 13: *Landscape with Pine Trees and Hut*, by Bunsei, fifteenth-century Japan.

moment, so that the reader's mind resonates with the poet's and 'tastes' the profound feeling of the moment of poetic expression.

A true Zen *haiku* must arise spontaneously, as can be seen from the story of Chiyo (1703–75), who had been given the subject of the night-flying cuckoo on which to perfect her *haiku*-writing skills (Suzuki, 1959: 224–6). One night, while listening to the bird in the distance, she struggled to produce a *haiku* that would be acceptable to her teacher. So enwrapped in this task was she that dawn crept up on her unexpectedly, and then the perfect *haiku* flowed from her writing brush:

> Calling 'cuckoo', 'cuckoo',
> All night long,
> Dawn at last!

This is not so much a poem on the cuckoo as on Chiyo-in-relation-to-the-cuckoo-at-the-moment-of-dawn. Even this is not quite correct, however, for the Zen perspective would just say that it expresses the thusness of a moment, without trying to split this up into subject and object at all.

CHAPTER 12

The Modern History of Buddhism in Asia

In the last two centuries, Buddhism has undergone a number of changes, and has had to respond to a range of pressures, coming from:

- Colonization of Asian countries by Western powers, which undermined political structures associated with Buddhism, but also led to Western scholarship on it, so helping its spread to the West, and to stimulating changes in Buddhism, both in colonized countries and in those influenced by them.
- Christianity: criticism of Buddhists by Christians was one element in stimulating increasing Buddhist social activism. Moreover, in South Korea and to some extent the Republic of China, Christianity and Buddhism are currently rivals for people's commitment.
- Communism: this has been something of a wet blanket on Buddhism in China (now including Tibet), North Korea, Vietnam, Laos, Cambodia and Mongolia. It remains most repressive in North Korea, though Cambodia and Mongolia have escaped from its rule in the last twenty years.
- Marxist-nationalism in Burma: not anti-Buddhist, as such, but it acts against Buddhist values.
- War or its after-effects, especially in Cambodia and Sri Lanka: Cambodia was affected by American bombing, then by the Khmer Rouge; Sri Lanka has been affected by a civil war between the Sinhalese and Tamils.
- Modern capitalism: originally brought with colonialism, though Japan developed its own capitalism as a foil to Western colonial threats. This has brought greater prosperity to many, but also undermined traditional value-structures.
- Consumerism: a particularly virulent form of capitalism, currently perhaps the greatest corrosive force undermining Buddhism in Japan, South Korea, Taiwan, Thailand and more recently mainland China. Its commodification of life and emphasis on possessions has heightened elements of greed in human nature and it accordingly encourages a reorientation of values.

- Modernity: democracy, egalitarianism, secularization, improved communication and ease of travel.

Buddhist monarchs still exist in Thailand, Bhutan and now again in Cambodia, and Buddhism remains the dominant or largest religion of Sri Lanka, Thailand, Burma, Cambodia, Laos, Vietnam, Bhutan, Tibet, Mongolia, China, Taiwan and Japan. It retains a strong presence in South Korea, and is reviving in Nepal and on a small scale in India. Outside Asia, it has broken entirely new ground.

SOUTHERN BUDDHISM

The number of Southern Buddhists in Asia are given in Table 5[1] (figures in brackets are percentages of total populations of each country), totalling 150 million.

Sri Lanka

The British took over the island of Laṅkā/Ceylon in 1815, and although they agreed to 'maintain and protect' Buddhism, the objections of Christian missionaries led to a gradual removal of the state's role in purifying the *Saṅgha* (Malalagoda, 1976). The missionaries ran all the officially approved schools, though they made few converts (Harris, 2009). They were annoyed when their attacks on Buddhism were at first only met by monks lending them Buddhist manuscripts and letting them stay in temples when on preaching tours. By 1865, however, monks began a counterattack by

Table 5 *Number of Southern Buddhists in Asia*

– Thailand, 61m. (94% of 65m.).	Minority populations exist in:
– Burma, 44.5m. (89% of 50m.).	– south-west China (Yunnan) bordering Laos and Burma, 1.2m.
– Sri Lanka, 15.05m. (70% of 21.5m.).	– southern Vietnam bordering Cambodia, 1m.
– Cambodia, 13.3m. (95% of 14m.).	– regions bordering Burma in Chittagong, Bangladesh, 1m., and India, 0·3m.
– Laos, 4.4m. (67% of 6.5m.).	– northern Malaysia, 0·07m.
	– recent converts in India, 7.1m., Indonesia, 0.3m.?, and Nepal, 0·3m.?

[1] Generally working from the figures in Wikipedia, 'Buddhism by country' (Wikipedia, 2010), checking their cited sources, and tending to take averages of variant estimates.

printing pamphlets and accepting Christian challenges to public debates. A famous one at Pānadura in 1873 saw the victory of the monk Guṇānanda before a crowd of 10,000 (Berkwitz, 2010: 165–9; Gombrich, 2006: 179–80). This much-publicized event signalled a resurgence in Buddhism, which borrowed certain techniques from the Christianity it was opposing.

By the last decade of the century, a new style of Buddhism was developing, at least among the newly affluent, English-educated middle classes of the capital, Colombo. It tended to see the Buddha as 'simply a human being', and Buddhism as a 'scientific', 'rational' philosophy, 'not a religion', as it did not depend on blind faith. Such ideas were influenced by English concepts and Western interpretations of Buddhism. This style of Buddhism also advocated the adoption of new organizational forms, such as lay societies (e.g. the Young Men's Buddhist Association), Buddhist-influenced modern schools, and the use of printing and newspapers. Heinz Bechert thus refers to it as 'Buddhist modernism'.[2] Richard Gombrich and Gananath Obeyesekere (1988: 6–7 and 204–40) prefer the more loaded term 'Protestant Buddhism'. This is because they emphasize that these developments were partly a protest against Christianity, and shared with Protestantism both a dislike of traditional 'ritualistic accretions' and an emphasis on the laity as individually responsible for their own salvation. The latter was aided by Western scholarship, which made the Pali Canon available in English translation: traditionally it was only conveyed to the laity from its Pali form by the monks.

An important event occurred in 1880, when Colonel H. S. Olcott (1832–1907) and Madame H. P. Blavatsky (1831–91) arrived in Colombo (Gombrich, 2006: 183–6). In 1875, this American journalist and Russian clairvoyant had founded the Hindu–Buddhist-leaning Theosophical Society in New York (see pp. 420–1). In 1879, they established the headquarters of this syncretistic religious movement in India. On arriving in Colombo, they appeared to embrace Buddhism by publicly taking the refuges and precepts, thus giving a great confidence-boost to some Buddhists, due to their being Westerners. Olcott set up a 'Buddhist Theosophical Society', which was in fact a vehicle of modernist Buddhism. He then organized a thriving Buddhist schools movement with a Western, English-language curriculum, in which the laity began to exercise leadership roles of a religious nature.

Out of this milieu arose Don David Hewavitarne (1864–1933), who reacted against an intolerant Christian schooling and was inspired by

[2] *Buddhismus, Staat und Gesellschaft in den Länden des Theravāda Buddhismus*, 3 vols., 1966, 1967 and 1973.

Guṇānanda and Olcott (Berkwitz, 2010: 174–6; Gombrich, 2006: 186–92). In 1881, he adopted the title Anagārika ('Homeless One') Dharmapāla ('Defender of *Dharma*'), and went on to become the hero of modern Sinhalese Buddhism, being regarded as a *Bodhisattva*. *Anagārika*-hood was a new status, mid-way between that of monk and layman, involving adherence to the eight precepts for life. While others did not follow his example in this respect, he was the model for lay activism in modernist Buddhism. In 1891, he went to India and visited Bodh-Gayā, the site of the Buddha's awakening, and was distressed by its dilapidated state and its ownership by a Hindu priest. He therefore founded the Mahā Bodhi Society, an international Buddhist organization whose aims were to win back the site for Buddhism by court action (achieved only in 1949) and to establish an international Buddhist monastery at Bodh-Gayā. For the rest of his life, Dharmapāla worked for the resurgence of Buddhism, linking this to Sinhalese nationalism and calls for independence. In this work, the missionary zeal which he had been subjected to as a child was directed back at the Christian British. He was also critical of caste, and even of recourse to gods, as un-Buddhist.

Christians and the influential modernist Buddhist minority criticized monks as not socially active enough. In time, this led to them highlighting and extending their traditional social welfare activities, acting as prison and even army chaplains, and as paid schoolteachers. In an influential book, *Bhiksuvage Urumaya* (1946),[3] Ven. Walpola Rāhula argued for the involvement of Buddhist monks in social and political matters. In a colonial context, this also talked of (Sinhalese-Buddhist) 'religio-nationalism' and 'religio-patriotism' (Tambiah, 1992: 27–8). Independence and the advent of democracy in 1948 brought monks increasingly into the political arena. Liberal, socialist and Marxist ideas encouraged political activity among all sections of the population, and some monks saw it as part of their duty to guide their parishioners politically. *Saṅgha* political pressure groups developed which are now split along party lines. For many laypeople, though, the activity of the 'political monk' is a distasteful expression of *Saṅgha* factionalism and secular involvement (Seneviratne, 1999).

The more traditional activity of monastic scholarship also flourished. There were many contributions to this by the small group of Western monks spearheaded by the German Nyānatiloka (1878–1956), who had ordained in 1904 in Burma. His pupil and fellow German, Nyānaponika (1901–94), helped found the Buddhist Publication Society in 1958, which he

[3] 1974 English version, *The Heritage of the Bhikkhu* (extract in *EB*.6.8.3).

headed until 1988, when the American Bhikkhu Bodhi took over until 2002. It has produced many English and Sinhala publications on Buddhism (www.bps.lk). The best of their 'Wheel' pamphlets have done much to show the modern implications of ancient Buddhist texts.

The re-emphasis on lay involvement in religion continues, and the desire for Buddhism to permeate life has now led to middle-class weddings having more Buddhist elements, sometimes even being held on monastery premises (Gombrich and Obeyesekere, 1988: 255–73). The middle classes also increasingly practise meditation, most often a Burmese form of *vipassanā* (Berkwitz, 2010: 203–4), and there is a trend for certain laypeople to live celibate lives. As the urban laity have become more active, and more educated, there has been an erosion of their respect for monks, most of whom are still from rural backgrounds and many of whom are less educated. Thus people may look more to a lay meditation teacher than a non-meditating monk for guidance. Increasingly, however, monasteries have become 'meditation centres' (Gombrich, 1983), an idea drawn from the West and Burma. Other developments have included a revival of the forest meditation tradition, whose monks are highly revered (Carrithers, 1983). They represent a 'reformist' trend, whose aim is closer conformity to the ideals of the early *Saṅgha*. The respect accorded to the nuns, a good number of whom have become *bhikkhunīs* since the revival of this order in 1998 (see pp. 301–2), is also due to their simple meditative life.

A new form of ritual, the *Bōdhi Pūjā*, was developed in the 1970s by Bhikkhu Ariyadhamma, and has since become very popular (see p. 245; Gombrich and Obeyesekere, 1988: 384–410). Centred on the *Bodhi*-tree, it uses chanting that is more like singing, so as to be more emotional in nature than traditional chanting, as well as involving more active participation by laypeople.

An important movement in Sri Lanka, of a clearly modernist type, is the Sarvodaya Śramadāna ('Giving of Energy for the Awakening of All'), an important example of 'socially engaged Buddhism', and Sri Lanka's largest non-governmental organization.[4] By the mid-1990s it had, since its inception, recruited more than 800,000 volunteers and touched the lives of over four million people in promoting the renewal of rural communities (Swearer, 1995: 117), and by 2006 it was active in around 15,000 of the island's 38,000 villages. Started in 1958 by A. T. Ariyaratne (Keown and Prebish, 2007: 43–5), this lay-led movement involves both laity and monks. Ariyaratne criticizes monastic activity aloof from society and

[4] Berkwitz, 2010: 196–9; Harvey, 2000: 225–34, 275–8; Queen and King, 1996: 121–46.

rejects forms of Buddhism that have primarily other-worldly goals, such as generating karmic fruitfulness for good rebirths (Bond, 1988: 255). He emphasizes that karma is only one factor that influences people's lives, so that they should do all they can to take charge of their lives in the present (Bond, 1988: 272). The movement's aim is to foster 'development' in the widest sense, by arousing villagers from their passivity and getting them involved in choosing and working on projects, such as building a road to their village or organizing a marketing co-operative. It draws on Buddhist ideals such as generosity and lovingkindness, and seeks to get *all* sections of the community to participate and work together so as to experience their individual and communal potential for changing their economic, social, natural and spiritual environments. It emphasizes 'ten basic needs for full human welfare and fulfilment' and an 'economics of sufficiency', and is critical of both capitalism and socialism as too focused on the purely economic aspects of life. Women are particularly encouraged to speak up and be more active, and the movement has also sought to foster better Sinhalese–Tamil relationships.

George Bond has described the Sarvōdaya as a 'Buddhist social liberation movement' (1996: 121) in which 'the path to individual liberation runs through social liberation', while Gombrich and Obeyesekere see it as simplifying the demanding other-worldly path into one of this-worldly activity (1988: 243–55). That said, Sarvōdaya activity exists alongside an increase in 'demanding' meditative activity in Sri Lanka by both monks and laity, and Sarvōdaya has stimulated other types of demanding activity in many who were unlikely to have engaged in meditation (other than chanting). Gombrich and Obeyesekere also see the movement as having an over-idealized image of traditional village life of the past, along with seeking to impose certain urban 'Protestant Buddhist' values on remaining village communities. Yet while Ariyaratne's vision is certainly idealistic, he clearly recognizes the vices of traditional village life and seeks to rectify these by drawing on neglected strengths that he, rightly or wrongly, sees as implicit in Sri Lankan village life. His glowing picture of certain ancient Sinhalese civilizations – broadly shared with some Sinhalese nationalists – certainly contains exaggerations, and is thus best treated as an inspiring vision, yet his movement certainly seems to be producing good results.

Since 1948, a population-boom[5] consequent on the eradication of malaria broke up traditional village communities by driving many peasants off the land to the cities. While there have been good improvements in health-care

[5] In 1946 6.7 million, 14.8m. by 1981 and 21.5m. by 2010.

and education, poor economic performance has led to mass unemployment and underemployment, and different communities have blamed each other for this, which is one of the roots of the long-running Tamil–Sinhalese ethnic conflict which erupted in 1983. The Sinhalese (74% of the population) have a long history of defending their culture against Tamil incursions from south India. In the post-war period, they sought to redress certain advantages which they saw the British as having given to the Tamils (18% of the population). In time these moves went too far, and led to Tamil demands for autonomy or independence for parts of the island where they predominate.

In the conflict, the Tamils came to be dominated by ruthless guerrillas fighting for an independent Tamil state in the north-east of the island: the LTTE, or 'Liberation Tigers of Tamil Eelam'. The conflict has been mainly rooted in the issues of language, peasant resettlement areas and regional devolution. The Sinhalese language has come to have a privileged status, and Tamil-speakers have felt that this has placed them at a disadvantage as regards education and government employment. Peasant resettlement schemes have involved the movement of Sinhalese people into once dry areas, which had been populated by the Sinhalese in earlier eras, but upsetting the population balance with the Tamils in such areas. Regional devolution for Tamil areas has been sought so as to overcome economic deprivation, though extremists have sought a completely separate state.

The conflict also has a religious dimension. The Sinhalese are mainly Buddhists, and Buddhism is a strong ingredient in their identity, due to the long history of the religion on the island, and the fact that the Sinhalese have done much to preserve and spread Theravāda Buddhism. The Tamils are mainly Hindu, but religion is not an emphasized part of their cultural identity. The Sinhalese Buddhists see themselves as an endangered minority protecting an ancient tradition. While a majority in their own country, a history of invasions by the much more numerous South Indian Tamils makes them feel insecure.

After independence, Sinhalese Buddhists rightly sought to revive and strengthen their culture after the colonial period. Yet in building their nationalism around a Buddhist identity rooted in perceptions of past Sinhalese Buddhist civilizations, a side-effect has been to exclude the non-Buddhist Tamils from this ideal. Buddhist values have become distorted as 'Buddhism' became increasingly identified, by some, with the Sinhalese people and the territory of the entire island.[6] While in the ancient

[6] Cf. the rise of 'Hindutva', a kind of Hindu fundamentalism, in India.

Mahāvaṃsa chronicle, the Buddha predicts that Buddhism would flourish in Sri Lanka, this has wrongly been taken by some into supporting a drive to restore all, and only, Buddhists to prominence (Bond, 1988: 9). This perspective has led to Buddhists exploiting their majority position and alienating Tamils, who are still perceived as a privileged minority. Sinhalese party politicians have 'played to the gallery' and made capital out of religion, producing a communalization of politics (Bond, 1988: 121–2). Often the party in opposition has objected when the party in power has made moves to address Tamil grievances. The division of the *Saṅgha* along political lines has not helped either.

But for extremists on both sides – including some Buddhist monks who have demonstrated against 'concessions to the Tamils' – moderates could have resolved the ethnic problem by taking into account the concerns of both sides and encouraging mutual forgiveness of past wrongs (Berkwitz, 2010: 177–81). In their drive to protect Buddhism, Sinhalese Buddhists have needed to pay more attention to the contents of what they are 'protecting', and less to the need for a strong political 'container' for it. A re-emphasis on Buddhist values of non-violence and tolerance has been needed, as has a more pluralistic model of Buddhist nationalism (Tambiah, 1992: 125). Stanley Tambiah argues that the idealizing of an ancient Sinhalese past has led to an overlooking of more recent medieval and pre-colonial times in which there was 'a multicultural and pluralistic civilization with a distinctively Buddhist stamp' (1992: 149).

The death toll over the years from the conflict has been around 90,000, military expenditure has taken up a quarter of government spending and the economy has become stunted. After various failed attempts at either peace talks or defeat of the Tamil Tigers, the army succeeded, in 2009, in defeating them and killing their leader. Many civilians were killed in the bombardments by both sides, and the underlying issues that lie behind the conflict still need to be addressed.

Given the above, it is ironic that Sinhala Buddhists have in fact been increasingly influenced by trends from Tamil Hinduism in the post-independence era. Perhaps their resistance to calls for more political power for Tamils is a way of externalizing elements of disquiet with this. The religious life of the Buddhists of Sri Lanka not only draws on Theravāda Buddhism, but also involves interaction with a range of deities, godlings and demons (*yakṣas*), the latter complex being referred to as 'spirit religion' by Gombrich and Obeyesekere (1988: 3). Buddhism is seen as the over-arching, superior tradition, and is looked to especially for liberation and a good rebirth; the spirit religion is looked to for help with the vicissitudes of life. These have increased as the population has increased, traditional village structures have been overcome, and the lacklustre economy – of course not helped by the ethnic conflict – has been unable to satisfy the increased aspirations raised by mass education. Hence people – whether businessmen, bureaucrats, politicians, slum dwellers or landless labourers – have looked more to less morally scrupulous deities for help than to the traditional 'Buddhist' ones, such as Viṣṇu (seen as a *Bodhisattva* and protector of Buddhism).

Particularly important is Kataragama (Gombrich and Obeyesekere, 1988: 99–101, 163–99), now the most popular deity on the island. He is named after the location of his main shrine in Sri Lanka, which is visited by people of all classes and nominal religious affiliations, including Christian, with 550,000 visiting in 1973. The shrine has a Buddhist *Stūpa* nearby, which is included in people's rituals, and has become a microcosm of the eclectic mingling of religious strands found in contemporary Sri Lanka. 'Protestant Buddhism', and its rather puritan, fundamentalist tone has been working its influence down the social classes from the middle classes, and has been meeting, and being influenced by, new aspects of the spirit religion, with much emotional deity-devotion, emanating from the urban working class (Gombrich and Obeyesekere, 1988: 9–11). While monks generally disbelieve in spirit-worship or are indifferent to it, sometimes popular pressure leads them to including new deity shrines in their temples.

Kataragama – another name for Skanda, 'son' of the key Hindu deity Śiva – was once seen as a war god, and was worshipped in Sri Lanka mainly by Tamils. He is now seen as a protector of Buddhism, with his main shrine mostly taken over by Buddhists (Gombrich and Obeyesekere, 1988: 411–44). In taking over the cult from the Tamil Hindus, and emphasizing its 'Buddhist' nature, Buddhists are assimilating Hindu values. Practices here and elsewhere are becoming more influenced by the emotional *bhakti*, or loving devotion, found in Hinduism, as well as by magical practices. Traditionally, Sinhala Buddhists looked to gods for help with material problems in life; now they are looking to them as personal guardian deities – as *iṣṭa devatās* (chosen deities) as in Hinduism – for 'constant guidance, consolation and love' (Gombrich and Obeyesekere, 1988: 455, cf. 32–3). At the main Kataragama shrine, people walk over glowing embers (originally a Śaiva Hindu practice) out of *bhakti* to a deity, perhaps to fulfil a vow, but certainly to renew their power to be possessed by the deity (Gombrich and Obeyesekere, 1988: 189–91).

The popularity of Kataragama means that he is becoming progressively Buddhicized, though his worship still involves a somewhat erotic and ecstatic mass dancing (*kāvaḍi*) in celebration of his dalliance with his mistress. As Kataragama becomes more ethicized, other deities are rising in popularity (Gombrich and Obeyesekere, 1988: 31–6, 112–62), especially: Hūniyam, personification of sorcery and indeed black magic, and thus seen as a protector against it; and the Hindu goddess Kālī, seen as having a terrifying aspect, but also as a source of protective power. Both were traditionally seen as demons by Buddhists. However, in an economically insecure context in which personal effort does not always bring rewards, partly due to the role played by trading in political influence, people have turned to non-rational means of looking after themselves and their families. Misfortunes may be diagnosed as due to sorcery perpetrated by a jealous neighbour, and seen as curable by counter-sorcery.

Traditionally, Buddhists usually saw possession as by demons or malign ancestral spirits (*preta*s), so as to require exorcism – or by minor gods, under limited and controlled conditions by priestly specialists. Increasingly, people are being seen as ecstatically possessed by a deity such as Kataragama (Gombrich and Obeyesekere, 1988: 28–9, 36–41), and as then able to do such things as make predictions, influence events or bring cures, all these being seen in an increasingly positive light. The 'Protestant Buddhist' validation of lay meditation, and the now often positive evaluation of possession states, especially in the lower classes, mean that a range of altered states of consciousness are being claimed. Of course, Buddhist meditative states differ from possession in that they are based on self-control and awareness, which seem absent in possession states. However, Gombrich and Obeyesekere (1988: 453–4) have noted a tendency for these two kinds of state to be merged in some cases. This may be because a state in which there is the strong concentration and sometimes body-shaking joy associated with *samatha* meditation, but without the usually emphasized mindfulness, may sometimes be akin to a possession state. In traditional Buddhist terms, this would be a form of 'wrong concentration'.

That said, there remains plenty of traditional Theravāda Buddhism in Sri Lanka!

Thailand

In the nineteenth century, Thailand (then called Siam) skilfully avoided being colonized by European powers, and had two enlightened, modernizing rulers: King Mongkut (r. 1851–68), inaccurately portrayed in the film *The King and I*, and his son King Chulalongkorn (r. 1868–1910). In his time in the *Saṅgha* before being king, Mongkut established the reformist

Dhammayutika monastic fraternity, and sought to spread a purified, ethically orientated Buddhism to the people. Since 1932, the country has had a constitutional monarchy and been ruled mostly by a parliamentary government guided by the military. Buddhism is the state religion, with the *Saṅgha* state-regulated, and royalty have continued to be much respected.

Since the 1960s, much economic development (and secularization) has taken place, though its unevenness caused the government, especially in the 1960s and 1970s, to ask the *Saṅgha* to co-operate with, encourage and lead community development projects in poorer regions (Suksamran, 1977; Swearer, 1995: 117–23). Development workers have always contacted the local abbot before initiating a project, as this could not succeed without his approval; for the villagers tend to be suspicious of government officials. The abbot can provide useful practical information on the locality. He may also, at the end of a sermon, encourage villagers to participate in the project, such as building a road. Monks may then take part in or help organize this, which further motivates the villagers by legitimating the action as generating karmic fruitfulness. The *Saṅgha* has also initiated training programmes to help monks, particularly graduates, to participate more effectively in community development activities. Both leaders of the programmes and the government have felt that the *Saṅgha* should help to ensure that material progress was not accompanied by moral and religious decline, or public disorder would ensue, and Communism would be more attractive to those in poorer regions. One of the activities of the monks has been to seek to encourage the laity to widen their notion of what actions generate karmic fruitfulness. Historically, these have come to be identified with acts beneficial to the *Saṅgha*, though early texts also refer to activities such as planting medicinal herbs and sinking wells as generating karmic fruitfulness (*S*.1.33). The training has given guidance in such matters as: effective leadership in the building of roads, bridges, clinics and wells; nutrition, first aid, sanitation, nature conservation, and mobilization of funds. The practical effects of such programmes have been reasonably encouraging, though the laity have often needed much persuasion to widen their notion of what generates karmic fruitfulness, and there are limits to what the rechannelling of traditionally haphazard karmic fruitfulness-related giving can achieve.

The involvement of monks in development work has not been without its critics. Those who support greater social activism on the part of the *Saṅgha* argue that, through it, the monks can 'reassert their traditional role' as community leaders in a changing world, and thus retain respect. Opponents are those of a more cautious and traditional outlook, particularly among the laity. They argue that, if monks become too involved in the affairs of secular society, then they will compromise their unique exemplary role of being spiritual specialists, this being to the detriment of society. Some have also criticized the government for making political use of the *Saṅgha* in work which has partly been an anti-Communist strategy. Both sides have a point, so that careful consideration is needed so as to work out the best practical accommodation in this area.

Somewhat different from most 'development' work is help given to poor urban dwellers who are heroin addicts. One monk, Phra Chamroon (1926–99), developed a curative regime of herbal medicine and moral discipline at his monastery, Thamkrabok (www.thamkrabok.net). Its high cure rate has attracted the interest of doctors in the West. Some Thais criticized him for involving monks too closely with disturbed laypeople, but others have seen his work as an extension of the meditative concern to purify the mind. Other monks have been very active in seeking to protect Thailand's dwindling forests, by such actions as 'ordaining' trees, and with Ajahn Pongsak Tejadhammo encouraging hill-tribe villagers to protect and enhance their forest environment, rather than cut it down in slash-and-burn agriculture (Harvey, 2000: 181–2; Swearer, 1995: 124–8). The *Saṅgha* as a whole is generally wary of innovators, and also of political monks, whether former Marxist student activists or the fervently anti-Communist Phra Kittivuddho, who in 1973 claimed (to much criticism) that there was no fault in killing Communists (Harvey, 2000: 260–1; Swearer, 1995: 112–14).

As in Burma, there are many fine meditation masters in Thailand (see p. 338), some of them lay, and meditation is increasingly popular among the educated urban classes. Some monks and laypeople downplay much of the conventional religion that is orientated to generating *bun* – 'merit' or karmic fruitfulness – to concentrate on matters pertaining to overcoming attachment and attaining *Nirvāṇa*, the ultimate goal. They stress the centrality of meditation, and the peripheral importance of ceremonies, as Chan had done in China. L. S. Cousins (1997a: 408–11) has coined the term 'ultimatism' to refer to such forms of Buddhism in Thailand and elsewhere.

Among the educated elite, one of the most well-known, if controversial, 'ultimatist' monks has been Buddhadāsa (1906–93[7]). His interpretation of the doctrine of rebirth, which has become influential with many Thai scientists (over half of whom no longer believe in life after death:

[7] Buddhadāsa, 1971, 1989; Jackson, 2003; Keown and Prebish, 2007: 160–1; Queen and King, 1996: 147–93; Swearer, 1995: 132–6.

Gosling, 1976), was that it only refers to a series of states within one life (Seeger, 2005). Each time the thought of 'I' arises, one is 'reborn', but one's aim should be to attain a new kind of selfless, Nirvāṇic living, beyond the birth and death of ego-thoughts. He criticized religious giving in order to get good karmic results in a future life as more like a business deal than real giving (*BP*.33). Buddhadāsa translated some Mahāyāna *Sūtras* into Thai, and the art he used for spiritual education was drawn from various Buddhist traditions and also from other religions. He said that both *Dhamma* and God, properly understood, refer to a reality beyond concepts. While his interpretation of Buddhism was a this-worldly one, he was critical of other this-worldly activities such as the involvement of monks in development projects, which he saw as inappropriate. He advocated a kind of spiritual 'Dhammic Socialism' and influenced other progressive Thai thinkers, such as the social critic Sulak Sivaraksa,[8] who have sought social justice and the protection of both traditional Siamese culture and the natural environment from corrosion by international capitalist trends. Opposing such people are those who have emphasized economic reliance on the West, close military links with the United States and a preference for strong, military-backed if not military-led government.

A leading, much-respected scholar-monk is Prayudh Payutto (1939–; Mackenzie, 2007: 51–2; Seeger, 2005), who is author of many studies that effectively present classical Theravāda Buddhist ideas and apply them to problems arising from modern life, with its need for greater co-operation and respect for nature.[9] Popular practice of Buddhism in terms of temporary ordination and attendance at the local *wat* (temple) has been in decline, but other, new activities and forms have flourished. Pilgrimage tours by bus have brought increased patronage to temples associated with famous monks, and radio talks and tapes have brought a national audience to certain monks (Baker and Phongpaichit, 2009: 225).

Two new Buddhist movements are Wat Phra Dhammakāya and Santi Asoke, which draw mainly urban followers (Mackenzie, 2007). Both seek a reinvigoration of Buddhist practice, and, while having a monastic core, offer greater scope for lay practice than in Thai Buddhism in general. The first has remained more mainstream, while the second has become relatively marginalized. Both have been criticized by the *Saṅgha* authorities and by Prayudh Payutto.

[8] Keown and Prebish, 2007: 692–3; Queen and King, 1996: 195–235.

[9] He has had various monastic titles (Swearer, 1995: 139–40); his works include Rājavaramuni, 1990; Payutto, 1993, 1994a, 1994b, 1995; see www.buddhanet/cmdsg/payutto.htm.

Wat Phra Dhammakāya is a fast-growing, efficiently organized modern movement that uses videos and a satellite TV channel to draw people to it, and attracts many donations from its often well-off followers, who include members of the political elite, the military and the royal family. It is very active in the Buddhist Associations of the major Thai universities and is centred on a large modern temple on the outskirts of Bangkok. This is part of an 800-acre site with the ability to cater for thousands of visitors at weekends and festivals, sometimes reaching 200,000. The temple is the largest in Thailand in terms of numbers of inhabitants: as of 2006, it had 600 monks, 300–400 novices,[10] 700 residential full-time lay-disciple volunteers, 1,000 paid officials, and many further volunteers that it can call on (Mackenzie, 2007: 41). It also has over 60,000 committed lay meditators (Mackenzie, 2007: 94).

Visitors and lay residents dress in white, and order, efficiency and convenience are emphasized. The movement focuses on a particular meditation technique and it is emphasized that it is best to meditate in a group, whether at Wat Phra Dhammakāya, linked up to it through the internet, or in a local Dhammkāya group (Mackenzie, 2007: 33–4). Training courses in ethics and in the meditation method are given, and there is an aspiration to spread Dhammakāya meditation around the world.

The meditation method used is a form of that taught by Luang Phaw Sot (1885–1959), abbot of Wat Paknam in Bangkok. He saw himself as having rediscovered the lost enlightenment method used in early Buddhism, focused on finding *Nirvāṇa* as a subtle, bright body hidden within the human body.[11] He taught the method from 1915, as well as emphasizing strict monastic discipline and having a reputation as a healer. One of his key disciples was the illiterate nun Khun Yai Chan, and among those she taught were two graduates, who ordained to become Phra Dhammachayo and Phra Dattacheewo. These two founded what was to became Wat Phra Dhammakāya in 1970, with Dhammachayo as its abbot, and later formed the lay Dhammakāya Foundation.

The Wat Phra Dhammakāya meditation method (Mackenzie, 2007: 102–4) makes much use of *samatha*-based techniques. It typically uses the *mantra Sammā Arahaṃ* (perfect *Arahat*) and visualization of a crystal sphere, initially in front of one, and then at a nostril and various points down to the 'centre' of the body at a place just above the navel. The first aim

[10] Respectively 800 and 1,000 during the annual 'rains' retreat.

[11] When the *Satipaṭṭhāna Sutta* talks of contemplating 'body (just) in (regard to) body' (*M*.I.56), he saw it as about contemplating a subtle body within the body.

is to suspend the hindrances and attain access concentration focused on a bright *nimitta* at this point (see p. 328). Focusing on the image's centre brings forth more refined images, then the first *jhāna* is attained, and some *vipassanā* stages. Then increasingly subtle inner bodies, like Buddha-images, are seen, which correspond to deeper levels of *samatha*, followed by bodies corresponding to the kinds of Noble persons, until finally an *Arahat*'s radiant, unconditioned *Dhamma-kāya*, or *Dhamma*-body, is said to be found within: an inner Buddha-nature, which allows experience of *Nirvāṇa*. The 'sphere (*āyatana*) of *Nirvāṇa*' is seen as a subtle physical realm, around 1,400 million miles across, but accessible by an *Arahat* from within his or her body, being where enlightened beings eternally exist as individuals with self-awareness. In a key monthly ritual, fruit is offered to them (Mackenzie, 2007: 46, 48, 98–9).[12] *Nirvāṇa* is controversially seen as one's true 'Self' (Williams, 2009: 125–8): the non-Self teaching being seen as about letting go of what is *not* Self, and finding what truly *is* Self, as in some interpretations of the *Tathāgata-garbha* doctrine in the Mahāyāna (see pp. 143–4). Indeed, a Dhammakāya website states: 'the Tathagata Garbha is The Dhammakaya or the Body of Enlightenment . . . inside our body'.[13]

A myth that some in Wat Phra Dhammakāya subscribe to is of an ongoing cosmic struggle between the forces of the 'Black *Dhammakāya*', led by Māra, and the 'White *Dhammakāya*', who sought to create our world as a good realm. The emphasis on large numbers of people meditating together is in part because this is seen to help overcome the influence of Māra in spoiling this world.

Wat Phra Dhammakāya offers success based on good karma generated by donating to the movement, belonging to an efficient, reforming organization that is working to overcome forces of evil in the world, and a meditation method that starts to bring its results fairly quickly (Mackenzie, 2007: 56–67). Rory Mackenzie characterizes it as 'a Buddhist prosperity movement with some millenarian and fundamentalist characteristics' (2007: 96). It is a form of 'Buddhist modernism', part of the 'revival of meditation', and has some continuities with esoteric or 'tantric' Theravāda' (see pp. 201–2; Mackenzie, 2007: 94–5).

As the movement grew, it came in for negative publicity (Swearer, 1995: 114–15; Mackenzie, 2007: 49–54) concerning:

- Too much emphasis on specified benefits of specific donations to the temple (Mackenzie, 2007: 43, 46), which seemed to critics like 'religious

[12] Though Luang Phaw Sot is only seen as reborn in the Tusita heaven (Mackenzie, 2007: 49).

[13] www.dhammakaya.net/en/docs/middle-way-and-dhammakaya.

consumerism', though donors are typically seen to derive great joy from their giving.

- Too much emphasis on land and grand buildings, such that it had assets of over $40 million by 1995. However, the temple runs a big operation and uses some of its funds to aid schools and temples in southern Thailand, an area of tension with the Muslim minority. It has been praised for helping people give up smoking and drinking, and in 1995 produced a CD-ROM of the Pali Canon, in co-operation with the Pali Text Society, Oxford.
- In 1999, Dhammachayo was charged with personally keeping various parcels of land which had been donated to the temple; but while he had to hand over abbotship of Wat Phra Dhammakāya to Dattacheewo, the charges then seem to have been dropped. Dhammachayo remains the president of the Dhammakāya Foundation, and is still regarded as leader of the movement.

While Wat Phra Dhammakāya has been controversial, it has reached an accommodation with mainstream Thai Buddhism, of which it remains one part, and has been helping to ensure this by offering administrative help to the aged monks of the *Saṅgha* authorities. Other forms of Luang Phaw Sot's Dhammakāya meditation are also practised at the continuing Wat Paknam and the Dhammakāya Buddhist Meditation Foundation and its Wat Luang Phaw Sot Dhammakāyaram, which was founded in 1991 by some who were dissatisfied with aspects of Wat Phra Dhammakāya.

Santi Asoke[14] is a smaller new Buddhist movement, with around 10,000 members. Its practice is not one that emphasizes formal meditation – though it includes brief periods of reflection, or of *samatha* to develop some calm. It focuses on morality, especially vegetarianism, and constant mindfulness: of actions, how they impact on the world and others, and any defilements that they may express. It aims at a peaceful life, free of suffering, which is associated with possessions, attachment and unjust practices in society, such as corruption. While it does not make much reference to Buddhist texts, the first seven factors of the Eight-factored Path are all seen as aspects of *sīla*, moral virtue, and the right concentration factor is seen as a peaceful state that arises from these, which then facilitates defilement-cutting insight. *Nirvāṇa*, regarded as attainable by laypeople, is seen as a peaceful, ego-free state of mind, enabling effortless work for others.

[14] Heikkilä-Horn, 1997; Mackenzie, 2007; Swearer, 1995: 136–9.

The movement is focused on temple-based communities, of which it had nine by 2007. These run vegetarian restaurants, grow their own organic food, manufacture such things as herbal medicines and tofu, and have shops selling goods at a low profit margin, with the original cost of the goods clearly marked (Mackenzie, 2007: 149–50). The emphasis is on a simple, moral life-style, in harmony with nature, and with daily tasks done with great care, and avoiding any waste. Community members, monastic or lay, mostly eat just once a day, and walk barefoot. Lay members dress in simple, blue peasant attire, though they are typically not poor peasants but better-off farmers, urban merchants and small businessmen/traders, especially of Chinese or Sino-Thai background.

Santi Asoke has its own printing press, is active on local radio stations, and runs schools which cover the normal syllabus as well as emphasizing collaborative working, art, music and Buddhist ethics, with much content negotiated between teachers and pupils. It also runs camps for children, where they learn self-discipline and helpfulness, and programmes for young adults emphasizing ecology, natural farming and Buddhism (Mackenzie, 2007: 136–8).

The movement has been influenced by Gandhian ideas of self-sufficiency and simple living (as has Sarvōdaya Śramadana in Sri Lanka), the Israeli *kibbutz* ideal and some of the ideas of Buddhadāsa, though it has also criticized him for insufficient attention to putting his ideas into practice. Unlike Wat Phra Dhammakāya, the movement is anti-capitalist and anti-consumerist. It is critical of the individualism and materialism present in Thai culture, and was thus pleased when, during the 1997 financial crisis, a televised speech by the king talked of a need for Thailand to be more self-sufficient and have a simpler economy. In general, consumerist materialism is now seen in a more critical light in Thailand than it had previously come to be seen.

Santi Asoke has a more communal approach than Dhammakāya, as well as being more open to outside enquirers, and less fundamentalist (Mackenzie, 2007: 189). It will only accept financial donations from those whom it knows well, and it has an egalitarian, democratic emphasis. Abbots of centres are appointed each year by their monks, and centres have quite flat hierarchies, each being run by an elected committee. The 'will of the group' is seen as important, and develops a strong atmosphere of discipline. Mackenzie characterizes Santi Asoke as a kind of 'ascetic/prophetic, utopian movement with legalistic tendencies', in whose communities members feel that they 'experience justice and support for living morally upright lives ... in contrast to their experience in mainstream Thai society' (Mackenzie, 2007: x, cf. 165, 172).

The 'legalistic', somewhat regimented aspects of the movement are seen in the fact that members have books in which they chart their ability to live up to, and failings from, the eight precepts (see p. 278), which are regarded as needing to be followed in both obvious and subtler ways to do with attitudes and mental states. This can arguably lead to 'grasping at rules and observances' and guilt feelings (Mackenzie, 2007: 165–7). Membership of a Santi Asoke community goes through seven formal stages, from temporary guest to ordination, which all takes a bare minimum of three years, three months (Mackenzie, 2007: 148–9). Unlike mainstream Buddhism, which sees possessions as unproblematic for laypeople if they are morally earnt, and shared with others, Santi Asoke sees possessions as tending to be problematic in themselves, and thus it has a simple, austere life-style for both monastics and laity.

In 2005, Santi Asoke had 105 *samaṇas*, their alternative name for their *bhikkhu* / monks, and 27 *sikkhamats*, or ten-precept nuns, with 9,929 registered members in 2001, and several thousand more in sympathy with it. Its size was stable rather than growing (Mackenzie, 2007: 136). The *sikhamats*, while being restricted in number to one-fifth of the ordained, have a much higher status than most Thai nuns, and have a very respected place in Santi Asoke (Mackenzie, 2007: 145–8).

Santi Asoke's founder is the monk Bodhirak, a hard-working, straight-talking and charismatic man of working-class Sino-Thai background (Mackenzie, 2007: 115–30). He is very accessible, much more so than the reclusive Dhammakāya leader Dhammachayo, and some see him as a *Bodhisattva*, and/or *Arahat*. He ordained in 1970 and soon had a reputation for strict discipline and being critical of those he saw as lacking this. Originally a Dhammayuttika Nikāya monk, then a Mahā Nikāya (see p. 293) monk, he became resistant to being labelled as either. He emphasized self-effort and reason, and was critical of what he saw as superstitious aspects of mainstream Thai Buddhism. By 1976 there were three centres of his 'Asoke group', and by 1979 the monastic authorities became critical of his approach, which did not fit well with mainstream, state-regulated Thai Buddhism.

A famous Santi Asoke member has been Major General Chamlong Srimuang, an ascetic character who was governor of Bangkok (1985–9 and 1990–2), strong on anti-corruption, and founder of the Phalang Dhamma political party. The association of Santi Asoke with a political party added to existing criticism of it and, in 1989, after Bodhirak had refused to come more into line with the regulations of the ecclesiastical authorities, they moved to disrobe him. He and his monastics agreed to wear dark brown robes, rather than ones of the usual colour, to stop using the honorific title Phra, used for monks, and 'lost' their existing identity cards as monks, but refused to go through a monastic disrobing ceremony. In 1995, he and his monastic followers were given suspended sentences for purporting to be monks when the state did not recognize them as such. The movement remains a somewhat marginalized, though accepted, part of the Thai religious scene.

Chamlong Srimuang, at one time the deputy prime minister, is now a prominent member of the People's Alliance for Democracy (the 'yellow shirts', yellow being a colour associated with the king), which opposes the return of the deposed former prime minister Thaksin Shinawatra, and the policies of his supporters. Thaksin, who became a billionaire through his telecommunication companies, was ousted by the military in 2006 on grounds of corruption. He had developed close links with Dhammakāya from 2001, and is supported by the 'red shirts', mainly working-class and rural people who value what he did for the reduction of rural poverty and the provision of health-care. In 2009, 'yellow shirt' protestors took over Bangkok airport, and in 2010, 'red shirt' ones took over areas of central Bangkok, demanding early elections.

The ill-health of the much-revered aged King Bhumibol (b. 1927, r. 1946–), who has often intervened to counsel moderation and compromise in Thai politics, is something that puts a question mark over the future stability of Thai politics, given that his son is less well respected. Among the factors making for a degree of conflict is some Muslim insurgency in Southern Thailand.

Burma[15]

The great Burmese ruler King Mindon (r. 1853–78) gave much support to Buddhism and presided over the 'fifth' Great Council (1868–71). At this, different editions of the Pali Canon were cross-checked, and an orthodox version was inscribed on 729 stone slabs. The British conquered lower Burma in 1853, and in 1885 they took over the whole country, leading to some weakening in monastic discipline, due to the ending of the royal prerogative of purging the *Saṅgha*. The 1920s saw both the development

[15] On this, see Bechert and Gombrich, 1984: 147–58; King, 1964; Spiro, 1971; Swearer, 1995.

of more accessible forms of *vipassanā* meditation (see p. 337), to teach to the laity, and agitation by monks in favour of independence. While monastic leaders saw political activity as against the *Vinaya*, it was difficult to prevent some of the younger monks from developing a taste for it. Discontented urban monks have therefore been active for or against certain parties or policies since this time. Leaders of the independence movement drew on a mix of socialism and nationalism, due to the dislike of Indian capitalists and landlords introduced by the British. After being ravaged by Japanese–British fighting in the Second World War, independence was gained in 1948, and U Nu, the first prime minister, favoured a form of socialism as a means to the Buddhist goal of a just and peaceful society which did not encourage greed.

In 1956, Southern Buddhists celebrated *'Buddha Jayanti'*, seen as 2,500 years since the Buddha's death, when a Buddhist revival had come to be expected. U Nu presided over the 'sixth' Great Council (1954–6), held to commemorate this. Monks from a number of Theravāda countries attended, a new edition of the Pali Canon was produced – the '*Chaṭṭha Saṅgāyana*' one – and efforts were made to stimulate Buddhist education, missionary endeavours and social welfare activities. Many 'meditation centres' for monks and laity were established, and this development later spread to Sri Lanka and Thailand. Of particular note was U Ba Khin (see p. 337), a layman who was a prominent and respected government official. Even in his seventies, he energetically combined his government work with the running of an International Meditation Centre, teaching *vipassanā* meditation to laypeople from Burma and abroad.

In 1962, a *coup* brought a semi-Marxist military government to power, which has expended much energy on warfare with various minority ethnic groups fighting for independence from the Burmese. The population is 68 per cent Bamar/Burmese, 9 per cent Shan and 7 per cent Karen/Kayin, but there are over a hundred recognized ethnic groups. Eighty-nine per cent of the population are Buddhist, with 4 per cent Christian and 4 per cent Muslim. Persecution of 'foreigners' by the military junta led to an exodus of 300,000 Burmese Indians around 1964, and persecution of the Rohingya Muslims has led to many fleeing to Bangladesh. Christians, who make up about a third of the Karen people, are also disadvantaged. The Karen have been the largest of twenty minority groups conducting insurgency against the government since 1950, with 140,000 mostly Karen refugees in Thailand by 2006.

The junta set up a one-party state which sought to control almost all aspects of the economy. It has not been overtly anti-Buddhist, though, and its isolationist policies may have helped to preserve a devoutly Buddhist culture from the forces of secularization and tourism. Nevertheless, increasing discontent with the country's poor economic performance, and the government's dictatorial methods, led to mass anti-government demonstrations in 1988. Monks took part in these, and the public placed the administration of many towns and cities in the hands of committees of monks, due to the breakdown of government authority there. The government crackdown on demonstrators killed thousands, and a new military government called itself the 'State Law and Order Restoration Council' (SLORC; from 1997, the 'State Peace and Development Council') and in 1989 changed the name of the country to the 'Union of Myanmar'. It later (2005) moved the capital from Rangoon/ Yangon to a new site it has constructed near a logging town. In 1990 free elections were held for the first time in thirty years, and the National League for Democracy, led by Aung San Suu Kyi (daughter of a hero who helped gain Burmese independence; Keown and Prebish, 2007: 68–9), won 80 per cent of the parliamentary seats. However, SLORC refused to step down, annulled the result and placed Aung San under strict house arrest, under which she has remained for most of the period since then until November 2010. She practises *vipassanā* meditation, is a revered figurehead of the democracy movement, and was awarded the Nobel Peace Prize in 1991, which she was only allowed to collect in 2012.

While, in the early 1990s, the government allowed limited economic liberalization and made ceasefire agreements with most of the ethnic guerrilla groups, it uses forced labour in its campaigns against the others. It runs what is in effect a police state, whose armed forces number almost half a million, and which spends the least percentage of its GDP on health-care of any country in the world. In 2007, there were again monk-led demonstrations, sparked by a sudden fuel-price increase, which were then suppressed. In 2008, a cyclone devastated parts of the country, and the government delayed United Nations help as it did not like foreign agencies operating in the country. The government has been writing a new constitution, under which new elections were held in November 2010, but with Aung San disqualified from participation, as she had been married to a foreigner, an English academic; the main opposition party boycotted the election. The patience of the population with its government has been severely strained, but Buddhists know that all conditioned things change. Recent relative liberalisation has meant that in 2012 Aung San was allowed to be elected to parliament and travel abroad.

Laos, Cambodia, Vietnam and Yunnan

From 1893, Vietnam, Cambodia and Laos were all colonies of France, forming the union of Indochina, until 1953 in Laos and Cambodia, and 1955 in Vietnam. In Laos (Harris, 1999: 153–72), most of the lowland Lao, around 60 per cent of the population, are Southern Buddhists, but most of the fifty or so other ethnic groups follow some form of animism. The Communist Pathet Lao came to power in 1975, after warring with the Royalist government. In this conflict, monks often joined the Pathet Lao as medics, porters and propaganda agents. The Pathet Lao have not subjected Buddhism to great repression, but have sought to control the *Saṅgha*, using it as a tool through which to spread and reinforce its ideology, as well as requiring monks to be teachers and health workers. Since the 1990s, the government has followed the Chinese lead of economic liberalization along with continuing political authoritarianism. Yet Buddhist ideas and practices remain strong in the country, such that politicians need to look to it for continuing sources of legitimacy, now mainly seen in nationalistic terms, and many political leaders retain an association with Buddhism. Buddhism is regaining its social position and influence, though the *Saṅgha* remains controlled by the ruling Lao People's Revolutionary Party.

In 1971, the Vietnam War spilt over into the once tranquil and gentle country of Cambodia (Harris, 2005, 1999: 54–78). Ninety-five per cent of the population follow Southern Buddhism, including a fair strand of 'tantric Theravāda' (see pp. 201–2). Independence brought regimes favouring 'Buddhist socialism', but the devastation wrought by American bombing helped usher in the Khmer Rouge terror of 1975–9, when this fanatical Communist regime sought to destroy previous civilization and start its own peasant-based 'utopia' from scratch. The cities were emptied and many people were murdered or died of starvation: over a million people were killed and half a million fled the country; 63 per cent of the monks died, and the rest were forced to disrobe or flee. Only 100 Cambodian-ordained monks had survived when invasion by the Vietnamese established a more tolerant government. From 1979 Cambodia had a Vietnamese-backed government, harassed by a range of Cambodian forces including remnants of the Khmer Rouge. In 1993, aided by the United Nations, it became a democracy and a constitutional monarchy. By 1990, there were 10,000 monks and 6,500 novices. Socially activist forms of Buddhism have flourished, with annual peace marches, once led by the charismatic Mahā Ghosānanda (1929–2007), supporting reconciliation and environmental protection (Harvey, 2000: 278–83; Keown and Prebish, 2007: 483–4).

In Vietnam, where the Buddhism is mainly Mahāyāna, Southern Buddhism is present as a minority, with sixty-four temples as of 1997, especially in the south, close to Cambodia. Numbers grew from the 1940s due to Buddhist modernization movements which developed an interest in the Pali Canon and Theravāda meditation. In the Yunnan province of China, Southern Buddhism is still found in an isolated region bordering Laos and Burma, among the 1.2 million Dai people. The main threat to their culture is their being swamped by an influx of Han Chinese.

India, Bangladesh and Nepal

Since the nineteenth century, both Western and Indian scholars studied the Buddhist heritage of India through archaeology and textual research. From the 1890s, popular works on Buddhism appeared, and the poet Rabindranath Tagore included Buddhist themes in his plays. Dharmapāla's Mahā Bodhi Society (MBS) developed centres in many cities and helped raise India's awareness of Buddhism. It gradually made some converts among educated Indians, and an ex-MBS member worked to convert some lower-caste people in the south. In the 1920s and 1930s, the MBS was associated with the scholarly and popular writings of three notable Indian scholar-monks, R. Sankrityayan, A. Kausalyayan and J. Kashyap.

The reawakening of Indian interest in Buddhism has led to the publication of many books on the religion. Some secularized intellectuals have become attracted to its 'rationalism' and its non-support of the caste system, but do not usually formally become Buddhists. Buddhism tends to be seen as part of Hinduism, whose strongly social nature retains its hold. The first prime minister of independent India, Jawaharlal Nehru, was such an 'intellectual' Buddhist. These are also found among the mainly middle-class people, of various religious affiliations, who attend ten-day 'meditation camps', which especially teach the *vipassanā* method of S. N. Goenka (see p. 337) as a means to a harmonious way of life, and this trend can be seen as a form of Buddhist modernism.

The most numerous 'new' Buddhists in India are ex-members of certain 'untouchable' castes, who are followers of Dr B. R. Ambedkar (1891–1956[16]). Such 'Ambedkar' Buddhists, numbering around 7.1 million, are mainly

[16] Berkwitz, 2010: 192–6; Keown and Prebish, 2007: 24–6; Ling, 1980: 67–135; Queen and King, 1996: 45–71.

concentrated in the western state of Maharashtra. The untouchable castes, known as 'scheduled castes' since 1935, comprise traditionally economically depressed and socially shunned groups, placed below even the *Śūdras* in the Hindu social system. They did dirty jobs such as street cleaning, and were looked down on, especially by Brahmins, as less than human. Ambedkar, though himself from this background, managed to get a good education, in India and abroad due to his intelligence, support from his father and winning a scholarship. He became a lawyer and, from the 1920s, worked for the emancipation of the untouchables from their degradation within Hinduism. He saw many social evils in India, and regarded the caste system as the root of them all. In 1936, he formed the Scheduled Castes Federation to help overcome Brahmin political power, which he saw as underpinning the caste system. As Minister of Law in the first post-independence government, he ensured that the constitution protected the rights of scheduled caste members, so that negative discrimination on grounds of caste became illegal. It still occurs, however, and members of scheduled castes now prefer to call themselves 'Dalits' or 'the Suppressed'.

In 1935, Ambedkar had declared he would convert from Hinduism to another religion, this being the way forward for scheduled caste members. He was courted by different religions, but rejected Christianity and Islam due to their non-Indian origin, and because their Indian members were affected by caste attitudes. He also found Christians rather individualistic and disliked Islam for its tendency to intolerance and its enforced seclusion of women in *purdah*. While he was also attracted to Sikhism, in 1950 he chose Buddhism, which he regarded as a rational and egalitarian religion, with emphases on love, equality and spiritual freedom. He wanted to avoid such things as expenditure on activities for generating karmic fruitfulness, however, and saw himself as a 'neo-Buddhist'. For him, Buddhism was a social gospel whose monks the Buddha had intended to be the torch-bearers of a new ideal society. They should therefore be 'social workers and social preachers', like Christian missionaries, and teach Buddhism as a means to human dignity and a democratic society. In 1956, Ambedkar and around 500,000 scheduled caste members converted to Buddhism at a mass public 'consecration' ceremony. Other mass conversions followed, and conversions still continue on a smaller scale, for example 5,000 in a 2007 ceremony in Mumbai. Ambedkar Buddhism focuses on the moral reform of the individual and society. It stresses devotion, but not meditation, and Ambedkar himself is taken as a fourth 'refuge', being regarded as a *Bodhisattva*. Its teachings are akin to those of modernist Southern Buddhism.

Ambedkar Buddhists are mostly ex-members of the Mahar and Jatav castes, and in fact now tend to be treated as a new (low) caste, such that they have not broken the mould in the eyes of others. Nevertheless, conversion has meant that they have overcome their sense of inferiority, and experienced a great enhancement of their dignity. They have been keen for educational advancement, and have experienced economic betterment, for example by greatly cutting down on the expense traditionally entailed by such things as weddings. These Buddhists have had the task of developing a knowledge of their newly adopted religion, a task which was not without its difficulties at first. The movement is mainly led by lay officials, who have undergone six months' training. By 1970, there were around forty monks, but training facilities for them were inadequate, so that few were learned. By around 2009, the number of monks had risen to around 1,000 (Berkwitz, 2010: 196). Since 1979, the Trailoka Bauddha Mahasangha Sahayaka Gana (in 2010 renamed Triratna Bauddha Mahasangha), an offshoot of the UK-based Friends of the Western Buddhist Order (see pp. 445–6), has also been working in India among Dalit Buddhists in social welfare and Buddhist education activities (Queen and King, 1996: 73–120).

The 2001 census for India showed that the 7.95 million Buddhists made up 0.8 per cent of the 1,028.6 million population. Their distribution is as follows, showing, for each area, their number, their percentage of the population there, and then their percentage of Buddhists in India:

- west, centre and north, where most Buddhists are Ambedkarites: Maharashtra 5.83m., 6% of population, 73.4% of Buddhists in India; Karnataka 0.3m., 0.6%, 3.8%; Madhya Pradesh 0.2m., 0.3%, 2.5%; Uttar Pradesh 0.3m., 0.2%, 3.8%.
- northern Himālayan regions where Northern Buddhists are mainly found: Ladakh (a region of Jammu and Kashmir) 0.128m., 47.4%, 1.6%; Himachal Pradesh 0.07m., 1%, 0.9% – its Lahaul-Spiti district is mainly Buddhist (33,224) and the Dalai Lama and some Tibetans live in Dharamsāla; Sikkim 0.15m., 28%, 2%; northern West Bengal 0.24m., 0.2%, 3%.
- North-eastern states close to Burma (Arunchal Pradesh, Tripura, Mizoram, Assam), where there are Southern Buddhists and a few of the Northern tradition (Ling, 1980: 50–8): 0.374m., 1.2%, 4.7%.

Buddhist pilgrims from many countries now visit sites associated with the Buddha's life in India, particularly Bodh-Gayā, the scene of the Buddha's enlightenment. Here there are temples or monasteries built by Buddhists from Bhutan, Burma, China, Japan, Nepal, Sikkim, Sri Lanka, Thailand, Tibet and Vietnam, in a variety of national styles, and a school for local children. The local villagers have also started to turn to Buddhism. In an important sense, Buddhism began at Bodh-Gayā, and it is fitting that this should now be a microcosm of the Buddhist world.

In Bangladesh there are about one million mainly Southern Buddhists (0.7 per cent of the 2009 population of 162.2m.), especially in a more thinly populated area, the Chittagong Hill Tracts (Berkwitz, 2010: 184–5). In recent years, however, these people have been suffering repression, being pushed off their land by hydro-electric schemes and settlement by the majority Muslim Bengalis, backed by the power of the Bangladeshi army. This may be due both to population pressures and to a response to harassment of Muslims by the Burmese government.

In Nepal, Buddhism has mostly remained as a junior partner in a syncretism of the tantric forms of Hinduism and Buddhism.[17] Renewal began in the 1930s, however, when Nepali Buddhists met monks from Burma and Sri Lanka working for the revival of Buddhism in India. In 1951, Nepal opened itself to the outside world, and the government pressure towards Hinduization abated. Southern Buddhist missions entered the country, so that the Theravāda is now a small but growing and very active religion, with an indigenous *Saṅgha* of monks, ten-precept and, since 1997, some *bhikkhunī* nuns. As of 2001, there were 78 monks, 94 novices and 118 Theravāda nuns in the country, with 81 monasteries and 17 nunneries (LeVine and Gellner, 2005: 13).

Malaysia and Indonesia

In Malaysia, Islam is the official religion, but Buddhism is the dominant element in the religious mix of the Chinese (76 per cent of whom are Buddhist), who make up 24 per cent of the population, having arrived mainly in the nineteenth century. Buddhism of a Thai variety also exists near the border with Thailand. Missionaries from Sri Lanka became active in the twentieth century, with converts being won especially since K. Sri Dhammananda arrived in 1951 (d. 2006) and became a driving force behind a Buddhist revival. Theravāda doctrine has been added to Chinese practice, and the 1980s saw a surge of interest in Burmese *vipassanā* practice, as well as the arrival of Tibetan, Taiwanese and Korean groups, the Order of Interbeing (see pp. 149, 412) and Sōka Gakkai. Malaysian Theravāda has a strong focus on education, youth and welfare activities, and an ecumenical engagement with non-sectarian lay groups (Drew, 2011). There are 600 to 700

[17] Bechert and Gombrich, 1984: 108–14; Berkwitz, 2010: 181–4, 203–4.

Buddhist monks of various traditions in the country, with the internet World Buddhist Directory listing, in June 2011, 197 groups, centres or temples: 66 Theravāda, 35 Mahāyāna (though many Chinese temples may not appear in the listing), 44 Vajrayāna and 52 non-sectarian/mixed.

The visit of Western Theosophists to Indonesia in 1883 reawakened an interest in Buddhism among both the Chinese, who make up about 3 per cent of the population, and the predominantly Muslim Indonesians, who have always had a taste for mysticism (Bechert, 1981). Buddhist missions followed from Sri Lanka (1929) and Burma (1934). In 1955 Ashin Jinarakkhita (1923–2002), a Chinese monk ordained in Burma, returned to Indonesia. Theravāda monasteries began to be built, helped by the interest aroused by the international celebration of *Buddha Jayanti*. Ordinations and many conversions followed from among the people of eastern Java who still adhered to the Śiva–Buddha syncretism, and also from the Chinese. In 1965, as a result of an attempted Communist coup, the government outlawed all organizations that doubted or denied the existence of God. This posed a problem for the 'non-theistic' Theravāda Buddhism. Jinarakkhita proposed that the Buddhist 'God' was the *Ādi*-Buddha, the primeval Buddha of the region's previous Mantranaya Buddhism, while more orthodox Theravādins said that *Nirvāṇa*, the 'unborn', was their 'God'. In general, the Buddhism favoured by Jinarakkhita has been somewhat syncretistic. While predominantly Theravādin in teaching, it uses some Sanskrit and Javanese texts, includes reference to some Mahāyāna Buddhas and *Bodhisattvas* in its devotion, and draws on elements of Chinese Buddhist ritual. The increase in Buddhist activity in Indonesia has led to greater activity among Chinese Buddhists, who make up the majority of Indonesian Buddhists, and a revival in Buddhist aspects of the Hindu-dominated syncretistic religion on the island of Bali. More traditional Theravāda was strengthened in 1970 by a Thai mission which started an indigenous *Saṅgha*. In the 2000 census, 3.5 per cent of the population were Buddhist or 'other', which will include Daoists – suggesting 8 million in 2009, when the estimated population of Indonesia was 230 million.

EASTERN BUDDHISM

It is difficult to give a figure for the number of 'Buddhists' of this tradition, due to traditional multi-religion allegiance, the different kinds of religious 'belonging', and the effects of Communism in China and North Korea. However, a round total of 360 million seems a reasonable estimate for Eastern Buddhism.

Table 6 *Number of Eastern Buddhists in Asia*

– Republic of China (excluding 5.4m. of Tibetans, 5.2m. Mongolians and Monguor, and 1.2m. Dai), 228m.?[a] (17.3% of the 1,319m. non-Tibetan/Mongol/Monguor or Dai population).	Minority populations exist in:
– Japan, 52m. (41% of 127.4m.).	– Indonesia, 4m.
– Vietnam, 43m. (50% of 85.3m.).	– The Philippines, 2.3m.
– South Korea, 10.9m. (23% of 47m.).	– Thailand, 1m.?
– Taiwan, 8m. (35% of 22.9m.).	– Brunei 0.03m.
– Malaysia, 5.5m. (19.2% of 28.25m.).	– Koreans in Uzbekistan, 0.055m.
– North Korea 2.5m.? (11%? of 23.3m.).	
– Singapore, 1.9m. (43% of 4.5m.).	
– Hong Kong, 0.7m. (10% of 7m.).	
– Macau, 0.14m. (30.7% of 0.46m.).	

[a] In July, 2010, Purdue University's Center on Religion and Chinese Society (www.purdue.edu/newsroom/research/2010/100726T-YangChina.html) reported that based on a 2007 survey, 18 per cent of the population is Buddhist: 239m.

Japan

In 1853, Japan was rudely awakened from an inward-looking period of its history by the gunboats of Admiral Perry, who demanded access for American traders. The Meiji restoration of 1868 led the country to end its feudal period, opening itself up to the outside world, and rapidly boosting its modernization. Shintō was separated from links with Buddhism, and a form of it known as 'State' or 'Shrine' Shintō was developed by the state, which saw it as the natural expression of Japanese life. In 1872, the government decreed that Buddhist clerics could marry (see p. 298). The end of state support, and attacks from Shintō, Christianity and Western science, stimulated a revival and modernization in some sections of Buddhism. Universities, schools and publishing houses were started, and monks and clergy visited Europe to study history and philosophy, and also for the critical study of Indian Buddhism, Sanskrit and Pali (Bechert and Gombrich, 1984: 229–30).

State Shintō was increasingly used as a vehicle for nationalism and militarism. The Japanese fought the Russians, colonized Taiwan and Korea, and then attacked China and finally America. Unfortunately, Buddhists sometimes supported such nationalistic excesses as a way in which Japan could oppose Western imperialism and 'revive' Asian cultures (Victoria, 1997). Defeat in the Second World War led to a discrediting of

State Shintō, and American occupation initiated a new, even more culturally and religiously open period of rapid social change and spiritual crisis.

Traditional Buddhism, which lost much income due to post-war land reforms, was initially slow to address the new situation. Nevertheless, many 'New Religions' have flourished or arisen to respond to the needs of the people (Hinnells, 1997: 497–504; Reader *et al.*, 1993: 121–52). These are lay-led movements which have their roots in Buddhism, Shintō or even Christianity. Their followers are mostly urban members of the upper lower classes, who feel economically and socially frustrated, dislike the anonymity of the sprawling cities, and feel the need for a modernized spiritual tradition to guide them in a confusing secularized world. The New Religions promise that religious practice will lead to health, wealth, personal fulfilment and success. Their leaders are focuses of great faith, a feature which draws on the traditional Japanese value of group loyalty. The major Buddhist New Religions give members both a sense of belonging and a sense of personal importance. They are organized into small discussion groups, where personal and social problems are discussed in the light of religious faith, but the groups are also part of well-organized and successful movements. The impressive headquarters of many of the New Religions are large and elegant structures of concrete and steel, which artistically blend traditional and modern forms.

A number of the most successful New Religions are based on the Nichiren sect. This is probably because of Nichiren's emphasis on reforming society, which appealed in the post-war period. The *Lotus Sūtra* also holds out the promise of earthly happiness to those who revere it, and gives prominence to the lay *Bodhisattva*. The most successful New Religion has been the Sōka Gakkai ('Value Creating Society'), founded in 1930.[18] It sees the teachings of Nichiren and the *Lotus Sūtra* as representing absolute truth, with Nichiren as the supreme Buddha, but regards values as having to be positively created, drawing on faith in the *Lotus Sūtra*. Basic values include respect for the dignity of all life, and the importance of karma.

The central practice of the movement is devout chanting, known as *gongyō*, for about half an hour in the morning and evening. The chanting is of sections of the *Lotus Sūtra* and especially of '*Nam-Myō-hō Ren-ge-kyō*' before the *gohonzon* (see p. 257), in which the presence of the 'Buddha Nichiren' is felt. Uttering *Nam* (adoration) is seen as summoning from within the revitalizing power of the universal law, or *Myō-hō* (True *Dharma*). *Ren-ge* (Lotus) is seen as the cause and effect of the emergence

[18] Prebish, 1999: 114–27; Queen and King, 1996: 365–400; Seager, 1999: 70–89.

of the Buddha-nature in terms of benefit, happiness and fulfilment. *Kyō* (*Sūtra*, literally a thread) is seen as the thread of eternal truth which links all life. Chanting is regarded as a way of overcoming obstacles in life, such as poverty, domestic disharmony and ill-health, and as a means to giving up drinking and smoking and to attaining happiness. It is seen as bringing out a person's Buddha-nature, in the form of enhanced compassion, courage, wisdom and vital life force, so as to generate a 'human revolution'. Practitioners say that it makes them more patient, clear-thinking, energetic, confident and positive. At first, chanting is for personal goals, but it then moves on towards helping to solve national and even world problems, such as an end to all war. Daily discussion meetings relate faith to everyday life.

The Sōka Gakkai sees all other religions and forms of Buddhism as false, and started off by seeing them as evil. Its rapid growth in the 1950s was due to the 'compassionate' urge to convert people from such errors, using an aggressive technique known as 'breaking and subduing' (*shakubuku*). In this, persuasion was followed by barrages of propaganda from a number of converters. Rival objects of worship were destroyed; dire warnings were given of troubles to come if the 'true faith' was not accepted, and economic sanctions were applied. Adverse reactions to this method have since led to its being progressively toned down. Daisaku Ikeda (1928–) became the movement's leader in 1960 and under him action for conversion was also directed beyond Japan. Sōka Gakkai sees its message as the hope of the world and herald of a new humanism, focusing on world peace, environmentalism, multiculturalism, religious dialogue and feminism.

The movement's original formal status was as a lay organization of the once small sub-sect Nichiren Shōshū ('True Nichiren Sect'), and it originally operated under the name 'Nichiren Shōshū' outside Japan. However, Nichiren Shōshū came to feel that its 'child' had become more powerful than it, and it was also critical of it for entering into dialogue with other religions, and no longer seeing them as evil teachings (Hinnells, 1997: 502–4). As a result, in 1991, a schism arose, so that the priests no longer provided *gohonzons* for Sōka Gakkai, in the form of certified copies of an original by Nichiren, and cut it off to fend for itself. Sōka Gakkai now sees such certified copies as unnecessary, and is known overseas as Sōka Gakkai International. SGI's website gives its 2005 membership as 1.723 million outside Japan, in 192 countries (1m. in Asia and Oceania, 352,000 in North America, 246,000 in South and Central America, 71,000 in Europe and 20,000 in Africa and the Middle East), and '8.72m households' in Japan. It does much to seek to foster peace and reconciliation in the world (Harvey, 2000: 273–4).

In line with Nichiren's ideal of the union of politics and religion, the Sōka Gakkai developed a political wing in 1964. This is known as the Kōmei-tō, or 'Clean Government' party, and has become the third or fourth largest in the Japanese Parliament. Since 1998, it has been known as the New Kōmei-tō party, after a 1994 split then reunification; it is now more centre-right than centre-left. While it severed formal links with Sōka Gakkai in 1970, it remains influenced by it, and attracts a similar membership. It has run Citizens' Livelihood Discussion Centres giving free legal counselling, and acts as a channel to government for grievances on such matters as housing, social security, education and pollution. Sōka Gakkai has also sponsored a labour union and student movement which seek to synthesize capitalist and socialist values.

In some ways Sōka Gakkai parallels the Thai Dhammakāya movement (Mackenzie, 2007: 67–74, 96). Both have a readily understood teaching, a prosperity now emphasis, excellent publicity, effective recruiting and fund-raising techniques, and offer a sense of belonging to a successful movement with global ambitions.

The Risshō-kōseikai, founded in 1938, combines faith in the *Lotus Sūtra* and Śākyamuni Buddha, honouring of ancestors and practice of ethical aspects of the Eight-factored Path and *Bodhisattva* perfections. In group counselling sessions, members confess their failings and receive guidance on life's problems, based on the *Lotus Sūtra* and the four True Realities for the Spiritually Ennobled. In 2010, it claimed 6.6 million members, with branches in twenty countries. Agon Shū focuses on early Buddhist teachings, as preserved in the Chinese *Āgama* texts, with an emphasis on liberation from bad karma through meditation. It also includes the idea of spirit possession, and has rituals in which sticks inscribed with prayers are burnt, for the benefit of ancestors and the participants (Hinnells, 1997: 501–2). Founded in 1978, it claims half a million members.

Aum Shinrikyo (now called Aleph), founded in 1986 by an ex-member of Agon Shū, is a syncretistic system drawing on elements of yoga, extreme asceticism, Hinduism, Vajrayāna Buddhism and Christianity, with prophecies of a coming world calamity.[19] A small cult, yet with very educated followers, it became infamous in 1995 when it killed twelve people by releasing sarin gas in the Tokyo subway system. In 2008, it was estimated to still have 1,650 members.

The older Buddhist sects, while still broadly serving the population through their conducting of funerals and memorial rites (Reader, 1991:

[19] Fowler, 1998; Hinnells, 1997: 506–8.

77–106), have to some extent been stimulated by the general atmosphere of modernization, and organized movements for the reinvigoration of lay practice. These include classes, lectures and discussions on Buddhism, organized pilgrimages, counselling services, kindergartens, Sunday schools, youth societies, Boy Scout troops and Zen meditation clubs. Many popular and scholarly Buddhist magazines and books exist, and there is much excellent scholarship on the historical and doctrinal roots of Buddhism.

Yet the consumer-orientation of contemporary Japanese society has produced much secularization. Most priests wear Western suits, and many do non-religious jobs to supplement their income. Especially in the countryside, support for Buddhism is currently on the decline, some temples are closing as priests' sons do not wish to continue the 'family business', perhaps because its income is reducing as local people move to the cities. Indeed even the city-focused 'New Religions' are now less thriving than they once were, partly due to the Aum Shinrikyo outrage (Reader, 2011).

A strand of thought which is evidence of a reformist questioning of traditional Buddhist beliefs has been 'Critical Buddhism' (see p. 145), led by two academics at a Sōtō Zen related university: Noriaki Hakamaya and Shirō Matsumoto (Hubbard and Swanson, 1997). They are very critical of a range of elements of Japanese Buddhism, along with the Chinese and to some extent Indian elements that have led to them, seeing the content of Buddhism as having been perverted in the process of attempts to preserve and transmit it. Consequently, they see much Zen as 'not Buddhism' – though Dōgen and aspects of Chinese Chan are less criticized. Their various targets are generally grouped under the heading of what they call '*dhātu-vāda*', a monistic view which sees everything as based on one fundamental substantial foundation. Key aspects of this are:

- The *Tathāgata-garbha* view, and related Japanese 'original/inherent enlightenment thought' (*hongaku shisō*; see p. 228), which the Critical Buddhists see as out of tune with the teachings of non-Self and Conditioned Arising, which they see as the marks of 'true Buddhism'.
- Rejection of discriminative thought and an emphasis on self-validating mystical experience, which the Critical Buddhists see as fostering a kind of authoritarianism that seeks to invalidate all criticism.
- The Japanese insistence on *Wa*, the harmony of all, which seems related to Huayan ideas, but which the Critical Buddhists see as fostering a smothering 'tolerance', conformism and social discrimination.

They are perhaps right in saying that Japanese Buddhism has undervalued the use of critical reasoning, but wrong in wanting to even reject elements of

Table 7 *Number of Buddhists in Japan by different criteria*

Criterion	*Result*	*Number of Buddhists*
1. Membership claimed by religious organizations	1985: *76%* of the 121m. population Buddhist, and also 95% Shintō (Reader, 1991: 6)	92m.
2. Have a Buddhist or Shintō shrine in the home	*61%* a Buddhist one, 60% a Shintō one, 45% both, 24% neither – so 80% of those with any home shrine have a Buddhist one (Reader, 1991: 7, from 1986 and 1988 sources)	73.8m.
3. Consider religious feelings important	~70% (Reader, 1991: 6, from a 1987 source)	Buddhists among 85m.
4. Professing a religious faith/belief	1983: *32%* of the 119.3m. population (Reader, 1991: 6). In a 1979 similar survey, for those who so professed, *78.4%* Buddhist, 3.3% Shintō (Hinnells, 1997: 493)	29.9m.
5. People who claimed active membership of a religious organization	1979 survey: *13.6%* (Hinnells, 1997: 492)	Buddhists among 15.6m.

early Buddhism that they feel do not accord with their somewhat narrow focus on non-Self and Conditioned Arising.

While there has been a decline in religious practice overall, Buddhism remains much the most influential religion. However, counting the number of 'Buddhists' is no easy matter, as this depends on the criterion used (see Table 7).

The figures in Table 7 show that many people draw on both Buddhism and Shintō. The high figures in row 1 arise because people may be counted as members simply due to traditional family affiliation; also they may be members of more than one Buddhist sect, whole families are counted when one member joins a religious group or temple, and these are not removed when affiliation ceases. Ian Reader (1991: 9) points out that the Sōtō Zen sect claimed 6,885,000 members in 1987, yet at the same time, only 287,000, approximately 4 per cent of this, could be counted as people who studied and expressed belief in Sōtō teachings. Similarly, 95 per cent of the population have some kind of Shintō affiliation, yet only 3 to 4 per cent can be counted as 'believers'. The Japanese level of religious activity – visiting shrines, collecting good luck charms there, praying and participating in religious events – is at a much higher level than religious cognitive belief (Reader, 1991: 9).

Given all this, if we take the average of 32 per cent (row 4: religious belief) and 70 per cent (row 3: religious feeling), then 51 per cent of the population is reasonably religious. If we then take 80 per cent (row 2: those with home shrines who have Buddhist ones) as the proportion of these who are Buddhist, then for the 2010 population of 127.4 million, this gives a figure of 52 million 'Buddhists'. In 2003, there were over 300,000 Buddhist clergy, and the number of Buddhist temples were: 30,000 Pure Land, 21,000 Zen, 15,000 Shingon, 14,000 Nichiren, 5,000 Tendai. Of the members claimed by the sects, the largest group was of the Nichiren sect.

The People's Republic of China

After the devastation of many temples and monasteries during the Christian-inspired Tai-ping (T'ai-p'ing) rebellion (1850–64), there was a modest revival in Chinese Buddhism. In the Republican period (1912–49), there was also something of an intellectual renaissance, led by Daixu (T'ai-hsü, 1899–1947), in an ideologically more open period free of Confucian dominance, and partly in response to well-organized Christian missionaries (Bechert and Gombrich, 1984: 211; Welch, 1968). There was revitalization in a number of monasteries, and contact was made with other Buddhists in Asia and the West. Dozens of urban lay Buddhist societies developed in the 1930s, concerned with education, social welfare and devotion. Buddhism remained very strong in some provinces, but new political ideas meant that young people often saw it as being irrelevant to the needs of modern China.

The triumph of the Communists in 1949 brought suppression and manipulation. *Saṅgha* numbers were decimated as all 'hereditary temples', and many large 'public monasteries', closed down because their income-producing lands were confiscated (Welch, 1972). Many of the monks had to support themselves by weaving, farming and running vegetarian restaurants. They were urged to see working in a Communist society as the true *Bodhisattva* way, and even to accept that killing the 'enemies of society' was compassionate. During the Cultural Revolution (1966–76), the Red Guards wrought great destruction, and all monasteries were closed, at least for a time. Since 1977, the general readjustment of policy in China has meant that temples have reopened, and, in 1980, ordination of monks (banned since 1957) was again permitted, with a state-funded Chinese Buddhist Academy opening to provide training seminaries (Sponberg, 1982). As of 1997, the country had around

200,000 Buddhist monks and nuns and 13,000 temples outside Tibetan areas.[20] In 1986, the cited number had been 28,000 monks and nuns, while in 1930, there had been 738,200 outside Tibet (Welch, 1967: 412–14). Lay activity has been renewed in certain regions, especially the provinces on the east coast. Buddhism has been seen as politically useful for making links with Buddhist countries, through the Chinese Buddhist Association, but Chinese universities now pursue the study of Buddhism, and Buddhists are increasingly coming to be valued for their contributions to society.[21] This is not the case, though, with Falun Gong, a new religious movement founded in 1992 that emphasizes *qigong* – a method of physical training and awareness-cultivation – the moral virtues of truthfulness, compassion and forbearance, and draws on Buddhist and Daoist ideas. By 1999, the government claimed it had seventy million followers, and banned it, no doubt as a locus of influence independent of government power. Its followers are predominantly female and elderly.

The *Saṅgha* has at times suffered from lack of income from land-rent, and at one time was not even allowed to charge for conducting rites for the dead. The government is now pushing for monasteries to be more self-sufficient, and their economies are becoming based on donations, invested endowment funds, small-scale businesses, entrance-fees (generally imposed by the government) and fees for such things as incense and rituals (e.g. Caple, 2010). In the context of the wholesale modernization of society, it is now the case that, 'Religion in China is thriving. The growth of Christianity is impressive [to 33m., 3.2 per cent] but Buddhist growth is extraordinary'.[22] The *China Daily* (7 Feb. 2007) said that 62 per cent of religious believers in the country were in the 16–39 age group, which indicates a good level of interest among younger people. In urban areas, new Buddhists are college-educated and upwardly mobile, looking for purpose in their lives and also ways to cope with the pressures of modernization. In 2007, on the site of a previous one in Changzhou, a 154-metre-high wooden pagoda was completed, the tallest in the world.

20 'Religious Statistics in the People's Republic of China', www2.kenyon.edu/Depts/Religion/Fac/Adler/Reln270/statistics.htm.

21 *China Daily*, 22 December 2006, 'Buddhists praised for contributions', www.chinadaily.com.cn/china/2006-12/22/content_765071.htm.

22 2010 Purdue University report: www.purdue.edu/newsroom/research/2010/100726T-YangChina.html.

Taiwan

On the island of Taiwan, the Nationalist Chinese government favours a revival of ancient Chinese culture, and Buddhism has benefited from this. New temples and monasteries have been built, Chan meditation is popular, there are Buddhist study groups in the universities and many Buddhist journals are published. There is a general stress on interpretations of Buddhism which see it as compatible with a modern outlook, and attempts to separate it from the 'superstitions' of popular folk religion. An influential trend is Renjian Fojiao, or 'Humanistic Buddhism', which emphasizes helping this world become a 'Pure Land' by compassionate action in it. A good example of this is the Tzu Chi Foundation, which is active in the fields of medicine, education and disaster relief (www.tzuchi.org/global; Jones, 2009): another example of modern 'socially engaged Buddhism'.

Vietnam[23]

In Vietnam, around half of the population of 85.3 million is broadly Buddhist, with 6 million Catholic and 0.75 million Protestant Christians. Confucian and Daoist ideas and practices are also common. In the 1930s, the ideas of the Chinese Buddhist reformist Daixu were influential, and there was a flourishing of popular Buddhist literature, especially of a Pure Land nature. There is also Hoa Hao, a new Buddhist movement founded in 1939, which is a home-focused millenarian movement that draws on Pure Land, Thien (Zen) and Confucianism, and has around 2 million followers. Cao Dai, founded in 1926, is a syncretistic monotheist religion that draws on Buddhism, Daoism, Confucianism and Christianity, and looks to God as a saviour from the round of rebirths.

Buddhists were active in the anti-colonial struggle, and joined the Communist-led revolution that arose from 1945. From 1955, the French-backed regime in the south favoured Catholicism, and sought to marginalize Buddhism, though the self-immolation of a Buddhist monk in 1963, as a witness against this, helped to rally Buddhists. During the Vietnam War (1964–75), Vietnamese monks were active in welfare work, and in encouraging deserters from the armies of the American-supported south and the Communist north, such that they were suspected by both sides. The north and south were unified in 1975, under the Communists. This brought the

[23] On this, see Harris, 1999: 254–83; Unger and Unger, 1997.

closure of a number of monasteries and temples, the state control of the *Saṅgha*, and the harassing of Buddhists, for example by political meetings being timed to clash with festivals (Keown and Prebish, 2007: 796–9). However, since 1986, there has been economic liberalization and a general rise of religious activity. Probably the most well-known Vietnamese Buddhist is Thich Nhat Hanh,[24] who formed the School of Youth for Social Services in the 1960s, which was active in helping those affected by the war. He coined the term 'socially engaged Buddhism', and in 1966 formed the Tiep Hien, or Order of Interbeing. Mainly exiled from Vietnam since 1973, he has been resident in France, and emphasized developing mindfulness of the many ways in which our actions impact on the inter-connected world, and the need to act in peaceful and ecologically sound ways (see p. 149, 435, 454).

Korea

In 1904, Japanese troops entered the country, and in the period 1910–45, Korea was a Japanese colony. Buddhism underwent a revival, but the Japanese wish to import and encourage its own forms of Buddhism caused tension, especially as regards an increase in the number of married clergy. Since the division of the country by the Korean War (1950–3), the north has been governed by a harsh, inward-looking, leader-worshipping Communist regime. However, perhaps 11 per cent of the population remain Buddhist, and while the government closely controls the *Saṅgha*, some limited support is given. Also of note is that in Uzbekistan, there are 55,560 Buddhists among the ethnic Koreans who were forcibly relocated there by the Soviets in 1937–8.

In South Korea, Buddhism remains in a Westernized and rapidly modernizing society, along with Christianity, Confucianism, Daoism and the native shamanism. Free of the oppression of the Confucian Yi dynasty, and of Japanese occupation, Korean Buddhism has undergone a definite revival. There are around 8,000 monks, 15,000 nuns and perhaps 2,300 married clerics. Young educated people continue to ordain, or go on meditation retreats to practise Seon (Zen) meditation. A renewal in Buddhist scholarship has developed, with the Chinese Canon being translated into modern Korean, and there is a general increase in interest in Buddhist philosophy, in a modernized form. The Buddhist Youth Organization is active in both study and social work.

[24] Keown and Prebish, 2007: 545–7; Nhat Hanh, 1967, 1991, 2008; Queen and King, 1996: 321–63.

A new form of Buddhism, which dates from 1924 and has blossomed since 1953, is the Won, or 'Round' school (Chung, 2003; Keown and Prebish, 2007: 834–5). This is a reformed, simplified school whose sole focus of worship is a black circle representing the *Dharma*-body or emptiness. Western influence is apparent in its religious services, which include *Sūtra*-readings, prayers, hymns and a sermon. It seeks to balance inner quiet with selfless social service, which has led to much charitable activity and the building of many schools. In 2005, it had 130,000 followers.

Christianity, present since the late seventeenth century, made many converts during the spiritual confusion of the post-war period, and is continuing to grow. In 2005, of the 47 million population, 10.9 million were Buddhist, 13.8 million were Christian, 22 million were non-religious, and 0.1 million were Confucian, though this has a wider general influence. Christians are influential in government circles, and some evangelical Protestant Christians are very anti-Buddhist and have sometimes set fire to or vandalized Buddhist temples.

Hong Kong, Macau, Singapore, Malaysia, Indonesia, Thailand and the Philippines

In Hong Kong, 56 per cent of the 6.9 million population are non-religious, while 10 per cent follow a mix of Buddhism and Daoism. In Macau, an ex-Portuguese colony, while the 1996 census indicated 60.9 per cent were non-religious, 16.8 per cent were Buddhist and 13.9 per cent followed a mix of Buddhism and Daoism. In Singapore, 43 per cent of the population practise some form of Buddhism: mainly Chinese Mahāyāna, but also some Thai Theravāda or Japanese Sōka Gakkai, and more recently Tibetan Buddhism. The situations in Malaysia and Indonesia are as described above under the Southern Buddhism section. Some of the Chinese in Thailand practise Eastern, rather than Southern Buddhism, and in the Philippines, Buddhism is practised by Filipino Chinese, Chinese, Japanese, Korean, Thai and Vietnamese communities.

NORTHERN BUDDHISM

The number of people belonging to Northern Buddhism totals only around 18.2 million (see Table 8).

Table 8 *Number of Northern Buddhists in Asia.*

– 5.4m. Tibetans in the People's Republic of China	– Buryat, Tuva and Kalmyk Republics of the Russian Federation, 0.7m. (70% of 1m.)
– ~5m. of the 5.81m. Mongols in northern and western China	Minority populations exist in:
– ~0.2m. of the 0.241m. Monguor or Tu people in Qinghai and Gansu	– north and north-east India, 0·4m.
– Mongolia, 2.7m. (90% of 3m.)	– Tibetan exiles in India, 0·15m.
– Nepal, 2.9m. (10% of 29.33m.)	– Pakistan, 0.16m.
– Bhutan, 0.49m. (70% of 0.7m.)	– Kazakhstan and Kyrgyzstan 0.1m.

Tibet

In 1950, the Communist Chinese invaded Tibet, claiming that they were reasserting a right over Chinese territory. The new Dalai Lama, enthroned not long before, continued to 'rule' in an uneasy co-existence with the Chinese until 1959, when an uprising against the Chinese was quashed, direct colonial rule was imposed, and the Dalai Lama fled to India. During the Red Guard period (1966–7), around 6,000 monasteries were destroyed, along with their art and libraries, in an attempt to wipe out Tibet's rich and ancient Buddhist culture (Powers, 2007b: 205–15). The Dalai Lama estimates that one million Tibetans died: in the rebellion, from the famine arising from inappropriate agricultural policies, and in persecutions (Bechert and Gombrich, 1984: 266–7).

From 1980, things became easier, and the Tibetan Buddhist Canon is being reprinted, much artistic restoration work has been done and the people retain a strong devotion to Buddhism (Lopez and Stearns, 1986; Samuel, 2012: 235–45). Ordinations have continued since 1959, but the past disruption of study has meant that at one time there was a severe shortage of learned Buddhist teachers. As of 1997, there were 120,000 monastics and 3,000 monasteries in Tibetan areas of China: mostly in the 'Tibetan Autonomous Region' and Tibetan autonomous prefectures and counties in Qinghai, Gansu, Sichuan and Yunnan provinces. These areas are roughly equivalent to the three provinces of ancient Tibet: Ü-Tsang in the West and centre, over which the current Dalai Lama had power, and Amdo and Kham in the east.

Tibetan culture is being diluted by an alien education system, the consumerism that the Chinese have begun to introduce, and by colonization by the Han Chinese. These outnumber Tibetans in the capital, Lhasa, and formed 6 per cent of the population in the Tibetan Autonomous

Region in 2000, with an increase since 2006, when a railway linked this with the rest of China. Tourism has been permitted since 1984, and while this may in time prove corrosive of the culture, at present it allows Tibetans contact with the outside world so as to protest at Chinese occupation. Anti-Chinese riots occurred in 1987, 1988 and 2008, involving young monks as well as laypeople. The Dalai Lama, who now lives in India, remains the focus of tremendous devotion. He supports demonstrations and civil disobedience if these are non-violent, and hopes that, if Tibet cannot be independent, it will be demilitarized and Han immigration will cease.

While the Chinese occupation of the country has brought devastating changes to its culture, along with the benefits and drawbacks of modernization, it also caused the spread of its religion to the four winds in Asia and beyond. Moreover, some Han are now turning to Tibetan Buddhism.

The Tibetan diaspora in India[25]

When the Dalai Lama fled from Tibet in 1959, thousands accompanied or followed him. Today, there are around 150,000 Tibetan exiles in India, 13,000 in Nepal and 1,500 in Bhutan (Powers, 2007b: 203). India granted land for refugee settlements and the Dalai Lama has an administrative centre at Dharamsāla in the northern state of Himachal Pradesh, which contains a third of the 120 or so monasteries established by the exiles. The largest Tibetan monastery in India has 4,700 monks (Gyatso, 2003: 219–21). Flourishing lay communities exist in Orissa and Mysore. The unfamiliar Indian climate has led to much ill-health among the Tibetans, however, and though many communities have become self-supporting, unemployment remains a problem; the Tibetans therefore partly subsist on Indian and foreign aid. The monks must support themselves by growing food, tending small herds of cattle and producing craftwork for sale, so that less time is available for study. The exiles are faced with the dual tasks of recording and passing on their rich cultural heritage, and physical survival. Nevertheless, Dharamsāla has the Library of Tibetan Works and Archives (www.ltwa.net), works of Tibetan Buddhism are being printed in India and monks and learned laypeople are studying at various universities in India, the West and Japan, thus stimulating an increase in studies of Tibetan Buddhist culture. The Tibetan diaspora has also led to around 20,000 refugees settling in the West, where they have been very active in spreading their tradition. A sign

[25] On this, see Berkwitz, 2010: 199–202; Gyatso, 2003; Keown and Prebish, 2007: 259–61.

of the vitality of Northern Buddhism was a gathering, in 1985, of more than 200,000 pilgrims at Bodh-Gayā, with 10,000 even coming from Tibet.

The present Dalai Lama (1935–) remains a revered figure among exiles and in Tibet, and his attempts at non-violent reconciliation with the Chinese, aimed at religious freedom in Tibet, with Tibet remaining part of China, won him the Nobel Peace Prize in 1989 (Keown and Prebish, 2007: 259–61). The Chinese, however, regard him as a dangerous person who aims at the splitting up of China, and pictures of him are banned in Tibet. An important question will be what happens when this 14th Dalai Lama dies: who will succeed him? Traditionally, the Panchen Lama identifies his successor, but there are now two candidates for the title 'Panchen Lama', one of whom is controlled by the Chinese. The present Dalai Lama, however, has said that he will not be reborn in a Tibet controlled by the Chinese, even if this means he is the last Dalai Lama. In 2011, he also declared that he would no longer be head of the Tibetan government in exile, wishing this to be democratic in form.

Overseas, many books on Buddhism by the Dalai Lama are available (e.g. Piburn, 1990), and his trips for Buddhist and diplomatic purposes have helped make him the most recognized and widely respected Buddhist in the world.

He has, though, been criticized by Tibetans supportive of the deity Dorje Shugden (rDo-rje Shugs-ldan; Dreyfus, 1998). This figure is a Gelugpa wrathful protector deity, regarded as a rebirth of a seventeenth-century *Lama* seen to have been a rival of the fifth Dalai Lama. Conflict between the two led to the former's suicide, in the hope that signs after his death would clear his name of certain 'slanders' on him; his supporters see these signs as having occurred. In time, he came to be seen as a minor '*Dharma* protector' deity, charged with protecting the Gelugpas against their enemies. Eventually, he was elevated in some people's eyes to the position of chief *Dharma* protector, after championing of him by Pabonka Rinpoche (Pha-bong-ka Rin-po-che; 1878–1941) and his student Trijang Rinpoche (Khri-byang Rin-po-che; 1901–83).

After the present Dalai Lama had a dream in which he saw Dorje Shugden in combat with Nechung (gNas-chung), the main *Dharma* protector of the Tibetan government-in-exile, he publicly announced that Tibetans should cease propitiating this deity, and that it was a 'worldly' deity, not a true Buddhist 'refuge' (such that the name prefix *Dorje*, or *Vajra*, was inappropriate). Though 'Dorje' Shugden had become a popular deity among Gelugpa *Lamas*, most then publicly renounced it. The most vocal exception to this has been Geshe Kelsang Gyatso (dGe-bshes bsKal-bzang rgyal-mtsho; 1931–), founder, in the UK, of the New Kadampa Tradition. Those who support the deity in India have accused the Dalai Lama of suppressing their religious freedom, and the bad feeling surrounding the issue may have led to the murder of a key supporter of the Dalai Lama. Lying behind the issue is that Dorje Shugden is seen as a protector specifically of the *Gelugpa* school, in a sectarian manner, while the Dalai Lama, though a Gelugpa, has a broad ecumenical outlook. The 'New Kadampa' (which was also the earliest name for the Gelugpas) sees itself as a reformed version of the Gelugpa school which has 'preserved the pure teaching' of its founder Tsongkh'apa and of Atiśa, founder of the Kadam-pa (bKa-gdams-pa) school on which it built.

Mongolia and related regions[26]

Mongolia was under Soviet dominance between 1924 and 1990, with strong repression of Buddhism, so that while there were 112,000 monks and 1,060 monasteries in the 1920s, from the 1940s to 1990 there were around 100 monks and only one monastery. However, Buddhism is now undergoing an enthusiastic revival, it mainly being of the Gelugpa form, and there are 3,000 monks and a growing number of nuns, aided by Tibetan *Lama*s from India (Kollmar-Paulenz, 2003), with 284 monasteries by 2009 (www.mongoliantemples.net). Buddhism is seen as an important part of national identity, as is Genghis Khan (1162–1227), once ruler of a huge Mongol empire. While he was not a Buddhist, he was religiously tolerant and came to be seen as a form of the *Bodhisattva* Vajrapāṇi.

Buddhism among the people of Inner Mongolia, part of China, is also benefiting from a more liberal attitude to the practice of religion. The same applies in the Buryat and Tuva Republics of the Russian Federation, to the north of Mongolia, and among the Mongolian people of Kalmykia, bordering the Caspian sea, in Europe.

Bhutan, northern India and Nepal

In the independent state of Bhutan, which has opened itself up to the outside world only since the 1970s, Northern Buddhism continues to flourish and be supported by both the people and government. Tourism is limited, to help protect Bhutanese culture, and the king is noted for favouring the 'Gross National Happiness' over the Gross National Product.

[26] On this, see Bechert and Gombrich, 1984: 267–8.

On the other hand, nearly 100,000 ethnic Nepalis have been expelled from the country, as they are seen as illegal immigrants.

Buddhism also exists in neighbouring Sikkim, a small state incorporated into India in 1975, and the Darjeeling and Jalpaiguru districts of northern West Bengal. In both, it has been strengthened by the influx of Tibetan refugees. Northern Buddhism exists in Ladakh, in the northern Indian state of Jammu and Kashmir (Norberg-Hodge, 2000), but it faces real problems from the rapidly increasing Muslim population of the state and the cutting off of communication with Tibet.

In Nepal, the growing minority presence of Theravāda Buddhism in this mainly Hindu land has also helped stimulate a general renaissance of Newar Vajrayāna Buddhism. Buddhism is also found among Tibetan refugees and Tibetan-influenced ethnic groups such as the Sherpas. Among the Gurkhas, who were originally Hindus from India, are ethnic groups which draw on elements of Nyingmapa Buddhism, Bön, shamanism and Hinduism.

CHAPTER 13

Buddhism Beyond Asia

As European powers expanded into Asia, knowledge of its religions became more soundly based. Changes in European thought also led to some receptivity to ideas from non-Christian religions. In the eighteenth century, the Enlightenment's emphasis on 'reason' and 'science' weakened reliance on authoritative 'revelation' in religious matters, and a number of people thought that they saw a 'natural religion' held in common by people of all cultures, though best expressed in Christianity. In the nineteenth century, advances in geology and Biblical studies led to a weakening of Biblical literalism, and the concept of biological evolution seemed, to many, to cast doubts on the 'revealed' Christian account of creation. In this context, the idea of making a 'scientific', 'comparative' study of all religions came to be advanced (Sharpe, 1986).

These elements came together in the last two decades of the nineteenth century, when there was something of a vogue for (modernist) Buddhism among sections of the middle classes in America, Britain and Germany.[1] Like Christianity, Buddhism had a noble ethical system, but it appeared to be a religion of self-help, not dependent on God or priests. Like science, it seemed to be based on experience, saw the universe as ruled by law, and did not regard humans and animals as radically distinct. Yet for those with a taste for mysticism, such as those touched by the Romantic movement, it offered more than science.

THE EARLY INFLUENCE OF BUDDHISM THROUGH LITERATURE, PHILOSOPHY AND PSYCHOLOGY

One channel through which Buddhism reached the West was the works of certain writers and thinkers. In Germany, Arthur Schopenhauer (1788–1860) saw parallels between his philosophy and the ideas of

[1] Almond, 1988; Clausen, 1973; Jackson, 1981; Lopez, 1995.

Buddhism and Hinduism (which he conflated to some extent). His key work, *The World as Will and Representation* (1818 and 1844, in German), contains many references to Buddhism, particularly in its second volume. Schopenhauer regarded Buddhism as the best religion, and while Christian missionaries criticized it for its 'pessimism', he saw this as its strength, realistically assessing the presence of suffering in the world (Batchelor, 1994: 250–71). In the 1830s and 1840s, the American Transcendentalist writers R. W. Emerson and H. D. Thoreau also drew on Indian themes (Seager, 1999: 34). In developing their individualist, intuitive and pantheistic philosophy, however, their Indian sources were mainly Hindu.

In England, Sir Edwin Arnold, who became editor of the *Daily Telegraph*, produced *The Light of Asia* (1879), a poem on the life of the Buddha. This led to quite a widespread interest in Buddhism among the middle classes in Britain and America, and aided the Buddhist renaissance in Sri Lanka. Arnold was a liberal Christian much attracted to Buddhism. His sympathetic account, in a somewhat rich, dramatic and sentimental style, portrayed the Buddha as a figure in some ways akin to Jesus. In 1885, he visited Bodh-Gayā and then travelled to Sri Lanka and Japan to rouse support for the restoration of it and other holy sites. This caused Anagārika Dharmapāla to visit the site, after which he founded the Mahā Bodhi Society.

The novels of the German writer Hermann Hesse used Buddhist themes, especially the influential *Siddhartha* (1922), and the Swiss psychoanalyst Carl Jung explored parallels between symbolic dreams and Tibetan *maṇḍalas* in the 1950s (Lopez, 1995: 197–250). Jack Kerouac's *On the Road* (1951) and *The Dharma Bums* (1958; Seager, 1999: 40–3) infused Zen themes into the anarchic Beat sub-culture, followed later by works of poets Allen Ginsberg and Gary Snyder. Aldous Huxley's *The Doors of Perception and Heaven and Hell* (1956) also stimulated an interest in Eastern meditation by (wrongly) comparing enlightenment to experiences had under the influence of mescaline. In the 1960s, this kind of association helped Buddhism catch the interest of people influenced by the Hippie movement.

THE THEOSOPHICAL SOCIETY: A BRIDGE BETWEEN EAST AND WEST

The first organized group in the West to advocate the adoption of Indian religious beliefs and practices was the Theosophical Society, founded in New York in 1875 (see p. 378; Campbell, 1980). This grew out of the American vogue for spiritualism, and mingled Neo-Platonic mysticism, other elements of the Western esoteric tradition, Hindu and Buddhist ideas and a religious version of 'evolution'. It saw individuals as spiritually evolving over many lives, through cycles of the universe, according to their 'karma' and knowledge. It did not accept that a human could be reborn at an animal level again, though. Ultimate reality was seen more in Hindu than in Buddhist terms: all beings were regarded as containing an inner *Ātman*, or Self, which was a portion of the universal One or *Brahman*.

The co-founder Helena Blavatsky (1831–91) was an eccentric, charismatic figure who had travelled widely, perhaps reaching an area of Tibetan Buddhist culture under Russian control. She later introduced to America and Europe the image of Tibet as a mysterious and wonderful land. She claimed that her books, such as *The Secret Doctrine* (1888), were clairvoyantly dictated to her by members of a 'Brotherhood' of spiritual 'Masters' who lived in Tibet. They had 'chosen' her to teach an ancient religion – Theosophy, or 'Divine Wisdom' – which was the inner essence and basis of all known religions. Jesus and the Buddha had been past 'Masters' of this esoteric tradition. The strengths of the other co-founder, Henry Steel Olcott (1832–1907), lay in his organizational abilities. It appears to have been he, though, who wished to go to what he saw as the 'holy land' of India: one of the first of many Western pilgrims who followed in later decades.

The Theosophical Society established branches in America, Britain, India and Sri Lanka. In the West, it attracted people who found the conventional structures of society inhibiting, for example intelligent, creative people with little formal education, or women chafing at their social position. From 1907, its President was Annie Besant (1847–1933), an Englishwoman who had previously been an atheist and socialist. The society was at the height of its influence in the 1920s, when it had groomed the Indian Jiddu Krishnamurti (1895–1986) as the vehicle of a Messiah figure, seen as both the returning Christ and Maitreya Buddha. In 1929, Krishnamurti publicly rejected this role, and the Society subsequently declined in influence. The Society had, however, been successful in introducing a number of key Buddhist and Hindu concepts to people unfamiliar with scholarly writings.

SCHOLARSHIP[2]

Other than the translation of passages from some Pali works from Siam (now Thailand) by Simon de La Loubère as early as 1691, the earliest

[2] See for example de Jong, 1986; Gombrich, 2005; Peiris, 1973.

Buddhist texts to be worked on were Sanskrit ones (mostly Mahāyāna) from Nepal, collected by the British resident B. H. Hodgson (1880–94). The French scholar Eugène Burnouf (Batchelor, 1994: 227–49) used these to produce his *Introduction à l'histoire du Bouddhisme indien* (1845), and a translation of the *Lotus Sūtra* (1852).

In Sri Lanka, missionaries began the study of Buddhism, though the best of their accounts still tended to give a distorted view of the Southern Buddhist tradition as a pessimistic, inadequate religion (Harris, 2009). From around 1850, this was rectified by the work of English, German and Scandinavian scholars, such as V. Fausboll, who edited the *Dhammapada* and translated it into Latin in 1855. Two influential and popular accounts of the Buddha's life and teachings, based on Pali materials, were *The Buddha, His Life, His Doctrine, His Community* (1881, in German), of Hermann Oldenberg (1854–1920), and *Buddhism* (1878), of T. W. Rhys Davids (1843–1922), who had spent eight years in the colonial civil service in Sri Lanka (Wickremeratne, 1984). Also in England, the German–English F. Max Müller edited the fifty-one volume Sacred Books of the East series (1879–1910), which contained translations of a number of Buddhist texts. In America, Henry Clarke Warren co-founded the Harvard Oriental Series (1891), and produced an excellent anthology of translations from the Pali Canon, *Buddhism in Translations* (1896). Particularly important was the work of the Pali Text Society, founded in England in 1881 by Rhys Davids. Its aim was to publish critical editions, in Roman characters, of the texts of the Pali Canon and its commentaries, along with translations. Interest in the Pali Canon arose because it was seen as preserving the 'original teachings' of the Buddha, who was regarded as a rational, ethical teacher, with ritual and supernatural elements of Buddhism being seen as later accretions. International co-operation enabled the PTS to publish most of the Pali texts of the Canon by 1910, and by 2009 it had produced 188 volumes of text, and 97 of translations, along with aids for textual study.

In the early twentieth century, Tibetan and Chinese texts were studied. In Russia, a team of scholars was led by Th. Stcherbatsky (1866–1942), who produced such works as *The Central Conception of Buddhism, and the Meaning of the Word Dharma* (1923), and *Buddhist Logic* (1930–2). Other scholars, mainly French and Belgian, also studied the religious and historical aspects of the Mahāyāna, with L. de La Vallée Poussin (1869–1938) producing translations of the *Abhidharma-kośa* and key Yogācāra works. L'École Française d'Extrême-Orient, founded in Hanoi in 1901, did much archaeological and epigraphic research, for example on the magnificent Angor Wat, and French scholars such as Paul Pelliot brought to light many artefacts and texts from Central Asia and China. Knowledge of Zen Buddhism was greatly aided by the scholarly and popular writings of D. T. Suzuki, for example his *Essays in Zen Buddhism, First Series* (1927).

After the Second World War, the Franco-Belgian school was continued by scholars such as Étienne Lamotte (1903–83) in his *Histoire du Bouddhisme indien* (1958), and advances in the study of Northern Buddhism were made by the travels and translations of the Italian Giuseppe Tucci (1894–1984). Heinz Bechert (1932–2005) explored the socio-political aspects of Buddhism in *Buddhismus, Staat und Gesellschaft in den Ländern des Theravāda Buddhismus* (1966, 1867 and 1973), while Indian and Japanese scholars have made important contributions to international Buddhology. The discovery of texts from such places as the sands of Central Asia, and the cave-temples of Dunhuang (Tun-huang) in China, have also opened up new areas of research. Edward Conze (1904–79) advanced the study of the Perfection of Wisdom literature, and his *Buddhism* (1951), *Buddhist Texts Through the Ages* (1954 (*BTTA*)), *Buddhist Scriptures* (1959 (*BS1*)) and *Buddhist Thought in India* (1967) did much to disseminate knowledge of Buddhism. From the 1960s, the study of Buddhism has become established in many Western universities, with important works including: Heinz Bechert and Richard Gombrich (eds.), *The World of Buddhism: Buddhist Monks and Nuns in Society and Culture* (1984), Richard Gombrich, *Theravāda Buddhism* (1988 and 2006), Paul Williams, *Mahāyāna Buddhism: The Doctrinal Foundations* (1989 and 2009), Bernard Faure, *The Rhetoric of Immediacy: A Cultural Critique of Chan/Zen Buddhism* (1991), Damien Keown, *The Nature of Buddhist Ethics* (1992), José Cabezón (ed.), *Buddhism, Sexuality and Gender* (1992), Geoffrey Samuel, *Civilized Shamans: Buddhism in Tibetan Societies* (1993), Reginald Ray, *Buddhist Saints in India: A Study in Buddhist Values and Orientations* (1994) and Gregory Schopen, *Bones, Stones, and Buddhist Monks: Collected Papers on Archaeology, Epigraphy and Texts of Monastic Buddhism in India* (1997). In 2005, Paul Williams edited an eight-volume collection of key papers on Buddhism, *Buddhism: Critical Concepts in Religious Studies.*

Western scholars have thus played a key role in bringing knowledge of Buddhism to the West (Prebish, 2007). This has been expressed both in scholarly and popular works and in exhibitions of Buddhist art and artefacts. Buddhist Studies journals include *The Eastern Buddhist* (*f.* 1921), *Journal of the International Association of Buddhist Studies* (*f.* 1978), *Pacific World* (*f.* 1982), *Buddhist Studies Review* (*f.* 1983) and *Contemporary Buddhism* (*f.* 2000). The International Association of Buddhist Studies was formed in 1976, the Buddhism section of the American Academy of

Religion in 1981 and the UK Association for Buddhist Studies in 1996. The study of Buddhism is also an established part of a range of university courses, and Charles Prebish estimates that in the USA perhaps half of the scholars of Buddhism are also Buddhists, half of these openly so, with such scholar-practitioners fulfilling a role akin to that of scholar-monks for the primarily lay Buddhism of the country (1999: 180, 198–200).

THE INTERNET, FILMS AND MUSIC

Buddhist practitioners and scholars have been quick to make good use of the internet.[3] There are the internet journals *Journal of Buddhist Ethics* (*f.* 1994) and *Global Buddhism* (*f.* 2000), the former having more than 1,500 subscribers (Prebish, 1999: 214). There are large, well-maintained websites for particular traditions, such as Access to Insight (Theravāda), the Berzin Archives (Vajrayāna) and Australian National University Zen Virtual Library. The International Dunhuang Project co-ordinates the study of texts and artefacts from the Eastern Silk Road, and there are web portals that link to a wide range of resources, such as on the DharmaNet and BuddhaNet websites (Prebish, 1999: 217–19). There are also scholarly e-lists such as Buddha-L and H-Buddhism (Prebish, 1999: 209–10). Most Buddhist organizations and centres also have a web presence. A Google search for 'Buddhism' brings up thirteen million results (twenty-eight million for Christianity).

Buddhism has also featured in television and radio documentaries and discussion programmes and in films such as *Little Buddha* (1994), *Red Corner*, *Kundun* (on the Dalai Lama's childhood), and *Seven Years in Tibet* (all 1997), and the Korean *Spring, Summer, Fall, Winter... Spring* (2003). It has also influenced the music of John Cage (1912–92; Prebish and Baumann, 2002: 371–2).

IMMIGRATION

In the 1860s and 1870s, hundreds of thousands of Chinese immigrants went to the West Coast of America and Canada to work in the gold mines and on the railroads. After 1882, when a US law curtailed Chinese immigration, Japanese labourers followed.[4] From 1868, significant numbers of Japanese

[3] On this, see Lancaster, 2007; Prebish, 1999: 203–32; Williams and Queen, 1999: 168–79. For a selection of such resources, see Appendix II.

[4] Prebish, 1999: 4–5; Prebish and Baumann, 2002: 107–8, 121–22, 192; Seager, 1999: 159–60.

and Chinese immigrants also went to work on the sugar plantations of Hawaii, which was annexed as an American territory in 1898. Asian immigration to California was halted in 1902, but continued in Hawaii, which thus became an important centre for the transmission of Buddhism to America. Japanese immigration to Brazil began in 1909 (Prebish and Baumann, 2002: 164).

Chinese religion at first kept a low profile in North America, though a Pure Land mission was active to some extent among the Chinese. Immigration increased in the 1950s, then the 1965 change to the US Immigration and Nationality Act led to an influx of Chinese people – non-religious, Christian or Buddhist – so that there were 921,000 people of this background in the country by 1990 (Prebish, 1999: 26). Chinese Buddhist groups have since become more active. They are less sectarian than Japanese Buddhists, and tend to emphasize devotional chanting and compassionate expressions of the *Bodhisattva* vows. Many temples serve the *Chinese* community, which tends to be split between working-class people living in Chinatowns, where temples may include both Buddhist and Daoist elements, and suburban professionals, but some have reached out to and attracted Euro-Americans. In Canada, immigration since the 1960s also led to Canada having, by 2000, over 600,000 Chinese immigrants, mainly from Hong Kong.

Japanese immigrants became overtly active in religious matters earlier than the Chinese, many coming from an area where the Jōdo-shin sect was strong.[5] This sect was also the most active in sending out missions. In 1889, the priest Sōryū Kagahi arrived in Hawaii and established the first Japanese temple there. He belonged to the Hompa Hongwanji sub-sect, which became for a long time the largest Buddhist denomination in Hawaii and North America. In 1899, Sokei Sonada came to San Francisco and established the sub-sect on the continent as the Buddhist Mission of North America. During the Second World War, when many Japanese were put in internment camps (Prebish and Baumann, 2002: 191–200), this was reorganized as the Buddhist Churches of America (BCA), and became independent of its Japanese parent body. To help pass on its traditions, the Mission and then Church organized a Young Men's Buddhist Association (1900), Sunday schools, Buddhist women's societies, and educational programmes. These Western-influenced activities had already begun to develop in Japan itself at this time, but increased in the 1920s to 1940s due to anti-Japanese pressure in North America. The title 'Church'

[5] On the Jōdo-shin in North America, see Prebish, 1999: 20–3, 127–38; Prebish and Tanaka, 1998: 31–47; Williams and Queen, 1999: 3–19; Seager, 1999: 51–69.

indicates further Westernization, as do the titles 'minister' and 'bishop' and the style of religious services, which are held on Sundays, use organs and have included the singing of hymns such as 'Buddha, lover of my soul . . .', though Christianized elements have reduced since the mid-1990s (Prebish and Baumann, 2002: 197; Seager, 1999: 63). While Japanese immigration to the US had been reduced by the 1924 Oriental Exclusion Act, which stopped new Japanese immigrants becoming citizens, it increased after changes to immigration laws in 1962 in Canada and 1965 in the USA (Prebish and Baumann, 2002: 114).

The Institute for Buddhist Studies, for training BCA priests, was established in 1966; one of the Church's members was an astronaut killed in the 1986 Challenger space-shuttle disaster and, in 1987, the US Defence Department allowed the Church to put forward chaplains to work in the military. However, membership has declined, from around 65,000 in 1977 to 50,775 in 1995, probably due to the BCA being seen as just for Japanese Americans, and rather undynamic and conformist (Prebish, 1999: 132–3). In 2010, it listed fifty-four temples on its website – down from sixty-three in 1987. In Canada, in 1985, the Buddhist Churches of Canada (now called Jodo Shinshu Buddhist Temples of Canada) had eighteen member Churches (thirteen in 2010) and a membership of around 10,000.

In Brazil, there are now around 1.26 million people of Japanese ancestry, 200,000 with Chinese ancestry and 80,000 with Korean ancestry. Various sects of Buddhism are found among them: Zen, Jōdo-shin, Jōdo, Shingon, Tendai and Nichiren, though Buddhism among families of Japanese descent seems to be declining over the generations (Prebish and Baumann, 2002: 167).

From 1975, refugees from Communist Vietnam, Laos and Cambodia, of whom around 60 per cent are Buddhist, have come to the West, their numbers reaching 884,000 by 1985: 561,000 in the USA, 94,000 in Canada (130,000 by 2002[6]), 97,000 in France, 91,000 in Australia, 22,000 in Germany (60,000 by 2002) and 19,000 in Britain. The Vietnamese have established a number of temples in the West, and the Cambodians have been building Buddhist centres and ordaining as monks. In Britain, a community of Indian Ambedkar Buddhists has developed around Birmingham, with around 14,000 Indian Buddhists in the 2001 census.

Some Buryats and Kalmyks, people of Monglian background, migrated to Western Russia and had a Gelugpa Buddhist temple and monastery built in St Petersburg in the period 1909–15. In the First World War, a Buddhist temple was also established in Warsaw to serve the needs of Buryat and

[6] Prebish and Baumann, 2002: 122–4.

Kalmyk troops in the Russian army, though the St Petersburg temple was desecrated in 1917, and there was persecution of Buddhists under Stalin from the 1930s (Prebish and Baumann, 2002: 90–1). The Chinese takeover of Tibet has, as noted above, had the side-effect of Tibetan refugees sharing their tradition with people in North America and Europe.

In Australia, Buddhism arrived in 1848 with some Chinese immigrants, then in 1882 with some from Sri Lanka. However, it did not start to develop among other sections of the population until the 1920s. By 1996, 31 per cent of Australian Buddhists were born in Vietnam, with 2 per cent born in Australia. Chinese immigrants entered New Zealand in 1863 (Prebish and Baumann, 2002: 140). In 1997, the largest ethnic group of New Zealand Buddhists, at 40 per cent, were the Chinese (Prebish and Baumann, 2002: 143).

From 1860 to 1913, low-caste Indians went as indentured labourers to South Africa, mainly to Natal. In the 1920s and 1930s, increasing discrimination led some of them to Westernize and convert to Christianity, while others explored their Indian roots, strengthening their Hinduism. Some turned to Buddhism, attracted by what they saw as its freedom from caste and superstition, its social ethic and its emphasis on the compassionate Buddha-nature within all. Links with Buddhists in south India led to the founding of a Buddhist Society in 1917. It was never a mass movement, however, its weakness being that it has had no temples or monks, and it has since declined. A Buddhist monastery was established in Tanzania in 1927 by immigrant labourers brought from Sri Lanka. It still exists, though the number of Buddhists seems to be dwindling. Immigrants from Sri Lanka also seem to be behind the existence of Mahā Bodhi Societies in Ghana and Zaire, and a Buddhist society in Zambia.

CATEGORIES OF BUDDHISTS, AND THEIR CHARACTERISTICS AND NUMBERS

In Europe as a whole in the late 1990s, there were around 650,000 Asian Buddhists of various kinds, around two-thirds of the Buddhists there (Prebish and Baumann, 2002: 95). The 2001 UK census indicated that there were 152,000 Buddhists in the UK (0.26%), of which 60 per cent were from Asian backgrounds (Bluck, 2004: 93, 2006: 15–16; 261,000 in 2011 census, 0.41%). In the 1990 US census, there were 500,000 to 750,000 Theravāda Buddhist immigrants (Prebish and Baumann, 2002: 115[7]), and Richard Seager (1999: 232) holds that:

[7] Of 6.9 million people of various Asian backgrounds. In the 2000 census, there were 10.24 million, including: 2.73m. Chinese, 0.14m. Taiwanese, 1.23m. Korean, 1.15m. Japanese, 1.22m. Vietnamese,

Perhaps as many as three quarters of America's Buddhists are new immigrant communities, whose contributions to the long-term development of the dharma remain particularly difficult to assess and are often overlooked – and, I think, highly underrated.

After the Second World War, an interest in Buddhism was developed by some American servicemen taking part in the occupation of Japan and in the Korean and Vietnam Wars, and by some of the young people who travelled overland to 'mystic' India and Nepal in the 1960s and 1970s. These helped open up a new era for Buddhism outside Asia. As in other Western countries, those new to Buddhism find their way to it through meditation (or, for SGI, chanting) practice, their interest perhaps aroused by the many popular books on Buddhism that are now widely available, or magazines such as *Tricyle: The Buddhist Review* (*f.* 1991). They then become involved in wider aspects of the tradition. In Asia, devotional practices and contact with monks are usually the starting point. In the USA non-Asian Buddhists tend to be in their late thirties to early fifties (averaging 46), college-educated, and with 31 per cent from a Protestant background, 25 per cent from a Catholic one, and 16.5 per cent from a Jewish[8] one, though Jews only make up around 1.2 per cent of the population (Williams and Queen, 1999: 94.5). Such converts feel uprooted to some extent, and see in Buddhism a non-traditional route to self-discovery and spiritual growth. Increasingly, Asian teachers have given Euro-Americans authority to hand on the tradition, there being around fifty such teachers by the 1980s.

Baumann estimates (1997: 198), for the mid-1990s, three to four million Buddhists in the USA (1.6 per cent of the population), with 800,000[9] being 'Euro-American'. For Europe, for the late 1990s he estimated 900,000 to one million, two-thirds of them Asian immigrants (Prebish and Baumann, 2002: 95–6): France ~350,000 (0.6% of population), Britain 180,000 (0.3%), Germany 170,000 (0.2%), Italy 70,000 (0.1%), the Netherlands 33,000 (0.2%), Switzerland 25,000 (0.3%). In 2007, he put the European figure at 'one or two million' (2007: 176).

For Canada, there are at least 300,000 Buddhists (1%; Prebish and Baumann, 2002: 120). In 1996 censuses, Australia had 199,812 Buddhists (1.1%) and New Zealand 28,131 (0.8%) (Prebish and Baumann, 2002: 139). In Brazil, the 1991 census indicated that there were 236,408 Buddhists

0.21m. Cambodian, 0.20m. Laotian, 0.19m. Hmong (from South-east Asian areas), 0.15m. Thai. In 2010, the overall figure was 14.67m.(4.75% of the population), a growth of 43.3% – the largest increase in a racial category.

[8] *EB*.10.2; Prebish and Baumann, 2002: 177–80.

[9] Though Seager (1999: 242) reported estimates of 100,000 to 800,000.

(0.14%), 89,971 of Asian origin (Prebish and Baumann, 2002: 164). In South Africa there are between 6,000 and 30,000 Buddhists (0.014%–0.07%; Prebish and Baumann, 2002: 153). In the Middle East, there are perhaps 800,000[10] Buddhist migrant workers, particularly from Sri Lanka, in Saudi Arabia, the United Arab Emirates and Kuwait. Overall, there are around seven million Buddhists outside Asia.

Perhaps the most obvious way that Buddhists beyond Asia can be divided is into:

- 'Ethnic' or perhaps 'Asian immigrant' Buddhists: various migrants (especially Chinese, Japanese and to some extent Thai and Sri Lankan) and refugee communities (especially Vietnamese, Cambodian and Laotian), who continue a range of Buddhist and associated traditions and practices of their lands of origin. Their focus is typically on such things as generating karmic fruitfulness for themselves and family members (alive and dead) by donations to monastics, devotional practices and such things as gaining prognostications through astrological or palmist readings. Community identity and preservation of their culture is important to them, but they generally have a low public profile. They are often monastic- or priest-focused, with activities centring round temples, but of course most are themselves lay (Numrich, 1996; Seager, 1999: 121, 234–5).
- 'Convert' Buddhists: those who have taken up Buddhism for the first time (often, though not only, from Asian teachers). Their Buddhism is typically of a modernist form, derived from modernist forms of Asian Buddhism. This tends to be focused on meditation and other practices that can be experienced to have psychological benefits in the short-to-medium term. They are more interested in texts and *Dharma*-teachings than ethnic Buddhists, place less emphasis on the lay/monastic division, with many laypeople doing meditative practices that in Asia tend to be done primarily by monastics, and are more concerned with gender equality and democratic principles.[11] Converts generally place less emphasis on rituals than ethnic Buddhists, though those attracted to Tibetan Buddhism value ritual, if seen more for its psychological benefits than to interact with beneficial forces in the cosmos. Ideas of karma and rebirth are much less central than with ethnic Buddhists, and may even

[10] Wikipedia page on 'Buddhism by country'.

[11] Prebish and Baumann, 2002: 145–6, 160–1, 259–84, 309–23; see Schedneck, 2009 for a range of attitudes to monasticism, and on gender, see: *EB*.10.4 and 10.7; Prebish, 1999: 75–81; Prebish and Baumann, 2002: 309–23; Prebish and Tanaka, 1998: 238–65; Seager, 1999: 185–200; 'Bibliography on Women and the Female in Buddhism': lhamo.tripod.com/8bibli.htm.

be abandoned or treated in an agnostic spirit (e.g. Batchelor, 1997). Converts tend to be well educated and well-off, form more organizations than ethnic Buddhists and are active spokespersons for Buddhism (Prebish and Baumann, 2002: 95, 100).

However, as an ethnic group settles and produces new generations, its characteristics change; this can be seen especially in the oldest groups, descendants of Chinese and Japanese migrants in the Americas, who are now fully integrated into their adopted land: Richard Seager identifies them as a third strand of Buddhists in the USA, 'old-line ethnic Buddhists' (1999: 9–10, 52; Prebish and Baumann, 2002: 106–9). Moreover, the children of converts are no longer true 'converts', but if they continue in the fold of Buddhism – though the proportion that do may not be high (Seager, 1999: 241) – they will most likely follow some form of modernist Buddhism, too. Hence Martin Baumann (Prebish and Baumann, 2002: 51–65) sees 'traditionalist' and 'modernist' as a better way of dividing Buddhists, whether in Asia or beyond. In some cases, though, there are temples with parallel congregations of convert and ethnic Buddhists (Numrich, 1996: 63; Prebish, 1999: 62–3), and figures such as the Dalai Lama have a wide influence.

Buddhist influence on people is something of varying degree.[12] There are 'lukewarm' Buddhists whose connection with the tradition is intermittent. Moreover, just as in Asia, where Buddhists have drawn on other traditions – such as Daoism, Shintō or Sri Lankan spirit religion – so in the West, modernist Buddhists draw on other traditions, such as humanistic psychology. And just as those in Asia who are not primarily 'Buddhist' draw on some aspects of Buddhism, so in the West there is a penumbra of Buddhist sympathizers or fellow-travellers who draw on some aspects of Buddhist practices and ideas but who might not call themselves 'Buddhists'. There are also scholars of Buddhism who respect the tradition and aid its understanding, as well as positive media-portrayals of Buddhism and Buddhists,[13] especially since the early 1990s, and aspects of popular culture that draw on Buddhist elements, such as in 'mind, body and spirit' books and Buddha-images as garden or home ornaments.

While Western countries now contain representatives of all or most Buddhist traditions, the extent to which they co-operate is patchy (Seager, 1999: 232–3). Besides various national and international networks of

[12] Prebish, 1999: 53–6; Prebish and Baumann, 2002: 17–33; Prebish and Tanaka, 1998: 184–8; Williams and Queen, 1999: 71–90. Seager, 1999: 249–65 gives profiles of influential Buddhists in the USA.

[13] Famous people who are now Buddhists also have an effect: see list for the USA at Prebish, 1999: 255–6.

affiliation of particular groups (Baumann, 2007: 37–79), there are, though, the Buddhist Sangha Council of Southern California, the American Buddhist Congress, and the Buddhist Council of the Midwest (Prebish, 1999: 92), founded in the 1980s or later. A Buddhist Union of Europe was formed in 1975, as a common forum for discussion, co-operation and publications. It had forty-five members in 2002 (Prebish and Baumann, 2002: 98–9). National Buddhist Unions are found in Germany (*f.* 1955), Australia (*f.* 1958), Austria and Switzerland (*f.* 1976), the Netherlands and Norway (*f.* 1979), Italy (*f.* 1985), France (*f.* 1986), Denmark (*f.* 1992), Belgium and Portugal (*f.* 1997; Baumann, 2007: 307), with the UK originally represented by the London Buddhist Society (*f.* 1943), later by the Network of Buddhist Organizations (*f.* 1993).

BUDDHIST MISSIONS AND ORGANIZATIONS

The USA[14]

An important platform for Buddhist missions to Westerners was created by the convening of the World Parliament of Religions, organized by liberal Christians as an adjunct to the 1893 Chicago World Fair (Seager, 1999: 35–7). The hope was to reveal the common elements in all religions, so as to foster brotherhood in worship, service to man, and opposition to materialism. The delegate who made the most impression was Swami Vivekānanda, a Vedāntic Hindu, but Anagārika Dharmapāla also made a very favourable impression. He and the Rinzai Zen abbot Sōen Shaku initiated a short surge of interest in Buddhism by their speeches at the Parliament. Dr Paul Carus resolved to publish works on Buddhism, especially Zen, through his Open Court Publishing Company, and himself produced *The Gospel of Buddha* (1894), a popular anthology of Buddhist texts (Prebish and Tanaka, 1998: 207–27).

In 1896, Dharmapāla returned to America for a year at the invitation of Carus, travelling widely and teaching Buddhist doctrine, psychology and meditation. He again returned in 1902–4. Carus also invited D. T. Suzuki (1870–1966), a lay student of Sōen Shaku, to work at his publishing company. After eleven years doing so, he returned to Japan in 1909, but he still kept up contacts with the West, publishing extensively in English on

[14] On this, see: Baumann, 2007: 561–5; Fields, 1992; Prebish, 1999; Prebish and Baumann, 2002; Prebish and Tanaka, 1998; Seager, 1999. Bechert and Gombrich, 1984: 272, 279–85 discusses Buddhism in the West. Baumann, 1997 surveys works on Buddhism in the West.

Zen from the late 1920s, and lecturing at Columbia University in the 1950s. His influential repackaging of Zen portrayed it as the purest, unmediated mystical experience of reality, associated with spontaneity and untrammelled by ritual and institutional religion. Sōen Shaku returned to America in 1905–6, at the invitation of supporters in San Francisco. His close disciple Nyogen Senzaki founded Zen groups in California from the 1920s to the 1950s. Another disciple, Ven. Sōkei-an, founded the Buddhist Society of America, in New York City in 1930. This later became the First Zen Institute of America. Zen became the first form of Buddhism to really catch on among Euro-Americans, who found it very amenable to the pragmatic, energetic American disposition.

In post-war America, Zen continued to develop in the 1950s 'Beat' period: then in the counterculture of the 1960s and 1970s, Buddhism in general started to really take off, mainly in its Zen and Tibetan forms. Almost all extant forms of Buddhism, including some new eclectic and syncretistic ones, now exist in the USA. In 2010, the number of entries for the USA in the web World Buddhist Directory were as in Table 9.[15]

Zen is now the most popular form of convert Buddhism among those who meditate (Seager, 1999: 92),[16] though Tibetan Buddhism has as many centres. While Rinzai was the first form of Zen established in America, Sōtō, which is popular in Hawaii, followed. In 1961, the Sōtō master Shunryu Suzuki (1904–71) opened the impressive San Francisco Zen Center and, in 1967, established the Tassajara Mountain monastery (Seager, 1999: 96–100); his 1970 *Zen Mind, Beginner's Mind* remains very influential. Sōtō Zen was also introduced by Peggy Kennett (1924–96), an Englishwoman born to Buddhist parents. After ordaining as a *bhikṣuṇī* of the Chinese *Saṅgha* in Malaysia, in 1962, she went to Japan and trained as the only woman in a Sōtō temple. In 1969, she went to America and, in 1970, she founded Shasta Abbey, in California, as the headquarters of the Zen Mission Society, from 1983 called the Order of Buddhist Contemplatives (Bluck, 2006: 6–8).

A particularly influential figure in US Zen was Hakuun Yasutani (1885–1974). He taught both Sōtō and Rinzai, in line with the approach of his teacher in Japan, Daiun Harada (1871–1961), who aimed to modernize and demystify Zen (Prebish, 1999: 16–20). One disciple of Yasutani (and of

[15] www.buddhanet.info/wbd/index.php, accessed 8 Sept. 2010. See also Morreale, 1998, which also covers Canada.

[16] For Japanese Zen in America, see: Prebish, 1999: 8–20; Prebish and Baumann, 2002: 218–29; Prebish and Tanaka, 1998: 49–78; Seager, 1999: 90–112; Williams and Queen, 1999: 20–35.

Table 9 *Buddhist groups, centres, monastery/temples and organizations in the USA*

Eastern Buddhism, 1,049:
Zen, 677: Thich Nhat Hanh Community of Mindful Living (199); Sōtō (138); non-specific or mixed Japanese Zen (136); Chan (60); Rinzai (45); Korean Kwan Um Zen (44); other Korean Zen (30); other Vietnamese Zen (25)
Pure Land, 145: Jōdo-shin (102); Chinese Pure Land (29); Jōdo (8); Vietnamese Pure Land (6)
General Mahāyāna, 113: Vietnamese (38); Chinese (13); Korean (10); Japanese (9); non-specified (43)
Nichiren, 53: Nichiren Shōshū and Nichiren Shū (24); Sōka Gakkai International (24); Risshō-kōseikai (5)
Other, 61: Chinese Humanistic Buddhism (25); Shingon (23); Tendai (8); Korean Won (3); Chinese Mantranaya (2)

Northern Buddhism, 656:
Gelugpa, 174: mainline Gelugpa (96); New Kadampa Tradition (78)
Kagyüdpa, 160
Nyingmapa, 141: general Nyingmapa (114); Dzogch'en (27)
Kagyüdpa/Nyingmapa, 84: Shambhala (64); other forms of this mix (20)
Non-specific or unidentified, 61
Other, 36: Ri-may (non-sectarian) (19); Sakyapa (13); Jonangpa (2); Sakyapa/Nyingmapa (1); Bon (1)

Southern Buddhism, 373:
Monastery/temples, 190: Thai (98); Thai Forest Sangha (5); Sri Lankan (28); Laotian (27); Cambodian (17); Burmese (7); Vietnamese (3); Bangladeshi (1); mixed (2); for nuns (2)
Vipassanā, 97
Non-specific, 63
National organizations, 12: Burmese (4); Cambodian (4); Indian (2); Sri Lankan (1); Vietnamese (1)
Other, 12: Thai Forest Tradition (9); Dhammakāya (2); Samatha Trust (1)

Mixed, 131:
General Buddhist, 115
Other, 16: Friends of the Western Buddhist Order (6); Engaged Buddhist (4); Vipassanā/Zen (3); Vipassanā/Vajrayāna (1); Chinese and Sri Lankan Forest Sanghas (1); Tendai/Vajrayāna (1)

other teachers) was Taizan Maezumi (1931–95), founder of the Zen Center of Los Angeles (1956), one of whose Dharma heirs was John Daido Loori (1931–2009) of the Zen Mountain monastery, which is for monks and nuns, and is also a lay retreat centre (Prebish, 1999: 96–107; Seager, 1999: 101–5). As with other Buddhist retreat centres, this is not a 'retreat' from life, but an opportunity to face and understand it. Loori emphasized ethical action and awareness in all actions, and developed a Prison Program and a Zen Environmental Studies Center. Two other influential Yasutani disciples were Philip Kapleau (1912–2004) and Robert Aitken (1917–2010). Kapleau was author of the influential *The Three Pillars of Zen* (1965), and founder of the Rochester Zen Center in New York (1966). Aitken, of Hawaii, was founder of the Diamond Sangha (1959), which in time spread to California, Australia and New Zealand (Baumann, 2007: 814–15).

In the late 1990s, there were nearly 150 Chinese Buddhist organizations in the US, with 68 in California and 25 in New York (Prebish, 1999: 27). The most notable ones are as follows.[17] Tripiṭaka Master Hsüan Hua (1918–96) came from Hong Kong in 1962 at the invitation of some Chinese-American disciples, and founded the Sino-American Buddhist Association (SABA) in San Francisco in 1968 (in 1984, renamed the Dharma Realm Buddhist Association). His reputation soon attracted Euro-American followers, who made up two-thirds of the SABA membership by 1971. By 1977, the Association's headquarters was 'The City of 10,000 Buddhas', a large former hospital in extensive grounds, in northern California, with the largest community of Buddhist celibate monastics – around 150 – in the USA. Here there is the Dharma Realm University, primary and secondary schools, and *Saṅgha* and lay training facilities. The Association emphasizes strict *Vinaya* for monks and nuns, meditation and study of Chinese Buddhist texts. Through the Buddhist Texts Translation Society, it also translates such texts, along with explanations by Hsüan Hua. Study is of Chan, Lü, Tiantai, Pure Land and Chen-yen, while meditation is Chan, and also Pure Land chanting. The head temple now has a dozen branch temples, monasteries and institutes.

The most recent, large and dynamic form of Chinese Buddhism in the USA is the Hsi Lai temple in California, an outreach of the Fo Kuang Shan temple in Taiwan. Founded and headed by the former abbot of this, Master Hsing-yün (1927–), and costing $30 million, it was opened in 1988. It now has over 100 monks and nuns, as well as running a university, a university press and the HQ of its lay wing, the Buddha's Light International Organization, which operates in fifty-one countries, with around a million members. It also facilitates the running of an informal Taiwanese embassy. Hsi Lai has over a hundred regional groups and a number of branch temples, serves both the Chinese community and Euro-Americans, and has forged links with Buddhists of non-Chinese traditions. It espouses 'Humanistic Buddhism' (see p. 411) and is working to make this world a 'Pure Land', partly through fostering greater cross-cultural understanding.

17 Prebish, 1999: 26–32, 139–48; Prebish and Tanaka, 1998: 13–30; Seager, 1999: 159–68; Williams and Queen, 1999: 36–56.

There is also the Buddhist Association of the United States (*f.* 1969) and its Chuang Yen monastery (New York State), the Institute of Chung-Hwa Buddhist Culture (*f.* 1985), dedicated to Chan meditation and the revitalization of Chinese Buddhism, and the Taiwanese Tzu Chi compassion relief organization has around 16,000 members in the US.

In the Korean tradition,[18] while there are devotion-focused temples for Korean immigrants, there are also Korean teachers of the wider community, such as Seung Sahn Sunim (1927–), a Seon (Korean Zen) teacher who founded the Kwan Um School of Zen in 1983. With its headquarters on Rhode Island, by 1998 it had sixty centres worldwide, mostly in the USA and Europe. It includes elements from Pure Land and Huayan practices, and repeated prostrations. It also allows non-celibate lay people to wear the robes of monks and nuns, and emphasizes an open 'don't know' attitude to life.

In the Vietnamese tradition,[19] there are around 160 temples in North America, with celibate monks and nuns who lead the Vietnamese community in such things as Pure Land chanting and Chan meditation. There are also teachers such as Thich Nhat Hanh (see pp. 149, 412, 454) who have reached out to converts, and indeed his Community of Mindful Living (and associated Order of Interbeing) has the largest number of Zen-related groups in the US.

Nhat Hanh's idea of 'socially engaged Buddhism' originated in the chaos of the Vietnam War, and since his 1973 exile in the West he has been a key inspiring focus of a number of Buddhist groups emphasizing meditating activists' engaged compassionate action in the world, to relieve suffering.[20] These include Nhat Hanh's own communities, the cross-tradition Buddhist Peace Fellowship, founded in 1978 by Zen teachers Robert and Anne Aitken (Prebish, 1999: 107–14), and Rōshi Bernard Glassman's Zen Peacemaker Order. These are 'committed to providing employment for the needy, the homeless, and unskilled, and to establishing facilities for the homeless, for childcare, and for job training (Prebish and Baumann, 2002: 41), and have engaged in work with refugees and 'boycotts, hospice work, tax resistance, ecological programs, voter mobilizations, prison reforms, letter writing campaigns' (Prebish, 1999: 82). In such groups, inspiration from Asian teachers such as Nhat Hahn flows together with that from liberal-left

[18] Prebish, 1999: 32–5; Prebish and Tanaka, 1998: 117–28; Seager, 1999: 168–73.
[19] Prebish, 1999: 35–7; Prebish and Tanaka, 1998: 129–46; Seager, 1999: 173–81.
[20] Batchelor, 1994: 353–69; Prebish, 1999: 81–5; Prebish and Baumann, 2002: 223–6, 324–47; Prebish and Tanaka, 1998: 266–86; Seager, 1999: 201–15.

concern for social justice and reformist Protestant tendencies in Western culture. There are also ethnic temples that do engaged work, such as a Thai one in California working with children in street gangs (*EB*.10.8).

In 1960 the Japanese-based Sōka Gakkai of America (see pp. 404–6),[21] soon known as Nichiren Shōshū of America, and then since 1991 as Sōka Gakkai International USA (SGI-USA), began to vigorously proselytize. From 1967, it worked beyond the Japanese-American community, so that 95 per cent of its members are now non-Asian. By 1970, it claimed 200,000 members in the USA, and by 1974 it had groups on over sixty university and college campuses. From 1976, it tailed off its street evangelism and went more for consolidation and steady growth. There are now around 300,000 Nichiren Buddhists in the USA (Prebish, 1999: 118). The majority are from the SGI, but some are from the smaller Nichiren Shōshū, from which SGI split, and the Nichiren Buddhist Church of America (Nichiren Shū). SGI practice is home based, and is spread by word of mouth. Its growth has been aided by its pyramidic national structure: units (structured according to age and gender) and groups, then districts, chapters, headquarters, territories and joint territories. In the 1990s, it democratized its organization, with ministerial roles played by unpaid volunteers on a rotating basis, and with women, who have always been a very active part of it, getting more of a role in its leadership. SGI membership includes more Hispanics and Blacks than other Buddhist groups – 30 per cent are non-white and non-Asian – and it has famous members such as the singer Tina Turner and musician Herbie Hancock – actor Patrick Swayze was also a member. The simplicity and power of its practice have drawn in those seeking to overcome frustration or negativity and to enhance their creativity, though its devotional emphasis has not been attractive to people of a countercultural background, who have been drawn more to Zen and Tibetan Buddhism. The main SGI draw is the qualities of members, and once people join they then come to value especially ethical motivation, intellectual satisfaction, personal confidence and happiness, and social involvement in a well-run organization. SGI does not have formalized moral norms, which is attractive to liberal Americans, but sees values as emerging from an individual's practice.

The four main schools of Tibetan Buddhism are all present in the USA, attracting a growing number of young people by their mixture of mysticism,

[21] Prebish, 1999: 23–26, 114–27; Prebish and Baumann, 2002: 42–3, 113–14, 311; Prebish and Tanaka, 1998: 79–97; Seager, 1999: 70–89.

symbolism, ritual and psychological insights.[22] 'The unique combination within Tibetan Buddhism of great complexity, prominent mystical and non-rational elements, and the flexibility to adapt to different temperaments, may explain much of its appeal to Westerners' (Bluck, 2006: 110). There are only around 10,000 Tibetan exiles and immigrants in the USA, so most followers of the tradition are converts, clustering around influential Tibetan teachers or their key Western disciples. There are three main focuses of activity in regard to Tibetan Buddhism in the USA (Seager, 1999: 114–28):

- Religious practice, in a network of practice centres focused on different teachers and lineages.
- The preservation of Tibet's rich heritage of Buddhist texts, and their dissemination and translation in the West, for example in the work of Jeffrey Hopkins at the University of Virginia, the Asian Classics Input Project of Gelugpa monk Geshe Michael Roach, and the activities of a cluster of Buddhist publishing houses, with the roots in different Tibetan schools: Shambhala Publications (1969, Kagyüdpa), Dharma Publishing (1971, Nyingmapa), Snow Lion Publications (1980) and Wisdom Publications (1983, both Gelugpa), and Tharpa (1985, New Kadampa) – except for the last of these, their publications are not confined to those of their own school.
- The campaign for Tibet to be free of Chinese domination and colonialism, as in the Students for a Free Tibet movement and New York's Tibet House (*f.* 1987), associated with Professor Robert Thurman and actors such as Richard Gere.

Kagyüdpa teachers have included Kalu Rinpoche (1905–89), though the most influential has been Chögyam Trungpa Rinpoche (1939–87), a charismatic figure of somewhat controversial behaviour, whose teachings and popular writings, such as *Cutting Through Spiritual Materialism* (1973), presented the Tibetan tradition in a way attractive to those, especially in the counterculture of the 1960s and 1970s, seeking new cultural horizons and 'psychological growth'. He was an ex-monk Karma Kagyüdpa *Lama,* but also part of the Ri-may movement (see pp. 209–10), and so also drew on Nyingmapa teachings. He established a thriving centre at Boulder, Colorado, in 1971, which became a key hub of the Vajradhatu organization (*f.* 1973), a network including many meditation centres and affiliated groups, and the more secular Nalanda Foundation (*f.* 1974). After

[22] Prebish, 1999: 40–6; Prebish and Baumann, 2002: 111–12; Prebish and Tanaka, 1998: 99–115; Seager, 1999: 113–35.

Trungpa's death, these were first led by Trungpa's regent Ösel Tendzin (Thomas Rich), who died of AIDS in 1990, and then by Trungpa's eldest son Mipham Rinpoche, who reorganized them under the name Shambhala International (*f.* 1992),[23] with its headquarters in Halifax, Nova Scotia. 'Shambhala' is the name of a mythical ideal land (from which the term Shangri-la derives), signalling Trungpa's aim of developing an enlightened society. The organization publishes the popular magazine *Shambhala Sun*, has six main residential contemplative communities, including Gampo Abbey (*f.* 1984) in Nova Scotia, with Thrangu Rinpoche as abbot and the American nun Pema Chödrön (1936–) as resident teacher, and has over a hundred centres round the world. It has three 'gates' or strands:

- The Vajradhatu path which, in various centres known as Dharmadhatus, emphasizes meditative training and study through a gradual programme which draws on Zen and Theravāda as well as Vajrayāna aspects.
- Shambhala Training, or the 'Sacred Path of the Warrior', a secular path of spiritual training for those of any or no religious tradition, emphasizing a mindful openness to life, fearlessly drawing on a basic human goodness and overcoming limiting habit-patterns.
- The Nalanda path (named after a famous Buddhist University in ancient north-east India), which emphasizes developing wisdom through artistic and cultural activities such as photography, dance, horsemanship, poetry and the tea ceremony, and includes the Naropa Institute (*f.* 1974), now a liberal arts university which also covers health, education, business and subjects such as Environmental Studies, Contemplative Psychology and Buddhist Studies.

In the Nyingmapa school, Tarthang Tulku Rinpoche (1935–) is a charismatic *Lama* who encourages study, publication of Buddhist works and help for the Tibetan refugees in India. Sogyal Rinpoche (1947–), author of the acclaimed *The Tibetan Book of Living and Dying* (1992), founded the Rigpa Fellowship in 1982, with a major centre in Santa Cruz. He teaches *Dzogch'en*, as does Lama Surya Das (Jeffrey Miller, 1950–), who has studied with Buddhist teachers of many traditions, founded the Dzogchen Foundation (1991) and is author of *Awakening the Buddha Within* (1997).

In the Gelugpa school, the Foundation for the Preservation of the Mahayana Tradition (FPMT), founded by Lama Thubten Yeshe (1935–84) in Nepal in 1975, has been led by Lama Thubten Zopa (1946–) since 1984, and oversees over fifty Buddhist centres around the world, with monasteries, nunneries, an Institute of Buddhist Studies, a prison

[23] Baumann, 2007: 818–19; Prebish, 1999: 158–71; Seager, 1999: 125–8.

programme, clinics and a hospice. Since it inception in 1991 in the UK, the more exclusive form of Gelugpa called the New Kadampa Tradition (see p. 445) has also spread to the USA.

The Theravāda tradition is relatively new in the USA,[24] its first temple-monastery being established by the Sinhalese in 1966 in Washington DC. In recent years, the tradition has grown considerably (Prebish, 1999: 38), and it is set to have a large impact on American Buddhism. While many of its temples are for immigrant communities, for whom the priority is conservation of culture while making necessary adaptations to American culture, there are also those who bridge the immigrant and convert communities. The Sri Lankan monk Henepola Gunaratana formed the Bhavana Society in 1982, this being a retreat centre for both monastics and laity. He is a moderate modernizer, upholding the monastic ideal, but supporting the revival of the Theravāda *bhikkhunī* ordination-line. The forest meditation tradition of Thailand is also present. In California, Abhayagiri monastery practises in the line of the Thai teacher Ajahn Chah, and there is a branch of this 'Forest Sangha' tradition in the UK, with mainly Western monks. Ajahn Ṭhānissaro is an American disciple of the Thai teacher Ajahn Fuang Jotiko, and is abbot of Metta Forest monastery in California, and many of his translations of Buddhist texts appear on the Access to Insight website. Both these monasteries also offer retreats for laypeople, and are supported by donations.

For the Theravāda convert community, the most notable trend, of considerable popularity, is the *Vipassanā*/Insight Meditation movement. It has many lay teachers who practised in Burma with Mahāsī Sayadaw (see p. 337) and his disciples, some as monks. They often transmit meditation in a largely de-traditionalized context – even more so than American Zen – as an awareness technique as a means to psychological development. They also draw on elements from Mahāyāna Buddhism and humanistic psychology. A key centre is the Insight Meditation Center in Barre, Massachusetts, founded in 1975 by Sharon Salzberg, Jack Kornfield, Joseph Goldstein and others. From 1989, it had a Center for Buddhist Studies, and Golstein's and Kornfield's *Seeking the Heart of Wisdom* (1987) has been of considerable influence. In 1988 the Spirit Rock centre was founded by Kornfield in California. Most of the around 150 US Theravāda meditation centres in 1997 were *vipassanā* ones (Seager, 1999: 149–50). As well as *vipassanā*, the movement has come to emphasize the practice of *mettā*, or lovingkindness meditation. The aim is to encompass the heart of monastic meditative

24 Prebish, 1999: 37–40, 148–58; Prebish and Baumann, 2002: 36–9, 285–306; Prebish and Tanaka, 1998: 147–80; Seager, 1999: 136–57; Williams and Queen, 1999: 57–68.

practice in a series of retreats for laypersons – with sitting and walking meditation, *Dhamma* talks and private and group interviews – though there are those, such as Goldstein, who fear a watering down of the tradition.

The approach of the Insight Meditation movement, as well as Korean Zen, is drawn on in the work of Jon Kabat-Zinn (Seager, 1999: 213–14), who established the approach of Mindfulness Based Stress Reduction in 1979 as a secular therapy. He published many books such as *Wherever You Go, There You Are: Mindfulness Meditation in Everyday Life* (1994), and in 1995 founded the University of Massachusetts Center for Mindfulness in Medicine, Healthcare and Society (http://umassmed.edu/cfm/index.aspx). This is part of a two-way interaction of Western Buddhism with aspects of Psychology,[25] as also reflected in books such as Mark Epstein's *Thoughts Without a Thinker: Psychotherapy from a Buddhist Perspective* (1995) and Harvey B. Aronson's *Buddhist Practice on Western Ground: Reconciling Eastern Ideals and Western Psychology* (2004), and the work of the Mind and Life Institute (www.mindandlife.org), which has organized seminars involving the Dalai Lama and brain scientists.

Canada[26]

In Canada, the development of Buddhism has been similar to that in the USA. Numbers rose fourfold in the 1970s, with approximately 50,000 Buddhists existing in the country by 1985, and around 300,000 by 2002. Much of this increase is due to immigration, but there has also been an increase in converts. In 1983, the multi-denominational Buddhist Council of Canada was formed, though it is mainly active in the Toronto area. The web World Buddhist Directory in 2010 had 306 listings for Canada: 119 'Mahāyāna', 94 Vajrayāna/Tibetan, 63 Theravāda and 30 Non-sectarian/Mixed, though buddhismcanada.com indicated a total of nearly 700 in 2002 (Prebish and Baumann, 2002: 120).

The United Kingdom and Ireland[27]

The first Buddhist missionary to the UK was Dharmapāla, who visited for five months in 1893, then in 1896 and 1904. On these occasions, he made

[25] Prebish and Tanaka, 1998: 228–37; Prebish and Baumann, 2002: 348–64.
[26] On this, see Matthews, 2006 and his entry in Prebish and Baumann, 2002: 120–38.
[27] On this, see Bluck, 2004, 2006; Harris and Kauth, 2004; Humphreys, 1968; Kay, 2004; Prebish and Baumann, 2002, 85–105; Waterhouse, 1997; Wilson and Dobbelaere, 1994.

contact with T. W. Rhys Davids, Edwin Arnold and the Theosophists. The first Westerner to ordain as a Buddhist monk may have been an Austrian working in Siam (Thailand; 1878). The first to gain any prominence were: Gordon Douglas (ordained in Siam in 1899 as Asoka), the Irish freethinker Laurence Colvin (or O'Rourke, ?1856–?1914), who ordained as Dhammaloka in Burma in 1900, and Allan Bennett (1872–1923), the first to return to the West in robes. Bennett was inspired by *The Light of Asia* and appears to have been influenced by Theosophy. In 1902 he went to Burma, ordained as Ānanda Metteyya, and then formed a missionary society (1903). In 1907, the Buddhist Society of Great Britain and Ireland was formed, with T. W. Rhys Davids as its president, to receive a mission, and in 1908 Ānanda Metteyya and three Burmese monks arrived in Britain (Bluck, 2006: 6–8).

The Society was interested in a modernist version of Southern Buddhism, as both a world-view and an ethic. At first, progress was slow, but from 1909 to 1922, the *Buddhist Review* was published. The First World War held up development, and afterwards the Society struggled on until it collapsed in 1924. In this year, however, the lawyer Christmas Humphreys (1901–83) founded the Buddhist Lodge of the Theosophical Society (Humphreys, 1968), which absorbed the remnants of the previous Society in 1926. In 1943, the Lodge became the Buddhist Society, and its journal (*Buddhism in England*) became *The Middle Way*, which is still going strong. Under Humphreys, interest turned more to Zen and meditation practice. For many, his paperback *Buddhism* (1951 and still in print) was their first book on Buddhism, though its interpretation is slanted by ideas of the 'One' and the 'Self', which are particular to Theosophy and some presentations of Zen. The Buddhist Society continues, offering classes in Theravāda, Tibetan and Zen traditions, and has an annual summer school.

Dharmapāla visited England from 1925 to 1927, to found a branch of the Mahā Bodhi Society (1926), and establish a monastery for Sinhalese monks (1928), which existed until 1939. In 1928 Chinese reformer Ven. Daixu (see p. 409) also visited, while in 1936, D. T. Suzuki came to the World Congress of Faiths, in London, and lectured on Zen and Japanese culture in several English cities.

After the Second World War (Bluck, 2006: 8–17), a Sinhalese *vihāra* was established in London in 1954, and a Thai one in 1966. From the 1970s, Buddhism started to put down firm roots, as seen by a more widespread commitment to Buddhist *practice*, as opposed to a still mostly intellectual interest, and by the development of a social dimension, with the establishment of an indigenous *Saṅgha* and many Buddhist centres. In 1979, the number of groups, centres, monastery/temples and organizations was

Table 10 *Buddhist groups, centres, monastery/temples and organizations in the UK and Ireland*

Eastern Buddhism: 161 (of which 20 monastery/temples):
Zen, 142 (of which 6 monastery/temples): Sōtō (59, 5 monastery/temples); Nhat Hanh Community of Interbeing (43); Chan (22, 1 monastery/temple); Sōtō/Rinzai (10); non-specific (6); Kwan Um (2)
Pure Land, 9 (of which 1 monastery/temple)
Other, 10 (of which 7 monastery/temples)

Northern Buddhism: 137 (of which 2 monastery/temples):
Karma Kagyüdpa (43, 2 monastery/temples); Dzogch'en/Nyingmapa (37); Kagyüd-Sakyapa (19); Kagyüd-Nyingmapa (17); Gelugpa (14); non-specific (6); Nepalese (1)

Southern Buddhism: 117 (of which 22 monastery/temples):
Forest Sangha (40, 4 monastery/temples); Samatha Trust (29); Vipassanā (13); Ambedkar (5, 4 monastery/temples); other (30, 14 monastery/temples)

Friends of the Western Buddhist Order/Triratna Buddhist Community 53

seventh-four (Prebish and Baumann, 2002: 93), while the 2007 Buddhist Society *Buddhist Directory* for the United Kingdom and Ireland (cf. Bluck, 2006: 14) showed 468, as in Table 10.

To these can be added the numbers for the New Kadampa Tradition (370, two monastery/temples) and Sōka Gakkai (544 'districts', as of June 2010, plus four centres), as the *Buddhist Directory* only lists their national headquarters.

Some of the more important elements of Buddhism in Britain are as follows. In 1954, William Purfhurst[28] travelled to Thailand to ordain under Luang Phaw Sot (see p. 389), becoming Ven. Kapilavaddho (Mackenzie, 2007: 36–7). In 1956, he returned to England and founded the English Sangha Trust, whose aim was to establish an indigenous *Saṅgha* of the Southern tradition. In 1957, he disrobed due to bad health, but his disciple Ven. Paññavaddho continued the work of teaching *vipassanā* meditation. There was, however, not much success in recruiting or retaining new monks. In 1962, a Thai-trained Canadian monk, Ānanda Bodhi, founded the Hampstead Buddhist Vihāra, under the auspices of the English Sangha Trust. Two years later, an invitation to his Thai teacher to visit England led to the establishment of a Thai *vihāra* in London, which opened in 1966. In 1967, Ānanda Bodhi moved on to found the Johnstone House Meditation Centre, in Dumfriesshire, Scotland, but Kapilavaddho reordained and

[28] Also known as Richard Randall.

returned as incumbent of the Hampstead Vihāra. By 1969, there were four monks at the *vihāra*, and there were regular meditation classes. In 1970, however, Kapilavaddho disrobed due to bad health, dying in 1971. The other monks also disrobed, but continued Buddhist activities, leading to the establishment of two *vipassanā* meditation centres.

In 1977, the well-known Thai meditation teacher Ajahn Chah (see p. 338) visited the Hampstead Vihāra, at the request of the English Sangha Trust. His Western pupil, the American monk Ajahn Sumedho (1934), stayed on and organized the introduction of a *Saṅgha* of Western monks, trained in the forest tradition of Thailand (Bluck, 2006: 25–48; Sumedho, 1984). This soon moved to a rural site developed from a near-derelict country house at Chithurst in Sussex, with a nearby 108-acre forest as an integral part of a monastic settlement. Branch monasteries were then opened in Northumberland (1981) and Devon (1984). In 1985, the Amaravati Buddhist Centre (amaravati.org) was opened near Hemel Hempstead, in a group of wooden buildings on a site which was formerly a camp school. This is the largest monastery of the group, and also acts as a centre for lay activities; an impressive main temple building was completed in 1999.

As of 2010, this 'Forest Sangha' tradition had seventy ordained members in the UK: forty-two monks, nine ten-precept nuns, three male novices, and nine male and seven female postulants (*anagārikas* and *anagārikās*). A few of the older monks, who trained in Thailand, come from North America, but half are British and the rest from fifteen European countries, five Asian ones, Australia, New Zealand and South Africa. Their leader up to 2010 has been Ajahn Sumedho. They live a simple life, emphasizing *Vinaya*, meditation and non-attachment in daily activities. For laypeople, they offer weekend and ten-day introductions to meditation, emphasizing *vipassanā* practice, and have regular teaching contacts with lay groups throughout the country. Senior monks travel to related monasteries now established in Australia, New Zealand, Italy, Switzerland and the USA and Canada, in which there are a further fifty monks and sixteen other monastics.

A lay-led organization of the Southern tradition is the Samatha Trust (http://samatha.org; Bluck, 2006: 49–64). This was set up in 1973 by pupils of a Thai meditation teacher, Nai Boonman Punyathiro (1932–), who had previously been a monk for fifteen years and then had links with the Hampstead Vihāra. It specializes in the teaching of *samatha* mindfulness of breathing in a progressive set of stages involving different breath lengths and ways of attending to the breath, as well as lovingkindness practice, mindfulness of walking, *vipassanā*, Pali (and more recently English) chanting and *Sutta* and *Abhidhamma* classes. As of 2010, it had eighty-two lay teachers, with classes in thirty-four towns and cities, a meditation centre in Manchester, and a national meditation centre in rural Wales (*f.* 1987) and four groups in the USA. In 2006, a group of Samatha Trust chanters went on a tour of Thailand, especially for chanting of the *Mahāsamaya Sutta* (*D. Sutta* 20), not normally chanted by laypeople.

Another lay-led organization of the Southern tradition is the International Meditation Centre in Heddington, Wiltshire. This was founded in 1978 to provide a facility to teach *vipassanā* meditation, through ten-day courses, using the approach of the Burmese teacher U Ba Khin (see p. 337). Other Southern-inspired groups offer *vipassanā* shorn of devotional accompaniments: The House of Inner Tranquillity in Wiltshire (*f.* 1980), Gaia House in Devon (*f.* 1983), and Dhamma Dipa, an S. N. Goenka centre in Herefordshire (*f.* 1991). The Thai Dhammakaya movement (see pp. 388–91) also has temples in London (*f.* 2007) and Newcastle-upon-Tyne (*f.* 2010).

All four schools of the Tibetan tradition are established in the UK. In 1967, Ānanda Bodhi invited the monk Chögyam Trungpa (see p. 437) and the married *Lama* Akong Tulku Rinpoche (1939–) to teach at Johnstone House. This led to its transformation into Kagyu Samye-Ling monastery and Tibetan Centre (www.samyeling.org; Bluck, 2006: 110–28). While Trungpa disrobed as a monk after a bad car-crash, and moved on to the USA in 1970, Samye-Ling has acted as a place of quiet retreat for people of various religious backgrounds, and has worked to pass on not only Buddhist teachings and practices, but also Tibetan arts, crafts and skills. Its workshops and Tibetan art school have also been utilized in the building of an impressive new temple (1988). Courses are run on Buddhism, meditation, yoga, T'ai-chi, art and gardening, and a number of people have done four-year retreats there, which can include long solitary stretches. Around sixty people – twenty or more being monks or nuns – live in this Karma Kagyüdpa community, which has been led since 1995 by Lama Yeshe Losal (1943–). The centre has connections with many others in Britain and elsewhere and in 1992 it bought Holy Island, off the west coast of Scotland, as a site for long-term retreats and an interfaith centre. It has also spawned the Rokpa Trust, which aims 'to promote Buddhism and to foster non-sectarian inter-religious dialogue and understanding. To provide medical care and therapy. To provide education. To relieve poverty'.

In the Gelugpa tradition, a key organization is the Foundation for the Preservation of the Mahayana Tradition (http://fpmt.org; see p. 438), which in 1976 set up the Manjushri Institute, situated on the edge of the English Lake District, as a college for the study and preservation of the Gelugpa tradition. However, in 1991, its then resident teacher, Geshe

Kelsang Gyatso (1931–), formed the view that the Gelugpa tradition in the West was becoming too open to influence from other Tibetan Buddhist schools, and so founded a new tradition which he called the New Kadampa Tradition, seeing this as the guardian of the pure Gelugpa tradition.[29] The NKT split from the FPMT, keeping control of Manjushri Institute (renamed Manjushri Kadampa Meditation Centre), and has been very active in developing centres and groups around the UK and beyond. While the Gelugpa leader the Dalai Lama has a very ecumenical spirit, and is concerned about the preservation of Tibetan culture, the NKT focuses on its 'pure transmission' of the *Dharma*, not Tibetan matters, and has fallen out with the Dalai Lama over his criticism of the NKT protector deity, Dorje Shugden (see pp. 416–17; Kay, 2004: 100–9). With its claimed 370 monasteries, centres and groups in the UK, it has far outgrown the FPMT, which has fourteen, the main one being the Jamyang Buddhist Centre in London. The NKT monks and nuns, of which there are perhaps fifty in the UK, and a claimed 700 worldwide, follow just the first five of the ten precepts of a novice (see p. 278), plus five others: 'I will practise contentment, reduce my desire for worldly pleasures, abandon engaging in meaningless activities, maintain commitments of refuge, and practise the three trainings of pure moral discipline, concentration and wisdom'. Most Tibetan monastics follow thirty-six precepts, while a few Tibetan monks take the higher ordination and follow 253 (see p. 296).

While Rinzai Zen is strong in the Buddhist Society, a key Sōtō centre is Throssel Hole Abbey, in Northumberland.[30] This was founded in 1972, as a branch monastery of Shasta Abbey, California (see p. 432). It acts as a training monastery for Western monks and nuns (also called 'monks', for egalitarian reasons) of the 'Order of Buddhist Contemplatives', and a retreat centre for intensive 'serene reflection meditation'. Throssel Hole's resident monks and lay visitors live a life emphasizing discipline, tidiness, meditation and hard work. The monks – numbering thirty in 2006 – are celibate, unlike the modern pattern of married priests in Japan. They visit various groups, conduct weddings and funerals, ordain people as lay Buddhists, and conduct a lay ministry programme. New priories were opened in Reading in 1990 and Telford in 1997, and in 2007 there were twenty-seven Serene Reflection Meditation groups in the UK and Ireland.

The Friends of the Western Buddhist Order (FWBO) is a lay movement which seeks to identify the 'essence' of Buddhism and teach it in a Western

[29] kadampa.org; Bluck, 2006: 129–51; Kay, 2004: 3–116, 211–14.
[30] throssel.org.uk; Bluck, 2006: 65–88; Kay, 2004: 117–207, 215–18.

context and manner.[31] In 2010, it changed its name to the Triratna (Three Jewels) Buddhist Community. It was founded in 1967 by Ven. Sangharakshita (Dennis Lingwood, 1925–; Batchelor, 1994: 323–40), an English monk with experience of the Southern, Northern and Eastern traditions. He had been a monk for fourteen years in India, ten of them working with the Ambedkar Buddhists. The FWBO consists of a network of four types of organizations: urban centres, offering meditation classes, retreats, and talks for the public; local groups; co-operatives, in which members work on a team basis with an emphasis on ethical livelihood which helps the personal development of the individual; and communities where many members live, often having a 'common purse'. The movement has spread from the UK to continental Europe, New Zealand, Australia and the USA, and especially to India (Queen and King, 1996: 73–120), where it has been known as the Trailoka Bauddha Mahasangha Sahayaka Gana (now Triratna Buddhist Community) and does educational, medical and spiritual work among the Ambedkar Buddhists. FWBO introductory practices are mindfulness of breathing and *mettā-bhāvanā* (the cultivation of lovingkindness), with later ones including refuge-taking, Zen 'Just Sitting' and the visualization of particular Buddhas and *Bodhisattvas* and use of their *mantras*. Chanting is done in Pali and English, and a devotional *pūjā*, adapted from that of Śāntideva (see pp. 115–16), is used. There is also the practice of yoga, T'ai chi and karate.

Sōka Gakkai International,[32] as it is now called (see pp. 404–6), entered Britain in the 1980s. By the end of 1986 it claimed 3,000 followers and as of 2010, its 544 local groups, with an average of twelve members, represent around 6,500 members, though it had around 11,000 names on its database. Many of its adherents work in the caring professions or performing or graphic arts, with many being self-employed. The mean age at which they join is 31/32 (Wilson and Dobbelaere, 1994: 45), not infrequently after some kind of personal crisis. Most value its chanting practice as a way to empower themselves to take control of, and responsibility for, their lives. In the UK, SGI headquarters is at Taplow Court, Maidenhead. In this elegant old house, the absence of any Buddhist art or imagery is striking for anyone who has visited other Buddhist centres. Only when one enters the chanting room and a small shrine is opened does one see the *gohonzon* scroll. The chanting of *Nam-Myō-hō Ren-ge-kyō* and of sections of the *Lotus Sūtra* is

[31] http://thebuddhistcentre.com/text/what-triratna-buddhist-community; Baumann, 2007: 815–16; Bluck, 2006: 152–78; Subhuti, 1994.
[32] sgi-uk.org; Bluck, 2006: 89–110; Wilson and Dobbelaere, 1994.

done tremendously fast, 'like a galloping horse', as they describe it. While it lacks the calm of much Buddhist chanting, it has a very energizing and concentrating effect.

Monks and nuns of the Nipponzan Myōhōji Order, a small Nichiren sub-sect founded by Nichidatsu Fujii (1885–1985) and dedicated to working for world peace, have also been very active (http://mkbuddhism.org.uk). A few monks of the Order first arrived in the late 1970s and became involved in marches of the Campaign for Nuclear Disarmament. They then moved on to building 'Peace Pagodas'. Since 1924, they have built sixty-one in Japan, including ones at Hiroshima and Nagasaki, seven in India, two in Nepal and one in Sri Lanka. In 1980, they opened the first consecrated Pagoda/*Stūpa* in the West, at Milton Keynes, UK. Ones in Vienna (1983), Massachusetts (1985) and London (1985) followed, then three more in the USA (1993, 1998, 2010) and one in Italy (1998). The London one is in Battersea Park, besides the Thames. It is 34 metres high and contains relics from Nepal, Burma, Sri Lanka and Japan. Unlike the Milton Keynes structure, which blends Japanese and ancient Indian designs, its form is primarily Japanese (see Frontispiece). The yellow and white robes of their monks and nuns can sometimes be glimpsed in television news reports dealing with matters relating to nuclear weapons in various parts of the world.

The Pure Land tradition also has a small following in the UK. In 1976, the Shin Buddhist Association of Great Britain was formed by Jack Austin (1917–93) and lecturer Hisau Inagaki. Inagaki's father had been largely responsible for the establishment of Jōdo-shin Buddhism in Europe, and Rev. Austin had also been active in this field. In 1977, people meeting at Rev. Inagaki's house also formed the non-sectarian Pure Land Buddhist Fellowship, which is now led by Quaker–Buddhist Jim Pym and publishes *Pure Land Notes*. There has also developed the Amida Trust (www.amidatrust.com), led by David and Caroline Brazier, which offers a course in Buddhist psychology and psychotherapy, and has an Order committed to social engagement. Another Japanese tradition with a small following is the Shingon school.

The different forms of British Buddhism, while from diverse Asian roots, all share the need to work out an accommodation with Western culture. In this, the Forest Sangha and the FWBO very broadly lie at the two ends of a spectrum – though the degree of adaption to Western culture is not uniform in any tradition, but varies within its dimensions (Bluck, 2006: 184–5). The Forest Sangha have sought to introduce a mostly traditional monastic life-style, with no deliberate attempt to adapt to Western conditions. Ajahn

Sumedho holds that 'If one trims the tradition down before planting the seed, one often severs or slightens its whole spirit'.[33] To those who criticize the importation of 'Asian' customs, such as Pali chanting, he replies that only dogmatically clinging to traditions for their own sake should be avoided. Rather than dogmatically rejecting traditions and conventions, he prefers the middle way of *using* them skilfully. This could be characterized as a non-dogmatic, pragmatic traditionalism.

As to institutional forms, the monks and nuns led by Ajahn Sumedho continue the monastic traditions of the Thai forest monasteries.[34] They have successfully introduced the close lay–monastic relationship of Thailand, and are supported by lay donations, from both Asian communities in the UK (and Thailand) and indigenous Britons. A monastic form for women has been evolved which goes beyond that of Thai *mae chi*s (see pp. 300–1) in that, while they still only formally take ten precepts, in practice they follow around 120 rules. Their role is gradually developing, though so far the reinstitution of the Theravāda full *bhikkhunī* ordination with 311 precepts, as has developed in Sri Lanka and more recently in Australia (2009), has not been accepted. Lay chanting is in both English and Pali. Fairly traditional teachings are given, though rebirth is seen primarily as something to be observed in changing states of mind. As regards life after death, a somewhat agnostic attitude tends to be conveyed.

The FWBO emphatically seeks to develop a Western form of Buddhism, and has criticized other Buddhist groups for importing what it sees as extraneous cultural accretions along with 'essential' Buddhism (Bell, 1996). It selects practices and teachings by the criterion of their contribution to the development of the individual. Of Buddhist groups, it has been the most antipathetic to certain features of Western culture, such as what it sees as 'pseudo-Liberalism', and is also very critical of Christianity, which it sees as both limited and harmful. On the other hand, it greatly admires the English mystic William Blake. The Western idea of an 'alternative society' has been influential, with the movement seeing itself as the nucleus of a 'New Society' in which the values of human growth are paramount. The emphasis is on the movement being an economically self-sufficient society-unto-itself. The economic base is provided by 'Right Livelihood' co-operatives such as vegetarian restaurants, wholefood shops, building teams, an Arts Centre, Windhorse trading and publishers, and Clear Vision Education, which produces materials on Buddhism for UK schools.

33 1984 *Middle Way* magazine (59, no. 1) interview cited in Bluck, 2006: 36.

34 Bell, 2000a; Prebish and Baumann, 2002: 245–54.

The FWBO is centred on the Western Buddhist Order (now called the Triratna Buddhist Order), which had 677 members in the UK in 2004 (Bluck, 2006: 156). They follow ten precepts (the first four of the usual five lay precepts, three more on speech and three on right thought), take a Sanskrit name and are united by their commitment to the Buddha, *Dharma* and Order. Order members, known as *Dharmacharis* and *Dharmacharinis* (male or female '*Dharma*-farers'), include both married people and those following a celibate, semi-monastic life. They live in communities (mostly single sex), alone or with their families. The FWBO has criticized the nuclear family form of married life, seeing it as spiritually restricting and 'neurotic', reflecting a fragmentation in modern society (Subhuti, 1994: 162–4, 177). Couples, whether heterosexual or homosexual, are seen as sometimes bound together in projection and dependency, tending to make each a half-person (Subhuti, 1994: 173–4). While at one stage of the FWBO's development, some Order members sought to 'keep clear of unhealthy attachment by happily enjoying a number of different sexual relationships' (Subhuti, 1983: 167), it is now emphasized that sexual desire should be gradually transcended (Subhuti, 1994: 171). Celibacy is not required of WBO members, though, and the FWBO is now seeking to ensure that members living with their family do not feel marginalized. The FWBO is welcoming of homosexuals, and some in the late 1970s and early 1980s had seen homosexual relationships as less prone to attachments and jealousy than heterosexual ones. Same-sex friendships are seen as usually the deepest, and as facilitating greater trust and spiritual communication and guidance (Subhuti, 1994: 155), but spiritual development is seen to entail a progressive transcendence of polarized identification with a person's masculinity or femininity (Subhuti, 1994: 171). In its early teachings, the FWBO sometimes emphasized the 'Higher Evolution' of the 'individual', with an associated ideal that seemed to be a kind of heroic, muscular, romantic superhumanism, influenced by some of the ideas of the philosopher Friedrich Nietzsche. In this, it seemed to neglect that aspect of the Buddhist path which ultimately aims at the transcending of I-ness and ego-attachment. However, such ideas now seem less influential, though it remains the case that *vipassanā* meditation is reserved only for the more committed. In the British press (1997) and in the internet 'FWBO-files' there have been attacks on the FWBO as cult-like and including sexual manipulation by some, but the FWBO has further matured as it has reflected on and responded to these criticisms (see e.g. Vishvapani, 2001). In 1994, a College of Public Preceptors was established to oversee ordinations, and in 2000 Sangharakshita passed leadership of the Order to this.

Since then, the movement has included some critical reflections on its founder and some of his teachings.

The FWBO, along with the NKT and SGI, can be seen as 'new Buddhist movements', and Sandra Bell (2000b: 398) has described them as 'closely bound, hierarchical organizations' with 'an undisguised commitment to recruitment and expansion'. Bluck (2006: 188) sees it as more helpful to see them as 'enthusiastic, with firm beliefs, and urgent message, commitment to a particular lifestyle and perhaps "charismatic leadership" '. Other British Buddhist groups have tended to view them with some suspicion – for example many groups left the Network of Buddhist Organizations when the NKT became a member – but as they have been maturing, this view has been reducing.

In terms of reasonably active members for the largest convert groups, Bluck reports: 1,500 for the Forest Sangha (2006: 27); around 500 members and another 500 with some contact with the Samatha Trust (2006: 50); 1,000 or more in the Sōtō Zen Serene Reflection Meditation tradition (2006: 68); around 6,500 members of Sōka Gakkai International (2006: 91); perhaps 5,000 associated with the Karma Kagyüd Samye Ling Tibetan centre (2006: 112); 3,000 New Kadampa Tradition members (2006: 132); and for the Friends of the Western Buddhist Order, 2,000 'core members' and 5,000 with 'regular involvement' (2006: 156): 23,000 in all. This leaves many of the approximately 62,000 converts belonging to smaller groups, or with no specific affiliation.

Those interested in Buddhism are likely to be exposed to several traditions, and adherents of these interact to a fair extent: probably more so than in Asia, due to geographical separation. There is a Buddhist prison chaplaincy organization (Angulimala), a Buddhist Hospice Trust, a Network of Engaged Buddhists (concerned with peace, ecology and the human rights of Buddhists abroad) and the Rokpa Trust charity (Bluck, 2006: 22–3, 124). The growth of Buddhist monasteries and meditation centres has helped stimulate something of a revival in Christian meditation, and Christian monks and nuns sometimes learn techniques from Buddhist ones.

Building on the work of Kabat-Zinn in the USA, Mark Williams and John Teasdale, from the UK, and Canadian Zindel Siegal developed Mindfulness Based Cognitive Therapy. In 2004, this was recognized by the National Health Service's National Institute for Health and Clinical Excellence as a recommended treatment for recurrent depression, and there are now MAs or MScs in the discipline at Oxford University's Mindfulness Centre, the University of Wales at Bangor, and Exeter and Aberdeen Universities. The country also has MA Buddhist Studies courses at the

University of Bristol, and the School of Oriental and African Studies, London. An online MA ran at the University of Sunderland 2002–11, to be taken up by the University of Wales at Newport, and one may be developed by the University of Oxford.

Continental Europe[35]

In 2010, the internet World Buddhist Directory listed 2,717 groups, centres, monastery/temples and organizations for the whole of Europe (Table 11): 1,216 (44.7%) 'Vajrayāna' or Tibetan ones; 985 (36.2%) 'Mahāyāna' ones, that is East Asian ones such as of the Zen, Pure Land, Nichiren/SGI and Vietnamese traditions; 319 (11.7%) 'Theravāda' ones; and 197 (7.2%) 'Non-sectarian/Mixed' ones. Countries with over fifty entries are listed in Table 11 (see Prebish and Baumann, 2002: 94).

Baumann reports that 'Interest in Buddhism has grown exponentially in Europe since the early 1990s' (Prebish and Baumann, 2002: 85), for example with an increase in Germany from forty groups in 1975 to more than 500 groups, centres or monasteries in 1999 (2002: 93), and with a growing interest in Eastern Europe since the political changes of 1989. Overall, interest in the Theravāda from the early twentieth century was complemented by a Zen boom in the 1960s and 1970s, then a surge of interest in Tibetan Buddhism (2002: 93–4). Moreover, the SGI, introduced from the 1970s, 'appears to be one of the numerically strongest Buddhist organizations in contemporary Europe' (2002: 92). The above figures include very few of the SGI groups, though, as their addresses are not publically available. Moreover, immigrant Buddhists (many from Theravāda lands) have fewer institutions, compared to their numbers, than do convert ones. The 60,000 Vietnamese immigrants in Germany, though, have built the largest pagoda in Europe in Hanover.[36]

In Germany (Baumann, 1995), interest was initially focused on the Southern tradition, which perhaps appeals to those from a Protestant culture. The first Buddhist society was started in 1903 by the Pali scholar Karl Seidenstücker (1876–1936), to promote Buddhist scholarship. Success was small, though. An influential figure in early German Buddhism was George Grimm (1868–1945), whose *The Doctrine of the Buddha, the Religion of Reason* (1915 in German) was one of the most widely read books on

[35] On this, see Baumann, 2007: 349–52; Prebish and Baumann, 2002: 85–105.

[36] 'Immigrant Buddhism in Germany: Vietnamese Buddhism': http://pluralism.org/resources/slideshow/thumbs.php?show=buddhagerm&shownumber=&from=1&to=18.

Table 11 *Buddhist groups, centres, monastery/temples and organizations in Europe*

Country	Theravāda	Mahāyāna (e.g. Zen, Pure Land, Nichiren)	Vajrayāna	Non-sectarian/ Mixed	Total
Germany	66 (9.8%)[a]	247 (36.6%)	332 (49.2%)	35 (5.2%)	675[b]
UK	100 (19.8%)	168 (33.3%)	138 (27.4%)	101 (20.0%)	504
France	24 (7.3%)	157 (47.4%)	139 (42.0%)	7 (2.1%)	331
Switzerland	19 (12.8%)	55 (37.2%)	69 (46.6%)	7 (4.7%)	148
Spain	4 (3.0%)	43 (32.3%)	82 (61.7%)	3 (2.3%)	133
Italy	28 (21.2%)	42 (31.8%)	56 (42.4%)	6 (4.5%)	132
Netherlands	12 (11.8%)	50 (49.0%)	34 (33.3%)	10 (9.8%)	102
Poland	1 (1.2%)	23 (27.0%)	56 (65.9%)	6 (7.0%)	85
Austria	7 (8.9%)	29 (36.7%)	44 (55.7%)	0 (0%)	79
Czech Republic	12 (17.1%)	14 (20.0%)	43 (61.4%)	1 (1.4%)	70
Belgium	7 (10.3%)	45 (66.2%)	11 (16.2%)	4 (5.9%)	68
Sweden	12 (20.7%)	22 (37.9%)	22 (37.9%)	6 (10.3%)	58
Denmark	5 (8.9%)	23 (41.0%)	26 (46.4%)	3 (5.4%)	56

[a] The percentages in parentheses for each country are the percentages of the Buddhist groups etc. in that country that are Theravāda, Mahāyana, Vajrayāna or mixed.
[b] The total figures in the column on the right reflect the fact that some of the groups etc. in the columns to the left are listed in more than one column in the World Buddhist Directory.

Buddhism, both in its original German, and in many translations. His interpretation of the *Suttas* saw the teaching that all phenomena are non-Self as a way to intuit the true Self, which lies beyond concepts. As he felt that the Buddhist tradition had misunderstood the Buddha, he called his interpretation 'Old Buddhism', meaning the 'original' teaching. In 1921, Grimm and Seidenstücker formed the Buddhist Community for Germany, which became the Old Buddhist Community in 1935, under Grimm's leadership. As most German Buddhists did not accept Grimm's views, 'Old Buddhism' became a kind of sect. Another key Buddhist was Paul Dahlke (1865–1928), who developed an interest in Buddhism while in Sri Lanka in 1900. He followed a modernist version of Southern Buddhism, well rooted in the Pali sources. He built the 'Buddhist House' in Berlin-Frohnau, a temple/meditation centre opened in 1924, and also published translations of a number of *Suttas*.

Several Germans became attracted to the monastic life in Asia. In Sri Lanka, Nyānatiloka (Anton Gueth; 1878–1957) ordained as a novice in 1903 (getting higher ordination in Burma, 1904), while his main pupil,

Nyānaponika (Siegmund Feniger; 1901–94), became a monk in 1937. Both produced much Buddhist literature, in English and German, which has been widely read by European Buddhists, such as Nyānatiloka's *The Word of the Buddha* (1906 in German; 1927 in English) and Nyānaponika's *The Heart of Buddhist Meditation* (1954). The first European Buddhist nun, the German Sister Uppalavannā (Else Buchholtz; 1886–1982), was ordained in Sri Lanka in 1926. In the post-war period, mission societies from Sri Lanka (1952) and Burma (1957) were established, and a *vipassanā* meditation centre was opened near Hamburg (1961). Ayya Khema (Ilse Kussel; 1923–97), of Jewish background like Nyānaponika, became a nun in Sri Lanka in 1979 and was very active in the movement to revive the Theravāda *bhikkhunī* ordination.

Between the wars, some studies of Zen were made, but it was still little known or appreciated. This changed after the Second World War, especially due to the influence of a small book by Eugen Herrigel, *Zen in the Art of Archery* (1948 in German; 1953 in English), the fruit of five years of studying a Zen martial art. From the 1970s, Zen centres sprang up, and Jōdo-shin also established a presence. The post-war period also saw the introduction in 1952 of the Arya Maitreya Mandala, which had centres in ten cities by 1970. This is a lay Order founded in 1933 in India by Lama Anagārika Govinda (Ernst Hoffman; 1898–1985), a German who had trained in both the Southern and Northern traditions, and was a follower of the Tibetan ecumenical Ris-may movement (see pp. 209–10). From the 1970s, other Tibetan groups have been established: of the 332 listed for Germany in the World Buddhist Directory in 2010, 38 are specifically Gelugpa, 10 New Kadampa, 37 Nyingmapa, 3 Sakyapa, but 197 Kagyüdpa, of which 79 belong to the Diamond Way Karma Kagyüdpa lineage, directed by Danish married *Lama* Ole Nydahl (1941–) and with its European headquarters in Immenstadt.

France (Lenoir, 1999) has been strong in Buddhist scholarship. Early popularizers were Alexandra David-Néel (1868–1969; Batchelor, 1994: 303–322) and Suzanne Karpelès (1890–1969). The former became an intrepid explorer and prolific writer, popularizing exotic aspects of Tibetan Buddhism decades before interest in it boomed. The revival of Buddhism in Cambodia and Laos, with Buddhist Institutes in their capitals, was greatly aided by pressure from Karpelès on the colonial authorities there. She supervised the printing of the Pali Canon and Khmer, was the General Secretary of both Institutes, and secretary of the L'École Française d'Extrême-Orient in Hanoi, Vietnam. She was also actively involved in Les Amis du Bouddhisme, France's first Buddhist society, which was founded in Paris in 1929 by the Chinese reformer Daixu (see p. 409) and expatriate American, Grace Constant Lounsberry (1876–1964). It included lectures on the Mahāyāna, but emphasized the Theravāda, as seen in a pioneer book on meditation by Lounsberry and R. and M. de Maratray's translation of the *Dhammapada*. From 1940, however, the fortunes of Les Amis declined. Later, Paul Arnold (1909–92) established the cross-tradition La Communauté Bouddhique de France (1986).

Among converts in France, Tibetan Buddhism has the most followers, then Zen. Jean-Pierre Schnetzler (1929–2009) supervised meditation and study circles in Grenoble (from 1972) and created one of the largest and most influential Tibetan Buddhist centres in France at a former Carthusian monastery, Karma Ling Institute in Arvillard (*f.* 1979). This is one of fifty-three Karma Kagyüdpa centres now in the country, many set up by Kalu Rinpoche (1905–89) from 1976. Another large Kagyüdpa one is Dhagpo Kundreul Ling (1984) in the Dordogne, founded by the Gwalya Karmapa (1902–81), which is perhaps the largest group of retreat centres and monastic hermitages in Europe. The Gelugpa and Nyingmapa traditions also established monasteries and centres. The most well-known French Buddhist is the Nyingmapa monk Matthieu Ricard (1945–), son of the famous philosopher Jean-François Revel, a dialogue with whom, *Le Moine et le Philosophe* (1997; *The Monk and the Philosopher*, 1998), has been a much-translated bestseller. After brain-scans on him at the University of Wisconsin-Madison, he has sometimes been dubbed the 'happiest person in the world'. Zen studies and practice have largely revolved round Japanese Sōtō Zen master Taisen Deshimaru (1914–82), who established L'Association Zen Internationale in Paris (*f.* 1970), a residential centre in a Loire chateau (*f.* 1979), and branches throughout the country and abroad.

There are now many refugees from Mahāyāna Vietnam and Theravāda Laos and Cambodia living in France. The Vietnamese have opened many centres, mainly in and around Paris, led by such monks as Huyên-vi and his Linh So'n association, and Thich Nhat Hanh (see pp. 412, 435). The latter has an international reputation as a peace activist, and has integrated Buddhist practice of mindfulness into many areas of life, enhanced by popular writings in English and in French, such as *The Miracle of Mindfulness* (1991). In 1982, he established Plum Village, a monastery and retreat centre in the Dordogne, which is the centre of his international Community of Mindful Living network. It hosts an annual four-week summer retreat, which by 2004 had an attendance of around 2,000. A set of four communities there respectively housed, in 2010: sixty-five monks and laymen, forty nuns and laywomen, twenty monks, and forty nuns and laywomen.

Cambodian, Laotian and Sinhalese Buddhists have also established a few monastery-temples, but as these primarily serve the needs of their countrymen, Theravāda Buddhism is poorly represented among converts. Compared to the English-speaking world, Germany and Italy, moreover, France has been less well served by publishers for translations of original texts, especially canonical scriptures.

In Italy, after the short-lived Società degli Amici del Buddhadhamma (1958–9), the Associazione Buddhista Italiana was founded in 1966 by Luigi Martinelli, a translator of Theravāda texts, and has a journal, *Buddhismo Scientifico*. Since the 1980s, Amadeo Solé-Leris has also supported the practice of *vipassanā* meditation through his writings and lecturing, and these developed the Associazone per la meditazione di consapevolezza (*vipassanā*). Theravāda is also present in nine Sri Lankan monastery-temples, six *vipassanā* groups, and Santacittarama monastery (*f.* 1990), 30 miles south of Rome, which follows the same tradition as the UK Forest Sangha, and has six associated groups.

The Zen tradition in Italy is somewhat larger, its main centre being Bukkosan Zenshinji, a Rinzai monastery near Orvieto, Umbria. Opened in 1975, it is directed by the married priest Luigi Mario, known as Engaki Taino. Two Italian monks direct the main Sōtō Zen establishment, Associazione Italiana Zen, in Milan. The Tibetan tradition has a greater appeal in Italy, no doubt due to the fact that its well-developed ritual, colourful art and 'catholic' outlook harmonize with people of a Roman Catholic background. Many towns have a Tibetan presence, most notably Pomaia (near Pisa), where the (Gelugpa, FPMT) Istituto Lama Tzong Khapa (*f.* 1977) has its headquarters, with around forty monastic and lay residents. Here and at other similar centres, Mahāyāna Buddhist texts are published in translation together with exegetical material in Italian. The SGI has also become popular in Italy, with perhaps 22,000 members, partly due to it being followed by soccer star Roberto Baggio and the actress Sabina Guzzanti (Prebish and Baumann, 2002: 103).

Since 1975, the Centro d'Informazione Buddhisti has facilitated knowledge of Buddhism and encouraged the development of retreat centres. During the 1980s there developed the Rome-based Centro di Cultura Buddhista (led by psychology Professor Riccardo Venturini), and the Fondazione Maitreya, with its quarterly journal *Paramita*, covering all aspects of Buddhism. A good representative selection of Buddhist material is now easily available from Italian commercial publishers, including the translation of almost all the *Suttas* of the Pali Canon.

In Switzerland (Baumann, 2000), the German Theravāda monk Nyānatolika was resident in 1909/10, and a monastery was built for him in Lausanne, at which the first Buddhist ordination in Europe, of a German

man as a novice, was conducted. There was a Theravāda group in Zurich from 1942 to 1961, and in 1968, the Monastic Tibet Institute was established to see to the needs of around a thousand Tibetan refugees in the country. Zen and other Tibetan groups were established in the 1970s, with the Gelugpa Rabten Choeling monastery established near Lausanne in 1977. *Vipassanā* groups were established, and in the 1980s Cambodian and Vietnamese refuges established centres. There is also the Dhammapala monastery, (*f.* 1988) of the Forest Sangha tradition, and a Thai temple (*f.* 1996). The largest number of groups are Tibetan, though.

In Spain, the Tibetan tradition has the largest number of Buddhist groups/centres (eighty-two), with fifty of these being Karma Kagyüdpa, and fourteen Gelugpa. Twenty-two of the Karma Kagyüdpa ones belong to the Diamond Way, and, in 2003, this built a 33-metre-high *Stūpa* in Benalmádena in Andalucia. In the Gelugpa, in 1986, a one-year-old Spanish boy, Osel Hita Torres, son of a couple running a Tibetan Buddhist centre, was recognized as the reincarnation of the FPMT founder Thubten Yeshe Rinpoche (see p. 438). The boy was then trained in Kopan monastery, Nepal, which was established by *Lama* Yeshe. He is currently at university in Spain and is exploring an open approach to spirituality. Of the thirty-seven Zen groups of various kinds, twenty-four are Sōtō.

Australia, New Zealand, Latin America, Africa and Israel

Since the mid-1920s, various short-lived Buddhist societies began to form in Australia, and from the 1950s in New Zealand.[37] The longest established are the Buddhist Societies of Victoria and New South Wales, founded in the 1950s. American Sister Dhammadinna came from Sri Lanka in 1952, the Burmese U Thittila in 1954, and the SGI leader Ikeda in 1964. From the early 1970s, Buddhism began to take root as other teachers arrived from Asia. These included the British monk Phra Khantipālo, trained in Thailand, who established a monastery, and FPMT *Lamas* Thubten Yeshe and Thubten Zopa (1974). The Tibetan, Theravāda, Zen, Chinese, Vietnamese and Sōka Gakkai traditions are now all present and active, with a large Fo Kuang Shan temple opened in 1996 in Wollongong, New South Wales. The Karma Kagyüdpa, FPMT, FWBO, Rinzai Zen and Diamond Sangha Zen traditions also arrived in New Zealand, with one Forest Sangha monastery established in 1986 and another in 2000. The Bodhinyana Forest

[37] Baumann, 2007: 69–71; Prebish and Baumann, 2002: 139–51; Rocha, 2007; Rocha and Barker, 2010.

Table 12 *Buddhist groups, centres, monastery/temples and organizations in Australia, New Zealand, Brazil, South Africa and Israel*

Country	Theravāda	Mahāyāna (e.g. Zen, Pure Land, Nichiren)	Vajrayāna	Non-sectarian/ Mixed	Total
Australia	128 (25.4%)	171 (34%), including 61 Vietnamese, 22 Pure Land, 10 Diamond Sangha Zen, 7 Sōtō Zen	146 (30%), including 48 Gelugpa, 31 Sakyapa, 24 Karma Kagyüdpa, 18 Nyingmapa, 4 New Kadampa	59 (11.7%)	504[a]
Brazil	16 (11.3%)	71 (50%)	52 (36.6%)	5 (3.5%)	142
New Zealand	30 (30%)	26 (26%)	31 (31%)	16 (16%)	100
South Africa	7 (14.3%)	17 (34.7%)	18 (36.7%)	9 (18.4%)	49
Israel	4 (14.3%)	16 (57.1%)	6 (21.4%)	2 (7.1%)	28

[a] The total figures in the column on the right reflect the fact that some groups etc. in the column to the left are listed in more than one column in the World Buddhist Directory.

Sangha monastery (*f.* 1983) in Serpentine, Western Australia, headed by Ajahn Brahmavamso, is notable in that in 2009 it accepted the re-establishment of the Theravāda *bhikkhunī* ordination-line, though as a result of doing this without proper consultation with other Forest Sangha leaders, it has been separated from this tradition. Refugees from Vietnam, Cambodia and Laos have also brought their Buddhism to both countries, and with Chinese immigrants, these make up the majority of Buddhists in both. Table 12 shows the entries for the World Buddhist Directory in 2010.

Buddhism did not spread beyond the Japanese community in countries such as Brazil until after the Second World War.[38] Since then, Tibetan and Western Zen Buddhism has established a small presence in Argentina, Brazil, Chile, Colombia and Venezuela, while Sōka Gakkai is active throughout the region, with a claimed 140,000 followers in Brazil, mostly non-Japanese. In Brazil, besides a number of Japanese sects, there are temples for Chinese and Korean immigrants, the Tibetan and Theravāda traditions, and a strand of academic interest in Buddhist philosophy.

In South Africa,[39] Buddhism has been developing among white people since 1970. In 1984 there were eight Tibetan centres and the influential

[38] Baumann, 2007: 709–10; Prebish and Baumann, 2002: 163–76.

[39] Baumann, 2007: 711–12; Prebish and Baumann, 2002: 152–62.

modernist Theravāda Buddhist Retreat Centre at Ixopo (*f.* 1980), specializing in *vipassanā* meditation, with further Tibetan Kagyüdpa and Gelugpa, Japanese and Korean Zen and Theravāda monastic Buddhism following in the 1990s. The Chinese Fo Kuang Shan school and the Sōka Gakkai are also active, and have been more successful in attracting black members. Sōka Gakkai has also been active in West Africa from around 1975, and Zen and *Vipassanā* are of some interest among Western-educated people in other African countries. The World Buddhist Directory had twenty entries for the rest of Africa in 2010. Buddhism has also started to develop in Israel (Prebish and Baumann, 2002: 177–88) from the 1990s, with some from the secularized liberal strata developing an interest in Tibetan Buddhism, Zen, *Vipassanā* and Sōka Gakkai.

Today, Buddhism has become a worldwide phenomenon. In Asia, it has suffered losses under Communist rule, but shows signs of recovery. It is also having to adapt to a secularizing environment. Beyond Asia, it is increasingly being established and recognized as one facet of a diverse religious scene.

APPENDIX I

Canons of Scriptures[1]

The scriptural canon of Southern Buddhism is generally known as the Pali Canon or, traditionally, as the *Tipiṭaka*, the 'Three Baskets/Collections' (see pp. xxi–xxviii for abbreviations). It consists of the *Vinaya-piṭaka*, or 'Basket of Monastic Discipline', the *Sutta-piṭaka*, or 'Basket of Discourses', and the *Abhidhamma-piṭaka*, or 'Basket of Further Teachings'. The contents of the *Vinaya* (six vols.) and *Abhidhamma* (seven texts in thirteen vols., in one edition) are discussed on pp. 289 and 90–2 respectively. The contents of the *Sutta-piṭaka* is as follows (the numbers of volumes are those of the PTS edition – www.palitext.com):

(i) *Dīgha Nikāya*, or 'Long Collection' of thirty-four discourses (three vols.).

(ii) *Majjhima Nikāya*, or 'Middle Length Collection' of 152 discourses (three vols.).

(iii) *Saṃyutta Nikāya*, or 'Connected Collection' of 7,762 discourses, grouped in fifty-six sections (*saṃyuttas*) according to subject matter (five vols.).

(iv) *Aṅguttara Nikāya*, or 'Incremental Collection' of 9,550 discourses, grouped according to the number of items occurring in lists (from one to eleven) which the discourses deal with (five vols.).

(v) *Khuddaka Nikāya*, or 'Small Collection' of 15 miscellaneous texts in 20 volumes, many in verse form, which contain both some of the earliest and some of the latest material in the Canon:

   (a) *Khuddaka-pāṭha*, a short collection of 'Little Readings' for recitation.

   (b) *Dhammapada*, or 'Verses on *Dhamma*', a popular collection of 423 pithy verses of a largely ethical nature. Its popularity is

[1] On these, see Ch'en, 1964: 365–78; Gethin, 1998: 39–45; Keown and Prebish, 2007: 195–205; Lancaster, 1979: 215–29; Pagel, 2001.

reflected in the many times it has been translated into Western languages.

(c) *Udāna*, eighty short *Suttas* based on inspired 'Verses of Uplift'.
(d) *Itivuttaka*, or 'As It Was Said': 112 short *Suttas*.
(e) *Sutta-nipāta*, the 'Group of Discourses', a collection of seventy-one verse *Suttas*, including some possibly very early material such as the *Aṭṭhakavagga*.
(f) *Vimāna-vatthu*, 'Stories of the Mansions', on heavenly rebirths.
(g) *Peta-vatthu*, 'Stories of the Departed', on ghostly rebirths.
(h) *Thera-gāthā*, 'Elders' Verses', telling how a number of early monks attained Arahatship.
(i) *Therī-gāthā*, the same as (h), for nuns.
(j) *Jātaka*, a collection of 547 'Birth Stories' of previous lives of the Buddha, with the aim of illustrating ethical points. The full stories are told in the commentary, based on verses, which are canonical; together they comprise six volumes. While this is a relatively late portion of the Canon, probably incorporating many Indian folk tales, it is extremely popular and is often used in sermons.
(k) *Niddesa*, an 'Exposition' on part of (e).
(l) *Paṭisambhidāmagga*, an *Abhidhamma*-style analysis of certain points of doctrine (two vols.).
(m) *Apadāna*, 'Stories of Actions and Their Results' on past lives of monks and nuns in (h) and (i).
(n) *Buddha-vaṃsa*, 'Chronicle of the Buddhas', on twenty-four previous Buddhas.
(o) *Cariyā-piṭaka*, 'Basket of Conduct', on the conduct of Gotama in previous lives, building up the 'perfections' of a *Bodhisattva*.

The Burmese tradition also includes in the *Khuddaka Nikāya*:

(p) *Suttasaṃgaha*, 'Compendium of Discourses'.
(q) and (r) *Peṭakopadesa*, '*Piṭaka* Disclosure', and *Nettippakaraṇa*, 'The Guide', both attributed to Kaccāna Thera and aimed at commentary writers.
(s) *Milindapañha*, 'Milinda's Questions': discussions between King Milinda and Nāgasena Thera.

The Chinese Canon is known as the *Dazangjing* (*Ta-tsang-ching*) or 'Great Scripture Store'. The standard modern edition, following a non-traditional order based on systematization by scholars, is the *Taishō Daizōkyō*, published in Japan from 1924 to 1929. It consists of fifty-five vols. containing 2,184 texts:

(i) Translations of the *Āgamas* (equivalent to the first four Pali *Nikāyas*, and part of the fifth) and the *Jātakas* (219 texts in four vols.).
(ii) Translations of Mahāyāna *Sūtras*, sometimes including several translations of the same text. These are grouped into sections on: the Perfection of Wisdom (see pp. 114–18), the *Lotus Sūtra* (see pp. 163–4), the *Avataṃsaka*, the *Ratnakūṭa* (a group of texts, some very early, such as the *Kāśyapa-parivarta*), the *Mahāparinirvāṇa* (on the last days of the Buddha, and the 'Buddha-nature'), the *Mahā-sannipāta* ('Great Assembly') and general '*Sūtras*' (mostly Mahāyāna) (627 texts in thirteen vols.).
(iii) Translations of *Tantras* (see p. 182; 572 texts in four vols.).
(iv) Translations of various early *Vinayas* (on monastic discipline) and some texts outlining 'discipline' for *Bodhisattvas* (eighty-six texts in three vols.).
(v) Translations of commentaries on the *Āgamas* and Mahāyāna *Sūtras* (thirty-one texts in three vols.).
(vi) Translations of various early *Abhidharmas* (see p. 94) (twenty-eight texts in four vols.).
(vii) Translations of Mādhyamika, Yogācāra and other *Śāstras*, or 'Treatises' (129 texts in three vols.).
(viii) Chinese commentaries on the *Sūtras*, *Vinaya* and *Śāstras* (twelve vols.).
(ix) Chinese sectarian writings (five vols.).
(x) Histories and biographies (95 texts in four vols.).
(xi) Encyclopaedias, dictionaries, non-Buddhist doctrines (Hindu, Manichaean, and Nestorian Christian), and catalogues of various Chinese Canons (sixty-four texts in three vols.).

As can be seen, the Chinese Canon includes types of material (such as commentaries, treatises and histories) which are treated as extra-canonical in the Southern, Pali tradition. By 1934, there was also a *Taishō Daizōkyō* supplement of forty-five volumes containing 736 further texts: Japanese texts, recently discovered Dunhuang texts, apocryphal texts composed in China, iconographies and bibliographical information.

The Tibetan Canon consists of the *Kangyur* (*bK'-'gyur*) and *Tengyur* (*bsTan-'gyur*). The former is the 'Translation of the Word of the Buddha', and consists in its Narthang (sNar thang) edition of ninety-eight volumes containing over 600 translated texts, grouped as follows:

(i) *Vinaya* (monastic discipline) (thirteen vols.).
(ii) Perfection of Wisdom (twenty-one vols.).
(iii) *Avataṃsaka* (six vols.).

(iv) *Ratnakūṭa* (forty-nine *Sūtras* in six vols.).
(v) *Sūtra* (three-quarters of which are Mahāyāna; 270 texts in thirty vols.).
(vi) *Tantra* (more than 300 texts in twenty-two vols.).

The *Tengyur* is the 'Translation of Treatises', consisting in its Peking edition of 3,626 texts in 224 volumes. These are grouped as follows:

(i) *Stotras*, or hymns of praise (sixty-four texts in one vol.).
(ii) Commentaries on the *Tantras* (3,055 texts in eighty-six vols.).
(iii) Other commentaries and treatises: commentaries on the Perfection of Wisdom *Sūtras* and the *Vinaya*; Mādhyamika and Yogācāra treatises, *Abhidharma* works, tales and dramas, treatises on such topics as logic, medicine, grammar and chemistry, and other miscellaneous works (567 texts in 137 vols.).

The *Tengyur* mainly consists of Indian works, but outside the above twofold Canon, there is an enormous literature written by Tibetans.

APPENDIX II

Web Resources

Please find an online version of these links to resources at: www.cambridge.org/harvey

GENERAL LINKS AND RESOURCES

- BuddhaNet: Buddhist Information and Education Network: www.buddhanet.net – including: e-Library, World Buddhist Directory (www.buddhanet.info/wbd) and audio resources.
- DharmaNet: www.dharmanet.org – including: learning resource centre, study centre and directory.
- Australian National University – Buddhist Studies Virtual Library: www.ciolek.com/WWWVL-Buddhism.html
- National Taiwan University Digital Library and Museum of Buddhist Studies: http://buddhism.lib.ntu.edu.tw/BDLM/copyright2E.htm
- LinksPitaka: www.pitaka.ch/intro.htm
- Buddhist Links and General Resources: www.academicinfo.net/buddhismmeta.html
- Sacred Texts site: www.sacred-texts.com/bud/index.htm – for out of copyright translations.
- Huntingdon Archive of Buddhist and Related Art: http://chnm.gmu.edu/worldhistorysources/d/104/whm.html
- International Dunhuang Project: http://idp.bl.uk
- Digital Dictionary of Buddhism: www.buddhism-dict.net/ddb
- *Buddhist Dictionary – Manual of Buddhist Terms and Doctrines*, by Nyanatiloka Mahathera: www.buddhanet.net/budsas/ebud/bud-dict/dic_idx.htm – explains Pali terminology.

FREE ONLINE JOURNALS AND E-TEXTS OF PRINT JOURNALS

- *Philosophy East and West*, *Japanese Journal of Religious Studies*, *Journal of Oriental Studies* and *Hsi Lai Journal of Humanistic Buddhism* – on website of the National Taiwan University, Center for Buddhist Studies: http://ccbs.ntu.edu.tw/FULLTEXT/e-journal.htm

  There are also selections from a range of other journals at: http://ccbs.ntu.edu.tw/DBLM/pg2-En/pg2_index_2.htm
- *Journal of Buddhist Ethics*: http://blogs.dickinson.edu/buddhistethics/
- *Journal of Global Buddhism*: www.globalbuddhism.org
- *Pacific World: Institute of Buddhist Studies*: www.shin-ibs.edu/academics/_pwj
- *Buddhist Himalaya*: http://buddhim.20m.com
- Bulletin of the Nanzan Institute for Religion and Culture: http://nirc.nanzan-u.ac.jp/welcome.htm
- *Shenpen Osel*: www.shenpen-osel.org – a Kagyüpa journal.
- *New Ch'an Forum*: http://westernchanfellowship.org/ncf
- *Western Buddhist Review* (Journal of the Friends of the Western Buddhist Order/Triratna Buddhist Community): www.westernbuddhistreview.com/index.html

SOUTHERN BUDDHISM

- Access to Insight: www.accesstoinsight.org/index.html – includes translations of many texts from the Pali Canon, teachings of Thai forest teachers, Buddhist Publication Society 'Wheel' booklets, other books and teachings, guidance on Pali and much more.
- Buddhist Publication Society, Sri Lanka: www.bps.lk – downloadable 'Wheel' booklets and other publications.
- The Works of Ven. P. A. Payutto: www.buddhanet.net/cmdsg/payutto.htm – e-books from this renowned Thai scholar-monk.
- BuddhaSasana: www.budsas.org/ebud/ebidx.htm – includes downloadable articles, books, selected *Sutta* and *Vinaya* translations.
- Chanting book – The Buddhist Society of Western Australia, on BuddhaSasana website: www.budsas.org/ebud/chant-bswa/chantbook.htm
- Abhidhamma Papers: www.samatha.org/images/stories/abhidhamma-papers-final.pdf
- Zolag on Theravāda Buddhism: www.zolag.co.uk/ – includes e-books by Nina van Gorkom on Abhidhamma topics.

- Forest Dhamma Books: www.forestdhammabooks.com – downloadable books.
- Insight Meditation Society, Barre: www.dharma.org
- The Bhāvanā Society: www.bhavanasociety.org
- Forest Sangha Newsletter: www.fsnewsletter.amaravati.org
- Suan Mokkh, The Garden of Liberation (Buddhadāsa's monastery): www.suanmokkh.org/
- Sulak Sivaraksa: www.sulak-sivaraksa.org/
- Sarvōdaya Śrāmadāna: www.sarvodaya.org/ – see also www.buddhanetz.org/texte/sarvoday.htm

GENERAL MAHĀYĀNA, ESPECIALLY TEXTS

- Mahāyāna Buddhist Sutras in English: www4.bayarea.net/~mtlee
- Buddhism.org Buddhist Sutras: www.buddhism.org/Sutras
- Dharma Realm Buddhist Association: www.drba.org/dharma
- Mahayana Buddhist Sutras and Mantras: www.sutrasmantras.info/sutrao.html
- Virtual Religion Index for links to translations: http://virtualreligion.net/vri/buddha.html
- Yogācāra Buddhism Research Association: www.acmuller.net/yogacara/ – which includes online articles.

NORTHERN BUDDHISM

- The Berzin Archives: www.berzinarchives.com/web/en/index.html
  A vast site including several e-books and covering many aspects of Tibetan Buddhism, by Gelugpa scholar Alexander Berzin.
- The Tibetan and Himalayan Library: www.thlib.org/
- The University of Virginia Library website on the Tibetan Book of the Dead: www.lib.virginia.edu/speccol/exhibits/dead/
- Tibetan Buddhist Chanting – Shar Gan-Ri Ma: www.youtube.com/watch?v=WaFUS4HVpGg
- Cornell University website, 'Exploring the Maṇḍala' – some aspects of the Vajrabhairava *maṇḍala*: www.graphics.cornell.edu/online/mandala/significance.html
- 'Mandala', Jytte Hansen website: www.jyh.dk/indengl.htm
- Rossi Collection, Early Tibetan Mandalas: www.asianart.com/mandalas/mandimge.html

- Foundation for the Preservation of the Mahayana Tradition (Gelugpa): www.fpmt.org/teachings/default.asp and Lama Yeshe Wisdom Archive: www.lamayeshe.com/index.php
- New Kadampa Tradition: http://kadampa.org
- Kagyu Samye Ling Tibetan Centre: www.samyeling.org (Kagyüdpa)
- Shambhala Sun Online: www.shambhalasun.com (Kagyüdpa) Buddhist-orientated newspaper/magazine.
- Dzogchen Center: www.dzogchen.org/

EASTERN BUDDHISM

- The Zensite: www.thezensite.com – academic essays etc. on Zen.
- Primary Zen Texts: www.zentexts.org/primary-texts.html
- The Gateless Gate *kōan* collection: www.ibiblio.org/zen/cgi-bin/koan-index.pl
- Awakening 101: http://webspace.webring.com/people/tt/the_wanderling/awakening101.html – includes a college-level course on Zen, and Zen texts.
- Links Pitaka-Jodo-Shinshu: www.pitaka.ch/indxshin.htm
- The Japanese Garden (Bowdoin College): http://academic.bowdoin.edu/zen/index.shtml?overview
- History of Haiku website: www.big.or.jp/~loupe/links/ehisto/ehisinx.shtml
- Bashō's Haikus in different translations: www.haikupoetshut.com/basho1.html
- Haiku site with articles and links: www.ahapoetry.com/haiku.htm
- Thich Nhat Hanh's Community of Mindful Living: www.parallax.org/about_cml.html
- *The Mindfulness Bell* – Magazine of Thich Nhat Hanh's Community of Mindful Living: www.mindfulnessbell.org
- Amida Net: www12.canvas.ne.jp/horai
- Nichiren Shū: www.nichiren-shu.org/
- Sōka Gakkai International USA: www.sgi-usa.org/
- Sōka Gakkai International USA, writings of Nichiren: www.sgilibrary.org/writings.php
- Risshō-kōsei-kai: www.rk-world.org/

OTHER ORGANIZATIONS

- Network of Buddhist Organisations (UK): www.nbo.org.uk

- Friends of the Western Buddhist Order (now called Triratna Buddhist Community): http://thebuddhistcentre.com/text/what-triratna-buddhist-community
- UK Buddhist Prison Chaplaincy Organisation, Angulimala: http://angulimala.org.uk
- Buddhist Peace Fellowship: www.bpf.org/default.aspx
- Tzu Chi Foundation, Buddhist compassion relief: www.tzuchi.org
- Dharma Net – Engaged Practice www.dharmanet.org/engaged.html
- Sakyadhita, International Association of Buddhist Women: www.sakyadhita.org/
- WAiB Pages, Resources on Women's Ordination: http://lhamo.tripod.com/40rdin.htm
- Ron Epstein's 'Buddhist Resources on Vegetarianism and Animal Welfare': http://online.sfsu.edu/~rone/Buddhism/BuddhismAnimalsVegetarian/BuddhistVegetarian.htm
- Mind and Life Institute: www.mindandlife.org/ – explores frontiers of psychology and Buddhism
- Oxford Mindfulness Centre: www.oxfordmindfulness.org
- Amida Trust: www.amidatrust.com – Buddhist-related therapy.

Bibliography

For abbreviations used below (BPS, *BSR*, *JBE*, *JIABS*, MB), see List of Abbreviations. In the following, reprints are only mentioned when they are by publishers other than the original ones.

Adam, M. T., 2006, 'Two Concepts of Meditation and Three Kinds of Wisdom in Kamalaśīla's *Bhāvanākramas*: A Problem of Translation', *BSR*, 23 (1): 71–92.

Aitken, R., 1984, *The Mind of Clover: Essays in Zen Buddhist Ethics*, Berkeley, Calif., North Point Press.

Almond, P. C., 1988, *The British Discovery of Buddhism*, Cambridge, Cambridge University Press.

Anālayo, 2003, *Satipaṭṭhāna: The Direct Path to Realization*, Birmingham, Windhorse.

Anderson, C., 1999, *Pain and its Ending: The Four Noble Truths in the Theravāda Buddhist Canon*, London, Curzon Press.

Appleton, N., 2010, *Jātaka Stories in Theravāda Buddhism: Narrating the Bodhisatta Path*, Farnham, Ashgate.

Arnold, E., 1978, *The Light of Asia: Or the Great Renunciation, Being the Life and Teaching of Gautama*, London, Routledge and Kegan Paul (orig. 1879).

Aronson, H. B., 2004, *Buddhist Practice on Western Ground*, Boston and London, Shambhala.

Ba Khin, U, 1981, *The Essentials of Buddha Dhamma in Meditative Practice*, Wheel booklet 231, Kandy, BPS: www.bps.lk/olib/wh/wh231.pdf

Baker, C. and Phongpaichit, P., 2009, *A History of Thailand*, 2nd edn, Cambridge, Cambridge University Press.

Bartholomeusz, T., 1992, 'The Female Mendicant in Buddhist Srī Laṅkā', in Cabezón, 1992: 37–61.

1994, *Women Under the Bo Tree: Buddhist Nuns in Sri Lanka*, Cambridge, Cambridge University Press.

Basham, A. L., 1981, *History and Doctrine of the Ājīvikas*, Delhi, MB.

1982, 'Asoka and Buddhism – a Re-examination', *JIABS*, 5 (1): 131–43.

2005, *The Wonder That Was India*, 3rd rev. edn, Delhi, Picador.

Basho, M. and Stryk, L., 2003, *On Love and Barley: The Haiku of Basho*, London, Penguin.

Bastow, D., 1995, 'The First Argument for Sarvāstivāda', *Asian Philosophy*, 5 (2): 109–26.

Batchelor, M. and Brown, K., eds., 1992, *Buddhism and Ecology*, London and New York, Cassell.

Batchelor, S., ed., 1987, *The Jewel in the Lotus: A Guide to the Buddhist Traditions of Tibet*, London and Boston, Wisdom.

1994, *The Awakening of the West: Encounters of Buddhism and Western Culture*, Berkeley, Parallax Press.

1997, *Buddhism Without Beliefs: A Contemporary Guide to Awakening*, London, Bloomsbury.

Baumann, Martin, 1995, *Deutsche Buddhisten: Geschichte und Gemeinschaften*, 2nd edn, Marburg, Diagonal-Verlag.

1997, 'The Dharma has Come to the West: A Survey of Recent Studies and Sources', *JBE*, 4: 194–211: http://blogs.dickinson.edu/buddhistethics/files/2010/04/baum2.pdf

2000, 'Buddhism in Switzerland', *Journal of Global Buddhism*, 1: 154–9: www.globalbuddhism.org/toc.html

2007, 'Buddhism and the Modern World' entries in D. Keown and C. S. Prebish, 2007: 69–71, 165–79, 180–1, 285–8, 306–7, 348–52, 378, 379, 542–3, 561–5, 709–12, 814–19.

Bays, G. 1983, *The Voice of the Buddha: The Beauty of Compassion*, Berkeley, Dharma Publishing. (Translation of P. E. Foucaux's 1884–92 French translation of the *Lalitavistara*.)

Bechert, H., 1981, 'The Buddhayāna of Indonesia: A Syncretistic Form of Theravāda', *Journal of the Pali Text Society*, 9: 10–21.

ed., 1991–2, *Dating of the Historical Buddha/Die Datierung des historischen Buddha, Parts 1–2*, Göttingen, Vandenhoeck und Ruprecht.

Bechert, H. and Gombrich, R., eds., 1984, *The World of Buddhism: Buddhist Monks and Nuns in Society and Culture*, London and New York, Thames & Hudson.

Bell, S., 1996, 'Change and Identity in the Friends of the Western Buddhist Order', *Scottish Journal of Religious Studies*, 17 (1): 87–107.

2000a, 'Being Creative With Tradition: Rooting Theravāda Buddhism in Britain', *Journal of Global Buddhism* 1: 1–23: www.globalbuddhism.org/toc.html

2000b, 'A Survey of Engaged Buddhism in Britain', in C. Queen, ed., *Engaged Buddhism in the West*, Boston, Wisdom, 397–422.

Benn, J. A., 2007, *Burning for the Buddha: Self-immolation in Chinese Buddhism*, Honolulu, Kuroda Institute.

Berkwitz, S. C., 2010, *South Asian Buddhism: A Survey*, London and New York, Routledge.

Berzin, A., 2002, *Buddha-Family Traits (Buddha-Families) and Aspects of Experience*, Berzin Archives: www.berzinarchives.com/tantra/buddha_family_traits.html

2003, *The Meaning and Use of a Mandala*, Berzin Archives: www.berzinarchives.com/tantra/meaning_use_mandala.html

Beyer, S., 1974, *The Buddhist Experience: Sources and Interpretations*, Encino, Calif., Dickenson.

Birnbaum, R., 1980, *The Healing Buddha*, London, Rider, and Boulder, Colo., Shambhala.

Blofeld, J., 1987, *The Tantric Mysticism of Tibet: A Practical Guide*, New York, Dutton, 1970; repr. Boston, Mass., Shambhala.

1988, *Bodhisattva of Compassion: The Mystical Tradition of Kuan Yin*, Boston, Mass., Shambhala.

Bloss, L. W., 1987, 'The Female Renunciants of Sri Lanka', *JIABS*, 10 (1): 7–32.

Bluck, R., 2002, 'The Path of the Householder', *BSR*, 19 (1): 1–18.

2004, 'Buddhism and Ethnicity in Britain: The 2001 Census Data', *Journal of Global Buddhism*, 5: 90–6: www.globalbuddhism.org/toc.html

2006, *British Buddhism: Teachings, Practice and Development*, London and New York, Routledge.

Blum, M. L., 2002, *The Origins and Development of Pure Land Buddhism*, Oxford, Oxford University Press.

Bodhi, Bhikkhu, 1980, *Transcendental Dependent Arising: A Translation and Exposition of the Upanisa Sutta*, Wheel booklet 277–8, Kandy, BPS: www.bps.lk/olib/wh/wh277.pdf

1981, *Going for Refuge and Taking the Precepts*, Wheel booklet 282–4, Kandy, BPS: www.bps.lk/olib/wh/wh282.pdf

tr., 1984, *The Great Discourse on Causation: The Mahā-nidāna Sutta and its Commentary*, Kandy, BPS.

1990, 'Merit and Spiritual Growth', pp. 13–17 in his *Nourishing the Roots: Essays on Buddhist Ethics*, Wheel booklet 259–60, Kandy, BPS: www.bps.lk/olib/wh/wh259.pdf

ed., 1993, *A Comprehensive Manual and Abhidhamma: The Abhidhammattha Sangaha: Pali Text, Translation and Explanatory Guide*, Kandy, BPS.

1994, *The Noble Eightfold Path: The Way to the End of Suffering*, Wheel booklet 308–11, Kandy, BPS: www.bps.lk/olib/wh/wh308.pdf

1996, *A Treatise on the Paramis, From the Commentary to the Cariyapiṭaka by Acariya Dhammapala*, Wheel booklet 409–11, Kandy, BPS: www.bps.lk/olib/wh/wh409.pdf

ed., 2003, *Dāna: The Practice of Giving*, 2nd edn, Wheel booklet 367–9, Kandy, BPS: www.bps.lk/olib/wh/wh367.pdf

Bond, G. D., 1988, *The Buddhist Revival in Sri Lanka: Religious Tradition, Reinterpretation and Response*, Columbia, University of South Carolina Press.

1996, 'A.T. Ariyaratne and the Sarvodaya Shramadana Movement in Sri Lanka', in Queen and King, 1996, 121–46.

Brahm, Ajahn, 2006, *Mindfulness, Bliss and Beyond: A Meditator's Handbook* Boston, Wisdom. [On *Samatha* meditation.]

Brinker, H., 1987, *Zen in the Art of Painting*, New York, Arkana.

Buddhadāsa, 1971, *Towards the Truth*, ed. D.K. Swearer, Philadelphia, Pa., Westminster.

1989, *Me and Mine*, ed. D. K. Swearer, Albany, State University of New York Press.

Buddharakkhita, Acharya, 1989, *Mettā: The Philosophy and Practice of Universal Love*, Wheel booklet 365–6, Kandy, BPS: www.bps.lk/olib/wh/wh365.pdf

Buddhist Society, 2007. *The Buddhist Directory*, 10th edn, London, The Buddhist Society.

Buddhist Text Translation Society, n.d., *The Brahma Net Sutra*, www.purifymind.com/BrahmaNetSutra.htm – accessed 30 April 2010.

Bunnag, J., 1973, *Buddhist Monk, Buddhist Layman: A Study of Urban Monastic Organization in Central Thailand*, Cambridge, Cambridge University Press.

Burtt, E. A., 1987, *The Teachings of the Compassionate Buddha* (originally New York, Mentor, 1955), repr. Camberwell, Australia, Penguin. [Anthology of texts.]

Cabezón, J. I., ed., 1992, *Buddhism, Sexuality and Gender*, New York, State University of New York Press.

Campbell, B. F., 1980, *Ancient Wisdom Revived, a History of the Theosophical Movement*, Berkeley, University of California Press.

Caple, Jane, 2010, 'Monastic Economic Reform at Rong-bo Monastery: Towards an Understanding of Contemporary Tibetan Monastic Revival and Development in A-mdo', *BSR*, 27 (2): 19–219.

Carlson, Rōshi Kyogen, 1982, 'The Meaning of Celibacy', in *Sexuality and Religious Training*, Hexham, Throssel Hole Priory.

Carrithers, M. B., 1983, *The Forest Monks of Sri Lanka: An Anthropological and Historical Study*, Delhi, Oxford University Press (India).

Carter, J. R., ed., 1982, *The Threefold Refuge in the Theravāda Buddhist Tradition*, Chambersburg, Pa., Anima Books.

Chah, Ajahn, 1997, *Bodhinyana: A Collection of Dhamma Talks*, Bung Wai Forest Monastery, and on Access to Insight website: www.accesstoinsight.org/lib/thai/chah/bodhinyana.html

Chang, G. C. C., 1970, *The Practice of Zen*, New York, Harper & Row.

Chapple, C. K., 1996, 'Abhidharma as Paradigm for Practice', in F. J. Hoffman and M. Deegalle, *Pāli Buddhism*, Richmond, Surrey, Curzon Press, 79–101.

Ch'en, K. K. S., 1964, *Buddhism in China: A Historical Survey*, Princeton, Princeton University Press.

1973, *The Chinese Transformation of Buddhism*, Princeton: Princeton University Press.

1976, 'The Role of Buddhist Monasteries in T'ang Society', *History of Religions*, 15 (3): 209–31.

Chun, Shi-Yong, ed., 1974, *Buddhist Culture in Korea*, Seoul, Cultural Foundation.

Chung, Bongkil, 2003, 'Won Buddhism: The Historical Context of Sot'aesan's Reformation of Buddhism for the Modern World', in S. Heine and C. S. Prebish, *Buddhism in the Modern World: Adaptations of an Ancient Tradition*, Oxford, Oxford University Press, 143–68.

Ciolek, M. T., 2005, 'Zen Buddhism Koan Study Pages', The World-Wide Web Virtual Library: www.ciolek.com/WWWVLPages/ZenPages/KoanStudy.html

Clausen, C., 1973, 'Victorian Buddhism and the Origins of Comparative Religion', *Religion*, 5: 1–15.

Cleary, T., 1983, *Entry Into the Inconceivable: An Introduction to Hua-yen Buddhism*, Honolulu, University of Hawaii Press.

1985, 1991, 1989, *The Flower Ornament Scripture: A Translation of the Avataṃsaka Sūtra*, Boulder, Colo., Shambhala, 3 vols. [Vol. II contains the *Daśabhūmika Sūtra*, and Vol. III is the *Gaṇḍavyūha Sūtra*. There is also a 1994 edition of all three volumes in one, along with *Entry into the Realm of Reality: The Guide*.]

1990, *Book of Serenity*, Hudson, N.Y., Lindisfarne Press.

1994, *Instant Zen – Waking Up in the Present*, Berkeley, Calif., North Atlantic Books.

1997, *Stopping and Seeing: A Comprehensive Course in Buddhist Meditation, by Chih-I*, Boston and London, Shambhala.

2000, *Record of Things Heard* [Dōgen], Berkeley, Calif., Shambhala.

n.d. Discussion of the *Amitābha-dhyāna Sūtra* and a commentary on it: www.sinc.sunysb.edu/Clubs/buddhism/mindseal/introamita.html

Collins, S., 1982, *Selfless Persons: Imagery and Thought in Theravāda Buddhism*, Cambridge, Cambridge University Press.

2010, *Nirvana: Concept, Imagery, Narrative*, Cambridge, Cambridge University Press.

Conze, E., 1958, *Buddhist Wisdom Books: The Diamond Sutra and the Heart Sutra*, London, George Allen and Unwin (repr. London, Vintage, 2001).

1967, *Buddhist Thought in India*, Ann Arbor, Mich., University of Michigan Press.

1972, *Buddhist Meditation*, London, Allen and Unwin (repr. Mineola, N.Y., Dover, 2003). [Anthology.]

1973, *The Short Prajñā-pāramitā Texts*, London, Luzac and Co.

1975, *The Large Sutra on Perfect Wisdom, with the Divisions of the Abhisamaālaṅkara*, Berkeley and London: University of California Press.

1993, *The Way of Wisdom: The Five Spiritual Faculties*, Wheel booklet 65–6, Kandy, BPS: www.bps.lk/olib/wh/wh065.pdf

Cook, F. H., 1977, *Hua-yen Buddhism: The Jewel Net of Indra*, University Park, Pennsylvania State University Press.

1983, 'Enlightenment in Dōgen's Zen', *JIABS*, 6 (1): 7–30.

1989, 'The Jewel Net of Indra', in J. B. Callicott and R. T. Ames, *Nature in Asian Traditions of Thought: Essays in Environmental Philosophy*, Albany, State University Press of New York, 213–30.

Corless, R. J., 1979, 'The Garland of Love: A History of the Religious Hermeneutics of Nembutsu Theory and Practice' in A. K. Narain, *Studies in Pali and Buddhism*, Delhi, B. R. Publishing Corp., 53–73.

Cornell University, n.d., 'Exploring the Mandala': www.graphics.cornell.edu/online/mandala Accessed May 18, 2010

Cousins, L. S., 1973, 'Buddhist Jhāna', *Religion*, 3: 115–31.
1984, '*Samatha-yāna* and *Vipassanā-yāna*' in D. Dhammapala *et al.*, *Buddhist Studies in Honour of Hammalava Saddhatissa*, Nugegoda, Sri Lanka, 56–68.
1991, 'The "Five Points" and the Origins of the Buddhist Schools', in T. Skorupski, *The Buddhist Forum Volume II*, London, School of Oriental and African Studies, 27–60.
1994, 'Person and Self', in *Buddhism into the Year 2000: International Conference Proceedings*, Bangkok and Los Angeles, Dhammakaya Foundation, 15–32.
1996a, 'The Origins of Insight Meditation', in T. Skorupski, *The Buddhist Forum, Volume 4*, London, School of Oriental and African Studies, 35–58.
1996b, 'Good or Skilful? Kusala in Canon and Commentary', *JBE*, 3: 136–64: http://blogs.dickinson.edu/buddhistethics/files/2010/04/cousins12.pdf
1996c, 'The Dating of the Historical Buddha: A Review Article', *Journal of the Royal Asiatic Society*, 6: 57–63.
1997a, 'Buddhism', in J. R. Hinnells, *A New Handbook of Living Religions*, Blackwell, Oxford, 369–444.
1997b, 'Aspects of Esoteric Southern Buddhism' in P. Connolly and S. Hamilton, *Indian Insights: Buddhism, Brahmanism and Bhakti*, London, Luzac Oriental, 185–208.
2001, 'On the Vibhajjavādins: The Mahiṃsāsaka, Dhammaguttaka, Kassapiya and Tambapaṇṇiya Branches of the Ancient Theriyas', *BSR*, 18 (2): 131–82.
Cowell, E. B., ed., 1985, *Buddhist Mahāyāna Texts*, Sacred Books of the East, Vol. 49 (Oxford, Clarendon Press, 1894), repr. Delhi, MB. [Contains trans. of three main Pure Land texts focused on Amitābha.]
Crosby, Kate, 2000, 'Tantric Theravāda: A Bibliographic Essay on the Writings of François Bizot and others on the Yogāvacara Tradition', *Contemporary Buddhism*, 1 (2): 141–98.
Cutler, Joshua W. C., 2002, *The Great Treatise on the Stages of Enlightenment: Lam Rim Chen Mo (of) Tsong-kha-pa*, 3 vols., Ithaca, N.Y., Snow Lion.
Dalai Lama, XIVth, Tenzin Gyatsho, 1971, *The Opening of the Wisdom-Eye*, Adyar, Theosophical Publishing House. [2nd rev. edn, *Opening the Eye of New Awareness* (tr. D. S. Lopez), 2005, Boston, Wisdom.]
Dayal, H., 1932, *The Bodhisattva Doctrine in Buddhist Sanskrit Literature*, London, Routledge and Kegan Paul (repr. Delhi, MB, 1970).
Deegalle, M., 1999, 'The Search for the Mahāyāna in Sri Lanka, *JIABS*, 22 (2): 343–57.
de Jong, J. W., 1986, *A Brief History of Buddhist Studies in Europe and America*, 2nd rev. edn, Delhi, Sri Satguru.
Dewaraja, L. S., 1994, *The Position of Women in Buddhism*, Wheel booklet 280, Kandy, BPS: www.bps.lk/olib/wh/wh280.pdf
Dhammadharo, Ajahn Lee, 1994, *The Craft of the Heart*: www.accesstoinsight.org/lib/thai/lee/craft.html
Dhammika, S., 1993, *The Edicts of King Asoka*, Wheel booklet 386–7, Kandy, BPS: www.bps.lk/olib/wh/wh386.pdf

Dharma Fellowship, n.d., 'Deepening Calm-abiding – The Nine Stages of Abiding', Dharma Fellowship of his Holiness the Gyalwa Karmapa website: www.dharmafellowship.org/library/essays/nine-stages-of-abiding.htm (accessed 1 June 2011).

Dorje, Gyurme, tr., 2005, *The Tibetan Book of the Dead (The Great Liberation by Hearing in the Intermediate State)*, London, Penguin.

Drew, T., 2011, 'Theravāda Buddhism in Malaysia: Transmission and Development of Practice in a Plural/Multicultural Southeast Asian Context', MA Buddhist Studies dissertation, University of Sunderland, UK.

Dreyfus, G., 1998, 'The Shuk-den Affair: History and Nature of the Quarrel', *JIABS*, 21 (2): 227–70.

Dumoulin, H., 2005a, *Zen Buddhism: A History: India and China* (tr. J. W. Heisig and P. Knitter), Bloomington, Ind., World Wisdom.

2005b, *Zen Buddhism: A History: Japan*, tr. J. W. Heisig and P. Knitter, Bloomington, Ind., World Wisdom.

Dutt, N., 1978, *Mahāyāna Buddhism*, Delhi, MB.

Earhart, H. B., 1974, *Religion in the Japanese Experience: Sources and Interpretations*, Encino and Belmont, Calif., Dickenson.

Ekvall, R. B., 1964, *Religious Observances in Tibet: Patterns and Functions*, Chicago, University of Chicago Press.

Evans-Wentz, W. Y., 1951, *Tibet's Great Yogī Milarepa: A Biography from the Tibetan*, 2nd edn, London, Oxford University Press.

1954, *The Tibetan Book of Great Liberation*, London, Oxford University Press.

Faure, B., 1991, *The Rhetoric of Immediacy: A Cultural Critique of Chan/Zen Buddhism*, New Jersey, Princeton University Press.

2003, *The Power of Denial: Buddhism, Purity and Gender*, Princeton and Oxford, Princeton University Press.

Fields, Rick, 1992, *How the Swans Came to the Lake: A Narrative History of Buddhism in America*, 3rd edn, Boston, Shambhala.

Fisher, Robert E., 1993, *Buddhist Art and Architecture*, London, Thames & Hudson.

Flood, Gavin, 1996, *An Introduction to Hinduism*, Cambridge, Cambridge University Press.

Foard, J., Solomon, M., and Payne, R. K., eds., 1996, *The Pure Land Tradition: History and Development*, Berkeley, Calif., Institute of Buddhist Studies, University of California.

Fowler, J., 1998, 'Aum Shinrikyo': www.bibliotecapleyades.net/sociopolitica/esp_sociopol_AUM01.htm

Fuller, P., 2005, *The Notion of Diṭṭhi in Theravāda Buddhism*, London and New York, RoutledgeCurzon.

Gethin, R. M. L., 1994, '*Bhavaṅga* and Rebirth According to the *Abhidhamma*', in T. Skorupski and U. Pagel, *The Buddhist Forum, Volume III*, London, School of Oriental and African Studies, 11–36.

1997, 'Cosmology and Meditation: from the *Aggañña Sutta* to the Mahāyāna', *History of Religions*, 36: 183–219.

1998, *The Foundations of Buddhism*, Oxford and New York, Oxford University Press.

2001, *The Buddhist Path to Awakening*, Oxford, Oneworld.

Getty, A., 1988, *The Gods of Northern Buddhism: Their History and Iconography* (Oxford, Clarendon Press, 1928), repr. New York, Dover.

Gokhale, B. G., 1994, *New Light on Early Buddhism*, Delhi, Sangam Books.

Gombrich, R. F., 1966, 'The Consecration of a Buddhist Image', *Journal of Asian Studies*, 26 (1): 23–36.

1971, *Precept and Practice: Traditional Buddhism in the Rural Highlands of Ceylon*, Oxford, Clarendon Press (2nd edn, Delhi, MB, 1998).

1981, 'A New Theravādin Liturgy', *Journal of the Pali Text Society*, 9: 7–73.

1983, 'From Monastery to Meditation Centre: Lay Meditation in Modern Sri Lanka', in P. Denwood and A. Piatigorsky, *Buddhist Studies, Ancient and Modern*, London, Curzon Press and Totowa, N.J., Barnes and Noble, 20–34.

1986, 'Buddhist Festivals', in S. Brown, *Festivals in World Religions*, London and New York, Longman, 31–59.

1991–2, 'Dating the Buddha: A Red Herring Revealed', in Bechert, 1991–2: II, 237–57.

1996, *How Buddhism Began: The Conditioned Genesis of the Early Teachings*, London and Atlantic Highlands, N.J., Athlone.

2000, 'Discovery of the Buddha's Date', in L. S. Perera, ed., *Buddhism for the New Millennium: Sri Saddhatissa International Buddhist Centre 10th Anniversary Celebratory Volume*, London, World Buddhist Foundation, 9–25.

2005, 'Fifty Years of Buddhist Studies in Britain', *BSR*, 22 (2): 141–54.

2006, *Theravāda Buddhism*, 2nd edn, London and New York, Routledge.

2009, *What the Buddha Thought*, London, Equinox.

Gombrich, R. F. and Obeyesekere, G., 1988, *Buddhism Transformed: Religious Change in Sri Lanka*, Princeton, N.J., Princeton University Press.

Gómez, Luis O., 1996, *The Land of Bliss: The Paradise of the Buddha of Measureless Light. Sanskrit and Chinese Versions of the Sukāvatīvyūha Sutras: Introductions and English Translations*, Honolulu, University of Hawaii Press.

Gosling, David, 1976, 'The Scientific and Religious Belief of Thai Scientists and the Inter-relationship', *Southeast Asian Journal of Social Science*, 4 (1): 1–18.

Gregory, P., ed., 1986, *Traditions of Meditation in Chinese Buddhism*, Kuroda Institute, Studies in East Asian Buddhism 4, Honolulu, University of Hawaii Press.

Griffiths, P. J., 1987, *On Being Mindless: Buddhist Meditation and the Mind–Body Problem*, La Salle, Ill., Open Court.

1994, *On Being Buddha: The Classical Doctrine of Buddhahood*, Albany, N.Y., State University of New York Press.

Gross, R. M., 1993, *Buddhism After Patriarchy: A Feminist History, Analysis, and Reconstruction of Buddhism*, Albany, N.Y., State University of New York Press.

Guenther, H. V., 1963, *The Life and Teaching of Nāropa*, Oxford, Clarendon Press.
tr., 1971, *The Jewel Ornament of Liberation* [of Gampopa], Berkeley, Calif., Shambhala.
1976, *Philosophy and Psychology in the Abhidharma*, Berkeley, Calif., Shambhala.
Gunaratana, H., 1980, *A Critical Analysis of the Jhānas in Theravāda Buddhist Meditation*, Washington, DC, The American University Library, and on Buddhanet website: www.buddhanet.net/pdf_file/scrnguna.pdf
1985, *The Path of Serenity and Insight: An Explanation of the Buddhist Jhānas*, Delhi, MB.
2006, *The Jhanas in Theravada Buddhist Meditation*, Wheel booklet 351–3, Kandy, BPS: www.bps.lk/olib/wh/wh351.pdf
Gyatso, S., 2003, 'Of Monks and Monasteries', in D. Bernstorff and H. von Welck, *Exile as Challenge: The Tibetan Diaspora*, New Delhi: Orient Longman, 213–43.
Habito, R. F. L. and Stone, J., eds., 1999, Revisiting Nichiren. Special edition of the *Japanese Journal of Religious Studies*, 26 (3/4): http://nirc.nanzan-u.ac.jp/publications/jjrs/pdf/546.pdf
Hakeda, Y. S., tr., 1967, *The Awakening of Faith in the Mahāyāna*, New York and London, Columbia University Press.
1972, *Kūkai and his Major Works*, New York and London, Columbia University Press.
Hall, D. G. E., 1981, *A History of Southeast Asia*, 4th edn, London, Macmillan.
Hall, F., 1902, *The Soul of a People*, London, Macmillan. [Observations on Burmese life.]
Harris, E. J., 1994, *Violence and Disruption in Society: A Study of the Early Buddhist Texts*, Wheel booklet 392–3, Kandy, BPS: www.bps.lk/olib/wh/wh392.pdf
2009, *Theravāda Buddhism and the British Encounter: Religious, Missionary and Colonial Experience in Nineteenth Century Sri Lanka*, London and New York, Routledge.
Harris, E. J., and Kauth, R., eds., 2004, *Meeting Buddhists*, Leicester, Christians Aware.
Harris, I., ed., 1999, *Buddhism and Politics in Twentieth-century Asia*, London and New York, Continuum.
2005, *Cambodian Buddhism: History and Practice*, Honolulu, University of Hawaii Press.
Harrison, P., 1978, 'Buddhānusmṛti in the Pratyutpannabuddha-saṃmukhāvasthita-samādhi Sūtra', *Journal of Indian Philosophy*, 9: 35–57.
1987, 'Who Gets to Ride in the Great Vehicle? Self-image and Identity Among the Followers of the Early Mahāyāna', *JIABS*, 10 (1): 67–89.
1990, *The Samādhi of Direct Encounter with the Buddhas of the Present: An Annotated English Translation of the Pratyutpanna-Buddhasaṃmukhāvasthita-Samādhi-Sūtra*, Tokyo, The International Institute for Buddhist Studies.
1992, 'Is the *Dharma-kāya* the Real "Phantom Body" of the Buddha?', *JIABS*, 15 (1): 44–94.

2000, 'Mañjuśrī and the Cult of the Celestial Bodhisattvas', *Chung-Hwa Buddhist Journal*, 13 (2): 157–93: http://ccbs.ntu.edu.tw/FULLTEXT/JR-BJ001/93605.htm

Harvey, P., 1986, 'Signless Samādhis in Pāli Buddhism', *JIABS*, 9 (1): 25–52.

1990, 'Venerated Objects and Symbols in Early Buddhism', in K. Werner, *Symbols in Art and Religion*, London, Curzon Press, and Glen Dale, Md., The Riverdale Company, 68–102.

1993, 'The Dynamics of *Paritta* Chanting in Southern Buddhism', in K. Werner, *Love Divine: Studies in Bhakti and Devotional Mysticism*, Richmond, Curzon Press, 53–84.

1995a, *The Selfless Mind: Personality, Consciousness and Nirvana in Early Buddhism*, London, Curzon Press.

1995b, 'Contemporary Characterisations of the "Philosophy" of Nikāyan Buddhism', *BSR*, 12 (2): 109–33.

1999, '*Vinaya* Principles for Assigning Degrees of Culpability', *JBE*, 6: 271–91: http://blogs.dickinson.edu/buddhistethics/files/2010/04/harvey991.pdf

2000, *An Introduction to Buddhist Ethics: Foundations, Values and Issues*, Cambridge, Cambridge University Press.

2001, 'Coming to be and Passing Away: Buddhist Reflections on Embryonic Life, Dying and Organ Donation', *BSR*, 18 (2): 183–215.

2007a, '*Dhammacakkappavattana Sutta*: The Discourse on the Setting in Motion of the Wheel (of Vision) of the Basic Pattern: The Four Realities for the Spiritually Ennobled Ones', translation, with notes, on Access to Insight Website: www.accesstoinsight.org/tipitaka/sn/sn56/sn56.011.harv.html

2007b, 'Avoiding Unintended Harm to the Environment and the Buddhist Ethic of Intention', *JBE*, 14: 1–34: http://blogs.dickinson.edu/buddhistethics/files/2010/05/harvey-article1.pdf

2007c, ' "Freedom of the Will" in the Light of Theravāda Buddhist Teachings', *JBE*, 14: 35–98. blogs.dickinson.edu/buddhistethics/files/2010/05/harvey2-article1.pdf

2007d, Eighteen entries on various aspects of 'The Buddha' in Keown and Prebish, 2007: 83–7, 92–102, 105–55, 161–5, 318–37, 568–75, 600–2. [These also appear, with fuller references, at: www.sunderland.ac.uk/buddhist/originaleob.pdf]

2008, 'Between Controversy and Ecumenism: Intra-Buddhist Relationships', in P. Schmidt-Leukel, *Buddhist Attitudes to Other Religions*, St Ottilien, EOS, 114–42.

2009a, 'The Four *Ariya-saccas* as "True Realities for the Spiritually Ennobled" – the Painful, its Origin, its Cessation, and the Way Going to This – Rather than "Noble Truths" Concerning These', *BSR*, 26 (2): 197–227.

2009b, 'The Approach to Knowledge and Truth in the Theravāda Record of the Discourses of the Buddha', 'Theravāda Philosophy of Mind and the Person', 'Theravāda Texts on Ethics', in W. Edelglass and J. L. Garfield, *Buddhist Philosophy: Essential Readings*, Oxford, Oxford University Press, 175–85, 265–74, 375–87.

2011, 'An Analysis of Factors Related to the *kusala/akusala* Quality of Actions in the Pali tradition', *JIABS*, 33: 175–209.
2014, 'The Nature of the Eight-factored *ariya, lokuttara magga* in the *Suttas* Compared to the Pali Commentarial Idea of it as Momentary', *Religions of South Asia*, 8: forthcoming
Havenick, H., 1991, *Tibetan Nuns Now: History, Cultural Norms and Social Reality*, Oslo, Norwegian University Press.
Hazra, K. L., 1982, *History of Theravāda Buddhism in South-East Asia, with special reference to India and Ceylon*, New Delhi, Munshiram Manoharlal.
Heikkilä-Horn, M., 1997, *Buddhism With Open Eyes: Belief and Practice of Santi Asoke*, Bangkok, Fah Apai.
Heirman, Ann, 2010, 'Fifth Century Chinese Nuns: An Exemplary Case', *BSR*, 27 (2): 61–76.
Heng-ching Shih, 1994, *The Sutra on Upasaka Precepts* (BDK English Tripitaka), Berkeley, Numata Center for Buddhist Translation and Research, Bukkyo Dendo Kyukai.
Herrigel, E., 2004, *Zen in the Art of Archery*, London, Penguin.
Hinnells, J. R., ed., 1997, *A New Handbook of Living Religions*, Oxford, Blackwell.
Hookham, Shenpen, 2004, 'Key Ideas Common to all Buddhist Traditions', in Harris and Kauth, 2004, 185–9.
Hopkins, J. and Lati Rinpoche, 1975, *The Precious Garland and Song of the Four Mindfulnesses* (Nāgārjuna's *Rāja-parikathā-ratnamālā* and a text of the seventh Dalai Lama), London, George Allen and Unwin.
Horii, Mitsutoshi, 2006, 'Deprofessionalisation of Buddhist Priests', in *Contemporary Japan, Electronic Journal of Contemporary Japanese Studies*: www.japanesestudies.org.uk/articles/2006/Horii.html
Horner, I. B., 1982, *Women in Early Buddhist Literature*, Wheel booklet 30, Kandy, BPS: www.bps.lk/olib/wh/wh030.pdf
1999, *Women Under Primitive Buddhism: Laywomen and Almswomen* (London, Routledge and Kegan Paul, 1930); repr. Delhi, MB.
Hua, H., 1974, *Sūtra of the Past Vows of Earth Store Bodhisattva*, New York, Institute for Advanced Studies of World Religions.
Hubbard, J. and Swanson, P., eds., 1997, *Pruning the Bodhi Tree: The Storm over Critical Buddhism*, Honolulu, University of Hawaii Press.
Humphreys, C., 1968, *Sixty Years of Buddhism in England (1907–1967)*, London, The Buddhist Society.
Hüsken, U., 2000, 'The Legend of the Establishment of the Buddhist Order of Nuns in the Theravāda Vinaya-piṭaka', *Journal of the Pali Text Society*, 26: 43–69.
Ingaki, H., 1995, *Three Pure Land Sutras*. Berkeley, Calif., Numata Center for Buddhist Translation and Research.
Jackson, C. T., 1981, *The Oriental Religions and American Thought – Nineteenth-Century Explorations*, Westport, Conn. and London, Greenwood Press.
Jackson, P., 2003, *Buddhadasa: Theravada Buddhism and Modernist Reform in Thailand*, Chiang Mai, Silkworm Books.

Jaffe, R. M., 2001, *Neither Monk nor Layman: Clerical Marriage in Modern Japanese Buddhism*, Princeton and Oxford, Princeton University Press.
James, A. and J., 1987, *Modern Buddhism*, Box, Wiltshire, Aukana.
Jiyu-Kennett, Roshi, 1999, *Zen is Eternal Life*, 4th edn, Mt Shasta, Calif., Shasta Abbey.
Johnston, E. H., 1972, *The Buddhacarita or Acts of the Buddha* [of Aśvaghosa; text and translation], 2nd edn, New Delhi, Oriental Books Reprint Corp.
Jones, C. B., 2009, 'Modernization and Traditionalism in Buddhist Almsgiving: The Case of the Buddhist Compassion Relief Tzu-chi Association in Taiwan', *Journal of Global Buddhism*, 10: 291–319: www.globalbuddhism.org/toc.html
Jones, K., 1981, *Buddhism and Social Action: An Exploration*, Wheel booklet 285–86, Kandy, BPS: www.bps.lk/olib/wh/wh285.pdf
Joshi, L., 1977, *Studies in the Buddhistic Culture of India*, 2nd edn, Delhi, MB.
Kabilsingh, C., 1991, *Thai Women in Buddhism*, Berkeley, Calif., Parallax Press.
Kapleau, P., 2000, *Three Pillars of Zen*, 4th edn, New York, Anchor Books.
Kasahara Kazuo, ed., 2001, *A History of Japanese Religion*, Tokyo, Kosei Publishing.
Kasulis, T. P., 1981, *Zen Action, Zen Person*, Honolulu, University of Hawaii Press.
Katz, N., 1980, 'Some Methodological Comments on the use of the Term "Hīnayāna" in the Study of Buddhism', *Religious Traditions*, 3 (1): 52–8.
1982, *Buddhist Images of Human Perfection: The Arahant of the Sutta Piṭaka Compared With the Bodhisattva and the Mahāsiddha*, Delhi, MB.
Kawanami, H., 1997, 'Buddhist Nuns in Transition: the case of Burmese *thila-shin*', in P. Connolly and S. Hamilton, *Indian Insights: Buddhism, Brahmanism and Bhakti*, London, Luzac Oriental, 209–24.
2007, 'The Bhikkhunī Ordination Debate: Global Aspirations, Local Concerns, with Special Emphasis on the Views of the Monastic Community in Burma', *BSR*, 24 (2): 226–44.
Kay, D. N., 2004, *Tibetan and Zen Buddhism in Britain: Transplantation, Development and Adaptation*, London and New York, RoutledgeCurzon.
Keenan, J. P., 1982, 'Original Purity and the Focus of Early Yogācāra', *JIABS*, 5 (1): 7–18.
Kent, S. A., 1982, 'A Sectarian Interpretation of the Rise of the Mahāyāna', *Religion*, 12: 311–32.
Keown, D., 1992, *The Nature of Buddhist Ethics*, London, Macmillan.
1995, *Buddhism and Bioethics*, London, Macmillan, and New York, St. Martin's Press.
ed., 1998, *Buddhism and Abortion*, London, Macmillan.
ed., 2000, *Contemporary Buddhist Ethics*, Richmond, Surrey, Curzon Press.
Keown, D. and Prebish, C. S., eds., 2007, *Encyclopedia of Buddhism*, London and New York, Routledge.
Khantipālo, Bhikkhu, 1979, *Banner of the Arahants: Buddhist Monks and Nuns from the Buddha's Time till Now* [in ancient and Southern Buddhism], Kandy, Sri Lanka, BPS.
1982, *Lay Buddhist Practice: The Shrine Room, Uposatha Day, Rains Residence*, Wheel booklet 206–7, Kandy, BPS: www.bps.lk/olib/wh/wh206.pdf

1986, *Practical Advice for Meditators*, Wheel booklet 116, Kandy, BPS: www.bps.lk/olib/wh/wh116.pdf

King, S. B., 1991, *Buddha Nature*, Albany, N.Y., State University Press of New York.

King, W. L., 1964, *In the Hope of Nibbana: An Essay on Theravada Buddhist Ethics*, LaSalle, Ill., Open Court.

1980, *Theravāda Meditation: The Buddhist Transformation of Yoga*, University Park, Pennsylvania State University Press (repr. Delhi, MB, 1998).

1981, 'A Christian and a Japanese Buddhist Work Ethic Compared', *Religion*, 11: 207–26.

Kitagawa, J. M., 1990, *Religion in Japanese History*, 2nd edn, New York, Columbia University Press.

Kiyota, M., ed., 1978a, *Mahāyāna Buddhist Meditation: Theory and Practice*, Honolulu, University Press of Hawaii (repr. Delhi, MB, 1998).

1978b, 'Buddhist Devotional Meditation: A Study of the *Sukhāvatīvyūhôpadeśa*', in Kiyota, 1978a, 249–96.

1978c, *Shingon Buddhism: Theory and Practice*, Los Angeles and Tokyo, Buddhist Books International.

Kodena, T. J., 1979, 'Nichiren and his Nationalistic Eschatology', *Religious Studies*, 15: 41–53.

Kollmar-Paulenz, K., 2003, 'Buddhism in Mongolia after 1990', *Journal of Global Buddhism*, 4: 18–34: www.globalbuddhism.org/toc.html

Kongtrul, J., 2002, *Creation and Completion: Essential Points of Tantric Meditation*, Boston, Wisdom.

Kornfield, J., 1995, *Living Dharma: Teachings of Twelve Buddhist Masters*, Boston, Shambhala.

Krey, Gisela, 2010, 'On Women as Teachers in Early Buddhism: Dhammadinnā and Khemā', *BSR*, 27 (1): 17–40.

Kuan, T., 2008, *Mindfulness in Early Buddhism: New Approaches Through Psychology and Textual Analysis of Pali, Chinese and Sanskrit Sources*, London and New York, Routledge.

LaFleur, W., 1992, *Liquid Life: Abortion and Buddhism in Japan*, Princeton, Princeton University Press.

Lamotte, E., 1976, *The Teaching of Vimalakīrti (Vimalakīrtinirdeśa)*, tr. from French *L'Enseignement de Vimalakīrti*, 1962 by Sara Webb, London, Pali Text Society.

1988, *History of Indian Buddhism*, tr. from French *Histoire du Bouddhisme Indien*, 1958 by Sara Boin-Webb, Leuven, Belgium, Peters Press.

Lancaster, L. R., 1979, 'Buddhist Literature: Its Canons, Scribes and Editors', in W. D. O'Flaherty, ed., *The Critical Study of Sacred Texts*, Berkeley Religious Studies Series, Berkeley, Calif., 215–29.

2007, 'Buddhism and technology' entries in Keown and Prebish, 2007, 241–4, 254–8, 288–99, 307–10, 726–33.

Lenoir, Frederic, 1999, *Le Bouddhisme en France*, Paris, Fayard.

Lester, R. C., 1973, *Theravada Buddhism in Southeast Asia*, Michigan, University of Michigan Press.

LeVine, S. and Gellner, D. N., 2005, *Rebuilding Buddhism: The Theravada Movement in Twentieth-Century Nepal*, Cambridge, Mass., Harvard University Press.

Ling, T., 1962, *Buddhism and the Mythology of Evil: A Study in Theravāda Buddhism*, London, George Allen and Unwin (repr. Oxford, One World, 1997).

1980, *Buddhist Revival in India: Aspects of the Sociology of Buddhism*, London, Macmillan.

Ling-pa, Jig-me, 1982, *The Dzogchen: Innermost Essence Preliminary Practice*, Dharamsala, Library of Tibetan Works and Archives.

Liu, Ming-Wood, 1982, 'The Doctrine of the Buddha-Nature in the Mahāyāna *Mahāparinirvāṇa Sūtra*', *JIABS*, 5 (2): 63–94.

Lodrö, G. G., 1998, *Calm Abiding and Special Insight*, New York, Snow Lion.

Lopez, D. S., ed., 1995, *Curators of the Buddha: Study of Buddhism Under Colonialism*, 2nd edn, Chicago, University of Chicago Press.

Lopez, D. S. and Stearns, C., 1986, 'A Report on Religious Activity in Central Tibet', *JIABS*, 9 (2): 101–8.

Mackenzie, R., 2007, *New Buddhist Movements in Thailand: Towards an Understanding of Wat Phra Dhammakāya and Santi Asoke*, London and New York, Routledge.

Maezumi, T. and Glassman, B., eds., 2002, *On Zen Practice: Body, Breath and Mind*, Boston, Wisdom.

Mahā Boowa Ñāṇasampanno, Ācariya, 2005, *Venerable Acariya Mun Bhuridatta Thera: A Spiritual Biography*, 3rd edn: www.abhayagiri.org/main/book/277/

Mahāsī Sayadaw, 1990, *Satipaṭṭhāna Vipassanā*, Wheel booklet 370–1, Kandy, BPS: www.bps.lk/olib/wh/wh370.pdf

1994, *The Progress of Insight (Visuddhiñāṇa-kathā): A Modern Treatise on Buddhist Satipatthana Meditation*, 3rd edn, Kandy, BPS, and on Access to Insight website: www.accesstoinsight.org/lib/authors/mahasi/progress.html

Malalagoda, K., 1976, *Buddhism in Sinhalese Society, 1750–1900: A Study of Religious Revival and Change*, Berkeley, Calif., University of California Press.

Malalasekera, G. P. *et al.*, eds., *Encyclopaedia of Buddhism*, Colombo, Government of Sri Lanka: Vol. I, fasc. 3 (1964), 363–8 ('Akṣobhya'), 434–63 ('Amita'); Vol. II, fasc. 3 (1967), 407–15 ('Avalokiteśvara'); Vol. II, fasc. 4 (1968), 661–6 ('Bhaiṣajya-guru').

Masunaga, Reihō, 1971, *A Primer of Sōtō Zen: A Translation of Dōgen's Shōbōgebzō Zuimonki*, Honolulu, University of Hawaii Press.

Matthews, Bruce, ed., 2006, *Buddhism in Canada*, London and New York, Routledge.

McDermott, J. P., 1984, *Development in the Early Buddhist Concept of Kamma/ Karma*, Delhi, MB.

McMahan, D. L., 2000, 'New Frontiers in Buddhism: Three Recent Works on Buddhism in America – A Review Article', *Journal of Global Buddhism*, 1: 116–35: www.globalbuddhism.org/toc.html

McQueen, G., 1981 and 1982, 'Inspired Speech in Mahāyāna Buddhism', *Religion*, 11: 303–19 and 12: 49–65.

Mendis, N. K. G., 1985, *The Abhidhamma in Practice*, Wheel booklet 322–3, Kandy, BPS: www.bps.lk/olib/wh/wh322.pdf

Miller, B. D., 1980, 'Views of Women's Roles in Buddhist Tibet', in A. K. Narain, *Studies in the History of Buddhism*, Delhi, B.R. Publishing Corp., 155–66.

Morreale, Don, ed., 1998, *The Complete Guide to Buddhist America*, Boston, Shambhala.

Mu Soeng Sunim, 1987, *Thousand Peaks: Korean Zen: Tradition and Teachers*, Berkeley, Calif., Parallax Press.

Mullin, G. H., 1996, *Tsongkhapa's Six Yogas of Naropa*, New York, Snow Lion.

Mun, Ajahn, 1995, *A Heart Released: The Teachings of Phra Ajaan Mun Bhuridatta Mahāthera*, Access to Insight website: www.accesstoinsight.org/lib/thai/mun/released.html

Nagao, G., 1991, *Mādhyamika and Yogācāra: A Study of Mahāyāna Philosophies: Collected Papers of G.M. Nagao*, Albany, N.Y., State University of New York Press.

Ñāṇamoli, Bhikkhu, 2003, *The Life of the Buddha: According to the Pali Canon*, Onalaska, Wash., Pariyatti Press.

Ñāṇamoli and Bodhi, Bhikkhus, 1991, *The Discourse on Right View: The Sammaditthi Sutta and its Commentary*, Wheel booklet 377–9, Kandy, BPS: www.bps.lk/olib/wh/wh377.pdf

Ñāṇamoli Thera and Khantipalo Bhikkhu, 1993, *The Buddha's Words on Kamma*, Wheel booklet 248–9, Kandy, BPS: www.bps.lk/olib/wh/wh248.pdf

Nash, J. and M., 1963, 'Marriage, Family and Population Growth in Upper Burma', *Anthropology*, 19: 151–66.

Nattier, J., 1991, *Once Upon a Future Time: Studies in a Buddhist Prophecy of Decline*, Berkeley, Calif., Asian Humanities Press.

1992, 'The *Heart Sūtra*: A Chinese apocryphal text?', *JIABS*, 15 (2): 153–219.

2000, 'The realm of Akṣobhya: A Missing Piece in the History of Pure Land Buddhism', *JIABS*, 23 (1): 71–102.

2003, *A Few Good Men: The Bodhisattva Path According to The Inquiry of Ugra (Ugraparipṛcchā): A Study and Translation*, Honolulu, University of Hawaii Press.

Nattier, J. J., and Prebish, C. S., 1976–7, 'Mahāsaṅghika Origins', *History of Religions*, 16: 237–72.

Nhat Hanh, Thich, 1967, *Vietnam: Lotus in a Sea of Fire*, London, SCM Press, and New York, Hill and Wang.

1991, *Peace is Every Step: The Path of Mindfulness in Everyday Life*, London, Rider.

2008, *The Miracle of Mindfulness*, London, Rider.

Nikam, N. A., and McKeon, R., 1959, *The Edicts of Aśoka*, Chicago, University of Chicago Press.

Norberg-Hodge, H., 2000, *Ancient Futures: Learning form Ladakh*, 2nd edn, London, Rider.

Norbu, N., 2000, *The Crystal and the Way of Light: Sutra, Tantra and Dzogchen*, Ithaca, N.Y., Snow Lion.

Norman, K. R., 1975, 'Asoka and Capital Punishment', *Journal of the Royal Asiatic Society*, Part I: 16–24.

1997, *A Philological Approach to Buddhism*, London, School of Oriental and African Studies.

Numrich, P., 1996, *Old Wisdom in the New World: Americanization in Two Immigrant Theravada Buddhist Temples*, Knoxville, University of Tennessee Press.

Nyanaponika Thera, 1965, *Abhidhamma Studies: Researches in Buddhist Psychology*, Kandy, BPS, and on Access to Insight website: www.buddhanet.net/pdf_file/abhistudy.pdf

1981, *Buddhism and the God-Idea*, Wheel booklet 47, Kandy, BPS: www.bps.lk/olib/wh/wh047.pdf

1983, *The Threefold Refuge*, Wheel booklet 76, Kandy, BPS: www.bps.lk/olib/wh/wh076.pdf

ed., 1990, *Kamma and its Fruit*, Wheel booklet 221–4, Kandy, BPS: www.bps.lk/olib/wh/wh221.pdf

1993, *The Five Mental Hindrances and Their Conquest*, Wheel booklet 26, Kandy, BPS: www.bps.lk/olib/wh/wh026.pdf

1996, *The Heart of Buddhist Meditation: A Handbook of Mental Training Based on the Buddha's Way of Mindfulness* (originally London, Rider, 1962), Newburyport, Mass., Red Wheel/Weiser.

1997, *The Power of Mindfulness: An Inquiry into the Scope of Bare Attention and the Principal Sources of its Strength*, Wheel booklet 121–2, Kandy, BPS: www.bps.lk/olib/wh/wh121.pdf

Nyanaponika Thera and Ñāṇamoli Thera, 1998, *The Four Sublime States: Contemplations on Love, Compassion, Sympathetic Joy and Equanimity, & The Practice of Lovingkindness (Mettā): As Taught by the Buddha in the Pali Canon*, Wheel booklet 6–7, Kandy, BPS: www.bps.lk/olib/wh/wh006.pdf

Nyanatiloka Mahāthera, 1994, 'Kamma and Rebirth', pp. 10–18 in *Fundamentals of Buddhism*, Wheel booklet 394–6, Kandy, BPS: www.bps.lk/olib/wh/wh394.pdf

Olivelle, Patrick, 1996, *Upaniṣads: A New Translation*, Oxford, Oxford University Press.

Ornatowski, G. K., 1996, 'Continuity and Change in the Economic Ethics of Buddhism: Evidence from the History of Buddhism in India, China and Japan', *JBE*, 3: 198–240: http://blogs.dickinson.edu/buddhistethics/files/2010/04/ornatow1.pdf

Pa-Auk Sayadaw, 2003, *Knowing and Seeing*: www.buddha.net/pdf_file/know-see.pdf

Pagel, U., 1995, *The Bodhisattvapiṭaka: Its Doctrines, Practices and their Position in Mahāyāna Literature*, Tring, UK, The Institute of Buddhist Studies.

2001, 'The Sacred Writings of Buddhism', in P. Harvey, *Buddhism*, London, Continuum, 29–63.

Pas, J. F., 1995, *Visions of Sukhāvatī*, Albany, N.Y., State University of New York Press.

Paul, D. Y., 1979, *Women in Buddhism: Images of the Feminine in Mahāyāna Tradition*, Berkeley, Calif., Asian Humanities Press. [Translations and discussion.]

Payutto, P. A., 1993, *Good, Evil and Beyond: Kamma in the Buddha's Teaching*, Bangkok, Buddhadhamma Foundation, and on Buddhanet website: www.buddhanet.net/cmdsg/kamma.htm

1994a, *Dependent Origination: The Buddhist Law of Causality*, Bangkok, Buddhadhamma Foundation, and on Buddhanet website: www.buddhanet.net/cmdsg/coarise.htm

1994b, *Buddhist Economics: A Middle Way for the Market Place*, Bangkok, Buddhadhamma Foundation, and on Buddhanet website: www.buddhanet.net/cmdsg/econ.htm

Payutto, Phra Pryudh, 1995, *Buddhadhamma: Natural Laws and Values for Life*, Albany, State University of New York Press.

Peiris, W., 1973, *The Western Contribution to Buddhism*, Delhi, MB.

Piburn, S., ed., 1990, *The Dalai Lama: A Policy of Kindness: An Anthology of Writings By and About the Dalai Lama*, Ithaca, N.Y., Snow Lion.

Piyadassi Thera, 1980, *The Seven Factors of Enlightenment*, Wheel booklet 1, Kandy, BPS: www.bps.lk/olib/wh/wh001.pdf

1999, *The Book of Protection: Paritta*, Kandy, BPS, and on Access to Insight website: www.accesstoinsight.org/lib/authors/piyadassi/protection.html

Powers, J., 1995, *Wisdom of the Buddha: The Saṃdhinirmocana Sūtra*, Berkeley, Dharma.

2000, *A Concise Encyclopedia of Buddhism*, Oxford, One World.

2007a, 'Other Emptiness and Self Emptiness in Tibetan Buddhism', in Keown and Prebish, 2007, 580–1.

2007b, *Introduction to Tibetan Buddhism*, rev. edn., Ithaca, N.Y., Boulder, Colo., Snow Lion.

Prebish, C. S., 1999, *Luminous Passage: The Practice and Study of Buddhism in America*, Berkeley, University of California Press.

2007, 'Academic study of Buddhism' entries in Keown and Prebish, 2007, 9–18, 30–3, 74–5, 244–5, 252–4, 262–3, 268–70, 393, 470–1, 493–5, 565–8, 596–7, 605–7, 614–15, 628–9, 678–80.

Prebish, C. S. and Baumann, M., eds., 2002, *Westward Dharma: Buddhism Beyond Asia*, Berkeley, University of California Press.

Prebish, C. S. and Tanaka, K. T., eds., 1998, *The Faces of Buddhism in America*, Berkeley: University of California Press.

Puri, B. N., 1987, *Buddhism in Central Asia*, Delhi, MB.

Putney, D., 1996, 'Some Problems of Interpretation: The Early and Late Writings of Dōgen', *Philosophy East and West*, 46 (4): 497–531, and on Buddhist Digital Library and Museum website: http://ccbs.ntu.edu.tw/FULLTEXT/JR-PHIL/putney1.htm

Pye, M., 2003, *Skilful Means: A Concept in Mahāyāna Buddhism*, 2nd edn, London and New York, Routledge.

Queen, C. S. and King, S. B., eds., 1996, *Engaged Buddhism: Buddhist Liberation Movements in Asia*, Albany, State University of New York Press.

Rahula, W., 1966, *History of Buddhism in Ceylon: The Anurādhapura Period, 3rd Century B.C. to 10th Century A.D.*, 2nd edn, Colombo, Gunasena.

1974, *What the Buddha Taught*, 2nd edn, New York, Grove.
Rājavaramuni, Phra, 1990, 'The Foundations of Buddhist Social Ethics', in R. F. Sizemore and D. K. Swearer, *Ethics, Wealth and Salvation: A Study of Buddhist Social Ethics*, Columbia, S.C., University of South Carolina Press, 29–53.
Ratnayaka, S., 1981, 'Metapsychology of the *Abhidharma*', *JIABS*, 4 (1): 76–88.
1985, 'The Bodhisattva Ideal of the Theravāda', *JIABS*, 8 (2): 85–110.
Ray, R., 1980, 'Accomplished Women in the Tantric Buddhism of Medieval India and Tibet', in N. A. Falk and R. Gross, *Unspoken Worlds: Women's Religious Lives in Non-Western Cultures*, San Francisco, Harper & Row, 227–42.
1989, 'The Mahāsiddha', in J. M. Kitagawa and M. Cummings, *Buddhism and Asian History: Religion, History and Culture*, New York, Macmillan and London, Collier Macmillan, 389–94.
1994, *Buddhist Saints in India: A Study in Buddhist Values and Orientations*, Oxford and New York, Oxford University Press.
Reader, I., 1991, *Religion in Contemporary Japan*, Honolulu, University of Hawaii Press.
2006, *Making Pilgrimages: Meaning and Practice in Shikoku*, Honolulu, University of Hawaii Press.
2011, 'Buddhism in Crisis? Institutional Decline and the Problems of Modernity in Japan', *BSR*, 28 (2): 233–63.
Reader, I., Andreasen, E. and Stefánsson, F., 1993, *Japanese Religions: Past and Present*, Honolulu, University of Hawaii Press.
Reynolds, F. E., 1977, 'Several Bodies of the Buddha: Reflections on a Neglected Aspect of Theravāda Tradition', *History of Religions*, 16: 374–88.
Rocha, C., ed., 2007, Special Issue on 'Buddhism in Oceania' of *Journal of Global Buddhism*, 8: www.globalbuddhism.org/toc.html
Rocha, C. and Barker, M., eds., 2010, *Buddhism in Australia: Traditions in Change*, London, Routledge.
Ronkin, N., 2005, *Early Buddhist Metaphysics: The Making of a Philosophical Tradition*, London and New York, RoutledgeCurzon. [On the Theravāda *Abhidhamma*.]
Rossi Collection, n.d., 'Early Tibetan Mandalas': www.asianart.com/mandalas/mandimge.html accessed 18 May 2010. [Fourteen *maṇḍalas*].
Rotman, A., tr., 2008, *Divine Stories: Divyāvadāna Part I*, Boston, Wisdom.
Rowlands, M., ed., 1982, *Abhidhamma Papers*, Manchester, Samatha Trust, and on Samatha Trust website: www.samatha.org/images/stories/abhidhamma-papers-final.pdf
Ruegg, D. S., 1969, *La Théorie du Tathāgatagarbha et du Gotra*, Paris, L'École Française D'Extrême-Orient.
1989a, 'The Buddhist Notion of an "Immanent Absolute" (*Tathāgatagarbha*) as a Problem in Hermeneutics', in T. Skorupski, *The Buddhist Heritage*, Tring, UK, The Institute of Buddhist Studies, 229–46.
1989b, *Buddha-nature, Mind and the Problem of Gradualism in a Comparative Perspective: On the Transmission and Reception of Buddhism in India and Tibet*, London, School of Oriental and African Studies.

Saddhatissa, H., 1970, *Buddhist Ethics: Essence of Buddhism*, London, George Allen and Unwin (repr. Boston, Wisdom, 1997).

Salzberg, S., 1995, *Lovingkindness: The Revolutionary Art of Happiness*, Boston and London, Shambhala.

Samuel, G., 1993, *Civilized Shamans: Buddhism in Tibetan Societies*, Washington DC and London, Smithsonian Institute.

2012, *Introducing Tibetan Buddhism*, London and New York, Routledge.

Sanderson, A., 1994, 'Vajrayāna: Origin and Function,' in *Buddhism into the Year 2000: International Conference Proceedings*, Bangkok and Los Angeles, Dhammakaya Foundation, 87–102.

Sasson, V. R., 2010, 'Peeling Back the Layers: Female Higher Ordination in Sri Lanka', *BSR*, 27 (1): 77–84.

Satō, G., 1973, *Unsui: A Diary of Zen Monastic Life*, ed. B. L. Smith, Honolulu, University Press of Hawaii.

Schedneck, B., 2009, 'Western Buddhist Perceptions of Monasticism', *BSR*, 26 (2): 229–46.

Schopen, G., 1997, *Bones, Stones, and Buddhist Monks: Collected Papers on the Archaeology, Epigraphy, and Texts of Monastic Buddhism in India*, Honolulu, University Press of Hawaii.

Schuster, N., 1981, 'Changing the Female Body: Wise Women and the Bodhisattva Career in Some *Mahāratnakṭastras*', *JIABS*, 4 (1): 24–69.

Seager, R. H., 1999, *Buddhism in America*, New York, Columbia University Press.

Seeger, M., 2005, 'How Long is a Lifetime? Buddhadāsa's and Phra Payutto's Interpretations of *paṭiccasamuppāda* in Comparison', *BSR*, 22: 107–30.

2006 (2008), 'The Bhikkhunī-Ordination Controversy in Thailand', *JIABS*, 29 (1): 155–83.

Sekida, K., 1975, *Zen Training: Methods and Philosophy*, New York and Tokyo, Weatherhill.

Seneviratne, H. L., 1999, *The Work of Kings: The New Buddhism in Sri Lanka*, Chicago and London, University of Chicago Press.

Sharpe. E. J., 1986, *Comparative Religion: A History*, 2nd edn, London, Duckworth.

Shaw, S., 2009, *Introduction to Buddhist Meditation*, London and New York, Routledge.

Skilling, P., 2009, 'Theravāda in History', *Pacific World*, 11: 61–93: www.uio.no/studier/emner/hf/ikos/SAS4014/v12/undervisningsmateriale/Skilling_Theravada%20in%20History%202009.pdf

Skilling, P., Carbine, J. A., Cicuzza, C., and Pakdeekam, S., eds., 2012, *How Theravadā is Theravāda?: Exploring Buddhist Identities*, Chiang Mai, Silkworm Books.

Skorupski, T., 2002, *The Six Perfections: An Abridged Version of E. Lamotte's French Translation of Nāgārjuna's Mahāprajñāpāramitāśastra Chapters XVI–XXX*, Tring, Institute of Buddhist Studies.

Snellgrove, D. L., 1987, 'Celestial Buddhas and Bodhisattvas', in M. Eliade, *The Encyclopaedia of Religion*, New York, Macmillan and London, Collier Macmillan, Vol. III, 133–44.

Snellgrove, D. L. and Richardson, H., 1968, *A Cultural History of Tibet*, London, Weidenfeld, and New York, Praeger.
Sogyal Rinpoche, 1992, *The Tibetan Book of Living and Dying*, London, Rider.
Soma Thera, 1981, *The Removal of Distracting Thoughts: Vitakka Santhana Sutta*, Wheel booklet 21, Kandy, BPS: www.bps.lk/olib/wh/wh021.pdf
1998, *The Way of Mindfulness: The Satipaṭṭhāna Sutta and Its Commentary*, 6th edn, A translation of the *Satipaṭṭhāna Sutta*, Kandy, BPS, and on Access to Insight website: www.accesstoinsight.org/lib/authors/soma/wayof.html
Sopa, Geshe, 1978, '*Śamatha-vipaśyanā-yuganaddha*: The Two Leading Principles of Buddhist Meditation', in Kiyota, 1978a, 46–65.
Spiro, M. E., 1971, *Buddhism and Society: A Great Tradition and its Burmese Vicissitudes*, London, Allen and Unwin.
Sponberg, A., 1982, 'Report on Buddhism in the People's Republic of China', *JIABS*, 5 (1): 109–17.
1992, 'Attitudes towards Women and the Feminine in Early Buddhism', in Cabezón, 1992, 3–36.
2007, 'Buddha-fields and Pure Lands', in Keown and Prebish, 2007, 155–58.
Sponberg, A. and Hardacre, H., eds., 1988, *Maitreya, the Future Buddha*, Cambridge, Cambridge University Press.
Stcherbatsky, T., 1956, *The Central Conception of Buddhism and the Meaning of the Word 'Dharma'* (London, Royal Asiatic Society, 1923), Calcutta, Susil Gupta.
Stevenson, D. B., 1986, 'The Four Kinds of Samādhi in Early Tiantai Buddhism', in Gregory, 1986, 45–98.
Stevenson, I., 1974, *20 Cases Suggestive of Reincarnation*, 2nd edn, Charlottesville, University of Virginia Press.
1987, *Children Who Remember Previous Lives*, Charlottesville, University of Virginia Press.
Stone, J. L., 1999, *Original Enlightenment and the Transformation of Medieval Japanese Buddhism*, Honolulu, University of Hawaii Press.
Strong, J. S., 1996, 'The Moves *Maṇḍalas* Make', *JIABS*, 19 (2). 301–12. [Edition on *maṇḍalas*.]
2001, *The Buddha: a Short Biography*, Oxford, One World.
2004, *Relics of the Buddha*, Princeton and Oxford, Princeton University Press.
tr., 2008, *The Legend of King Aśoka: A Study and Translation of the Aśokāvadāna*, 2nd edn, Delhi, MB.
Subhuti, Dharmachari, 1983, *Buddhism for Today: A Portait of a New Buddhist Movement*, Salisbury, Wiltshire, Element Books.
1994, *Sangharakshita: A New Voice in the Buddhist Tradition*, Birmingham, Windhorse.
Suksamran, S., 1977, *Political Buddhism in Southeast Asia: The Role of the Sangha in the Modernization of Thailand*, London, Hurst.
Sumedho, Ajahn, 1984, *Cittaviveka: Teachings from the Silent Mind*, Hemel Hempstead, Amaravati Publications. Online at: www.what-buddha-taught.net/Books2/Ajahn_Sumedho_Cittaviveka.htm
Suzuki, D. T., 1959, *Zen and Japanese Culture*, New York, Princeton University Press.

1969, *The Zen Doctrine of No Mind*, London, Rider.

1970a, b, c, *Essays in Zen Buddhism*, First, Second and Third Series, 2nd edn (orig. London, Luzac and Co., 1927, 1933 and 1934), London, Rider.

Suzuki, S., 1999, *Zen Mind, Beginner's Mind*, New York, Weatherhill.

Swanson, Paul L., 1989, *T'ien-t'ai Philosophy*, Berkeley, Calif., Asian Humanities Press.

Swearer, D. K., 1995, *The Buddhist World of Southeast Asia*, Albany, N.Y., State University of New York Press.

Tambiah, S. J., 1984, *The Buddhist Saints of the Forest and the Cult of Amulets*, Cambridge, Cambridge University Press.

1992, *Buddhism Betrayed? Religion, Politics and Violence in Sri Lanka*, Chicago and London, University of Chicago Press.

Tatz, M., 1986, *Asanga's Chapter on Ethics, With the Commentary of Tsong-Kha-Pa*, Studies in Asian Thought and Religion, Vol. iv, Lewiston/Queenston, Edwin Mellen.

1994, *Skill in Means, Upāyakauśalya, Sūtra*, Delhi, MB.

Tay, N., 1976–7, 'Kuan-yin: The Cult of Half Asia', *History of Religions*, 16: 144–77.

Ṭhānissaro Bhikkhu, 1996, *The Wings to Awakening: An Anthology from the Pali Canon*, Barre, Mass., Barre Center for Buddhist Studies, also on the Access to Insight website: www.accesstoinsight.org/lib/authors/thanissaro/wings/index.html

1999a, *The Mind Like Fire Unbound*, Barre, Mass., Dhamma Dana Publications, and on Access to Insight website: www.accesstoinsight.org/lib/modern/thanissaro/likefire/index.html

1999b, 'The Custom of the Noble Ones', on Access to Insight website: www.accesstoinsight.org/lib/authors/thanissaro/customs.html

2007, *The Buddhist Monastic Code*, 2nd edition; 2 vols., California, Metta Forest Monastery, and on Access to Insight website: www.accesstoinsight.org/lib/authors/thanissaro/bmc1/bmc1.intro.html

Thien-An, Thich, 1975, *Buddhism and Zen in Vietnam in Relation to the Development of Buddhism in Asia*, Rutland, Vt. and Tokyo, C. E. Tuttle.

Thomas, E. J., 1949, *The Life of Buddha as Legend and History*, 3rd edn, London, Routledge and Kegan Paul (repr. Dover, 2000).

Tribe, A. H. F., 1997, 'Mañjuśrī: Origins, Role and Significance', Parts i and ii, *Western Buddhist Review*, 2: 49–123: www.westernbuddhistreview.com/vol2/manjusri_parts_1_and_2.html

Trungpa, Chogyam 1973, *Cutting Through Spiritual Materialism*, Berkeley, Calif., Shambhala.

1994a, 'Tilopa, "The Union of Joy and Happiness" (*Mahāmudropadeśa*)', in S. Bercholz and S. Kohn, *Entering the Stream: An Introduction to the Buddha and his Teachings*, Boston, Shambhala, 266–72.

1994b, 'Jigme Lingpa, "Ati: the innermost essence"', in S. Bercholz and S. Kohn, *Entering the Stream: An Introduction to the Buddha and his Teachings*, Boston, Shambhala, 283–8.

Tsai, K. A., 1994, *Lives of the Nuns: Biographies of Chinese Buddhist Nuns from the Fourth to Sixth Centuries*, Honolulu, University of Hawaii Press.

Tsomo, K. L., ed., 1988, *Sakyadhītā: Daughters of the Buddha*, Ithaca, N.Y., Snow Lion.
2010, 'Lao Buddhist Women: Quietly Negotiating Religious Authority', *BSR*, 27 (1): 8–106.
Tucker, M. E. and Williams, D. R., eds., 1997, *Buddhism and Ecology: The Interconnection of Dharma and Deeds*, Cambridge, Mass., Harvard University Center for the Study of World Religions.
Uchino, K., 1986, 'The Status Elevation Process of Sōtō Sect Nuns in Modern Japan', in D. L. Eck and D. Jain, *Speaking of Faith: Cross-cultural Perspectives on Women, Religion and Social Change*, London, The Women's Press, 149–63.
Unger, A. H. and Unger, W., 1997, *Pagodas, Gods and Spirits of Vietnam: Popular Religion, Sacred Buildings and Religious Art in Vietnam*, New York, Thames & Hudson.
van Gorkom, N., 1990, *Abhidhamma in Daily Life*, London, Triple Gem Press, and on Abhidhamma.org website: www.Abhidhamma.org/abhid.html
Victoria, B., 1997, *Zen at War*, New York and Tokyo, Weatherhill.
Vishvapani, Dharmachari, 2001, 'Perceptions of the FWBO in British Buddhism', *Western Buddhist Review*: www.westernbuddhistreview.com/vol3/Perceptions.htm
Waddell, N. and Abe, M., trs., 2002, *The Heart of Dōgen's Shōbōgenzō*, New York, State University of New York Press.
Waldron, W. S., 2003, *The Buddhist Unconscious: The ālaya-vijñāna in the Context of Indian Buddhist Thought*, London and New York, RoutledgeCurzon.
Wallace, B. A., ed., 2003, *Buddhism and Science: Breaking New Ground*, New York, Columbia University Press.
Waterhouse, H., 1997, *Buddhism in Bath: Adaptation and Authority*, Leeds, Community Religions Project, University of Leeds.
Watts, A., 1962, *The Way of Zen*, London, Pelican.
Wayman, A., 1991, *Ethics of Tibet: Bodhisattva Section of Tsong-Kha-Pa's Lam Rim Chen Mo*, Albany, State University of New York Press.
1996, 'A Defence of Yogācāra Buddhism', *Philosophy East and West*, 46 (4): 447–76, and on Buddhist Digital Library and Museum website: http://ccbs.ntu.edu.tw/FULLTEXT/JR-PHIL/alex1.htm
Webster, D., 2005, *The Philosophy of Desire in the Buddhist Pali Canon*, London and New York, RoutledgeCurzon.
Weeraratne, D. A., n.d., 'Revival of the Bhikkhuni Order in Sri Lanka', www.buddhanet.net/nunorder.htm – accessed 30 April 2010.
Wei-an, Cheng, 2000, *Taming the Monkey Mind: A Guide to Pure Land Practice*: www.buddhanet.net/pdf_file/monkeym.pdf
Welch, H., 1967, *The Practice of Chinese Buddhism*, Cambridge, Mass., Harvard University Press.
1968, *The Buddhist Revival in China*, Cambridge, Mass., Harvard University Press.
1972, *Buddhism Under Mao*, Cambridge, Mass., Harvard University Press.
Welter, Albert, 2000, 'Mahākāśyapa's Smile: Silent Transmission and the *Kung-an* (*Kōan*) Tradition', in S. Heine and D. S. Wright, *The Kōan: Texts and Contexts in Zen Buddhism*, Oxford and New York, Oxford University Press, 75–109.

Westerhoff, J., 2009, *Nāgārjuna's Madhyamaka: A Philosophical Introduction*, Oxford, Oxford University Press.

Wickremeratne, Ananda, 1984, *The Genesis of an Orientalist: Thomas William Rhys Davids in Sri Lanka*, Delhi, MB.

Wijayaratna, M., 1990, *Buddhist Monastic Life According to the Texts of the Theravāda Tradition*, Cambridge, Cambridge University Press.

Wijeratne, R. P. and Gethin, R., trs., 2002, *Summary of the Topics of Abhidhamma (Abhidhammaahasaṅgaha) by Anuruddha. Exposition of the Topics of Abhidhamma (Abhidhammatthavibhāvinī) by Sumaṅgala, being a commentary on Anuruddha's Summary of the Topics of Abhidhamma*, Oxford, Pali Text Society.

Wikipedia, 2010, 'Buddhism by Country': http://en.wikipedia.org/wiki/Buddhism_by_country – accessed 26 May 2010.

Willemen, C., Dessein, B. and Cox, C., 1998, *Sarvāstivāda Buddhist Scholasticism*, Leiden, Brill.

Williams, D. R., and Queen, C. S., eds., 1999, *American Buddhism: Methods and Findings in Recent Scholarship*, Richmond, Curzon Press.

Williams, L., 2000, 'A Whisper in the Silence: Nuns Before Mahāpajāpatī', *BSR*, 17 (2): 167–74.

Williams, P., 2004, *Songs of Love, Poems of Sadness: The Erotic Verses of the Sixth Dalai Lama*, London and New York, I.B. Tauris.

ed., 2005, *Buddhism: Critical Concepts in Religious Studies*, 8 vols., London and New York, Routledge.

2009, *Mahāyāna Buddhism: The Doctrinal Foundations*, 2nd edn, London and New York, Routledge and Kegan Paul.

Williams, P. with Tribe, A. and Wynne, A., 2012, *Buddhist Thought: A Complete Introduction to the Indian Tradition*, 2nd edn, London and New York, Routledge and Kegan Paul.

Williams, P., and Ladwig, P., eds., 2012, *Buddhist Funeral Cultures of Southeast Asia and China*, Cambridge, Cambridge University Press.

Willis, J., 1989, *Feminine Ground: Essays on Women and Tibet*, Ithaca, N.Y., Snow Lion.

Wilson, B. and Dobbelaere, K., 1994, *A Time to Chant: The Soka Gakkai Buddhists in Britain*, Oxford, Clarendon Press.

Wright, D. S., 1993, 'The Discourse of Awakening: Rhetorical Practice in Classical Cha'n Buddhism', *Journal of the American Academy of Religion*, 61 (1): 23–40.

1998, *Philosophical Meditations on Zen Buddhism*, Cambridge, Cambridge University Press.

Xing, Guang, 2005a, *The Concept of the Buddha: Its Evolution from Early Buddhism to the Trikāya Theory*, London and New York, RoutledgeCurzon.

2005b, 'Filial Piety in Early Buddhism', *JBE*, 12: 82–106: http://blogs.dickinson.edu/buddhistethics/files/2010/04/xing1228.pdf

Zürcher, E., 1959, *The Buddhist Conquest of China*, 2 vols., Leiden, Brill.

1989, 'The Impact of Buddhism on Chinese Culture in Historical Perspective', in T. Skorupski, *The Buddhist Heritage*, Tring, UK, The Institute of Buddhist Studies, 117–28.

Index

Chinese terms are given in Pinyin form, with the older Wade-Giles form in brackets. Where a term in the latter starts with a different letter, it also has its own entry directing the reader to the Pinyin entry. Tibetan terms are given in pronounceable form, with fuller Wylie forms in brackets. Primary entries in bold. Italicised items are non-English words, or names of texts.